NEW MERMAIDS

General editors:
William C. Carroll, Boston University
Brian Gibbons, University of Münster
Tiffany Stern, University of Oxford

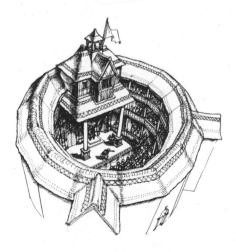

Reconstruction of an Elizabethan theatre
by C. Walter Hodges

NEW MERMAIDS

NEW MERMAIDS

BEN JONSON

FOUR PLAYS

VOLPONE
EPICOENE, OR THE SILENT WOMAN
THE ALCHEMIST
BARTHOLMEW FAIR

Introduction by Robert N. Watson

Methuen Drama • London

Bloomsbury Methuen Drama
An imprint of Bloomsbury Publishing Plc

50 Bedford Square
London
WC1B 3DP
UK

1385 Broadway
New York
NY 10018
USA

www.bloomsbury.com

Bloomsbury is a registered trade mark of Bloomsbury Publishing Plc

Copyright © 2014 Bloomsbury Publishing Plc

Volpone
© 2003 Bloomsbury Publishing Ltd

Epicoene, or the Silent Woman
© 1979 Ernest Benn Ltd
©2002 Bloomsbury Publishing Ltd

The Alchemist
©2010 A&C Black Publishers Ltd

Bartholmew Fair
©2007 A&C Black Publishers Ltd

British Library Cataloguing-in-Publication Data
A catalogue record for this book is available from the British Library.

ISBN: PB: 978-1-4081-7962-8
ePub: 978-1-4081-7964-2
ePDF: 978-1-4081-7963-5

Library of Congress Cataloging-in-Publication Data
A catalog record for this book is available from the Library of Congress.

Typeset by Country Setting, Kingsdown, Kent CT14 8ES
Printed and bound in India

CONTENTS

ACKNOWLEDGEMENTS

This anthology brings together the texts and commentaries from the most recent single-play versions of four Ben Jonson comedies in the New Mermaids series: my edition of *Volpone*, Roger Holdsworth's edition of *Epicoene*, Elizabeth Cook's edition of *The Alchemist*, and Alexander Leggatt and G. R. Hibbard's edition of *Bartholmew Fair*. The Notes on the Texts from those editions appear at the end of the collection. Although I have made a few small corrections and reconciliations of format, and updated line numbers and cross-references in the original editions to match the lineation in this anthology, I have not attempted to override the different approaches and emphases of my fellow New Mermaids editors, and my chief debt is of course to them.

The volume begins with a new introduction offering a brief biography of Jonson and an overview of what I believe makes these plays still so interesting and so important; Dana Cairns Watson and Dan Hugh-Jones helped me trim this introduction down to size and sharpen its focus.

I am very grateful for the guiding wisdom of the excellent General Editors of this series and the extraordinarily diligent and intelligent work of Simon Trussler and Jane Armstrong in overseeing and copy-editing the text, as well as Claire Cooper and ultimately Margaret Bartley in bringing this book into being.

INTRODUCTION

Biographical Sketch

The world has seldom seen anything like Ben Jonson – so big, brilliant, and stubborn, rocketing up from the lower realms of society and repeatedly tumbling back down again, and contradictory in so many aspects of his life. He was a passionate man with no apparent interest in love, a working-class child who became the exemplar of high court culture, a decorous classicist given to extreme drunkenness and murderous violence, a self-proclaimed Stoic driven by violent appetites for praise and pleasure, and a dedicated social climber who repeatedly sabotaged his own advancement. He was a moralistic writer who always seemed to side with his rogues, and a genius of comic drama who repeatedly withdrew bitterly from the theatre. Ironically, Jonson has now become a victim of his own success: having used the mantles of classical literature and royal employment to conceal his common origins and wild tendencies, Jonson has convinced many potential modern readers to mistake him for yet another formal snob in the literary establishment.

Jonson's father, a minister, died before his son was born in 1572; Jonson's stepfather was a bricklayer. Intelligence and diligence won the boy a scholarship and success at the prestigious Westminster School in London, but he was then unhappily apprenticed to his stepfather's trade. In a society that assumed intellect, taste, and learning were exclusively the property of the upper classes, his literary rivals often sneered that Jonson was better suited to bricklaying than to any more sophisticated creations. So it is not surprising that he became hyper-competitive and sensitive to insults. This elite intellectual was simultaneously proud of his earthier side and embarrassed by it, and the comedies in this volume thrive on the mixture of affection and disdain he apparently felt toward ordinary human life, in all its richness and stupidity.

Jonson was physically gigantic for his era – extremely tall and eventually extremely fat – and he lived an outsized life. He volunteered for the wars in Flanders, where he reportedly challenged an enemy soldier to single combat, and killed him. All we really know about his wife Anne is that, in his alcohol-fuelled 'Conversations' with William Drummond, Jonson called her 'a shrew, yet honest'. Despite the efforts of most biographers to take that as a hedged compliment, the comment suggests a familiar male-chauvinist combination of demeaning her as a mere annoyance and insisting that nobody ever cuckolded him, as he bragged of cuckolding others. They had several children together; the deaths of his first daughter and first son are lamented movingly in his *Epigrams*, and there is no evidence that any of his legitimate offspring survived to adulthood.

By 1597 he was acting and writing in the nascent theatre industry – and heading for jail. He had played the lead in Thomas Kyd's *Spanish Tragedy*, and was called one of England's best tragic playwrights in Francis Meres's 1598 survey, though neither Jonson nor anyone else preserved any of the plays on which that judgement must have been based. In August of 1597 he was imprisoned for his part in finishing a satiric play called *The Isle of Dogs* (also now lost). The next year, within a few days of the opening performance of his hit comedy *Every Man In His Humour*, with William Shakespeare in the cast, Jonson killed another fellow-actor in a duel. Luckily for us, the victim was Gabriel Spencer, who had previously been in prison with Jonson, rather than Shakespeare. Jonson escaped execution – any man able to read Latin could claim exemption as a clergyman – but had his thumb branded and his belongings confiscated. To make things worse, while in jail he announced his conversion to Catholicism, which was then essentially illegal. Released from prison, Jonson channelled his characteristic pugnacity into scholarly arrogance, launching a prolonged literary and sometimes physical brawl – now hyperbolically known as the War of the Theatres, and reflected in the Prologue to *Volpone* – against his fellow playwrights.

Despite disgrace and debt (or perhaps because of them) Jonson used his literary skills and scholarly reputation to gain the patronage of power-ful aristocrats, whom he followed to their country houses – leaving his family back in London, at risk of bubonic plague, which killed his first son. He wrote intricate elegies of praise to anyone who supported him, and brutally nasty epigrams against anyone who crossed him. When the Scottish King James succeeded Queen Elizabeth in 1603, Jonson co-authored a play called *Eastward Ho!* that briefly satirized the Scots and landed him again in prison. After the notorious Gunpowder Plot was thwarted, Jonson was discovered to have dined with the main con-spirators only a few nights before they attempted to blow up England's monarch and Parliament as part of a Catholic coup.

Jonson emerged from that dark period to write a series of great and popular comedies, including *Volpone, Epicoene, The Alchemist,* and *Bartholmew Fair,* as well as the best of his surviving tragedies (*Sejanus,* based on ancient Roman history) and a number of his great lyric poems. He became James's leading author of masques: elaborately produced ceremonial allegories designed to instruct and flatter the high-ranking persons who watched and often performed them. But he feuded bitterly with the architect Inigo Jones, who created spectacular designs for these productions, and James's successor, Charles I, turned to other authors. Jonson's theatrical achievements were often social liabilities: along with the instances already mentioned, the early *Poetaster*, the mid-career *Sejanus* and *Epicoene*, and the late *Devil is an Ass* each landed him in trouble with the authorities. Jonson was even hired by Sir Walter Ralegh to tutor Ralegh's son – until the drunken Jonson was carted mockingly through the streets of Paris by his pupil as an 'image of the Crucifix'.

Jonson's lifelong struggle to construct and project a dignified self through his literary art culminated in the 1616 Folio of his *Works*. Although this publication provoked some mockery of the presumption involved in presenting mere 'plays' under the grand traditional title of 'Works', Jonson had become a revered figure: a kind of poet laureate, winning honorary degrees, state employment, and a pension (including an annual barrel of wine). The 'Tribe of Ben', a loose association of leading Cavalier poets, worshipped him as their 'father' at many bibulous occasions. But a fire destroyed his books and unpublished works in 1623, and a stroke in 1628 rendered him paraplegic – and a far less successful comic playwright – until his death in 1637. His grave in Westminster Abbey is a diamond-shaped stone that says only, 'O rare Ben Jonson' – a stone so small that it seems to confirm the rumour that this giant was buried vertically. The rumour that he was also buried upside down suggests an apt ending for such an endlessly contradictory character.

Jonson's Comedies

That human life is largely driven by greed for food, sex, money, and status is hardly news. Nor is it news that people are made selfish, hypocritical, and gullible by those desires. But no one has ever made those facts more hilariously visible than Jonson does in his comedies. They are consistently funnier onstage than those of Shakespeare, and more subversive too: Jonson refuses to conclude with heartwarming affirmations of social decorum and literary convention.

As the war raged within Jonson between his intense emotions and appetites on the one hand and his high aesthetic intellect on the other, satiric comedy allowed him to work through the conflicts productively. In his poems and masques he is often obsequious, seeking the favour of potential patrons among the aristocracy and monarchy. But the rancorous, rebellious side of his personality, which he acted out destructively so many times in his life, could sometimes be diverted into this popular theatrical genre.

Comedy tends to focus on the lowest common denominators of

human life, showing pretensions deflated by the ordinary demands of the body. Even Jonson's poems ruefully observe that his lovely lines of verse cannot erase the unlovely swellings and pockmarks of his aging physique. His comedies often culminate in an inconvenient but incontrovertible physical fact crushing a grandiose scheme. Mistress Epicoene's body and voice ruin Morose's recruitment of a perfect bride. What wrecks Volpone's thriving swindle is first that his body is lustful, and then that it is still alive at all. Surly's lustful and violent body, and Dapper's exhausted and hungry one, bring crashing down the masterfully orchestrated frauds in *The Alchemist*. In *Bartholmew Fair*, Mistress Overdo's need to urinate spoils her husband's ambitions as a great reforming magistrate, Busy's gluttony undermines his pose as a Puritan saint, and brawls and sexual banter degrade everything else.

Jonson also systematically humiliates his literary rivals. Ordinary parodists would simply stage ridiculous versions of the plays they wanted to attack, but Jonson shows his foolish characters striving to live out roles drawn from those rival works within the more realistic environment of city comedy. Jacobean London was as predatory towards naive persons as Jonson was towards the works of his naive fellow-playwrights. As Jonson makes the formulaic, egoistical fantasies of his gullible characters collide with each other, creating his own triumphant satiric plot out of their collision, the audience's conventional expectations of plot are similarly aroused, exploited, and overruled. By allowing a satirist resembling himself to exploit and defeat all these pretenders and pretensions, Jonson claims victory over his conventional-minded competitors. The values of money and romantic love, in which Jonson was generally poor, yield to the value of theatrical wit, which he had in abundance.

In *Volpone* (1605–6), the title character seems to think he inhabits a beast fable – the fox tricking some birds of prey — while Celia and Bonario over-confidently await a sentimental melodrama, and Corvino fears a cuckolding fabliau rather than the kind of humiliation actually awaiting him. Having the servant Mosca outwit them all must have been satisfying for Jonson, who always felt he was unjustly in servitude to people of superior birth but inferior mind. Truewit's plot in *Epicoene, or the Silent Woman* (1609) similarly exploits the self-conceptions other characters have drawn from classical and scriptural sources. In *The Alchemist* (1610), Dapper can be manipulated because he believes himself the hero of a fairy tale, Kastril because he's proudly playing the roaring-boy role then often seen onstage, and Drugger because he believes himself the earnest hero of the kind of rising-middle-class citizen comedy popular at the time. In a double twist, Surly can be tricked because he thinks the story is a cony-catching pamphlet in which his type would expose the cheaters preying on such fantasies. *Bartholmew Fair* (1614) shows Justice Overdo assuming the story is about his clever ploy of disguising himself as an ordinary citizen to discover criminal conspiracies – this disguised-magistrate plot was also popular at the time – while Wasp anticipates a prodigal-son story, Dame Pliant a dynastic-marriage plot, and so on.

These self-fashioned imitators of literary characters show that people are made by language, as much as the other way around. In the critical notebook called his *Discoveries*, Jonson argues that verbal style is the best clue to a person's true character – '*Language* most shewes a man: speake that I may see thee' – and his comedies show his ear for characteristic speech habits at its finest. No writer takes a more observant and exuberant joy in the quirks of his characters' speech, or in the sheer momentum of rhetoric and the sheer multiplicity of items that can be conjured into presence by words. The lists spun out by Jonson's characters call up these material riches even faster than the burgeoning commodity culture that Jonson recognized in Jacobean London could do.

The four plays in this volume have the rare and wonderful quality of making an audience think not just in between but actually through its laughter. What is most amusing is often what is most profound, not just a way of cajoling the audience into awaiting the next development of plot or theme. In a world simultaneously compressed by urbanization and expanded by colonial ventures, money talked louder than ever, and Jonson listened sceptically to its seductive lies. His comedies are brilliantly local, grounded in the specifics of his time and place. Yet they somehow remain stunningly insightful about the tendencies that still corrupt the collective human project: narcissism and the gullibility and greed it generates, consumer capitalism and the waste it encourages and the pious hypocrites it empowers. For such a sick society, Jonson prescribed laughter – including the harsh kind signalling ridicule – as the best medicine.

Volpone

Volpone is the sharpest, funniest Renaissance comedy about money and morals, and it has lost none of its zing and sting in the twenty-first century. It depicts unprincipled selfishness thinly covered by sanctimonious speeches, lust and possessiveness masquerading as love and marriage, cynical legalism passing itself off as justice, boastful name-dropping passing for cultural sophistication, and greed deluding itself that it is really prudence and even religion. As his clever servant Mosca knows, Volpone likes to be flattered that he is not like the misers despised in medieval literature. But he does resemble a more modern version of the figure: the Wall Street mogul who makes money breed more money without actually producing anything useful, unaccountably determined to acquire further millions, whatever the ethical and social costs, if only to outdo his fellow plutocrats. This modern self is defined by its performances and its acquisitions, surrounded by a sterile caricature of family, and protected by the illusion that wealth can claim priority even over death. It is a game for the man who has everything except a life or a heart, and Volpone plays it well.

The competitors scheming to inherit Volpone's estate have prominent sources in classical literature (Horace, Petronius, Lucian, Juvenal), but they emerge here as venture capitalists, investing more and more of their considerable wealth in flattering Volpone, in hopes of inheriting even greater wealth when he dies. As capitalism took hold in the Renaissance, the old, feudal rules of social order collapsed, and money became a primary measure of status, an idol to be worshipped for its own sake. In this sense, Jonson's *Volpone* conveys the same warning as Marlowe's *Doctor Faustus*: that the modern world – though it may lack the explicitly diabolical tempters of the old morality plays – offers to buy our souls in exchange for some superficial power and glory that never really transcend the banal and the mundane. Gold replaces God, as it does for Volpone in the play's opening lines, and opulent possessions become the new form of demonic possession. Greed, the vice driving many moral tales, stands in for all sorts of insatiable desires and grandiose fantasies.

Jonson chose to set this play in Venice: a place English authors liked to depict as an epitome of corruption. What makes that city-state such an apt locale for this play (and for Shakespeare's *Merchant of Venice*) is its lack of any fundamental values – literally a lack of grounding. In the absence of land and other natural resources, Venice built its economy and identity entirely around exchange. So it provides a perfect setting for a sophisticated understanding of greed as desire that has broken loose from real objects and real needs. Even the naive heroine Celia seems to be more a marker in men's competition than a person whose inner qualities matter.

As in the 'humours' plays Jonson had been writing during the preceding years, various characters in *Volpone* are led astray by over-confidence in the flattering scripts they have unconsciously adopted and adapted. Mosca comments that each of the legacy-hunters 'is so possessed, and stuffed with his own hopes, / That anything unto the contrary, / Never so true, or never so apparent, / Never so palpable, they will resist it' (V.ii.24–7). They assume they are the stars of the show. If the story of Sir

Politic Would-Be and his wife seems irrelevant to the centre of the play, that may itself be Jonson's point: the Would-Be subplot is a would-be main plot.

Celia and Bonario are exiles from the world of sentimental melodrama, where their sort of virtue might have relevance and force. Samuel Taylor Coleridge revealingly suggested that 'a most delightful comedy might be produced, by making Celia the ward or niece of Corvino, instead of his wife, and Bonario her lover'. Since then, scholars have repeatedly puzzled over the fact that Jonson neglects to propel this pair into a conventional romantic union; the pair themselves appear to be similarly baffled. But a morality-play tradition in which Virtue (Bonario) rescues Innocent Humanity (Celia) from the clutches of the Vice (Volpone) rings deliberately hollow on Jonson's stage. If we try to perceive Celia and Bonario as heroes, the play calls us fools.

Yet if we try to perceive them as merely fools, the play calls us scoundrels. While deluding their victims, the satiric manipulators also delude themselves. Jonson's audience, meanwhile, is rebuffed for confidently awaiting either the victory of goodness that concludes most popular comedies, or else the victory of cleverness that concludes so many other Jonsonian comedies. If the critics Jonson attacks in the Epistle to this play (pp. 169–78) demand a moral ending, they will receive it only in the harsh discordant form of the court's official sentences, where power and money crush playfulness. Those critics will then have to decide whether they really prefer that to the comic spirit that survives in Volpone's Epilogue, and in Jonson's other comedies.

Volpone leans heavily on the tradition of Aesop's beast-fables, especially the legends of Reynard the Fox, many of whose adventures – extremely popular in Renaissance European folklore – suggest parallels to Volpone. Reynard too is tried by a corrupt court for attempted rape and for feigning death in an attempt to capture the crow's wife. Like Volpone (and like some real foxes), Reynard often plays dead in order to trap the predatory birds who gather to feed on his corpse. The vulture (here, the lawyer Voltore) is a notorious carrion-seeker, so it makes sense that he hovers hungrily over Volpone's supposedly dying body. The crow (the jealous merchant Corvino) is another scavenger, and ironically a bird traditionally associated with marital fidelity. Flies also feed on the dead, and were associated (as Mosca is here) with demonic possession; in the 1952 production in Stratford-upon-Avon, England, Anthony Quayle's fabulously unctuous Mosca not only wore shiny black clothes and rubbed his hands together like a fly, but emitted a strange buzzing laugh, and (thanks to matching table legs) appeared to have six black legs as he took inventory of Volpone's treasures. Sir Pol displays the parrot's devotion to loud, mindless mimicry, and is hunted down by the sharper hawk Peregrine. The fable thus conjoins with the overall ethical thrust of the play: as traditional social and religious principles yield to rapacious appetites, human beings inevitably sink to the level of beasts.

Volpone offers the thrill of witnessing swift manoeuvres in a tight space, of watching the protagonists improvise and integrate an ever-increasing number of subplots, each reflecting some character's vain fantasy. Mosca – who seemingly envisions himself as the all-conquering wily servant of the ancient mode still known as New Comedy — must keep all these incompatible story lines running on the same stage, without collisions. This juggling act earns gasps of admiration as it endures through mounting complications and several near falls, and provides a satisfying series of crashes when Jonson brings it all tumbling to earth at the end.

Volpone opened at the Globe in 1606, with the same company that performed Shakespeare's masterpieces of that period. For one hundred and eighty years following that successful debut (except when the theatres were closed from 1642 to 1660), it was frequently in performance – long after most other Jacobean plays had been forgotten. Since its revival at the Lyric Theatre Hammersmith in 1921 (which won a rave review from T. S. Eliot), *Volpone* has been produced more often than any other non-Shakespearean play of the period, and more often than several of Shakespeare's. It has also inspired opera and musical-comedy versions, film adaptations such as a 1936 French version that followed a 1926 socialist reworking of the play by Stefan Zweig in which Mosca shares the hoarded wealth with the poor, and the 1967 feature film *The Honey Pot*, where Cecil Fox tests three money-hungry mistresses. If these adaptations have anything in common, it is the effort to make *Volpone* a more conventional comedy, softening the cruelty, allowing at least a glimmer of romance and the possibility of a happy ending. But efforts to make this play less cynical and theatrical have usually spoiled it. *Volpone* needs to be savage and stagey to evoke the cut-throat, hypocritical world Jonson saw emerging alongside consumer capitalism.

Epicoene, or the Silent Woman

Four years passed after *Volpone* before Jonson produced another play: *Epicoene, or The Silent Woman*, written and performed in 1609–10. The plot again centres on competition over an inheritance, but it is even harder to blame the characters of *Epicoene* for failing to understand the kind of comedy they are in than it was to blame the gulls in *Volpone*. In the early seventeenth century, comedies almost always built towards a concluding marriage, with the implied promise of renewed life. This promise was accompanied by an atmosphere of forgiveness that restored social cohesion by acknowledging how much human beings finally have in common, through our bodily appetites and our psychological foibles. Who therefore could have expected a vivacious comedy to culminate instead in the undoing of a marriage, with no romantic story to take its place, no normalization of disrupted gender roles, and with its isolated hero wishing the uncle he has scammed a short and lonely life?

Jonson himself repeatedly employed the standard plot of classical New Comedy, in which a wily slave or servant helps a young nobleman marry the young woman he loves by snatching her away from the wealthy old man who covets her. But Jonson is remarkably incapable of depicting romantic tenderness, and here the young aristocrat Dauphine has no interest in getting married. The chief premise of *Epicoene* is that the noise-phobic Morose, angry at his nephew Dauphine, is determined to 'thrust him out' of an inheritance by thrusting himself into a wife. Dauphine – similarly driven by a love of money and mastery rather than love of another person – will subvert that marriage to preserve his inheritance.

This shift changes the play from a reflection of the ancient literary past to the invention of an imminent literary future. Few plays have ever transformed their genre as radically and lastingly as *Epicoene* did. Like most important artistic innovations, it endured some harsh commentary from its original audiences. Yet within a few decades the discerning John Dryden called it 'the greatest and most noble of any pure unmixed comedy in any language', and in his famous diary Samuel Pepys called it 'the best comedy, I think, that ever was wrote'. When King Charles II allowed England's theatres to reopen in 1660 following the collapse of Puritan control, *Epicoene* was apparently the first play performed, and the masterpieces of what is now called Restoration drama were mostly direct descendants of *Epicoene*: witty but cynical comedies of manners in which suave but ruthlessly calculating aristocratic heroes, moving through a decadent world of fools and hypocrites, manoeuvre themselves into opulent legacies.

'Epicoene' means 'having the characteristics of both sexes', and when these Jonsonian fools misunderstand their roles, gender is a major aspect of their errors. Sexual confusion certainly occurs in other comedies, notably in the cross-dressing of Shakespeare's mid-career heroines, but those stories culminate in a restoration of the conventional male-female binary. In *Epicoene*, everyone but the master manipulator has some stubborn form of gender trouble. Mistress Otter violently dominates her husband. The intellectual 'Collegiate' ladies similarly trespass on traditional male authority and female modesty. Within the play's first twenty-three lines, the gender-identity of Clerimont's boy-servant is multiply violated. Later, two rather effeminate men claim to have had sexual intercourse with a woman who isn't a woman, and Morose, seeking to annul his marriage, declares himself sexually impotent. A key fact to bear in mind while following these sexual identity crises is that Jonson wrote in an era when female roles were played by boys, and *Epicoene* was specifically written for one of the all-boy acting companies that were a fad around the start of the seventeenth century (as Shakespeare's hero complains in *Hamlet*).

As in Jonson's other comedies, many characters delude themselves by imagining that they are playing lead roles in some genre other than the satiric comedy Jonson and his clever exploiters are actually staging. Morose seems to fantasize a dumbshow, Mistress Otter insists on being called Princess, and La Foole and Daw are tricked into thinking themselves Damon and Pythias – the classical story of true friendship and love-rivalry that Jonson will mock in the puppet-show at the end of *Bartholmew Fair*. As the master-manipulator Dauphine comments, 'They have nothing, not the use of their senses, but by tradition' (III.iii.82–3). Truewit – whose name convinces himself as well as the audience that he should triumph in Jonson's witty drama – argues that the way to seduce any woman is to 'perform always the second parts to her' (IV.i.105). If all the world's a stage, then playwrights are the ultimate masters.

Several of these characters are humiliated by their 'parts' in another sense as well. Dauphine is broken down by the lustful 'Collegiates' into a *blason* of body parts. Daw and Morose are threatened with amputations. Mistress Otter's 'teeth were made i' the Blackfriars, both her eyebrows i' the Strand, and her hair in Silver Street . . . She takes herself asunder still when she goes to bed, into some twenty boxes, and about next day noon is put together again, like a great German clock' (IV.ii.79–85). Eventually the private parts become essential to the play's plot as well as to its commentary on social and theatrical conventions. The shifting relationship between the living body and its social performances launches a whole new era of English comedy.

The Alchemist

The Alchemist exposes the modern world as a cynical scam worked on a crowd of dreamers. The dupes surrender their money, their honesty, even their perceptions, in exchange for the conspirators' promise to fulfil their secret fantasies. Jonson thus encourages his audience to identify instead with Lovewit, forgiving their wily, naughty servant Jonson as Lovewit forgives his wily, naughty servant Jeremy who (disguised as Face) uses

Lovewit's house to stage ridiculous but profitable little dramas. The promises of Face and his ally Subtle to convert lead into gold are actually a cover for a more realistic project of converting human follies into profit; Jonson's representation of that alchemical fraud is similarly a cover for an effort to transform the base drama of his time profitably into something resembling its classical Golden Age.

Like the theatres of Elizabethan London, Lovewit's house was supposed to be closed when the frequency of deaths from the plague reached a certain threshold. The conspirators there (according to the acrostic Argument preceding the play) form something like an Elizabethan theatre company: 'they here contract, / Each for a share, and all begin to act. / Much company they draw, and much abuse,' until 'they, and all in fume are gone.' The house of glories is merely a grimy shed once the enchantment of language has ceased to fill it (V.v.38–42). Even the location of the house, in Blackfriars, suggests a connection with the private theatre the King's Men had taken over in 1608, where many of Jonson's and Shakespeare's later works were performed.

As Jonson converts the stage into Lovewit's house, Face/Jeremy converts Lovewit's house into an over-populated Jacobean stage. There the conspirators produce a kind of classic farce of increasingly frantic efforts to keep various lies concealed by keeping the people who have been told those lies from encountering each other. Coleridge declared it to be one of the three best-designed plots in all of literature. The house is full of tales of the sort that packed Elizabethan theatres and bookstalls: versions of Marlowe's dramas of extravagant riches and supernatural pleasures, Webster's and Middleton's dramas of dynastic marriage, Shakespeare's and Spenser's adult fairy tales, even Deloney's chronicles of triumphant middle-class commercial diligence.

The first victim, Dapper, makes a good example. The conspirators easily convince him that he is the hero of a fairy tale, embraced by a doting Fairy Queen. Ten years earlier London audiences had laughed at the egotistical Bottom's easy acceptance of his ludicrous match with Titania in Shakespeare's *Midsummer Night's Dream*; now that same literary fantasy makes an ass of Dapper. As the gulling continues, Dapper's will to believe induces him to accept a stinking privy as 'Fortune's privy lodgings' (III.v.79), a dead mouse as a delicacy from the Fairy Queen's private trencher (III.v.65), pickpockets as fairies, a mugging as a purifying ritual, the prostitute Dol Common as the Queen herself, and an instruction to 'Kiss her departing part' (V.iv.57) as evidence of her favour.

What makes Dapper's pitiful cry near the end of the play so funny – 'For God's sake, when will her Grace be at leisure?' (V.iii.65) – is our recognition that this pathetic figure has been clinging to his ridiculous dream all this time amidst the choking stench, and speaks up only in a mannerly way that seeks not to offend the goddess who offered him this lodging and this provender. The fact that he has been long forgotten, and must shout his plea from somewhere backstage, extends the joke about his fairy-tale delusions: the play he imagines is simply not being performed on this stage on this day. Similar fates befall the aspiring shopkeeper Drugger, the aspiring roaring boy Kastril, his aspiring international-noblewoman sister Dame Pliant, and the aspiring Puritan prophet Ananias.

Sir Epicure Mammon deludes himself with even greater romantic and pietistic fantasies, as if he were a Marlowe protagonist: a Tamburlaine in his thirst for universal conquest, a Barabas in his absolute greed, a Faustus in his determination magically to reshape the world according to his desires. Even his visions of pleasure are actually a string of allusions to Seneca, Aristophanes, Juvenal, Pliny, and several other classical authors. And his poses as a Neoplatonic, Petrarchan, and Metaphysical love-poet look all the more ridiculous because the wealthy widow he believes he is courting is really only Dol Common in a fancy gown.

Surly recognizes these deceits, but complacently casts himself as the fraud-busting hero of a moral comedy. Face wisely concentrates instead on casting Surly as the villain of the formulaic dramas various other characters have playing in their minds. Surly's choice of a dandified Spanish costume is unfortunate, because it encourages Drugger to interpret him as a rival for Dame Pliant, Kastril to interpret him as a competing quarreller, and Ananias to interpret him as a Catholic and therefore as the Satanic enemy against whom Puritans directed their internal allegories. Surly had planned to call an end to all their plays by injecting truth and common sense into Lovewit's house, but he finds himself absorbed into those plays instead. What would serve as the conclusion of many more ordinary didactic plays – Surly's detection of the abuses and his gallant rescue of the maiden – thus becomes merely an interruption that serves to emphasize Jonson's insight into self-dramatizing human nature. Surly's failure compels him to discover bitterly that people would rather be told grand ridiculous lies about their own splendour than plain moral truths about their own folly.

In the final act, the conspirators are still busy sorting the pelf they gained by playing to the hackneyed fantasies of a seemingly unlimited supply of gulls who dream of pirate voyages and sudden transformations into the aristocracy (V.iv.110–16). The mob that gathers outside Lovewit's house shouts so many different accusations about what occurred there that the officers would have to arrest the whole costume-shop to investigate them; and even then the evidence would be hard to find, since the illusions were finally provided as much by the desiring imaginations of the gulls as by the shreds of disguise used by the conspirators.

Jonson's audience is left with an easy choice between identifying with these fools in demanding a conventional resolution of the plot, or identifying instead with the aptly named Lovewit, who comes home and promptly and playfully seizes all the sexual and financial profits. He replaces the conspirators not because he is more socially ethical than they are, which wouldn't be difficult, but because he is even more self-aware as a theatrical improviser. There is still an alchemist at work in the house in Blackfriars; he is named Ben Jonson, and he mocks the naive Londoners who gather there, even while he transforms the leaden formulas they bring to him into his own satiric gold.

Bartholmew Fair

Bartholmew Fair shows Jonson in a far more accepting mood. It celebrates the energies of life and the varieties of art rather than those who exploit or condemn them. Instead of mortifying all forms of play other than Jonson's own, as the previous comedies do, this conclusion seems to say: let the shows go on, let the world be playful. In the final words before the Epilogue, the formerly overbearing judge overseeing the fair invites his community to 'have the rest of the play at home', and Jonson finally seems willing to allow art to infiltrate life for his audience also.

This change probably reflects a shift in cultural conditions, rather than any radical mellowing of Jonson's bumptious personality. When rival playwrights were the chief threat to his artistic career, he ridiculed those playwrights. By 1613, however, the chief threat to any English playwright was the Puritan movement, which was already campaigning to close down the theatres, and would succeed in doing so completely a few decades later. Perhaps Jonson recognized that, by deriding characters for naively mimicking actions they had seen onstage, he had unwittingly been playing into the hands of those censors. The Puritan accusation that theatre encouraged idolatry was close kin to Plato's warning that drama encouraged imitation of the often corrupt actions it portrayed. Both arguments assumed that people could not keep track of the difference between a representation and an absolute reality.

So, once Jonson realized he had become an unwitting witness for the prosecution of theatre, he created *Bartholmew Fair*, in which a Puritan named Zeal-of-the-Land Busy at first condemns stage shows but is then converted into a man who wants the puppet-show to 'go on. For I am changed, and will become a beholder with you' (V.v.101–2). Instead of humiliating even his silliest dramatic competitors, Jonson uses this comedy to humiliate censorious authority-figures: at one point the Puritan ranter Busy, the irritable tutor Wasp, and Justice Overdo, who tries to control the 'enormities' of the Fair, are all sitting humiliated in the stocks together onstage. Everyone who passes judgement on others ends up vulnerable to judgement, as the Lord's Prayer would have warned.

Jonson thus establishes a middle ground: *Bartholmew Fair* endorses neither these condemners, nor the similarly indiscriminate enthusiasts, of popular entertainments. The petty Wasp is as foolish to reject the fair completely as his childish student Bartholomew Cokes is to embrace it completely. But, finally forced to choose between narrow-minded enemies of plays, such as Busy, and nearly mindless popularizing playwrights, such as Littlewit, who give those censors so much ammunition, Jonson chooses vitality over purity. His huge hunger for life and his fascination with the endless objects of the world triumph over his satiric recognition that these things are grotesque, that they ruin any claim to high classical dignity. Jonson thus comes to accept three forms of mindlessness he had spent decades trying to condemn and suppress: lowbrow popular theatre, common human appetites, and the boisterous side of his own personality. No wonder this comedy radiates such a warm release of energy.

The repudiation of authorities throws open the question of authorship. The marriage licence – the licence, in effect to write a comedy – passes chaotically from Cokes to Wasp to Edgworth to Winwife. Control of the puppet-show similarly tumbles along from Littlewit to Leatherhead to Busy to Dionysius to Overdo to Quarlous. But Jonson has been in control all along, and he is still testifying to the 'enormities' of life in seventeenth-century London. The stage becomes a wildly overpopulated, almost nightmarishly carnal scene, like a Brueghel painting, where everything is up for grabs. Before the play really even begins, it invites us to question whether the authority of money is legitimate, through a contract the stage-keeper offers the audience allowing them to judge the play proportionately to how much they paid for their tickets. The play that follows becomes a crescendo of commerce that exposes almost everyone as cheaters, fools, hypocrites, and/or madmen, but this time we laugh at them affectionately.

Jonson still mocks the tendency of his characters to mistake themselves for famous heroes of some other genre. Because of his name, Bartholmew Cokes thinks the fair celebrates him, and he sets about buying it. When he suffers setbacks in that project, he sees himself as the martyr St Bartholomew. The ranting Busy depicts himself as Odysseus leading his crew safely past the allures of the Sirens and Circe, or as the holy man leading Progressing Pilgrims through Vanity Fair, safe from the idolatry of gingerbread-men and puppets. Overdo envisions himself as Hercules wrapped up in Columbus and Magellan; and his trick of disguising himself so he can spy on misconduct and then use that information when he resumes his official role was a common plot device in works such as Shakespeare's *Measure for Measure*, and had actually been recently attempted by London's Lord Mayor.

The way Jonson sets up his fairground would have recalled the late-medieval mystery cycles – which, like the fair, were annual occasions that utilised booths to play distinctive 'scenes'. The puppet-show that concludes this play is inane, yet it also resembles Jonson's comedies in several important ways. It recasts classical literary formulas into their Jacobean equivalents; it reduces people into mere puppets of their humoral fluids and their formulaic literary fantasies; it degrades human life towards creaturely scatology (yet again, Jonson depicts love as a mix of competition and base appetites); and it sets the ideals of poetic language against the cruder fascinations of spontaneous contemporary speech.

Teeming with life in all its exuberance and corruption, rousing joy in the human spirit and creative imagination right alongside sorrow at the narrow earthbound materialism into which those virtues are diverted, *Bartholmew Fair* is the play in which this great comic playwright most fully embraces the crazy spectacle of the world.

Jonson surely believed he was writing these comedies to come to life on the stage for his London contemporaries, not to be studied on the page by people in distant times and places for whom the local references would require footnotes. In performance, these plays are certainly among the most hilarious ever written. They are less heartwarming than Shakespeare's, but their ruthless exposure of human greed, vanity, and stupidity generates far more laughter. See them on stage when you get the chance. For now, read them with the stage in mind, or act them out, and prepare to find, miraculously woven together, a profound lamentation and even more profound celebration of the human race.

FURTHER READING

Editions
Ben Jonson, *Ben Jonson*, ed. C. H. Herford, Percy Simpson, and Evelyn Simpson, 1925–52.
————, *The Cambridge Edition of the Works of Ben Jonson*, ed. David Bevington, Martin Butler, and Ian Donaldson, 2012.

For individual plays, the New Mermaids series, the Revels series, and the Yale Ben Jonson are generally very good, with informative introductions.

Biography
David Riggs, *Ben Jonson: A Life*, 1989.
Ian Donaldson, *Ben Jonson: A Life*, 2011.

General Studies
Brian Gibbons, *Jacobean City Comedy*, 1980.
Anne Barton, *Ben Jonson: Dramatist*, 1984.
Robert N. Watson, *Ben Jonson's Parodic Strategy: Literary Imperialism in the Comedies*, 1987.
Russ McDonald, *Shakespeare & Jonson, Jonson & Shakespeare*, 1988.
The Ben Jonson Journal. 1994–.
Robert N. Watson, ed., *Critical Essays on Ben Jonson*, 1997.
Melinda Gough, 'Jonson's Siren Stage', *SP* 96.1 (Winter 1999), 68–95.
Richard Cave, Elizabeth Schafer, and Brian Woolland, *Ben Jonson and Theatre: Performance, Practice and Theory*, 1999.
Jeffrey Masten, 'Ben Jonson's Head', *Shakespeare Studies* 28 (2000), 160–8.
Jeffrey Knapp, 'Jonson, Shakespeare, and the Religion of Players', *Shakespeare Survey: An Annual Survey of Shakespeare Studies and Production* 54 (2001), 57–70.
Joseph Loewenstein, *Ben Jonson and Possessive Authorship*, 2002.
Lorna Hutson, 'Liking Men: Ben Jonson's Closet Opened', *ELH* 71.4 (Winter 2004), 1065–96.
Mark Albert Johnston, 'Prosthetic Absence in Ben Jonson's *Epicoene, The Alchemist*, and *Bartholomew Fair*', *English Literary Renaissance* 37.3 (Autumn 2007), 401–28.
Sean McEvoy, *Ben Jonson, Renaissance Dramatist*, 2008.
Julie Sanders, *Ben Jonson in Context*, 2010.

Volpone

Harold Bloom, ed., *Ben Jonson's 'Volpone, or the Fox'; Modern Critical Interpretations*, 1988.

Jonathan Gil Harris, '"I Am Sailing to My Port, Uh! Uh! Uh! Uh!": The Pathologies of Transmigration in *Volpone*', *Literature and Medicine* 20.2 (Fall 2001), 109–32.

Katharine Eisaman Maus, 'Idol and Gift in *Volpone*', *ELR* 35.3 (Autumn 2005), 429–53.

Richard Dutton, *'Volpone' and the Gunpowder Plot*, 2008.

Oliver Hennessey, 'Jonson's Joyless Economy: Theorizing Motivation and Pleasure in *Volpone*', *ELR* 38.1 (Winter 2008), 83–105.

Lisa Klotz, 'Ben Jonson's Legal Imagination in *Volpone*', *SEL* 51.2 (Spring 2011), 385–408.

Robert N. Watson, 'The Fox and his Pause: Punctuating Consciousness in Jonson's *Volpone*', *Close-Reading the Renaissance* (2012), 199–207.

Epicoene

Marjorie Swann, 'Refashioning Society in Ben Jonson's *Epicoene*', *SEL* 38.2 (Spring 1998), 297–315.

Adam Zucker, 'The Social Logic of Ben Jonson's *Epicoene*', *Renaissance Drama* 33 (2004), 37–62.

Reuben Sanchez, '"Things Like Truths, Well Feigned": Mimesis and Secrecy in Jonson's *Epicoene*', *Comparative Drama* 40.3 (Fall 2006), 313–36.

Mimi Yiu, 'Sounding the Space between Men: Choric and Choral Cities in Ben Jonson's *Epicoene; or, The Silent Woman*', *PMLA* 122.1 (2007), 72–88.

Mathew Martin, 'Wasting Time in Ben Jonson's *Epicoene*', *SP* 105.1 (Winter 2008), 83–102.

Adrian Curtin, 'Dumb Reading: The Noise of the Mute in Jonson's *Epicoene*', *Comparative Drama* 43.1 (Spring 2009), 45–62.

Blaine Greteman, 'Coming of Age on Stage: Jonson's *Epicoene* and the Politics of Childhood in Early Stuart England', *ELH* 79.1 (Spring 2012), 135–60.

The Alchemist

Cheryl Lynn Ross, 'The Plague of *The Alchemist*', *Renaissance Quarterly* 41.3 (Autumn 1988), 439–58.

Richard Levin, 'Another "Source" for *The Alchemist* and Another Look at Source Studies', *ELR* 28.2 (Spring 1998), 210–30.

Anthony J. Ouellette, '*The Alchemist* and the Emerging Adult Private Playhouse', *SEL* 45.2 (Spring 2005), 375–99.

John Shanahan, 'Ben Jonson's *Alchemist* and Early Modern Laboratory Space', *Journal for Early Modern Cultural Studies* 8.1 (Spring–Summer 2008), 35–66.

Erin Julian and Helen Ostovich, eds, *The Alchemist: A Critical Reader*, 2013.

Bartholmew Fair

G. M. Pinciss, '*Bartholomew Fair* and Jonsonian Tolerance', *SEL* 35.2 (Spring 1995), 345–59.

Kathleen Lynch, 'The Dramatic Festivity of *Bartholomew Fair*', *Medieval and Renaissance Drama in England: An Annual Gathering of Research, Criticism and Reviews* 8 (1996), 128–45.

Paul A. Cantor, 'In Defense of the Marketplace: Spontaneous Order in Jonson's *Bartholomew Fair*', *Ben Jonson Journal: Literary Contexts in the Age of Elizabeth, James and Charles* 8 (2001), 23–64.

David Weil Baker, '"Master of the Monuments": Memory and Erasure in Jonson's *Bartholomew Fair*', *ELR* 31.2 (Spring 2001), 266–87.

Alison A. Chapman, 'Flaying Bartholomew: Jonson's Hagiographic Parody', *Modern Philology: A Journal Devoted to Research in Medieval and Modern Literature* 101.4 (May 2004), 511–41.

Ian McAdam, 'The Puritan Dialectic of Law and Grace in *Bartholomew Fair*', *SEL* 46.2 (Spring 2006), 415–33.

Kirsty Milne, 'Reforming *Bartholomew Fair*: Bunyan, Jonson, and the Puritan Point of View', *Huntington Library Quarterly: Studies in English and American History and Literature* 74.2 (2011), 289–308.

ABBREVIATIONS

Works by Ben Jonson

Alch.	*The Alchemist*
B.F.	*Bartholmew Fair*
Cat.	*Catiline his Conspiracy*
C.R.	*Cynthia's Revels*
D. is A.	*The Devil is an Ass*
Disc	*Timber, or Discoveries*
E.M.I.	*Every Man In His Humour*
E.M.O.	*Every Man Out Of His Humour*
Epig.	*Epigrams*
Hym.	*Hymenaei*
M.L.	*The Magnetic Lady, or Humours Reconciled*
M.V.	*Mercury Vindicated from the Alchemists*
N.I.	*The New Inn, or The Light Heart*
N.N.W.	*News from the New World*
N.T.	*Neptune's Triumph*
Poet.	*The Poetaster*
Sej.	*Sejanus*
S.N.	*The Staple of News*
T.T.	*The Tale of a Tub*
Und.	*Underwood*
Volp.	*Volpone*

References

Abbott	E. A. Abbott, *A Shakespearian Grammar*, 2nd edn, 1870.
Beaurline	L. A. Beaurline, ed., *Epicoene*, 1966.
Chambers	E. K. Chambers, *The Elizabethan Stage*, 4 vols, 1923.
Delrio	Martin Delrio, *Disquisitiones Magicae*, 1608.
ELH	*English Literary History.*
ELR	*English Literary Renaissance.*
F	Folio.
Gerritsen	Johann Gerritsen, 'Stansby and Jonson Produce a Folio: A Preliminary Account', *English Studies* 40 (1959), 52–5.
Gifford	William Gifford, ed., *The Works of Ben Jonson*, 9 vols, 1816.
H&S	C. H. Herford, Percy Simpson, and Evelyn Simpson, eds, *Ben Jonson*, 1925–52.
Henry	Aurelia Henry, ed., *Epicoene or The Silent Woman*, *Yale Studies in English* XXXI, 1906.

Horsman	E. A. Horsman, ed., *Bartholomew Fair*, The Revels Plays, 1960.
Kernan	Alvin B. Kernan, ed., *Volpone*, The Yale Ben Jonson, 1962.
Nares	Robert Nares, *A Glossary, or Collection of Words, Phrases and Names*, 1822.
Nashe	*The Works of Thomas Nashe*, ed. R. B. McKerrow, 5 vols; 1904–10 (*B.F.*); rev. edn 1966 (*Alch.*).
OED	*Oxford English Dictionary.*
Parker	Brian Parker ed., *Volpone*, rev. edn, The Revels Plays, 1999.
Partridge	Edward Partridge, ed., *Epicoene*, The Yale Ben Jonson, 1971.
PMLA	*Publication of the Modern Language Association of America.*
Q	Quarto.
s.d.	stage direction.
SEL	*Studies in English Literature, 1500–1900.*
s.p.	speech prefix.
SP	*Studies in Philology.*
Spencer	Hazelton Spencer, ed., *Elizabethan Plays*, 1933.
Stow	John Stow, *A Survey of London*, 1598, ed. Henry B. Wheatley, 1912 (*B.F.*); rev. edn 1603, ed. C. L. Kingsford, 1908 (*Alch.*); continued by A. Munday, 1618 (*Epicoene*).
Sugden	E. H. Sugden, *A Topographical Dictionary to the Works of Shakespeare and his Fellow Dramatists*, 1925.
T.C.B.	*Theatrum Chemicum Britannicum*, ed. Elias Ashmole, 1652.
Tilley	M. P. Tilley, *A Dictionary of the Proverbs in England in the Sixteenth and Seventeenth Centuries*, 1950.
Upton	John Upton, *Remarks on Three Plays of Benjamin Jonson, viz Volpone, Epicoene, and The Alchimist*, 1749.
Waith	Eugene M. Waith, ed., *Bartholomew Fair*, The Yale Ben Jonson, 1963.

BEN: IONSON

his

VOLPONE

Or

THE FOXE.

—Simul & iucunda, & idonea dicere vitæ.

Printed for *Thomas Thorppe.*
1607.

THE ARGUMENT

V *olpone, childless, rich, feigns sick, despairs,*
O *ffers his state to hopes of several heirs,*
L *ies languishing; his parasite receives*
P *resents of all, assures, deludes; then weaves*
O *ther cross-plots, which ope' themselves, are told.*   5
N *ew tricks for safety are sought; they thrive; when, bold,*
E *ach tempts th'other again, and all are sold.*

The Argument
As in the comedies of Plautus, the first letters form an acrostic of the play's title.

2   *state* estate, property.
5   *ope'* open.
      told exposed.
7   *sold* betrayed, ruined

The Persons of the Comedy

VOLPONE, *a Magnifico* Volpone meant 'an old fox' and hence 'an old craftie, slie, subtle companion, sneaking lurking wily deceiver' (according to a popular 1598 dictionary, *A Worlde of Wordes*, by John Florio, to whom Jonson sent a copy of Q thanking him for 'the aid of his Muses'). A *Magnifico* was a name for a Venetian magnate or plutocrat, and also an alternative name for the Pantalone character in the *commedia dell'arte*. Though Jonson's Epistle warns against such 'applications', and editors have generally dismissed this one, several commentators in Jonson's own time suspected that Volpone was based on Thomas Sutton, the wealthiest commoner in London, and a controversial figure whose lack of direct heirs apparently allowed him to profit by manipulating those who were scheming to gain his legacy, which eventually founded the Charterhouse hospital (as Volpone's wealth finally goes to 'the hospital of the *Incurabili* at V.xii.120).

MOSCA, *his Parasite* Mosca meant a kind of fly, and became thereby a term for human parasites, those who live and feed on others (usually by servile flattery); as references to demonic possession accumulate later in the play, we may also suspect a reference to Beelzebub, 'Lord of the Flies'.

VOLTORE, *an Advocate* Voltore meant 'a ravenous bird called a vultur' (Florio), and – because vultures feed on dead animals – the name was applied to legacy-hunters. It was also applied to persuasive lawyers; an Advocate was the equivalent of an English barrister or American defence attorney.

CORBACCIO Italian for a raven, a bird believed (as in Psalm 147, Proverbs 30:17, and Luke 12:24) to neglect its offspring, who (like Bonario) therefore had to rely on heaven for protection; its croaking was thought to signal death.

CORVINO Italian for a small crow – an emblem of marital fidelity, and an enemy of the fox.

NANO Italian for dwarf; dwarves were popular as court jesters.

CASTRONE 'a gelded man' (Florio), one who has been castrated, often to preserve a high singing voice or to preclude sexual intercourse.

ANDROGYNO 'he that is both male and female' (Florio).

POLITIC WOULD-BE a would-be schemer in affairs of state, one who wishes (like many English Renaissance travellers) to be thought important, clever, prudent and worldly. Shortened to Pol, his name links him to the parrot, which suits his mindless efforts to mimic the fashionable phrases and sophisticated schemes of those around him.

PEREGRINE a traveller; also a kind of hawk, birds which Jonson's Epigram LXXXV says 'strike ignorance' and 'make fools their quarry'; an emblematic tradition made them the opposite of the tortoise.

CELIA literally, 'heavenly one', celestial; sometimes the name of the heroine in the *commedia dell'arte*.

BONARIO 'debonaire, honest, good, uncorrupt' (Florio), though it can also thereby imply 'naive'.

FINE MADAM WOULD-BE cf. Jonson's satiric Epigram LXII 'To Fine Lady Would-Be'; she probably has a large red beak of a nose that emphasizes her kinship to Pol the parrot.

AVOCATORI Venetian officials who served as prosecutors and sometimes (as in Jonson's version) as judges.

COMMANDATORI lower officials who enforced subpoenas summoning witnesses and malefactors to court hearings.

THE PERSONS OF THE COMEDY

[*in order of appearance*]

VOLPONE, *a Magnifico*
MOSCA, *his Parasite*
VOLTORE, *an Advocate*
CORBACCIO, *an old Gentleman*
CORVINO, *a Merchant*
NANO, *a Dwarf*
CASTRONE, *an Eunuch*
ANDROGYNO, *a Hermaphrodite*
POLITIC WOULD-BE, *a Knight* [*from England*]
PEREGRINE, *a Gentleman-traveller* [*from England*]
CROWD
CELIA, *the Merchant's wife*
SERVATOR[I], *Servant*[*s*]
BONARIO, *a young Gentleman,* [Corbaccio's son]
FINE MADAM WOULD-BE, *the Knight's wife*
WOMEN, [*Attendants waiting on* Lady Would-Be]
AVOCATORI, *four Magistrates*
NOTARIO, *the Court clerk*
COMMANDATORI, *Officers*
MERCATORI, *Merchants*

The Scene: Venice

PROLOGUE

Now, luck God send us, and a little wit
  Will serve, to make our play hit,
According to the palates of the season:
  Here is rhyme, not empty of reason.
This we were bid to credit, from our poet,   5
  Whose true scope, if you would know it,
In all his poems, still, hath been this measure:
  To mix profit, with your pleasure;
And not as some (whose throats their envy failing)
  Cry hoarsely, 'All he writes, is railing',   10
And, when his plays come forth, think they can flout them,
  With saying, 'He was a year about them'.
To these there needs no lie, but this his creature,
  Which was, two months since, no feature;
And, though he dares give them five lives to mend it,   15
  'Tis known, five weeks fully penned it,
From his own hand, without a co-adjutor,
  Novice, journeyman, or tutor.
Yet, thus much I can give you, as a token
  Of his play's worth: no eggs are broken;   20

Prologue
This Prologue may be spoken by Nano, Androgyno, and/or Castrone, since it shares the clunky
poetic meter of their show in I.ii, and Mosca and Volpone will be needed onstage in character
as soon as the Prologue ends.

   1   *God* This word was changed to a meaningless 'yet' in F, probably because of the 1606
        Act against Blasphemy.
   5   *credit* believe, understand.
   6   *scope* intention.
   8   *profit* didactic value, as in Horace's formula of *utile dolci*; but perhaps quipping also
        on the playwright's financial motive in writing for the public theatre.
   10   *railing* a tirade of abuse, complaint, and criticism; theatrical rivals such as Dekker
        and Marston voiced this objection to Jonson.
   12   *about them* in writing them; Jonson proudly contrasted his careful workmanship
        with the hasty play-writing of his competitors, including Shakespeare, but here he
        boasts that he can also outdo them in writing quickly.
   13   *To these . . . creature* To refute these critics requires no lie, only this play he has
        created; or, he does not need to call them liars – 'give the lie' – only show this play.
   17–18 *co-adjutor . . . tutor* Various kinds of assistant, each common in the play-factory that
        was the Elizabethan public theatre, ranging from a full collaborator to an apprentice,
        a hack assistant and scene doctor, or a mentor and corrector.

Nor quaking custards with fierce teeth affrighted,
  Wherewith your rout are so delighted;
Nor hales he in a gull, old ends reciting,
  To stop gaps in his loose writing,
With such a deal of monstrous, and forced action,   25
  As might make Bedlam a faction;
Nor made he his play for jests stol'n from each table,
  But makes jests, to fit his fable.
And so presents quick comedy, refined,
  As best critics have designed: 30
The laws of time, place, persons he observeth,
  From no needful rule he swerveth.
All gall, and copp'ras, from his ink he draineth,
  Only, a little salt remaineth;
Wherewith, he'll rub your cheeks, till, red with laughter, 35
  They shall look fresh, a week after.

21 *quaking custards* the stock cowards of comedy, with reference also to pie-in-the-face
    slapstick and the fool's leap into a giant custard at the Lord Mayor's banquet; here,
    as in *Poetaster,* V.iii.525, Jonson mocks the phrase 'Let custards quake' from his rival
    Marston's *Scourge of Villainy* (1599), an example of what was called 'biting satire'.
22 *your rout* the rabble, 'your basic mob'.
23–4 *Nor hales . . . writing* Nor will this playwright haul in a gullible fool reciting stock
    phrases or bits from other plays.
    make Bedlam a faction add a new group to the madhouse, or competitor to the show
    people went to see there, or possibly, gain the endorsement of madmen; Bedlam was
    the common name of the insane asylum of St Mary of Bethlehem in London.
27 *jests stol'n from each table* jokes stolen like random leftovers from a feast, or picked
    up as table-talk, or plagiarized from a jest-book.
29 *quick* lively.
31 *The laws of time, place, persons* Sixteenth-century Italian critics developed precepts
    from Aristotle's *Poetics* into an insistence on the dramatic unities, which lent
    verisimilitude and thus believability to a play by having it all occur in a single day
    and area, with suitable and consistent character-types (since *Volpone* has a distinct
    subplot, Jonson conveniently omits the law governing unity of action here); Jonson
    often used his adherence to these laws to attack his theatrical rivals, who generally
    did not observe them.
33 *gall, and copp'ras* substances used to make ink, but standing here for animosity
    (attributed to the gall-bladder) and bitterness (ferrous sulphate, known as copperas,
    tastes extremely harsh).
34 *salt* sediment; edible salt was a metaphor for pungent wit, and was also used in
    cleaning and food preservation, leading to 'fresh' in line 36.

ACT I, SCENE i

[Enter] MOSCA, *[pulling back the curtains to discover]*
VOLPONE *[in bed]*

VOLPONE
Good morning to the day; and, next, my gold:
Open the shrine, that I may see my saint.

*[*MOSCA *uncovers the treasure]*

Hail the world's soul, and mine. More glad than is
The teeming earth, to see the longed-for sun
Peep through the horns of the celestial Ram,   5
Am I, to view thy splendour, darkening his;
That, lying here, amongst my other hoards,
Show'st like a flame by night; or like the day
Struck out of chaos, when all darkness fled
Unto the centre. O thou son of Sol,   10
But brighter than thy father, let me kiss,
With adoration, thee, and every relic
Of sacred treasure in this blessed room.

---

  0   s.d. Though his entrance could be delayed until just before he speaks, Mosca prob-
       ably enters here, perhaps opening the curtains around Volpone's bed, or opening
       curtains to admit the morning sun. Bracketed stage directions are merely editorial
       suggestions, The other stage directions were mostly added, probably by Jonson
       himself, in the 1616 Folio.
  2   *shrine ... saint* Volpone asks Mosca to open curtains concealing the gold, to which
       Volpone then addresses a kind of matins prayer, which would normally have been
       addressed to God in praise of the morning sun. His subsequent speeches are per-
       meated with religious language blasphemously redirected toward gold.
  3   *world's soul* the Platonic *anima mundi*, but punning on *sol* – the French word for the
       sun; Volpone sees gold (which alchemists called 'the son of Sol', as at line 10 below)
       as the soul of worldly desires; *sol* was also the name of a French coin (as at IV.v.97
       below).
  4   *teeming* full of life, and ready to give birth.
  5   *horns ... Ram* Aries in the zodiac, the beginning of spring, when the increasing
       sunlight nurtures renewed life.
  6   *thy splendour ... his* the gold's splendour making the sun seem dim by comparison.
  7   *hoards* secret treasures, presumably including jewels and silver plate.
9–10   *Struck ... centre* Established amid the primal Chaos, driving all darkness to the
       centre of the earth (described in the opening of Genesis).
 10   *son of Sol* in alchemy, the sun was described as the father of gold.

Well did wise poets, by thy glorious name,
Title that age which they would have the best,   15
Thou being the best of things, and far transcending
All style of joy, in children, parents, friends,
Or any other waking dream on earth.
Thy looks when they to Venus did ascribe,
They should have giv'n her twenty thousand Cupids;   20
Such are thy beauties, and our loves! Dear saint,
Riches, the dumb god that giv'st all men tongues;
That canst do nought, and yet mak'st men do all things;
The price of souls; even hell, with thee to boot,
Is made worth heaven! Thou art virtue, fame,   25
Honour, and all things else! Who can get thee,
He shall be noble, valiant, honest, wise –

MOSCA

And what he will, sir. Riches are in fortune
A greater good than wisdom is in nature.

VOLPONE

True, my beloved Mosca. Yet, I glory   30
More in the cunning purchase of my wealth,
Than in the glad possession, since I gain

14–15   *thy glorious name ... best* The great poets called the first and best period in human
        history 'the Golden Age' – the classical equivalent of the Christian Garden of Eden;
        e.g. Ovid's *Metamorphoses*, I.89–112 and XV.96 ff.
16–20   When Seneca translated the portion of Euripides' *Danae* on which this passage is
        based (*Epistles* CXV.14), he reported that Euripides had to placate the original
        audience by assuring them that this impious greedy speaker would be punished –
        very much the same promise Jonson makes in the Epistle accompanying *Volpone*
        (lines 121–4) (Parker).
19–20   *Venus ... Cupids* the goddess often called golden – *aurea Venus* – by Homer and
        classical Latin poets would need to have many supplementary beauties (typified by
        the son she produced, the god of love) to be worthy of that adjective; but Volpone
        is also unwittingly confessing that he has perverted the love inspired (in the classical
        tradition) by Cupid into the greed defined (in the Christian tradition) as *cupiditas*.
   22   *dumb* mute. Compare the proverbs 'when gold speaks every tongue is silent' (Tilley
        G295) and 'silence is golden'.
   23   *That ... things* Recalling Aristotle's definition of divinity as the unmoved mover
        (Parker).
   24   *with thee to boot* with gold as a compensation (playing perhaps also on 'booty', stolen
        treasure); where Christ's sacrifice had paid 'the price of souls', gold can buy them
        back for damnation.
   28   *what he will* whatever he desires.
28–9   *Riches ... nature* It is better to be wealthy than wise (playing on a conventional
        debate about the relative importance of nature and fortune).

No common way: I use no trade, no venture;
I wound no earth with ploughshares; fat no beasts
To feed the shambles; have no mills for iron,   35
Oil, corn, or men, to grind 'em into powder;
I blow no subtle glass; expose no ships
To threat'nings of the furrow-facèd sea;
I turn no monies, in the public bank;
Nor usure private.

MOSCA   No, sir, nor devour   40
Soft prodigals. You shall ha' some will swallow
A melting heir, as glibly as your Dutch
Will pills of butter, and ne'er purge for't;
Tear forth the fathers of poor families
Out of their beds, and coffin them, alive,   45
In some kind, clasping prison, where their bones
May be forthcoming, when the flesh is rotten.
But your sweet nature doth abhor these courses:
You loathe, the widow's, or the orphan's tears
Should wash your pavements; or their piteous cries   50
Ring in your roofs, and beat the air for vengeance.

VOLPONE
Right, Mosca, I do loathe it.

MOSCA   And besides, sir,
You are not like a thresher, that doth stand
With a huge flail, watching a heap of corn,
And, hungry, dares not taste the smallest grain,   55

---

33   *venture* speculative business scheme.
35   *shambles* slaughterhouse.
37   *subtle glass* Venice was (and still is) famous for its artistic glass-blowers.
38   *furrow-facèd* covered with dangerous waves.
39   *turn* exchange.
40   *usure private* loan-sharking; as Shakespeare also shows, Venice was a hot-bed of usury in the Renaissance.
41   *Soft prodigals* Gullible spendthrifts; foolish heirs are often cheated by clever urban operators in the plays of this period, especially Jonson's.
42   *melting* wasteful (continuing also the play on their 'soft' edibility, one of countless cannibalistic metaphors in the play).
42–3 *Dutch . . . butter* The Dutch appetite for butter was notorious.
43   *purge* suffer diarrhoea or vomiting, or possibly, need a laxative.
44–7 *Tear . . . rotten* Hold men in debtors' prison, letting them out only when they have been reduced to mere bones.

But feeds on mallows, and such bitter herbs;
Nor like the merchant, who hath filled his vaults
With *Romagnia*, and rich Candian wines,
Yet drinks the lees of Lombard's vinegar;
You will not lie in straw, whilst moths, and worms   60
Feed on your sumptuous hangings and soft beds.
You know the use of riches, and dare give, now,
From that bright heap, to me, your poor observer,
Or to your dwarf, or your hermaphrodite,
Your eunuch, or what other household trifle   65
Your pleasure allows maint'nance.

VOLPONE   Hold thee, Mosca,
   Take, of my hand: [*Gives him money*]
                    thou strik'st on truth, in all;
And they are envious, term thee parasite.
Call forth my dwarf, my eunuch, and my fool,
And let 'em make me sport.

                              [*Exit* MOSCA]
                    What should I do,   70
But cocker up my genius, and live free
To all delights my fortune calls me to?
I have no wife, no parent, child, ally,
To give my substance to; but whom I make,
Must be my heir; and this makes men observe me,   75
This draws new clients, daily, to my house,
Women, and men, of every sex, and age,
That bring me presents, send me plate, coin, jewels,
With hope, that when I die, which they expect

---

56   *mallows* a common plant family which Pliny (among others) believed to be medicinal.
     Cf. Horace's *Satires* II.3.111–21: 'If beside a huge corn-heap a man were to lie out-
     stretched, keeping ceaseless watch with a big cudgel, yet never dare, hungry though
     he be and owner of it all, to touch one grain thereof, but rather feed like a miser on
     bitter herbs' (Parker).
58   *Romagnia . . . wines* sweet wines from Greece and Crete.
59   *Lombard's vinegar* The wines of Lombardy were notoriously harsh.
63   *observer* lowly, worshipful follower.
66   *Hold thee* Stop talking, and/or, You may hold this coin or jewel.
68   *term* [who] call.
71   *But cocker up my genius* Except indulge my natural talents and tendencies (with a
     suggestion of rousing his genital powers to pleasure).
74   *substance* wealth; *whom I make* whomever I designate.
75   *observe me* treat me reverently.
76   *clients* persons depending on patronage, as in the decadent phase of ancient Rome.
78   *plate* gold or silver dishes.

Each greedy minute, it shall then return   80
Tenfold upon them; whilst some, covetous
Above the rest, seek to engross me, whole,
And counterwork, the one, unto the other,
Contend in gifts, as they would seem, in love;
All which I suffer, playing with their hopes,   85
And am content to coin 'em into profit,
And look upon their kindness, and take more,
And look on that; still, bearing them in hand,
Letting the cherry knock against their lips,
And draw it by their mouths, and back again.   90
How now!

ACT I, SCENE ii

[*Enter* MOSCA,] NANO, ANDROGYNO, CASTRONE

NANO

Now, room for fresh gamesters, who do will you to know,
    They do bring you neither play, nor university show;
And therefore do entreat you, that whatsoever they rehearse,
    May not fare a whit the worse, for the false pace of the verse.

82–4   *engross me ... love* take over my wealth wholesale, and undermine each other, competing in gifts that masquerade as true affection.

85   *suffer* allow.

88   *bearing them in hand* leading them on.

89   *cherry knock against their lips* This refers to a tantalizing game called chop-cherry, much like bobbing for apples.

Act I, Scene ii Like many Renaissance play-texts, the printed *Volpone* seems too long to have been acted in two hours; this scene is often cut by modern directors who favour rapid plot-development over arcane set-pieces.

1   *room* make room.

2   *neither play, nor university show* neither from the public theatre, nor from the academic pastimes or classical revivals performed by the Cambridge and Oxford students Jonson addresses in his Epistle. The cluster of learned references in this scene seem better suited to a university than a general audience.

4   *whit* the slightest bit (with a pun on 'wit', on which the academic plays especially depended).
       false pace Nano is speaking in an awkward old-fashioned type of verse, familiar from medieval drama: rhymed tetrameter couplets, with varying numbers of unstressed syllables.

If you wonder at this, you will wonder more, ere we pass,   5
    For know, here [*Indicating* ANDROGYNO] is enclosed the
      soul of Pythagoras,
That juggler divine, as hereafter shall follow;
    Which Soul (fast, and loose, sir) came first from Apollo,
And was breathed into Aethalides, Mercurius his son,
    Where it had the gift to remember all that ever was done.   10
From thence it fled forth, and made quick transmigration
    To goldy-locked Euphorbus, who was killed, in good fashion,
At the siege of old Troy, by the cuckold of Sparta.
    Hermotimus was next (I find it, in my charta)
To whom it did pass, where no sooner it was missing,   15
    But with one Pyrrhus of Delos, it learned to go a-fishing:
And thence did it enter the Sophist of Greece.
    From Pythagore, she went into a beautiful piece,
Hight Aspasia, the meretrix; and the next toss of her
    Was, again, of a whore, she became a philosopher,   20

---

5   *ere we pass* before we are finished.

6   *Pythagoras* a famous ancient Greek philosopher, whose followers believed in re-incarnation, including across species. The cynical version Volpone's freakish servants perform here echoes Lucian's parody of those beliefs in *The Dream, or The Cock* – a parody which warns against worshipping wealth. So there is a warning for Volpone here, especially since people degrade themselves into lower animals throughout this play. The rest of the speech echoes many Pythagorean doctrines, including the musical order of the cosmos, and the silence and bean-free vegetarianism he demanded from his followers (lines 26–40) (Parker).

7   *juggler* Often a pejorative term for any kind of cheater in this period, though juggling in the modern sense would fit the tricky series of hand-offs that follows.

8   *fast, and loose* hard to pin down; based on a tricky game of guessing whether a belt was actually knotted around a dagger, and hence held fast, or could simply be pulled loose.

9   *Aethalides, Mercurius his son* the herald for Jason's argonauts, Mercury's son (Jonson liked this form of the possessive, though it is based on a false etymology).

12 *goldy-locked Euphorbus* According to *The Iliad*, the Trojan Euphorbus bound up his hair with gold, wounded Patroclus, and was killed by the Spartan king Menelaus (the theft of whose wife provoked the Trojan wars).

14 *Hermotimus* ancient Greek philosopher who probably lived shortly after Pythagoras. *charta* charter, written script or history.

16 *Pyrrhus* perhaps the Greek philosopher who was 'a fisherman of Delos' (Parker).

17 *Sophist of Greece* Pythagoras.

19 *Hight Aspasia, the meretrix* Called Aspasia the courtesan; she was the mistress of the ancient Greek king Pericles.

20 *again* This may refer ahead syntactically to becoming again a philosopher.

Crates the Cynic (as itself doth relate it);
    Since, kings, knights, and beggars, knaves, lords and fools
      gat it,
Besides, ox, and ass, camel, mule, goat, and brock,
    In all which it hath spoke, as in the cobbler's cock.
But I come not here to discourse of that matter,   25
    Or his one, two, or three, or his great oath, 'by quater',
His musics, his trigon, his golden thigh,
    Or his telling how elements shift; but I
Would ask, how of late, thou hast suffered translation,
    And shifted thy coat, in these days of reformation?   30

ANDROGYNO

Like one of the reformed, a fool, as you see,
    Counting all old doctrine heresy.

NANO

But not on thine own forbid meats hast thou ventured?

ANDROGYNO

On fish, when first a Carthusian I entered.

NANO

Why, then thy dogmatical silence hath left thee?   35

ANDROGYNO

Of that an obstreperous lawyer bereft me.

NANO

O wonderful change! When Sir Lawyer forsook thee,
    For Pythagore's sake, what body then took thee?

21   *Crates* a student of Diogenes, who disdained material pleasures.
     itself The neuter pronoun here may refer to the soul itself, the source text, the cock
     narrator in Lucian, or Androgyno, whose name indicates mixed gender.
22   *gat it* temporarily held this soul.
23   *brock* badger.
24   *the cobbler's cock* In the Lucian text, a rooster tells its tale to a greedy shoemaker.
26   *quater* Pythagoras's musical and mathematical model of the universe was based on
     symmetrical permutations of the numbers 1–4, as in the balanced triangle (the
     'trigon' of the next line).
27   *golden thigh* a legend about Pythagoras's body.
30   *shifted . . . reformation* changed allegiance (hence the expression 'turn-coat' for a
     traitor) since Protestantism gained power.
31   *reformed, a fool* One of Jonson's many attacks on the radical Protestants, now known
     as Puritans, whom he would have hated as enemies of three things very important
     to him at this time: theatre, bodily pleasures, and Catholicism.
32   *Counting* Considering.
34   *Carthusian* an austere order of monks, forbidden meat and speech, but allowed fish.

ANDROGYNO

A good dull mule.

NANO   And how! by that means,

Thou wert brought to allow of the eating of beans?   40

ANDROGYNO

Yes.

NANO   But, from the mule, into whom didst thou pass?

ANDROGYNO

Into a very strange beast, by some writers called an ass;

By others, a precise, pure, illuminate brother,

Of those devour flesh, and sometimes one another,

And will drop you forth a libel, or a sanctified lie,   45

Betwixt every spoonful of a Nativity pie.

NANO

Now quit thee, for heaven, of that profane nation;

And gently report thy next transmigration.

ANDROGYNO

To the same that I am.

NANO   A creature of delight?

And (what is more than a fool) an hermaphrodite?   50

Now 'pray thee, sweet soul, in all thy variation,

Which body wouldst thou choose, to take up thy station?

ANDROGYNO

Troth, this I am in, even here would I tarry.

NANO

'Cause here, the delight of each sex thou canst vary?

ANDROGYNO

Alas, those pleasures be stale, and forsaken;   55

No, it is your fool wherewith I am so taken,

The only one creature that I can call blessed,

For all other forms I have proved most distressed.

---

39   *how!* an exclamation of surprise and inquiry.

43   *precise, pure, illuminate brother* a Puritan, one who claims to have seen the light.

44   *those* those who; cf. Galatians V.14–15.

46   *Nativity* an alternative term for Christmas used by Puritans, who mistrusted any residue of the term 'Mass'.

47   *quit thee* get out.
     for heaven for heaven's sake.

51   *'pray thee* [I] prithee tell me.

52   *take up thy station* stay in.

53   *Troth* I swear by my honesty

NANO

    Spoke true, as thou wert in Pythagoras still.

      This learned opinion we celebrate will,   60

    Fellow eunuch, as behooves us, with all our wit, and art,

      To dignify that, whereof ourselves are so great, and special
          a part.

VOLPONE

    Now very, very pretty! Mosca, this

    Was thy invention?

MOSCA   If it please my patron,

    Not else.

VOLPONE   It doth, good Mosca.

MOSCA   Then it was, sir.   65

Song

    Fools, they are the only nation

    Worth men's envy, or admiration;

    Free from care, or sorrow-taking,

    Themselves, and others merry making;

    All they speak, or do, is sterling.   70

    Your Fool, he is your great man's dearling,

    And your lady's sport, and pleasure:

    Tongue and bable are his treasure.

    His very face begetteth laughter,

    And he speaks truth, free from slaughter;   75

    He's the grace of every feast,

    And, sometimes, the chiefest guest;

    Hath his trencher, and his stool,

    When wit shall wait upon the Fool:

      O, who would not be   80

      He, he, he?

One knocks without

62   *that* the folly.

65   s.d. *Song* probably sung by Nano and Castrone in high-pitched eunuch voices.

70   *sterling* excellent, valuable.

73   *bable* both the fool's sceptre (called a bauble) with its clear phallic suggestions, and
      babble, rapid meaningless speech.

75   *free from slaughter* immune from punishment.

78   *trencher* plate for eating.

79   *wait upon* several simultaneous meanings: serves as a food-waiter for, acts as a
      subservient courtier to, and waits for his turn after.

81   s.d. *without* outside, offstage.

VOLPONE
Who's that? Away, look Mosca.

[*Exit* NANO *and* CASTRONE]

MOSCA   Fool, be gone,

[*Exit* ANDROGYNO]

'Tis Signior Voltore, the advocate,
I know him by his knock.
VOLPONE   Fetch me my gown,
My furs, and night-caps. Say, my couch is changing,   85
And let him entertain himself, awhile,
Within i' th' gallery.

[*Exit* MOSCA]

                    Now, now, my clients
Begin their visitation! Vulture, kite,
Raven, and gorcrow, all my birds of prey,
That think me turning carcass, now they come;   90
I am not for 'em yet.

[*Enter* MOSCA *carrying* VOLPONE'*s disguise*]

                    How now? The news?
MOSCA
A piece of plate, sir.
VOLPONE   Of what bigness?
MOSCA   Huge,
Massy, and antique, with your name inscribed,
And arms engraven.
VOLPONE   Good! And not a fox
Stretched on the earth, with fine delusive sleights,   95
Mocking a gaping crow? ha, Mosca?
MOSCA   Sharp, sir.
VOLPONE
Give me my furs. Why dost thou laugh so, man?
MOSCA
I cannot choose, sir, when I apprehend

---

85   *couch is changing* bed is being made.
89   *gorcrow* flesh-eating crow.
91   *not for* not ready for – not yet disguised, but also, not yet decayed.
93   *Massy* Massive, Heavy.
94–6 *And not . . . crow?* Volpone jokes that the coat of arms engraved on the plate ought
       to refer to the tactics (such as playing dead) by which the fox consumes the crow who
       was hoping to consume him.
98   *choose* resist.

What thoughts he has within now, as he walks:
That this might be the last gift he should give;   100
That this would fetch you; if you died today,
And gave him all, what he should be tomorrow;
What large return would come of all his ventures;
How he should worshipped be, and reverenced;
Ride, with his furs, and foot-cloths; waited on   105
By herds of fools, and clients; have clear way
Made for his mule, as lettered as himself;
Be called the great and learned advocate:
And then concludes, there's nought impossible.
VOLPONE
  Yes, to be learnèd, Mosca.
MOSCA   O no: rich   110
  Implies it. Hood an ass with reverend purple,
So you can hide his two ambitious ears,
And he shall pass for a cathedral doctor.
VOLPONE
  My caps, my caps, good Mosca, fetch him in.
MOSCA
  Stay, sir, your ointment for your eyes.
VOLPONE   That's true;   115
  Dispatch, dispatch: I long to have possession
Of my new present.
MOSCA   That, and thousands more,
  I hope, to see you lord of.
VOLPONE   Thanks, kind Mosca.
MOSCA
  And that, when I am lost in blended dust,
And hundred such as I am, in succession –   120
VOLPONE
  Nay, that were too much, Mosca.

---

103   *What large ... ventures* What a profit he would make on his investment in expensive
       gifts designed to win the dying man's favour.
105   *foot-cloths* richly ornamented fabric draped over an aristocrat's horse.
107   *lettered* learned.
111–13 *Hood ... doctor* Erasmus makes this joke repeatedly in *Praise of Folly*, based on the
       purple hood worn by Doctors of Philosophy.
114   *caps* nightcaps; but perhaps with an unwitting ironic resemblance to the ass's hood
       in the previous lines.
116   *Dispatch* Hurry.

MOSCA You shall live,
Still, to delude these harpies.
VOLPONE Loving Mosca,
'Tis well, my pillow now, and let him enter.

Exit MOSCA

Now, my feigned cough, my phthisic, and my gout,
My apoplexy, palsy, and catarrh,   125
Help, with your forced functions, this my posture,
Wherein, this three year, I have milked their hopes.
He comes, I hear him – uh, uh, uh, uh – oh.

ACT I, SCENE iii

MOSCA [*brings in*] VOLTORE [*clutching the plate*]

MOSCA
You still are, what you were, sir. Only you,
Of all the rest, are he, commands his love;
And you do wisely to preserve it, thus,
With early visitation, and kind notes
Of your good meaning to him, which, I know,   5
Cannot but come most grateful. [*To* VOLPONE] Patron, sir.
Here's Signior Voltore is come –
VOLPONE   What say you?
MOSCA
Sir, Signior Voltore is come, this morning,
To visit you.
VOLPONE   I thank him.

122 *harpies* mythological creatures with the face of a woman and the body of a fierce
bird of prey.
124 *phthisic* tuberculosis, or possibly asthma.
125 *apoplexy, palsy, and catarrh* stroke or seizure, paralysis or quivering, and mucus flow.
126 *forced* feigned.
posture imposture, deluding performance (though perhaps referring directly to his
sickly sprawl in the bed).
128 *uh* Jonson probably intended the 'h' to sound like the German guttural 'ch',
simulating a shallow cough (Parker).

2 *he . . . love* the man who has Volpone's favour.
6 *Cannot . . . grateful* Must be very welcome.

MOSCA   And hath brought
  A piece of antique plate, bought of St Mark,   10
  With which he here presents you.
VOLPONE   He is welcome.
  Pray him, to come more often.
MOSCA   Yes.
VOLTORE   What says he?
MOSCA
  He thanks you, and desires you see him often.
VOLPONE
  Mosca.
MOSCA   My patron?
VOLPONE   Bring him near, where is he?
  I long to feel his hand.
MOSCA [*Guiding his hand*] The plate is here, sir.   15
VOLTORE
  How fare you, sir?
VOLPONE   I thank you, Signior Voltore.
  Where is the plate? Mine eyes are bad.
VOLTORE [*Putting the plate in* VOLPONE's *hands*] I am sorry,
  To see you still thus weak.
MOSCA [*Aside*]   That he is not weaker.
VOLPONE
  You are too munificent.
VOLTORE   No, sir, would to heaven
  I could as well give health to you, as that plate.   20
VOLPONE
  You give, sir, what you can. I thank you. Your love
  Hath taste in this, and shall not be unanswered.
  I pray you see me often.
VOLTORE   Yes, I shall, sir.
VOLPONE
  Be not far from me.
MOSCA [*Aside to* VOLTORE] Do you observe that, sir?
VOLPONE
  Hearken unto me, still. It will concern you.   25
MOSCA [*Aside to* VOLTORE]
  You are a happy man, sir, know your good.

---

10 *St Mark* Venice's Piazza San Marco was famous for its goldsmiths.
22 *Hath taste* Can be sensed.

VOLPONE

    I cannot now last long.

MOSCA [*Aside to* VOLTORE] You are his heir, sir.

VOLTORE [*Aside to* MOSCA]

    Am I?

VOLPONE I feel me going – uh, uh, uh, uh –

    I am sailing to my port – uh, uh, uh, uh! –

    And I am glad I am so near my haven.   30

MOSCA

    Alas, kind gentleman, well, we must all go.

VOLTORE

    But, Mosca.

MOSCA   Age will conquer.

VOLTORE   'Pray thee hear me.

    Am I inscribed his heir, for certain?

MOSCA   Are you?

    I do beseech you, sir, you will vouchsafe

    To write me i' your family. All my hopes   35

    Depend upon your worship: I am lost,

    Except the rising sun do shine on me.

VOLTORE

    It shall both shine, and warm thee, Mosca.

MOSCA   Sir.

    I am a man that have not done your love

    All the worst offices: here I wear your keys,   40

    See all your coffers, and your caskets locked,

    Keep the poor inventory of your jewels,

    Your plate, and monies, am your steward, sir.

    Husband your goods here.

VOLTORE   But am I sole heir?

MOSCA

    Without a partner, sir, confirmed this morning;   45

    The wax is warm yet, and the ink scarce dry

    Upon the parchment.

---

35   *write . . . family* include me in your household (when Volpone's death ends my employment there).

37   *rising sun* This plays on Voltore's hope to become an inheriting 'son' to Volpone, and Mosca's hope to become 'son' to Voltore (as well as recalling the play's opening lines).

39–40   *that have . . . offices* who has not rewarded your kindness with such bad services.

44   *Husband* Manage prudently.

46   *wax* the stamped sealing wax that marked the will as legitimate.

VOLTORE   Happy, happy me!
By what good chance, sweet Mosca?
MOSCA   Your desert, sir;
I know no second cause.
VOLTORE   Thy modesty
Is loath to know it; well, we shall requite it.   50
MOSCA
He ever liked your course, sir: that first took him.
I oft have heard him say, how he admired
Men of your large profession, that could speak
To every cause, and things mere contraries,
Till they were hoarse again, yet all be law;   55
That, with most quick agility, could turn,
And return; make knots, and undo them;
Give forked counsel; take provoking gold
On either hand, and put it up. These men,
He knew, would thrive, with their humility.   60
And (for his part) he thought, he should be blest
To have his heir of such a suffering spirit,
So wise, so grave, of so perplexed a tongue,
And loud withal, that would not wag, nor scarce
Lie still, without a fee; when every word   65
Your worship but lets fall, is a chequin.

                             Another knocks

Who is that? One knocks, I would not have you seen, sir.
And yet – pretend you came, and went in haste;
I'll fashion an excuse. And, gentle sir,
When you do come to swim, in golden lard,   70
Up to the arms, in honey, that your chin
Is borne up stiff with fatness of the flood,
Think on your vassal; but remember me:
I have not been your worst of clients.
VOLTORE   Mosca –

---

51   *He ever . . . him* He always liked your manner, or path of life; that was what first won
      his affection.
54   *mere contraries* totally contradictory.
58   *forked* ambiguous; but the term has diabolical associations. Mosca keeps thinly
      disguising his insults.
59   *On . . . up* From both sides, and pocket it (as if for safekeeping).
62   *suffering* patiently enduring.
63   *perplexed* intricate, with an implication of double-dealing
66   *chequin* a gold coin used in Renaissance Venice.

MOSCA

When will you have your inventory brought, sir? 75
Or see a copy of the will?
                    [*More knocking, and* MOSCA *shouts toward the door*]
                                Anon!
[*To* VOLTORE] I'll bring 'em to you, sir. Away, be gone,
Put business i' your face.

                                                    [*Exit* VOLTORE]

                    [VOLPONE *sits up in bed*]

VOLPONE   Excellent, Mosca!
Come hither, let me kiss thee.
MOSCA   Keep you still, sir.
Here is Corbaccio.
VOLPONE   Set the plate away, 80
The vulture's gone, and the old raven's come.

ACT I, SCENE iv

MOSCA

[*To* VOLPONE] Betake you to your silence, and your sleep;
[*To the silver plate*] Stand there, and multiply. Now shall we see
A wretch, who is, indeed, more impotent,
Than this can feign to be; yet hopes to hop
Over his grave.

                    [*Enter* CORBACCIO]

                    Signior Corbaccio 5
You're very welcome, sir.
CORBACCIO   How does your patron?

76   *Anon!* In just a moment (to the person knocking).
78   *Put . . . face* Look hurried, and/or look as if you were here on business.

2   *multiply* Mosca encourages the precious metal to breed more like itself, as he is about
      to make it do; the way greed replaces natural human reproduction with unnatural
      or perverted reproduction is a persistent theme of the play.
4   *this* Volpone.

MOSCA

    Troth, as he did, sir, no amends.

CORBACCIO   What? Mends he?

MOSCA

    No, sir: he is rather worse.

CORBACCIO   That's well. Where is he?

MOSCA

    Upon his couch sir, newly fall'n asleep.

CORBACCIO

    Does he sleep well?

MOSCA   No wink, sir, all this night,   10

    Nor yesterday, but slumbers.

CORBACCIO   Good! He should take

    Some counsel of physicians: I have brought him

    An opiate here, from mine own doctor –

MOSCA

    He will not hear of drugs.

CORBACCIO   Why? I myself

    Stood by while't was made; saw all th' ingredients;   15

    And know, it cannot but most gently work.

    My life for his, 'tis but to make him sleep.

VOLPONE [*Aside*]

    Ay, his last sleep, if he would take it.

MOSCA   Sir,

    He has no faith in physic.

CORBACCIO   Say you? Say you?

MOSCA

    He has no faith in physic: he does think   20

    Most of your doctors are the greater danger,

    And worse disease, t' escape. I often have

    Heard him protest that your physician

    Should never be his heir.

CORBACCIO   Not I his heir?

MOSCA

    Not your physician, sir.

CORBACCIO   O, no, no, no,   25

    I do not mean it.

---

11   *but slumbers* only dozes.

19   *physic* medicine.

21   *your doctors* doctors in general (a common Renaissance construction); the complaints against this profession that follow, like those against lawyers in the previous scene, were familiar from classical as well as Renaissance commentators.

MOSCA   No sir, nor their fees
He cannot brook: he says, they flay a man,
Before they kill him.
CORBACCIO   Right, I conceive you.
MOSCA
And then, they do it by experiment,
For which the law not only doth absolve them,   30
But gives them great reward; and, he is loath
To hire his death so.
CORBACCIO   It is true, they kill
With as much licence as a judge.
MOSCA   Nay, more;
For he but kills, sir, where the law condemns,
And these can kill him, too.
CORBACCIO   Ay, or me;   35
Or any man. How does his apoplex?
Is that strong on him, still?
MOSCA   Most violent.
His speech is broken, and his eyes are set,
His face drawn longer, than 'twas wont –
CORBACCIO   How? how?
Stronger, than he was wont?
MOSCA   No, sir: his face   40
Drawn longer, than 'twas wont.
CORBACCIO   O, good.
MOSCA   His mouth
Is ever gaping, and his eyelids hang.
CORBACCIO   Good.
MOSCA
A freezing numbness stiffens all his joints,
And makes the colour of his flesh like lead.
CORBACCIO   'Tis good.
MOSCA
His pulse beats slow, and dull.

---

27   *brook* tolerate.
       flay take the skin off.
28   *conceive* understand.
29   *by experiment* by trying out medicines on their patients.
35   *these can kill him* doctors can safely kill a judge.
39   *wont* formerly accustomed to being.
40   Q gives this line to Mosca, but that is clearly a technical error, corrected by F.

CORBACCIO   Good symptoms, still.   45
MOSCA
  And, from his brain –
CORBACCIO   Ha? How? Not from his brain?
MOSCA
  Yes, sir, and from his brain –
CORBACCIO   I conceive you, good.
MOSCA
  Flows a cold sweat, with a continual rheum,
  Forth the resolvèd corners of his eyes.
CORBACCIO
  Is't possible? Yet I am better, ha!   50
  How does he, with the swimming of his head?
MOSCA
  O, sir, 'tis past the scotomy: he now
  Hath lost his feeling, and hath left to snort;
  You hardly can perceive him, that he breathes.
CORBACCIO
  Excellent, excellent, sure I shall outlast him: 55
  This makes me young again, a score of years.
MOSCA
  I was a-coming for you, sir.
CORBACCIO   Has he made his will?
  What has he giv'n me?
MOSCA   No, sir.
CORBACCIO   Nothing? ha?
MOSCA
  He has not made his will, sir.
CORBACCIO   Oh, oh, oh.
  But what did Voltore, the lawyer, here?   60
MOSCA
  He smelled a carcass, sir, when he but heard
  My master was about his testament;

---

46   *from his brain* Though the hard-of-hearing Corbaccio again misunderstands at first,
     thinking perhaps Mosca is talking about whether Volpone is out of his mind, he
     soon gleefully recognizes that Mosca is describing the final stages of apoplexy, in
     which the drainage of brain fluid was thought to lead to death.
49   *resolved* drooping and/or watery.
50   *Yet I am better* I am even better off (because Volpone is even worse).
52   *scotomy* dizziness, accompanied by dimness of sight (OED).
53   *left* ceased.
62   *about his testament* working on composing his will.

As I did urge him to it, for your good –

CORBACCIO
He came unto him, did he? I thought so.

MOSCA
Yes, and presented him this piece of plate.   65

CORBACCIO
To be his heir?

MOSCA   I do not know, sir.

CORBACCIO   True,
I know it too.

MOSCA   By your own scale, sir.

CORBACCIO   Well,
I shall prevent him, yet. See, Mosca, look,
Here, I have brought a bag of bright chequins,
Will quite weigh down his plate.

MOSCA   Yea, marry, sir.   70
This is true physic, this your sacred medicine,
No talk of opiates, to this great elixir.

CORBACCIO
'Tis *aurum palpabile*, if not *potabile*.

MOSCA
It shall be ministered to him, in his bowl?

CORBACCIO
Ay, do, do, do.

MOSCA   Most blessed cordial,   75
This will recover him.

CORBACCIO   Yes, do, do, do.

MOSCA
I think, it were not best, sir.

CORBACCIO   What?

MOSCA   To recover him.

CORBACCIO
O, no, no, no; by no means.

MOSCA   Why, sir, this
Will work some strange effect if he but feel it.

70   *weigh down* outweigh.
     marry indeed (a common form of the oath, '[I swear by the Virgin] Mary').
72   *No talk . . . elixir* Opiates can't compare to this great medicine, gold, which is like the
     alchemists' elixir, the 'philosopher's stone', that was rumoured to bestow eternal life.
73   *'Tis . . . potabile* It is gold which can be felt, if not drunk. A liquid solution of gold
     was widely believed to be a health-giving miracle drug.
75   *cordial* medicine for the heart.

CORBACCIO
    'Tis true, therefore forbear; I'll take my venture: 80
    Give me't again.
MOSCA   At no hand, pardon me;
    You shall not do your self that wrong, sir. I
    Will so advise you, you shall have it all.
CORBACCIO
    How!
MOSCA   All, sir, 'tis your right, your own; no man
    Can claim a part; 'tis yours, without a rival,   85
    Decreed by destiny.
CORBACCIO   How? How, good Mosca?
MOSCA
    I'll tell you, sir. This fit he shall recover –
CORBACCIO
    I do conceive you.
MOSCA   And, on first advantage
    Of his gained sense, will I re-importune him
    Unto the making of his testament;   90
    And show him this. [*Indicates the money*]
CORBACCIO   Good, good.
MOSCA   'Tis better yet,
    If you will hear, sir.
CORBACCIO   Yes, with all my heart.
MOSCA
    Now, would I counsel you, make home with speed;
    There, frame a will; whereto you shall inscribe
    My master your sole heir.
CORBACCIO   And disinherit   95
    My son?
MOSCA   O, sir, the better: for that colour
    Shall make it much more taking.
CORBACCIO   O, but colour?

---

80   *venture* speculative investment, in this case the gold he brought Volpone.
81   *At no hand* By no means.
84   *How!* Perhaps a question, as two lines later, but probably here an exclamation, much like the modern 'What!'.
88–9   *advantage . . . sense* opportunity of Volpone's recovering consciousness.
93   *make* go.
96–7   *that colour . . . taking* that pretence will make your overall pretence toward Volpone much more convincing; a similar trick appears in Lucian's *Dialogues of the Dead*, XVIII (Parker).

MOSCA
    This will, sir, you shall send it unto me.
    Now, when I come to enforce (as I will do)
    Your cares, your watchings, and your many prayers,   100
    Your more than many gifts, your this day's present,
    And, last, produce your will; where – without thought,
    Or least regard, unto your proper issue,
    A son so brave, and highly meriting –
    The stream of your diverted love hath thrown you   105
    Upon my master, and made him your heir;
    He cannot be so stupid, or stone dead,
    But, out of conscience, and mere gratitude –
CORBACCIO
    He must pronounce me, his?
MOSCA   It is true.
CORBACCIO   This plot
    Did I think on before.
MOSCA   I do believe it.   110
CORBACCIO
    Do you not believe it?
MOSCA   Yes, sir.
CORBACCIO   Mine own project.
MOSCA
    Which when he hath done, sir –
CORBACCIO   Published me his heir?
MOSCA
    And you so certain to survive him.
CORBACCIO   Ay.
MOSCA
    Being so lusty a man.
CORBACCIO   It is true.
MOSCA   Yes, sir.
CORBACCIO
    I thought on that too. See, how he should be   115
    The very organ to express my thoughts!

99   *enforce* emphasize, impress on Volpone.
103   *proper issue* own true offspring.
114   *lusty* healthy, robust, energetic.
115   *he* Mosca.
116   *very organ* true instrument.

MOSCA
You have not only done yourself a good –
CORBACCIO
But multiplied it on my son?
MOSCA   It is right, sir.
CORBACCIO
Still, my invention.
MOSCA   'Las, sir, heaven knows,
It hath been all my study, all my care –   120
I e'en grow grey withal – how to work things –
CORBACCIO
I do conceive, sweet Mosca.
MOSCA   You are he,
For whom I labour, here.
CORBACCIO   Ay, do, do, do:
I'll straight about it.
MOSCA   Rook go with you, raven.
CORBACCIO
I know thee honest.
MOSCA   You do lie, sir.
CORBACCIO   And –   125
MOSCA
Your knowledge is no better than your ears, sir.
CORBACCIO
I do not doubt, to be a father to thee.
MOSCA
Nor I, to gull my brother of his blessing.
CORBACCIO
I may ha' my youth restored to me, why not?
MOSCA
Your worship is a precious ass –
CORBACCIO   What say'st thou?   130
MOSCA
I do desire your worship, to make haste, sir.

---

119   *Still, my invention* This, too, is what I had planned.
124   *straight* immediately.
       Rook . . . raven May you be cheated (with a pun on 'rook', which means both 'swindle' and 'a kind of raven').
128   *Nor I . . . blessing* And I intend to steal, by trickery, this father's legacy. Mosca is alluding to Jacob's theft of the paternal blessing from his brother Esau in Genesis.

CORBACCIO
    'Tis done, 'tis done, I go.   [*Exit*]
VOLPONE   O, I shall burst;
    Let out my sides, let out my sides –
MOSCA   Contain
    Your flux of laughter, sir: you know, this hope
    Is such a bait, it covers any hook.   135
VOLPONE
    O, but thy working, and thy placing it!
    I cannot hold; good rascal, let me kiss thee;
    I never knew thee in so rare a humour.
MOSCA
    Alas, sir, I but do as I am taught:
    Follow your grave instructions; give 'em words;   140
    Pour oil into their ears; and send them hence.
VOLPONE
    'Tis true, 'tis true. What a rare punishment
    Is avarice, to itself!
MOSCA   Ay, with our help, sir.
VOLPONE
    So many cares, so many maladies,
    So many fears attending on old age,   145
    Yea, death so often called on, as no wish
    Can be more frequent with 'em, their limbs faint,
    Their senses dull, their seeing, hearing, going,
    All dead before them; yea, their very teeth,
    Their instruments of eating, failing them: 150
    Yet this is reckoned life! Nay, here was one,
    Is now gone home, that wishes to live longer!
    Feels not his gout, nor palsy, feigns himself
    Younger, by scores of years, flatters his age,
    With confident belying it, hopes he may   155

---

134   *flux* flood.
        this hope the hope of inheriting Volpone's estate.
137   *hold* hold back.
138   *so rare a humour* so excellent a state of inspired wit.
140   *grave* wise.
141   *Pour . . . ears* Flatter them with pleasing words (from a Latin proverb) (Parker).
142   *'Tis true* Even while laughing at Corbaccio for believing Mosca's flattery, Volpone
        here believes an almost identical flattery – that he is really the one who conceived the
        plots he sees Mosca executing, supposedly on his behalf.
148   *going* walking.
155   *belying* denying.

With charms, like Aeson, have his youth restored,
And with these thoughts so battens, as if fate
Would be as easily cheated on, as he,
And all turns air!

Another knocks

Who's that, there, now? A third?

MOSCA

Close, to your couch again; I hear his voice.   160
It is Corvino, our spruce merchant.

VOLPONE [*Lying down*]   Dead.

MOSCA

Another bout, sir, with your eyes.   [*Applies more ointment*]
Who's there?

ACT I, SCENE v

[*Enter*] CORVINO

MOSCA

Signior Corvino! Come most wished for! O,
How happy were you, if you knew it, now!

CORVINO

Why? What? Wherein?

MOSCA   The tardy hour is come, sir.

CORVINO

He is not dead?

MOSCA   Not dead, sir, but as good;
He knows no man.

CORVINO   How shall I do then?

MOSCA   Why, sir?   5

---

156   *Aeson* The evil magic of Medea restored the youth of Aeson, the father of Jason (see
      the note to I.ii.9 above).
157   *battens* feeds himself into fatness   .
159   *And all turns air* Though all his hopes will turn out to be empty; or perhaps, As if
      the material fact of Corbaccio's decaying body meant nothing.
160   *Close* Hush, resume your secrecy.
161   *spruce* trim, dapper.
162   *bout* dose (of the substance used to make Volpone's eyes appear sickly) .

  1   *Come* You have come when you were.

CORVINO
  I have brought him, here, a pearl.
MOSCA   Perhaps he has
  So much remembrance left, as to know you, sir;
  He still calls on you: nothing but your name
  Is in his mouth. Is your pearl orient, sir?
CORVINO
  Venice was never owner of the like.   10
VOLPONE [*Faintly*]
  Signior Corvino.
MOSCA   Hark.
VOLPONE   Signior Corvino.
MOSCA
  He calls you, step and give it him.
  [*Aloud to* VOLPONE]   He's here, sir,
  And he has brought you a rich pearl.
CORVINO   How do you, sir?
  Tell him, it doubles the twelfth carat.
MOSCA   Sir,
  He cannot understand, his hearing's gone;   15
  And yet it comforts him, to see you –
CORVINO   Say,
  I have a diamond for him, too.
MOSCA   Best show't, sir,
  Put it into his hand: 'tis only there
  He apprehends; he has his feeling, yet.
                        [VOLPONE *seizes the pearl*]
  See, how he grasps it!
CORVINO   'Las, good gentleman!   20
  How pitiful the sight is!
MOSCA   Tut, forget, sir.
  The weeping of an heir should still be laughter,
  Under a visor.
CORVINO   Why, am I his heir?
MOSCA
  Sir, I am sworn, I may not show the will,

----

   8   *still* always.
   9   *orient* The most lustrous and hence valuable pearls came from the East. Since 'stones'
       was common slang for testicles, the fact that Corvino here gives Volpone two stones
       may foreshadow the sexual advantage he will give Volpone later.
  14   *doubles . . . carat* The pearl measures twenty-four carats, hence extremely valuable.
  23   *visor* mask – in this case, of feigned mourning.

Till he be dead. But, here has been Corbaccio, 25
Here has been Voltore, here were others too,
I cannot number 'em, they were so many,
All gaping here for legacies; but I,
Taking the vantage of his naming you –
[*Mimicking* VOLPONE] 'Signior Corvino, Signior Corvino' –
took 30
Paper, and pen, and ink, and there I asked him,
Whom he would have his heir? Corvino. Who
Should be executor? Corvino. And,
To any question he was silent to,
I still interpreted the nods he made 35
Through weakness for consent; and sent home th' others,
Nothing bequeathed them, but to cry, and curse.

CORVINO

O, my dear Mosca. *They embrace*
Does he not perceive us?

MOSCA

No more than a blind harper. He knows no man,
No face of friend, nor name of any servant, 40
Who't was that fed him last, or gave him drink;
Not those he hath begotten, or brought up
Can he remember.

CORVINO Has he children?

MOSCA Bastards,
Some dozen, or more, that he begot on beggars,
Gypsies, and Jews, and black-moors, when he was drunk. 45
Knew you not that, sir? 'Tis the common fable.
The dwarf, the fool, the eunuch are all his:
He's the true father of his family,
In all, save me; but he has giv'n 'em nothing.

CORVINO

That's well, that's well. Art sure he does not hear us? 50

MOSCA

Sure, sir? Why look you, credit your own sense.

---

39   *blind harper* Proverbial for insensibility: cf. Tilley H175, 176.
46   *'Tis the common fable* This is widely known. Again the play stresses the perversion
     of Volpone's reproductive powers.
51   *credit* believe.

[*Aloud to* VOLPONE] The pox approach, and add to your
    diseases,
If it would send you hence the sooner, sir.
For, your incontinence, it hath deserved it
Throughly, and throughly, and the plague to boot.   55
[*To* CORVINO] You may come near, sir.
[*Aloud to* VOLPONE]   Would you would once close
Those filthy eyes of yours, that flow with slime,
Like two frog-pits; and those same hanging cheeks,
Covered with hide, instead of skin.
[*To* CORVINO]   Nay, help, sir,
[*Aloud to* VOLPONE] That look like frozen dish-clouts, set
   on end.   60
CORVINO
Or, like an old smoked wall, on which the rain
Ran down in streaks.
MOSCA   Excellent, sir, speak out;
You may be louder yet: a culverin,
Discharged in his ear would hardly bore it.
CORVINO
His nose is like a common sewer, still running.   65
MOSCA
'Tis good! And, what his mouth?
CORVINO   A very draught.
MOSCA [*Taking up a pillow to smother* VOLPONE]
O stop it up –
CORVINO   By no means.
MOSCA   'Pray you let me.
Faith, I could stifle him, rarely, with a pillow,
As well as any woman that should keep him.

---

52   *pox* either smallpox or (as line 54 hints) syphilis. The series of insults that follow
     offers several layers of irony, as Corvino thinks they are making fun of Volpone,
     Volpone thinks they are actually making fun of that delusion of Corvino's, and
     Mosca may actually be taking advantage of the situation to insult Volpone after all.
53   *send you hence* kill you off.
54   *your incontinence . . . deserved it* your sexual promiscuity and other indulgences
     should have earned you the pox.
58   *frog-pits* stagnant puddles, or possibly 'frogspit', the froth around insect larvae.
60   *clouts* rags.
63–4   *culverin, / Discharged* handgun fired.
66   *draught* sewer drain, or possibly, chimney flue.
68   *Faith* a common condensation of the oath, '[I swear by my] faith'.
     rarely skilfully.
69   *that should keep him* who would be his caretaker.

CORVINO

Do as you will, but I'll be gone.

MOSCA   Be so: 70

It is your presence makes him last so long.

CORVINO

I pray you, use no violence.

MOSCA   No, sir? Why?

Why should you be thus scrupulous? 'Pray you, sir.

CORVINO

Nay, at your discretion.

MOSCA   Well, good sir, be gone.

CORVINO

I will not trouble him now, to take my pearl?   75

MOSCA

Puh, nor your diamond. [*Taking the jewels*]
                    What a needless care

Is this afflicts you? Is not all, here, yours?

Am not I here? whom you have made? your creature?

That owe my being to you?

CORVINO   Grateful Mosca!

Thou art my friend, my fellow, my companion,   80

My partner, and shalt share in all my fortunes.

MOSCA

Excepting one.

CORVINO   What is that?

MOSCA   Your gallant wife, sir.

                     [*Exit* CORVINO *hurriedly*]

Now is he gone: we had no other means,

To shoot him hence, but this.

VOLPONE   My divine Mosca!

Thou hast today outgone thyself.   *Another knocks*

                 Who's there?   85

I will be troubled with no more. Prepare

Me music, dances, banquets, all delights:

The Turk is not more sensual, in his pleasures,

Than will Volpone.

---

73   *'Pray you* I ask you, pray tell me.

74   *Nay . . . discretion* Well, I'll leave it up to you.

83–4 *we had . . . but this* the only way to get him to leave was to remind him that he has left his wife alone.

85   *outgone* outdone.

88   *The Turk* Either Turks in general, or Mahomet III, Sultan of the Ottoman empire; in either case, a person devoted to sensual pleasures.

[Exit MOSCA]

        Let me see, a pearl?
A diamond? Plate? Chequins? Good morning's purchase!   90
Why this is better than rob churches, yet;
Or fat, by eating, once a month, a man.

[Enter MOSCA]

Who is't?
MOSCA   The beauteous Lady Would-Be, sir,
Wife to the English knight, Sir Politic Would-Be,
(This is the style, sir, is directed me),   95
Hath sent to know, how you have slept tonight,
And if you would be visited.
VOLPONE   Not now.
Some three hours hence –
MOSCA   I told the squire so much.
VOLPONE
When I am high with mirth, and wine: then, then.
'Fore heaven, I wonder at the desperate valour   100
Of the bold English, that they dare let loose
Their wives, to all encounters!
MOSCA   Sir, this knight
Had not his name for nothing, he is politic,
And knows, howe'er his wife affect strange airs,
She hath not yet the face to be dishonest.   105
But had she Signior Corvino's wife's face –
VOLPONE
Has she so rare a face?
MOSCA   O, sir, the wonder,
The blazing star of Italy! A wench
O' the first year, a beauty, ripe, as harvest!

---

90   *Good morning's purchase!* A profitable morning!
92   *fat* grow fat; the line may imply cannibalism in monthly communion.
95   *This is . . . directed me* That is how she told me to identify her.
98   *squire* attendant, but sometimes with a suggestion of 'pimp'.
101 *bold English* By Venetian standards, English husbands gave their wives an unusual
     and risky degree of freedom.
104 *affect strange airs* probably a pun on 1) visiting foreign countries, 2) putting on
     pretentious behaviour, and possibly 3) producing unusual odours.
105 *She hath . . . dishonest* She is no longer pretty enough to commit adultery, and/or, She
     nonetheless lacks the nerve to commit adultery.
109 *O' the first year* Of the best vintage, and/or, In the innocent first bloom of
     womanhood.

Whose skin is whiter than a swan, all over!   110
Than silver, snow, or lilies! A soft lip,
Would tempt you to eternity of kissing!
And flesh, that melteth, in the touch, to blood!
Bright as your gold, and lovely, as your gold!

VOLPONE
Why had not I known this, before?

MOSCA   Alas, sir.   115
Myself but yesterday discovered it.

VOLPONE
How might I see her?

MOSCA   O, not possible:
She's kept as warily as is your gold;
Never does come abroad, never takes air,
But at a window. All her looks are sweet,   120
As the first grapes, or cherries; and are watched
As near as they are.

VOLPONE   I must see her –

MOSCA   Sir.
There is a guard, of ten spies thick, upon her:
All his whole household, each of which is set
Upon his fellow, and have all their charge –   125
When he goes out, when he comes in – examined.

VOLPONE
I will go see her, though but at her window.

MOSCA
In some disguise, then?

VOLPONE   That is true, I must
Maintain mine own shape, still, the same: we'll think.

                                                              [*Exeunt*]

---

113   *melteth . . . to blood* blushes when touched, or responds with passionate heat to
       touch, or is as yielding to the touch as warm liquid. 'Touch' was also a term for testing
       the quality of gold, and so leads to Mosca's next line, which shows his understanding
       of Volpone's deepest desires.

119   *abroad* outside.

122   *near* closely. The fruit comparisons recall Aesop's fable of the fox and the grapes,
       and Volpone's earlier reference to the game of bob-cherry; Volpone again fails to
       notice that Mosca is doing to him what he does to the legacy-hunters.

124–6 *each . . . examined* each of whom is assigned to spy on the others, and is interrogated
       about his responsibilities (or, about Corvino's wife) every time Corvino departs or
       returns home.

129   *Maintain mine own shape* Maintain the appearance that I am confined to my death-
       bed.

[Enter Sir] POLITIC WOULD-BE, PEREGRINE

SIR POLITIC

Sir, to a wise man, all the world's his soil.
It is not Italy, nor France, nor Europe,
That must bound me, if my fates call me forth.
Yet, I protest, it is no salt desire
Of seeing countries, shifting a religion, 5
Nor any disaffection to the state
Where I was bred and unto which I owe
My dearest plots, hath brought me out; much less,
That idle, antique, stale, grey-headed project
Of knowing men's minds and manners, with Ulysses; 10
But, a peculiar humour of my wife's,
Laid for this height of Venice, to observe,
To quote, to learn the language, and so forth –
I hope you travel, sir, with licence?

PEREGRINE   Yes.

SIR POLITIC

I dare the safelier converse – How long, sir, 15
Since you left England?

PEREGRINE   Seven weeks.

---

4   *salt* intense, with connotations of sexual appetite and a possible pun on the saltiness of sea voyages.

5   *shifting* changing; recusant Englishmen (and Jonson may have been one) sometimes fled that Protestant country so that they could practise openly in Catholic Italy.

8   *plots* plans (of which Sir Pol has many).

10   *knowing . . . Ulysses* The opening lines of Homer's *Odyssey* describe the hero as one who 'learned the minds of many distant men' (trans. Robert Fitzgerald).

11   *humour* whim or obsession; Jonson wrote two comedies about characters controlled by 'humours' – four bodily fluids whose balance was believed to dictate psychological tendencies.

12   *Laid for this height* Aimed for this place; 'height' may refer to latitude, it may reflect Pol's folly, since Venice is decidedly at sea-level, or it may refer to the famous arched bridge of the Rialto (from *rivo alto*) where (as a common meeting-place) this scene may be set.

13   *quote* take note of things, whether mentally or in writing.

14   *licence* a kind of passport or visa, required by the Privy Council for overseas travel, and often excluding Catholic countries as dangerous to the traveller's soul and England's safety.

SIR POLITIC   So lately!
  You ha' not been with my lord ambassador?
PEREGRINE
  Not yet, sir.
SIR POLITIC   'Pray you, what news, sir, vents our climate?
  I heard, last night, a most strange thing reported
  By some of my lord's followers, and I long   20
  To hear how 'twill be seconded!
PEREGRINE   What was't, sir?
SIR POLITIC
  Marry, sir, of a raven, that should build
  In a ship royal of the King's.
PEREGRINE [*Aside*]   This fellow,
  Does he gull me, trow? or is gulled?
  [*To* SIR POLITIC]   Your name, sir?
SIR POLITIC
  My name is Politic Would-Be.
PEREGRINE [*Aside*]   O, that speaks him.   25
  [*To* SIR POLITIC] A knight, sir?
SIR POLITIC   A poor knight, sir.
PEREGRINE   Your lady
  Lies here in Venice for intelligence
  Of tires, and fashions, and behaviour,
  Among the courtesans? The fine Lady Would-Be?
SIR POLITIC
  Yes, sir: the spider and the bee, ofttimes,   30
  Suck from one flower.

17   *my lord ambassador* Sir Pol may be partly a caricature of England's crafty ambassador
    to Venice in this period, Sir Henry Wotton, a close friend of John Donne's.
18   *vents our climate* blows in from our home country, or is breathily reported about it.
21   *seconded* confirmed by some other source.
22   *Marry . . . build* I swear by Mary, news of a raven that was said to build. (Birds
    building nests were bad omens on a ship, as Shakespeare suggests at IV.xii.4 of
    Antony and Cleopatra.)
24   *Does . . . gulled?* Is he trying to make a fool of me, I wonder, or is he fooled himself
    (by this grandiose gossip)?
25   *speaks* defines.
27   *Lies* Stays (but with possible sexual connotations).
    for intelligence to gather information.
28   *Of tires* About attire, clothing.
29   *courtesans* high-class prostitutes, for which Venice was famous.
30–1 *the spider . . . flower* A common proverb (Tilley B208); Sir Pol means that, as one kind
    of creature can draw sweetness from the same place another kind draws poison, so
    his wife could use virtuously the Venetian arts the courtesans use sinfully.

PEREGRINE   Good Sir Politic!
I cry you mercy: I have heard much of you.
'Tis true, sir, of your raven.
SIR POLITIC   On your knowledge?
PEREGRINE
Yes, and your lion's whelping, in the Tower.
SIR POLITIC
Another whelp?
PEREGRINE   Another, sir.
SIR POLITIC   Now heaven!   35
What prodigies be these? The fires at Berwick!
And the new star! These things concurring, strange!
And full of omen! Saw you those meteors?
PEREGRINE
I did, sir.
SIR POLITIC Fearful! 'Pray you, sir, confirm me:
Were there three porpoises seen, above the bridge,   40
As they give out?
PEREGRINE   Six, and a sturgeon, sir.
SIR POLITIC
I am astonished.
PEREGRINE   Nay, sir, be not so:
I'll tell you a greater prodigy than these –
SIR POLITIC
What should these things portend!
PEREGRINE   The very day
(Let me be sure) that I put forth from London,   45
There was a whale discovered, in the river,
As high as Woolwich, that had waited there,

32   *I cry you mercy* I beg your pardon (for not recognizing you sooner).
33   *your raven* the aforementioned raven; as in the next line, the 'your' is impersonal.
34   *lion's whelping* A lioness kept in the Tower of London bore cubs in 1604 and 1605.
36   *fires at Berwick* Armies were reported seen fighting in the sky near Scotland in 1604,
     perhaps an effect of the *aurora borealis*.
37   *the new star* a supernova observed by Kepler in 1604.
38   *meteors* Meteors were believed ominous, since they evinced disruption in the
     heavens.
40   *porpoises* According to Stow's *Annals*, early in 1606 'a great Porpus was taken alive
     at Westham ... and within a few dayes after, a very great whale came up within 8 mile
     of London'; this reference suggests that Jonson did not finish *Volpone* until 1606.
     the bridge London Bridge.
41   *sturgeon* Peregrine is making fun of Sir Pol here, since sturgeon were common in the
     Thames (Parker).

Few know how many months, for the subversion
Of the Stode fleet.
SIR POLITIC   Is't possible? Believe it,
'Twas either sent from Spain, or the Archdukes!   50
Spinola's whale, upon my life, my credit!
Will they not leave these projects? Worthy sir,
Some other news.
PEREGRINE   Faith, Stone, the fool, is dead;
And they do lack a tavern fool, extremely.
SIR POLITIC
Is Mas' Stone dead?
PEREGRINE   He's dead sir; why? I hope   55
You thought him not immortal? [*Aside*] O this knight,
Were he well known, would be a precious thing
To fit our English stage. He that should write
But such a fellow should be thought to feign
Extremely, if not maliciously.
SIR POLITIC   Stone dead?   60
PEREGRINE
Dead. Lord, how deeply, sir, you apprehend it!
He was no kinsman to you?
SIR POLITIC   That I know of.
Well; that same fellow was an unknown fool.
PEREGRINE
And yet you know him, it seems?
SIR POLITIC   I did so. Sir,
I knew him one of the most dangerous heads   65
Living within the state, and so I held him.

---

49   *the Stode fleet* the ships of the English Merchant Adventurers, near the mouth of the
       Elbe river
51   *Spinola* a Spanish general feared in England for his ingenious secret weapons,
       including a whale 'hir'd to have drown'd London by snuffling up the Thames and
       spouting it upon the City' (Charles Herle, *Worldly Policy and Moral Prudence*
       [1654]).
53   *Stone* a London clown who had been whipped in 1605 for 'a blasphemous speech'.
55   *Stone dead* Here, and again at line 60, playing off the sense 'completely dead'; see
       I.iv.107.
62   *That I know of* Not that I know of.
63   *that . . . unknown fool* Stone's actual cleverness was successfully concealed; ironically,
       Sir Pol, who is a fool fancying himself a clever spy, believes Stone was a clever spy
       masquerading as a fool.
66   *held* considered.

PEREGRINE

Indeed, sir?

SIR POLITIC While he lived, in action.

He has received weekly intelligence,

Upon my knowledge, out of the Low Countries,

For all parts of the world, in cabbages;   70

And those dispensed again t' ambassadors,

In oranges, musk-melons, apricots,

Lemons, pome-citrons, and such-like; sometimes,

In Colchester oysters, and your Selsey cockles.

PEREGRINE

You make me wonder!

SIR POLITIC   Sir, upon my knowledge.   75

Nay, I have observed him, at your public ordinary,

Take his advertisement from a traveller

(A concealed statesman) in a trencher of meat;

And, instantly, before the meal was done,

Convey an answer in a toothpick.

PEREGRINE   Strange!   80

How could this be, sir?

SIR POLITIC   Why, the meat was cut

So like his character, and so laid, as he

Must easily read the cipher.

PEREGRINE   I have heard,

He could not read, sir.

SIR POLITIC   So 'twas given out,

In polity, by those that did employ him;   85

But he could read, and had your languages,

And to't, as sound a noddle –

PEREGRINE   I have heard, sir,

That your baboons were spies; and that they were

A kind of subtle nation, near to China.

---

67   *in action* while active, or, in actuality.
70   *cabbages* England imported cabbage from Holland; Sir Pol's paranoid fantasies echo
      many that were produced by the failed Gunpowder Plot of 1605.
76   *ordinary* tavern/restaurant.
77   *advertisement* information, instructions.
82   *character* writing or code; Shakespeare's *Cymbeline* describes a similarly intricate
      cutting of food.
87   *And to't, as sound a noddle* And in addition to that ability, he had as healthy a brain.
89   *subtle* crafty.

SIR POLITIC
    Ay, ay, your *Mamaluchi*. Faith, they had   90
    Their hand in a French plot, or two; but they
    Were so extremely given to women, as
    They made discovery of all. Yet I
    Had my advices here, on Wednesday last,
    From one of their own coat, they were returned,   95
    Made their relations (as the fashion is)
    And now stand fair, for fresh employment.
PEREGRINE [*Aside*]   'Heart!
    This Sir Pol will be ignorant of nothing.
    [*To* SIR POLITIC] It seems, sir, you know all?
SIR POLITIC   Not all, sir. But,
    I have some general notions; I do love   100
    To note, and to observe; though I live out,
    Free from the active torrent, yet I'd mark
    The currents, and the passages of things,
    For mine own private use; and know the ebbs,
    And flows of state.
PEREGRINE   Believe it, sir, I hold   105
    Myself, in no small tie, unto my fortunes,
    For casting me thus luckily, upon you;
    Whose knowledge, if your bounty equal it,
    May do me great assistance, in instruction
    For my behaviour, and my bearing, which   110
    Is yet so rude, and raw –
SIR POLITIC   Why, came you forth
    Empty of rules for travel?
PEREGRINE   Faith, I had
    Some common ones, from out that vulgar grammar,

---

90   *Mamaluchi* slaves who seized power in Egypt in the thirteenth century; the irrele-
      vance emphasizes Sir Pol's ridiculous efforts to sound knowledgeable.
91   *hand in a French plot* role in a French conspiracy, but probably with an unwitting
      sexual implication.
92   *given* susceptible (Topsell claimed baboons were so 'lustful' that they tried 'to defile
      all sorts of women' [Parker]).
93   *made discovery of all* disclosed all their secrets.
94   *advices* news dispatches.
95   *coat* faction.
96   *relations* reports.
97   *stand . . . employment* are ready to resume their spying
      'Heart! I swear by God's heart.
105–7 *I hold . . . upon you* I count myself very lucky to have run into you.
108 *bounty* generosity.

Which he that cried Italian to me taught me.
SIR POLITIC
    Why, this it is that spoils all our brave bloods,   115
    Trusting our hopeful gentry unto pedants,
    Fellows of outside, and mere bark. You seem
    To be a gentleman, of ingenuous race –
    I not profess it, but my fate hath been
    To be where I have been consulted with,   120
    In this high kind, touching some great men's sons,
    Persons of blood, and honour –
PEREGRINE   Who be these, sir?

ACT II, SCENE ii

[Enter MOSCA *and* NANO, *disguised as*
mountebank's assistants and carrying the makings
of a scaffold stage, followed by a CROWD]

MOSCA
    Under that window, there't must be. The same.
SIR POLITIC
    Fellows to mount a bank! Did your instructor
    In the dear tongues never discourse to you
    Of the Italian mountebanks?
PEREGRINE   Yes, sir.
SIR POLITIC   Why,
    Here shall you see one.

114   *cried* taught.
115   *brave bloods* aristocratic young men.
116   *hopeful* promising.
118   *ingenuous race* noble lineage.
121   *touching* concerning.
122   *blood* noble birth.

2   *mount a bank* 'An itinerant quack who from an elevated platform appealed to his audience by means of stories, tricks, juggling, and the like' (OED). Such figures were common in Venice, and had probably appeared in London as well. The travelling show dispensing patent medicines in rural America was a more recent equivalent. This set-up also strongly resembles the travelling scaffold stage on which most English drama had been performed in Jonson's youth (Kernan).
3   *dear* valuable.

PEREGRINE   They are quacksalvers,   5
Fellows that live by venting oils, and drugs?
SIR POLITIC
Was that the character he gave you of them?
PEREGRINE
As I remember.
SIR POLITIC   Pity his ignorance.
They are the only knowing men of Europe!
Great, general scholars, excellent physicians,   10
Most admired statesmen, professed favourites,
And cabinet counsellors, to the greatest princes!
The only languaged men of all the world!
PEREGRINE
And, I have heard, they are most lewd impostors;
Made all of terms, and shreds; no less beliers   15
Of great men's favours, than their own vile med'cines;
Which they will utter upon monstrous oaths,
Selling that drug for two pence, ere they part,
Which they have valued at twelve crowns, before.
SIR POLITIC
Sir, calumnies are answered best with silence: 20
Yourself shall judge.
[*To* MOSCA *and* NANO] Who is it mounts, my friends?
MOSCA
Scoto of Mantua, sir.
SIR POLITIC   Is't he? Nay, then
I'll proudly promise, sir, you shall behold
Another man than has been fant'sied to you.
I wonder, yet, that he should mount his bank   25
Here, in this nook, that has been wont t' appear

6   *venting* advertising and selling (vending).
7   *Was that . . . them?* Was that how your instructor characterized mountebanks?
9   *knowing* truly knowledgeable.
12   *cabinet* private.
15   *terms, and shreds* impressive jargon, and bits of undigested learning.
15–16 *no less . . . med'cines* as dishonest in claiming great patrons as in claiming that their
        disgusting potions are healthy (or, possibly, as treacherous to their great patrons as
        the supposed medicines are).
17   *utter* offer for sale.
19   *crowns* silver coins stamped with a crown (Parker).
22   *Scoto of Mantua* A famous Italian juggler and sleight-of-hand performer who visited
        Elizabethan England, and whose name became a by-word for a skilful deceiver.
26   *wont* accustomed. Sir Pol believes Scoto normally rates a grander setting.

In face of the Piazza! Here, he comes.

[*Enter* VOLPONE, *disguised as a mountebank*]

VOLPONE [*To* NANO]
Mount, zany.
CROWD   Follow, follow, follow, follow, follow.
SIR POLITIC
See how the people follow him! He's a man
May write ten thousand crowns, in bank, here.

[VOLPONE *climbs onto the platform*]

                                        Note,   30
Mark but his gesture; I do use to observe
The state he keeps, in getting up!
PEREGRINE   'Tis worth it, sir.
VOLPONE
Most noble gentlemen and my worthy patrons, it may seem
strange, that I, your Scoto Mantuano, who was ever wont to fix
my bank in face of the public Piazza, near the shelter of the   35
portico to the *Procuratia*, should, now, after eight months'
absence from this illustrious city of Venice, humbly retire myself
into an obscure nook of the Piazza.
SIR POLITIC
Did not I, now, object the same?
PEREGRINE   Peace, sir.

---

28   *zany* the clownish assistant of a performer.
31–2   *I do use . . . getting up* I always admire the dignity Scoto maintains in climbing on to the stage.
33–233 Throughout this scene, Jonson not only builds on standard episodes from the beast-fable and *commedia dell'arte* traditions, but also builds an extended metaphor that makes Volpone/Scoto a playful parody of Jonson himself (as Kernan has shown): a proud intellectual selling his goods now at a lower price to a public audience (at the Globe) instead of his usual aristocratic private one (at Blackfriars), after being jailed for offending a powerful man (Jonson angered King James, a Scot, by satirizing Scots in *Eastward Ho!*). Scoto and Jonson alike scorn their less scholarly competitors (whom they dismiss as poor imitators of their work, and purveyors of stale material), while trying to argue that their products have the power to cure their audience (notice the ways Jonson's boastful Prologue and Epistle resemble Scoto's sales pitch). Many of the Londoners from whom Jonson was now trying to coax the occasional sixpence (the likely cost of admission to *Volpone*) would surely have appreciated the in-joke.
36   *portico to the Procuratia* arcade of the residence of senior Venetian officials on the Piazza San Marco.

VOLPONE

> Let me tell you: I am not (as your Lombard proverb saith) cold   40
> on my feet, or content to part with my commodities at a cheaper
> rate than I accustomed: look not for it. Nor, that the calumnious
> reports of that impudent detractor, and shame to our profession
> (Alessandro Buttone, I mean) who gave out, in public, I was
> condemned *a sforzato* to the galleys, for poisoning the Cardinal   45
> Bembo's – cook, hath at all attached, much less dejected me. No,
> no, worthy gentlemen, to tell you true, I cannot endure to see
> the rabble of these ground *ciarlitani*, that spread their cloaks on
> the pavement, as if they meant to do feats of activity, and then
> come in, lamely, with their mouldy tales out of Boccaccio, like   50
> stale Tabarin, the fabulist; some of them discoursing their travels,
> and of their tedious captivity in the Turk's galleys, when indeed,
> were the truth known, they were the Christian's galleys, where
> very temperately they ate bread, and drunk water, as a whole-
> some penance, enjoined them by their confessors, for base   55
> pilferies.

SIR POLITIC

> Note but his bearing, and contempt of these.

VOLPONE

> These turdy-facey-nasty-patey-lousy-fartical rogues, with one
> poor groatsworth of unprepared antimony, finely wrapped up
> in several *scartoccios*, are able, very well, to kill their twenty a   60
> week, and play; yet these meagre starved spirits, who have half
> stopped the organs of their minds with earthy oppilations, want

40–1   *cold on my feet* stage-frightened, or, desperate to sell.
45   *a sforzato* by force (into enslavement).
45–6   *Cardinal Bembo's – cook* Bembo was a great Venetian Renaissance humanist; the
  dash suggests a hesitation about naming a more scandalous relationship (perhaps,
  'mistress').
48   *ground ciarlitani* lowly charlatans who lack a bank or bench to mount.
49   *feats of activity* gymnastics.
50   *Boccaccio* fourteenth-century author whose *Decameron* provided plots for many
  later writers, including Shakespeare.
51   *Tabarin, the fabulist* a travelling Venetian zany, contemporary with Scoto, here
  identified as a story-teller as well as comic performer; also a stock minor character
  in the *commedia*.
55   *enjoined them* prescribed for them.
59   *groatsworth of unprepared antimony* fourpence worth of native bisulphide (known
  as monksbane).
60   *several scartoccios* separate paper bins.
61   *play* keep their show running.
62   *earthy oppilations* mundane thoughts, which function like constipating foods.

not their favourers among your shrivelled, salad-eating artisans,
who are overjoyed that they may have their half-pe'rth of physic,
though it purge them into another world, makes no matter.   65

SIR POLITIC

Excellent! Ha' you heard better language, sir?

VOLPONE

Well, let 'em go. And gentlemen, honourable gentlemen, know,
that for this time, our bank, being thus removed from the clamours of the *canaglia*, shall be the scene of pleasure, and delight;
for I have nothing to sell, little or nothing to sell.   70

SIR POLITIC

I told you, sir, his end.

PEREGRINE   You did so, sir.

VOLPONE

I protest, I and my six servants are not able to make of this
precious liquor so fast as it is fetched away from my lodging, by
gentlemen of your city; strangers of the *terra-firma*; worshipful
merchants; ay, and senators too – who, ever since my arrival,   75
have detained me to their uses, by their splendidous liberalities.
And worthily. For what avails your rich man to have his magazines stuffed with *moscadelli*, or the purest grape, when his
physicians prescribe him (on pain of death) to drink nothing
but water, cocted with anise-seeds? O health! health! the   80
blessing of the rich, the riches of the poor! Who can buy thee at
too dear a rate, since there is no enjoying this world, without
thee? Be not then so sparing of your purses, honourable gentlemen, as to abridge the natural course of life –

PEREGRINE

You see his end?

SIR POLITIC   Ay, is't not good?   85

VOLPONE

For, when a humid flux, or catarrh, by the mutability of air, falls
from your head, into an arm or shoulder, or any other part, take
you a ducat, or your chequin of gold, and apply to the place

64   *half-pe'rth of physic* halfpenny worth of medicine.
69   *canaglia* rabble.
74   *terra-firma* mainland, especially the parts owned by Venice.
77–8 *magazines . . . moscadelli* storehouses full of muscatel wines.
80   *cocted* boiled.
86   *humid flux* Scoto/Volpone here uses the Renaissance theory of 'humours', which
      linked bodily and spiritual conditions to the balance of four fluids, to warn that
      inclement weather could send dampness from the head down into the body.

affected: see what good effect it can work. No, no, 'tis this blessed
unguento, this rare extraction, that hath only power to disperse   90
all malignant humours, that proceed, either of hot, cold, moist
or windy causes –

PEREGRINE

I would he had put in dry too.

SIR POLITIC   'Pray you, observe.

VOLPONE

To fortify the most indigest, and crude stomach – ay, were it of
one that, through extreme weakness, vomited blood – applying   95
only a warm napkin to the place, after the unction, and fricace;
for the *vertigine* in the head, putting but a drop into your nostrils,
likewise, behind the ears; a most sovereign and approved remedy:
the *mal caduco*, cramps, convulsions, paralyses, epilepsies,
tremor cordia, retired nerves, ill vapours of the spleen, stoppings   100
of the liver, the stone, the strangury, *hernia ventosa, iliaca passio*;
stops a *dysentaria*, immediately; easeth the torsion of the small
guts; and cures *melancholia hypocondriaca*, being taken and
applied, according to my printed receipt. (*Pointing to his bill and
his glass.*) For, this is the physician, this the medicine; this   105
counsels, this cures; this gives the direction, this works the
effect; and, in sum, both together may be termed an abstract of
the theoric and practic in the Aesculapian art. 'Twill cost you
eight crowns. [*Aloud to* NANO] And, Zan Fritada, 'pray thee sing
a verse, extempore, in honour of it.   110

SIR POLITIC

How do you like him, sir?

PEREGRINE   Most strangely, I!

SIR POLITIC

Is not his language rare?

---

90   *unguento* ointment.
96   *fricace* massage.
97–101 Scoto/Volpone claims to cure a variety of common medical problems – *vertigine*:
        vertigo, dizziness; *mal caduco*: epilepsy; *tremor cordia*: heart palpitations; *retired
        nerves*: shrunken sinews; *stone*: kidney stone; *strangury*: difficult urination; *iliaca
        passio*: intestinal cramps.
104   *receipt* recipe, prescription.
104–5   *his bill and his glass* Volpone points alternately to his prescription list and his beaker
        of medicinal oil.
108   *the Aesculapian art* medicine, of which Aesculapius was the classical god.
109   *Zan Fritada* Volpone calls on Nano by the name of a well-known zany.
111   *strangely* exceptionally, but not necessarily in a positive sense.

PEREGRINE   But alchemy,
I never heard the like; or Broughton's books.

Song [*by* VOLPONE'S SERVANTS]

> Had old Hippocrates, or Galen,
> That to their books put med'cines all in,   115
> But known this secret, they had never
> (Of which they will be guilty ever)
> Been murderers of so much paper,
> Or wasted many a hurtless taper;
> No Indian drug had e'er been famed,   120
> Tobacco, sassafras not named;
> Ne yet, of guacum one small stick, sir,
> Nor Raymond Lully's great elixir;
> Ne had been known the Danish Gonswart,
> Or Paracelsus, with his long-sword.   125

PEREGRINE

All this, yet, will not do: eight crowns is high.

VOLPONE

No more. Gentlemen, if I had but time to discourse to you the
miraculous effects of this my oil, surnamed *Oglio del Scoto*, with
the countless catalogue of those I have cured of th' aforesaid,
and many more diseases, the patents and privileges of all the   130
princes and commonwealths of Christendom; or but the depo-
sitions of those that appeared on my part, before the signiory of
the *Sanita*, and most learned college of physicians, where I was
authorized, upon notice taken of the admirable virtues of my
medicaments, and mine own excellency in matter of rare and   135

---

113   *Broughton* Hugh Broughton, a scholarly Puritan minister whose eccentric works
       Jonson mocks in *The Alchemist* (IV.v.1–32).
113   s.d. *Song* This song, and the one at line 181, are sung by some combination of Nano,
       as the zany, and perhaps Mosca (since Volpone refers to their 'voices'); it is also
       possible that Castrone appears and sings, since a primary purpose of castration was
       to preserve a pure soprano singing-voice.
114   *Hippocrates, or Galen* revered masters of ancient medicine, and inventor and
       propagator respectively, of the theory of humours.
122   *guacum* The wood and resin of the West Indian guaiacum tree were used medically.
123   *Lully* a Medieval astrologer later rumoured to have discovered the alchemical elixir
       of life.
125   *Paracelsus* a revolutionary Renaissance theorist of the body-chemistry of health, said
       to keep his medicines inside a sword handle.
128   *Oglio del Scoto* Scoto's Oil.
132–3 *signiory of the Sanita* Venetian medical board.

unknown secrets, not only to disperse them publicly in this
famous city, but in all the territories that happily joy under the
government of the most pious and magnificent states of Italy.
But may some other gallant fellow say, 'O, there be divers, that
make profession to have as good, and as experimented receipts, 140
as yours.' Indeed, very many have assayed, like apes, in imitation
of that which is really and essentially in me, to make of this oil;
bestowed great cost in furnaces, stills, alembics, continual fires,
and preparation of the ingredients, (as indeed there goes to it six
hundred several simples, beside some quantity of human fat, for 145
the conglutination, which we buy of the anatomists); but, when
these practitioners come to the last decoction, blow, blow, puff,
puff, and all flies *in fumo*: ha, ha, ha! Poor wretches! I rather pity
their folly, and indiscretion, than their loss of time, and money;
for those may be recovered by industry, but to be a fool born is 150
a disease incurable. For myself, I always from my youth have
endeavoured to get the rarest secrets, and book them, either in
exchange or for money; I spared nor cost, nor labour, where
anything was worthy to be learned. And gentlemen, honourable
gentlemen, I will undertake, by virtue of chemical art, out of 155
the honourable hat that covers your head, to extract the four
elements; that is to say, the fire, air, water, and earth, and return
you your felt without burn or stain. For, whilst others have been
at the *balloo*, I have been at my book; and am now past the craggy
paths of study, and come to the flowery plains of honour, and 160
reputation.

SIR POLITIC
I do assure you, sir, that is his aim.

VOLPONE
But, to our price.

PEREGRINE   And that withal, Sir Pol.

VOLPONE
You all know, honourable gentlemen, I never valued this *ampulla*,

139   *divers* many other people.
145   *several simples* separate herbs.
146   *conglutination* gluing together.
147   *decoction* boiling down.
147–8 *blow, blow, puff, puff* Volpone imitates alchemists trying to increase the heat of their
       fires with breath or bellows.
148   *in fumo* up in smoke; a similar catastrophe is reported in *The Alchemist*.
159   *balloo* a Venetian ball-game.
163   *that withal* Peregrine points out that Scoto is also aiming at money.

or vial, at less than eight crowns, but for this time, I am content 165
to be deprived of it for six: six crowns is the price, and less in
courtesy I know you cannot offer me; take it, or leave it, howsoever, both it, and I am at your service. I ask you not as the
value of the thing, for then I should demand of you a thousand
crowns: so the Cardinals Montalto, Fernese, the great Duke of 170
Tuscany, my gossip, with divers other princes have given me; but
I despise money. Only to show my affection to you, honourable
gentlemen, and your illustrious state here, I have neglected the
messages of these princes, mine own offices, framed my journey
hither, only to present you with the fruits of my travels. Tune 175
your voices once more, to the touch of your instruments, and
give the honourable assembly some delightful recreation.

PEREGRINE

What monstrous, and most painful circumstance
Is here, to get some three or four gazets?
Some threepence, i' th' whole; for that 'twill come to. 180

Song [by VOLPONE'S SERVANTS, *during which*
CELIA *appears at a window above]*

> You that would last long, list to my song,
> Make no more coil, but buy of this oil.
> Would you be ever fair? and young?
> Stout of teeth? and strong of tongue?
> Tart of palate? quick of ear? 185
> Sharp of sight? of nostril clear?
> Moist of hand? and light of foot?
> Or – I will come nearer to't –
> Would you live free from all diseases?
> Do the act your mistress pleases; 190

170 *Montalto, Fernese* sixteenth-century popes; but Jonson may also be alluding to the
contrast between the inexpensive tickets to *Volpone* and his well-paid work writing
single-performance masques for powerful Jacobean courtiers.
171 *gossip* godfather or close friend.
174 *offices* duties.
178 *painful circumstance* careful and elaborate set-up.
179 *gazets* Venetian pennies.
182 *coil* fuss.
185 *Tart* Keen.

> Yet fright all aches from your bones?
> Here's a med'cine, for the nones.

VOLPONE

Well, I am in a humour, at this time, to make a present of the
small quantity my coffer contains: to the rich, in courtesy, and
to the poor, for God's sake. Wherefore, now mark: I asked you 195
six crowns, and six crowns, at other times, you have paid me.
You shall not give me six crowns; nor five, nor four, nor three,
nor two, nor one; nor half a ducat; no, nor a *moccenigo*. Six pence
it will cost you, or six hundred pound – expect no lower price,
for by the banner of my front, I will not bate a *bagatine*, that I 200
will have, only, a pledge of your loves, to carry something from
amongst you, to show I am not contemned by you. Therefore,
now, toss your handkerchiefs, cheerfully, cheerfully; and be adver-
tised, that the first heroic spirit, that deigns to grace me with a
handkerchief, I will give it a little remembrance of something, 205
beside, shall please it better than if I had presented it with a
double pistolet.

PEREGRINE

Will you be that heroic spark, Sir Pol?

CELIA *at the window throws down her handkerchief*

O, see! The window has prevented you.

VOLPONE

Lady, I kiss your bounty; and, for this timely grace you have 210
done your poor Scoto of Mantua, I will return you, over and
above my oil, a secret of that high and inestimable nature, shall
make you for ever enamoured on that minute wherein your eye
first descended on so mean (yet not altogether to be despised)

191   *aches from your bones* possibly arthritis, but more likely venereal disease; 'aches' is two
      syllables, probably pronounced 'aitches'.
192   *nones* nonce, occasion.
198   *moccenigo* small Venetian coin.
200   *banner of my front* a sheet advertising the mountebank's cures.
      bate a bagatine drop the price by even the tiniest amount.
202   *contemned* scorned.
203   *handkerchiefs* Payments were often tossed to mountebanks, and the purchase tossed
      back, in tied handkerchiefs. But – as Shakespeare's *Othello* demonstrates – hand-
      kerchiefs could also serve as symbols of erotic interest.
207   *pistolet* valuable Spanish coin.
208   *spark* gallant.
209   *The window has prevented you* Someone above has beaten you to it; the Jacobean stage
      set had an upper level where at some unspecified point Celia appears at a window.

an object. Here is a powder, concealed in this paper, of which, if 215
I should speak to the worth, nine thousand volumes were but as
one page, that page as a line, that line as a word; so short is this
pilgrimage of man (which some call life) to the expressing of it.
Would I reflect on the price? Why, the whole world were but as
an empire, that empire as a province, that province as a bank, 220
that bank as a private purse, to the purchase of it. I will only tell
you: it is the powder that made Venus a goddess, given her by
Apollo, that kept her perpetually young, cleared her wrinkles,
firmed her gums, filled her skin, coloured her hair; from her,
derived to Helen, and at the sack of Troy, unfortunately, lost; till 225
now, in this our age, it was as happily recovered, by a studious
antiquary, out of some ruins of Asia, who sent a moiety of it to
the Court of France (but much sophisticated) wherewith the
ladies there now colour their hair. The rest, at this present,
remains with me, extracted, to a quintessence; so that, wherever 230
it but touches, in youth it perpetually preserves, in age restores
the complexion; seats your teeth, did they dance like virginal jacks,
firm as a wall; makes them white, as ivory, that were black, as –

ACT II, SCENE iii

[Enter] CORVINO [shouting up to CELIA]

CORVINO

Blood of the devil, and my shame. Come down, here;
Come down! No house but mine to make your scene?
Signor Flaminio, will you down sir? down?

222–4   *made Venus . . . colour their hair* The decreasing dignity of the powder's roles parallels
the history of Pythagoras's soul in I.ii.
227   *antiquary* scholar who studies the ancient world.
moiety portion.
228   *sophisticated* adulterated.
232   *did they dance like virginal jacks* even if they danced like little piano keys.

1   Corvino's line plausibly completes Scoto/Volpone's phrase, 'black, as'; F reads, 'Spite
of the devil', meaning the seducible woman, the devil's spite against man.
3–8   *Flaminio . . . Besogniosi* Among the play's many references to the *commedia dell'arte*
tradition, these names of actors and stock characters reflect Corvino's fear that he
has been put in the role of laughable old cuckold.

He beats away the mountebank, etc.

What, is my wife your Franciscina? sir?
No windows on the whole Piazza, here,   5
To make your properties, but mine? but mine?
Heart! ere tomorrow, I shall be new christened,
And called the *Pantalone di Besogniosi*,
About the town.   [*Exit*]
PEREGRINE   What should this mean, Sir Pol?
SIR POLITIC
Some trick of state, believe it. I will home.   10
PEREGRINE
It may be some design on you.
SIR POLITIC   I know not.
I'll stand upon my guard.
PEREGRINE   'Tis your best, sir.
SIR POLITIC
This three weeks, all my advices, all my letters,
They have been intercepted.
PEREGRINE   Indeed, sir?
Best have a care.
SIR POLITIC   Nay, so I will.   [*Exit*]
PEREGRINE   This knight,   15
I may not lose him, for my mirth, till night.   [*Exit*]

ACT II, SCENE iv

[*Enter*] VOLPONE, MOSCA

VOLPONE
O, I am wounded.
MOSCA   Where, sir?
VOLPONE   Not without:
Those blows were nothing; I could bear them ever.

6   *properties* stage props, but punning on the way Scoto has impinged on Corvino's
      property – his house, and perhaps also his wife.
11   *design on* plot against.

1   *without* on the outside.

But angry Cupid, bolting from her eyes,
Hath shot himself into me, like a flame;
Where, now, he flings about his burning heat,   5
As in a furnace, some ambitious fire,
Whose vent is stopped. The fight is all within me.
I cannot live, except thou help me, Mosca:
My liver melts, and I, without the hope
Of some soft air, from her refreshing breath,   10
Am but a heap of cinders.

MOSCA   'Las, good sir,
Would you had never seen her.

VOLPONE   Nay, would thou
Hadst never told me of her.

MOSCA   Sir, 'tis true:
I do confess, I was unfortunate,
And you unhappy; but I am bound in conscience,   15
No less than duty, to effect my best
To your release of torment, and I will, sir.

VOLPONE
Dear Mosca, shall I hope?

MOSCA   Sir, more than dear,
I will not bid you to despair of aught,
Within a human compass.

VOLPONE   O, there spoke   20
My better angel. Mosca, take my keys,
Gold, plate, and jewels, all's at thy devotion;
Employ them, how thou wilt; nay, coin me, too;
So thou, in this, but crown my longings. Mosca?

MOSCA
Use but your patience.

VOLPONE   So I have.

MOSCA   I doubt not   25
To bring success to your desires.

VOLPONE   Nay, then,
I not repent me of my late disguise.

MOSCA
If you can horn him, sir, you need not.

---

3   *bolting* shooting like an arrow, often called a 'bolt'; cf. Anacreon's Odes 14 and 16.
9   *liver* believed to be the location of violent emotions.
19–20   *aught, / Within a human compass* anything within human reach (or imagination).
24   *So . . . longings* If you can fulfil my desires in this regard.
28   *horn* cuckold (betrayed husbands were said to grow horns).

VOLPONE   True;
  Besides, I never meant him for my heir.
  Is not the colour of my beard, and eyebrows,   30
  To make me known?
MOSCA   No jot.
VOLPONE   I did it well.
MOSCA
  So well, would I could follow you in mine,
  With half the happiness; and, yet, I would
  Escape your epilogue.
VOLPONE   But, were they gulled
  With a belief, that I was Scoto?
MOSCA   Sir,   35
  Scoto himself could hardly have distinguished!
  I have not time to flatter you, we'll part;
  And, as I prosper, so applaud my art.
                                                     [*Exeunt*]

ACT II, SCENE v

[*Enter*] CORVINO, CELIA

CORVINO
  Death of mine honour, with the city's fool?
  A juggling, tooth-drawing, prating mountebank?
  And, at a public window? where whilst he,
  With his strained action, and his dole of faces,
  To his drug-lecture draws your itching ears,   5

29–31 *Besides . . . known* Perhaps reminded by his use of the word 'heir', Volpone worries
       that his (fox-red?) hair ruined his disguise.
  31   *No jot* Not in the slightest.
  32   *mine* my role in this trickery.
33–4   *I would / Escape your epilogue* I would like to avoid the beating you took from
       Corvino. The line is also another oblique signal that Mosca intends to come out
       better than Volpone when their show ends.

   2   *tooth-drawing* Mountebanks sometimes performed dental extractions.
   4   *his strained action . . . faces* his exaggerated gestures, and his poor repertoire of masks
       or facial expressions.

A crew of old, unmarried, noted lechers,
Stood leering up, like satyrs; and you smile,
Most graciously! and fan your favours forth,
To give your hot spectators satisfaction!
What, was your mountebank their call? their whistle?   10
Or were you enamoured on his copper rings?
His saffron jewel, with the toad-stone in't?
Or his embroidered suit, with the cope-stitch,
Made of a hearse-cloth? or his old tilt-feather?
Or his starched beard? Well! you shall have him, yes.   15
He shall come home, and minister unto you
The fricace, for the mother. Or, let me see,
I think, you'd rather mount? would you not mount?
Why, if you'll mount, you may; yes truly, you may;
And so, you may be seen, down to th' foot.   20
Get you a cittern, Lady Vanity,
And be a dealer with the virtuous man:
Make one; I'll but protest myself a cuckold,
And save your dowry. I am a Dutchman, I!
For, if you thought me an Italian,   25
You would be damned ere you did this, you whore:
Thou'dst tremble to imagine that the murder
Of father, mother, brother, all thy race,
Should follow, as the subject of my justice.

10 *their call? their whistle?* Apparently a reference to bird-calls, with hints of prosti-
    tution, and resonance in the extended bird-metaphors of the play as a whole.
11–12 *copper rings ... saffron jewel* cheap simulations of the colour of gold.
12 *toad-stone* a jewel with magical curative properties believed hidden between the eyes
    of toads.
14–15 *hearse-cloth ... starched beard* The Scoto costume was evidently garish, with fancy
    draperies used in funerals, a large feather from a jousting helmet, and a fashionably
    shaped and waxed beard.
17 *fricace, for the mother* massage for hysteria, believed to arise from the womb; hence,
    a thinly disguised metaphor for sexual ministrations.
19 *mount* perform as a mountebank, but also implying sexual mounting with the
    mountebank.
21 *cittern* zither, sometimes played by mountebanks' assistants or prostitutes.
    Lady Vanity a stock sinister character in English morality plays.
22 *be a dealer* transact business, presumably prostitution.
23 *Make one* Make a deal, join a company, or perform a sexual act.
24 *save your dowry* An unfaithful wife legally forfeited her dowry.
    Dutchman Englishmen considered Dutchmen oddly sluggish, apathetic, and
    tolerant.

CELIA

    Good sir, have patience.

CORVINO [*Drawing a weapon*] What couldst thou propose   30
    Less to thyself, than, in this heat of wrath,
    And stung with my dishonour, I should strike
    This steel into thee, with as many stabs
    As thou wert gazed upon with goatish eyes?

CELIA

    Alas sir, be appeased: I could not think   35
    My being at the window should more, now,
    Move your impatience, than at other times.

CORVINO

    No? Not to seek and entertain a parley
    With a known knave? before a multitude?
    You were an actor, with your handkerchief;   40
    Which he, most sweetly, kissed in the receipt,
    And might, no doubt, return it, with a letter,
    And 'point the place where you might meet: your sister's,
    Your mother's, or your aunt's might serve the turn.

CELIA

    Why, dear sir, when do I make these excuses?   45
    Or ever stir abroad but to the church?
    And that, so seldom –

CORVINO   Well, it shall be less;
    And thy restraint, before, was liberty,
    To what I now decree; and therefore, mark me.
    First, I will have this bawdy light dammed up;   50
    And, till't be done, some two, or three yards off,
    I'll chalk a line; o'er which, if thou but chance
    To set thy desp'rate foot, more hell, more horror,
    More wild, remorseless rage shall seize on thee,

---

34   *goatish* lustful.
38   *parley* conversation or negotiation.
40   *actor* an active participant, and perhaps a deceptive one.
43   *'point* appoint, designate.
44   *turn* purpose.
49   *To* Compared to.
        mark me listen carefully, mark my words.
50   *light* window.

Than on a conjurer, that had heedless left   55
His circle's safety, ere his devil was laid.
Then [*Showing a chastity belt*], here's a lock, which I will hang
    upon thee;
And, now I think on't, I will keep thee backwards:
Thy lodging shall be backwards, thy walks backwards,
Thy prospect – all be backwards; and no pleasure   60
That thou shalt know, but backwards. Nay, since you force
My honest nature, know, it is your own
Being too open, makes me use you thus.
Since you will not contain your subtle nostrils
In a sweet room, but, they must snuff the air   65
Of rank and sweaty passengers –

                                                          Knock within
                              One knocks.
Away, and be not seen, pain of thy life;
Not look toward the window: if thou dost –

                                        [CELIA *begins to exit*]
Nay, stay, hear this – let me not prosper, whore,
But I will make thee an anatomy,   70
Dissect thee mine own self, and read a lecture
Upon thee, to the city, and in public.
Away.

                                                          [*Exit* CELIA]
        Who is there?

                        [*Enter* SERVANT]

SERVANT   'Tis Signior Mosca, sir.

55–6   *conjurer . . . laid* It was believed that, if a necromancer stepped outside his protective
        chalk-circle before sending the demons he was commanding back to hell, they would
        tear him to pieces.
60   *prospect* future, or, view.
61   *backwards* Corvino vows to keep Celia away from the public edges of his house, but
        by this fifth use, the word has taken on sexual implications, probably related to some
        stage business with the chastity belt.
64   *subtle* crafty (for sniffing out sexual interest), or (sarcastically) delicate.
67   *pain* on pain.
70   *anatomy* Autopsies became popular public events in this period.

ACT II, SCENE vi

CORVINO
Let him come in, his master's dead. There's yet
Some good, to help the bad.

[*Exit* SERVANT]

[*Enter* MOSCA]

My Mosca, welcome;
I guess your news.
MOSCA   I fear you cannot, sir.
CORVINO
Is't not his death?
MOSCA   Rather the contrary.
CORVINO
Not his recovery?
MOSCA   Yes, sir.
CORVINO   I am cursed,   5
I am bewitched, my crosses meet to vex me.
How? how? how? how?
MOSCA   Why, sir, with Scoto's oil!
Corbaccio and Voltore brought of it,
Whilst I was busy in an inner room –
CORVINO
Death! that damned mountebank! but for the law,   10
Now, I could kill the rascal; 't cannot be
His oil should have that virtue. Ha' not I
Known him a common rogue, come fiddling in
To th' *osteria*, with a tumbling whore,
And, when he has done all his forced tricks, been glad   15
Of a poor spoonful of dead wine, with flies in't?
It cannot be. All his ingredients
Are a sheep's gall, a roasted bitch's marrow,
Some few sod earwigs, pounded caterpillars,

---

6   *crosses* afflictions.
14   *osteria* inn.
16   *dead* stale.
19   *sod* boiled.

A little capon's grease, and fasting spittle: 20
I know 'em, to a dram.
MOSCA   I know not, sir;
But some on't, there, they poured into his ears,
Some in his nostrils, and recovered him,
Applying but the fricace.
CORVINO   Pox o' that fricace.
MOSCA
And since, to seem the more officious,   25
And flatt'ring of his health, there, they have had,
At extreme fees, the college of physicians
Consulting on him how they might restore him;
Where, one would have a cataplasm of spices,
Another a flayed ape clapped to his breast,   30
A third would ha' it a dog, a fourth an oil
With wild cats' skins. At last, they all resolved
That, to preserve him, was no other means,
But some young woman must be straight sought out –
Lusty, and full of juice – to sleep by him;   35
And, to this service (most unhappily,
And most unwillingly) am I now employed,
Which, here, I thought to pre-acquaint you with,
For your advice, since it concerns you most,
Because I would not do that thing might cross   40
Your ends, on whom I have my whole dependence, sir.
Yet if I do it not, they may delate
My slackness to my patron, work me out
Of his opinion; and there, all your hopes,
Ventures, or whatsoever, are all frustrate.   45
I do but tell you, sir. Besides, they are all
Now striving, who shall first present him. Therefore –
I could entreat you, briefly, conclude somewhat:

20   *fasting spittle* the saliva of a starving man – probably Scoto himself.
21   *to a dram* down to the most miniscule portion.
22   *on't* of it.
29   *cataplasm* poultice.
34   *straight* immediately.
34–5 *some young woman . . . sleep by him* King David is similarly cured in I Kings 1.
40–1 *cross / Your ends* interfere with your goals.
42   *delate* report.
44   *opinion* favour.
48   *I could . . . somewhat* I beg you to make a quick decision.

Prevent 'em if you can.

CORVINO   Death to my hopes!
This is my villainous fortune! Best to hire   50
Some common courtesan?

MOSCA   Ay, I thought on that, sir.
But they are all so subtle, full of art,
And age again doting, and flexible,
So as – I cannot tell – we may perchance
Light on a quean may cheat us all.

CORVINO   'Tis true.   55

MOSCA

No, no; it must be one that has no tricks, sir,
Some simple thing, a creature made unto it;
Some wench you may command. Ha' you no kinswoman?
Godso – Think, think, think, think, think, think, think, sir.
One o' the doctors offered, there, his daughter.   60

CORVINO

How!

MOSCA

       Yes, Signior Lupo, the physician.

CORVINO

His daughter?

MOSCA   And a virgin, sir. Why? Alas,
He knows the state of's body, what it is:
That nought can warm his blood, sir, but a fever;
Nor any incantation raise his spirit: 65
A long forgetfulness hath seized that part.
Besides, sir, who shall know it? Some one, or two –

CORVINO

I pray thee give me leave.   [*Moves away, talking to himself*]
                      If any man
But I had had this luck – The thing in't self,
I know, is nothing – Wherefore should not I   70
As well command my blood, and my affections,
As this dull doctor? In the point of honour,

---

53   *age . . . flexible* old men, moreover, tend to become infatuated and thereby manipulated.
55   *quean* whore.
59   *Godso* An exclamatory oath, probably short for 'By God's soul'.
61   *Lupo* Italian for a wolf.

The cases are all one, of wife and daughter.

MOSCA [*Aside*]

    I hear him coming.

CORVINO   She shall do't. 'Tis done.

    'Slight, if this doctor, who is not engaged,   75

    Unless 't be for his counsel (which is nothing)

    Offer his daughter, what should I, that am

    So deeply in? I will prevent him: wretch!

    Covetous wretch! [*To* MOSCA] Mosca, I have determined.

MOSCA

    How, sir?

CORVINO   We'll make all sure. The party you wot of,   80

    Shall be mine own wife, Mosca.

MOSCA   Sir. The thing –

    But that I would not seem to counsel you –

    I should have motioned to you at the first;

    And, make your count, you have cut all their throats.

    Why, 'tis directly taking a possession!   85

    And, in his next fit, we may let him go.

    'Tis but to pull the pillow from his head,

    And he is throttled: 't had been done before,

    But for your scrupulous doubts.

CORVINO   Ay, a plague on't,

    My conscience fools my wit. Well, I'll be brief,   90

    And so be thou, lest they should be before us:

    Go home, prepare him, tell him, with what zeal,

    And willingness, I do it; swear it was

    On the first hearing (as thou mayst do, truly),

    Mine own free motion.

MOSCA   Sir, I warrant you,   95

    I'll so possess him with it, that the rest

    Of his starved clients shall be banished, all;

    And only you received. But come not, sir,

---

73   *all one* equal.

74   *coming* coming around, deciding to cooperate.

75   *'Slight* an exclamatory oath, short for 'I swear by God's light'.
     not engaged does not have a monetary investment at stake.

80   *party you wot of* person you were seeking.

83   *motioned* suggested.

84   *make your . . . throats* count on it, begin inventory of your grand inheritance, because
     you have thus defeated your rivals for it.

90   *fools my wit* has caused my intelligence to fail.

Until I send, for I have something else
To ripen, for your good – you must not know't.   100
CORVINO
But do not you forget to send, now.
MOSCA   Fear not.   [*Exit* MOSCA]

ACT II, SCENE vii

CORVINO
Where are you, wife? my Celia? wife?

[*Enter* CELIA, *weeping*]

                              What, blubbering?
Come, dry those tears. I think, thou thought'st me in earnest?
Ha? By this light, I talked so but to try thee.
Methinks the lightness of the occasion
Should ha' confirmed thee. Come, I am not jealous.   5
CELIA
No?
CORVINO Faith, I am not, I, nor never was:
It is a poor, unprofitable humour.
Do not I know, if women have a will,
They'll do 'gainst all the watches o' the world?
And that the fiercest spies are tamed with gold?   10
Tut, I am confident in thee, thou shalt see't;
And see, I'll give thee cause too, to believe it.
Come, kiss me. Go, and make thee ready straight,
In all thy best attire, thy choicest jewels,
Put 'em all on, and, with 'em, thy best looks: 15

99–100   *something else* / *To ripen* a plot to bring to fruition – tricking Corbaccio into making
         Volpone, rather than his own son Bonario, his heir.

   3   *try* test.
 4–5   *the lightness . . . confirmed thee* the triviality of the cause of my outburst should
         have assured you I wasn't serious.
   6   *Faith* In faith.
   7   *humour* emotion.
   9   *do 'gainst* cheat despite.
  11   *Tut* Nonsense, don't be silly.

We are invited to a solemn feast,
At old Volpone's, where it shall appear
How far I am free from jealousy or fear.

[*Exeunt*]

ACT III, SCENE i

[*Enter*] MOSCA

MOSCA
I fear I shall begin to grow in love
With my dear self, and my most prosp'rous parts,
They do so spring, and burgeon; I can feel
A whimsy i' my blood. I know not how,
Success hath made me wanton. I could skip   5
Out of my skin, now, like a subtle snake,
I am so limber. O! your parasite
Is a most precious thing, dropped from above,
Not bred 'mongst clods and clodpolls here on earth.
I muse the mystery was not made a science,   10
It is so liberally professed! Almost
All the wise world is little else, in nature,
But parasites, or sub-parasites. And yet,
I mean not those, that have your bare town-art,
To know who's fit to feed 'em; have no house,   15
No family, no care, and therefore mould
Tales for men's ears, to bait that sense; or get
Kitchen-invention, and some stale receipts
To please the belly, and the groin; nor those,
With their court-dog-tricks, that can fawn and fleer,   20
Make their revenue out of legs and faces,
Echo my lord, and lick away a moth.

2   *parts* qualities – but also body-parts and stage-parts.
4   *whimsy* giddiness, or whirling.
5   *wanton* wild, playful, sensual.
9   *clods and clodpolls* dull, stupid persons.
10   *mystery* craft.
     science field of knowledge in higher education.
14   *bare town-art* crude skills of street-hustlers; here and in line 19 the commas after
     'those' are dropped by most modern editors, but they may mark opportunities for
     Mosca to point to members of the audience.
20   *court-dog-tricks* obsequious service, begging favours (as opposed to the more prac-
     tical offerings of town-parasites).
21   *legs and faces* either elaborate bows and smiles, or (as under King James) physical
     attractiveness.
22   *moth* any small vermin; minute grooming was a common servile behaviour at court,
     and licking would presumably be an even more dog-like form of that service.

But your fine, elegant rascal, that can rise
And stoop, almost together, like an arrow;
Shoot through the air, as nimbly as a star; 25
Turn short, as doth a swallow; and be here,
And there, and here, and yonder, all at once;
Present to any humour, all occasion;
And change a visor swifter than a thought!
This is the creature had the art born with him; 30
Toils not to learn it, but doth practise it
Out of most excellent nature; and such sparks
Are the true parasites, others but their zanies.

ACT III, SCENE ii

[*Enter*] BONARIO

MOSCA
Who's this? Bonario? Old Corbaccio's son?
The person I was bound to seek. Fair sir,
You are happ'ly met.

BONARIO   That cannot be, by thee.

MOSCA
Why sir?

BONARIO   Nay, 'pray thee, know thy way, and leave me:
I would be loath to interchange discourse 5
With such a mate as thou art.

MOSCA   Courteous sir,
Scorn not my poverty.

BONARIO   Not I, by heaven;
But thou shalt give me leave to hate thy baseness.

MOSCA
Baseness?

24   *together* simultaneously.
28   *Present ... occasion* Ready to respond pleasingly to any mood or event, or, Ready to
       offer justification for any mood, or, Ready to satisfy any whim.
29   *visor* mask, facial expression, personality.

 2   *bound* on my way.
 6   *mate* lowly companion.

BONARIO   Ay, answer me, is not thy sloth
   Sufficient argument? Thy flattery?   10
   Thy means of feeding?
MOSCA   Heaven, be good to me.
   These imputations are too common, sir,
   And eas'ly stuck on virtue, when she's poor.
   You are unequal to me, and howe'er
   Your sentence may be righteous, yet you are not,   15
   That ere you know me, thus, proceed in censure;
   St Mark bear witness 'gainst you, 'tis inhuman.
BONARIO [*Aside*]
   What? Does he weep? The sign is soft, and good;
   I do repent me, that I was so harsh.
MOSCA
   'Tis true that, swayed by strong necessity,   20
   I am enforced to eat my careful bread
   With too much obsequy; 'tis true, beside,
   That I am fain to spin mine own poor raiment
   Out of my mere observance, being not born
   To a free fortune; but that I have done   25
   Base offices, in rending friends asunder,
   Dividing families, betraying counsels,
   Whispering false lies, or mining men with praises,
   Trained their credulity with perjuries,
   Corrupted chastity, or am in love   30
   With mine own tender ease, but would not rather
   Prove the most rugged and laborious course
   That might redeem my present estimation,
   Let me here perish, in all hope of goodness.
BONARIO
   This cannot be a personated passion.   35
   I was to blame, so to mistake thy nature;

10   *argument* evidence.
14   *unequal* unfair.
      howe'er however much.
21   *careful* full of cares.
23–4 *fain . . . observance* obliged to earn the clothes on my back by nothing more heroic
      than dutiful service.
29   *Trained* Led on.
32   *Prove* Attempt, endure.
33   *estimation* reputation.
35   *personated* impersonated, feigned.

'Pray thee forgive me, and speak out thy business.

MOSCA

    Sir, it concerns you; and though I may seem,
    At first, to make a main offence in manners,
    And in my gratitude unto my master,   40
    Yet, for the pure love which I bear all right,
    And hatred of the wrong, I must reveal it.
    This very hour, your father is in purpose
    To disinherit you –

BONARIO   How!

MOSCA   And thrust you forth,
    As a mere stranger to his blood; 'tis true, sir,   45
    The work no way engageth me, but as
    I claim an interest in the general state
    Of goodness, and true virtue, which I hear
    T' abound in you; and, for which mere respect,
    Without a second aim, sir, I have done it.   50

BONARIO

    This tale hath lost thee much of the late trust
    Thou hadst with me: it is impossible.
    I know not how to lend it any thought,
    My father should be so unnatural.

MOSCA

    It is a confidence that well becomes   55
    Your piety; and formed, no doubt, it is
    From your own simple innocence; which makes
    Your wrong more monstrous, and abhorred. But, sir,
    I now will tell you more. This very minute,
    It is, or will be doing; and, if you   60
    Shall be but pleased to go with me, I'll bring you –
    I dare not say where you shall see, but – where
    Your ear shall be a witness of the deed:
    Hear yourself written bastard, and professed
    The common issue of the earth.

---

41   *bear all right* feel towards the good and just.
46   *engageth* holds advantage for.
49   *for which mere respect* for this reason only.
51   *late* recent.
53   *lend it any thought* even imagine the possibility that.
56   *piety* filial love (the Latin *pietas*).
58   *Your wrong* The way you are being wronged.
65   *common issue of the earth* child with no acknowledged parent (the Latin *terrae filius*).

BONARIO   I'm mazed.   65
MOSCA
    Sir, if I do it not, draw your just sword,
    And score your vengeance, on my front, and face:
    Mark me your villain. You have too much wrong,
    And I do suffer for you, sir. My heart
    Weeps blood, in anguish –
BONARIO   Lead. I follow thee.   70

                                              [*Exeunt*]

ACT III, SCENE iii

[*Enter*] VOLPONE, NANO, ANDROGYNO, CASTRONE

VOLPONE
    Mosca stays long, methinks. Bring forth your sports
    And help to make the wretched time more sweet.
NANO
    Dwarf, fool, and eunuch, well met here we be.
        A question it were now, whether of us three –
    Being, all, the known delicates of a rich man –   5
        In pleasing him, claim the precedency can?
CASTRONE
    I claim for myself.
ANDROGYNO   And so doth the fool.
NANO
    'Tis foolish indeed: let me set you both to school.
    First, for your dwarf, he's little and witty,
        And everything, as it is little, is pretty;   10
    Else, why do men say to a creature of my shape
        So soon as they see him, 'It's a pretty little ape'?
    And, why a pretty ape, but for pleasing imitation
        Of greater men's action, in a ridiculous fashion?
    Beside, this feat body of mine doth not crave   15

----

    4   *whether* which.
    5   *delicates* favourites; this competition for Volpone's favour parallels that among the
         legacy-hunters.
    8   *set you both to school* instruct you both.
    15   *feat* dainty.

Half the meat, drink, and cloth, one of your bulks will have.
Admit, your fool's face be the mother of laughter,
   Yet, for his·brain, it must always come after;
And, though that do feed him, it's a pitiful case,
   His body is beholding to such a bad face.   20

One knocks

VOLPONE

Who's there? My couch, away, look, Nano, see:
Give me my caps, first – go, inquire.
        [*Exeunt* NANO, ANDROGYNO, *and* CASTRONE]
              Now, Cupid
Send it be Mosca, and with fair return.

      [VOLPONE *lies on bis bed;* NANO *enters*]

NANO

It is the beauteous madam –

VOLPONE   Would-Be – is it?

NANO

The same.

VOLPONE   Now, torment on me! Squire her in;   25
For she will enter, or dwell here forever.
Nay, quickly, that my fit were past.

                 [*Exit* NANO]

           I fear
A second hell too, that my loathing this
Will quite expel my appetite to the other:
Would she were taking, now, her tedious leave.   30
Lord, how it threats me, what I am to suffer!

---

19   *that* his face.
22   s.d. *Exeunt* NANO No re-entry is marked for Nano before his next line; perhaps he
       speaks through the doorway.
22–3 *Now, Cupid . . . return* may Cupid grant my wish that it is Mosca knocking, and
       bringing good news.
27   *that my fit were past* so that I can get it over with.
29   *the other* the other woman, Celia.

ACT III, SCENE iv

[*Enter* NANO, *bringing*] LADY WOULD-BE

LADY WOULD-BE [*To* NANO]
  I thank you, good sir. 'Pray you signify
  Unto your patron, I am here. This band
  Shows not my neck enough – I trouble you, sir,
  Let me request you, bid one of my women
  Come hither to me –

                          [*Exit* NANO]
                  In good faith, I, am dressed   5
  Most favourably, today, it is no matter,
  'Tis well enough.

       [*Enter* NANO *with first* SERVING-WOMAN]

           Look, see, these petulant things,
  How they have done this!
VOLPONE [*Aside*]   I do feel the fever
  Ent'ring, in at mine ears: O, for a charm
  To fright it hence.
LADY WOULD-BE   Come nearer: is this curl   10
  In his right place? or this? Why is this higher
  Than all the rest? You ha' not washed your eyes, yet?
  Or do they not stand even in your head?
  Where is your fellow? Call her.
             [*Exit first* SERVING-WOMAN]
NANO [*Aside*]   Now, St Mark
  Deliver us: anon, she'll beat her women,   15
  Because her nose is red.

      [*Enter first* SERVING-WOMAN *with* ANOTHER]

---

  2   *band* ruff or collar; this line may refer to what the English considered shockingly
       low necklines on Italian dresses (Coryat 1, 399–400, cited by Parker); it may also
       refer to the band around the neck of a parrot, a bird the English commonly called
       'Pol' or 'Polly', thus extending the avian metaphor to this fourth legacy-hunter.
5–6 *In good . . . today* Lady Would-Be is speaking sarcastically.
  9   *charm* magic spell.
 13 *do they . . . head?* can't you see straight?.
 15 *anon* in a moment.

LADY WOULD-BE   I pray you, view
  This tire, forsooth; are all things apt, or no?
1ST WOMAN
  One hair a little, here, sticks out, forsooth.
LADY WOULD-BE
  Does't so, forsooth? And where was your dear sight
  When it did so, forsooth? What now? Bird-eyed?   20
  And you too? 'Pray you both approach, and mend it.
  Now, by that light, I muse you are not ashamed!
  I, that have preached these things so oft unto you,
  Read you the principles, argued all the grounds,
  Disputed every fitness, every grace,   25
  Called you to counsel of so frequent dressings –
NANO [Aside]
  More carefully, than of your fame, or honour.
LADY WOULD-BE
  Made you acquainted what an ample dowry
  The knowledge of these things would be unto you,
  Able, alone, to get you noble husbands   30
  At your return; and you, thus, to neglect it?
  Besides, you seeing what a curious nation
  Th' Italians are, what will they say of me?
  'The English lady cannot dress herself':
  Here's a fine imputation, to our country.   35
  Well, go your ways, and stay i' the next room.
  This fucus was too coarse too, it's no matter.
  Good sir, you'll give 'em entertainment?
                            [Exit NANO with SERVING-WOMEN]
VOLPONE [Aside]
  The storm comes toward me.
LADY WOULD-BE   How does my Volp?
VOLPONE
  Troubled with noise, I cannot sleep: I dreamt   40
  That a strange fury entered, now, my house,

---

17   *tire* head-dress.
22   *I muse* I am amazed.
23–6 *preached . . . counsel* Lady Would-Be invokes the high language of theological, logical,
     rhetorical, aesthetic, and legal education.
27   *fame* reputation.
31   *return* return to England.
32   *curious* attentive to details.
37   *fucus* a paste or paint used as a cosmetic base.

And, with the dreadful tempest of her breath,
Did cleave my roof asunder.

LADY WOULD-BE   Believe me, and I
Had the most fearful dream, could I remember't –

VOLPONE [*Aside*]
Out on my fate! I ha' giv'n her the occasion   45
How to torment me: she will tell me hers.

LADY WOULD-BE
Methought, the golden mediocrity,
Polite and delicate –

VOLPONE   O, if you do love me,
No more: I sweat, and suffer, at the mention
Of any dream; feel, how I tremble yet.   50

LADY WOULD-BE
Alas, good soul, the passion of the heart!
Seed-pearl were good now, boiled with syrup of apples,
Tincture of gold, and coral, citron-pills,
Your elecampane root, myrobalanes –

VOLPONE [*Aside*]
Ay me, I have ta'en a grasshopper by the wing.   55

LADY WOULD-BE
Burnt silk, and amber, you have muscadel
Good i' the house –

VOLPONE   You will not drink, and part?

LADY WOULD-BE
No, fear not that. I doubt, we shall not get

---

45   *Out* Curses.
      occasion opportunity.
47   *golden mediocrity* Lady Would-Be's characteristically protracted and mannered term
      (out of Theophrastus) for the Horatian 'golden mean', and also a reminder that gold
      is what diverts all the play's characters from safe moderation. Unlike modern editors,
      neither Q nor F (both usually generous with commas) places a comma at the end
      of this line; so if Lady Would-Be's dream was indeed 'fearful', she may be preparing
      (after a 'but') to describe the shocking transformation of this supposedly decorous
      'mediocrity' into something monstrous.
52–4 *Seed-pearl . . . myrobalanes* A medley of popular remedies, mostly stimulants and
      cures for melancholy.
55   *ta'en a grasshopper by the wing* Volpone here complains about the constant whining
      noise of Lady Would-Be's voice, but may also have in mind a Renaissance locution:
      'someone *seizes the grasshopper by the wing* when he incites and prompts someone
      else to do something, which the latter is prepared to do even more promptly and
      readily on his own initiative' (Parker, citing Stephanus's gloss to Erasmus's *Adagia*).
56   *Burnt silk* a treatment for smallpox.
58   *doubt* fear.

Some English saffron – half a dram would serve –
Your sixteen cloves, a little musk, dried mints,   60
Bugloss, and barley-meal –
VOLPONE [*Aside*]   She's in again;
Before I feigned diseases, now I have one.
LADY WOULD-BE
And these applied with a right scarlet cloth –
VOLPONE [*Aside*]
Another flood of words! A very torrent!
LADY WOULD-BE
Shall I, sir, make you a poultice?
VOLPONE   No, no, no: 65
I'm very well; you need prescribe no more.
LADY WOULD-BE
I have, a little, studied physic; but, now,
I'm all for music – save, i' the forenoons,
An hour, or two, for painting. I would have
A lady, indeed, to have all, letters and arts,   70
Be able to discourse, to write, to paint,
But principal (as Plato holds) your music
(And, so does wise Pythagoras, I take it)
Is your true rapture: when there is concent
In face, in voice, and clothes; and is, indeed,   75
Our sex's chiefest ornament.
VOLPONE   The poet,
As old in time as Plato, and as knowing,
Says that your highest female grace is silence.
LADY WOULD-BE
Which o' your poets? Petrarch? or Tasso? or Dante?
Guarini? Ariosto? Aretine?   80
Cieco di Hadria? I have read them all.

---

61   *Bugloss* recommended (as are many of Lady Would-Be's remedies) in Burton's
       Anatomy of Melancholy, this one as a heart stimulant.
63   *scarlet cloth* Smallpox patients were sometimes wrapped in scarlet cloth.
70, 75   *indeed* Apparently a familiar pretentious verbal tic in Jacobean society; overuse of
       'indeed' is mocked in Marston's *What You Will*, III.iii.136 (Parker).
74   *concent* harmony.
76   *The poet* Sophocles (*Ajax*, line 293, Loeb edition), or possibly Euripides (*Children of
       Hercules*, lines 476–7, Loeb edition).
79–81   *Petrarch ... Hadria* Yet another degrading downward succession, since Aretine was
       a notorious (if skilful) pornographer, and Cieco di Hadria far below the others in
       literary merit.

VOLPONE [*Aside*]
  Is every thing a cause, to my destruction?
LADY WOULD-BE
  I think I ha' two or three of 'em about me.
VOLPONE [*Aside*]
  The sun, the sea will sooner, both, stand still,
  Then her eternal tongue: nothing can scape it.   85
LADY WOULD-BE [*Holding up a book*]
  Here is *Pastor Fido* –
VOLPONE [*Aside*]   Profess obstinate silence,
  That's, now, my safest.
LADY WOULD-BE   All our English writers,
  I mean such as are happy in th' Italian,
  Will deign to steal out of this author, mainly –
  Almost as much, as from Montagni –   90
  He has so modern, and facile a vein,
  Fitting the time, and catching the court-ear.
  Your Petrarch is more passionate, yet he,
  In days of sonneting, trusted 'em with much;
  Dante is hard, and few can understand him.   95
  But, for a desperate wit, there's Aretine;
  Only, his pictures are a little obscene –
  You mark me not?
VOLPONE   Alas, my mind's perturbed.
LADY WOULD-BE
  Why, in such cases we must cure ourselves,
  Make use of our philosophy –

---

82   *cause* Again the comma allows a first meaning – *causa*, the classical term for a topic
     for debate – to emerge before being subsumed in the more conventional modern
     notion of cause and (destructive) effect, implying a sequence of thought and verbal
     association in the speaker.
86   Guarini's 1590 play appeared in English as *The Faithful Shepherd* in 1602 and,
     though widely popular, was condemned by Jonson in the *Conversations with
     Drummond* (H&S I, 134).
94   *sonneting* Jonson also criticizes Petrarch's sonnets in the *Conversations* (H&S
     I, 133–4).
     trusted 'em with much entrusted his successors (Wyatt, Surrey, Sidney, and Spenser)
     with a legacy worth imitating.
96   *desperate* outrageous.
98   *You mark me not?* Are you listening to me? (though Jonson sometimes used the
     question mark in place of an exclamation mark, so this could be a more direct
     accusation).

VOLPONE [*Aside*]　　　　　　　　O'ay me!　　　　　　　　100

LADY WOULD-BE

And, as we find our passions do rebel,
Encounter them with reason; or divert them,
By giving scope unto some other humour
Of lesser danger; as, in politic bodies,
There's nothing more doth overwhelm the judgement,　　　105
And clouds the understanding, than too much
Settling, and fixing, and (as 'twere) subsiding
Upon one object. For the incorporating
Of these same outward things, into that part
Which we call mental, leaves some certain faeces,　　　110
That stop the organs, and as Plato says,
Assassinates our knowledge.

VOLPONE [*Aside*]　　　　　　　Now, the spirit
Of patience help me.

LADY WOULD-BE　　　　Come, in faith, I must
Visit you more, a-days; and make you well:
Laugh, and be lusty.

VOLPONE [*Aside*]　　　My good angel save me.　　　115

LADY WOULD-BE

There was but one sole man, in all the world,
With whom I e'er could sympathize; and he
Would lie you often three, four hours together,
To hear me speak: and be, sometime, so rapt,
As he would answer me quite from the purpose,　　　120
Like you, and you are like him, just. I'll discourse
(And't be but only, sir, to bring you asleep)
How we did spend our time, and loves, together,
For some six years.

100　　*O'ay me* A cry of anguish, like 'Alas'; perhaps a version of the Italian *Ohime,* which
Parker substitutes here; compare 'O me!' or 'Ay me!' several times later in this play
(and in Milton's 'Lycidas', lines 56 and 154).

104　　*politic bodies* Lady Would-Be seems to mean wise persons, though the term would
normally refer to kingdoms.

107　　*Settling . . . subsiding* terms from alchemy – aptly, since all the characters here are
diseased by their obsession with acquiring gold.

115　　*lusty* merry, but the modern sexual sense begins to impinge.

118　　*lie you* lie.

119　　*rapt* enraptured, or lost in thought.

120　　*quite from the purpose* entirely off the topic; her supposed paramour does not seem
to have been listening.

VOLPONE   Oh, oh, oh, oh, oh, oh.

LADY WOULD-BE

For we were *coaetanei*, and brought up –   125

VOLPONE [*Aside*]

Some power, some fate, some fortune rescue me.

ACT III, SCENE v

[*Enter*] MOSCA

MOSCA

God save you, madam.

LADY WOULD-BE   Good sir.

VOLPONE   Mosca? Welcome,

Welcome to my redemption.

MOSCA   Why, sir?

VOLPONE   O,

Rid me of this my torture, quickly, there:

My madam, with the everlasting voice.

The bells, in time of pestilence, ne'er made   5

Like noise, or were in that perpetual motion;

The cock-pit comes not near it. All my house,

But now, steamed like a bath, with her thick breath.

A lawyer could not have been heard; nor scarce

Another woman, such a hail of words   10

She has let fall. For hell's sake, rid her hence.

MOSCA

Has she presented?

VOLPONE   O, I do not care,

I'll take her absence, upon any price,

With any loss.

---

125   *coaetanei* of the same age.

5–6   *The bells . . . noise* The church-bells, even when the plague had them ringing death-knells constantly, never made so much noise.

7   *cock-pit* Cock fights were fashionable in this period – King James liked them – and were always raucous.

8   *But now* Just a moment ago.

12   *presented* given a present; Volpone's reply puns on 'presents' and 'presence'.

MOSCA   Madam.
LADY WOULD-BE   I ha' brought your patron
  A toy, a cap here, of mine own work –
MOSCA   'Tis well;   15
  I had forgot to tell you, I saw your knight,
  Where you'd little think it –
LADY WOULD-BE   Where?
MOSCA   Marry,
  Where yet, if you make haste, you may apprehend him,
  Rowing upon the water in a gondole,
  With the most cunning courtesan of Venice.   20
LADY WOULD-BE
  Is't true?
MOSCA   Pursue 'em, and believe your eyes;
  Leave me to make your gift.
                              [*Exit* LADY WOULD-BE]
                    I knew't would take.
  For lightly they, that use themselves most licence,
  Are still most jealous.
VOLPONE   Mosca, hearty thanks,
  For thy quick fiction, and delivery of me.   25
  Now, to my hopes, what sayst thou?

                  [*Enter* LADY WOULD-BE]

LADY WOULD-BE   But do you hear, sir?
VOLPONE
  Again! I fear a paroxysm.
LADY WOULD-BE   Which way
  Rowed they together?
MOSCA   Toward the Rialto.
LADY WOULD-BE
  I pray you, lend me your dwarf.
MOSCA   I pray you, take him –
                              [*Exit* LADY WOULD-BE]
  Your hopes, sir, are like happy blossoms, fair,   30
  And promise timely fruit, if you will stay
  But the maturing: keep you at your couch,
  Corbaccio will arrive straight, with the will;

15   *toy* silly trifle.
23   *lightly* readily; with slight provocation.
24   *still* always.

82

When he is gone, I'll tell you more.   [*Exit*]
VOLPONE   My blood,
My spirits are returned: I am alive;   35
And like your wanton gamester, at primero,
Whose thought had whispered to him not go less,
Methinks I lie, and draw – for an encounter.

ACT III, SCENE vi

[MOSCA *brings in* BONARIO *and hides him*]

MOSCA
Sir, here concealed, you may hear all. But 'pray you
                              One knocks
Have patience, sir; the same's your father, knocks:
I am compelled to leave you.
BONARIO   Do so. Yet,
Cannot my thought imagine this a truth.

ACT III, SCENE vii

[MOSCA *opens the door, enter*] CORVINO, CELIA

MOSCA
Death on me! You are come too soon, what meant you?
Did not I say, I would send?
CORVINO   Yes, but I feared
You might forget it, and then they prevent us.

---

36   *wanton gamester, at primero* reckless gambler playing a popular card-game; Volpone
     uses technical terms of the game – go less, lie, draw, encounter – as metaphors for
     his anticipated seduction of Celia.

4   *Cannot . . . truth* I cannot believe my father would really disinherit me as Mosca
     claims.

1   *Death on me!* Apparently an exclamatory curse, like 'Damn it!', but oddly parallel to
     Corvino's 'Death of mine honour' at the beginning of II.v.

MOSCA [*Aside*]
  Prevent? Did e'er man haste so, for his horns?
  A courtier would not ply it so, for a place.   5
  [*To* CORVINO] Well, now there is no helping it, stay here;
  I'll presently return.

                              [MOSCA *goes to* BONARIO]
CORVINO   Where are you, Celia?
  You know not wherefore I have brought you hither?
CELIA
  Not well, except you told me.
CORVINO   Now, I will:
  Hark hither.
MOSCA (*To* BONARIO) Sir, your father hath sent word,   10
  It will be half an hour, ere he come;
  And therefore, if you please to walk, the while,
  Into that gallery – at the upper end,
  There are some books, to entertain the time;
  And I'll take care, no man shall come unto you, sir.   15
BONARIO
  Yes, I will stay there. [*Aside*] I do doubt this fellow.   [*Exit*]
MOSCA
  There, he is far enough: he can hear nothing;
  And, for his father, I can keep him off.

                              [*Goes to* VOLPONE]
CORVINO
  Nay, now, there is no starting back; and therefore,
  Resolve upon it: I have so decreed.   20
  It must be done. Nor would I move't afore,
  Because I would avoid all shifts and tricks
  That might deny me.
CELIA   Sir, let me beseech you,
  Affect not these strange trials. If you doubt
  My chastity, why, lock me up, for ever;   25
  Make me the heir of darkness. Let me live,

  4   *horns* marks of the cuckold.
  5   *ply it so, for a place* strive so diligently for appointment to a higher office.
  9   *except you told me* unless you tell me, or possibly, except what little you have told me.
  10   *Hark hither* Listen here.
  19   *no starting back* no turning back, or possibly, no use drawing back startled.
  21   *Nor would I move't afore* Nor was I willing to suggest this plan earlier.
  22   *shifts* evasions.
  24   *Affect not* Do not attempt, or pretend to attempt.

Where I may please your fears, if not your trust.

CORVINO

    Believe it, I have no such humour, I.

    All that I speak, I mean; yet I am not mad –

    Not horn-mad, see you? Go to, show yourself   30

    Obedient, and a wife.

CELIA   O heaven!

CORVINO   I say it,

    Do so.

CELIA   Was this the train?

CORVINO   I've told you reasons:

    What the physicians have set down; how much

    It may concern me; what my engagements are;

    My means; and the necessity of those means,   35

    For my recovery. Wherefore, if you be

    Loyal, and mine, be won, respect my venture.

CELIA

    Before your honour?

CORVINO   Honour? tut, a breath;

    There's no such thing, in nature: a mere term

    Invented to awe fools. What is my gold   40

    The worse, for touching? clothes, for being looked on?

    Why, this 's no more. An old, decrepit wretch,

    That has no sense, no sinew; takes his meat

    With others' fingers; only knows to gape,

    When you do scald his gums; a voice; a shadow;   45

    And what can this man hurt you?

CELIA   Lord! what spirit

    Is this hath entered him?

CORVINO   And for your fame,

---

27   *please your fears, if not your trust* allay your jealous fears, if not earn your actual trust.
30   *horn-mad* sexually jealous, or (almost the opposite), eager to be cuckolded.
32   *train* plan, trap.
33   *set down* recorded as their prognosis (for Volpone's sexual impotence and imminent death).
34   *engagements* investments (in courting Volpone), perhaps also consequent debts to others.
35   *means* method, means to the end, which is winning Volpone's inheritance.
37   *venture* risky commercial undertaking.
38   *tut, a breath* nonsense, an empty word.
43   *no sense, no sinew* no sensory awareness, no physical strength.

That's such a jig; as if I would go tell it,
Cry it, on the Piazza! Who shall know it?
But he, that cannot speak it; and this fellow,   50
Whose lips are i' my pocket; save yourself –
If you'll proclaim't, you may – I know no other
Should come to know it.

CELIA   Are heaven and saints then nothing?
Will they be blind, or stupid?

CORVINO   How?

CELIA   Good sir,
Be jealous still, emulate them; and think   55
What hate they burn with, toward every sin.

CORVINO
I grant you; if I thought it were a sin,
I would not urge you. Should I offer this
To some young Frenchman, or hot Tuscan blood,
That had read Aretine, conned all his prints,   60
Knew every quirk within lust's labyrinth,
And were professed critic in lechery,
And I would look upon him, and applaud him,
This were a sin; but here, 'tis contrary,
A pious work, mere charity, for physic,   65
And honest polity, to assure mine own.

CELIA
O heaven! canst thou suffer such a change?

VOLPONE [*Aside to* MOSCA]
Thou art mine honour, Mosca, and my pride,
My joy, my tickling, my delight! Go, bring 'em.

MOSCA
Please you draw near, sir.

CORVINO   Come on, what –   70
          [CELIA *resists as he drags her toward the bed*]
You will not be rebellious? By that light –

48   *jig* farcical diversion, silly excuse.
51   *Whose lips are i' my pocket* Whose silence I have purchased.
      save except.
60   *conned all his prints* studied all Aretine's pornographic illustrations.
62   *professed critic* expert scholar.
63   *And* If.
66   *polity, to assure mine own* stratagem to secure the fortune that is rightfully mine.
71   *You will not be rebellious?* Are you really going to disobey me? or, Didn't you promise
      to be an obedient wife?

MOSCA
  Sir, Signior Corvino, here, is come to see you.
VOLPONE
  Oh.
MOSCA And, hearing of the consultation had,
  So lately, for your health, is come to offer,
  Or rather, sir, to prostitute –
CORVINO   Thanks, sweet Mosca.   75
MOSCA
  Freely, unasked, or unentreated –
CORVINO   Well.
MOSCA
  As the true, fervent instance of his love,
  His own most fair and proper wife: the beauty,
  Only of price, in Venice –
CORVINO   'Tis well urged.
MOSCA
  To be your comfortress, and to preserve you.   80
VOLPONE
  Alas, I'm past already. 'Pray you, thank him,
  For his good care, and promptness. But for that,
  'Tis a vain labour, e'en to fight, 'gainst heaven:
  Applying fire to a stone – uh, uh, uh, uh –
  Making a dead leaf grow again. I take   85
  His wishes gently, though; and, you may tell him,
  What I've done for him. Marry, my state is hopeless.
  Will him to pray for me; and t' use his fortune,
  With reverence, when he comes to't.
MOSCA   Do you hear, sir?
  Go to him, with your wife.
CORVINO   Heart of my father!   90
  Wilt thou persist thus? Come, I pray thee, come.
  Thou seest 'tis nothing, Celia. By this hand,

---

78   *proper* Three meanings simultaneously: respectable, attractive, and privately owned.
78–9 *the beauty, / Only of price* the most prized and precious beauty (but with a reminder
      that even she can be bought).
81–9 *Alas . . . to't* The heavy punctuation in this speech (both in Q and in F) suggests
      Volpone struggling for breath as he speaks.
84   *Applying fire to a stone* A proverb for futility (Tilley S892), but Volpone is also playing
      slyly on 'stone' as Renaissance slang for 'testicle'.
92   *By this hand* A familiar oath, short for 'I swear by this hand', but also suggesting that
      Corvino raises his hand threateningly here.

I shall grow violent. Come, do't, I say.

CELIA

Sir, kill me, rather: I will take down poison,
Eat burning coals, do anything –

CORVINO   Be damned!   95
Heart, I will drag thee hence, home, by the hair;
Cry thee a strumpet through the streets; rip up
Thy mouth, unto thine ears; and slit thy nose,
Like a raw rotchet – do not tempt me, come;
Yield, I am loath – Death, I will buy some slave,   100
Whom I will kill, and bind thee to him, alive;
And, at my window, hang you forth; devising
Some monstrous crime, which I, in capital letters,
Will eat into thy flesh, with *aquafortis*,
And burning cor'sives, on this stubborn breast.   105
Now, by the blood thou hast incensed, I'll do't.

CELIA

Sir, what you please, you may: I am your martyr.

CORVINO

Be not thus obstinate, I ha' not deserved it.
Think who it is entreats you. 'Pray thee, sweet:
Good faith, thou shalt have jewels, gowns, attires,   110
What thou wilt think, and ask – do but go kiss him.
Or touch him, but. For my sake. At my suit.
This once. No? Not? I shall remember this.
Will you disgrace me, thus? Do you thirst my undoing?

MOSCA

Nay, gentle lady, be advised.

CORVINO   No, no.   115

---

95   *Eat burning coals* Portia, wife of Brutus and legendary for her virtue and loyalty,
     chose this method of suicide.
97   *Cry* Proclaim.
99   *rochet* a reddish fish; Jonson had been threatened with judicial nose-slitting for
     mocking Scots in *Eastward Ho!*
104 *aquafortis* nitric acid, used for etching; Corvino threatens to engrave his false
     accusation against Celia in her flesh with corrosives.
111 *What thou wilt think, and ask* Anything you can imagine and ask for, or, Think of
     anything you wish for, and ask me for it.
     but merely.
112 *At my suit* Because I am begging you.
115 *be advised* take your husband's advice, believe his warning.

She has watched her time. God's precious, this is scurvy;
'Tis very scurvy; and you are –
MOSCA   Nay, good, sir.
CORVINO
An errant locust, by heaven, a locust. Whore,
Crocodile, that hast thy tears prepared,
Expecting how thou'lt bid 'em flow.
MOSCA   Nay, 'pray you, sir,   120
She will consider.
CELIA   Would my life would serve
To satisfy –
CORVINO   'Sdeath, if she would but speak to him,
And save my reputation, 'twere somewhat;
But, spitefully to affect my utter ruin –
MOSCA
Ay, now you've put your fortune in her hands.   125
Why, i' faith, it is her modesty, I must 'quit her:
If you were absent, she would be more coming;
I know it, and dare undertake for her.
What woman can, before her husband? 'Pray you,
Let us depart, and leave her here.
CORVINO   Sweet Celia,   130
Thou mayst redeem all, yet; I'll say no more:
If not, esteem yourself as lost –

                              [CELIA *tries to exit*]
                    Nay, stay there.
                    [*Exeunt* CORVINO *and* MOSCA]

CELIA
O God, and his good angels! Whither, whither,
Is shame fled human breasts? that, with such ease,

116   *watched her time* waited for the opportunity to do me the most damage.
      God's precious I swear by God's precious blood.
118   *errant* arrant, notorious; or possibly, erring, devious.
      locust a Biblical plague, a pest that swallows up the harvest.
119–20 *Crocodile . . . flow* Crocodiles were believed to lure their victims with false tears.
120   *Expecting* Anticipating, plotting.
121–2 *Would my life . . . satisfy* I would be happy to be killed if only that would solve the
      problem.
123   *'twere somewhat* that would count for something.
124   *affect* attempt.
126   *'quit* acquit, excuse; or possibly, leave her in privacy.
127   *coming* forthcoming, agreeable, perhaps with sexual connotations.
129   *can, before* can (commit adultery) in sight of.

Men dare put off your honours, and their own? 135
Is that, which ever was a cause of life,
Now placed beneath the basest circumstance?
And modesty an exile made, for money?

He [VOLPONE] *leaps off from his couch*

VOLPONE
Ay, in Corvino, and such earth-fed minds,
That never tasted the true heav'n of love. 140
Assure thee, Celia, he that would sell thee,
Only for hope of gain, and that uncertain,
He would have sold his part of Paradise
For ready money, had he met a cope-man.
Why art thou mazed, to see me thus revived? 145
Rather, applaud thy beauty's miracle:
'Tis thy great work, that hath, not now alone,
But sundry times, raised me, in several shapes,
And, but this morning, like a mountebank,
To see thee at thy window. Ay, before 150
I would have left my practice for thy love,
In varying figures, I would have contended
With the blue Proteus, or the hornèd flood.
Now, art thou welcome.

CELIA   Sir!

VOLPONE   Nay, fly me not;
Nor let thy false imagination 155
That I was bed-rid, make thee think, I am so:
Thou shalt not find it. I am, now, as fresh,
As hot, as high, and in as jovial plight,

---

135 *put off your honours* ignore or betray the divine principles of honour, or, dishonour
      the divine by doing so.
136–7 *Is that . . . circumstance?* Is honour, which has always been considered a cause worth
      dying for, now valued less than the lowliest and most trivial advantage?
142 *and that uncertain* when the gain is not even guaranteed.
144 *cope-man* suitable merchant.
145 *mazed* amazed, bewildered.
151 *practice for* scheming to win.
152 *figures* disguises, shapes.
153 *blue Proteus, or the hornèd flood* Proteus was a sea-god who could change shape at
      will; the hornèd flood is the river-god Achelous who turned himself into various
      animals while battling Hercules for a woman's love.
158 *jovial plight* thriving condition, with some reference to Jove's persistent courting of
      beautiful mortal women.

As when (in that so celebrated scene,
At recitation of our comedy,   160
For entertainment of the great Valois)
I acted young Antinous; and attracted
The eyes and ears of all the ladies present,
To admire each graceful gesture, note, and footing.

Song

    Come, my Celia, let us prove,   165
    While we can, the sports of love:
    Time will not be ours forever,
    He, at length, our good will sever;
    Spend not then his gifts, in vain.
    Suns that set may rise again;   170
    But if, once, we lose this light,
    'Tis with us perpetual night.
    Why should we defer our joys?
    Fame and rumour are but toys.
    Cannot we delude the eyes   175
    Of a few poor household-spies?
    Or his easier ears beguile,
    Thus removèd by our wile?
    'Tis no sin, love's fruits to steal,
    But the sweet thefts to reveal;   180
    To be taken, to be seen,
    These have crimes accounted been.

161   *Valois* Henry Valois, later King Henry III of France, was lavishly entertained in Venice in 1574.

162   *Antinous* either the manly chief suitor to Odysseus's chaste wife Penelope, or the boy beloved by the Emperor Hadrian; considering how often Jonson traps this play's characters into self-aggrandizing masculine poses that can be ironically reinterpreted as signs of sterility and perversion (which was evidently his view of homosexuality), the ambiguity may be deliberate.

164   *footing* dance step.

164   s.d. *Song* Jonson based this *carpe diem* song on Catullus's Ode V, had his friend Antonio Ferrabosco set it to music, and later reprinted it in his poetry collection *The Forest*.

165   *prove* experience, try out.

168   *our good will sever* will cut off our good times.

174   *toys* silly trifles.

177   *his* Corvino's.

178   *Thus removed by our wile* Since we have cleverly got him out of the room.

181   *taken* caught.

CELIA

    Some serene blast me, or dire lightning strike
    This my offending face.

VOLPONE   Why droops my Celia?

    Thou hast, in place of a base husband, found   185
    A worthy lover: use thy fortune well,
    With secrecy, and pleasure. See, behold,   [*Shows the treasure*]
    What thou art queen of; not in expectation,
    As I feed others, but possessed, and crowned.
    See, here, a rope of pearl; and each more orient   190
    Than that the brave Egyptian queen caroused:
    Dissolve, and drink 'em. See, a carbuncle,
    May put out both the eyes of our St Mark;
    A diamond, would have bought Lollia Paulina,
    When she came in, like starlight, hid with jewels,   195
    That were the spoils of provinces. Take these,
    And wear, and lose 'em; yet remains an earring
    To purchase them again, and this whole state.
    A gem but worth a private patrimony
    Is nothing: we will eat such at a meal.   200
    The heads of parrots, tongues of nightingales,
    The brains of peacocks, and of ostriches

183   *Some serene blast me* I wish some poisonous mist would destroy me.
184   *offending* Her beauty has committed an offence, she feels, in provoking this sinful proposal.
190   *orient* rare, fine, precious; see the note at I.v.9.
191   *the brave Egyptian queen caroused* The glamorous Cleopatra, according to Pliny, was challenged by her lover Antony to spend a fortune on a meal, which she did by dissolving a pearl in vinegar and drinking it.
192   *carbuncle* a round red gem.
193   *put out both the eyes of our St Mark* Perhaps Venice, known to possess some precious rubies, had a statue of its patron saint with carbuncles for the eyes. Volpone (possibly echoing Pietro Aretino) offers a jewel that will either put to shame, or bribe into looking the other way, the grand patron saint of the city. In any case – as when Volpone's worship of gold 'darkens' the sun in the opening scene – Jonson suggests monetary values eclipsing religious ones (Kernan).
194   *Lollia Paulina* consort of the Emperor Caligula; Pliny describes her as covered with jewels. Volpone neglects to mention that her opulent story, like that of Cleopatra, ends in suicide.
196   *spoils of provinces* greatest treasures stolen from conquered territories.
197–8   *yet remains . . . whole state* there would still be left an earring that would purchase all the aforementioned jewellery, and all of Venice too.
199   *but worth a private patrimony* worth only as much as a single person's estate.

Shall be our food; and, could we get the phoenix,
Though nature lost her kind, she were our dish.

CELIA

Good sir, these things might move a mind affected   205
With such delights; but I, whose innocence
Is all I can think wealthy, or worth th' enjoying,
And which, once lost, I have nought to lose beyond it,
Cannot be taken with these sensual baits.
If you have conscience –

VOLPONE   'Tis the beggar's virtue;   210
If thou hast wisdom, hear me, Celia.
Thy baths shall be the juice of July-flowers,
Spirit of roses, and of violets,
The milk of unicorns, and panthers' breath
Gathered in bags, and mixed with Cretan wines.   215
Our drink shall be preparèd gold, and amber;
Which we will take, until my roof whirl round
With the vertigo; and my dwarf shall dance,
My eunuch sing, my fool make up the antic.
Whilst, we, in changèd shapes, act Ovid's tales,   220
Thou, like Europa now, and I like Jove,
Then I like Mars, and thou like Erycine,
So, of the rest, till we have quite run through
And wearied all the fables of the gods.
Then will I have thee, in more modern forms,   225
Attired like some sprightly dame of France,
Brave Tuscan lady, or proud Spanish beauty;
Sometimes, unto the Persian Sophy's wife;
Or the Grand Signior's Mistress; and, for change,

203   *phoenix* a mythical bird, supposedly reborn from its own ashes every five hundred
        years; Volpone is willing to render the species ('kind') extinct by eating it.
210   *'Tis the beggar's virtue* Conscience is good only for those so poor they can't afford
        great pleasures anyway.
212   *July-flowers* gillyflowers, or clove-scented pinks, which Perdita in Shakespeare's
        Winter's Tale (IV.iv) mistrusts as an exotic graft.
214   *panthers' breath* Panthers were supposed to lure their prey with sweet breath (as
        Volpone is luring Celia with sweet words).
219   *antic* strange dance.
220   *Ovid's tales* Ovid's *Metamorphoses* recounts many transformations and seductions,
        such as Zeus disguising himself as a bull to capture Europa; Jonson mocks the male
        appetite for such pornographic role-playing in several of his works.
222   *Erycine* Venus.
228   *Persian Sophy* Shah of Iran.
229   *Grand Signior* Sultan of Turkey.

To one of our most artful courtesans,   230
Or some quick Negro, or cold Russian;
And I will meet thee, in as many shapes,
Where we may, so, transfuse our wand'ring souls,
Out at our lips, and score up sums of pleasures,
[*Sings*]   That the curious shall not know,   235
                How to tell them, as they flow;
                And the envious, when they find
                What their number is, be pined.

CELIA

If you have ears, that will be pierced – or eyes,
That can be opened – a heart, may be touched –   240
Or any part, that yet sounds man, about you –
If you have touch of holy saints – or Heaven –
Do me the grace, to let me 'scape – if not,
Be bountiful, and kill me – you do know,
I am a creature, hither ill betrayed,   245
By one whose shame I would forget it were –
If you will deign me neither of these graces,
Yet feed your wrath, sir, rather than your lust –
It is a vice, comes nearer manliness –
And punish that unhappy crime of nature,   250
Which you miscall my beauty – flay my face,
Or poison it, with ointments, for seducing
Your blood to this rebellion – rub these hands,
With what may cause an eating leprosy,
E'en to my bones and marrow – anything,   255

231   *quick* lively, hot-blooded.
233   *transfuse* cause to flow from one to another (OED); this exotic but finally pathetic
        wandering through many identities recalls the degrading transmigration of
        Pythagoras's soul in I.ii.1–62.
236   *tell* count.
238   *pined* pained, caused to pine away with envy.
239–59 Q's punctuation of Celia's speech with dashes suggests breathless panic, or struggles
        to escape Volpone's embraces or his bedchamber; F provides grammatically and
        logically accurate punctuation instead. This edition, trusting the theatrical wisdom
        of Jonson in 1606 and recognizing that the 1616 version may reflect Jonson's effort
        to impose a consistent form on the page rather than a rethinking of Celia's
        demeanour on the stage here, preserves Q's dashes. Still, it is worth acknowledging
        a feminist argument for the F version, which would create a much stronger Celia –
        less a wide-eyed damsel in distress than a well-spoken, cool-headed defender of her
        chastity, appealing eloquently to what little is left of Volpone's reason and (though
        this immediately backfires) to his manly pride.
241   *yet sounds man* still retains some echo of manly honour or humane mercy.

That may disfavour me, save in my honour –
And I will kneel to you, pray for you, pay down
A thousand hourly vows, sir, for your health –
Report, and think you virtuous –
VOLPONE   Think me cold,
Frozen, and impotent, and so report me?   260
That I had Nestor's hernia, thou wouldst think.
I do degenerate, and abuse my nation,
To play with opportunity thus long:
 · I should have done the act, and then have parleyed.
Yield, or I'll force thee.
CELIA   O, just God!
VOLPONE   In vain –   265

He [BONARIO] *leaps out from where*
Mosca had placed him

BONARIO
Forbear, foul ravisher, libidinous swine!
Free the forced lady, or thou diest, impostor.
But that I am loath to snatch thy punishment
Out of the hand of justice, thou shouldst yet
Be made the timely sacrifice of vengeance,   270
Before this altar, and this dross,
[*Gesturing toward the gold*]   thy idol.
Lady, let's quit the place: it is the den
Of villainy. Fear nought, you have a guard;
And he, ere long, shall meet his just reward.
VOLPONE
Fall on me, roof, and bury me in ruin,   275
Become my grave, that wert my shelter.
O! I am unmasked, unspirited, undone,
Betrayed to beggary, to infamy –

---

256   *disfavour* disfigure, destroy whatever makes me sexually appealing.
261   *Nestor's hernia* impotence; Nestor was the aged Greek commander in Homer's *Iliad*
        (cf. Juvenal's *Satires* VI, 326).
262   *abuse my nation* dishonour the reputation of Italians for ferocious virility.
271   *dross* a dismissive term for Volpone's gold.
274   *he* presumably Volpone; but the situation conventionally suggests (though this play
        stubbornly refuses to fulfil the expectation) that Bonario should be rewarded with
        the hand of the young woman he has saved.

ACT III, SCENE viii

[Enter] MOSCA, *[bleeding]*

MOSCA
  Where shall I run, most wretched shame of men,
  To beat out my unlucky brains?
VOLPONE   Here, here.
  What! dost thou bleed?
MOSCA   O, that his well-driven sword
  Had been so courteous to have cleft me down
  Unto the navel, ere I lived to see   5
  My life, my hopes, my spirits, my patron, all
  Thus desperately engagèd, by my error.
VOLPONE
  Woe on thy fortune.
MOSCA   And my follies, sir.
VOLPONE
  Th' hast made me miserable.
MOSCA   And myself, sir.
  Who would have thought he would have hearkened so?   10
VOLPONE
  What shall we do?
MOSCA   I know not; if my heart
  Could expiate the mischance, I'd pluck it out.
  Will you be pleased to hang me? Or cut my throat?
  And I'll requite you, sir. Let's die like Romans,
  Since we have lived like Grecians.
                       They knock without
VOLPONE   Hark, who's there?   15
  I hear some footing: officers, the *Saffi*,

---

7   *engagèd* entrapped, entangled, or thrown into debt.
10 *he would have hearkened* Bonario would have eavesdropped.
14 *requite* repay you in kind.
     Romans Ancient Rome had a Stoic tradition of answering adversity and preserving
     honour by suicide.
15 *like Grecians* craftily, and (above all) for high pleasures.
16 *Saffi* bailiffs assigned to make arrests.

Come to apprehend us! I do feel the brand
Hissing, already, at my forehead; now,
Mine ears are boring.
MOSCA   To your couch, sir; you
Make that place good, however,

            [VOLPONE *gets into bed*]
                    Guilty men   20
Suspect what they deserve still.   [*Opens the door*]
                    Signior Corbaccio!

ACT III, SCENE ix

[*Enter*] CORBACCIO;
VOLTORE [*enters unnoticed behind him*]

CORBACCIO
Why, how now, Mosca?
MOSCA   O, undone, amazed, sir.
Your son (I know not by what accident)
Acquainted with your purpose to my patron,
Touching your will, and making him your heir,
Entered our house with violence, his sword drawn,   5
Sought for you, called you wretch, unnatural,
Vowed he would kill you.
CORBACCIO   Me?
MOSCA   Yes, and my patron.
CORBACCIO
This act shall disinherit him indeed:
Here is the will.
MOSCA   'Tis well, sir.
CORBACCIO   Right, and well.

17–19   *brand . . . boring* permanently disfiguring punishments with hot or sharp metal;
Jonson himself had been branded on the thumb for killing a fellow-actor.
20   *Make that place good, however* Try to resume playing the dying man convincingly, in
whatever way you can, or whatever happens.
21   *Suspect what they deserve still* Always expect, with dread, their due punishment.

1   *undone, amazed* ruined, bewildered.
3–4   *your purpose . . . will* your intention toward Volpone, regarding your last will and
testament.

Be you as careful, now, for me.

MOSCA   My life, sir,   10
Is not more tendered; I am only yours.

CORBACCIO
How does he? Will he die shortly, think'st thou?

MOSCA   I fear
He'll outlast May.

CORBACCIO   Today?

MOSCA   No, last out May, sir.

CORBACCIO
Couldst thou not gi' him a dram?

MOSCA   O, by no means, sir.

CORBACCIO
Nay, I'll not bid you.

VOLTORE   This is a knave, I see.   15

MOSCA [*Aside*]
How, Signior Voltore! Did he hear me?

VOLTORE   Parasite!

MOSCA
Who's that? O, sir, most timely welcome –

VOLTORE   Scarce,
To the discovery of your tricks, I fear.
You are his, only? and mine, also? are you not?

MOSCA
Who? I, sir?

VOLTORE   You, sir. What device is this   20
About a will?

MOSCA   A plot for you, sir.

VOLTORE   Come,
Put not your foists upon me, I shall scent 'em.

MOSCA
Did you not hear it?

VOLTORE   Yes, I hear, Corbaccio
Hath made your patron, there, his heir.

MOSCA   'Tis true;
By my device, drawn to it by my plot,   25

11   *tendered* tenderly cared for.
14   *dram* drug, presumably a fatal overdose or poison.
15   *This* Mosca.
17   *Scarce* Hardly welcome, or, Just in time.
22   *foists* tricks, but with a secondary meaning of 'odours of decay', which a vulture
     would be attuned to notice.

With hope –
VOLTORE　　　Your patron should reciprocate?
And you have promised?
MOSCA　　　　　　　For your good, I did, sir.
Nay, more, I told his son, brought, hid him here,
Where he might hear his father pass the deed;
Being persuaded to it by this thought, sir:　　　　　　　30
That the unnaturalness, first, of the act,
And then, his father's oft disclaiming in him,
Which I did mean t' help on, would sure enrage him
To do some violence upon his parent,
On which the law should take sufficient hold,　　　　　　35
And you be stated in a double hope.
Truth be my comfort, and my conscience,
My only aim was, to dig you a fortune
Out of these two, old, rotten sepulchres –
VOLTORE
I cry thee mercy, Mosca.
MOSCA　　　　　　　Worth your patience,　　　　　　40
And your great merit, sir. And, see the change!
VOLTORE
Why? what success?
MOSCA　　　　　　Most hapless! You must help, sir.
Whilst we expected th' old raven, in comes
Corvino's wife, sent hither by her husband –
VOLTORE
What, with a present?
MOSCA　　　　　　No, sir, on visitation　　　　　45
(I'll tell you how, anon); and, staying long,
The youth, he grows impatient, rushes forth,
Seizeth the lady, wounds me, makes her swear –
Or he would murder her, that was his vow –
T' affirm my patron would have done her rape –　　　　50
Which how unlike it is, you see! – and, hence,
With that pretext, he's gone t' accuse his father;

32　*oft disclaiming in him* repeatedly disowning him.
35　*sufficient hold* severe enough penalty to make Bonario ineligible for Corbaccio's
　　inheritance.
36　*stated in a double hope* instated with both inheritances
40　*cry thee mercy* beg your pardon.
42　*what success?* how successful was this?.
　　hapless unlucky.

Defame my patron; defeat you –
VOLTORE   Where's her husband?
Let him be sent for, straight.
MOSCA   Sir, I'll go fetch him.
VOLTORE
Bring him to the *Scrutineo.*
MOSCA   Sir, I will.   55
VOLTORE
This must be stopped.
MOSCA   O, you do nobly, sir.
Alas, 'twas laboured all, sir, for your good;
Nor was there want of counsel in the plot;
But fortune can, at any time, o'erthrow
The projects of a hundred learned clerks, sir.   60
CORBACCIO
What's that?
VOLTORE   Will't please you, sir, to go along?
                              [*Exeunt* VOLTORE *and* CORBACCIO]
MOSCA
Patron, go in, and pray for our success.
VOLPONE
Need makes devotion: heaven your labour bless.
                                                              [*Exeunt*]

55   *Scrutineo* The law court in the Venetian Senate House.
58   *want of counsel* lack of deliberation.
60   *clerks* learned men.

ACT IV, SCENE i

[Enter] POLITIC, PEREGRINE

SIR POLITIC
  I told you, sir, it was a plot: you see
  What observation is. You mentioned me
  For some instructions: I will tell you, sir,
  Since we are met, here, in this height of Venice,
  Some few particulars I have set down   5
  Only for this meridian, fit to be known
  Of your crude traveller; and they are these.
  I will not touch, sir, at your phrase, or clothes,
  For they are old.
PEREGRINE   Sir, I have better.
SIR POLITIC   Pardon,
  I meant, as they are themes.
PEREGRINE   O, sir, proceed: 10
  I'll slander you no more of wit, good sir.
SIR POLITIC
  First, for your garb, it must be grave, and serious;
  Very reserved, and locked; not tell a secret,
  On any terms, not to your father; scarce
  A fable, but with caution; make sure choice   15
  Both of your company, and discourse; beware
  You never speak a truth –
PEREGRINE   How!
SIR POLITIC   Not to strangers,
  For those be they you must converse with most;

1–2   *I told you . . . what observation is* You see how observant I was to suspect (at II.iii.10–12) that the mountebank scene was all a plot to entrap me.

  2   *mentioned* asked.

  4   *height of Venice* Cf. II.i.12 and the explanatory note there.

  7   *crude* raw (implying inexperience and also, perhaps, vulgarity).

  8   *touch, sir, at your phrase* make mention, sir, of your style of speech; but Peregrine mischievously pretends to mistake the sense of 'touch' as well as the referent of 'old' here.

 11   *slander you no more of wit* never again mistakenly think you capable of a witty insult.

 12   *garb* bearing, demeanour; like Polonius's advice to Laertes in *Hamlet*, Sir Pol's advice emphasizes shallow social tactics rather than deep moral sense.

 14   *not* not even.

14–15   *scarce . . . caution* hardly even risk telling a fictional story without caution.

Others I would not know, sir, but, at distance,
So as I still might be a saver in 'em: 20
You shall have tricks, else, passed upon you, hourly.
And then, for your religion, profess none;
But wonder, at the diversity of all;
And, for your part, protest, were there no other
But simply the laws o' th' land, you could content you: 25
Nick Machiavel and Monsieur Bodin, both,
Were of this mind. Then, must you learn the use,
And handling of your silver fork, at meals;
The metal of your glass – these are main matters,
With your Italian – and to know the hour,   30
When you must eat your melons, and your figs.
PEREGRINE
Is that a point of state, too?
SIR POLITIC   Here it is.
For your Venetian, if he see a man
Preposterous in the least, he has him straight;
He has: he strips him. I'll acquaint you, sir,   35
I now have lived here, 'tis some fourteen months;
Within the first week of my landing here,
All took me for a citizen of Venice;
I knew the forms so well –
PEREGRINE [*Aside*]   And nothing else.
SIR POLITIC
I had read Contarine, took me a house,   40
Dealt with my Jews, to furnish it with movables –

---

19   *Others* presumably, other travellers from your own country.
20   *be a saver in 'em* be safer around them (by being an acquaintance) or save time and
      money (by not becoming close enough to be asked for favours or loans).
26   *Nick Machiavel and Monsieur Bodin* Sir Pol has a characteristically fashionable
      misunderstanding of Niccolo Machiavelli (whose book arguably advocated putting
      political considerations ahead of religious ones) and Jean Bodin (who argued for
      religious toleration, a cause that might have appealed to Jonson, himself a convert
      to the banned Catholicism).
28   *fork* Forks were still uncommon silverware in Jacobean England.
29   *metal* material.
34   *Preposterous* Disordered, incorrect.
      has him straight instantly sees through his pretences and takes advantage of him.
35   *strips him* exposes him to ridicule.
40   *Contarine* Cardinal Gasparo Contarini's book on Venice was translated into English
      in 1599.
41   *Jews* Venice supported a Jewish community to handle the money-lending business
      which was forbidden to Christians but necessary for their capitalist economy;

Well, if I could but find one man – one man,
To mine own heart, whom I durst trust – I would –

PEREGRINE
What? What, sir?

SIR POLITIC   Make him rich; make him a fortune:
He should not think again. I would command it.   45

PEREGRINE
As how?

SIR POLITIC With certain projects, that I have;
Which, I may not discover.

PEREGRINE [*Aside*]   If I had
But one to wager with, I would lay odds, now,
He tells me, instantly.

SIR POLITIC   One is – and that
I care not greatly who knows – to serve the state   50
Of Venice with red herrings, for three years,
And at a certain rate, from Rotterdam,
Where I have correspondence. There's a letter,
Sent me from one o' th' States, and to that purpose;

                              [*Shows a letter*]

He cannot write his name, but that's his mark.   55

PEREGRINE
He is a chandler?

SIR POLITIC   No, a cheesemonger.
There are some other too, with whom I treat
About the same negotiation;
And I will undertake it. For, 'tis thus,

---

cf. Shakespeare's misrepresentation of this relationship in *The Merchant of Venice*,
    movables furniture other than fixtures.

46   *projects* In this period, the word connotes highly speculative schemes; Jonson mocks
      such ingenious 'projectors' again in *The Devil is an Ass*.

47   *may not discover* must not reveal.

51   *red herrings* a basic cheap food in England, but considered a dainty in Venice; the
      modern meaning of strategic diversion or delusion was not yet common, but seems
      relevant, especially in parallel with the same three-year period Volpone has been
      misleading the legacy-hunters (Parker).

54   *th' States* Holland.

56   *chandler* candle-maker or retailer of provisions; Peregrine may be joking about the
      messiness of the paper or the size of the seal.
      cheesemonger Sir Pol has settled on an illiterate cheese-seller as his source for
      correspondence and herrings; a further joke lies in the standard English mockery of
      the Dutch fondness for butter and cheese.

I'll do't with ease, I've cast it all: your hoy   60
Carries but three men in her, and a boy;
And she shall make me three returns, a year;
So, if there come but one of three, I save,
If two, I can defalk. But this is now
If my main project fail.
PEREGRINE   Then, you have others?   65
SIR POLITIC
I should be loath to draw the subtle air
Of such a place without my thousand aims.
I'll not dissemble, sir: where'er I come,
I love to be considerative; and, 'tis true,
I have, at my free hours, thought upon   70
Some certain goods unto the state of Venice,
Which I do call my cautions; and, sir, which
I mean (in hope of pension) to propound
To the Great Council, then unto the Forty,
So to the Ten. My means are made already –   75
PEREGRINE
By whom?
SIR POLITIC Sir, one, that though his place be obscure,
Yet, he can sway, and they will hear him. He's
A *commandatore*.
PEREGRINE   What, a common sergeant?
SIR POLITIC
Sir, such as they are, put it in their mouths,
What they should say, sometimes, as well as greater.   80
I think I have my notes, to show you –
PEREGRINE   Good, sir.

60   *cast* calculated.
       hoy small boat for coastal transportation; probably not adequate for safe voyaging
       between Venice and Rotterdam.
63–4 *if there come . . . defalk* The sense of this seems to be that Sir Pol can afford to have
       only one of his three shiploads arrive safely, and that if two arrive he can reduce his
       debt, or maybe his price; but Jonson may not intend Sir Pol's plans to make perfect
       sense.
64   *now* only.
66   *draw the subtle air* breathe the atmosphere of intrigue.
71   *goods* benefits; Sir Pol intends to offer such valuable precautionary schemes to the
       three highest levels of the Venetian government that they will pay him a pension.
78   *commandatore* officer charged with bringing offenders to court – the disguise
       Volpone will later assume.
79–80 *such as . . . greater* lowly officials such as sergeants, as well as more exalted ones,
       sometimes advise these authorities what to say.

SIR POLITIC

    But, you shall swear unto me, on your gentry,
    Not to anticipate –

PEREGRINE   I, sir?

SIR POLITIC   Nor reveal

    A circumstance – My paper is not with me.

PEREGRINE

    O, but, you can remember, sir.

SIR POLITIC   My first is   85
    Concerning tinderboxes. You must know,
    No family is, here, without its box.
    Now sir, it being so portable a thing,
    Put case, that you or I were ill affected
    Unto the state: sir, with it in our pockets,   90
    Might not I go into the Arsenale?
    Or you? Come out again? And none the wiser?

PEREGRINE

    Except yourself, sir.

SIR POLITIC   Go to, then. I, therefore,
    Advertise to the state how fit it were
    That none, but such as were known patriots,   95
    Sound lovers of their country, should be suffered
    T' enjoy them in their houses; and even those,
    Sealed, at some office, and at such a bigness,
    As might not lurk in pockets.

PEREGRINE   Admirable!

SIR POLITIC

    My next is, how t' enquire, and be resolved   100
    By present demonstration, whether a ship,
    Newly arrived from *Soria*, or from
    Any suspected part of all the Levant,
    Be guilty of the plague: and, where they use
    To lie out forty, fifty days, sometimes,   105

82–3   *swear unto . . . anticipate* swear, on your good name, not to use my ideas before I do.

89   *Put case, that* What if, suppose hypothetically.

91   *Arsenale* the place Venice kept its ships and weapons, where a spark from a tinderbox could have devastating effects; it had exploded and burnt in 1568–9, and a Jacobean audience might again have been reminded of the 1605 Gunpowder Plot.

96   *suffered* allowed; Sir Pol's scheme would make it impossible for most Venetians to maintain the fires they need for cooking and heating.

98   *Sealed* Licensed, perhaps sealed shut.

101   *present* immediate.

102   *Soria* Sir Pol suavely employs the Italian name for Syria.

About the Lazaretto, for their trial,
I'll save that charge and loss unto the merchant,
And, in an hour, clear the doubt.

PEREGRINE   Indeed, sir?

SIR POLITIC

Or –1 will lose my labour.

PEREGRINE   My faith, that's much.

SIR POLITIC

Nay, sir, conceive me. 'Twill cost me, in onions,   110
Some thirty *livres* –

PEREGRINE   Which is one pound sterling.

SIR POLITIC

Beside my waterworks. For this I do, sir:
First, I bring in your ship, 'twixt two brick walls
(But those the state shall venture); on the one
I strain me a fair tarpaulin; and, in that,   115
I stick my onions, cut in halves; the other
Is full of loopholes, out at which, I thrust
The noses of my bellows; and those bellows
I keep, with waterworks, in perpetual motion
(Which is the easiest matter of a hundred).   120
Now, sir, your onion, which doth naturally
Attract th' infection, and your bellows, blowing
The air upon him, will show, instantly,
By his changed colour, if there be contagion;
Or else, remain as fair as at the first.   125
Now 'tis known, 'tis nothing.

PEREGRINE   You are right, sir.

SIR POLITIC

I would I had my note.

PEREGRINE   Faith, so would I;

---

106   *About the Lazaretto* Near Venice's quarantine areas for those suspected of bubonic
      plague or leprosy; as a world port, Venice had various schemes to prevent importation
      of disease, including lengthy quarantines and purifying incoming goods with vinegar.
109   *that's much* Peregrine is unimpressed, to the point of sarcasm, with the 'labour' that
      must have gone into Pol's scheme.
111   *livres* French coins.
114   *venture* invest in.
115   *strain* stretch.
126   *Now 'tis known . . . right, sir* With false humility, Pol acknowledges that the idea may
      seem obvious once it has been explained; but Peregrine exploits Pol's wording to
      suggest (with characteristic suave irony) that the idea is worthless rather than obvious.

But, you ha' done well, for once, sir.

SIR POLITIC   Were I false,
Or would be made so, I could show you reasons,
How I could sell this state, now, to the Turk;   130
Spite of their galleys, or their –

PEREGRINE   'Pray you, Sir Pol.

SIR POLITIC
I have 'em not, about me.

PEREGRINE   That I feared.
They're there, sir?

SIR POLITIC   No. This is my diary,
Wherein I note my actions of the day.

PEREGRINE
'Pray you, let's see, sir. What is here? '*Notandum,*   135
A rat had gnawn my spur leathers; notwithstanding,
I put on new, and did go forth; but, first,
I threw three beans over the threshold. *Item,*
I went and bought two toothpicks, whereof one
I burst, immediately, in a discourse   140
With a Dutch merchant, 'bout *ragion' del stato.*
From him, I went and paid a *moccenigo,*
For piecing my silk stockings; by the way,
I cheapened sprats; and at St Mark's, I urined'.
Faith, these are politic notes!

SIR POLITIC   Sir, I do slip   145
No action of my life, thus, but I quote it.

PEREGRINE
Believe me, it is wise!

SIR POLITIC   Nay, sir, read forth.

---

128 *false* treacherous.
131 *'Pray you* Probably, a version of 'Please', either asking Pol to finish his sentence, or
     asking him to show his papers, or asking him to forget about his papers: throughout
     the scene Jonson suggests stage business in which Pol fumbles with miscellaneous
     documents.
133 *diary* Travellers in this period (like bloggers today) were notorious for assuming that
     the trivia of their daily lives was worth recording.
138 *threw three beans* a superstition (drawn from Theophrastus).
141 *ragion' del stato* reasons of state, politics.
142 *moccenigo* small coin.
143 *piecing* mending, piecing together.
144 *cheapened sprats* bargained for herring.
145 *slip* allow to pass.

ACT IV, SCENE ii

[*Enter*] LADY WOULD-BE, NANO, SERVING-WOMEN

LADY WOULD-BE
Where should this loose knight be, trow? Sure he's housed.
NANO
  Why, then he's fast.
LADY WOULD-BE   Ay, he plays both with me.
  I pray you, stay. This heat will do more harm
  To my complexion than his heart is worth.
  I do not care to hinder, but to take him.   5
  [*Rubbing her cheeks*] How it comes off!
1ST WOMAN   My master's yonder.
LADY WOULD-BE   Where?
1ST WOMAN
  With a young gentleman.
LADY WOULD-BE   That same's the party,
  In man's apparel! 'Pray you, sir, jog my knight.
  I will be tender to his reputation,
  However he demerit.
SIR POLITIC   My lady!
PEREGRINE   Where?   10
SIR POLITIC
  'Tis she indeed, sir, you shall know her. She is,
  Were she not mine, a lady of that merit,
  For fashion, and behaviour; and, for beauty
  I durst compare –
PEREGRINE   It seems you are not jealous,
  That dare commend her.
SIR POLITIC   Nay, and for discourse –   15

1   *loose* promiscuous, wandering.
     housed hidden away, presumably in a house of prostitution, maybe in the prostitute herself.
2   *fast* caught, with a pun on the game of fast-and-loose, referred to at I.ii.8.
5   *take him* catch him in the act.
6   *How it comes off* Perspiration is making Lady Would-Be's heavy make-up run.
8   *man's apparel* Lady Would-Be's error here is partly explained by a tradition of Venetian courtesans dressing as men.
     jog nudge (to get his attention).
10 *However he demerit* Even though, or even if, he doesn't deserve it.

PEREGRINE
  Being your wife, she cannot miss that.
SIR POLITIC [*Approaching* LADY WOULD-BE *to introduce* PEREGRINE]
                              Madam,
  Here is a gentleman, 'pray you, use him fairly,
  He seems a youth, but he is –
LADY WOULD-BE   None?
SIR POLITIC   Yes, one
  Has put his face, as soon, into the world –
LADY WOULD-BE
  You mean, as early? But today?
SIR POLITIC   How's this?   20
LADY WOULD-BE
  Why, in this habit, sir: you apprehend me.
  Well, Master Would-Be, this doth not become you.
  I had thought, the odour, sir, of your good name
  Had been more precious to you; that you would not
  Have done this dire massacre on your honour –   25
  One of your gravity, and rank, besides –
  But, knights, I see, care little for the oath
  They make to ladies; chiefly their own ladies.
SIR POLITIC
  Now, by my spurs, the symbol of my knighthood –
PEREGRINE [*Aside*]
  Lord, how his brain is humbled for an oath!   30
SIR POLITIC
  I reach you not.
LADY WOULD-BE Right, sir, your polity
  May bear it through thus.
  [*To* PEREGRINE]   Sir, a word with you.
  I would be loath, to contest, publicly,
  With any gentlewoman or to seem

---

21   *habit* clothing; Lady Would-Be is sardonically suggesting that Peregrine is new in
      the world because the supposed courtesan had only newly assumed this male
      'disguise'.
26   *gravity* seriousness.
30   *humbled* brought low – down to the level of his spurs, which seem to be an impor-
      tant item to Sir Pol, and probably notable in his costume.
31   *reach* understand.
31–2 *your polity / May bear it through* sustaining your clever bluff may spare you having
      to confess your adultery.

Froward, or violent: as *The Courtier* says, 35
It comes too near rusticity, in a lady,
Which I would shun, by all means; and, however
I may deserve from Master Would-Be, yet,
To have one fair gentlewoman, thus, be made
The unkind instrument to wrong another, 40
And one she knows not; ay, and to persever;
In my poor judgement, is not warranted
From being a solecism in our sex,
If not in manners.
PEREGRINE   How is this?
SIR POLITIC   Sweet madam,
Come nearer to your aim.
LADY WOULD-BE   Marry, and will, sir. 45
Since you provoke me, with your impudence,
And laughter of your light land-siren, here,
Your Sporus, your hermaphrodite –
PEREGRINE   What's here?
Poetic fury, and historic storms?
SIR POLITIC
The gentleman, believe it, is of worth, 50
And of our nation.
LADY WOULD-BE   Ay, your Whitefriars nation!
Come, I blush for you, Master Would-Be, I;
And am ashamed you should ha' no more forehead

---

35   *Froward* Ill-humoured, unreasonable.
     The Courtier Castiglione's famous sixteenth-century courtesy manual.
36   *rusticity* crude country-bumpkin conduct.
41   *persever* persist (in denying involvement?); accented on second syllable.
42   *warranted* exempted.
43   *solecism* breach of propriety (usually in grammar).
47   *light land-siren* immoral temptress.
48   *Sporus* a young man whom the emperor Nero, finding him attractive, had castrated, and dressed as a woman; this recalls Volpone's attachment to Androgyno and Castrone.
49   *Poetic fury* Peregrine plays off Plato's term for poetic inspiration (in the *Ion* dialogue).
     historic Now Peregrine balances 'poetic' with the historical Sporus reference, and perhaps plays off 'hysterical' and 'histrionic'.
51   *Whitefriars* an area of London (called a 'liberty') which was exempt from the City's jurisdiction, and therefore became a haven for criminals and prostitutes; Q ends this line with a question mark.
53   *forehead* sense of shame, ability to blush.

Than thus to be the patron or St George
To a lewd harlot, a base fricatrice,   55
A female devil, in a male outside.
SIR POLITIC   Nay,
And you be such a one, I must bid adieu
To your delights! The case appears too liquid.   [*Exit*]
LADY WOULD-BE
Ay, you may carry't clear, with your state-face!
But, for your carnival concupiscence,   60
Who here is fled for liberty of conscience,
From furious persecution of the marshal,
Her will I disc'ple.
PEREGRINE   This is fine, i' faith!
And do you use this, often? Is this part
Of your wit's exercise, 'gainst you have occasion?   65
Madam –
LADY WOULD-BE Go to, sir.
PEREGRINE   Do you hear me, lady?
Why, if your knight have set you to beg shirts,
Or to invite me home, you might have done it
A nearer way, by far.
LADY WOULD-BE   This cannot work you
Out of my snare.

54   *St George* England's patron saint was also a patron saint of Venice, and was famous
      for rescuing a princess from a dragon.
55   *fricatrice* masseuse, prostitute.
57   *you* either Peregrine, whom Sir Pol (always looking for obscure plots) now suspects
      may actually be the courtesan his wife claims, or perhaps Lady Would-Be herself.
58   *liquid* transparent, or perhaps hard to grasp; Sir Pol may also be punning on his
      wife's sweat and tears ('case' often meant 'mask').
59   *state-face* calculated, dignified public demeanour.
61   *liberty of conscience* religious freedom, for which Venice was famous, here turned
      into an ironic euphemism for sexual licentiousness (playing on the previous
      reference to the Whitefriars liberty).
63   *disc'ple* discipline; in many productions, Lady Would-Be here attacks Peregrine
      physically.
64   *use this* behave this way.
65   *'gainst you have occasion* to keep your wit in practice, so it will be ready when really
      needed; or possibly, whenever you have an opportunity.
67   *beg shirts* Lady Would-Be may be tugging at Peregrine's shirt here (trying to expose
      a courtesan's breasts?), or Peregrine may be referring to a common cover-story for
      sexual solicitation.
69   *nearer* more direct.

PEREGRINE   Why, am I in it, then?   70
   Indeed, your husband told me you were fair,
   And so you are; only, your nose inclines
   (That side, that's next the sun) to the queen-apple.
LADY WOULD-BE
   This cannot be endured, by any patience.

ACT IV, SCENE iii

[*Enter*] MOSCA

MOSCA
   What's the matter, madam?
LADY WOULD-BE   If the Senate
   Right not my quest in this, I will protest 'em,
   To all the world, no aristocracy.
MOSCA
   What is the injury, lady?
LADY WOULD-BE   Why, the callet
   You told me of, here I have ta'en disguised.   5
MOSCA
   Who? This? What means your ladyship? The creature
   I mentioned to you is apprehended, now,
   Before the Senate, you shall see her –
LADY WOULD-BE   Where?
MOSCA
   I'll bring you to her. This young gentleman,
   I saw him land, this morning, at the port.   10
LADY WOULD-BE
   Is't possible? How has my judgement wandered!
   Sir, I must, blushing, say to you, I have erred;
   And plead your pardon.

---

73   *queen-apple* large red fruit; Peregrine plays off the common idealization of 'fair'
     (pale) complexion, which Lady Would-Be's heavy make-up has failed to sustain.

2   *Right not . . . protest 'em* Does not enforce my complaint against this courtesan, I will
    proclaim that they are; Machiavelli argued that the leading Venetians were not truly
    aristocrats, since they were merchants.
4   *callet* prostitute.

PEREGRINE   What, more changes, yet?
LADY WOULD-BE
   I hope y' ha' not the malice to remember
   A gentlewoman's passion. If you stay   15
   In Venice here, please you to use me, sir –
MOSCA
   Will you go, madam?
LADY WOULD-BE   'Pray you, sir, use me. In faith,
   The more you use me the more I shall conceive
   You have forgot our quarrel.
            [*Exeunt* LADY WOULD-BE, SERVING-WOMEN,
                          MOSCA, NANO]
PEREGRINE   This is rare!
   Sir Politic Would-Be? No, Sir Politic Bawd!   20
   To bring me, thus, acquainted with his wife!
   Well, wise Sir Pol: since you have practised, thus,
   Upon my freshmanship, I will try your salt-head,
   What proof it is against a counter-plot.   [*Exit*]

ACT IV, SCENE iv

[*Enter*] VOLTORE, CORBACCIO, CORVINO, MOSCA

VOLTORE
   Well, now you know the carriage of the business,
   Your constancy is all that is required
   Unto the safety of it.
MOSCA   Is the lie
   Safely conveyed amongst us? Is that sure?
   Knows every man his burden?

16   *use me* let me be helpful, find me useful; but the common sense of sexual use comes
     through strongly, especially in conjunction with 'conceive' in the next line.
21   *acquainted* Since Peregrine suspects Sir Pol of being a wittol who abets his wife's
     adulteries, there may be a pun here on 'quaint', Jacobean slang for a woman's
     genitalia.
22–4 *practised . . . proof it is* plotted thus to take advantage of my inexperience here, I'll
     test how well your more seasoned mind can defend you.

1   *the carriage* the management, how to carry it off.
5   *burden* the refrain of a song; hence, his part in the group performance.

CORVINO	Yes.	
MOSCA	Then, shrink not.	5

CORVINO [*Taking* MOSCA *aside*]
    But, knows the advocate the truth?
MOSCA   O, sir,
    By no means. I devised a formal tale,
    That salved your reputation. But, be valiant, sir.
CORVINO
    I fear no one but him: that this his pleading
    Should make him stand for a co-heir –

MOSCA	Co-halter.	10

    Hang him: we will but use his tongue, his noise,
    As we do Croaker's here.
CORVINO   Ay, what shall he do?
MOSCA
    When we have done, you mean?
CORVINO   Yes.
MOSCA   Why, we'll think:
    Sell him for mummia, he's half dust already.

(*To* VOLTORE) Do not you smile, to see this buffalo,		15

    How he does sport it with his head? [*To himself*] I should
    If all were well, and past. (*To* CORBACCIO) Sir, only you
    Are he that shall enjoy the crop of all,
    And these not know for whom they toil.
CORBACCIO   Ay, peace.
MOSCA (*To* CORVINO)
    But you shall eat it. [*To himself*] Much!

(*To* VOLTORE)	Worshipful sir,	20

    Mercury sit upon your thund'ring tongue,
    Or the French Hercules, and make your language

---

7   *formal tale* elaborate fiction (to conceal Corvino's attempt to prostitute his wife – a thematic connection to the Would-Be scene that has just ended).
12   *Croaker* Corbaccio, whose voice may have been crow-like.
14   *mummia* a supposedly medicinal substance derived from preserved corpses.
15   *buffalo* Mosca is now confiding in Voltore instead, joking about the cuckold's horns Corvino has earned.
20   *Much!* Probably an ironic exclamation, like the sarcastic, 'that's likely' or 'fat chance'; Mosca may be speaking to Voltore to assure him that the previous assurances to Corvino and Corbaccio were merely ploys. Mosca's handling of these three rival suitors in the same room at the same time is a bravura juggling act.
21   *Mercury* the god of eloquence, but also associated with thievery.
22   *French Hercules* Late in life Hercules was believed to have fathered the Celts in Gaul, and to have compensated for his lost physical strength with oratorical powers.

As conquering as his club, to beat along,
As with a tempest, flat, our adversaries;
But, much more, yours, sir.

VOLTORE   Here they come, ha' done.   25

MOSCA
I have another witness, if you need, sir,
I can produce.

VOLTORE   Who is it?

MOSCA   Sir, I have her.

ACT IV, SCENE v

[*Enter*] *four* AVOCATORI, BONARIO, CELIA, NOTARIO,
COMMANDATORI

1ST AVOCATORE
The like of this the Senate never heard of.

2ND AVOCATORE
'Twill come most strange to them, when we report it.

4TH AVOCATORE
The gentlewoman has been ever held
Of unreprovèd name.

3RD AVOCATORE   So has the youth.

4TH AVOCATORE
The more unnatural part that of his father.   5

2ND AVOCATORE
More of the husband.

1ST AVOCATORE   I not know to give
His act a name, it is so monstrous!

4TH AVOCATORE
But the impostor, he is a thing created
T' exceed example!

1ST AVOCATORE   And all after-times!

25 *yours* your adversaries.
     ha' done stop, be quiet.
27 *her* Lady Would-Be.

9   *example* precedent.

115

2ND AVOCATORE
    I never heard a true voluptuary   10
    Described but him.

3RD AVOCATORE   Appear yet those were cited?

NOTARIO
    All but the old *magnifico*, Volpone.

1ST AVOCATORE
    Why is not he here?

MOSCA   Please your fatherhoods,
    Here is his advocate. Himself's so weak,
    So feeble –

4TH AVOCATORE What are you?

BONARIO   His parasite,   15
    His knave, his pander! I beseech the court
    He may be forced to come, that your grave eyes
    May bear strong witness of his strange impostures.

VOLTORE
    Upon my faith, and credit with your virtues,
    He is not able to endure the air.   20

2ND AVOCATORE
    Bring him, however.

3RD AVOCATORE   We will see him.

4TH AVOCATORE   Fetch him.
          [*Exit* COMMANDATORE]

VOLTORE
    Your fatherhoods' fit pleasures be obeyed,
    But sure, the sight will rather move your pities,
    Than indignation. May it please the court,
    In the meantime, he may be heard in me;   25
    I know this place most void of prejudice,
    And therefore crave it, since we have no reason
    To fear our truth should hurt our cause.

3RD AVOCATORE   Speak free.

VOLTORE
    Then know, most honoured fathers, I must now
    Discover, to your strangely abused ears,   30

---

11   *cited* subpoenaed, summoned.
12   *magnifico* nobleman.
13   *fatherhoods* As Kernan points out, this is not only a technically correct form of
      address, but also a rhetorically advantageous one, since it inclines the judges to side
      with the father Corbaccio.

The most prodigious, and most frontless piece
Of solid impudence, and treachery,
That ever vicious nature yet brought forth
To shame the state of Venice. This lewd woman,
                              [*Pointing to* CELIA]
That wants no artificial looks, or tears,   35
To help the visor, she has now put on,
Hath long been known a close adulteress,
To that lascivious youth there;   [*Pointing to* BONARIO]
                         not suspected,
I say, but known; and taken, in the act;
With him; and by this man,   [*Pointing to* CORVINO]
                   the easy husband,   40
Pardoned; whose timeless bounty makes him, now,
Stand here, the most unhappy, innocent person
That ever man's own virtue made accused.
For these, not knowing how to owe a gift
Of that dear grace but with their shame, being placed   45
So above all powers of their gratitude,
Began to hate the benefit; and, in place
Of thanks, devise t' extirp the memory
Of such an act. Wherein, I pray your fatherhoods,
To observe the malice, yea, the rage of creatures   50
Discovered in their evils; and what heart
Such take, even from their crimes. But that, anon,
Will more appear. This gentleman,   [*Pointing to* CORBACCIO]
                   the father,
Hearing of this foul fact, with many others,
Which daily struck at his too tender ears,   55
And, grieved in nothing more than that he could not
Preserve himself a parent (his son's ills
Growing to that strange flood), at last decreed

31   *frontless* shameless.
35   *wants* lacks.
36   *visor* mask; either Celia has now modestly masked herself, or Voltore is implying
     that her appearance of anguished innocence is merely a disguise.
37   *close* secret.
40   *easy* lenient.
44–7   *For these . . . benefit* Celia and Bonario do not know how to respond to such
     generosity except by feeling shamed, since it goes beyond their sadly limited capacity
     for gratitude, and so they began to resent the gift.
48   *extirp* eradicate.
51   *heart* audacity, encouragement.

To disinherit him.

1ST AVOCATORE   These be strange turns!

2ND AVOCATORE

The young man's fame was ever fair and honest.   60

VOLTORE

So much more full of danger is his vice,
That can beguile so, under shade of virtue.
But as I said, my honoured sires, his father
Having this settled purpose – by what means
To him betrayed, we know not – and this day   65
Appointed for the deed, that parricide
(I cannot style him better), by confederacy
Preparing this his paramour to be there,
Entered Volpone's house – who was the man
Your fatherhoods must understand, designed   70
For the inheritance – there, sought his father.
But, with what purpose sought he him, my sires?
I tremble to pronounce it, that a son
Unto a father, and to such a father,
Should have so foul, felonious intent: 75
It was, to murder him. When, being prevented
By his more happy absence, what then did he?
Not check his wicked thoughts; no, now new deeds –
Mischief doth ever end, where it begins –
An act of horror, fathers! He dragged forth   80
The aged gentleman, that had there lain, bed-rid,
Three years and more, out off his innocent couch,
Naked upon the floor, there left him; wounded
His servant in the face; and, with this strumpet,
The stale to his forged practice, who was glad   85
To be so active (I shall here desire
Your fatherhoods to note but my collections,
As most remarkable), thought at once to stop
His father's ends; discredit his free choice
In the old gentleman; redeem themselves,   90

65   *To him betrayed* Revealed to Bonario.
70   *designed* designated, intended.
77   *his more happy* Corbaccio's fortunate.
85   *The stale . . . practice* The prostitute used as a lure for his deceptive plot.
87   *collections* conclusions, inferences.
89   *ends* intentions.
90   *the old gentleman* Volpone, whom Corbaccio had chosen as his heir.

By laying infamy upon this man
To whom, with blushing, they should owe their lives.

1ST AVOCATORE
What proofs have you of this?

BONARIO   Most honoured fathers,
I humbly crave there be no credit given
To this man's mercenary tongue.

2ND AVOCATORE   Forbear.   95

BONARIO
His soul moves in his fee.

3RD AVOCATORE   O, sir.

BONARIO   This fellow,
For six sols more, would plead against his Maker.

1ST AVOCATORE
You do forget yourself.

VOLTORE   Nay, nay, grave fathers,
Let him have scope: can any man imagine
That he will spare 's accuser, that would not   100
Have spared his parent?

1ST AVOCATORE   Well, produce your proofs.

CELIA
I would I could forget I were a creature.

VOLTORE
Signior Corbaccio.

4TH AVOCATORE   What is he?

VOLTORE   The father.

2ND AVOCATORE
Has he had an oath?

NOTARIO   Yes.

CORBACCIO   What must I do now?

NOTARIO
Your testimony's craved.

CORBACCIO   Speak to the knave?   105
I'll ha' my mouth, first, stopped with earth! My heart
Abhors his knowledge; I disclaim in him.

---

91   *this man* Corvino.
97   *sols* low-value French coins.
102 *I would ... creature* I wish I could forget that I am created by God (so I could choose
     suicide), or, I wish I could separate myself totally from these beasts.
105 *Speak to the knave?* The half-deaf Corbaccio has misheard the Notario's response.
107 *Abhors his knowledge* Hates to acknowledge him, or, Hates even to think about him.

1ST AVOCATORE
  But, for what cause?
CORBACCIO   The mere portent of nature.
  He is an utter stranger to my loins.
BONARIO
  Have they made you to this?
CORBACCIO   I will not hear thee,   110
  Monster of men, swine, goat, wolf, parricide;
  Speak not, thou viper.
BONARIO   Sir, I will sit down,
  And rather wish my innocence should suffer,
  Than I resist the authority of a father.
VOLTORE
  Signior Corvino.
2ND AVOCATORE   This is strange!
1ST AVOCATORE   Who's this?   115
NOTARIO
  The husband.
4TH AVOCATORE Is he sworn?
NOTARIO   He is.
3RD AVOCATORE   Speak, then.
CORVINO
  This woman, please your fatherhoods, is a whore,
  Of most hot exercise, more than a partridge,
  Upon record –
1ST AVOCATORE   No more.
CORVINO   Neighs like a jennet.
NOTARIO
  Preserve the honour of the court.
CORVINO   I shall,   120
  And modesty of your most reverend ears.
  And yet I hope that I may say, these eyes
  Have seen her glued unto that piece of cedar,

---

108   *The mere portent* An absolute freak; unnatural births were considered portentous,
     and Corbaccio is distancing himself from his natural fatherhood of Bonario.
110   *made you* forced you, or, put you up.
118   *partridge* nature's most lecherous creature, according to Pliny's *Natural History*.
119   *jennet* small, lively Spanish horse.
124   *well-timbered gallant* well-built young man (Bonario).

That fine well-timbered gallant; and that, here,
[*Pointing to his forehead*]
The letters may be read, thorough the horn,   125
That make the story perfect.
MOSCA [*Aside to* CORVINO]   Excellent, sir!
CORVINO [*Aside to* MOSCA]
   There is no shame in this, now, is there?
MOSCA [*Aside to* CORVINO]   None.
CORVINO
   Or if I said, I hoped that she were onward
   To her damnation, if there be a hell
   Greater than whore, and woman: a good Catholic   130
   May make the doubt.
3RD AVOCATORE   His grief hath made him frantic.
1ST AVOCATORE
   Remove him, hence.

[CELIA] *swoons*

2ND AVOCATORE   Look to the woman.
CORVINO   Rare!
   Prettily feigned! Again!
4TH AVOCATORE   Stand from about her.
1ST AVOCATORE
   Give her the air.
3RD AVOCATORE [*To* MOSCA] What can you say?
MOSCA   My wound,
   May it please your wisdoms, speaks for me, received   135
   In aid of my good patron, when he missed
   His sought-for father, when that well-taught dame

124–6   *here . . . perfect* here on my forehead is legible the letter V that makes the shape of
        cuckold's horns – or maybe the word 'cuckold' that can be read through the
        transparent horn that covered the printed sheets on which Elizabethan school-
        children were taught their letters – that completes the story of my betrayal.
127   *There is . . . None* Corvino wants reassurance that he has not humiliated himself by
        claiming to have been cuckolded; Mosca gives the desired answer, but (by changing
        Q's 'harm' to F's 'shame' here) Jonson allows him a sly implication that Corvino's
        performance was shameless.
128   *onward* well on her way.
131   *make the doubt* suspect that women and whores are themselves hell; Jonson was
        apparently no longer a Catholic at the time of F, allowing him to replace Q's 'a good
        Christian' with a more pointed implication about Catholicism's powerful ambiva-
        lence toward women.
136   *he* Bonario.

Had her cue given her, to cry out a rape.

BONARIO

O, most laid impudence! Fathers –

3RD AVOCATORE   Sir, be silent,

You had your hearing free, so must they theirs.   140

2ND AVOCATORE

I do begin to doubt th' imposture, here.

4TH AVOCATORE

This woman has too many moods.

VOLTORE   Grave fathers,

She is a creature of a most professed

And prostituted lewdness.

CORVINO   Most impetuous!

Unsatisfied, grave fathers!

VOLTORE   May her feignings   145

Not take your wisdoms; but this day, she baited

A stranger, a grave knight, with her loose eyes,

And more lascivious kisses. This man saw them

Together, on the water, in a gondola.

MOSCA

Here is the lady herself, that saw 'em too,   150

Without; who then had in the open streets

Pursued them, but for saving her knight's honour.

1ST AVOCATORE

Produce that lady.

2ND AVOCATORE   Let her come.

                                        [*Exit* MOSCA]

4TH AVOCATORE   These things,

They strike with wonder!

3RD AVOCATORE   I am turned a stone!

---

139   *most laid* deeply plotted.
141   *doubt th' imposture* suspect fraud by Celia and Bonario.
146   *take* take in, deceive, charm.
        but this day this very day.
151   *Without* Outside.

ACT IV, SCENE vi

[*Enter*] MOSCA [*with*] LADY WOULD-BE

MOSCA
Be resolute, Madam.

LADY WOULD-BE [*Pointing at* CELIA]
           Ay, this same is she.
Out, thou chameleon harlot; now thine eyes
Vie tears with the hyena. Dar'st thou look
Upon my wrongèd face?
[*To the* AVOCATORI]   I cry your pardons.
I fear I have, forgettingly, transgressed   5
Against the dignity of the court –

2ND AVOCATORE   No, madam.

LADY WOULD-BE
And been exorbitant –

2ND AVOCATORE   You have not, lady.

4TH AVOCATORE
These proofs are strong.

LADY WOULD-BE   Surely, I had no purpose,
To scandalise your honours, or my sex's.

3RD AVOCATORE
We do believe it.

LADY WOULD-BE Surely, you may believe it.   10

---

2   *chameleon* creature famous for its changing camouflage; Lady Would-Be now assumes that Celia was the woman disguised as a man she heard was accompanying her husband.

3   *hyena* Lady Would-Be confuses the hyena, which was thought to capture people by imitating a human voice, with the crocodile, which was thought to use unfelt tears for the same purpose; in fact, in her make-up and shifting stories, her destructive voice and eagerness to feed on Volpone's moribund flesh, she herself becomes both chameleon and hyena, extending Jonson's fable of human beings who degrade themselves into beasts.

7   *exorbitant* excessive or disorderly.

    s.p. *2ND AVOCATORE* Both parts of the reply are given to the 4th Avocatore by Q and F, but with separate speech headings, so this edition (like others) follows F3 (Jonson's 1692 *Works*) in giving the first part to the 2nd Avocatore; in any case, the judges (like Volpone earlier) seem desperate throughout the scene to forestall, by futile interruptions, any long explanations from Lady Would-Be.

2ND AVOCATORE
Madam, we do.

LADY WOULD-BE Indeed, you may: my breeding
Is not so coarse –

4TH AVOCATORE We know it.

LADY WOULD-BE To offend
With pertinacy –

3RD AVOCATORE Lady.

LADY WOULD-BE Such a presence;
No, surely.

1ST AVOCATORE We well think it.

LADY WOULD-BE You may think it.

1ST AVOCATORE
Let her o'ercome.
[*To* CELIA *and* BONARIO] What witnesses have you,   15
To make good your report?

BONARIO Our consciences.

CELIA
And heaven, that never fails the innocent.

4TH AVOCATORE
These are no testimonies.

BONARIO Not in your courts,
Where multitude and clamour overcomes.

1ST AVOCATORE
Nay, then you do wax insolent.

VOLPONE *is brought in, as impotent*

VOLTORE Here, here,   20
The testimony comes, that will convince,
And put to utter dumbness, their bold tongues.
See here, grave fathers, here is the ravisher,
The rider on men's wives, the great impostor,
The grand voluptuary! Do you not think,   25

---

13   *pertinacy* pertinacity, stubborness; or possibly Lady Would-Be's mistake for 'impertinence'.
15   *o'ercome* conquer – either by believing her testimony against Celia, or by letting her characteristic verbal persistence grant her the last word in the exchange of courteous remarks.
19   *multitude and clamour* the larger number of witnesses, and louder ones.
20   s.d. *as impotent* seemingly devoid of bodily strength; Volpone is presumably carried in draped on a litter or stretcher.

These limbs should affect venery? or these eyes
Covet a concubine? 'Pray you, mark these hands:
Are they not fit to stroke a lady's breasts?
Perhaps, he doth dissemble.

BONARIO   So he does.

VOLTORE

Would you have him tortured?

BONARIO   I would have him proved.   30

VOLTORE

Best try him, then, with goads, or burning irons;
Put him to the *strappado*! I have heard,
The rack hath cured the gout: 'faith, give it him,
And help him of a malady, be courteous.
I will undertake, before these honoured fathers,   35
He shall have, yet, as many left diseases,
As she has known adulterers, or thou strumpets.
O, my most equal hearers, if these deeds –
Acts of this bold and most exorbitant strain –
May pass with sufferance, what one citizen   40
But owes the forfeit of his life, yea, fame,
To him that dares traduce him? Which of you
Are safe, my honoured fathers? I would ask,
With leave of your grave fatherhoods, if their plot
Have any face, or colour like to truth?   45
Or if, unto the dullest nostril here,
It smell not rank, and most abhorrèd slander?
I crave your care of this good gentleman,
Whose life is much endangered by their fable;
And, as for them, I will conclude with this: 50
That vicious persons when they are hot, and fleshed

26   *affect venery* pursue sexual pleasure.
30   *proved* tested.
32   *strappado* hoisting prisoners by a rope tied to their wrists behind their back and then dropping them; all these forms of torture were practised by the Venetian republic.
34   *help* relieve.
38   *equal* fair-minded.
39   *strain* type.
40–2   *May pass . . . traduce him?* May occur and be tolerated, can any citizen defend his life or even his reputation against anyone who has the nerve to slander him?
44   *leave* permission.
45   *face, or colour* resemblance; but the irony is that Voltore's own case consists entirely of face (surface and shamelessness) and colour (rhetorical devices).
51   *fleshed* initiated (as in the passion of a hunt).

In impious acts, their constancy abounds:
Damned deeds are done with greatest confidence.

1ST AVOCATORE

Take 'em to custody, and sever them.

[CELIA *and* BONARIO *are led out separately*]

2ND AVOCATORE

'Tis pity two such prodigies should live.   55

1ST AVOCATORE

Let the old gentleman be returned, with care;
I'm sorry, our credulity wronged him.

[VOLPONE *is carried out*]

4TH AVOCATORE

These are two creatures!

3RD AVOCATORE   I have an earthquake in me!

2ND AVOCATORE

Their shame, even in their cradles, fled their faces.

4TH AVOCATORE [*To* VOLTORE]

You've done a worthy service to the state, sir,   60
In their discovery.

1ST AVOCATORE   You shall hear, ere night,
What punishment the court decrees upon 'em.

VOLTORE

We thank your fatherhoods.

[*Exeunt* AVOCATORI, NOTARIO, *and all other officials*]
                    How like you it?

MOSCA   Rare.

I'd ha' your tongue, sir, tipped with gold, for this;
I'd ha' you be the heir to the whole city;   65
The earth I'd have want men, ere you want living!
They're bound to erect your statue, in St Mark's.
Signior Corvino, I would have you go
And show yourself, that you have conquered.

CORVINO   Yes.

MOSCA

It was much better that you should profess   70
Yourself a cuckold, thus, than that the other

52   *constancy* resolution.
54   *sever them* keep them separate.
55   *prodigies* ominous monsters.
63   *Rare* Unusually good; Jonson's tombstone reads simply, 'O Rare Ben Jonson'.
66   *The earth . . . living* I would rather have the earth lack human beings than have you lack a lawyer's livelihood.
71   *the other* that Corvino had deliberately prostituted his own wife.

Should have been proved.

CORVINO   Nay, I considered that:
Now, it is her fault:

MOSCA   Then, it had been yours.

CORVINO
True. I do doubt this advocate, still.

MOSCA   I' faith,
You need not, I dare ease you of that care.   75

CORVINO
I trust thee, Mosca.

MOSCA   As your own soul, sir.

                                       [*Exit* CORVINO]

CORBACCIO   Mosca.

MOSCA
Now for your business, sir.

CORBACCIO   How? Ha' you business?

MOSCA
Yes, yours, sir.

CORBACCIO   O, none else?

MOSCA   None else, not I.

CORBACCIO
Be careful, then.

MOSCA   Rest you, with both your eyes, sir.

CORBACCIO
Dispatch it.

MOSCA   Instantly.

CORBACCIO   And look that all,   80
Whatever, be put in: jewels, plate, moneys,
Household stuff, bedding, curtains.

MOSCA   Curtain-rings, sir.
Only, the advocate's fee must be deducted.

CORBACCIO
I'll pay him now: you'll be too prodigal.

MOSCA
Sir, I must tender it.

CORBACCIO   Two chequins is well?   85

---

74   *I do . . . still* I still don't trust this lawyer Voltore.
79   *Rest . . . eyes* Relax completely.
80   *Dispatch it* Quickly begin an inventory of Volpone's property.
85   *tender* give.

MOSCA
   No, six, sir.

CORBACCIO   'Tis too much.

MOSCA   He talked a great while;
   You must consider that, sir.

CORBACCIO [*Giving* MOSCA *coins*]
                     Well, there's three –

MOSCA
   I'll give it him.

CORBACCIO   Do so, and there's for thee.
                   [*Gives* MOSCA *a small tip and exits*]

MOSCA
   Bountiful bones! What horrid strange offence
   Did he commit 'gainst nature, in his youth,   90
   Worthy this age? [*To* VOLTORE] You see, sir, how I work
   Unto your ends; take you no notice.

VOLTORE   No,
   I'll leave you.

MOSCA   All is yours –
                       [*Exit* VOLTORE]
              the devil and all,
   Good advocate.
   [*To* LADY WOULD-BE] Madam, I'll bring you home.

LADY WOULD-BE
   No, I'll go see your patron.

MOSCA   That you shall not.   95
   I'll tell you why. My purpose is, to urge
   My patron to reform his will; and, for
   The zeal you've shown today, whereas before
   You were but third or fourth, you shall be now
   Put in the first; which would appear as begged,   100
   If you be present. Therefore –

LADY WOULD-BE   You shall sway me.
                     [*Exeunt*]

---

89   *Bountiful bones* A sarcastic exclamation associating Corbaccio's stinginess with his shrunken, skeletal physique; the connection between moral and physical condition is important throughout the play.

91   *Worthy this age* To have earned such an ugly old age.

92   *take you no notice* don't worry that I seem to be conspiring with your rivals, or, don't acknowledge what I am doing for or saying to you (because Lady Would-Be is still present).

101   *sway* persuade, perhaps (as often with Lady Would-Be) with a secondary sexual meaning.

ACT V, SCENE i

[Enter VOLPONE]

VOLPONE

Well, I am here; and all this brunt is past!
I ne'er was in dislike with my disguise,
Till this fled moment: here, 'twas good, in private,
But in your public – *cavè*, whilst I breathe.
'Fore God, my left leg 'gan to have the cramp;   5
And I appre'nded, straight, some power had struck me
With a dead palsy! Well, I must be merry,
And shake it off. A many of these fears
Would put me into some villainous disease,
Should they come thick upon me: I'll prevent 'em.   10
Give me a bowl of lusty wine, to fright
This humour from my heart – hum, hum, hum;   *(He drinks)*
'Tis almost gone already: I shall conquer.
Any device, now, of rare, ingenious knavery,
That would possess me with a violent laughter,   15
Would make me up, again! So, so, so, so.   *(Drinks again)*
This heat is life; 'tis blood, by this time! Mosca!

ACT V, SCENE ii

[Enter] MOSCA

MOSCA

How now, sir? Does the day look clear again?

---

1   *brunt* stress, attack, crisis.
3   *fled* past.
4   *cavè* beware; Volpone is reminding himself, and perhaps asking the audience, to make sure he isn't seen standing up.
6   *appre'nded, straight* thought immediately.
7   *dead palsy* total paralysis; Jonson suffered some kind of palsy later in life.
16 s.d. *Drinks again* Some productions emphasize Volpone's over-indulgence here to explain his rash decision to play dead; Tilley, F651, records 'foxed' as a euphemism for 'drunk' (Parker).

Are we recovered? And wrought out of error,
Into our way? To see our path before us?
Is our trade free once more?
VOLPONE   Exquisite Mosca!
MOSCA
Was it not carried learnedly?
VOLPONE   And stoutly.   5
Good wits are greatest in extremities.
MOSCA
It were a folly, beyond thought, to trust
Any grand act unto a cowardly spirit.
You are not taken with it enough, methinks?
VOLPONE
O, more than if I had enjoyed the wench!   10
The pleasure of all womankind's not like it.
MOSCA
Why, now you speak, sir. We must here be fixed;
Here, we must rest; this is our masterpiece;
We cannot think to go beyond this.
VOLPONE   True,
Thou hast played thy prize, my precious Mosca.
MOSCA   Nay sir,   15
To gull the court –
VOLPONE   And quite divert the torrent
Upon the innocent.
MOSCA   Yes, and to make
So rare a music out of discords –
VOLPONE   Right.
That, yet, to me's the strangest! How thou'st borne it!
That these, being so divided 'mongst themselves,   20
Should not scent somewhat, or in me, or thee,
Or doubt their own side.
MOSCA   True. They will not see it:
Too much light blinds them, I think; each of 'em

7   *beyond thought* unthinkable.
9   *taken* pleased.
15   *prize* masterpiece; but Mosca may have another prize in view.
16   *gull* trick, make fools of (as in 'gullible').
18   *discords* the conflicting testimonies, and/or the feuding rival heirs.
19   *borne* managed.
23   *light* hope, perhaps with a gesture toward the gleaming treasure, as in the play's opening line.

Is so possessed, and stuffed with his own hopes,
That anything unto the contrary,   25
Never so true, or never so apparent,
Never so palpable, they will resist it –
VOLPONE
Like a temptation of the devil.
MOSCA   Right, sir.
Merchants may talk of trade, and your great signiors
Of land that yields well; but if Italy   30
Have any glebe more fruitful than these fellows,
I am deceived. Did not your advocate rare?
VOLPONE [*Mimicking* VOLTORE]
'O, my most honoured fathers, my grave fathers,
Under correction of your fatherhoods,
What face of truth is, here? If these strange deeds   35
May pass, most honoured fathers' – I had much ado
To forbear laughing.
MOSCA   'T seemed to me, you sweat, sir.
VOLPONE
In troth, I did a little.
MOSCA   But confess, sir,
Were you not daunted?
VOLPONE   In good faith, I was
A little in a mist; but not dejected;   40
Never, but still myself.
MOSCA   I think it, sir.
Now (so truth help me) I must needs say this, sir,
And, out of conscience, for your advocate:
He's taken pains, in faith, sir, and deserved,
In my poor judgement (I speak it, under favour,   45
Not to contrary you, sir), very richly –
Well – to be cozened.
VOLPONE   Troth, and I think so too,
By that I heard him in the latter end.

24   *possessed* The word (like much about Mosca) hovers between material and demonic
      possessions.
31   *glebe* agricultural field.
32   *rare* extremely well.
45   *under favour* with your permission. Mosca may be parodying the lawyer Voltore's
      obsequious grandiloquence here.
47   *cozened* cheated.
48   *By that I heard him* Judging by what I heard him say.

MOSCA
    O, but before, sir; had you heard him, first,
    Draw it to certain heads, then aggravate,   50
    Then use his vehement figures – I looked still,
    When he would shift a shirt; and, doing this
    Out of pure love, no hope of gain –
VOLPONE   'Tis right.
    I cannot answer him, Mosca, as I would,
    Not yet; but, for thy sake, at thy entreaty,   55
    I will begin, even now, to vex 'em all;
    This very instant.
MOSCA   Good, sir.
VOLPONE   Call the dwarf
    And eunuch forth.
MOSCA   Castrone, Nano.

             [*Enter* CASTRONE, NANO]

NANO   Here.
VOLPONE
    Shall we have a jig now?
MOSCA   What you please, sir.
VOLPONE   Go,
    Straight, give out, about the streets, you two,   60
    That I am dead; do it, with constancy,
    Sadly, do you hear? Impute it to the grief
    Of this late slander.

             [*Exeunt* CASTRONE, NANO]

MOSCA   What do you mean, sir?
VOLPONE   O,
    I shall have, instantly, my vulture, crow,
    Raven, come flying hither, on the news,   65

---

50   *Draw . . . aggravate* Gather his arguments into specific topics, then emphasize.
51   *figures* rhetorical tropes (figures of speech), or gestures.
51–2 *I looked . . . shirt* I kept expecting him to change his clothing (because his extreme efforts must have made him sweat).
54   *answer* repay.
59   *jig* a lively dance, often performed at the end of an Elizabethan play; but Volpone seems to be using it as a metaphor for the final satiric dance of death he intends to choreograph for the legacy-hunters.
60   *Straight . . . about* Immediately report throughout.
61   *with constancy* with conviction and straight faces.
63   *mean* intend.

To peck for carrion; my she-wolf, and all,
Greedy, and full of expectation –
MOSCA
And then, to have it ravished from their mouths?
VOLPONE
'Tis true, I will ha' thee put on a gown,
And take upon thee as thou wert mine heir;   70
Show 'em a will. Open that chest, and reach
Forth one of those, that has the blanks. I'll straight
Put in thy name.
MOSCA   It will be rare, sir.
VOLPONE   Aye,
When they e'en gape, and find themselves deluded –
MOSCA
Yes.
VOLPONE And thou use them scurvily. Dispatch,   75
Get on thy gown.
MOSCA   But, what, sir, if they ask
After the body?
VOLPONE   Say, it was corrupted.
MOSCA
I'll say it stunk, sir; and was fain t' have it
Coffined up instantly, and sent away.
VOLPONE
Anything, what thou wilt. Hold, here's my will.   80
Get thee a cap, a count-book, pen and ink,
Papers afore thee; sit, as thou wert taking
An inventory of parcels. I'll get up,
Behind the curtain, on a stool, and hearken;
Sometime, peep over; see, how they do look;   85
With what degrees, their blood doth leave their faces!
O, 'twill afford me a rare meal of laughter.
MOSCA
Your advocate will turn stark dull upon it.
VOLPONE
It will take off his oratory's edge.

70   *take upon thee as* act as if.
78   *fain* eager, compelled.
81   *count-book* account-book, financial ledger.
88   *turn stark dull* be struck dumb; Volpone's reply puns on another meaning of 'dull'.

MOSCA

But your *clarissimo*, old round-back, he   90
Will crump you, like a hog-louse, with the touch.

VOLPONE

And what Corvino?

MOSCA   O, sir, look for him,
Tomorrow morning, with a rope, and a dagger,
To visit all the streets: he must run mad.
My lady too, that came into the court,   95
To bear false witness for your worship.

VOLPONE   Yes,
And kissed me 'fore the fathers; when my face
Flowed all with oils.

MOSCA   And sweat – sir. Why, your gold
Is such another med'cine, it dries up
All those offensive savours! It transforms   100
The most deformèd, and restores 'em lovely,
As 'twere the strange poetical girdle. Jove
Could not invent, t' himself, a shroud more subtle,
To pass Acrisius' guards. It is the thing
Makes all the world her grace, her youth, her beauty.   105

VOLPONE

I think she loves me.

MOSCA   Who? The lady, sir?
She is jealous of you.

VOLPONE   Dost thou say so?

---

90   *clarissimo* high-ranking Venetian.

90–1 *old round-back . . . touch* Corbaccio, who evidently stoops with age, will curl (or crumple) up like a wood-louse (pill-bug) from the impact of this development.

93   *rope, dagger* These were standard symbols of suicidal madness, ones Jonson would have used as props when he played the grieving Hieronimo in Kyd's *Spanish Tragedy*.

98   *And sweat – sir* Mosca needles Volpone with a reminder that he was panicked, not just performing, at the trial; the dash may suggest a pause before reverting to deference with 'sir'.

99   *such another* so great a.

102 *girdle* F inserts '*Cestus*' in the margin at the end of this line, probably to clarify the reference to Venus's girdle of that name, which is capable (according to Homer's *Iliad*, XIV) of transforming ugliness to beauty and reviving passion in the aged.

104 *Acrisius* the father of Danae, who locked her in a brazen tower to forestall a prophecy that her son would kill him; but Jove descended on her in a shower of gold and impregnated her with Perseus.

106 *The lady* Perhaps Lady Would-Be, and some commentators suggest Celia, but the previous lines feminize the gold itself, which is the thing Volpone seeks love from, and which proves to be his jealous god.

>   [*A knock at the door*]
MOSCA   Hark,
  There's some already.
VOLPONE   Look.
MOSCA   It is the vulture:
  He has the quickest scent.
VOLPONE   I'll to my place,
  Thou, to thy posture.
MOSCA   I'm set.
VOLPONE   But, Mosca,   110
  Play the artificer now, torture 'em, rarely.

ACT V, SCENE iii

[*Enter* VOLTORE]

VOLTORE
  How now, my Mosca?
MOSCA   Turkey carpets, nine –
VOLTORE
  Taking an inventory? That is well.
MOSCA
  Two suits of bedding, tissue –
VOLTORE   Where's the will?
  Let me read that, the while.

[CORBACCIO *is carried in*]

CORBACCIO   So, set me down;
  And get you home.
                              [*Exeunt* CHAIR-BEARERS]
VOLTORE   Is he come, now, to trouble us?   5

---

110   *posture* pose, imposture.
111   *Play the artificer* Perform craftily and elaborately.

  1   *Turkey carpets* imported through Italy, and used as table covers or wall hangings.
  3   *suits of bedding* sets of bed covers in expensive fabrics
       tissue cloth with silver or gold.
  4   *the while* while you are completing the inventory.

MOSCA
    Of cloth of gold, two more –
CORBACCIO   Is it done, Mosca?
MOSCA
    Of several vellets, eight –
VOLTORE   I like his care.
CORBACCIO
    Dost thou not hear?

[Enter CORVINO]

CORVINO   Ha? Is the hour come, Mosca?
                   VOLPONE *peeps from behind a traverse*
VOLPONE
    Ay, now they muster.
CORVINO   What does the advocate here?
    Or this Corbaccio?
CORVINO   What do these here?

[Enter LADY WOULD-BE]

LADY WOULD-BE   Mosca?   10
    Is his thread spun?
MOSCA   Eight chests of linen –
VOLPONE   O,
    My fine Dame Would-Be, too!
CORVINO   Mosca, the will,
    That I may show it these, and rid 'em hence.
MOSCA
    Six chests of diaper, four of damask – There.
                   [Points to papers on a table]
CORBACCIO
    Is that the will?
MOSCA   Down-beds, and bolsters –
VOLPONE   Rare!   15
    Be busy still. Now they begin to flutter;
    They never think of me. Look, see, see, see!

---

7   *several vellets* separate velvet hangings.
11 *Is his thread spun* Lady Would-Be alludes to the myth of the Three Fates to ask, in
     characteristically pompous fashion, whether Volpone is dead; she may also sub-
     consciously be responding to the sight of all these expensive fabrics.
14 *diaper* linen woven into a diamond pattern.
     damask intricately woven table-linen.

How their swift eyes run over the long deed,
Unto the name, and to the legacies,
What is bequeathed them there –
MOSCA   Ten suits of hangings –   20
VOLPONE
Ay, i' their garters, Mosca. Now their hopes
Are at the gasp.
VOLTORE   Mosca the heir!
CORBACCIO   What's that?
VOLPONE
My advocate is dumb. Look to my merchant,
He has heard of some strange storm, a ship is lost:
He faints. My lady will swoon. Old glazen-eyes,   25
He hath not reached his despair, yet.
CORBACCIO   All these
Are out of hope, I'm sure the man.
CORVINO   But, Mosca –
MOSCA
Two cabinets.
CORVINO   Is this in earnest?
MOSCA   One
Of ebony –
CORVINO   Or, do you but delude me?
MOSCA
The other, mother of pearl – I am very busy.   30
Good faith, it is a fortune thrown upon me –
Item, one salt of agate – not my seeking.
LADY WOULD-BE
Do you hear, sir?
MOSCA   A perfumed box – 'pray you forbear,
You see I'm troubled – made of an onyx –
LADY WOULD-BE   How!
MOSCA
Tomorrow, or next day, I shall be at leisure   35
To talk with you all.
CORVINO   Is this my large hope's issue?

20   *suits of hangings* sets of draperies for poster-beds.
21   *i' their garters* Volpone puns on a jeering Elizabethan invitation to suicide, 'Hang
       yourself in your own garters' (Tilley G42).
22   *gasp* last gasp.
32   *salt* salt-cellar.

LADY WOULD-BE
 Sir, I must have a fairer answer.
MOSCA   Madam!
 Marry, and shall: 'pray you, fairly quit my house.
 Nay, raise no tempest with your looks; but, hark you:
 Remember what your ladyship offered me,   40
 To put you in, an heir; go to, think on't.
 And what you said e'en your best madams did
 For maintenance, and why not you? Enough.
 Go home, and use the poor Sir Pol, your knight, well,
 For fear I tell some riddles: go, be melancholic.   45
                              [*Exit* LADY WOULD-BE]
VOLPONE
 O, my fine devil!
CORVINO   Mosca, 'pray you a word.
MOSCA
 Lord! Will not you take your dispatch hence, yet?
 Methinks, of all, you should have been th' example.
 Why should you stay here? With what thought? What promise?
 Hear you: do not you know, I know you an ass?   50
 And that you would, most fain, have been a wittol,
 If fortune would have let you? That you are
 A declared cuckold, on good terms? This pearl,
 You'll say, was yours? Right. This diamond?
 I will not deny't, but thank you. Much here else?   55
 It may be so. Why, think that these good works
 May help to hide your bad; I'll not betray you;
 Although you be but extraordinary,
 And have it only in title, it sufficeth.
 Go home; be melancholic too, or mad.   60
                              [*Exit* CORVINO]

38   *fairly* simply, completely; but with a sense of poetic justice, a play off her preceding
     line, and another dig at her compromised cosmetic 'fairness' (cf. IV.ii.73).
40   *what . . . me* Lady Would-Be has offered herself sexually to Mosca, either by her
     salacious double-entendres, as at IV.vi.101, or by a more explicit offer we are now
     invited to imagine.
47   *dispatch* sending off.
51   *fain . . . wittol* eagerly have been a pimp to your own wife.
56–7 *think that . . . bad* think of these unrewarded gifts of yours as charity to expiate your
     evil deeds.
58–9 *Although . . . sufficeth* Although you are unusual in being a cuckold in public name
     rather than physical fact, that is bad enough.

VOLPONE
  Rare, Mosca! How his villainy becomes him!
VOLTORE
  Certain, he doth delude all these for me.
CORBACCIO
  Mosca the heir?
VOLPONE   O, his four eyes have found it.
CORBACCIO
  I'm cozened, cheated, by a parasite slave;
  Harlot, th'ast gulled me.
MOSCA   Yes, sir. Stop your mouth,   65
  Or I shall draw the only tooth is left.
  Are not you he – that filthy covetous wretch,
  With the three legs – that, here, in hope of prey,
  Have, any time this three year, snuffed about,
  With your most grov'ling nose; and would have hired   70
  Me to the pois'ning of my patron? Sir?
  Are not you he, that have, today, in court,
  Professed the disinheriting of your son?
  Perjured yourself? Go home, and die, and stink;
  If you but croak a syllable, all comes out: 75
  Away, and call your porters, go, go stink.
                                         [*Exit* CORBACCIO]
VOLPONE
  Excellent varlet!
VOLTORE   Now, my faithful Mosca,
  I find thy constancy.
MOSCA   Sir?
VOLTORE   Sincere.
MOSCA   A table
  Of porphyry – I mar'l you'll be thus troublesome.
VOLTORE
  Nay, leave off now, they are gone.
MOSCA   Why, who are you?   80
  What? Who did send for you? O, cry you mercy,

63   *four eyes* Corbaccio evidently wears spectacles.
65   *Harlot* Rogue, low-born man; not yet exclusively a synonym for female prostitute.
68   *three legs* Corbaccio walks with a cane.
69   *any time this three year* constantly during the past three years.
79   *mar'l* marvel, am astonished.
81   *cry you mercy* I beg your pardon.

Reverend sir! Good faith, I am grieved for you,
That any chance of mine should thus defeat
Your (I must needs say) most deserving travails;
But, I protest, sir, it was cast upon me,   85
And I could, almost, wish to be without it,
But that the will o' th' dead must be observed.
Marry, my joy is, that you need it not,
You have a gift, sir, (thank your education)
Will never let you want, while there are men,   90
And malice to breed causes. Would I had
But half the like, for all my fortune, sir.
If I have any suits – as I do hope,
Things being so easy and direct, I shall not –
I will make bold with your obstreperous aid –   95
Conceive me, for your fee, sir. In meantime,
You, that have so much law, I know ha' the conscience
Not to be covetous of what is mine.
Good sir, I thank you, for my plate: 'twill help
To set up a young man. Good faith, you look   100
As you were costive: best go home, and purge, sir.
                              [*Exit* VOLTORE]

VOLPONE

Bid him eat lettuce well! My witty mischief,
Let me embrace thee. O, that I could now
Transform thee to a Venus – Mosca, go,
Straight, take my habit of *clarissimo*,   105
And walk the streets; be seen, torment 'em more:
We must pursue, as well as plot. Who would
Have lost this feast?

---

83   *chance* luck.
91   *causes* lawsuits.
95–6   *I will . . . fee* will not hesitate to enlist your strong voice (in any litigation over
        Volpone's will) – and, please understand, I will pay your usual fee.
99   *my plate* the valuable piece Voltore gave Volpone at I.iii.10.
101   *costive* constipated.
102   *lettuce* considered a good laxative.
104   *Venus* Flies were believed to be bisexual (Parker). This wish renews the Venus allegory
        and the hermaphroditic theme that have surfaced several times in the play.
105   *habit of clarissimo* The strict Venetian dress code dictated that such gentlemen should
        wear black gowns edged with black taffeta, and a brimless black felt cap (Parker).
107–8   *Who would . . . feast?* Would anyone willingly miss out on this delicious opportunity
        to gloat and taunt?.

MOSCA   I doubt it will lose them.

VOLPONE

O, my recovery shall recover all.
That I could now but think on some disguise,   110
To meet 'em in; and ask 'em questions.
How I would vex 'em still, at every turn!

MOSCA

Sir, I can fit you.

VOLPONE   Canst thou?

MOSCA   Yes. I know

One o' th' *commandatori*, sir, so like you;
Him will I straight make drunk, and bring you his habit.   115

VOLPONE

A rare disguise, and answering thy brain!
O, I will be a sharp disease unto 'em.

MOSCA

Sir, you must look for curses –

VOLPONE   Till they burst;

The fox fares ever best when he is cursed.

                             [*Exeunt*]

ACT V, SCENE iv

[*Enter*] PEREGRINE [*in disguise, and three* MERCHANTS]

PEREGRINE

Am I enough disguised?

1ST MERCHANT   I warrant you.

108   *I doubt it will lose them* either (as Volpone understands it), I'm afraid it will make it impossible to exploit these gulls any further; or possibly, I'm afraid it won't get rid of them.
110   *That* I wish that.
113   *fit you* fit you out for that, provide what you asked for.
114   *commandatori* officers charged with bringing offenders to court (cf. IV.i.78).
116   *answering* worthy of.
118   *look for* expect.
119   *The fox . . . cursed* This proverb (Tilley F632) probably meant that hunters curse the fox when they cannot catch him.

1   *warrant* assure.

PEREGRINE

All my ambition is to fright him, only.

2ND MERCHANT

If you could ship him away, 'twere excellent.

3RD MERCHANT

To Zant, or to Aleppo?

PEREGRINE　　　　　　Yes, and ha' his

Adventures put i' th' *Book of Voyages*,　　　　　　　5

And his gulled story registered for truth?

Well, gentlemen, when I am in a while,

And that you think us warm in our discourse,

Know your approaches.

1ST MERCHANT　　　　　　Trust it to our care.

[*Exeunt* MERCHANTS]

[*Enter* WOMAN]

PEREGRINE

'Save you, fair lady. Is Sir Pol within?　　　　　　　10

WOMAN

I do not know, sir.

PEREGRINE　　　　　　'Pray you, say unto him,

Here is a merchant, upon earnest business,

Desires to speak with him.

WOMAN　　　　　　I will see, sir.　　　[*Exit* WOMAN]

PEREGRINE　　　　　　　　　　'Pray you.

I see, the family is all female, here.

[*Enter* WOMAN]

WOMAN

He says, sir, he has weighty affairs of state,　　　　　　　15

That now require him whole; some other time,

You may possess him.

PEREGRINE　　　　　　'Pray you say again,

4　*Zant* an Ionian island, controlled at that time by Venice.

5　*Book of Voyages* probably one of the travel books (such as Hakluyt's) popular in this period.

6　*gulled story* Previous editors have assumed this means the story of Pol's humiliating gulling; but Peregrine may be warning that Sir Pol's grandiose version of his downfall might end up recorded as heroic historical truth. Jonson may thus be scoffing at the other grandiose tales so recorded.

9　*Know your approaches* Remember exactly how and when to enter.

16　*require him whole* demand his complete attention.

If those require him whole, these will exact him,
Whereof I bring him tidings.

[Exit WOMAN]

                    What might be
His grave affair of state, now? How to make   20
Bolognian sausages, here, in Venice, sparing
One o' th' ingredients?

[Enter WOMAN]

WOMAN   Sir, he says he knows
By your word 'tidings' that you are no statesman,
And therefore, wills you stay.
PEREGRINE   Sweet, 'pray you return him,
I have not read so many proclamations,   25
And studied them, for words, as he has done,
But – here he deigns to come.

[Enter SIR POLITIC]

[Exit WOMAN]

SIR POLITIC   Sir, I must crave
Your courteous pardon. There hath chanced, today,
Unkind disaster 'twixt my Lady and me;
And I was penning my apology   30
To give her satisfaction, as you came, now.
PEREGRINE
Sir, I am grieved, I bring you worse disaster:
The gentleman you met at th' port, today,
That told you he was newly arrived –
SIR POLITIC   Ay, was
A fugitive punk?
PEREGRINE   No, sir, a spy, set on you,   35
And he has made relation to the Senate,
That you professed to him to have a plot
To sell the state of Venice to the Turk.

18–19   *these . . . tidings* the state affairs of which I bring him news will draw him out;
         Peregrine here mocks Pol's pretentious phrasing.
   24   *wills you stay* says – because you said 'tidings' instead of the sophisticated spy-jargon,
         'intelligences' – you are not dangerous and may stay, or (almost the opposite), are
         not important and must wait.
         return him say to him in response.
   35   *punk* prostitute.
   36   *made relation to* told (Peregrine again adopts Pol's overblown lingo, cf. II.i.96).

SIR POLITIC
  O me!
PEREGRINE For which, warrants are signed by this time,
  To apprehend you, and to search your study,   40
  For papers –
SIR POLITIC   Alas, sir. I have none, but notes,
  Drawn out of play-books –
PEREGRINE   All the better, sir.
SIR POLITIC
  And some essays. What shall I do?
PEREGRINE   Sir, best
  Convey yourself into a sugar-chest,
  Or, if you could lie round, a frail were rare;   45
  And I could send you aboard.
SIR POLITIC   Sir, I but talked so,
  For discourse sake, merely.
PEREGRINE   Hark, they are there.

                                        They knock without

SIR POLITIC
  I am a wretch, a wretch.
PEREGRINE   What will you do, sir?
  Ha' you ne'er a currant-butt to leap into?
  They'll put you to the rack, you must be sudden.   50
SIR POLITIC
  Sir, I have an engine –
3RD MERCHANT [*From off-stage*] Sir Politic Would-Be?
2ND MERCHANT [*From off-stage*]
  Where is he?
SIR POLITIC   – that I have thought upon beforetime.
PEREGRINE
  What is it?
SIR POLITIC [*Aside*] I shall ne'er endure the torture.
  [*To PEREGRINE*] Marry, it is, sir, of a tortoise-shell,
  Fitted for these extremities; 'pray you sir, help me.   55

42   *Drawn . . . better, sir* As in the Epistle accompanying this play (lines 55–65), Jonson
     often complained that he was persecuted by the government because people insisted
     on reading sinister political implications into his plays.
45   *lie round . . . rare* curl up, a basket of rushes (such as figs were packed in) would be ideal.
49   *currant-butt* cask or small barrel used to hold currants or currant-wine.
50   *sudden* quick.
55   *Fitted for these extremities* Prepared (Q 'apted') for emergencies like this, but perhaps
     also, Made to fit my limbs; tortoises were sold in the Venetian markets, and (as
     Peregrine's remark at line 80 suggests) were a symbol of wise policy.

[*Climbs into the tortoise shell*]
Here, I've a place, sir, to put back my legs;
Please you to lay it on, sir. With this cap,
And my black gloves, I'll lie, sir, like a tortoise,
Till they are gone.

PEREGRINE   And call you this an engine?

SIR POLITIC
Mine own device – Good sir, bid my wife's women   60
To burn my papers.

[*Exit* PEREGRINE]

[THE MERCHANTS] *rush in*

1ST MERCHANT   Where's he hid?
3RD MERCHANT   We must,
And will, sure, find him.
2ND MERCHANT   Which is his study?

[*Enter* PEREGRINE]

1ST MERCHANT   What
Are you, sir?
PEREGRINE   I'm a merchant, that came here
To look upon this tortoise.
3RD MERCHANT   How?
1ST MERCHANT   St Mark!
What beast is this?
PEREGRINE   It is a fish.
2ND MERCHANT   Come out here.   65
PEREGRINE
Nay, you may strike him, sir, and tread upon him:
He'll bear a cart.
1ST MERCHANT   What, to run over him?
PEREGRINE   Yes.
3RD MERCHANT
Let's jump upon him.
2ND MERCHANT   Can he not go?
PEREGRINE   He creeps, sir.
[1ST MERCHANT *prods* SIR POLITIC *through the openings
in the shell*]

59   *engine* piece of engineering.
68   *go* move.

145

1ST MERCHANT
Let's see him creep.
PEREGRINE   No, good sir, you will hurt him.
2ND MERCHANT
'Heart, I'll see him creep; or prick his guts.   70
3RD MERCHANT
Come out here.
PEREGRINE [*Aside to* SIR POLITIC] 'Pray you, sir. Creep a little.
1ST MERCHANT   Forth.
2ND MERCHANT
Yet further.
PEREGRINE [*Aside to* SIR POLITIC] Good sir. Creep.
2ND MERCHANT   We'll see his legs.
3RD MERCHANT
Godso, he has garters!
                    They pull off the shell and discover him.
1ST MERCHANT   Ay, and gloves!
2ND MERCHANT   Is this
Your fearful tortoise?
PEREGRINE [*Taking off his own disguise*]
                    Now, Sir Pol, we are even;
For your next project, I shall be prepared!   75
I am sorry for the funeral of your notes, sir.
1ST MERCHANT
'Twere a rare motion, to be seen in Fleet Street!
2ND MERCHANT
Ay, i' the term.
1ST MERCHANT Or Smithfield, in the fair.
3RD MERCHANT
Methinks, 'tis but a melancholic sight!
PEREGRINE
Farewell, most politic tortoise.
                    [*Exeunt* PEREGRINE *and* MERCHANTS]

---

74   *even* Peregrine still seems to believe that Pol's pretensions were partly some kind of
      plot against him, deserving vengeance.
76   *funeral* burning, as on a pyre; smoke was sometimes released from trap doors on
      the Jacobean stage.
77   *motion* puppet-show.
78   *i' the term* when law courts were in session, which drew crowds to Fleet Street, where
      puppet-shows were often performed.
      Smithfield Jonson's play *Bartholmew Fair,* set in Smithfield, culminates with a
      puppet-show.

[*Enter* WOMAN]

SIR POLITIC   Where's my lady?   80
  Knows she of this?
WOMAN   I know not, sir.
SIR POLITIC   Inquire.

                              [*Exit* WOMAN]

  O, I shall be the fable of all feasts;
  The freight of the *gazetti*; ship-boys' tale;
  And, which is worst, even talk for ordinaries.

                 [*Enter* WOMAN]

WOMAN
  My lady's come most melancholic home,   85
  And says, sir, she will straight to sea, for physic.
SIR POLITIC
  And I, to shun this place and clime forever;
  Creeping, with house on back; and think it well
  To shrink my poor head, in my politic shell.

                       [*Exeunt*]

ACT V, SCENE v

[*Enter*] VOLPONE, MOSCA; *the first, in the habit
of a commandatore; the other, of a clarissimo*

VOLPONE
  Am I then like him?
MOSCA   O, sir, you are he:
  No man can sever you.
VOLPONE   Good.

---

79   s.d. *Enter* WOMAN Alternatively, the waiting woman could have remained on stage
     instead of exiting at line 27 above; her ongoing reactions to Sir Pol's humiliation
     would present interesting theatrical opportunities.
83   *freight of the gazetti* material for the newspapers.
84   *ordinaries* taverns.
86   *physic* health, medical purposes.

1   *him* the *commandatore*.
2   *sever* distinguish.

MOSCA   But, what am I?

VOLPONE

'Fore heav'n, a brave *clarissimo*; thou becom'st it!

Pity, thou wert not born one.

MOSCA   If I hold

My made one, 'twill be well.

VOLPONE   I will go, and see   5

What news, first, at the court.

MOSCA   Do so.

[*Exit* VOLPONE]

My fox

Is out on his hole, and, ere he shall re-enter,

I will make him languish, in his borrowed case,

Except he come to composition with me.

Androgyno, Castrone, Nano!

[*Enter* ANDROGYNO, CASTRONE, NANO]

ALL   Here.   10

MOSCA

Go, recreate yourselves, abroad; go, sport!

[*Exeunt* ANDROGYNO, CASTRONE, NANO]

So, now I have the keys, and am possessed.

Since he will needs be dead, afore his time,

I'll bury him, or gain by him. I'm his heir;

And so will keep me, till he share at least.   15

To cozen him of all, were but a cheat

Well placed; no man would construe it a sin.

Let his sport pay for't; this is called the fox-trap.   [*Exit*]

---

3   *becom'st it* fill the role handsomely.

4–5 *If . . . one* If I can maintain my assumed role. What sounds like Mosca's modesty
     actually reveals his intentions.

6–7 *My fox . . . hole* Volpone has made himself vulnerable (by playing dead and then
     leaving his house); 'Fox in the Hole' was a game in which the players hop and strike
     each other with gloves and a piece of leather.

8   *case* disguise.

9   *Except he come to composition* Unless he negotiates a wealth-sharing agreement.

12   *possessed* in possession of the riches; but Jonson again (as at V.ii.24 and many other
     places in the play) uses the word to remind us that gold is a demonic possessor, a
     notion which will become explicit in V.xii.

13   *will needs be* insists on being.

15   *keep me* remain.

16–17 *were but . . . placed* would only be poetic justice.

18   *Let his sport pay for't* Let his amusement at this latest trick compensate him for what
     it will cost him.

ACT V, SCENE vi

[Enter] CORBACCIO, CORVINO

CORBACCIO
They say the court is set.

CORVINO   We must maintain
Our first tale good, for both our reputations.

CORBACCIO
Why, mine's no tale: my son would, there, have killed me.

CORVINO
That's true, I had forgot; mine is, I am sure.
But, for your will, sir.

CORBACCIO   Ay, I'll come upon him   5
For that, hereafter, now his patron's dead.

[Enter VOLPONE, *disguised as a commandatore]*

VOLPONE
Signor Corvino! And Corbaccio! Sir,
Much joy unto you.

CORVINO   Of what?

VOLPONE   The sudden good,
Dropped down upon you –

CORBACCIO   Where?

VOLPONE   – and none knows how –
From old Volpone, sir.

CORBACCIO   Out, errant knave.   10

VOLPONE
Let not your too much wealth, sir, make you furious.

CORBACCIO
Away, thou varlet.

VOLPONE   Why, sir?

CORBACCIO   Dost thou mock me?

1–2   *maintain . . . good* stick to the story we told the court the first time.
5   *come upon him* make a demand to Mosca.
10   *errant* As at III.vii.118, possibly Jonson's version of 'arrant', meaning 'notorious', but more likely 'erring', combining the accusation that he is mistaken with a dismissive view of the *commandatore's* itinerant occupation.

VOLPONE
    You mock the world, sir: did you not change wills?
CORBACCIO
    Out, harlot.
VOLPONE   O! Belike you are the man,
    Signor Corvino? 'Faith, you carry it well: 15
    You grow not mad withal; I love your spirit.
    You are not over-leavened with your fortune.
    You should ha' some would swell, now, like a wine-vat,
    With such an autumn – Did he gi' you all, sir?
CORVINO
    Avoid, you rascal.
VOLPONE   Troth, your wife has shown   20
    Herself a very woman; but, you are well,
    You need not care, you have a good estate,
    To bear it out sir, better by this chance.
    Except Corbaccio have a share?
CORVINO   Hence, varlet.
VOLPONE
    You will not be a'known, sir. Why, 'tis wise,   25
    Thus do all gamesters, at all games, dissemble:
    No man will seem to win.
                            [*Exeunt* CORVINO *and* CORBACCIO]
                    Here comes my vulture,
    Heaving his beak up i' the air, and snuffing.

---

13   *You mock the world* You are trying to conceal the truth from everyone, or perhaps,
      You can laugh at everyone.
      change exchange (by naming each other as heirs).
14   *Belike* Perhaps.
17   *over-leavened* puffed up.
18   *You should ha' some* There would be some people who.
19   *autumn* large harvest.
21   *very* true.
24   *Except* Unless.
25   *a'known* acknowledged (as heir).
26   *gamesters* gamblers.
27   *seem to win* acknowledge he is winning.

ACT V, SCENE vii

[*Enter*] VOLTORE

VOLTORE

Out-stripped thus, by a parasite? a slave?
Would run on errands? and make legs, for crumbs?
Well, what I'll do –

VOLPONE   The court stays for your worship.

I e'en rejoice, sir, at your worship's happiness,
And that it fell into so learnèd hands,   5
That understand the fingering.

VOLTORE   What do you mean?

VOLPONE

I mean to be a suitor to your worship,
For the small tenement, out of reparations:
That, at the end of your long row of houses,
By the *Piscaria*. It was, in Volpone's time,   10
Your predecessor, ere he grew diseased,
A handsome, pretty, customed bawdy-house
As any was in Venice – none dispraised –
But fell with him; his body and that house
Decayed together.

VOLTORE   Come, sir, leave your prating.   15

VOLPONE

Why, if your worship give me but your hand,
That I may ha' the refusal, I have done.

---

2   *make legs* bow.
3   *stays* waits.
5   *it* the inheritance.
6   *fingering* manipulation, how to handle it (playing off the reference to 'learnèd
      hands').
8   *out of reparations* needing repairs.
10   *Piscaria* Fish-market.
12   *customed* well supplied with customers (or, possibly, permitted, either because bribes
      have been paid as 'customs', or because it has been established by custom)
      bawdy-house house of prostitution.
13   *none dispraised* not to say anything bad of the others (Kernan).
16–17 *Why . . . done* Well, if your honoured self will just give me your handshake
      (or handwriting) promising me first refusal on the property, I won't ask any more
      favours.

'Tis a mere toy, to you, sir: candle-rents;
As your learned worship knows –

VOLTORE   What do I know?

VOLPONE

Marry, no end of your wealth, sir, God decrease it.   20

VOLTORE

Mistaking knave! What, mock'st thou my misfortune?

VOLPONE

His blessing on your heart, sir, would 'twere more.

[Exit VOLTORE]

Now to my first again, at the next corner.

ACT V, SCENE viii

[Enter] CORBACCIO, CORVINO; MOSCA
[*walking across the stage dressed as a clarissimo*]

CORBACCIO

See, in our habit! See the impudent varlet!

CORVINO

That I could shoot mine eyes at him, like gunstones.

[Exit MOSCA]

VOLPONE

But, is this true, sir, of the parasite?

CORBACCIO

Again, to afflict us? Monster!

VOLPONE   In good faith, sir,
I'm heartily grieved a beard of your grave length   5
Should be so over-reached. I never brooked
That parasite's hair, methought his nose should cozen:

18   toy trifle.
      candle-rents rents from deteriorating property.
20   *decrease* A deliberate slip for 'increase'; Volpone plays the sergeant like a Shake-
      spearean comic constable, such as the malapropist Dogberry.
22   *would 'twere more* Under the guise of politely wishing Voltore's fortune were even
      greater, Volpone can tauntingly wish that Voltore's misfortune were even greater.

1   *in our habit* dressed like us (despite his lower birth).
5–6   *a beard . . . over-reached* that someone of your advanced age has been so outsmarted.
6   *brooked* could tolerate.

There still was somewhat, in his look, did promise
The bane of a *clarissimo*.
CORBACCIO   Knave –
VOLPONE   Methinks
Yet you, that are so traded i' the world,   10
A witty merchant, the fine bird, Corvino,
That have such moral emblems on your name,
Should not have sung your shame, and dropped your cheese,
To let the fox laugh at your emptiness.
CORVINO
Sirrah, you think the privilege of the place,   15
And your red saucy cap, that seems, to me,
Nailed to your jolt-head with those two chequins,
Can warrant your abuses. Come you, hither:
You shall perceive, sir, I dare beat you. Approach.
VOLPONE
No haste, sir, I do know your valour, well,   20
Since you durst publish what you are, sir.
CORVINO   Tarry,
I'd speak with you.
VOLPONE   Sir, sir, another time –
CORVINO
Nay, now.
VOLPONE   O God, sir! I were a wise man,
Would stand the fury of a distracted cuckold.
CORBACCIO
What! Come again?

---

8   *still* always.
9   *bane* poison.
10   *traded* experienced (playing on Corvino's occupation).
12–14   *That have . . . emptiness* Volpone here refers explicitly to one of the Aesop's fables that
        have informed the entire play: the fox who flatters the crow into dropping his cheese.
        Horace (*Satires* II.v.55–7) alludes to this tale when describing a legacy-hunter much
        like Corvino: one who married his daughter to an old man, but was left out of the
        old man's will anyway.
14   *emptiness* the now-empty beak, but also the empty head that made it so.
15   *place* either his role as a court official or the physical proximity to the high court.
17   *jolt-head* block-head.
       chequins probably coin-like gold buttons on the cap.
20–1   *I do know . . . sir* I don't doubt your courage, since you were brave enough to
        announce publicly that you are a cuckold.
23–4   *I were . . . cuckold* I'd have to be very wise to stand still and endure the fury of an
        insane cuckold (spoken sarcastically).

MOSCA *walks by 'em*

VOLPONE [*Aside*]   Upon 'em, Mosca: save me.   25
CORBACCIO
The air's infected where he breathes.
CORVINO   Let's fly him.
                    [*Exeunt* CORVINO *and* CORBACCIO]
VOLPONE
Excellent basilisk! Turn upon the vulture.

ACT V, SCENE ix

[*Enter*] VOLTORE

VOLTORE
Well, flesh-fly, it is summer with you now;
Your winter will come on.
MOSCA   Good advocate,
'Pray thee, not rail, nor threaten out of place, thus:
Thou'lt make a solecism (as Madam says).
Get you a biggin more: your brain breaks loose.   5
VOLTORE
Well, sir.
VOLPONE   Would you have me beat the insolent slave?
Throw dirt upon his first good clothes?
VOLTORE   This same
Is, doubtless, some familiar!
VOLPONE   Sir, the court,
In troth, stays for you. I am mad a mule,
That never read Justinian, should get up,   10
And ride an advocate. Had you no quirk

27   *basilisk* a mythical serpent that could kill with just its glance.

1   *flesh-fly* the meaning of 'Mosca' – a fly that plants its eggs in dead flesh (OED).
4   *Madam* Lady Would-Be (cf. IV.ii.43).
5   *biggin* lawyer's cap.
8   *familiar* evil spirit (renewing the theme of demonic possession).
9   *I am mad* It drives me crazy.
9–11   *a mule ... advocate* Lawyers traditionally rode mules; Justinian was the great Roman codifier of law.
11   *quirk* trick.

To avoid gullage, sir, by such a creature?
I hope you do but jest; he has not done't.
This's but confederacy, to blind the rest.
You are the heir?
VOLTORE   A strange, officious,   15
Troublesome knave! Thou dost torment me.
VOLPONE   I know –
It cannot be, sir, that you should be cozened:
'Tis not within the wit of man, to do it;
You are so wise, so prudent – and 'tis fit
That wealth and wisdom still should go together –   20

                                        [*Exeunt*]

ACT V, SCENE x

[*Enter four*] AVOCATORI, NOTARIO, COMMANDATORI
[*including the disguised* VOLPONE], BONARIO, CELIA,
                    CORBACCIO, CORVINO

1ST AVOCATORE
Are all the parties here?
NOTARIO   All but the advocate.
2ND AVOCATORE
And here he comes.

                    [*Enter* VOLTORE]

1ST AVOCATORE   Then bring 'em forth to sentence.
VOLTORE
O, my most honoured fathers, let your mercy
Once win upon your justice, to forgive –

12   *gullage* being made a fool of.
14   *confederacy* a conspiratorial subterfuge (with Mosca – but Volpone himself is
      dangerously blind to the possibility that he no longer has such a conspiracy with
      Mosca).

 2   *And here he comes* Here, and at line 20, F gives the speech to 'AVO', Q to 'AVOC',
      which might indicate the lines are spoken by several of the judges together; but
      editorial tradition has reasonably assigned these lines to individual judges.
      'em Celia and Bonario.
 4   *win upon* take precedence over.

I am distracted –
VOLPONE [*Aside*]   What will he do now?
VOLTORE   O,   5
I know not which t' address myself to first,
Whether your fatherhoods, or these innocents –
CORVINO [*Aside*]
Will he betray himself?
VOLTORE   Whom, equally,
I have abused, out of most covetous ends –
CORVINO [*Aside*]
The man is mad!
CORBACCIO [*Aside*] What's that?
CORVINO [*Aside*]   He is possessed.   10
VOLTORE
For which, now struck in conscience, here I prostrate
Myself, at your offended feet, for pardon.
                                    [*Throws himself down*]
1ST, 2ND AVOCATORI
Arise.
CELIA   O heaven, how just thou art!
VOLPONE [*Aside*]   I'm caught
I' mine own noose –
CORVINO [*Aside to* CORBACCIO] Be constant, sir: nought now
Can help but impudence.
1ST AVOCATORE   Speak forward.
COMMANDATORE   Silence.   15
VOLTORE
It is not passion in me, reverend fathers,
But only conscience – conscience, my good sires –
That makes me, now, tell truth. That parasite,
That knave hath been the instrument of all.
1ST AVOCATORE
Where is that knave? Fetch him.
VOLPONE   I go.   [*Exit*]
CORVINO   Grave fathers,   20
This man is distracted, he confessed it now;
For, hoping to be old Volpone's heir,

5   *distracted* mad, out of my wits.
9   *out of most covetous ends* because of extremely greedy motives.
15   *impudence* shamelessness (in sticking to their earlier lie).
16   *passion* frenzy.

    Who now is dead –
3RD AVOCATORE   How?
2ND AVOCATORE   Is Volpone dead?
CORVINO
    Dead since, grave fathers –
BONARIO   O, sure vengeance!
1ST AVOCATORE   Stay –
    Then he was no deceiver?
VOLTORE   O, no, none;   25
    The parasite, grave fathers –
CORVINO   He does speak
    Out of mere envy, 'cause the servant's made
    The thing he gaped for. Please your fatherhoods,
    This is the truth; though, I'll not justify
    The other, but he may be somewhere faulty.   30
VOLTORE
    Ay, to your hopes, as well as mine, Corvino;
    But I'll use modesty. Pleaseth your wisdoms
    To view these certain notes, and but confer them:
                 [*Gives papers to the* AVOCATORI]
    As I hope favour, they shall speak clear truth.
CORVINO
    The devil has entered him!
BONARIO   Or bides in you.   35
4TH AVOCATORE
    We have done ill, by a public officer
    To send for him, if he be heir.
2ND AVOCATORE   For whom?
4TH AVOCATORE
    Him that they call the parasite.
3RD AVOCATORE   'Tis true:
    He is a man of great estate now left.
4TH AVOCATORE [*To* NOTARIO]
    Go you, and learn his name; and say, the court   40
    Entreats his presence here, but to the clearing
    Of some few doubts.

32   *modesty* restraint, moderation.
33   *certain* particular, or, offering reliable proof.
       but confer simply compare them, or confer about them.
35   *bides* abides, remains.
40   *you* the Notario, a more decorous emissary.
41   *but to* only for.

[*Exit* NOTARIO]

2ND AVOCATORE   This same's a labyrinth!

1ST AVOCATORE
  Stand you unto your first report?

CORVINO   My state,
  My life, my fame –

BONARIO   Where is't?

CORVINO   Are at the stake

1ST AVOCATORE [*To* CORBACCIO]
  Is yours so too?

CORBACCIO   The advocate is a knave: 45
  And has a forkèd tongue –

2ND AVOCATORE   Speak to the point.

CORBACCIO
  So is the parasite, too.

1ST AVOCATORE   This is confusion.

VOLTORE
  I do beseech your fatherhoods, read but those –

CORVINO
  And credit nothing the false spirit hath writ:
  It cannot be, my sires, but he is possessed.   50

                              [*Exeunt*]

ACT V, SCENE xi

[*Enter*] VOLPONE

VOLPONE
  To make a snare for mine own neck! and run
  My head into it, wilfully! with laughter!
  When I had newly 'scaped, was free, and clear!

43   *Stand you unto* Do you hold to?
      state estate.
44   *fame* reputation.
49   *credit* believe.
50   *It cannot be . . . but* There is no possible explanation except that.

 1   *snare* noose; but the same term would have been used for a fox-trap.

Out of mere wantonness! O, the dull devil
Was in this brain of mine, when I devised it;   5
And Mosca gave it second: he must now
Help to sear up this vein, or we bleed dead.

[*Enter* NANO, ANDROGYNO, *and* CASTRONE]

How now! Who let you loose? Whither go you, now?
What? To buy gingerbread? Or to drown kitlings?

NANO

Sir, Master Mosca called us out of doors,   10
And bid us all go play, and took the keys.

ANDROGYNO   Yes.

VOLPONE

Did Master Mosca take the keys? Why, so!
I am farther in. These are my fine conceits!
I must be merry, with a mischief to me!
What a vile wretch was I, that could not bear   15
My fortune soberly? I must ha' my crotchets!
And my conundrums! Well, go you, and seek him;
His meaning may be truer than my fear.
Bid him, he straight come to me, to the court;
Thither will I, and, if 't be possible,   20
Unscrew my advocate, upon new hopes:
When I provoked him, then I lost myself.

4   *wantonness* playful enthusiasm, careless self-indulgence.
6   *gave it second* seconded the idea.
7   *sear* cauterize.
9   *kitlings* kittens; Volpone suggests the pastimes of naughty or cruel children.
13   *farther in* in even more trouble than I realized; Volpone now suspects Mosca's true
      intentions, so the remainder of the line is spoken sarcastically.
      conceits schemes.
14   *I must . . . to me* I had to enjoy myself with something that would do me harm.
16   *My fortune soberly* My wealth, or my good luck in court, wisely.
16–17 *my crotchets . . . my conundrums* my perverse and clever whims.
18   *truer* more honest and loyal.
19   *Bid* Instruct, ask.
21   *Unscrew* Reverse the course of, or perhaps, Calm the fierce resolution of.
      upon by offering him.

ACT V, SCENE xii

[*Enter*] AVOCATORI, [NOTARIO, COMMANDATORI,
BONARIO, CELIA, VOLTORE, CORBACCIO, CORVINO]

1ST AVOCATORE [*Studying* VOLTORE'*s notes*]
    These things can ne'er be reconciled. He here
    Professeth, that the gentleman was wronged;
    And that the gentlewoman was brought thither,
    Forced by her husband; and there left.
VOLTORE   Most true.
CELIA
    How ready is heaven to those that pray!
1ST AVOCATORE   But, that   5
    Volpone would have ravished her, he holds
    Utterly false, knowing his impotence.
CORVINO
    Grave fathers, he is possessed; again I say,
    Possessed; nay, if there be possession
    And obsession, he has both.
3RD AVOCATORE   Here comes our officer.   10

[*Enter* VOLPONE, *still disguised*]

VOLPONE
    The parasite will straight be here, grave fathers.
4TH AVOCATORE
    You might invent some other name, sir varlet.
3RD AVOCATORE
    Did not the notary meet him?
VOLPONE   Not that I know.
4TH AVOCATORE
    His coming will clear all.
2ND AVOCATORE   Yet it is misty.

---

  1   *He* Voltore.
  5   *ready* promptly responsive.
 10 *obsession* a devil's assault on a person from the outside (as opposed to possession,
      which is from the inside).
 12 *invent* find, choose (because Mosca's wealth makes him suddenly worthy of a nobler
      term).
 14 *Yet it is misty* Still, up to this moment, it remains unclear.

VOLTORE
    May't please your fatherhoods –
               VOLPONE *whispers* [*to*] *the advocate* [VOLTORE]
VOLPONE   Sir, the parasite   15
    Willed me to tell you that his master lives;
    That you are still the man; your hopes the same;
    And this was only a jest –
VOLTORE   How?
VOLPONE   Sir, to try
    If you were firm, and how you stood affected.
VOLTORE
    Art sure he lives?
VOLPONE   Do I live, sir?
VOLTORE   O me!   20
    I was too violent.
VOLPONE   Sir, you may redeem it.
    They said you were possessed; fall down, and seem so:
                    VOLTORE *falls*
    I'll help to make it good. [*Aloud*] God bless the man!
    [*Aside to* VOLTORE] Stop your wind hard, and swell.
    [*Aloud*]   See, see, see, see!
    He vomits crooked pins! His eyes are set,   25
    Like a dead hare's, hung in a poulter's shop!
    His mouth's running away! Do you see, Signor?
    Now 'tis in his belly!
CORVINO   Ay, the devil!
VOLPONE
    Now, in his throat.
CORVINO   Ay, I perceive it plain.

---

19   *stood affected* truly felt (about Volpone).
20   *Do I live* This normally means something like, 'as surely as I am here talking to you',
       with an added irony in this situation; but Volpone may also lift off his disguise
       momentarily for Voltore here, which would explain Voltore's instant change of
       tactics, though it does not explain how he would hope to inherit anytime soon from
       such a radically revived man.
23   *good* convincing.
24   *Stop your wind* Hold your breath.
25–31   *He vomits . . . bat's wings* Similar phenomena were reported during Jacobean
       exorcisms (of which King James became a prominent debunker).
26   *poulter* seller of poultry and small game such as hares.
27   *running away* moving wildly – perhaps twitching side to side, perhaps silently
       imitating rapid speech.

VOLPONE
> 'Twill out, 'twill out: stand clear. See, where it flies!   30
> In shape of a blue toad, with a bat's wings!
> Do not you see it, sir?

CORBACCIO   What? I think I do.

CORVINO
> 'Tis too manifest.

VOLPONE   Look! He comes t' himself!

VOLTORE
> Where am I?

VOLPONE   Take good heart, the worst is past, sir.
> You are dispossessed.

1ST AVOCATORE   What accident is this?   35

2ND AVOCATORE
> Sudden, and full of wonder!

3RD AVOCATORE   If he were
> Possessed, as it appears, all this is nothing.

CORVINO
> He has been, often, subject to these fits.

1ST AVOCATORE
> Show him that writing. [*To* VOLTORE] Do you know it, sir?

VOLPONE [*Aside to* VOLTORE]
> Deny it, sir, forswear it, know it not.   40

VOLTORE
> Yes, I do know it well, it is my hand;
> But all that it contains is false.

BONARIO   O practice!

2ND AVOCATORE
> What maze is this!

1ST AVOCATORE   Is he not guilty, then,
> Whom you there name the parasite?

VOLTORE   Grave fathers,
> No more than his good patron, old Volpone.   45

4TH AVOCATORE
> Why, he is dead!

---

34   *Take good heart* Cheer up, be encouraged.
35   *accident* unforeseen event.
37   *this* Probably indicating Voltore's notes to the court.
41   *hand* handwriting.
42   *O practice!* This is a treachery!

VOLTORE   O no, my honoured fathers,
He lives –
1ST AVOCATORE How! Lives?
VOLTORE   Lives.
2ND AVOCATORE   This is subtler yet!
3RD AVOCATORE
You said he was dead!
VOLTORE   Never.
3RD AVOCATORE [*To* CORVINO] You said so!
CORVINO   I heard so.
4TH AVOCATORE
Here comes the gentleman, make him way.

[*Enter* MOSCA]

3RD AVOCATORE   A stool.
4TH AVOCATORE
A proper man! And, were Volpone dead,   50
A fit match for my daughter.
3RD AVOCATORE   Give him way.
VOLPONE [*Aside to* MOSCA]
Mosca, I was almost lost, the advocate
Had betrayed all; but now it is recovered:
All's on the hinge again – say I am living.
MOSCA
What busy knave is this! Most reverend fathers,   55
I sooner had attended your grave pleasures,
But that my order for the funeral
Of my dear patron did require me –
VOLPONE [*Aside*]   Mosca!
MOSCA
Whom I intend to bury like a gentleman –
VOLPONE [*Aside*]
Ay, quick, and cozen me of all.

---

47   *subtler* trickier.
50   *proper* handsome.
53   *recovered* revived, repaired, or covered up again.
54   *on the hinge* working properly.
55   *busy* meddling, officious.
56   *sooner . . . pleasures* would have responded sooner to the summons from you important men.
60   *quick* alive.

2ND AVOCATORE	Still stranger!	60

More intricate!

1ST AVOCATORE And come about again!

4TH AVOCATORE
It is a match, my daughter is bestowed.

MOSCA [*Aside to* VOLPONE]
Will you gi' me half?

VOLPONE   First I'll be hanged.

MOSCA [*Aside to* VOLPONE]   I know,
Your voice is good, cry not so loud.

1ST AVOCATORE   Demand
The advocate. Sir, did not you affirm   65
Volpone was alive?

VOLPONE   Yes, and he is;
This gent'man told me so.
[*Aside to* MOSCA]   Thou shalt have half.

MOSCA
Whose drunkard is this same? Speak, some that know him:
I never saw his face. [*Aside to* VOLPONE] I cannot now
Afford it you so cheap.

VOLPONE [*Aside to* MOSCA] No?

1ST AVOCATORE [*To* VOLTORE] What say you?   70

VOLTORE
The officer told me.

VOLPONE   I did, grave fathers,
And will maintain he lives with mine own life,
And that this creature told me. [*Aside*] I was born
With all good stars my enemies.

MOSCA   Most grave fathers,
If such an insolence as this must pass   75
Upon me, I am silent; 'twas not this
For which you sent, I hope.

2ND AVOCATORE [*Indicating* VOLPONE] Take him away.

VOLPONE [*Aside to* MOSCA]
Mosca.

---

61   *come about* reversed (because Volpone is reported dead after all).
64   *cry* shout; Mosca is apparently warning Volpone that his exasperated reply in the
       previous line was dangerously audible.
72   *And will . . . lives* I would bet my life he is alive (repeating the joke from line 20).
74   *With all good stars my enemies* Under a bad astrological sign; hence, unlucky.
75–6 *pass / Upon me* will be tolerated against me.

3RD AVOCATORE Let him be whipped.

VOLPONE [*Aside to* MOSCA]   Wilt thou betray me?
    Cozen me?

3RD AVOCATORE And taught to bear himself
    Toward a person of his rank.

4TH AVOCATORE   Away.   80

          [*Officers begin to drag* VOLPONE *away*]

MOSCA
    I humbly thank your fatherhoods.

VOLPONE   Soft, soft. [*Aside*] Whipped?
    And lose all that I have? If I confess,
    It cannot be much more.

4TH AVOCATORE [*To* MOSCA] Sir, are you married?

VOLPONE
    They'll be allied, anon: I must be resolute;
    The fox shall, here, uncase.

          He puts off his disguise

MOSCA [*Aside to* VOLPONE]   Patron.

VOLPONE   Nay, now,   85
    My ruins shall not come alone. Your match
    I'll hinder sure; my substance shall not glue you,
    Nor screw you, into a family.

MOSCA [*Aside to* VOLPONE]   Why, patron!

VOLPONE
    I am Volpone, and this [*Indicating* MOSCA] is my knave;
    This, his own knave; this, avarice's fool;   90
    This [*Indicating* CORVINO], a chimera of wittol, fool, and knave;
    And, reverend fathers, since we all can hope
    Nought but a sentence, let's not now despair it.
    You hear me brief.

---

80   *his* Mosca's.
81   *Soft* Take it easy, wait a minute.
84   *allied, anon* made allies (by marriage) soon.
85   *uncase* drop his disguise, and perhaps also (like a hunted fox) break from his cover,
      or, possibly, (like a captured fox) have his coat flayed off.
86–7 *Your match . . . sure* I'll definitely ruin your plans to marry into the aristocracy.
89   *knave* low-ranking servant, with a connotation of low ethics.
90   *avarice's fool* a person duped by greed; the 'knave' is probably Voltore and the 'fool'
      Corbaccio, as some editors stipulate, but it could be the other way around.
91   *chimera* a mythical beast combining lion, goat, and serpent.
93   *let's . . . despair it* don't disappoint us (spoken with bitter irony).
94   *brief* keeping my remarks brief (to get this over with).

CORVINO   May it please your fatherhoods –

COMMANDATORI   Silence.

1ST AVOCATORE

   The knot is now undone, by miracle!   95

2ND AVOCATORE

   Nothing can be more clear.

3RD AVOCATORE   Or can more prove

   These innocent.

1ST AVOCATORE   Give 'em their liberty.

BONARIO

   Heaven could not, long, let such gross crimes be hid.

2ND AVOCATORE

   If this be held the high way, to get riches,

   May I be poor.

3RD AVOCATORE This's not the gain, but torment.   100

1ST AVOCATORE

   These possess wealth, as sick men possess fevers,

   Which, trulier, may be said to possess them.

2ND AVOCATORE

   Disrobe that parasite.

CORVINO, MOSCA   Most honoured fathers –

1ST AVOCATORE

   Can you plead aught to stay the course of justice?

   If you can, speak.

CORVINO, VOLTORE We beg favour.

CELIA   And mercy.   105

1ST AVOCATORE

   You hurt your innocence, suing for the guilty.

   Stand forth; and, first, the parasite. You appear

   To have been the chiefest minister, if not plotter,

   In all these lewd impostures; and now, lastly,

   Have, with your impudence, abused the court,   110

   And habit of a gentleman of Venice,

   Being a fellow of no birth or blood;

   For which, our sentence is, first thou be whipped;

   Then live perpetual prisoner in our galleys.

---

100   *This's . . . torment* This one gained nothing but torment, or, This is not profit but
      torment.

109   *lewd impostures* wicked falsehoods.

VOLPONE

    I thank you, for him.

MOSCA   Bane to thy wolfish nature.   115

1ST AVOCATORE

    Deliver him to the *Saffi*. Thou, Volpone,

    By blood and rank a gentleman, canst not fall

    Under like censure; but our judgement on thee

    Is, that thy substance all be straight confiscate

    To the hospital of the *Incurabili*;   120

    And, since the most was gotten by imposture,

    By feigning lame, gout, palsy and such diseases,

    Thou art to lie in prison, cramped with irons,

    Till thou be'st sick and lame indeed. Remove him.

VOLPONE

    This is called mortifying of a fox.   125

1ST AVOCATORE

    Thou, Voltore, to take away the scandal

    Thou hast giv'n all worthy men of thy profession,

    Art banished from their fellowship, and our state.

    Corbaccio, bring him near. We here possess

    Thy son of all thy estate; and confine thee   130

    To the monastery of *San' Spirito*;

    Where since thou knew'st not how to live well here,

    Thou shalt be learned to die well.

CORBACCIO   Ha! What said he?

COMMANDATORE

    You shall know anon, sir.

115   VOLPONE F and Q give this line to Voltore, but – considering Mosca's immediate
       response, and the vengeful parallel with line 81 – it fits better spoken by Volpone.
       This is particularly true if the scene is staged with each miscreant led offstage
       immediately after his sentencing.
       Bane Mosca is cursing Volpone; wolf's-bane was a powerful poison.

116   *Saffi* bailiffs.

119   *substance* wealth, material goods.

120   *Incurabili* incurables – mostly victims of venereal disease.

125   *mortifying* a quintuple pun – the word means not only 'humiliation' and 'bringing
       toward death', but also 'tenderizing animal meat', 'teaching sinners, by punishment,
       to overcome their worldly appetites', and even 'disposing of property for charitable
       purposes' (Parker).

126–7 *the scandal . . . profession* the disgrace you have brought on all honourable lawyers;
       the Dedication and Epistle suggest that Jonson was aiming his play at an audience
       which included many legal scholars.

133   *die well* The arts of dying well – the *ars moriendi* – were a central religious practice
       throughout the Renaissance.

1ST AVOCATORE   Thou Corvino, shalt
  Be straight embarked from thine own house, and rowed   135
  Round about Venice, through the Grand Canal,
  Wearing a cap, with fair, long ass's ears,
  Instead of horns; and so to mount, a paper
  Pinned on thy breast, to the *Berlino* –

CORVINO   Yes,
  And have mine eyes beat out with stinking fish,   140
  Bruised fruit and rotten eggs – 'Tis well. I'm glad
  I shall not see my shame, yet.

1ST AVOCATORE   And to expiate
  Thy wrongs done to thy wife, thou art to send her
  Home, to her father, with her dowry trebled;
  And these are all your judgements –

ALL   Honoured fathers.   145

1ST AVOCATORE
  Which may not be revoked. Now you begin,
  When crimes are done, and past, and to be punished,
  To think what your crimes are; away with them.
  Let all that see these vices thus rewarded
  Take heart, and love to study 'em. Mischiefs feed   150
  Like beasts, till they be fat, and then they bleed.

                             [*Exeunt*]

---

135   *embarked* sent out on a boat.
137–8   *ass's ears . . . horns* Because Corvino behaved like an ass but was never actually a cuckold.
138   *so to mount* to climb in that costume.
139   *Berlino* the pillory, where malefactors were exposed to public humiliation.
142   *I shall not see my shame, yet* I still won't be forced to witness my own humiliation, not even such a prominent humiliation (since my eyes will be smashed by the garbage that people throw at those in the pillory).
150   *Take heart . . . study 'em* Be encouraged, and love to practice those vices (spoken ironically).

[*Enter*] VOLPONE [*as* EPILOGUE]

The seasoning of a play is the applause.
Now, though the fox be punished by the laws,
He yet doth hope there is no suff'ring due
For any fact which he hath done 'gainst you.
If there be, censure him; here he doubtful stands.   5
If not, fare jovially, and clap your hands.

THE END

---

4   *fact* crime.
6   *fare jovially* be cheerful; Jonson here translates a standard closing plea for applause
     from classical comedies, and alters the familiar phrase 'farewell' to invoke the sup-
     posedly happy planetary influence of Jupiter.

TO

THE MOST

NOBLE AND

MOST EQVALL

SISTERS

THE TWO FAMOVS

VNIVERSITIES

FOR THEIR LOVE

A**N**D

ACCEPTANCE

SHEW'N TO HIS POEME IN THE

P**RESENTATION**

B**EN.** I**ONSON**

THE GRATEFVLL ACKNOWLEDGER

D**EDICATES**

BOTH IT AND HIMSELFE.

EQUAL equal to each other in quality, and fair (equitable) in their judgements; Jonson was granted honorary degrees from both Oxford and Cambridge, partly perhaps in appreciation of this play.

UNIVERSITIES Oxford and Cambridge.

POEM Volpone, which was performed at Oxford and Cambridge between its early 1606 London premiere and its early 1607 Quarto printing.

Jonson's dedicatory letter to the 'sister' universities Oxford and Cambridge defends literature (Jonson uses the term 'poetry' broadly) against its accusers (including, implicitly, Puritans), though it concedes that sloppy and slanderous writers have recently injured literature's ancient prestige. The Epistle draws its didactic justification of literary art from Jonson's own 'Apologetical Dialogue' in *Poetaster* five years earlier, as well as from Erasmus, Minturno, and Jonson's perennial favourite, Horace.

Jonson strives for an erudite elegance of style in addressing his university audience, which makes for interesting but difficult reading for more modern audiences. His rich and varied sentences provide some sense of how the best literary minds of Jacobean England chose ceremoniously to communicate their beliefs. The Epistle is so convoluted in syntax and so mannered in diction, however, that a single modern paraphrase (following the original text on page 177) seemed preferable to dozens of piecemeal glosses, and I have added footnotes only where they add substance, not where they merely provide translation.

THE EPISTLE

Never, most equal Sisters, had any man a wit so presently excellent, as that it could raise itself; but there must come both matter, occasion, commenders, and favourers to it. If this be true, and that the fortune of all writers doth daily prove it, it behooves the careful to provide well towards these accidents; and, having acquired them, to preserve that part of reputation most tenderly, wherein the bene- 5
fit of a friend is also defended. Hence is it that I now render myself grateful, and am studious to justify the bounty of your act; to which, though your mere authority were satisfying, yet, it being an age wherein poetry and the professors of it hear so ill on all sides, there will a reason be looked for in the subject. 10

It is certain, nor can it with any forehead be opposed, that the too much licence of poetasters in this time hath much deformed their mistress; that, every day, their manifold and manifest ignorance doth stick unnatural reproaches upon her. But for their petulancy, it were an act of the greatest injustice, either to let the learned suf- 15
fer, or so divine a skill – which indeed should not be attempted with unclean hands – to fall under the least contempt. For, if men will impartially, and not asquint, look toward the offices and function of a poet, they will easily conclude to themselves the impossibility of any man's being the good poet, without first being 20
a good man. He that is said to be able to inform young men to all good disciplines, inflame grown men to all great virtues, keep old men in their best and supreme state, or, as they decline to child-hood, recover them to their first strength; that comes forth the interpreter and arbiter of nature, a teacher of things divine no less 25
than human, a master in manners; and can alone, or with a few, effect the business of mankind: this, I take him, is no subject for pride and ignorance to exercise their railing rhetoric upon. But it will here be hastily answered, that the writers of these days are other things; that not only their manners, but their natures, 30
are inverted; and nothing remaining with them of the dignity of poet, but the abused name, which every scribe usurps; that now,

---

7   *the bounty of your act* your generous patronage (which Jonson is trying to repay by explaining to the world why support of literature is justified).

13   *their mistress* poetry; 'poetasters' are weak, pretentious, dilettante poets, whose failings oblige true poets to defend their profession.

especially in dramatic, or (as they term it) stage-poetry, nothing
but ribaldry, profanation, blasphemy, all licence of offence to God
and man is practised. I dare not deny a great part of this, and   35
am sorry I dare not, because in some men's abortive features – and
would they had never boasted the light – it is over-true. But, that all
are embarked in this bold adventure for hell, is a most uncharitable
thought, and, uttered, a more malicious slander. For my particular,
I can (and from a most clear conscience) affirm, that I have ever   40
trembled to think toward the least profaneness; have loathed the
use of such foul and unwashed bawdry, as is now made the food of
the scene. And, howsoever I cannot escape, from some, the imputation of sharpness, but that they will say, I have taken a pride, or
lust, to be bitter, and not my youngest infant but hath come into   45
the world with all his teeth; I would ask of these supercilious
politics, what nation, society, or general order or state I have
provoked? What public person? Whether I have not in all these
preserved their dignity, as mine own person, safe? My works are
read, allowed, (I speak of those that are entirely mine). Look   50
into them: what broad reproofs have I used? where have I been
particular? where personal? except to a mimic, cheater, bawd, or
buffoon – creatures, for their insolencies, worthy to be taxed? Or to
which of these so pointingly, as he might not either ingenuously
have confessed, or wisely dissembled his disease? But it is not   55
rumour can make men guilty, much less entitle me to other men's
crimes. I know that nothing can be so innocently writ or carried,
but may be made obnoxious to construction; marry, whilst I bear

33–5   *especially ... practised* Jonson here echoes some of the Puritans' principal objections
        to the English theatre.
36   *features* plays, though it also suggests a condemnation of the authors' faces.
39–43   Jonson's rowdy conduct throughout his life – including persistent drunkenness,
        nasty insults, censored plays, brawling, killing a fellow-actor, and fathering illegiti-
        mate children – makes this claim that he 'can (and from a most clear conscience)
        affirm, that I have ever trembled to think toward the least profaneness' seem like a
        wildly self-serving falsehood. If it were not for the context of a serious defence of
        poetic morality, it would be tempting to read it as a self-deprecating in-joke designed
        to elicit mocking whoops of laughter from an audience.
50   *entirely mine* Jonson must make an exception for collaborations such as *The Isle of
        Dogs, Eastward Ho!* and perhaps the first version of *Sejanus*, which landed Jonson
        in serious trouble with the authorities.
52   *particular* aiming at a specific person; satirists traditionally defended themselves by
        claiming they were attacking the faults, not any actual individual person; and that
        for anyone to complain of slander was foolishly to confess to the vices the satires
        depicted.

mine innocence about me, I fear it not. Application is now grown a trade with many; and there are that profess to have a key for the   60
deciphering of every thing: but let wise and noble persons take heed how they be too credulous, or give leave to these invading interpreters to be over-familiar with their fames, who cunningly, and often, utter their own virulent malice, under other men's simplest meanings.   65

As for those that will – by faults which charity hath raked up, or common honesty concealed – make themselves a name with the multitude, or, to draw their rude and beastly claps, care not whose living faces they entrench with their petulant styles, may they do it without a rival, for me: I choose rather to live graved in obscurity,   70
than share with them in so preposterous a fame. Nor can I blame the wishes of those grave and wiser patriots, who providing the hurts these licentious spirits may do in a state, desire rather to see fools and devils, and those antique relics of barbarism retrieved, with all other ridiculous and exploded follies, than behold the   75
wounds of private men, of princes and nations: for, as Horace makes Trebatius speak, in these,

– *Sibi quisque timet, quanquam est intactus, et odit.*

And men may justly impute such rages, if continued, to the writer, as his sports. The increase of which lust in liberty, together with the   80
present trade of the stage, in all their miscellane interludes, what learned or liberal soul doth not already abhor, where nothing but the garbage of the time is uttered, and that with such impropriety of phrase, such plenty of solecisms, such dearth of sense, so bold prolepses, so racked metaphors, with brothelry able to violate the ear   85
of a pagan, and blasphemy to turn the blood of a Christian to water?

I cannot but be serious in a cause of this nature, wherein my fame, and the reputation of diverse honest and learned are the

59   *Application* Interpretation designed to apply the satire to specific persons or events, the seeking out of personal allusions and political allegories; Volpone himself was apparently taken as a caricature of the wealthy Thomas Sutton.

68–9   *whose living faces . . . petulant styles* what actual persons' public image they mutilate with their writing (punning on 'stiles', meaning pens); writers convicted of slandering royalty sometimes had their faces scarred in punishment, and Jonson himself had been in danger of that disfigurement, though he here insists he would never compete with such gossip-columnists.

72   *providing* foreseeing; Jonson here provisionally sides with those who, for the good of society, prefer old-fashioned entertainments to the current trends in satire.

78   *Sibi . . . odit* Horace, *Satires*, II.1.23, which Jonson translates (in *Poetaster*, III.v.41) as 'In satires, each man, though untouched, Complains / As he were hurt; and hates such biting strains'.

question; when a name so full of authority, antiquity, and all great mark, is, through their insolence, become the lowest scorn of the 90 age; and those men subject to the petulancy of every vernaculous orator, that were wont to be the care of kings and happiest monarchs. This it is that hath not only rapt me to present indignation, but made me studious heretofore, and by all my actions, to stand off from them; which may most appear in this my latest work, which 95 you, most learned arbitresses, have seen, judged, and to my crown, approved; wherein I have laboured for their instruction and amendment, to reduce not only the ancient forms, but manners of the scene, the easiness, the propriety, the innocence, and last, the doctrine, which is the principal end of poesy, to inform men in the best 100 reason of living.

And though my catastrophe may, in the strict rigour of comic law, meet with censure, as turning back to my promise, I desire the learned and charitable critic to have so much faith in me to think it was done of industry: for, with what ease I could have varied it 105 nearer his scale (but that I fear to boast my own faculty) I could here insert. But my special aim being to put the snaffle in their mouths, that cry out, We never punish vice in our interludes, etc., I took the more liberty; though not without some lines of example, drawn even in the ancients themselves, the goings-out of whose 110 comedies are not always joyful, but oft-times the bawds, the servants, the rivals, yea, and the masters are mulcted; and fitly, it being the office of a comic poet to imitate justice, and instruct to life, as well as purity of language, or stir up gentle affections; to which, upon my next opportunity toward the examining and digesting of 115 my notes, I shall speak more wealthily, and pay the world a debt.

In the meantime, most reverenced Sisters, as I have cared to be thankful for your affections past, and here made the understanding acquainted with some ground of your favours, let me not despair

---

91 *vernaculous* ill-bred, probably also implicating those who accuse in the vernacular language because they (and their low-class audience) lack the ability to use Latin.

96 *to my crown* to my credit and glory (playing on the laureate crown granted to great poets).

98 *reduce* restore; Jonson often claims to be reviving the forms and mores of the classics.

102 *catastrophe* denouement, final act; Jonson concedes that *Volpone* lacks the happy ending traditional to the genre.

106 *his scale* the traditional measurements used by a learned critic (with a pun on the variations that can be played on a musical scale).

112 *mulcted* punished; the classical precedents Jonson broadly claims here for his harsh ending have been hard for modern scholars to find.

their continuance, to the maturing of some worthier fruits; where- 120
in, if my muses be true to me, I shall raise the despised head of
poetry again, and stripping her out of those rotten and base rags
wherewith the times have adulterated her form, restore her to her
primitive habit, feature, and majesty, and render her worthy to be
embraced and kissed of all the great and master-spirits of our world. 125

As for the vile and slothful, who never affected an act worthy of
celebration, or are so inward with their own vicious natures as they
worthily fear her, and think it a high point of policy to keep her in
contempt, with their declamatory and windy invectives: she shall
out of just rage incite her servants (who are *genus irritabile*) to 130
spout ink in their faces, that shall eat farther than their marrow into
their fames; and not Cinnamus the barber, with his art, shall be able
to take out the brands; but they shall live, and be read, till the
wretches die, as things worst deserving of themselves in chief, and
then of all mankind. 135

From my House in the Black-Friars, this 11th of February, 1607

Since no writer is great enough to succeed without favourable circumstances, including
admirers, writers should especially defend themselves when that entails defending their
admirers also. So, while the endorsement of you great universities should be enough in itself,
further justification is called for in an era when writers are so widely condemned.

Undisciplined writers have certainly damaged the reputation of literature; otherwise
these accusations would be completely outrageous. Good writers have to be good men, and
anyone who can provide the benefits true literature provides should be spared snobbish, ill-
informed accusations. But the accusers will object that modern writers hardly correspond to
the high dignity traditionally associated with literature; many people claim the title of author,
while (especially in drama) producing only stupid and offensive works. I cannot deny that,
but it is unfair to judge all writers by these bad pretenders. I have always tried to avoid
blasphemy or bawdiness; and though my satires are considered biting, what society have I
offended, what public person have I insulted? My works are licensed, because I avoid excessive or personal criticisms, attacking only bad kinds of people, who richly deserve it. Any text
can be wilfully misinterpreted, and it is unfair to blame me if malicious commentators try to
interpret my works as attacks on individuals (whom the commentators themselves want to
attack indirectly).

Those writers who seek popularity by recklessly slandering people will get no competition from me: I would rather go unread than become famous that way. Nor can I blame
the government who, recognizing the damage slander can do, would rather see stupid, old-
fashioned slapstick comedies and morality plays than satires on individuals, leaders, or
nations. As Horace writes, 'Everyone is afraid and angry, even if personally uninjured'.

132   *Cinnamus* cf. Martial, *Epigrams* VI, 24–6; barbers were surgeons in the Renaissance,
and Jonson, whose thumb had been branded for killing a fellow-actor, would have
had reason to ponder the permanence of such marks of disgrace.

Some writers seem to enjoy that; but all worthy observers already abhor it, as they abhor the chaotic practices of the popular theatre, and the ugly, incorrect, nonsensical writing that offends anyone who cares about language, morality, or Christianity.

I am naturally concerned when my own reputation, and that of many virtuous scholars, is at risk; when the traditionally noble title of author is made scornful by these bad imitators; when those traditionally honoured by monarchs must endure the insults of every loud-mouthed, self-appointed preacher. That is what compels me to write this defence, and what always made me careful to distinguish myself from those bad writers. Therefore, in this new play *Volpone*, which you have honoured me by approving, I have tried to teach them all a lesson by copying the virtues of ancient literature: the structure, the style, the decorum, and finally the moral instruction, which is the principal purpose of literature – to teach people how to live, and why.

And though the ending of the play may be criticized as diverging from the traditions of comedy, strictly defined, I ask the knowledgeable and generous reader to recognize that it was done deliberately (except that I do not want to seem boastful, I could show here how easily I could have followed those traditional rules). But, because I was especially concerned to stifle those who claim that plays never punish sin, I took some liberty (though even my variations have precedents in the classics, where comedies often end with some characters appropriately punished, about which I will write more adequately soon).

Meanwhile, since I have been careful to show my gratitude for your support, and to show the world, in this epistle, why your support was justified, I hope I can count on that patronage continuing, which will give me time to complete even better works, which will restore the great ancient reputation of literature which has lately been besmirched.

As for those nasty and lazy commentators who have never tried to do anything positive, or who know themselves so sinful that they fear literature's ability to reveal truth, and therefore, as a precaution, defend themselves by long-winded attacks on it: they will find that literature's servants (whose feelings are easily aroused) will throw some ink at them that will disfigure their reputations more deeply than acid would disfigure their bodies; and not even a skilful plastic surgeon will be able to remove the scars, which will remain until death, announcing their unworthiness.

EPICOENE,

OR

The silent VVoman.

A Comœdie.

Acted in the yeere 1609. By
the Children of her Maiesties
REVELLS.

The Author B. I.

HORAT.

*Vt sis tu similis Cæli, Byrrhiq, latronum,
Non ego sim Capri, neq̃, Sulci. Cur metuas me?*

LONDON,

Printed by VVILLIAM STANSBY.

M. DC. XVI.

EPICOENE. Having the characteristics of both sexes. Jonson is fond of the word; cf. *N.N.W.*, 276, and *N.T.*, 260; in 'An Epigram on the Court Pucelle' *(Und.*, XLIX), 7, it is used of masculine behaviour in a woman: see note to II.ii.99–100.

The silent Woman. The play's second title, by which it has always been better known, can be seen as a tongue-in-cheek version of a popular type of play-title in the period, the title which offers an arresting paradox; e.g. *The Honest Whore, The Honest Lawyer, A Chaste Maid in Cheapside, Wit in a Constable.* Coupled with *'Epicoene'* the effect is to imply that a silent woman is a contradiction: sexual abnormality must be what makes such a creature possible.

Ut . . . me. From Horace's defence of satire in *Satires,* I.iv.69–70: 'Though you are like Caelius and Birrius, the robbers, I need not be like Caprius or Sulcius [described earlier as professional informers, hoarse from bawling their accusations in the courts]: why should you fear me?'

DEDICATION

TO THE TRULY
NOBLE, BY ALL
TITLES,
Sir Francis Stuart:

Sir,   5

My hope is not so nourished by example, as it will conclude this
dumb piece should please you by cause it hath pleased others before,
but by trust, that when you have read it, you will find it worthy to
have displeased none. This makes that I now number you not only
in the names of favour but the names of justice to what I write, and   10
do presently call you to the exercise of that noblest and manliest
virtue, as coveting rather to be freed in my fame by the authority
of a judge than the credit of an undertaker. Read therefore, I pray
you, and censure. There is not a line or syllable in it changed from
the simplicity of the first copy. And, when you shall consider,   15
through the certain hatred of some, how much a man's innocency
may be endangered by an uncertain accusation, you will, I doubt
not, so begin to hate the iniquity of such natures as I shall love the
contumely done me, whose end was so honourable as to be wiped
off by your sentence.   20

Your unprofitable but true lover,

BEN JONSON

4   *Sir Francis Stuart.* 'He was a learned gentleman, and one of the club at the
     Mermayd, in Fryday street, with Sir Walter Ralegh, etc., of that sodalitie: heroes and
     witts of that time' (John Aubrey, *Brief Lives*, ed. A. Clark, 2 vols., Oxford, 1898, II,
     239).

6   *example* authorizing instances in the past.

7   *dumb piece,* (i) silent play (because the authorities had suppressed *Epicoene* in
     1610); (ii) silent woman (regarded sexually; cf. *Troilus and Cressida,* IV.ii.63, where
     Helen is called 'a flat and tamed piece').
     by cause because.

9   *makes* is the reason.

11 *presently* at this time.

12 *fame* reputation (Latin *fama*).

13 *undertaker.* Guarantor, sponsor: according to *OED*, sb., 7, a sense first used by
     Jonson (in the dedication to *Poet.*); here with the pejorative associations of a
     political 'fixer* who influences voting in Parliament (see *OED*, sb., 4.b).

14 *censure* judge.

15 *simplicity.* Openness, straightforwardness, ingenuousness (Latin *simplicitas*).
     But perhaps Jonson himself is being covertly disingenuous, since *Epicoene* is a
     highly sophisticated play, in which simplicity is itself a leading theme; see I.i.88.

1   MOROSE Latin *morosus* means 'peevish, stubborn' (from *mos*, custom, habit), which is the sense here. *OED* has only one example of the word, from a Latin–English dictionary of 1565, before this one.

2   DAUPHINE EUGENIE The immediate meaning is 'well-born heir', but Dauphine's name also associates him with the ideas of effeminate fashionableness and sexual ambivalence embodied in the more obviously satirized characters. It connects him with things French (since the Dauphin was the heir apparent to the King of France), and in the play France, fashion, and sexual unnaturalness are linked (cf. II.ii.57, II.v.68, IV.iii.20–1, IV.vi.25–6, and the name 'La Foole'); also, it is given an 'incorrect', indeed impossible, feminine form by the addition of the *e* (cf. 'La Foole' and 'Centaure'). As well as representing the Greek for 'well-born', *Eugenie* points to *genie*, French for 'wit'.

3   CLERIMONT Another French name; cf. Marlowe, *Edward II*, V.v.68–9. Partridge suggests an echo of French *clairement*, clearly, plainly, in view of Clerimont's championing of simplicity against artifice in the debate with Truewit in I.i.

6   JOHN DAW The daw is the jackdaw, a bird 'noted for its loquacity and thievish propensities' (*OED*), and *daw* commonly meant 'noodle, dolt'; cf. the proverb 'As wise as a daw' (Tilley, D50).
   servant lover devoted to the service of his lady.

7   AMOROUS LA FOOLE Cf. Thomas Overbury's character 'An Amorist': 'his fashion exceeds the worth of his weight. He is never without verses, and muske comfects: and sighes to the hazard of his buttons . . . His imagination is a foole . . ., shortly hee is translated out of a man into folly; his imagination is the glasse of lust, and himselfe the traitor to his own discretion' (*Characters*, 1614, sig. E1^r).

8   OTTER '*Animal amphibium*' (I.iv.22), which suits with Otter's captaincy of 'land and sea'. The Otters' name also suggests their sexual topsy-turviness, since the creature was a byword for the unclassifiable: '[is the otter] a beast or a fish? . . . I have heard, the question hath been debated among many great Clerks, and they seem to differ about it; yet most agree that his tail is Fish' (Izaac Walton, *The Complete Angler*, 1653, chap. ii). Cf. Falstaff on the Hostess in *1 Henry IV*, III.iii.123–8: she is 'an otter . . . she's neither fish nor flesh, a man knows not where to have her'.

12   CENTAURE The classical monster, half human, half horse, characteristically savage and lustful. 'For the Greeks Centaurs are representative of wild life, animal desires, and barbarism' (*Oxford Classical Dictionary*). Despite IV.v.41, and Zeuxis' famous painting of a Centaur family scene, female Centaurs do not exist in classical mythology. Centaurs mated with mares, or, usually by raping them, women.
   collegiates. Belonging to a college (collective body, society). For the plural adjective in official phrases cf. 'letters patents'.

13   MAVIS 'Song-thrush', adding another to the multitude of birds in the play, though in this case the name is comically inappropriate to its owner. A more learned sense, Italian 'Maviso, *for* Malviso, *an ill face*' (J. Florio, *Queen Anna's New World of Words*, 1611, p. 304), is punned on at V.ii.31.

14-15   *pretenders* aspirants (to membership of the college)

THE PERSONS OF THE PLAY

MOROSE, *a gentleman that loves no noise*
DAUPHINE EUGENIE, *a knight, his nephew*
CLERIMONT, *a gentleman, his friend*
TRUEWIT, *another friend*
EPICOENE, *a young gentleman, supposed the silent woman*   5
JOHN DAW, *a knight, her servant*
AMOROUS LA FOOLE, *a knight also*
THOMAS OTTER, *a land and sea captain*
CUTBEARD, *a barber*
MUTE, *one of Morose his servants*   10
MADAME HAUGHTY ⎫
MADAME CENTAURE ⎬ *ladies collegiates*
MISTRESS MAVIS ⎭
MISTRESS TRUSTY, *the Lady Haughty's woman* ⎫ *pretenders*
MISTRESS OTTER, *the Captain's wife*   ⎭   15
Parson, Pages, Servants, [*Musicians*]

The Scene: London

Act 2 s.2   Truewit tells Morose to kill himself rather than marry

Act 2 s.3   Clerimont & Dauphine poke fun at Daw who proclaims himself a poet.

Act 2 s.4   Morose meet Epicoene
Act 2 s.5   Clerimont & Dauphine & Truewit decide to bring guests to celebrate th marrage

183

1   *Truth says* In particular Terence, in the opening lines of the prologue to *Andria*, which Jonson is echoing.

3   *bays* Acclaim, fame (from the bay laurel, the leaves of which formed the poet's garland).

4   *sect of writers* Possibly Jonson had in mind such dramatists as George Chapman and John Marston, his collaborators in *Eastward Ho!* (1604), who wrote exclusively for the private-theatre companies.

5   *particular* Restricted to a set of persons; cf. 'these domestic and particular broils' (*King Lear*, V.i.30).

6   *popular* Pertaining to the common people, or the people as a whole.

8   *those make* those who make.

9   *not . . . guests'* The comparison is common, deriving from Martial, *Epigrams*, IX.lxxxi, though it is interesting that it is developed with similar elaborateness in the epilogue to another Queen's Revels' play, Chapman's *All Fools* (c. 1604). Jonson, who was intensely interested in food, and fond of describing literary and moral discrimination in terms of culinary, no doubt found the simile especially significant and appealing; cf. *C.R.*, Induction, 185–8; the dialogue between the Poet and Cook in *N.T.*

10   *cunning* learned, sophisticated

11   *entreaty* entertainment (*OED*'s first example of this sense)

12   *all relish not* everything is not to their taste
     some some parts (of the play)

14   *so* i.e. making every piece to the taste of the 'cunning palates'; cf. *Volp.*, Dedication, 111–14.

15   *this . . . way.* The opposite of Jonson's earlier attitude; cf. the revised conclusion in the quarto text of *E.M.O.* (H&S, III, 603–4): 'We know (and we are pleas'd to know so much) / The Cates that you have tasted were not season'd / For every vulgar Pallat, but prepar'd / To banket pure and apprehensive eares: / Let then their Voices speake for our desert'; also *Disc*, 409–12.

16   *custard* open pie containing meat or fruit

17   *meats* dishes

18   *coarse.* Punning on '(food) course', the spelling in F.

20   *cates* choice victuals, usually bought

21–2 *none . . . ladies.* Proverbial: 'dear bought and far fetched are dainties for ladies' (Tilley, D12).

23   *city-wires.* Fashionable gentlewomen of the city, who used wire to support their ruffs and hair.

24   *men . . . Whitefriars.* Both the audience of the Whitefriars theatre, where the play was performed, and the residents of the district between Fleet Street and the Thames where the theatre was situated. The sense implied by this latter reference is 'thieves and prostitutes', since Whitefriars at this date, because it enjoyed privilege of sanctuary, was a notorious centre of crime and vice. It is a haunt of Lieutenant Shift, the pimp of *Epig.*, XII, and in *Volp.*, IV.ii.51 Lady Would-be calls Peregrine one of 'your *white-Friers* nation' when she mistakes him for 'a lewd harlot'.

27   *ord'naries* eating-houses, taverns
     broken meat fragments of food left after a meal

29   *her* herself

PROLOGUE

Truth says, of old the art of making plays
    Was to content the people, and their praise
    Was to the Poet money, wine, and bays.
But in this age a sect of writers are,
    That only for particular likings care   5
    And will taste nothing that is popular.
With such we mingle neither brains nor breasts;
    Our wishes, like to those make public feasts,
    Are not to please the cook's tastes, but the guests'.
Yet if those cunning palates hither come,   10
    They shall find guests' entreaty and good room;
    And though all relish not, sure there will be some
That, when they leave their seats, shall make 'em say,
    Who wrote that piece could so have wrote a play,
    But that he knew this was the better way.   15
For to present all custard or all tart
    And have no other meats to bear a part,
    Or to want bread and salt, were but coarse art.
The Poet prays you, then, with better thought
    To sit, and when his cates are all in brought,   20
    Though there be none far-fet, there will dear-bought
Be fit for ladies; some for lords, knights, squires,
    Some for your waiting-wench and city-wires,
    Some for your men and daughters of Whitefriars.
Nor is it only while you keep your seat   25
    Here that his feast will last, but you shall eat
    A week at ord'naries on his broken meat,
            If his Muse be true,
            Who commends her to you.

0   *Occasioned . . . exception* F^b (om. F^4).

    impertinent probably 'inappropriate, irrelevant', or more loosely 'absurd, silly' (*OED*, a., 2, 3), rather than the modern sense, which is not common before the eighteenth century.

    exception objection, fault-finding

1–2   *The . . . delight.* The Horatian maxim (*Ars Poetica*, 343–4). It was 'a fixed article in Jonson's literary creed: he is never tired of repeating it' (H&S, IX, 420, who cite numerous examples).

1   *scene* stage (Latin *scena*)

3   *still* always

    praise subject of praise

4   *So . . . crimes.* Another favourite maxim of Jonson's, from Martial, *Epigrams*, X.xxxiii; cf. *Und.*, XII, 28, and the Apologetical Dialogue appended to *Poet.*, 84–5: 'My Bookes have still been taught / To spare the persons, and to speake the vices'.

4   *So* provided

7   *true* real, describing an actual occurrence

    On . . . yourselves Cf. the stage-keeper's agreement with the audience in *B.F.*, Induction, 145–8, concerning anyone caught associating the characters with real people: 'that such person, or persons so found, be left discovered to the mercy of the *Author*, as a forfeiture to the *Stage*, and your laughter, aforesaid'.

8   *maker.* 'A Poet is that, which by the *Greeks* is call'd κατ' 'εξοχήν, ὁ Ποιητής, a Maker, or a fainer' (*Disc*, 2347–8).

9–10 *poet . . . feigned.* From Horace, *Ars Poetica*, 338; often echoed by Jonson: e.g. *Disc*, 2351–4; The Prologue for the Court in *S.N.*, 11–14.

11–14 The standard protest of the Elizabethan and Jacobean satirist. The *locus classicus* is Marston's 'To Him that hath Perused Me', appended to *The Scourge of Villainy* (1598): 'If thou hast perused me, what lesser favour canst thou graunt then not to abuse me with unjust application? Yet I feare me, I shall be much, much injuried by two sorts of readers: the one being ignorant, not knowing the nature of Satyre, (which is under fained private persons, to note generall vices,) will needes wrest each fayned name to a private unfained person. The other too subtile, bearing a private malice to some greater personage then he dare in his owne person seeme to maligne, will strive by a forced application of my generall reproofes to broach his private hatred . . . Let this protestation satisfie our curious readers'. Jaques makes the same disclaimer in *As You Like It*, II.vii.70ff., and Jonson, at considerable length, in Chorus II of *M.L.*, where he explicitly recalls the present prologue (H&S, VI, 544).

11   *particular* Personal, relating in detail to an individual; cf. *Volp.*, Dedication, 56–7: '*Where have I beene particular? Where personall?*'

    sleight cunning device, jugglery

12   *wrest* twist, misinterpret

13   *or . . . or* either . . . or

ANOTHER
Occasioned by some person's impertinent exception

The ends of all who for the scene do write
   Are, or should be, to profit and delight.
And still 't hath been the praise of all best times,
   So persons were not touched, to tax the crimes.
Then, in this play which we present tonight,   5
   And make the object of your ear and sight,
On forfeit of yourselves, think nothing true,
   Lest so you make the maker to judge you.
For he knows, poet never credit gained
   By writing truths, but things like truths well feigned.   10
If any yet will, with particular sleight
   Of application, wrest what he doth write,
And that he meant or him or her will say,
   They make a libel which he made a play.

ACT I, SCENE i

[*Enter*] CLERIMONT. *He comes out making himself ready,*
[*followed by*] BOY

CLERIMONT
Ha' you got the song yet perfect I ga' you, boy?
BOY
Yes, sir.
CLERIMONT
Let me hear it.
BOY
You shall, sir, but i' faith let nobody else.
CLERIMONT
Why, I pray?   5
BOY
It will get you the dangerous name of a poet in town, sir, besides
me a perfect deal of ill will at the mansion you wot of, whose
lady is the argument of it, where now I am the welcom'st thing
under a man that comes there.
CLERIMONT
I think, and above a man too, if the truth were racked out of   10
you.
BOY
No, faith, I'll confess before, sir. The gentlewomen play with me
and throw me o' the bed, and carry me in to my lady, and she
kisses me with her oiled face, and puts a peruke o' my head, and
asks me an' I will wear her gown, and I say no; and then she hits   15

---

0 s.d. *making . . . ready* dressing.
1 *perfect* perfectly memorized.
6 *dangerous . . . poet* Because poets (at this time the term included playwrights) satirize
  folly and vice, and were regarded, in Jonson's view, with scorn: 'now, letters onely
  make men vile. Hee is upbraidingly call'd a *Poet*, as if it were a most contemptible
  Nick-name' (*Disc*, 280–2).
7 *wot* know.
8 *argument* subject
  where whereas.
9 *under a man* With a sexual pun; cf. 'ingle' (l. 22) and 'Mistress Underman' in
  Middleton's *A Chaste Maid in Cheapside*, II.iii.17.
10 *above* (i) better than; (ii) taller than (as a result of being stretched on the rack); (iii)
  continuing the sexual joke in *under*.
15 *an'* if.

me a blow o' the ear and calls me innocent, and lets me go.

CLERIMONT

No marvel if the door be kept shut against your master, when
the entrance is so easy to you. Well, sir, you shall go there no
more, lest I be fain to seek your voice in my lady's rushes a fortnight hence. Sing, sir.   20

BOY *sings*

[*Enter* TRUEWIT]

TRUEWIT

Why, here's the man that can melt away his time, and never feels
it! What between his mistress abroad and his ingle at home,
high fare, soft lodging, fine clothes, and his fiddle, he thinks the
hours ha' no wings or the day no post-horse. Well, sir gallant,
were you struck with the plague this minute or condemned to   25
any capital punishment tomorrow, you would begin then to
think and value every article o' your time, esteem it at the true
rate, and give all for't.

CLERIMONT

Why, what should a man do?

TRUEWIT

Why, nothing, or that which, when 'tis done, is as idle. Hearken   30
after the next horse-race, or hunting-match; lay wagers, praise
Puppy, or Peppercorn, Whitefoot, Franklin; *Horses o' the time* swear
upon Whitemane's party, spend aloud that my lords may hear
you; visit my ladies at night and be able to give 'em the character
of every bowler or bettor o' the green. These be the things   35
wherein your fashionable men exercise themselves, and I for
company.

16   *innocent* simpleton.
17–18   *door . . . entrance* For the innuendo see note to V.i.65.
19   *fain* obliged.
      rushes green rushes strewn on the floor of houses.
20   s.d. The song is that at l. 81. Jonson delays printing it until then so that it can be
      read in conjunction with Truewit's disquisition on artifice.
22   *abroad* away from home.
      ingle boy kept for homosexual purposes, catamite.
27   *article o' your time* moment (Latin *articulus temporis*).
30   *idle* vain, useless.
      Hearken inquire.
32   *Horses . . . time* F^b (om. F^a).
33   *aloud* ostentatiously.
35   *bettor* OED's first example of the word.

CLERIMONT

Nay, if I have thy authority, I'll not leave yet. Come, the other are considerations when we come to have grey heads and weak hams, moist eyes and shrunk members. We'll think on 'em then; then we'll pray and fast.   40

TRUEWIT

Ay, and destine only that time of age to goodness which our want of ability will not let us employ in evil?

CLERIMONT

Why then 'tis time enough.

TRUEWIT

Yes, as if a man should sleep all the term and think to effect his   45
business the last day. Oh, Clerimont, this time, because it is an incorporeal thing and not subject to sense, we mock ourselves the fineliest out of it, with vanity and misery indeed, not seeking an end of wretchedness, but only changing the matter still.

CLERIMONT

Nay, thou'lt not leave now –   50

TRUEWIT

See but our common disease! With what justice can we complain that great men will not look upon us nor be at leisure to give our affairs such dispatch as we expect, when we will never do it to ourselves, nor hear nor regard ourselves.

CLERIMONT

Foh, thou hast read Plutarch's *Morals* now, or some such tedious   55
fellow, and it shows so vilely with thee, 'fore God, 'twill spoil thy wit utterly. Talk me of pins, and feathers, and ladies, and rushes, and such things, and leave this stoicity alone till thou mak'st sermons.

---

38   *leave* leave off.

43   *ability* capacity, or perhaps 'bodily power, strength' (*OED*, sb., 3).

45   *term* one of the four periods of the year during which the London law-courts were in session.

48   *fineliest* most perfectly. Partridge suggests that this old-fashioned form of the adverb, used only by Truewit (cf. II.ii.87), may be Jonson's way of calling attention to his elaborate language.

49   *still* ever, continually.

51   *common disease* 'Discontent, the nobleman's consumption' (*The Revenger's Tragedy*, I.i.126), caused by lack of patronage and neglect at court; *common* = common to all.

54   *nor hear* F[b] (not heare F[a]).

55   *Plutarch* In fact the stoic philosopher Seneca, *De Brevitate Vitae*, III.v; see II.iii.40–1.

57   *rushes* Suggesting triviality; cf. 'Not worth a rush' (Tilley, S918).

58   *stoicity* stoicism (Clerimont's coinage).

TRUEWIT

Well, sir, if it will not take, I have learned to lose as little of my   60
kindness as I can. I'll do good to no man against his will, certainly.
When were you at the college?

CLERIMONT

What college?

TRUEWIT

As if you knew not!

CLERIMONT

No, faith, I came but from court yesterday.   65

TRUEWIT

Why, is it not arrived there yet, the news? A new foundation,
sir, here i' the town, of ladies that call themselves the Collegiates,
an order between courtiers and country madams, that live from
their husbands and give entertainment to all the Wits and
Braveries o' the time, as they call 'em, cry down or up what they   70
like or dislike in a brain or a fashion with most masculine or
rather hermaphroditical authority, and every day gain to their
college some new probationer.

CLERIMONT

Who is the president?

TRUEWIT

The grave and youthful matron, the Lady Haughty.   75

CLERIMONT

A pox of her autumnal face, her pieced beauty! There's no man
can be admitted till she be ready nowadays, till she has painted
and perfumed and washed, and scoured, but the boy here, and
him she wipes her oiled lips upon like a sponge. I have made a
song, I pray thee hear it, o' the subject.   80

---

60   *sir, if* ed. (sir. If F).
     take take effect.
67   *Collegiates* OED's first example of the noun.
68   *from* apart from.
69–70   *Wits and Braveries*, i.e. gallants who set the fashion in talk and dress respectively. Cf.
     Und., XLII, 33–6: '[I] Have eaten with the Beauties, and the wits, / And braveries of
     Court . . . and came so nigh to know / Whether their faces were their owne, or no'.
70   *cry down or up* decry or extol.
76   *pieced* (i) mended, patched; (ii) made up of pieces (cf. IV.ii.79–85).
77   *ready* properly attired, having finished one's toilet (*OED*, a., 1.b); cf. I.i.1 s.d.
78   *scoured* Fb (sour'd Fa). Scrubbed, with the idea of the hard rubbing of stone or metal
     with detergent. The first of several such associations in the play. Clerimont's list
     reverses the order of the stages of preparation, as though stripping off the layers of
     artifice.

[BOY *sings*]

Song

Still to be neat, still to be dressed,
As you were going to a feast;
Still to be powdered, still perfumed:
Lady, it is to be presumed,
Though art's hid causes are not found,   85
All is not sweet, all is not sound.

Give me a look, give me a face,
That makes simplicity a grace;
Robes loosely flowing, hair as free:
Such sweet neglect more taketh me   90
Than all th' adulteries of art:
They strike mine eyes, but not my heart.

TRUEWIT

And I am clearly o' the other side: I love a good dressing before
any beauty o' the world. Oh, a woman is then like a delicate
garden; nor is there one kind of it: she may vary every hour, take   95
often counsel of her glass and choose the best. If she have good
ears, show 'em; good hair, lay it out; good legs, wear short clothes;
a good hand, discover it often; practise any art to mend breath,
cleanse teeth, repair eyebrows, paint, and profess it.

CLERIMONT

How! publicly?   100

TRUEWIT

The doing of it, not the manner: that must be private. Many
things that seem foul i' the doing, do please, done. A lady should
indeed study her face when we think she sleeps; nor when the
doors are shut should men be inquiring; all is sacred within,

---

81   *Still* always.
88   *simplicity* Absence of ornament or decoration (*OED*'s first example), and suggesting
      also, in view of 'adulteries', the moral senses of the Dedication, 15.
90   *taketh* captivate, catch the fancy of; a sense coined by Jonson in *Volp.*, I.ii.56.
91   *adulteries* adulterations. The first of *OED*'s two instances, the second being a remin-
      iscence of this one.
92   *They* F[a] (*Thy* F[b]).
93   *dressing* pun on (i) attire; (ii) ornamentation (used of technical processes in arts
      and manufactures).
98   *discover* reveal, as at l. 107.
99   *profess* declare, acknowledge.
100   *How* exclamation of surprise.

then. Is it for us to see their perukes put on, their false teeth, 105
their complexion, their eyebrows, their nails? You see gilders
will not work but enclosed. They must not discover how little
serves with the help of art to adorn a great deal. How long did
the canvas hang afore Aldgate? Were the people suffered to see
the city's *Love* and *Charity* while they were rude stone, before 110
they were painted and burnished? No. No more should servants
approach their mistresses but when they are complete and
finished.

CLERIMONT

Well said, my Truewit.

TRUEWIT

And a wise lady will keep a guard always upon the place, that she 115
may do things securely. I once followed a rude fellow into a
chamber, where the poor madam, for haste, and troubled,
snatched at her peruke to cover her baldness and put it on the
wrong way.

CLERIMONT

Oh prodigy! 120

TRUEWIT

And the unconscionable knave held her in compliment an hour,
with that reversed face, when I still looked when she should talk
from the tother side.

CLERIMONT

Why, thou shouldst ha' relieved her.

---

106   *complexion* A deft play on two senses: (i) natural colour, texture, and appearance of
         the face; (ii) cosmetic application; cf. *Alch.*, I.i.29, and J. Bullokar, *An English Expo-*
         sitor, 1616, sig. D8^V: '*Complexion* . . . painting used by women'.
107   *enclosed* shut up in a room.
108–11 *How . . . burnished* Aldgate, the main eastern gate in the old city wall, was pulled
         down in 1606 and rebuilt. On the new gate, completed in 1609, were set 'two
         Feminine personages, the one South-ward, appearing to be Peace, with a silver Dove
         upon her one hand, and a guilded wreath or Garland in the other. On the North
         side standeth Charity, with a child at her brest, and another led in her hand. Implying
         (as I conceive) that where Peace, and Love or Charity do prosper, and are truely
         embraced, that Citie shall be for ever blessed' (J. Stow's *Survey of London*, continued
         by A. Munday, 1618, p. 231).
111   *servants* lovers.
121   *compliment* 'Courtiers . . . do nothing but sing the gamuth A-re of complementall
         courtesie' (T. Dekker, *The Gull's Horn Book*, 1609, p. 2). The stock expressions are
         listed in *King John*, I.i.184 ff.
123   *tother* common form of other.

TRUEWIT

No, faith, I let her alone, as we'll let this argument, if you please,   125
and pass to another. When saw you Dauphine Eugenie?

CLERIMONT

Not these three days. Shall we go to him this morning? He is
very melancholic, I hear.

TRUEWIT

Sick o' the uncle, is he? I met that stiff piece of formality, his
uncle, yesterday, with a huge turban of nightcaps on his head,   130
buckled over his ears.

CLERIMONT

Oh, that's his custom when he walks abroad. He can endure no
noise, man.

TRUEWIT

So I have heard. But is the disease so ridiculous in him as it is
made? They say he has been upon divers treaties with the fish-   135
wives and orange-women, and articles propounded between
them. Marry, the chimney-sweepers will not be drawn in.

CLERIMONT

No, nor the broom-men: they stand out stiffly. He cannot endure
a costardmonger, he swoons if he hear one.

TRUEWIT

Methinks a smith should be ominous.   .   140

CLERIMONT

Or any hammerman. A brazier is not suffered to dwell in the
parish, nor an armourer. He would have hanged a pewterer's
'prentice once upon a Shrove Tuesday's riot for being o' that

---

125   *argument* topic.
129   *Sick . . . uncle* Adapting 'sick of the mother' (hysteria).
130   *nightcaps* Worn in the daytime by the elderly and infirm.
135   *made* made out to be.
      been entered.
138   *broom-men* Either 'street-sweepers' (*OED*'s only sense) or 'broom-sellers' (Henry,
      H&S, who quote their cries).
139   *costardmonger* fruit-seller.
141   *hammerman* metal-worker.
      brazier worker in brass.
142   *pewterer* Cf. Middleton's *Women Beware Women*, III.i.77–9: 'she hates the name of
      pewterer / More than sick men the noise, or diseased bones / That quake at fall
      o'th'hammer'.
143   *upon* vp/on F^b (on F^a).
      Shrove Tuesday When the apprentices went on the rampage, wrecking brothels and
      sometimes playhouses. The authorities reacted sharply if the fun got out of hand:

trade, when the rest were quit.

TRUEWIT

A trumpet should fright him terribly, or the hau'boys? 145

CLERIMONT

Out of his senses. The waits of the city have a pension of him
not to come near that ward. This youth practised on him one
night like the bellman, and never left till he had brought him
down to the door with a long sword, and there left him flourish-
ing with the air. 150

BOY

Why, sir, he hath chosen a street to lie in so narrow at both ends
that it will receive no coaches nor carts nor any of these common noises, and therefore we that love him devise to bring him
in such as we may, now and then, for his exercise, to breathe
him. He would grow resty else in his ease. His virtue would rust 155
without action. I entreated a bearward one day to come down
with the fogs of some four parishes that way, and I thank him
he did, and cried his games under Master Morose's window till
he was sent crying away with his head made a most bleeding
spectacle to the multitude. And another time a fencer, marching 160
to his prize, had his drum most tragically run through for taking
that street in his way, at my request.

in 1617 'The Prentizes on Shrove Tewsday last, to the number of 3. or 4000 comitted
extreame insolencies . . . such of them as are taken his Majestie hath commaunded
shal be executed for example sake' (quoted by A. Gurr, *The Shakespearean Stage
1574–1642*, Cambridge, 1970, pp. 13–14).

144   *quit* acquitted.
145   *trumpet* Anticipating Truewit's device in II.ii.
       hau'boys oboes (French *hautbois*).
146   *waits* band of street musicians maintained at the public charge.
147   *ward* district of the city.
       This youth Clerimont's boy.
       practised played a trick, imposed.
148   *bellman* night-watchman, who called the hours, ringing a bell.
151   *lie* live.
154   *in* F^b (om. F^a).
       breathe exercise briskly (said of horses).
155   *resty* sluggish (said of horses that refuse to go forward).
       virtue special quality, and glancing at the sense 'manly vigour' (Latin *virtus*).
156   *bearward* Keeper of a bear for baiting by dogs. Henry quotes the bearward of W.
       Cavendish's *The Humorous Lovers* (1667), V.i: 'fetch me a Bag-pipe, we will walk the
       streets in triumph, and give the people notice of our sport'.
160   *marching* F^b (going F^a).
161   *prize* fencing-match. Fencers were often drummed through the streets to publicize
       their matches.

TRUEWIT

A good wag. How does he for the bells?

CLERIMONT

Oh, i' the Queen's time he was wont to go out of town every
Saturday at ten o'clock or on holiday eves. But now, by reason of   165
the sickness, the perpetuity of ringing has made him devise a
room with double walls and treble ceilings, the windows close
shut and caulked, and there he lives by candlelight. He turned
away a man last week for having a pair of new shoes that
creaked, and this fellow waits on him now in tennis-court socks,   170
or slippers soled with wool, and they talk each to other in a
trunk. – See who comes here!

ACT I, SCENE ii

[Enter] DAUPHINE

DAUPHINE

How now! What ail you, sirs? Dumb?

TRUEWIT

Struck into stone almost, I am here, with tales o' thine uncle!
There was never such a prodigy heard of.

DAUPHINE

I would you would once lose this subject, my masters, for my

---

163   *wag* mischievous boy.

165–6   *now . . . sickness* An up-to-date allusion. In 1609 the virulence of the plague 'was far
more severe than in any other year between 1603 and 1625, and the total mortality
was [4,240,] greater by 2,000 than in any year from 1604 to 1623' (F.P. Wilson, *The
Plague in Shakespeare's London*, Oxford, 1927, p. 121).

166   *ringing* London was famous for its bells, and their sound was impossible to escape
during time of plague, when the city's 114 churches tolled for their dead. Cf. Volpone
on Lady Wouldbe's voice: 'The bells, in time of pestilence, ne're made / Like noise,
or were in that perpetuall motion; / The cock-pit comes not neere it' (*Volp.*,
III.v.5–7).

        sickness plague.

168–9   *turned away a man* dismissed a servant.

172   *trunk* speaking-tube (see note to II.i.2).

2   *I am here* as I stand here.

4   *once* once for all.

sake. They are such as you are that have brought me into that   5
predicament I am with him.

TRUEWIT

How is that?

DAUPHINE

Marry, that he will disinherit me, no more. He thinks I and my
company are authors of all the ridiculous acts and moniments
are told of him.   10

TRUEWIT

'Slid, I would be the author of more to vex him; that purpose
deserves it: it gives thee law of plaguing him. I'll tell thee what I
would do. I would make a false almanac, get it printed, and then
ha' him drawn out on a coronation day to the Tower-wharf, and
kill him with the noise of the ordinance. Disinherit thee! He   15
cannot, man. Art not thou next of blood, and his sister's son?

DAUPHINE

Ay, but he will thrust me out of it, he vows, and marry.

TRUEWIT

How! That's a more portent. Can he endure no noise, and will
venture on a wife?

CLERIMONT

Yes. Why, thou art a stranger, it seems, to his best trick yet. He   20
has employed a fellow this half year all over England to hearken
him out a dumb woman, be she of any form or any quality,
so she be able to bear children. Her silence is dowry enough,
he says.

---

9   *acts and moniments* The first English edition (1563) of John Foxe's *The Book of
Martyrs* was entitled *Acts and Monuments*; 'moniments' follows Latin *monimentum*.
Cf. III.vii.10.
11   *'Slid* God's (eye)lid, a common oath.
that purpose Morose's purpose to disinherit Dauphine.
12   *gives thee law* authorizes you.
14   *coronation day* Anniversary of James I's coronation, 25 July, when the Tower guns
fired a salute.
15   *ordinance* ordnance, cannon (the original form and pronunciation).
16   *next* nearest.
18   *more* greater. Marriage might produce children, whereas disinheriting seems illegal
(Partridge). This archaic usage, appropriate to a conservative stylist like Truewit, is
paralleled in *Cat.*, IV, 46.
19   *venture on* dare to take (*OED*, v., 9.b).
21–2   *hearken . . . out* find by inquiry.
23   *quality* rank.

TRUEWIT

But I trust to God he has found none.   25

CLERIMONT

No, but he has heard of one that's lodged i' the next street to him, who
is exceedingly soft-spoken, thrifty of her speech, that spends but six
words a day. And her he's about now and shall have her.

TRUEWIT

Is't possible! Who is his agent i' the business?

CLERIMONT

Marry, a barber, one Cutbeard, an honest fellow, one that tells   30
Dauphine all here.

TRUEWIT

Why, you oppress me with wonder! A woman, and a barber, and love
no noise!

CLERIMONT

Yes, faith. The fellow trims him silently and has not the knack with
his shears or his fingers, and that continence in a barber he thinks so   35
eminent a virtue as it has made him chief of his counsel.

TRUEWIT

Is the barber to be seen? or the wench?

CLERIMONT

Yes, that they are.

TRUEWIT

I pray thee, Dauphine, let's go thither.

DAUPHINE

I have some business now; I cannot i' faith.   40

TRUEWIT

You shall have no business shall make you neglect this, sir. We'll make
her talk, believe it; or if she will not, we can give out at least so much
as shall interrupt the treaty. We will break it. Thou art bound in conscience, when he suspects thee without cause, to torment him.

DAUPHINE

Not I, by any means. I'll give no suffrage to't. He shall never ha' that   45

---

30   *one Cutbeard* F^b (om. F^a).
32   *oppress* overwhelm (Latin *opprimere*).
34   *knack* (i) know-how, trick; (ii) sharp snap, crack: cf. J. Cooke, *Greene's Tu Quoque*, 1614, sig.
       D3^r: 'the Barber . . . can snacke his fingers with dexteritie'.
42   *give out* report, put about.
43   *interrupt the treaty* hinder the negotiation (the legal metaphors continue to l. 52).
45   *suffrage* consent.

plea against me that I opposed the least fant'sy of his. Let it lie
upon my stars to be guilty, I'll be innocent.

TRUEWIT

Yes, and be poor, and beg; do, innocent, when some groom
of his has got him an heir, or this barber, if he himself cannot. Innocent! – I pray thee, Ned, where lies she? Let him be   50
innocent still.

CLERIMONT

Why, right over against the barber's, in the house where Sir John
Daw lies.

TRUEWIT

You do not mean to confound me!

CLERIMONT

Why?   55

TRUEWIT

Does he that would marry her know so much?

CLERIMONT

I cannot tell.

TRUEWIT

'Twere enough of imputation to her, with him.

CLERIMONT

Why?

TRUEWIT

The only talking sir i' th' town! Jack Daw! And he teach her not   60
to speak – God b' w' you. I have some business too.

CLERIMONT

Will you not go thither then?

TRUEWIT

Not with the danger to meet Daw, for mine ears.

CLERIMONT

Why? I thought you two had been upon very good terms.

---

46 *fant'sy* fancy; and so pronounced, but full contraction obscures the range of meaning
    available: e.g. caprice, amorous passion, delusion (Partridge).
46–7 *Let . . . stars* though I be fated.
48 *innocent* playing on the sense of I.i.16.
    groom servant.
49 *got* begot.
52 *over against* opposite.
54 *confound* dumbfound.
58 *to her* against her (that she is talkative).
60 *only* pre-eminent.
    sir Mockingly for 'gentleman'; cf. 'a proud, and spangled sir', *C.R.*, III.iv.12.

TRUEWIT

Yes, of keeping distance.   65

CLERIMONT

They say he is a very good scholar.

TRUEWIT

Ay, and he says it first. A pox on him, a fellow that pretends only
to learning, buys titles, and nothing else of books in him.

CLERIMONT

The world reports him to be very learned.

TRUEWIT

I am sorry the world should so conspire to belie him.   70

CLERIMONT

Good faith, I have heard very good things come from him.

TRUEWIT

You may. There's none so desperately ignorant to deny that:
would they were his own. God b' w' you, gentlemen.   [*Exit*]

CLERIMONT

This is very abrupt!

ACT I, SCENE iii

DAUPHINE

Come, you are a strange open man to tell everything thus.

CLERIMONT

Why, believe it, Dauphine, Truewit's a very honest fellow.

DAUPHINE

I think no other, but this frank nature of his is not for secrets.

CLERIMONT

Nay, then, you are mistaken, Dauphine. I know where he
has been well trusted, and discharged the trust very truly and   5
heartily.

67–8   *pretends . . . to* makes a claim to.
68   *titles* Cf. J. Earle's 'A Pretender to Learning', *Microcosmography*, 1628, sig. G2ʳ: 'Hee
       is a great Nomen-clator of Authors, which hee has read in generall in the Catalogue,
       and in particular in the Title, and goes seldome so farre as the Dedication'.

6   *heartily* earnestly.

DAUPHINE

I contend not, Ned, but with the fewer a business is carried, it is ever the safer. Now we are alone, if you'll go thither, I am for you.

CLERIMONT

When were you there? 10

DAUPHINE

Last night, and such a *Decameron* of sport fallen out! Boccace never thought of the like. Daw does nothing but court her, and the wrong way. He would lie with her, and praises her modesty; desires that she would talk and be free, and commends her silence in verses, which he reads and swears are the best that 15 ever man made. Then rails at his fortunes, stamps, and mutines why he is not made a councillor and called to affairs of state.

CLERIMONT

I pray thee, let's go. I would fain partake this. – Some water, boy.

[*Exit* BOY]

DAUPHINE

We are invited to dinner together, he and I, by one that came thither to him, Sir La Foole. 20

CLERIMONT

Oh, that's a precious manikin!

DAUPHINE

Do you know him?

CLERIMONT

Ay, and he will know you too, if e'er he saw you but once, though you should meet him at church in the midst of prayers. He is one of the Braveries, though he be none o' the Wits. He 25 will salute a judge upon the bench and a bishop in the pulpit, a lawyer when he is pleading at the bar, and a lady when she is

---

7   *contend not* do not dispute it.
      carried managed.
8   *thither* i.e. to visit Epicoene.
11   *Decameron* Boccaccio's collection of a hundred tales, much concerned with amorous folly.
      fallen out come about, happened.
16–17 *mutines why* mutinies because.
18   *fain partake* gladly have some of. *OED*, v., l.b, has no example before 1617, but in view of the gallants' detachment, and the frequency with which Jonson images folly as a feast, this sense is preferable to 'take part in'.
21   *manikin* little model of a man, puppet; perhaps suggested by *Twelfth Night*, III.ii.53, where Sir Andrew Aguecheek is called 'a dear manikin'.

dancing in a masque, and put her out. He does give plays and
suppers, and invites his guests to 'em aloud out of his window
as they ride by in coaches. He has a lodging in the Strand for the 30
purpose, or to watch when ladies are gone to the china-houses
or the Exchange, that he may meet 'em by chance and give 'em
presents, some two or three hundred pounds' worth of toys,
to be laughed at. He is never without a spare banquet or sweetmeats in his chamber, for their women to alight at and come up 35
to, for a bait.

DAUPHINE

Excellent! He was a fine youth last night, but now he is much
finer! What is his christian name? I ha' forgot.

[*Enter* BOY]

CLERIMONT

Sir Amorous La Foole.

BOY

The gentleman is here below that owns that name. 40

CLERIMONT

'Heart, he's come to invite me to dinner, I hold my life.

DAUPHINE

Like enough. Pray thee, let's ha' him up.

CLERIMONT

Boy, marshal him.

BOY

With a truncheon, sir?

28   *put her out* make her forget her part; cf. V.iii.12.
30   *Strand* Where many of the gentry lived.
31   *purpose, or* ed. (purpose: or F^a purpose. Or F^b).
31   *china-houses* Shops selling oriental goods, fashionable meeting-places.
32   *Exchange* The New Exchange on the south side of the Strand, opened in 1609; its
      milliners' shops made it a fashionable resort for ladies (Sugden).
33   *toys* trifles, trumpery.
34   *to . . . at* i.e. (i) for the ladies' entertainment; or (ii) which only makes the ladies
      laugh at him scornfully.
      banquet Course of sweetmeats, fruit, and wine.
35   *for their* F^b (om. for F^a).
      their women the maidservants of the ladies of l. 31.
      alight descend from their coaches.
36   *bait* (i) refreshment, snack; (ii) food as a lure (using the women to catch the ladies).
40   *below* F^b (om. F^a).
      owns F^b (owes F^a).
43   *marshal him* show him in.
44   *truncheon* (i) marshal's baton; (ii) cudgel.

CLERIMONT

Away, I beseech you.   45

                                                    [*Exit* BOY]

– I'll make him tell us his pedigree now, and what meat he has
to dinner, and who are his guests, and the whole course of his
fortunes, with a breath.

ACT I, SCENE iv

[*Enter*] LA FOOLE

LA FOOLE

'Save, dear Sir Dauphine, honoured Master Clerimont.

CLERIMONT

Sir Amorous! You have very much honested my lodging with
your presence.

LA FOOLE

Good faith, it is a fine lodging, almost as delicate a lodging as
mine.   5

CLERIMONT

Not so, sir.

LA FOOLE

Excuse me, sir, if it were i' the Strand, I assure you. I am come,
Master Clerimont, to entreat you wait upon two or three ladies
to dinner today.

CLERIMONT

How, sir! Wait upon 'em? Did you ever see me carry dishes?   10

LA FOOLE

No, sir, dispense with me; I meant to bear 'em company.

CLERIMONT

Oh, that I will, sir. The doubtfulness o' your phrase, believe it,

46   *meat* food.

1   *'Save* affectedly for 'God save you'.
2   *honested* honoured (Latin *honestare*); becoming archaic at this date, and used by
     Clerimont to mock La Foole's affected courtliness.
11   *dispense with me* affectedly for 'excuse me'.
12   *that I will* Referring to La Foole's 'dispense with me' as well as what he says next, and
     playing on the sense 'do away with' or 'do without'.
     phrase way of talking.

sir, would breed you a quarrel once an hour with the terrible
boys, if you should but keep 'em fellowship a day.

LA FOOLE

It should be extremely against my will, sir, if I contested with   15
any man.

CLERIMONT

I believe it, sir. Where hold you your feast?

LA FOOLE

At Tom Otter's, sir.

DAUPHINE

Tom Otter? What's he?

LA FOOLE

Captain Otter, sir; he is a kind of gamester, but he has had com-   20
mand both by sea and by land.

DAUPHINE

Oh, then he is *animal amphibium*?

LA FOOLE

Ay, sir. His wife was the rich china-woman that the courtiers
visited so often, that gave the rare entertainment. She commands
all at home.   25

CLERIMONT

Then she is Captain Otter?

LA FOOLE

You say very well, sir. She is my kinswoman, a La Foole by the
mother side, and will invite any great ladies for my sake.

DAUPHINE

Not of the La Fooles of Essex?

LA FOOLE

No, sir, the La Fooles of London.   30

CLERIMONT [*Aside to* DAUPHINE]

Now h'is in.

13–14 *terrible boys* Gangs of swaggering bullies, Kastril's 'angry boys' in *Alch.*, usually called
 roarers or roaring boys; an amusingly unlikely fellowship for the perfumed and
 affected La Foole.

14 *but* F^b (om. F^a).

20 *gamester* player of a game (here, bear-baiting).

23 *china-woman* owner of a china-house, but through 'doubtfulness of phrase' (cf.
 visited, entertainment) La Foole manages to imply that his kinswoman was a high-
 class prostitute.

24 *rare* excellent, but (because of *often*) suggesting 'infrequent, scant'. Cf. II.iii.29, where
 Dauphine uses the same pun consciously.

28 *mother side* mother's side.

31 *in* underway.

LA FOOLE

They all come out of our house, the La Fooles o' the north, the
La Fooles of the west, the La Fooles of the east and south – we
are as ancient a family as any is in Europe – but I myself am
descended lineally of the French La Fooles – and we do bear for   35
our coat yellow, or or, checkered azure and gules, and some
three or four colours more, which is a very noted coat and has
sometimes been solemnly worn by divers nobility of our house
– but let that go, antiquity is not respected now – I had a brace
of fat does sent me, gentlemen, and half a dozen of pheasants,   40
a dozen or two of godwits, and some other fowl, which I would
have eaten while they are good, and in good company – there
will be a great lady or two, my Lady Haughty, my Lady Centaure,
Mistress Dol Mavis – and they come a' purpose to see the silent
gentlewoman, Mistress Epicoene, that honest Sir John Daw   45
has promised to bring thither – and then Mistress Trusty, my
Lady's woman, will be there too, and this honourable knight,
Sir Dauphine, with yourself, Master Clerimont – and we'll be
very merry and have fiddlers and dance – I have been a mad wag
in my time, and have spent some crowns since I was a page in   50
court to my Lord Lofty, and after my Lady's gentleman-usher,
who got me knighted in Ireland, since it pleased my elder
brother to die – I had as fair a gold jerkin on that day as any
was worn in the Island Voyage or at Caliz, none dispraised, and

32   *house* family, lineage.
35   *for* F^b (om. F^a).
36   *coat* coat-of-arms.
36   *or ... gules* yellow ... red (in heraldry).
36–7   *some ... more* Like Sogliardo in *E.M.O.*, III.iv.57, La Foole unwittingly suggests the
       motley coat of the fool or jester.
38   *sometimes* in former times (with an unfortunate ambiguity).
40   *does* 'Doves' has been proposed as the correct reading, but 'does' is confirmed by
       III.iii.70 and IV.v.170 (a typical example of Jonson's attentiveness to the smallest
       and apparently most random detail of his design). For comment on La Foole's extra-
       vagant feast, and the moral and social failings it symbolizes, see W. Trimpi, *Ben
       Jonson's Poems: A Study of the Plain Style* (Stanford, 1962), pp. 187–8.
41   *godwits* marsh-birds, a delicacy.
51   *after*, i.e. after that I was; *who* presumably = 'my Lady'. Throughout this speech La
       Foole's verbal ineptness continually leaves his sense open to ludicrous misinter-
       pretations; e.g. 'that day', which could mean the day of his brother's death.
       gentleman-usher gentleman who serves a person of high rank.
52   *Ireland* A dubious place to be knighted. In 1599, during his Irish campaign, the Earl of
       Essex had been sharply criticized for cheapening the title by bestowing it too liberally.
54   *Island Voyage* Another unfortunate boast. Gallants had flocked to join the disastrous

I came over in it hither, showed myself to my friends in court and   55
after went down to my tenants in the country and surveyed my
lands, let new leases, took their money, spent it in the eye o' the
land here, upon ladies – and now I can take up at my pleasure.

DAUPHINE

Can you take up ladies, sir?

CLERIMONT

Oh, let him breathe, he has not recovered.   60

DAUPHINE

Would I were your half in that commodity –

LA FOOLE

No, sir, excuse me: I meant money, which can take up anything.
I have another guest or two to invite and say as much to, gentlemen. I'll take my leave abruptly, in hope you will not fail – Your
servant.   [*Exit* LA FOOLE]   65

DAUPHINE

We will not fail you, sir precious La Foole; but she shall that
your ladies come to see, if I have credit afore Sir Daw.

CLERIMONT

Did you ever hear such a wind-fucker as this?

DAUPHINE

Or such a rook as the other, that will betray his mistress to be
seen! Come, 'tis time we prevented it.   70

CLERIMONT

Go.

                                                        [*Exeunt*]

expedition led by Essex, Howard, and Raleigh against the Spanish in the Azores in
1597, many of them dressed, according to one English captain, 'rather like Maskers
then Souldiers' (H&S).
Caliz Cadiz, captured by Essex and Howard in 1596.

57   *eye* centre.
58   *take up* borrow (at interest).
59–61   *take up ... commodity* Referring to money-lenders' practice, in order to circumvent
the rates of interest fixed by the government, of making clients accept part of their
loan in goods. These would either be greatly overpriced, or would be bought back
by the money-lender much more cheaply than he parted with them.
61   *half* partner.
62   s.p. LA FOOLE F^b (CLE. F^a).
62   *take up* purchase.
67   *have credit afore* take precedence to (the metaphor refers back to ll. 61–2).
68   *wind-fucker* 'The kistrilles or windfuckers that filling themselves with winde, fly
against the winde evermore' (T. Nashe, *Lenten Stuff*, 1599, sig. H1^r).
69   *rook* gull, simpleton (as often, but here glancing at Daw's name).

ACT II, SCENE i

[Enter] MOROSE, MUTE

MOROSE

Cannot I yet find out a more compendious method than by this
trunk to save my servants the labour of speech and mine ears
the discord of sounds? Let me see. All discourses but mine own
afflict me, they seem harsh, impertinent, and irksome. Is it not
possible that thou shouldst answer me by signs, and I appre-   5
hend thee, fellow? Speak not, though I question you. You have
taken the ring off from the street door, as I bade you? Answer
me not by speech but by silence, unless it be otherwise. – Very
good.

       At the breaches, still the fellow makes legs or signs
And you have fastened on a thick quilt or flock-bed on the   10
outside of the door, that if they knock with their daggers or with
brickbats, they can make no noise? But with your leg, your
answer, unless it be otherwise. – Very good. This is not only fit
modesty in a servant, but good state and discretion in a master.
And you have been with Cutbeard, the barber, to have him   15
come to me? – Good. And he will come presently? Answer me
not but with your leg, unless it be otherwise; if it be otherwise,
shake your head or shrug. –

                   [MUTE *makes a leg*]
So. Your Italian and Spaniard are wise in these, and it is a frugal
and comely gravity. How long will it be ere Cutbeard come?   20
Stay, if an hour, hold up your whole hand; if half an hour, two
fingers; if a quarter, one. –

            [MUTE *holds up one finger bent*]

1   *compendious* expeditious, direct.
2   *trunk* A pipe in the wall for communicating with different parts of the house, such
       as Dol uses in *Alch.*, I.iv.5.
4   *impertinent* irrelevant.
7   *ring* (circular) door-knocker.
9   s.d. *breaches* breaks (in the text).
       s.d. *makes legs* bows (by drawing back one leg and bending the other).
10   *flock-bed* mattress stuffed with wool or cotton waste.
12   *brickbats* pieces of brick.
14   *state* dignity of demeanour.
      discretion judgement.
21   *your* F[b] (you F[a]).

Good; half a quarter? 'Tis well. And have you given him a key to
come in without knocking? – Good. And is the lock oiled, and
the hinges, today? – Good. And the quilting of the stairs nowhere   25
worn out and bare? – Very good. I see by much doctrine and
impulsion, it may be effected. Stand by. The Turk in this divine
discipline is admirable, exceeding all the potentates of the earth;
still waited on by mutes, and all his commands so executed, yea,
even in the war, as I have heard, and in his marches, most of his   30
charges and directions given by signs and with silence: an exquisite art! And I am heartily ashamed and angry oftentimes that
the princes of Christendom should suffer a barbarian to transcend 'em in so high a point of felicity. I will practise it hereafter.
                                    One winds a horn without

How now? Oh! oh! What villain, what prodigy of mankind is   35
that? – Look.

                    [Exit MUTE. *Horn sounds again]*
– Oh! cut his throat, cut his throat! What murderer, hell-hound,
devil can this be?

                    [Enter MUTE*]*

MUTE

It is a post from the court –

MOROSE

Out, rogue! And must thou blow thy horn too?   40

MUTE

Alas, it is a post from the court, sir, that says he must speak with
you, pain of death –

MOROSE

Pain of thy life, be silent!

---

25 *quilting* padding (*OED* has no example before 1710). Another sign of Morose's
    oddity: floor carpets did not begin to be widely used in England before the
    eighteenth century.
26 *doctrine* teaching (Latin *doctrina*).
27 *impulsion* influence, instigation.
    by to one side.
28 *discipline* branch of instruction.
29 *still* always.
31 *charges . . . directions* orders . . . instructions for the deployment of troops.
34 s.d. *winds* blows.
35 *prodigy* monster.
39 *post* express messenger (who often announced his arrival by blowing a horn).
40 *Out* exclamation expressing reproach.
41 *with* F^b (om. F^a).

ACT II, SCENE ii

[*Enter*] TRUEWIT [*carrying a post-horn and a halter*]

TRUEWIT

By your leave, sir – I am a stranger here – is your name Master
Morose? – [*To* MUTE] Is your name Master Morose? Fishes,
Pythagoreans all! This is strange! What say you, sir? Nothing?
Has Harpocrates been here with his club among you? – Well, sir,
I will believe you to be the man at this time; I will venture upon   5
you, sir. Your friends at court commend 'em to you, sir –

MOROSE [*Aside*]

Oh men! Oh manners! Was there ever such an impudence?

TRUEWIT

And are extremely solicitous for you, sir.

MOROSE

Whose knave are you?

TRUEWIT

Mine own knave and your compeer, sir.   10

MOROSE

Fetch me my sword –

TRUEWIT

You shall taste the one half of my dagger if you do, groom, and
you the other if you stir, sir. Be patient, I charge you in the
King's name, and hear me without insurrection. They say you
are to marry? To marry! Do you mark, sir?   15

MOROSE

How then, rude companion!

---

2   *Fishes* 'As mute as a fish' (Tilley, F300).
3   *Pythagoreans* Ironically inappropriate to Morose. The religious society founded by
     Pythagoras vowed itself to silence for the purpose of self-examination.
4   *Harpocrates* The god of silence, represented with a finger over his mouth, and
     occasionally with a club (acquired from Hercules, by confusion).
5   *venture upon* hazard an approach to.
7   *Oh men! Oh manners!* Echoing Cicero's famous 'O tempora, O mores' (*In Catilinam*,
     I.2). An ironic self-identification, in view of Cicero's reputation as the paragon of
     learned eloquence.
     impudence Probably '(instance of) shamelessness' (Latin *impudentia*) rather than
     the modern sense, which is not common before the eighteenth century.
10   *knave* menial; *compeer* equal.
16   *companion* fellow (expressing contempt).

TRUEWIT

Marry, your friends do wonder, sir, the Thames being so near,
wherein you may drown so handsomely; or London Bridge at a
low fall with a fine leap, to hurry you down the stream; or such
a delicate steeple i' the town as Bow, to vault from; or a braver   20
height as Paul's; or if you affected to do it nearer home and
a shorter way, an excellent garret window into the street; or a
beam in the said garret, with this halter, (*He shows him a halter*)
which they have sent, and desire that you would sooner commit
your grave head to this knot than to the wedlock noose; or take   25
a little sublimate and go out of the world like a rat, or a fly, as
one said, with a straw i' your arse: any way rather than to follow
this goblin matrimony. Alas, sir, do you ever think to find a chaste
wife in these times? Now? When there are so many masques,
plays, Puritan preachings, mad folks, and other strange sights   30
to be seen daily, private and public? If you had lived in King
Etheldred's time, sir, or Edward the Confessor's, you might perhaps have found in some cold country hamlet, then, a dull frosty
wench would have been contented with one man; now, they will
as soon be pleased with one leg or one eye. I'll tell you, sir, the   35
monstrous hazards you shall run with a wife.

MOROSE

Good sir! Have I ever cozened any friends of yours of their land?
bought their possessions? taken forfeit of their mortgage?
begged a reversion from 'em? bastarded their issue? What have

17   *Marry* Quibbling on the exclamation of surprise; as if the verb 'to marry' were itself
       an expression of surprise, indignation, and 'wonder' (Partridge).
18–19 *at ... fall* At a low ebb-tide, when it would be difficult to drown from the bank. The
       water gushed with great force from under the bridge, because of the bridge-piers
       which impeded the stream.
20   *Bow* St Mary-le-Bow, in Cheapside.
       braver more splendid, more excellent.
26   *sublimate* mercury sublimate (mercuric chloride, used as rat-poison).
26–7 *fly ... arse* In fly and spider fights, a popular diversion, a straw was thrust into the
       fly's tail.
30   *preachings* F^b (parleys F^a).
       mad folks Viewing the inmates of Bedlam was a popular amusement; a small fee was
       charged.
32   *Etheldred* Ethelred the Unready (978–1016), the father of Edward the Confessor
       (1042–66).
34   *would* who would.
37   *cozened* cheated.
39   *reversion* right of succession to an estate or office.
       from away from.
       bastarded rendered illegitimate.

I done that may deserve this? 40

TRUEWIT

Nothing, sir, that I know, but your itch of marriage.

MOROSE

Why, if I had made an assassinate upon your father, vitiated your mother, ravished your sisters –

TRUEWIT

I would kill you, sir, I would kill you if you had.

MOROSE

Why, you do more in this, sir. It were a vengeance centuple for 45 all facinorous acts that could be named, to do that you do –

TRUEWIT

Alas, sir, I am but a messenger: I but tell you what you must hear. It seems your friends are careful after your soul's health, sir, and would have you know the danger – but you may do your pleasure for all them; I persuade not, sir. If after you are married 50 your wife do run away with a vaulter, or the Frenchman that walks upon ropes, or him that dances the jig, or a fencer for his skill at his weapon, why, it is not their fault; they have discharged their consciences when you know what may happen. Nay, suffer valiantly, sir, for I must tell you all the perils that you are 55 obnoxious to. If she be fair, young, and vegetous, no sweetmeats ever drew more flies; all the yellow doublets and great roses i' the town will be there. If foul and crooked, she'll be with them and buy those doublets and roses, sir. If rich and that you marry her dowry, not her, she'll reign in your house as imperious as 60 a widow. If noble, all her kindred will be your tyrans. If fruitful, as proud as May and humorous as April; she must have her

42   *assassinate* murderous attack.
      vitiated corrupted.
46   *facinorous* wicked, infamous.
51–3 *vaulter ... jig ... weapon* with sexual innuendoes.
52   *ropes* The skill of the French at tightrope-walking is mentioned in *Women Beware Women*, III.iii.122.
53   *discharged* relieved.
56   *obnoxious* open, liable (Latin *obnoxius*).   *to* ed. (too F).
      vegetous lively (Latin *vegetus*).
58–9 *be with them and buy* seek their company and pay for.
59   *roses* rosettes, worn on shoes by gallants, often very ornate.
61   *tyrans* tyrants (Latin *tyrannus*).
62   *proud* (i) exuberant (cf. Shakespeare's Sonnet 98 and *Hamlet*, III.iii.81, 'as flush as May'); (ii) haughty, arrogant; (iii) sexually excited, said of 'a female ... in her heate' (example dated 1615 in *OED*, a., 8.b). Cf. l. 98.

doctors, her midwives, her nurses, her longings every hour, though it be for the dearest morsel of man. If learned, there was never such a parrot; all your patrimony will be too little for the 65 guests that must be invited to hear her speak Latin and Greek, and you must lie with her in those languages too, if you will please her. If precise, you must feast all the silenced brethren once in three days, salute the sisters, entertain the whole family or wood of 'em, and hear long-winded exercises, singings, and 70 catechizings, which you are not given to and yet must give for, to please the zealous matron your wife, who for the holy cause will cozen you over and above. You begin to sweat, sir? But this is not half, i' faith; you may do your pleasure notwithstanding, as I said before; I come not to persuade you. – 75

The MUTE *is stealing away*

Upon my faith, master servingman, if you do stir, I will beat you.

MOROSE

Oh, what is my sin, what is my sin?

TRUEWIT

Then, if you love your wife, or rather dote on her, sir, oh, how she'll torture you and take pleasure i' your torments! You shall 80 lie with her but when she lists; she will not hurt her beauty, her complexion; or it must be for that jewel or that pearl when she does; every half hour's pleasure must be bought anew, and with the same pain and charge you wooed her at first. Then you must keep what servants she please, what company she will; that 85 friend must not visit you without her licence; and him she loves

---

62   *humorous* capricious.
64   *morsel* with a sexual innuendo.
65   *parrot* Cf. the learned Lady Would-be, wife of Sir Pol, in *Volp.*
68   *precise* a Puritan.
      silenced brethren Puritan clergy who refused to conform to the canons passed at the Hampton Court conference of 1604 and lost their licences to preach; Tribulation Wholesome's 'silenced saints' in *Alch.*, III.i.38.
70   *wood* Latin *silva* could mean a crowd or collection of anything, not only trees. Punning on *wood* = 'mad', as *in Alch.*, III.ii.98.
      exercises religious observances.
73   *over and above* into the bargain.
75   *before*; ed. (before, F).
82   *complexion* face make-up, as at I.i.106.
84   *pain and charge* trouble and cost.

most she will seem to hate eagerliest, to decline your jealousy;
or feign to be jealous of you first, and for that cause go live with
her she-friend or cousin at the college, that can instruct her in
all the mysteries of writing letters, corrupting servants, taming   90
spies; where she must have that rich gown for such a great day,
a new one for the next, a richer for the third; be served in silver;
have the chamber filled with a succession of grooms, footmen,
ushers, and other messengers, besides embroiderers, jewellers,
tire-women, sempsters, feathermen, perfumers; while she feels   95
not how the land drops away, nor the acres melt, nor foresees
the change when the mercer has your woods for her velvets;
never weighs what her pride costs, sir, so she may kiss a page
or a smooth chin that has the despair of a beard; be a stateswoman, know all the news; what was done at Salisbury, what at the   100
Bath, what at court, what in progress; or so she may censure poets
and authors and styles, and compare 'em, Daniel with Spenser,

87   *eagerliest* most fiercely.
       decline avert.
89   *she-friend or cousin* Both terms could mean 'mistress' or 'strumpet', and *cousin* was
       also a euphemism for 'lover'; Jonson's substitution for Juvenal's 'wife's mother'.
91   *spies* Cf. Volpone to Celia: 'Cannot we delude the eyes / Of a few poore household-
       spies?' (*Volp.*, III.vii.175–6).
92   *silver* A mark of Bianca's finicky upper-classness in *Women Beware Women*, III.i.76,
       is the demand to be 'served all in silver' rather than the normal household pewter.
94   *and . . . messengers* Implying that all these servants would be there to act as go-
       betweens in amorous intrigues.
95   *tire-women* dressmakers.
       sempsters men or women who sew.
       feathermen dealers in feathers and plumes.
97   *change* punning on 'exchange'.
       mercer dealer in fabrics, especially silk and velvet.
98   *so* as long as.
99   *despair of a beard* The accusations of sexual unnaturalness here and down to l. 107
       are paralleled in Jonson's attack on Cecilia Bulstrode (d. 1609), 'An Epigram on the
       Court Pucelle', 7–12: 'What though with Tribade [= lesbian] lust she force a Muse,
       / And in an Epicoene fury can write newes / Equall with that, which for the best
       newes goes, / . . . What though she talke, and can at once with them, / Make State,
       Religion, Bawdrie, all a theame?'
99–100 *stateswoman* Jonson's satiric coinage for a Jacobean impossibility: a female politician.
100–1   *Salisbury . . . Bath* Fashionable places for race-meetings and medicinal bathing
       respectively.
101   *progress* monarch's state visit to the provinces.
       censure judge.
102   *Daniel . . . Spenser* H&S cite several instances of contemporaries comparing them,
       and Jonson reviews them together, very uncomplimentarily, in a conversation with
       Drummond (H&S, I, 132).

Jonson with the tother youth, and so forth; or be thought
cunning in controversies or the very knots of divinity, and have
often in her mouth the state of the question, and then skip to   105
the mathematics and demonstration, and answer in religion to
one, in state to another, in bawdry to a third.

MOROSE

Oh, oh!

TRUEWIT

All this is very true, sir. And then her going in disguise to that
conjuror and this cunning woman, where the first question is,   110
how soon you shall die? next, if her present servant love her?
next that, if she shall have a new servant? and how many? which
of her family would make the best bawd, male or female? what
precedence she shall have by her next match? And sets down the
answers, and believes 'em above the scriptures. Nay, perhaps   115
she'll study the art.

MOROSE

Gentle sir, ha' you done? Ha' you had your pleasure o' me? I'll
think of these things.

TRUEWIT

Yes, sir; and then comes reeking home of vapour and sweat
with going afoot, and lies in a month of a new face, all oil and   120

---

103   *tother youth* Probably Shakespeare: by 1609 it must have been as commonplace to
       compare the two leading dramatists of the time as it became after the Restoration.
       Jonson had much to say about Shakespeare, who had acted in two of his plays and
       may have assisted the start of his career; here he humorously makes Truewit unable
       to remember his name. However, the joke is affectionate, not hostile: neither
       Shakespeare nor Jonson was a 'youth' in 1609. In Juvenal the comparison is between
       Virgil and Homer.
104   *cunning* skilful.
       knots essential (and most difficult) points.
105   *state* in rhetoric, the principal point at issue (Latin *status*); cf. V.iii.31.
106   *demonstration* making evident by reasoning.
107   *state* politics.
110   *conjuror* wizard, astrologer.
       cunning woman or wise woman, who told fortunes.
112   *servant* in the amatory sense of The Persons of the Play, l. 6.
113   *bawd* pander.
114   *precedence* right of preceding others at formal social occasions.
       match marriage.
116   *study* i.e. practise (the art of fortune-telling).
119   *reeking* (i) steaming; (ii) stinking (a sense not recorded in *OED* before 1710).
120   *lies . . . of* i.e. before giving birth to.

birdlime, and rises in asses' milk, and is cleansed with a new
fucus. God b' w' you, sir. One thing more, which I had almost
forgot. This too, with whom you are to marry may have made a
conveyance of her virginity aforehand, as your wise widows do
of their states, before they marry, in trust to some friend, sir.   125
Who can tell? Or if she have not done it yet, she may do, upon
the wedding day, or the night before, and antedate you cuckold.
The like has been heard of in nature. 'Tis no devised, impossible
thing, sir. God b' w' you. I'll be bold to leave this rope with you,
sir, for a remembrance. – Farewell, Mute.   [*Exit*]   130

MOROSE

Come, ha' me to my chamber, but first shut the door.

The horn again

Oh, shut the door, shut the door. Is he come again?

[*Enter* CUTBEARD]

CUTBEARD

'Tis I, sir, your barber.

MOROSE

Oh, Cutbeard, Cutbeard, Cutbeard! here has been a cutthroat
with me: help me in to my bed, and give me physic with thy   135
counsel.

[*Exeunt*]

---

121   *birdlime*, 'i.e. viscous and glutinous unguents and cataplasms for beautifying the
face' (Upton).
rises Like Venus rising from the waves at her birth. Many editors have suppressed this
ironic parallel by emending to 'rinses', on the grounds that this is the sense in Juvenal,
but Juvenal's *fovetur* does not clearly mean this, and anyway Jonson is not tied in this
pedestrian way to his sources. Cf. Belinda's toilet in *The Rape of the Lock*, 140: 'The
fair each moment rises in her charms'.
122   *fucus* Wash or colouring for the face (Latin *fucus*), coined by Jonson in *C.R.*, V.ii.391.
124   *conveyance* legal transference of property from one person to another.
125   *states* estates.
friend punning on the sense 'lover'.
128   *devised* invented, contrived.
130   *remembrance* reminder (*OED*, sb., 8.c; earliest example, 1617).

ACT II, SCENE iii

[*Enter*] DAW, CLERIMONT, DAUPHINE, EPICOENE

DAW

Nay, and she will, let her refuse at her own charges; 'tis nothing
to me, gentlemen. But she will not be invited to the like feasts or
guests every day.

CLERIMONT

Oh, by no means, she may not refuse – (*they dissuade her
privately*) to stay at home if you love your reputation. 'Slight,   5
you are invited thither o' purpose to be seen and laughed at by
the lady of the college and her shadows. This trumpeter hath
proclaimed you.

DAUPHINE

You shall not go; let him be laughed at in your stead, for not
bringing you, and put him to his extemporal faculty of fooling   10
and talking loud to satisfy the company.

CLERIMONT

He will suspect us, talk aloud. – Pray, Mistress Epicoene, let's see
your verses; we have Sir John Daw's leave; do not conceal your
servant's merit and your own glories.

EPICOENE

They'll prove my servant's glories if you have his leave so soon.   15

DAUPHINE [*Aside to* EPICOENE]

His vainglories, lady!

DAW

Show 'em, show 'em, mistress, I dare own 'em.

EPICOENE

Judge you what glories!

1	*and* if.
	charges cost.
7	*shadows* parasites, toadies.
	This trumpeter Daw.
10	*fooling* acting foolishly.
11	*satisfy* i.e. with an explanation.
15	*glories* (i) triumphs; (ii) boasts.
17	*own* acknowledge as my own.

DAW

Nay, I'll read 'em myself too: an author must recite his own
works. It is a madrigal of modesty. 20
     'Modest and fair, for fair and good are near
               Neighbours, howe'er' –

DAUPHINE

Very good.

CLERIMONT

Ay, is't not?

DAW

     'No noble virtue ever was alone, 25
           But two in one.'

DAUPHINE

Excellent!

CLERIMONT

That again, I pray, Sir John.

DAUPHINE

It has something in't like rare wit and sense.

CLERIMONT

Peace. 30

DAW

     'No noble virtue ever was alone,
           But two in one.
    Then, when I praise sweet modesty, I praise
           Bright beauty's rays:
   And having praised both beauty' and modestee, 35
           I have praised thee.'

DAUPHINE

Admirable!

CLERIMONT

How it chimes, and cries tink i' the close, divinely!

20   *madrigal of* love lyric concerning.
21 ff. Daw's 'own works' in fact comprise two platitudes; cf. P. Charron, *Of Wisdom*, 1612,
       p. 18, '*Faire* and good are neere neighbours', and Anon., *England's Parnassus, or The*
       Choicest Flowers of our Modern Poets, 1600, p. 292, 'The simple vertue may consist
       alone, / But better are two vertues joynd in one'.
35   *beauty'* indicating the elision of a syllable.
38   *chimes* The word suggested for Jonson the mechanical and overemphatic rhymes of
       ballads; in *N.T.*, 162, contrasting poetry and ballads, he compares 'Musick with the
       vulgars chime'.
       close Conclusion of a musical phrase, continuing the ballad comparison; cf. the
       prisoners' drinking-song in W. Cartwright's *The Royal Slave* (1636), I.i.19: 'And make
       our hard Irons cry clinke in the Close'.

DAUPHINE

    Ay, 'tis Seneca.

CLERIMONT

    No, I think 'tis Plutarch.   40

DAW

    The dor on Plutarch, and Seneca, I hate it: they are mine own
    imaginations, by that light. I wonder those fellows have such
    credit with gentlemen!

CLERIMONT

    They are very grave authors.

DAW

    Grave asses! Mere essayists! A few loose sentences, and that's all.   45
    A man would talk so his whole age; I do utter as good things
    every hour, if they were collected and observed, as either of 'em.

DAUPHINE

    Indeed, Sir John!

CLERIMONT

    He must needs, living among the Wits and Braveries too.

DAUPHINE

    Ay, and being president of 'em as he is.   50

DAW

    There's Aristotle, a mere commonplace fellow; Plato, a dis-
    courser; Thucydides and Livy, tedious and dry; Tacitus, an entire
    knot, sometimes worth the untying, very seldom.

39–40   *Seneca . . . Plutarch* Whose essays were regarded as storehouses of moral wisdom.
           Part of the joke lies in the suggestion that the poem is prosaic enough to be mistaken
           for a prose essay (Partridge).

41   *The dor on* I scoff at, a set phrase. An audience could also understand *daw*, as though
           Daw were using his own name as a term of abuse.

42   *imaginations* inventions.
           by that light variant of 'By God's light' (cf. ' 'Slight', l. 5).

44   *grave* weighty (Latin *gravis*).

45   *essayists* Jonson himself voices a low opinion of modern essayists, 'even their Master
           Mountaigne', in *Disc*, 719 ff. Punning on 'asses'.
           sentences maxims (Latin *sententiae*).

51–3   As Partridge notes, Daw's comments have an appositeness of which he is unaware.
           Aristotle, whom Jonson hails in *Disc*, 2569, as one who 'understood the Causes of
           things', could be accurately described as the great philosopher of the 'common place'
           (Latin *locus communis*), the universal truth; Plato wrote dialogues which exemplified
           the art of learning through discourse; 'tedious' is close in sound to 'Thucydides';
           'Livy' suggests 'livid' (Latin *liveo*), the colour of melancholy, the 'dry' humour; *tacitus*
           in Latin means 'secret, hidden', which goes well with 'knot' in the sense at II.ii.104.

51   *There's* F corr. (There is F uncorr.).
           commonplace fellow ed. (common place-fellow F).

CLERIMONT

What do you think of the poets, Sir John?

DAW

Not worthy to be named for authors. Homer, an old, tedious,   55
prolix ass, talks of curriers and chines of beef; Virgil, of dunging
of land and bees; Horace, of I know not what.

CLERIMONT

I think so.

DAW

And so Pindarus, Lycophron, Anacreon, Catullus, Seneca the
tragedian, Lucan, Propertius, Tibullus, Martial, Juvenal, Ausonius,   60
Statius, Politian, Valerius Flaccus, and the rest –

CLERIMONT

What a sackful of their names he has got!

DAUPHINE

And how he pours 'em out! Politian with Valerius Flaccus!

CLERIMONT

Was not the character right of him?

DAUPHINE

As could be made, i' faith.   65

DAW

And Persius, a crabbed coxcomb not to be endured.

DAUPHINE

Why, whom do you account for authors, Sir John Daw?

DAW

Syntagma juris civilis, Corpus juris civilis, Corpus juris canonici,
the King of Spain's Bible.

56   *curriers and chines* groomers of horses and backbones (because horses figure pro-
      minently in *The Iliad*, and at VII, 321 Agamemnon gives Ajax 'the whole length of
      the chine' of an ox). Daw's slack syntax also permits the senses 'groomers of cattle'
      and 'makers of beef curry'.

56–7 *dunging . . . bees* In *Georgics*, I, 79–81 and IV respectively; there are also some famous
      similes concerning bees in the *Aeneid*. More ambiguous syntax.

57   *of . . . what* Appropriately, in view of Jonson's description of Horace as 'the best
      master, both of vertue, and wisdome' (*Disc*, 2592).

59–61 A chaotic jumble of major, minor, and very obscure classical poets, with an Italian
      humanist, Politian (Angelo Poliziano, 1454–94), absurdly included. 'Seneca the
      tragedian' implies that Daw thinks this writer is different from the Seneca of ll. 39, 41
      (a common mistake at this time).

62–5 Probably spoken ironically in Daw's hearing.

64   *character* character sketch (at I.ii.66 ff.).

68–9 *Syntagma . . . Bible* Titles which Daw has seen on the spines of books and mistaken
      for names of authors. The first two are the same book, the standard collection of
      Roman law, since *syntagma* is Greek for *corpus;* the third is the collection of canon
      law, the fourth the polyglot Bible sponsored by Philip II, known as the *Biblia Regia.*

DAUPHINE

Is the King of Spain's Bible an author? 70

CLERIMONT

Yes, and *Syntagma*.

DAUPHINE

What was that *Syntagma*, sir?

DAW

A civil lawyer, a Spaniard.

DAUPHINE

Sure, *Corpus* was a Dutchman.

CLERIMONT

Ay, both the Corpuses, I knew 'em: they were very corpulent 75
authors.

DAW

And then there's Vatablus, Pomponatius, Symancha; the other
are not to be received within the thought of a scholar.

DAUPHINE

'Fore God, you have a simple learned servant, lady, in titles.

CLERIMONT

I wonder that he is not called to the helm and made a coun- 80
cillor!

DAUPHINE

He is one extraordinary.

CLERIMONT

Nay, but in ordinary! To say truth, the state wants such.

DAUPHINE

Why, that will follow.

CLERIMONT

I muse a mistress can be so silent to the dotes of such a servant. 85

DAW

'Tis her virtue, sir. I have written somewhat of her silence too.

DAUPHINE

In verse, Sir John?

---

72   *What* who.
74   *Dutchman* The English thought of the Dutch as chronically fat, due to a diet largely
      composed of butter and alcohol.
77   *Vatablus, Pomponatius, Symancha* Minor sixteenth-century continental scholars.
79   *simple* purely, absolutely (with an ironic pun).
82   *extraordinary* outside the regular staff (with an ironic pun).
83   *in ordinary* full-time, belonging to the regular staff.
      wants requires, punning ironically on 'lacks'.
85   *dotes* natural gifts, endowments (Latin *dotes*), glancing at *dote*, 'to act stupidly'.

CLERIMONT

What else?

DAUPHINE

Why, how can you justify your own being of a poet, that so
slight all the old poets?   90

DAW

Why, every man that writes in verse is not a poet; you have of
the Wits that write verses and yet are no poets: they are poets
that live by it, the poor fellows that live by it.

DAUPHINE

Why, would not you live by your verses, Sir John?

CLERIMONT

No, 'twere pity he should. A knight live by his verses? He did not   95
make 'em to that end, I hope.

DAUPHINE

And yet the noble Sidney lives by his, and the noble family not
ashamed.

CLERIMONT

Ay, he professed himself; but Sir John Daw has more caution:
he'll not hinder his own rising i' the state so much! Do you   100
think he will? Your verses, good Sir John, and no poems.

DAW

'Silence in woman is like speech in man,
Deny't who can.'

DAUPHINE

Not I, believe it; your reason, sir.

DAW

'Nor is't a tale   105
That female vice should be a virtue male,

91–3   *every . . . it* Daw is making a standard distinction between two sorts of poet, the
professional, such as Spenser, Drayton, and Jonson himself, who made a living from
his pen by having his work printed, and the gentleman amateur, such as Sidney or
Greville, who wrote for a small circle of friends and shunned print as socially
lowering. However, Daw fogs the issue by combining with it his own topsy-turvy
distinction between the poet and the verser. For Daw, who, like Hedon in *C.R.*,
II.i.48–9, regards himself as 'a rimer, and thats a thought better then a poet', 'poets'
are contemptible fellows who get a living from their work, whereas those who just
write verse are your true wits.

97   *lives by* Sidney had died in 1586, and his work had been published, with his family's
permission, during the 1590s.

99   *professed* openly declared.

104   s.p. *DAW* ed. (*DAV.* F).

105–11 *tale . . . peace . . . conceive* Unconscious sexual puns.

222

Or masculine vice, a female virtue be:
          You shall it see
          Proved with increase,
    I know to speak, and she to hold her peace.'   110
  Do you conceive me, gentlemen?

DAUPHINE

  No, faith; how mean you 'with increase', Sir John?

DAW

  Why, 'with increase' is when I court her for the common cause
  of mankind, and she says nothing, but *consentire videtur*, and in
  time is *gravida*.   115

DAUPHINE

  Then this is a ballad of procreation?

CLERIMONT

  A madrigal of procreation; you mistake.

EPICOENE

  Pray give me my verses again, servant.

DAW

  If you'll ask 'em aloud, you shall.

                          [*Walks apart with* EPICOENE]

CLERIMONT

  See, here's Truewit again!   120

ACT II, SCENE iv

[*Enter*] TRUEWIT [*with his post-horn*]

CLERIMONT

  Where hast thou been, in the name of madness, thus accoutred
  with thy horn?

TRUEWIT

  Where the sound of it might have pierced your senses with
  gladness had you been in ear-reach of it. Dauphine, fall down

---

114   *consentire videtur* she seems to consent.
115   *gravida* pregnant.
116   *ballad* Jonson, like many of his literary contemporaries, detested 'th' abortive, and
        extemporall dinne / Of balladrie' (*N.T.*, 163–4).
119   *you'll* ed. (you you'll F).

  2   *accoutred* equipped.

and worship me: I have forbid the banns, lad. I have been with   5
thy virtuous uncle and have broke the match.

DAUPHINE
You ha' not, I hope.

TRUEWIT
Yes, faith; and thou shouldst hope otherwise, I should repent
me. This horn got me entrance, kiss it. I had no other way to get
in but by feigning to be a post; but when I got in once, I proved   10
none, but rather the contrary, turned him into a post or a stone
or what is stiffer, with thund'ring into him the incommodities
of a wife and the miseries of marriage. If ever Gorgon were seen
in the shape of a woman, he hath seen her in my description.
I have put him off o' that scent forever. Why do you not applaud   15
and adore me, sirs? Why stand you mute? Are you stupid? You
are not worthy o' the benefit.

DAUPHINE
Did not I tell you? mischief! –

CLERIMONT
I would you had placed this benefit somewhere else.

TRUEWIT
Why so?   20

CLERIMONT
'Slight, you have done the most inconsiderate, rash, weak thing
that ever man did to his friend.

DAUPHINE
Friend! If the most malicious enemy I have had studied to inflict
an injury upon me, it could not be a greater.

TRUEWIT
Wherein, for God's sake? Gentlemen, come to yourselves again.   25

DAUPHINE
But I presaged thus much afore to you.

CLERIMONT
Would my lips had been soldered when I spake on't. 'Slight, what
moved you to be thus impertinent?

---

5   *forbid the banns* made a formal objection to the intended marriage.
12   *incommodities* hurtful disadvantages.
13   *Gorgon* One of the three female monsters of classical legend; anyone who met their
      gaze was turned to stone.
16   *stupid* stupefied (Latin *stupidus*), glancing also at the current sense.
26   *presaged* gave warning of (see I.iii.1–9).

TRUEWIT

My masters, do not put on this strange face to pay my courtesy;
off with this visor. Have good turns done you and thank 'em   30
this way?

DAUPHINE

'Fore heav'n, you have undone me. That which I have plotted
for and been maturing now these four months, you have blasted
in a minute. Now I am lost, I may speak. This gentlewoman was
lodged here by me o' purpose, and, to be put upon my uncle,   35
hath professed this obstinate silence for my sake, being my
entire friend, and one that for the requital of such a fortune
as to marry him, would have made me very ample conditions;
where now all my hopes are utterly miscarried by this unlucky
accident.   40

CLERIMONT

Thus 'tis when a man will be ignorantly officious, do services
and not know his why. I wonder what courteous itch possessed
you! You never did absurder part i' your life, nor a greater trespass to friendship, to humanity.

DAUPHINE

Faith, you may forgive it best; 'twas your cause principally.   45

CLERIMONT

I know it; would it had not.

[*Enter* CUTBEARD]

DAUPHINE

How now, Cutbeard, what news?

CUTBEARD

The best, the happiest that ever was, sir. There has been a mad
gentleman with your uncle this morning – [*seeing* TRUEWIT]
I think this be the gentleman – that has almost talked him out   50
of his wits with threat'ning him from marriage –

DAUPHINE

On, I pray thee.

32–4   *That . . . minute* The metaphor is provided by *plot* = 'plot out land', as in Marvell's
        'An Horatian Ode', 31.
34   *Now . . . speak* 'Give losers leave to speak' (Tilley, L458).
35   *put upon* combining two senses: to trick, by being imposed upon him.
37–8   *for . . . him* in return for the fortune she would gain by marrying him.
38   *conditions* provisions, settlement.
43   *did* played.
45   *your cause* i.e. your fault.

CUTBEARD

> And your uncle, sir, he thinks 'twas done by your procurement; therefore he will see the party you wot of presently, and if he like her, he says, and that she be so inclining to dumb as I have told him, he swears he will marry her today, instantly, and not defer it a minute longer. 55

DAUPHINE

> Excellent! Beyond our expectation!

TRUEWIT

> Beyond your expectation? By this light, I knew it would be thus.

DAUPHINE

> Nay, sweet Truewit, forgive me. 60

TRUEWIT

> No, I was 'ignorantly officious, impertinent'; this was the 'absurd, weak part'.

CLERIMONT

> Wilt thou ascribe that to merit now, was mere fortune?

TRUEWIT

> Fortune? Mere providence. Fortune had not a finger in't. I saw it must necessarily in nature fall out so: my genius is never false 65 to me in these things. Show me how it could be otherwise.

DAUPHINE

> Nay, gentlemen, contend not; 'tis well now.

TRUEWIT

> Alas, I let him go on with 'inconsiderate', and 'rash', and what he pleased.

CLERIMONT

> Away, thou strange justifier of thyself, to be wiser than thou wert 70 by the event.

TRUEWIT

> Event! By this light, thou shalt never persuade me but I foresaw it as well as the stars themselves

DAUPHINE

> Nay, gentlemen, 'tis well now. Do you two entertain Sir John

---

54   *wot* know.
       presently immediately.
55   *dumb* dumbness (a common idiom).
63   *was* which was.
64   *Mere* nothing short of, sheer.
       providence foreknowledge.
65   *genius* attendant spirit.
71   *event* outcome.

Daw with discourse while I send her away with instructions.　　75

TRUEWIT

I'll be acquainted with her first, by your favour.

[They approach EPICOENE *and* DAW]

CLERIMONT

Master Truewit, lady, a friend of ours.

TRUEWIT

I am sorry I have not known you sooner, lady, to celebrate this
rare virtue of your silence.

CLERIMONT

Faith, an' you had come sooner, you should ha' seen and heard　80
her well celebrated in Sir John Daw's madrigals.

[Exeunt DAUPHINE, EPICOENE, *and* CUTBEARD]

TRUEWIT

Jack Daw, God save you, when saw you La Foole?

DAW

Not since last night, Master Truewit.

TRUEWIT

That's miracle! I thought you two had been inseparable.

DAW

He's gone to invite his guests.　　85

TRUEWIT

Gods so, 'tis true! What a false memory have I towards that man!
I am one: I met him e'en now upon that he calls his delicate fine
black horse, rid into a foam with posting from place to place
and person to person to give 'em the cue –

CLERIMONT

Lest they should forget?　　90

TRUEWIT

Yes; there was never poor captain took more pains at a muster
to show men than he at this meal to show friends.

DAW

It is his quarter-feast, sir.

CLERIMONT

What, do you say so, Sir John?

79　　*rare* (i) excellent; (ii) very uncommon.
87　　*delicate* exquisite.
91　　*poor* The corruptness of officers' recruiting methods at this time, for motives of
　　　profit, was notorious.
93　　*quarter-feast* Daw's sarcastic coinage from *quarter-day*, one of the four days of the
　　　year on which rents fall due.

TRUEWIT

Nay, Jack Daw will not be out, at the best friends he has, to the   95
talent of his wit. Where's his mistress, to hear and applaud him?
Is she gone?

DAW

Is Mistress Epicoene gone?

CLERIMONT

Gone afore with Sir Dauphine, I warrant, to the place.

TRUEWIT

Gone afore! That were a manifest injury, a disgrace and a half,   100
to refuse him at such a festival time as this, being a Bravery and
a Wit too.

CLERIMONT

Tut, he'll swallow it like cream: he's better read in *jure civili* than
to esteem anything a disgrace is offered him from a mistress.

DAW

Nay, let her e'en go; she shall sit alone and be dumb in her   105
chamber a week together, for Sir John Daw, I warrant her. Does
she refuse me?

CLERIMONT

No, sir, do not take it so to heart: she does not refuse you, but
a little neglect you. Good faith, Truewit, you were too blame to
put it into his head that she does refuse him.   110

TRUEWIT

She does refuse him, sir, palpably, however you mince it. An'
I were as he, I would swear to speak ne'er a word to her today
for't.

DAW

By this light, no more I will not.

TRUEWIT

Nor to anybody else, sir.   115

DAW

Nay, I will not say so, gentlemen.

95–6   *out ... wit* 'he wil sooner lose his best friend, then his least jest' (*Poet.*, IV.iii.110–11).
103   *jure civili* civil law, one of Daw's 'authors' at II.iii.68.
106   *for* as far as ... is concerned.
109   *too blame*. The phrase was commonly understood as adverb plus adjective.
111   *mince* make light of.

CLERIMONT

It had been an excellent happy condition for the company if you could have drawn him to it.

DAW

I'll be very melancholic, i' faith.

CLERIMONT

As a dog, if I were as you, Sir John.   120

TRUEWIT

Or a snail or a hog-louse: I would roll myself up for this day; in troth, they should not unwind me.

DAW

By this picktooth, so I will.

CLERIMONT

'Tis well done: he begins already to be angry with his teeth.

DAW

Will you go, gentlemen?   125

CLERIMONT

Nay, you must walk alone if you be right melancholic, Sir John.

TRUEWIT

Yes, sir, we'll dog you, we'll follow you afar off.

[*Exit* DAW]

CLERIMONT

Was there ever such a two yards of knighthood, measured out by time, to be sold to laughter?

TRUEWIT

A mere talking mole! Hang him, no mushroom was ever so fresh.   130
A fellow so utterly nothing, as he knows not what he would be.

---

117   *condition* (i) item in an agreement; (ii) state.

117–18, 124   Spoken ironically in Daw's hearing.

120   *dog* Using the proverb 'As melancholy as a dog' (Tilley, D438) to screen the common term of abuse; cf. IV.ii.5–6.

121   *hog-louse* wood-louse.

121–2   *day; in troth*, ed. (day, introth, F).

123   *picktooth* Toothpick, a mark of the affected gallant; Fastidious Brisk, the fashion-fixated courtier of *E.M.O.*, has a case-full (IV.i.39).

124   *teeth* Glancing at the proverb 'Good that the teeth guard the tongue' (Tilley, T424).

127   *dog* follow, covertly implying 'hound, torment'.

130   *mere* absolute.

        mole Cf. 'As blind as a mole' (Tilley, M1034).

        mushroom Cf. 'these mushrompe gentlemen, / That shoot up in a night to place, and worship' (*E.M.O.*, I.ii.162–3). Jonson often likens social climbers to fungi; cf. *Cat.*, II, 136, and the character Fungoso in *E.M.O.*

CLERIMONT
Let's follow him, but first let's go to Dauphine; he's hovering
about the house to hear what news.
TRUEWIT
Content.

[*Exeunt*]

ACT II, SCENE v

[*Enter*] MOROSE, EPICOENE, CUTBEARD, MUTE

MOROSE
Welcome, Cutbeard; draw near with your fair charge, and in her
ear softly entreat her to unmask,

[CUTBEARD *whispers to* EPICOENE, *who removes her mask*]
So. Is the door shut? –

[MUTE *makes a leg*]
Enough. Now, Cutbeard, with the same discipline I use to my
family, I will question you. As I conceive, Cutbeard, this gentle-   5
woman is she you have provided and brought, in hope she will
fit me in the place and person of a wife? Answer me not but with
your leg, unless it be otherwise. – Very well done, Cutbeard. I
conceive besides, Cutbeard, you have been pre-acquainted with
her birth, education, and qualities, or else you would not prefer   10
her to my acceptance, in the weighty consequence of marriage.
– This I conceive, Cutbeard. Answer me not but with your leg,
unless it be otherwise. – Very well done, Cutbeard. Give aside
now a little, and leave me to examine her condition and apti-
tude to my affection. (*He goes about her and views her*) She is   15
exceeding fair and of a special good favour; a sweet composition or harmony of limbs; her temper of beauty has the true
height of my blood. The knave hath exceedingly well fitted me

1   *your* ed. (you F).
5   *family* household servants (Latin *familia*).
10   *prefer* recommend.
16   *favour* comeliness, beauty.
17–18   *her . . . blood* A roundabout and distinctly unpassionate way of saying 'her beauty is
of exactly the sort which excites my passion'.

without: I will now try her within. – Come near, fair gentlewoman; let not my behaviour seem rude, though unto you, 20
being rare, it may haply appear strange. (*She curtsies*) Nay, lady,
you may speak, though Cutbeard and my man might not: for
of all sounds only the sweet voice of a fair lady has the just
length of mine ears. I beseech you, say, lady; out of the first fire
of meeting eyes, they say, love is stricken: do you feel any such 25
motion suddenly shot into you from any part you see in me?
Ha, lady? (*Curtsy*) Alas, lady, these answers by silent curtsies
from you are too courtless and simple. I have ever had my
breeding in court, and she that shall be my wife must be
accomplished with courtly and audacious ornaments. Can you 30
speak, lady?

EPICOENE

Judge you, forsooth. *She speaks softly*

MOROSE

What say you, lady? Speak out, I beseech you.

EPICOENE

Judge you, forsooth.

MOROSE

O' my judgement, a divine softness! But can you naturally, lady, 35
as I enjoin these by doctrine and industry, refer yourself to
the search of my judgement and, not taking pleasure in your
tongue, which is a woman's chiefest pleasure, think it plausible
to answer me by silent gestures, so long as my speeches jump
right with what you conceive? (*Curtsy*) Excellent! Divine! If it 40
were possible she should hold out thus! Peace, Cutbeard, thou
art made forever, as thou hast made me, if this felicity have
lasting; but I will try her further. Dear lady, I am courtly, I tell
you, and I must have mine ears banqueted with pleasant and

---

19   *try her within* Morose's courtly idiom is continually slipping unconsciously into
     crude sexual innuendo; cf. ll. 29–30, 60–2.
21   *rare* of uncommon excellence.
     haply perhaps.
28   *courtless* affectedly for 'uncourtly' (*OED*'s only example).
30   *audacious* 'Spirited, confident', but suggesting inadvertently 'shameless, brazen'.
35   *softness* Cf. *King Lear*, V.iii.273–4: 'Her voice was ever soft, / Gentle, and low, an
     excellent thing in woman'.
36   *these* Cutbeard and Mute.
     doctrine instruction.
38   *plausible* pleasantly acceptable.
39–40   *jump right* agree.

witty conferences, pretty girds, scoffs, and dalliance in her that   45
I mean to choose for my bed-fere. The ladies in court think it a
most desperate impair to their quickness of wit and good carriage if they cannot give occasion for a man to court 'em, and
when an amorous discourse is set on foot, minister as good
matter to continue it as himself; and do you alone so much   50
differ from all them that what they, with so much circumstance,
affect and toil for, to seem learned, to seem judicious, to seem
sharp and conceited, you can bury in yourself with silence, and
rather trust your graces to the fair conscience of virtue than to
the world's or your own proclamation?   55

EPICOENE

I should be sorry else.

MOROSE

What say you, lady? Good lady, speak out.

EPICOENE

I should be sorry, else.

MOROSE

That sorrow doth fill me with gladness! Oh, Morose, thou art
happy above mankind! Pray that thou mayst contain thyself. I   60
will only put her to it once more, and it shall be with the utmost
touch and test of their sex. – But hear me, fair lady; I do also
love to see her whom I shall choose for my heifer to be the first
and principal in all fashions, precede all the dames at court by a
fortnight, have her council of tailors, lineners, lace-women,   65
embroiderers, and sit with 'em sometimes twice a day upon
French intelligences, and then come forth varied like Nature, or

45   *girds* gibes.
46   *bed-fere* bedfellow.
47   *impair* impairment, injury.
47–8   *carriage* demeanour.
49   *minister* supply.
51   *circumstance* ceremony, to do.
52   *affect* aim at.
53   *conceited* witty.
54   *conscience* inward knowledge.
60   *happy* fortunate.
62   *touch* trial.
63   *heifer* A young cow that has not had a calf, hence 'yoke-mate, bride'. *OED*'s only
       example, apart from the proverb 'To plow with another's heifer' (Tilley, H395).
65   *lineners* linen-drapers.
67   *French intelligences* i.e. news of the latest fashions. Fitzdottrel in *D. is A.* wishes to be
       rich enough to allow his wife 'to sit with your foure women / In councell, and receive
       intelligences. / From forraigne parts, to dress you at all pieces' (II.vii.35–7).

oft'ner than she, and better by the help of Art, her emulous
servant. This do I affect. And how will you be able, lady, with
this frugality of speech, to give the manifold, but necessary,   70
instructions for that bodice, these sleeves, those skirts, this cut,
that stitch, this embroidery, that lace, this wire, those knots, that
ruff, those roses, this girdle, that fan, the tother scarf, these
gloves? Ha? What say you, lady?

EPICOENE

I'll leave it to you, sir.   75

MOROSE

How, lady? Pray you, rise a note.

EPICOENE

I leave it to wisdom and you, sir.

MOROSE

Admirable creature! I will trouble you no more; I will not sin
against so sweet a simplicity. Let me now be bold to print on
those divine lips the seal of being mine. [*Kisses her*] Cutbeard, I   80
give thee the lease of thy house free; thank me not, but with thy
leg. – I know what thou wouldst say, she's poor and her friends
deceased: she has brought a wealthy dowry in her silence, Cutbeard, and in respect of her poverty, Cutbeard, I shall have her
more loving and obedient, Cutbeard. Go thy ways and get me a   85
minister presently, with a soft, low voice, to marry us, and pray
him he will not be impertinent, but brief as he can; away; softly,
Cutbeard.

[*Exit* CUTBEARD]

Sirrah, conduct your mistress into the dining room, your now-
mistress.   90

[*Exeunt* MUTE *and* EPICOENE]

Oh my felicity! How I shall be revenged on mine insolent kinsman and his plots to fright me from marrying! This night I will

---

67–9   *and . . . servant* Sir Epicure Mammon really desires this transformation for Dol:
        'thou shalt ha' thy wardrobe, / Richer then *Natures*, still, to change thy selfe, / And
        vary oftener, for thy pride, then sheer / Or *Art*, her wise, and almost-equall servant'
        (*Alch.*, IV.i.166–9).

69   *affect* love.

71   *cut* ornamental slash in a garment exposing the lining.

72   *wire* frame of wire to support the hair or the ruff.

73   *roses* shoe-roses; see II.ii.59.
        girdle belt.

86   *presently* at once.

87   *impertinent* irrelevant.

get an heir and thrust him out of my blood like a stranger. He
would be knighted, forsooth, and thought by that means to
reign over me, his title must do it: no, kinsman, I will now make   95
you bring me the tenth lord's and the sixteenth lady's letter,
kinsman, and it shall do you no good, kinsman. Your knighthood itself shall come on its knees, and it shall be rejected;
it shall be sued for its fees to execution, and not be redeemed;
it shall cheat at the twelvepenny ordinary, it knighthood, for its   100
diet all the term time, and tell tales for it in the vacation, to
the hostess; or it knighthood shall do worse, take sanctuary in
Coleharbour, and fast. It shall fright all it friends with borrowing letters, and when one of the fourscore hath brought it
knighthood ten shillings, it knighthood shall go to the Cranes   105
or the Bear at the Bridge-foot and be drunk in fear; it shall not
have money to discharge one tavern-reckoning, to invite the old
creditors to forbear it knighthood, or the new that should be,
to trust it knighthood. It shall be the tenth name in the bond, to
take up the commodity of pipkins and stone jugs, and the part   110
thereof shall not furnish it knighthood forth for the attempting of a baker's widow, a brown baker's widow. It shall give it
knighthood's name for a stallion to all gamesome citizens'
wives, and be refused, when the master of a dancing school or –
how do you call him? – the worst reveller in the town is taken;   115

96   *letter* i.e. letter of commendation, character reference.
99   *to execution* as far as execution of the writ of seizure of debtors' goods.
100   *twelvepenny ordinary* One of the more expensive London eating-houses frequented
       by gallants, where gambling was common (hence 'cheat').
       it Archaic form of its, *his*, used in talking to babies.
101   *term time* see I.i.45.
       tell tales 'The wife of the ordinarie gives him his diet, to maintaine her table in
       discourse' (*C.R.*, II.iii.93–4).
103   *Coleharbour* Or Coldharborough, a seedy maze of tenements on Upper Thames
       Street. 'In some obscure way it had acquired the right of sanctuary' (Sugden).
103–4 *borrowing* i.e. begging.
105–6 *Cranes . . . Bear* The Three Cranes on Upper Thames Street and the Bear at the
       Southwark end of London Bridge, well-known taverns.
109–10 *tenth . . . jugs* See I.iv.59–61 and note. As tenth in the list of borrowers forced to
       accept their loan in the form of worthless goods, Dauphine could expect to receive
       only a small share ('part') of the cash when they were sold.
110   *pipkins* small earthenware pots.
112   *brown* (i) coarse and inferior bread; (ii) of (unfashionable) dark complexion, ill-
       favoured; cf. 'brown wench' in *Henry VIII*, III.ii.295.
115   *how* (*How* F). F's capital and italics indicate a reference to Edmund Howes, the public
       chronicler. Jonson repeats the joke in *S.N.*, I.v.32.

it shall want clothes, and by reason of that, wit, to fool to lawyers. It shall not have hope to repair itself by Constantinople,
Ireland, or Virginia; but the best and last fortune to it knighthood shall be to make Dol Tearsheet or Kate Common a lady,
and so it knighthood may eat.   120

                                                            [*Exit*]

ACT II, SCENE vi

[*Enter*] TRUEWIT, DAUPHINE, CLERIMONT

TRUEWIT
Are you sure he is not gone by?

DAUPHINE
No, I stayed in the shop ever since.

CLERIMONT
But he may take the other end of the lane.

DAUPHINE
No, I told him I would be here at this end; I appointed him
hither.   5

TRUEWIT
What a barbarian it is to stay then!

[*Enter* CUTBEARD]

DAUPHINE
Yonder he comes.

CLERIMONT
And his charge left behind him, which is a very good sign,
Dauphine.

---

116   *fool to* Probably 'play the fool in front of, as at IV.v.11, with the idea of 'make up to',
       rather than 'deceive'.
117–18 *Constantinople, Ireland, or Virginia* Places where younger brothers, wastrels, and
       criminals might go to rescue their fortunes or escape the law (Partridge).
119   *Dol Tearsheet or Kate Common* Type names for whores; cf. Dol Tearsheet in *2 Henry
       IV* and Dol Common in *Alch*.

4   *appointed him hither* arranged to meet him here.
6   *barbarian* A bad pun on 'barber'.
       it i.e. he.

235

DAUPHINE

How now, Cutbeard, succeeds it or no?   10

CUTBEARD

Past imagination, sir, *omnia secunda*; you could not have prayed
to have had it so well. *Saltat senex*, as it is i' the proverb; he does
triumph in his felicity, admires the party! He has given me the
lease of my house too! And I am now going for a silent minister
to marry 'em, and away.   15

TRUEWIT

'Slight, get one o' the silenced ministers; a zealous brother would
torment him purely.

CUTBEARD

Cum privilegio, sir.

DAUPHINE

Oh, by no means; let's do nothing to hinder it now; when 'tis
done and finished, I am for you, for any device of vexation.   20

CUTBEARD

And that shall be within this half hour, upon my dexterity,
gentlemen. Contrive what you can in the meantime, *bonis avibus*.
                                                                  [*Exit*]

CLERIMONT

How the slave doth Latin it!

TRUEWIT

It would be made a jest to posterity, sirs, this day's mirth, if
ye will.   25

CLERIMONT

Beshrew his heart that will not, I pronounce.

DAUPHINE

And for my part. What is't?

11–12   *omnia secunda . . . Saltat senex* Roman proverb, here meant literally: 'All's well, the
old boy is cutting capers' (H&S).

16   *silenced ministers* Cf. II.ii.68.

17   *purely* (i) perfectly; (ii) in the true Puritan manner.

18   *Cum privilegio* with authority.

19   *now; when* ed. (now when F).

21   *upon my dexterity* A suitable oath for a barber (H&S); see note to I.ii.34.

22   *bonis avibus* the omens being favourable.

23   *Latin it* lard his talk with scraps of Latin; no doubt a common affectation among
barbers at this time, since they were also surgeons; cf. Middleton's Sweetball in
Anything for a Quiet Life.

TRUEWIT

To translate all La Foole's company and his feast hither today, to celebrate this bridal.

DAUPHINE

Ay, marry, but how will't be done?   30

TRUEWIT

I'll undertake the directing of all the lady guests thither, and then the meat must follow.

CLERIMONT

For God's sake, let's effect it; it will be an excellent comedy of affliction, so many several noises.

DAUPHINE

But are they not at the other place already, think you?   35

TRUEWIT

I'll warrant you for the college-honours: one o' their faces has not the priming colour laid on yet, nor the other her smock sleeked.

CLERIMONT

Oh, but they'll rise earlier than ordinary to a feast.

TRUEWIT

Best go see and assure ourselves.   40

CLERIMONT

Who knows the house?

TRUEWIT

I'll lead you. Were you never there yet?

DAUPHINE

Not I.

CLERIMONT

Nor I.

TRUEWIT

Where ha' you lived then? Not know Tom Otter!   45

---

28   *translate* transfer.
32   *meat* food.
34   *several* different.
35   *the other place* Otter's house.
36   *I'll warrant you for* I can guarantee you about
37   *priming* As though painting a house. *OED*'s first example *ol priming* applied to painting. *smock* Apart from the suggestion of female sexuality which this word often carries (cf. V.i.44 and *Alch.*, V.iv.126, where Dol is called a 'smock-rampant'), the point is that many layers of clothing would remain to go over the smock.
38   *sleeked* smoothed.

CLERIMONT

No. For God's sake, what is he?

TRUEWIT

An excellent animal, equal with your Daw or La Foole, if not transcendent, and does Latin it as much as your barber. He is his wife's subject; he calls her princess, and at such times as these follows her up and down the house like a page, with his hat off, 50 partly for heat, partly for reverence. At this instant he is marshalling of his bull, bear, and horse.

DAUPHINE

What be those, in the name of Sphinx?

TRUEWIT

Why, sir, he has been a great man at the Bear Garden in his time, and from that subtle sport has ta'en the witty denomination of 55 his chief carousing cups. One he calls his bull, another his bear, another his horse. And then he has his lesser glasses, that he calls his deer and his ape, and several degrees of 'em too, and never is well, nor thinks any entertainment perfect, till these be brought out and set o' the cupboard. 60

CLERIMONT

For God's love, we should miss this if we should not go!

TRUEWIT

Nay, he has a thousand things as good that will speak him all day. He will rail on his wife, with certain commonplaces, behind her backhand to her face –

DAUPHINE

No more of him. Let's go see him, I petition you. 65

[*Exeunt*]

---

53   *Sphinx* Who asked riddles.
54   *Bear Garden* Next to Paris Garden on the Bankside, the centre for bull- and bear-baiting; 'the sport was as popular as football is now' (Sugden).
56   *cups* Their lids are in the shape of the animals' heads; cf. IV.ii.117–21.
58   *degrees* sizes.
59   *well* content.
62   *speak* describe, reveal.

ACT III, SCENE i

[*Enter*] OTTER, MISTRESS OTTER.
TRUEWIT, CLERIMONT, DAUPHINE
[*presently follow, unobserved*]

OTTER

Nay, good princess, hear me *pauca verba*.

MISTRESS OTTER

By that light, I'll ha' you chained up with your bull-dogs and
bear-dogs, if you be not civil the sooner. I'll send you to kennel,
i' faith. You were best bait me with your bull, bear, and horse!
Never a time that the courtiers or collegiates come to the house,   5
but you make it a Shrove Tuesday! I would have you get your
Whitsuntide velvet cap and your staff i' your hand to entertain
'em; yes, in troth, do.

OTTER

Not so, princess, neither, but under correction, sweet princess,
gi' me leave – these things I am known to the courtiers by. It is   10
reported to them for my humour, and they receive it so, and do
expect it. Tom Otter's bull, bear, and horse is known all over
England, in *rerum natura*.

MISTRESS OTTER

'Fore me, I will 'na-ture' 'em over to Paris Garden and 'na-ture'
you thither too, if you pronounce 'em again. Is a bear a fit beast,   15
or a bull, to mix in society with great ladies? Think i' your discretion, in any good polity?

1   *pauca verba* Few words, a catch-phrase; appropriate to Otter, since it was 'the
     Benchers [= bar-fly's] phrase' (*E.M.I.*, IV.ii.40), meaning 'drink more, and talk less'.
4   *were best* had best.
     with along with.
6   *Shrove Tuesday* See I.i.143 and note.
7   *velvet cap* Worn during holidays, such as Whitsun-week.
9   *under correction* subject to correction (common expression of deference).
11   *humour* Characteristic oddity, special trick of disposition; here an affectation of a
     humour, as Jonson distinguishes it in *E.M.O.*, Induction, 75 ff.
13   *rerum natura* The phrase often meant 'the universe, the world', but here a more literal
     sense seems intended: 'the natural order of things'.
14   *'Fore me* before me, a common asseveration.
16–17 *discretion* judgement.
17   *good polity* affectedly for 'well-run community' (*OED* has no example of this sense
     of *polity* before 1650).

OTTER

The horse then, good princess.

MISTRESS OTTER

Well, I am contented for the horse; they love to be well horsed,
I know. I love it myself. 20

OTTER

And it is a delicate fine horse this. *Poetarum Pegasus.* Under
correction, princess, Jupiter did turn himself into a – *taurus*, or
bull, under correction, good princess.

MISTRESS OTTER

By my integrity, I'll send you over to the Bankside, I'll commit
you to the master of the Garden, if I hear but a syllable more. 25
Must my house, or my roof, be polluted with the scent of bears
and bulls, when it is perfumed for great ladies? Is this according
to the instrument when I married you? That I would be princess and reign in mine own house, and you would be my subject
and obey me? What did you bring me, should make you thus 30
peremptory? Do I allow you your half-crown a day to spend
where you will among your gamesters, to vex and torment me
at such times as these? Who gives you your maintenance, I pray
you? Who allows you your horse-meat and man's meat? Your
three suits of apparel a year? Your four pair of stockings, one 35
silk, three worsted? Your clean linen, your bands and cuffs,
when I can get you to wear 'em? 'Tis mar'l you ha' 'em on now.
Who graces you with courtiers or great personages, to speak to
you out of their coaches, and come home to your house? Were
you ever so much as looked upon by a lord, or a lady, before I 40
married you, but on the Easter or Whitsun holidays, and then

---

19   *horsed* Glancing at the sexual senses of *ride* and *mount*.
21   *Poetarum Pegasus* The poets' Pegasus. Cf. Jonson's poem on the Apollo room, 12–14:
      'Wine it is the Milk of Venus, / And the Poets' Horse accounted. / Ply it, and you all
      are mounted' (H&S, VIII, 657).
22–3 *Jupiter . . . bull* When he seduced Europa.
28   *instrument* formal legal agreement.
31   *peremptory* Self-willed (*OED*, a., 3), and glancing at the legal term *peremptory
      challenge*, 'an objection without showing any cause' (a., 1).
34   *horse-meat* horse-fodder.
35–6 *three suits . . . worsted* This associates Otter with domestic servants, who were allowed
      this number of suits and wore worsted stockings; cf. *King Lear*, II.ii.17, III.iv.135–6.
36   *bands* collars.
37   *mar'l* marvel.

out at the Banqueting House window, when Ned Whiting or
George Stone were at the stake?

TRUEWIT [*Aside*]

For God's sake, let's go stave her off him.

MISTRESS OTTER

Answer me to that. And did not I take you up from thence in an   45
old greasy buff-doublet, with points, and green vellet sleeves out
at the elbows? You forget this.

TRUEWIT [*Aside*]

She'll worry him, if we help not in time.

[*They come forward*]

MISTRESS OTTER

Oh, here are some o' the gallants! Go to, behave yourself distinctly,
and with good morality, or I protest, I'll take away your exhibition.   50

ACT III, SCENE ii

TRUEWIT

By your leave, fair Mistress Otter, I'll be bold to enter these
gentlemen in your acquaintance.

MISTRESS OTTER

It shall not be obnoxious or difficil, sir.

---

42   *Banqueting House* At Whitehall. Bear-baiting, outside in the courtyard, was among
         the entertainments.

42–3   *Ned Whiting . . . George Stone* Champion bears, the second particularly famous; he
        died in 1606, being baited before the King of Denmark.

44–8   *stave her off . . . him* As in bear-baiting.

46   *buff-doublet* leather jerkin, as worn by common soldiers.
         points laces.
         vellet velvet.

49–50   *distinctly . . . with good morality* Affected phrases for 'well'; *distinctly* is a nonce-usage
        (Latin *distincte*) and this is *OED*'s first example of *morality* = 'moral conduct'.

50   *exhibition* allowance.

3   *obnoxious or difficil* Offensive or troublesome; 'Mrs. Otter's affectation of what she
         thinks is courtly idiom' (Partridge). *OED* does not give this sense of *obnoxious* before
         1675, and *difficil* keeps close to Latin *difficilis*.

241

TRUEWIT

How does my noble captain? Is the bull, bear, and horse in *rerum natura* still?   5

OTTER

Sir, *sic visum superis.*

MISTRESS OTTER

I would you would but intimate 'em, do. Go your ways in, and get toasts and butter made for the woodcocks. That's a fit province for you.

[*Exit* OTTER]

CLERIMONT [*Aside to* TRUEWIT *and* DAUPHINE]

Alas, what a tyranny is this poor fellow married to!   10

TRUEWIT

Oh, but the sport will be anon, when we get him loose.

DAUPHINE

Dares he ever speak?

TRUEWIT

No Anabaptist ever railed with the like licence: but mark her language in the meantime, I beseech you.

MISTRESS OTTER

Gentlemen, you are very aptly come. My cousin, Sir Amorous,   15
will be here briefly.

TRUEWIT

In good time, lady. Was not Sir John Daw here, to ask for him and the company?

MISTRESS OTTER

I cannot assure you, Master Truewit. Here was a very melancholy knight in a ruff, that demanded my subject for somebody,   20
a gentleman, I think.

CLERIMONT

Ay, that was he, lady.

4–5   *in rerum natura* i.e. in existence.

6   *sic visum superis* as those above decree.

7   *intimate* become intimate with, go and join (your animals). Another of Mistress Otter's coinages.

8–9   *get . . . you* The right way to serve woodcock, and 'fit' because a *toast and butter* was a milksop (cf. *1 Henry IV*, IV.ii.21) and a *woodcock* a fool.

13   *Anabaptist* here loosely for 'Puritan'.

    licence (i) lack of restraint; (ii) licence to preach (denied the 'silenced brethren').

16   *briefly* soon.

20   *in a ruff* Suggests that Daw is sporting one of the very large ruffs fashionable among gallants.

    my subject Otter.

MISTRESS OTTER

But he departed straight, I can resolve you.

DAUPHINE

What an excellent choice phrase this lady expresses in!

TRUEWIT

Oh, sir, she is the only authentical courtier that is not naturally   25
bred one, in the city.

MISTRESS OTTER

You have taken that report upon trust, gentlemen.

TRUEWIT

No, I assure you, the court governs it so, lady, in your behalf.

MISTRESS OTTER

I am the servant of the court and courtiers, sir.

TRUEWIT

They are rather your idolaters.   30

MISTRESS OTTER

Not so, sir.

[*Enter* CUTBEARD. DAUPHINE, TRUEWIT *and* CLERIMONT
converse with him apart]

DAUPHINE

How now, Cutbeard? Any cross?

CUTBEARD

Oh, no, sir, *omnia bene.* 'Twas never better o' the hinges, all's
sure. I have so pleased him with a curate that he's gone to't
almost with the delight he hopes for soon.   35

DAUPHINE

What is he for a vicar?

CUTBEARD

One that has catched a cold, sir, and can scarce be heard six
inches off, as if he spoke out of a bulrush that were not picked,
or his throat were full of pith; a fine quick fellow and an excellent barber of prayers. I came to tell you, sir, that you might   40

---

23   *I . . . you* Often singled out by Jonson as an affected phrase; see H&S, IX, 317.
25   *authentical* genuine (*OED*'s only example of this sense).
28   *governs* determines.
32   *cross* hindrance.
33   *omnia bene* all's well.
      o' the hinges on the hinges, running smoothly.
36   *What . . . vicar* what sort of a vicar is he.
38   *as . . . picked* i.e. he has a thin reedy voice.

omnem movere lapidem, as they say, be ready with your vexation.

DAUPHINE

Gramercy, honest Cutbeard; be thereabouts with thy key to let us in.

CUTBEARD

I will not fail you, sir: *ad manum.*   [*Exit*]   45

TRUEWIT

Well, I'll go watch my coaches.

CLERIMONT

Do, and we'll send Daw to you if you meet him not.

[*Exit* TRUEWIT]

MISTRESS OTTER

Is Master Truewit gone?

DAUPHINE

Yes, lady, there is some unfortunate business fallen out.

MISTRESS OTTER

So I judged by the physiognomy of the fellow that came in, and   50
I had a dream last night too of the new pageant and my Lady
Mayoress, which is always very ominous to me. I told it my Lady
Haughty t'other day, when her honour came hither to see some
China stuffs, and she expounded it out of Artemidorus, and
I have found it since very true. It has done me many affronts.   55

CLERIMONT

Your dream, lady?

MISTRESS OTTER

Yes, sir, anything I do but dream o' the city. It stained me a
damask table-cloth, cost me eighteen pound at one time, and
burnt me a black satin gown as I stood by the fire at my Lady
Centaure's chamber in the college another time. A third time, at   60
the lord's masque, it dropped all my wire and my ruff with wax
candle, that I could not go up to the banquet. A fourth time, as

---

41   *omnem movere lapidem* leave no stone unturned.
43   *Gramercy* thanks.
45   *ad manum* (I'm) at hand.
51   *pageant* Entertainment marking the installation of the new Lord Mayor.
54   *Artemidorus.* Second-century Greek author of a treatise on the interpretation of
      dreams.
55   *it* Mistress Otter's confused pronoun references reveal the confusion of her mind
      (Partridge).
61   *lord's* ed. (Lords F).
      wire See II.v.72.

I was taking coach to go to Ware to meet a friend, it dashed me
a new suit all over – a crimson satin doublet and black velvet
skirts – with a brewer's horse, that I was fain to go in and shift   65
me, and kept my chamber a leash of days for the anguish of it.

DAUPHINE

These were dire mischances, lady.

CLERIMONT

I would not dwell in the city, and 'twere so fatal to me.

MISTRESS OTTER

Yes, sir, but I do take advice of my doctor, to dream of it as little
as I can.   70

DAUPHINE

You do well, Mistress Otter.

[*Enter* DAW; CLERIMONT *takes him aside*]

MISTRESS OTTER

Will it please you to enter the house farther, gentlemen?

DAUPHINE

And your favour, lady; but we stay to speak with a knight, Sir
John Daw, who is here come. We shall follow you, lady.

MISTRESS OTTER

At your own time, sir. It is my cousin Sir Amorous his feast –   75

DAUPHINE

I know it, lady.

MISTRESS OTTER

And mine together. But it is for his honour, and therefore I take
no name of it, more than of the place.

DAUPHINE

You are a bounteous kinswoman.

MISTRESS OTTER

Your servant, sir.   [*Exit*]   80

63   *Ware* 20 miles north of London, a favourite spot for assignations; cf. V.i.53.
      friend a common euphemism for 'lover'.
64   *crimson satin* Fashionable and very expensive. Both the colour and the cloth were
      usually associated with the nobility; see M. C. Linthicum, *Costume in the Drama of
      Shakespeare and his Contemporaries*, Oxford, 1936, pp. 123, 151 n.4, 198.
      doublet Normally a man's garment.
65–6 *shift me* change my clothes.
66   *leash* in hunting, a set of three.
68   *fatal* ominous.
75   *Amorous his feast* Jonson calls this form of the genitive 'monstrous Syntaxe' in his
      English Grammar (H&S, VIII, 511).
78   *name* credit.
      the place i.e. its taking place in my house.

ACT III, SCENE iii

[CLERIMONT *comes forward with* DAW]

CLERIMONT

Why, do not you know it, Sir John Daw?

DAW

No, I am a rook if I do.

CLERIMONT

I'll tell you then: she's married by this time! And whereas you
were put i' the head that she was gone with Sir Dauphine, I
assure you Sir Dauphine has been the noblest, honestest friend   5
to you that ever gentleman of your quality could boast of.
He has discovered the whole plot, and made your mistress so
acknowledging and indeed so ashamed of her injury to you, that
she desires you to forgive her, and but grace her wedding with
your presence today – she is to be married to a very good fortune,   10
she says, his uncle, old Morose; and she willed me in private to
tell you that she shall be able to do you more favours, and with
more security now than before.

DAW

Did she say so, i' faith?

CLERIMONT

Why, what do you think of me, Sir John? Ask Sir Dauphine.   15

DAW

Nay, I believe you. Good Sir Dauphine, did she desire me to
forgive her?

DAUPHINE

I assure you, Sir John, she did.

DAW

Nay, then, I do with all my heart, and I'll be jovial.

---

4   *put i' the head* made to think.
6   *of your quality* Ambiguously implying 'someone like you deserves far worse'.
15   s.p. DAW ed. (*DAVP.* F).
18   s.p. DAUPHINE ed. (*CLE.* F).
19   *jovial* Italicized throughout F, probably to indicate Daw's affected use of a word only
     recently coined into English. Partridge suggests that the gallants take it up in ironic
     awareness of its astrological sense (lit. 'pertaining to Jupiter'), since Daw is the
     helplessly susceptible victim of their 'influence'.

CLERIMONT

Yes, for look you, sir, this was the injury to you. La Foole 20
intended this feast to honour her bridal day, and made you the
property to invite the college ladies and promise to bring her;
and then at the time she should have appeared, as his friend, to
have given you the dor. Whereas now, Sir Dauphine has brought
her to a feeling of it, with this kind of satisfaction, that you shall 25
bring all the ladies to the place where she is, and be very jovial;
and there she will have a dinner which shall be in your name,
and so disappoint La Foole, to make you good again and, as it
were, a saver i' the man.

DAW

As I am a knight, I honour her and forgive her heartily. 30

CLERIMONT

About it then presently. Truewit is gone before to confront the
coaches, and to acquaint you with so much if he meet you. Join
with him, and 'tis well.

[*Enter* LA FOOLE]

See, here comes your antagonist, but take you no notice, but be
very jovial. 35

LA FOOLE

Are the ladies come, Sir John Daw, and your mistress?

[*Exit* DAW]

Sir Dauphine! You are exceeding welcome, and honest Master
Clerimont. Where's my cousin? Did you see no collegiates,
gentlemen?

DAUPHINE

Collegiates! Do you not hear, Sir Amorous, how you are abused? 40

LA FOOLE

How, sir!

---

22   *property* tool, mere means.
24   *the dor* A snub; cf. II.iii.41. Methods of 'giving the dor' in situations of sexual rivalry
       are elaborated in *C.R.*, V.ii.
25   *feeling of* sensitivity to.
29   *i' the man* i.e. of your manhood; with a pun on main = (i) the main or overall
       consideration; (ii) the fixed score in the dice game of hazard, which if thrown by
       one player enables the others to be 'savers' (recoup their losses). Most editors emend
       to *main*, but Clerimont's preliminary 'as it were' indicates, as it still does today, that
       he is about to make precisely this kind of verbal joke.
40   *abused* deceived.

CLERIMONT

Will you speak so kindly to Sir John Daw, that has done you such an affront?

LA FOOLE

Wherein, gentlemen? Let me be a suitor to you to know, I beseech you! 45

CLERIMONT

Why, sir, his mistress is married today to Sir Dauphine's uncle, your cousin's neighbour, and he has diverted all the ladies and all your company thither, to frustrate your provision and stick a disgrace upon you. He was here now to have enticed us away from you too, but we told him his own, I think. 50

LA FOOLE

Has Sir John Daw wronged me so inhumanly?

DAUPHINE

He has done it, Sir Amorous, most maliciously, and treacherously; but if you'll be ruled by us, you shall quit him, i' faith.

LA FOOLE

Good gentlemen, I'll make one, believe it! How, I pray?

DAUPHINE

Marry, sir, get me your pheasants, and your godwits, and your 55 best meat, and dish it in silver dishes of your cousin's presently, and say nothing, but clap me a clean towel about you, like a sewer, and bare-headed march afore it with a good confidence – 'tis but over the way, hard by – and we'll second you, where you shall set it o' the board, and bid 'em welcome to't, which 60 shall show 'tis yours and disgrace his preparation utterly; and for your cousin, whereas she should be troubled here at home with care of making and giving welcome, she shall transfer all that labour thither and be a principal guest herself, sit ranked with the college-honours, and be honoured, and have her health 65 drunk as often, as bare, and as loud as the best of 'em.

---

48 *provision* preparations.
50 *his own* his true character.
51 *inhumanly* (in-humanely F). The two words did not become separate until the eighteenth century.
53 *quit* repay.
54 *make one* join in.
58 *sewer* chief servant at a meal who superintended the seating and serving of guests.
66 *bare* Bare-headed, as a sign of respect; with a pun, reinforced by *loud*, on 'shamelessly'.

LA FOOLE

I'll go tell her presently. It shall be done, that's resolved.   [*Exit*]

CLERIMONT

I thought he would not hear it out, but 'twould take him.

DAUPHINE

Well, there be guests and meat now; how shall we do for music?

CLERIMONT

The smell of the venison going through the street will invite one   70
noise of fiddlers or other.

DAUPHINE

I would it would call the trumpeters thither.

CLERIMONT

Faith, there is hope; they have intelligence of all feasts. There's
good correspondence betwixt them and the London cooks. 'Tis
twenty to one but we have 'em.   75

DAUPHINE

'Twill be a most solemn day for my uncle, and an excellent fit of
mirth for us.

CLERIMONT

Ay, if we can hold up the emulation betwixt Foole and Daw, and
never bring them to expostulate.

DAUPHINE

Tut, flatter 'em both, as Truewit says, and you may take their   80
understandings in a purse-net. They'll believe themselves to be
just such men as we make 'em, neither more nor less. They have
nothing, not the use of their senses, but by tradition.

> [LA FOOLE] *enters like a sewer*

CLERIMONT

See! Sir Amorous has his towel on already. Have you persuaded
your cousin?   85

LA FOOLE

Yes, 'tis very feasible: she'll do anything, she says, rather than the
La Fooles shall be disgraced.

---

71   *noise* band.
76   *solemn* (i) ceremonious; (ii) gloomy.
78   *emulation* ambitious rivalry.
79   *expostulate* set forth their grievances to one another.
81   *purse-net* bag-shaped net, the mouth of which can be drawn together with cords;
         used especially for catching rabbits.
83   *tradition* i.e. handing over (Latin *traditio*).
         s.d. [LA FOOLE] ed. (*He* F).

DAUPHINE

She is a noble kinswoman. It will be such a pestling device, Sir
Amorous! It will pound all your enemy's practices to powder
and blow him up with his own mine, his own train.   90

LA FOOLE

Nay, we'll give fire, I warrant you.

CLERIMONT

But you must carry it privately, without any noise, and take no
notice by any means –

[Enter OTTER]

OTTER

Gentlemen, my princess says you shall have all her silver dishes,
festinate; and she's gone to alter her tire a little and go with you –   95

CLERIMONT

And yourself too, Captain Otter.

DAUPHINE

By any means, sir.

OTTER

Yes, sir, I do mean it; but I would entreat my cousin Sir Amorous,
and you gentlemen, to be suitors to my princess, that I may
carry my bull and my bear, as well as my horse.   100

CLERIMONT

That you shall do, Captain Otter.

LA FOOLE

My cousin will never consent, gentlemen.

DAUPHINE

She must consent, Sir Amorous, to reason.

LA FOOLE

Why, she says they are no decorum among ladies.

OTTER

But they are *decora*, and that's better, sir.   105

---

88   *pestling* crushing, as with a pestle.
89   *practices* plots.
90   *train* (i) line of gunpowder conveying fire to a mine; (ii) snare, trick.
92   *carry* manage.
95   *festinate* with despatch
     tire head-dress.
105 *decora* Beautiful; and 'better' also because, if La Foole's 'decorum' is taken as Latin,
     decora is the grammatically correct form.

250

CLERIMONT

Ay, she must hear argument. Did not Pasiphae, who was a queen, love a bull? And was not Callisto, the mother of Areas, turned into a bear and made a star, Mistress Ursula, i' the heavens?

OTTER

Oh God, that I could ha' said as much! I will have these stories painted i' the Bear Garden, *ex Ovidii Metamorphosi.* 110

DAUPHINE

Where is your princess, captain? Pray be our leader.

OTTER

That I shall, sir.

CLERIMONT

Make haste, good Sir Amorous.

[*Exeunt*]

ACT III, SCENE iv

[*Enter*] MOROSE, EPICOENE, PARSON, CUTBEARD

MOROSE

Sir, there's an angel for yourself, and a brace of angels for your cold. Muse not at this manage of my bounty. It is fit we should thank fortune double to nature, for any benefit she confers upon us; besides, it is your imperfection, but my solace.

PARSON

I thank your worship, so is it mine now. 5

The PARSON *speaks as having a cold*

106–7   *Pasiphae . . . bull* Their offspring was the Minotaur.
107   *Callisto* Loved by Jupiter and changed by Juno into a bear, and after her death into a constellation, *Ursa Major*, the Great Bear, by Jupiter; recounted in *Metamorphoses*, II, 401–507.
110   *ex . . . Metamorphosi* Out of Ovid's *Metamorphoses*. The story of Pasiphae, who loved a real bull (not Jupiter; cf. III.i.22–3), and was not transformed, is in fact told in Ovid's *Ars Amatoria*, I, 295–326.

1   *angel* gold coin – worth at this time about ten shillings.
2   *manage* management.
3   *double to* twice as much as we do.

MOROSE
What says he, Cutbeard?

CUTBEARD
He says *praesto*, sir: whensoever your worship needs him, he can be ready with the like. He got this cold with sitting up late and singing catches with cloth-workers.

MOROSE
No more. I thank him.   10

PARSON
God keep your worship and give you much joy with your fair spouse. Umh, umh.   *He coughs*

MOROSE
Oh, oh! Stay, Cutbeard! Let him give me five shillings of my money back. As it is bounty to reward benefits, so is it equity to mulct injuries. I will have it. What says he?   15

CUTBEARD
He cannot change it, sir.

MOROSE
It must be changed.

CUTBEARD [*Aside to* PARSON]
Cough again.

MOROSE
What says he?

CUTBEARD
He will cough out the rest, sir.   20

PARSON
Umh, umh, umh.   [*Coughs*] *again*

MOROSE
Away, away with him, stop his mouth, away, I forgive it –
                                                [*Exit* CUTBEARD *with* PARSON]

EPICOENE
Fie, Master Morose, that you will use this violence to a man of the church.

7   *praesto* Latin for 'at your service'.
9   *catches* part-songs for three or four, in which the second singer begins the first line as the first begins the second line, and so on.
     cloth-workers Who sang while they sat at their work. Many were Puritans, much given to hymn-singing; cf. *1 Henry IV*, II.iv.133–4: 'I would I were a weaver, I could sing psalms, or anything'.
14   *benefits* acts of kindness (an archaic use at this date).
15   *mulct* punish by a fine.

MOROSE

How!   25

EPICOENE

It does not become your gravity or breeding – as you pretend in
court – to have offered this outrage on a waterman, or any more
boist'rous creature, much less on a man of his civil coat.

MOROSE

You can speak then!

EPICOENE

Yes, sir.   30

MOROSE

Speak out, I mean.

EPICOENE

Ay, sir. Why, did you think you had married a statue? or a
motion only? one of the French puppets with the eyes turned
with a wire? or some innocent out of the hospital, that would
stand with her hands thus, and a plaice-mouth, and look upon   35
you?

MOROSE

Oh immodesty! A manifest woman! What, Cutbeard!

EPICOENE

Nay, never quarrel with Cutbeard, sir, it is too late now. I confess
it doth bate somewhat of the modesty I had, when I writ simply
maid; but I hope I shall make it a stock still competent to the   40
estate and dignity of your wife.

MOROSE

She can talk!

26   *pretend* profess to have.
27   *waterman* The Thames boatmen were notorious for their loud cries to attract
      passengers.
28   *civil coat* sober profession.
33   *motion* puppet.
34   *innocent* half-wit.
      hospital Bethlehem Hospital (Bedlam), rather than Christ's.
35   *hands thus* Loosely placed one over the other and hanging down limply in front, to
      indicate placid obedience, or idiocy. Beaurline compares Dürer's drawings of a rustic
      couple and a Turkish woman (E. Panofsky, *The Life and Art of Albrecht Dürer*,
      Princeton, 1955, plates 43, 256).
      plaice-mouth small, puckered mouth, like the fish's.
37   *A manifest woman* As one might say, 'a manifest villain'.
39   *it* her speaking out.
      bate lessen.
40   *competent* appropriate, sufficient.
41   *estate* status, rank.

EPICOENE

Yes, indeed, sir.

MOROSE

What sirrah! None of my knaves there?

[*Enter* MUTE]

Where is this impostor, Cutbeard?   45

[MUTE *makes signs*]

EPICOENE

Speak to him, fellow, speak to him. I'll have none of this coacted, unnatural dumbness in my house, in a family where I govern.

[*Exit* MUTE]

MOROSE

She is my regent already! I have married a Penthesilea, a Semiramis, sold my liberty to a distaff!

ACT III, SCENE v

[*Enter*] TRUEWIT

TRUEWIT

Where's Master Morose?

MOROSE

Is he come again? Lord have mercy upon me!

TRUEWIT

I wish you all joy, Mistress Epicoene, with your grave and honourable match.

EPICOENE

I return you the thanks, Master Truewit, so friendly a wish   5
deserves.

---

44   *knaves* servants.
46   *coacted* enforced.
47   *family* household.
48   *Penthesilea* Amazon queen who fought against the Greeks at Troy; cf. III.v.35.
49   *Semiramis* Warrior queen of the Assyrians who after her husband's death disguised herself in men's clothes, in order to govern.
      distaff The insignia of the sexes were the sword and the distaff; see *OED*, sb., 3.b.

3   *grave* (i) worthy of respect, dignified; (ii) sombre.

MOROSE

She has acquaintance too!

TRUEWIT

God save you, sir, and give you all contentment in your fair
choice here. Before I was the bird of night to you, the owl, but
now I am the messenger of peace, a dove, and bring you the glad   10
wishes of many friends, to the celebration of this good hour.

MOROSE

What hour, sir?

TRUEWIT

Your marriage hour, sir. I commend your resolution, that, notwithstanding all the dangers I laid afore you, in the voice of a
night-crow, would yet go on, and be yourself. It shows you are a   15
man constant to your own ends, and upright to your purposes,
that would not be put off with left-handed cries.

MOROSE

How should you arrive at the knowledge of so much?

TRUEWIT

Why, did you ever hope, sir, committing the secrecy of it to a
barber, that less than the whole town should know it? You might   20
as well ha' told it the conduit, or the bakehouse, or the infantry
that follow the court, and with more security. Could your gravity
forget so old and noted a remnant as *lippis et tonsoribus notum*
Well, sir, forgive it yourself now, the fault, and be communicable
with your friends. Here will be three or four fashionable ladies   25
from the college to visit you presently, and their train of minions
and followers.

5–6   *return . . . thanks* Probably the second of two kisses is exchanged here; *friendly* glances
        tauntingly at *friend* = 'lover'.
9, 15 *owl . . . night-crow* Conventional bearers of evil omen, the latter not denoting a
        specific bird.
17   *left-handed* ill-omened, sinister (*OED*'s first example). In Latin literature birds of ill
        omen conventionally cry on one's left.
21   *conduit . . . bakehouse* Centres of gossip, since people gathered there each morning
        to get water and bread.
21–2   *infantry . . . court* The 'Blacke guard' of *M.V.*, 86, i.e. the army of lower domestic ser-
        vants employed by the court. *Follow* means literally 'follow' as well as 'serve', since
        these servants would bring up the rear on royal progresses.
22   *your gravity* Truewit's mocking variation of 'your honour'.
23   *remnant* Scrap of quotation. Jonson's coinage, in *E.M.I.*, III.iv.75 (Quarto version).
        lippis . . . notum 'Known to the bleary-eyed [i.e. frequenters of apothecary shops] and
        to barbers'; a compression of Horace, *Satires*, I.vii.3.
24   *communicable* communicative.

MOROSE

Bar my doors! Bar my doors! Where are all my eaters, my mouths now?

[*Enter* SERVANTS]

Bar up my doors, you varlets!   30

EPICOENE

He is a varlet that stirs to such an office. Let 'em stand open. I would see him that dares move his eyes toward it. Shall I have a barricado made against my friends, to be barred of any pleasure they can bring in to me with honourable visitation?

[*Exit* SERVANTS]

MOROSE

Oh Amazonian impudence!   35

TRUEWIT

Nay, faith, in this, sir, she speaks but reason, and methinks is more continent than you. Would you go to bed so presently, sir, afore noon? A man of your head and hair should owe more to that reverend ceremony, and not mount the marriage-bed like a town bull or a mountain goat, but stay the due season, and   40
ascend it then with religion and fear. Those delights are to be steeped in the humour and silence of the night; and give the day to other open pleasures and jollities of feast, of music, of revels, of discourse: we'll have all, sir, that may make your hymen high and happy.   45

MOROSE

Oh, my torment, my torment!

TRUEWIT

Nay, if you endure the first half hour, sir, so tediously, and with this irksomeness, what comfort or hope can this fair gentlewoman make to herself hereafter, in the consideration of so many years as are to come –   50

MOROSE

Of my affliction. Good sir, depart and let her do it alone.

---

35   *impudence* shamelessness.
38   *head and hair* judgement and character, glancing ironically at Morose's appearance.
40   *stay* await.
42   *humour* (i) moisture (cf. 'steeped'); (ii) inclination, fancy.
44   *hymen* wedding.
47   *tediously* (i) irritatedly; (ii) tiresomely (cf. IV.ii.128).

TRUEWIT

I have done, sir.

MOROSE

That cursed barber!

TRUEWIT

Yes, faith, a cursed wretch indeed, sir.

MOROSE

I have married his cittern, that's common to all men. Some   55
plague above the plague –

TRUEWIT

All Egypt's ten plagues –

MOROSE

Revenge me on him.

TRUEWIT

'Tis very well, sir. If you laid on a curse or two more, I'll assure
you he'll bear 'em. As, that he may get the pox with seeking to   60
cure it, sir? Or, that while he is curling another man's hair, his
own may drop off? Or, for burning some male bawd's lock, he
may have his brain beat out with the curling-iron?

MOROSE

No, let the wretch live wretched. May he get the itch, and his
shop so lousy as no man dare come at him, nor he come at no   65
man.

TRUEWIT

Ay, and if he would swallow all his balls for pills, let not them
purge him.

MOROSE

Let his warming-pan be ever cold.

TRUEWIT

A perpetual frost underneath it, sir.   70

MOROSE

Let him never hope to see fire again.

---

55   *cittern* Instrument like a lute kept in barbers' shops for customers to amuse them-
      selves with.
57   *ten plagues* Sent by God to persuade Pharaoh to release the Israelites (Exodus, vii–xii).
61   *cure it* At this date barbers were also surgeons.
62   *lock* love-lock, often large and ribanded.
64   *the itch* contagious skin disease, scabies.
67   *balls* of soap.
70   *perpetual frost* A reference to the Great Frost of 1608, when the Thames froze for six
      weeks.

TRUEWIT

But in hell, sir.

MOROSE

His chairs be always empty, his scissors rust, and his combs mould in their cases.

TRUEWIT

Very dreadful that! And may he lose the invention, sir, of   75
carving lanterns in paper.

MOROSE

Let there be no bawd carted that year to employ a basin of his, but let him be glad to eat his sponge for bread.

TRUEWIT

And drink lotium to it, and much good do him.

MOROSE

Or, for want of bread –   80

TRUEWIT

Eat ear-wax, sir. I'll help you. Or, draw his own teeth and add them to the lute-string.

MOROSE

No, beat the old ones to powder and make bread of them.

TRUEWIT

Yes, make meal o' the millstones.

MOROSE

May all the botches and burns that he has cured on others break   85
out upon him.

TRUEWIT

And he now forget the cure of 'em in himself, sir; or, if he do remember it, let him ha' scraped all his linen into lint for't, and have not a rag left him to set up with.

MOROSE

Let him never set up again, but have the gout in his hands   90
forever. Now no more, sir.

---

76   *lanterns in paper* 'Oild Lanterne-paper . . . every Barber . . . has it' (*T.T.*, V.ii.31–2).
77   *basin* Metal basins, hired from barbers, were beaten before sexual offenders as they were carted through the streets (H&S, who quote a contemporary account).
79   *lotium* stale urine used by barbers as hair-lotion.
      to with.
81   *ear-wax . . . teeth* Barbers cleaned ears and pulled teeth, which they hung on strings as a form of advertising.
85   *botches* boils.
89–90   *set up . . . set up* set up business . . . set hair.

TRUEWIT

Oh, that last was too high set! You might go less with him, i'
faith, and be revenged enough; as, that he be never able to new-
paint his pole –

MOROSE

Good sir, no more. I forgot myself.   95

TRUEWIT

Or, want credit to take up with a comb-maker –

MOROSE

No more, sir.

TRUEWIT

Or, having broken his glass in a former despair, fall now into a
much greater, of ever getting another –

MOROSE

I beseech you, no more.   100

TRUEWIT

Or, that he never be trusted with trimming of any but chimney-
sweepers –

MOROSE

Sir –

TRUEWIT

Or, may he cut a collier's throat with his razor by chance-
medley, and yet hang for't.   105

MOROSE

I will forgive him, rather than hear any more. I beseech you, sir.

---

92   *set . . . go less* the metaphor is from gambling.
96   *want . . . with* not to be able to obtain supplies on credit from.
101–2   *chimney-sweepers* With colliers, the least desirable customers, because likely to be
        the dirtiest.
104   *collier* Colliers (coalmen) were proverbially dishonest.
104–5   *chance-medley* homicide by misadventure.

ACT III, SCENE vi

[*Enter*] DAW, HAUGHTY, CENTAURE, MAVIS, TRUSTY

DAW

This way, madam.

MOROSE

Oh, the sea breaks in upon me! Another flood! An inundation!
I shall be o'erwhelmed with noise. It beats already at my shores.
I feel an earthquake in myself for't.

DAW [*Kissing* EPICOENE]

'Give you joy, mistress.   5

MOROSE

Has she servants too!

DAW

I have brought some ladies here to see and know you.

She kisses them severally as he presents them

My Lady Haughty, this my Lady Centaure, Mistress Dol Mavis,
Mistress Trusty, my Lady Haughty's woman. Where's your husband? Let's see him: can he endure no noise? Let me come to him.   10

MOROSE

What nomenclator is this!

TRUEWIT

Sir John Daw, sir, your wife's servant, this.

MOROSE

A Daw, and her servant! Oh, 'tis decreed, 'tis decreed of me, and
she have such servants.   [*Makes to go out*]

TRUEWIT

Nay, sir, you must kiss the ladies, you must not go away now;   15
they come toward you to seek you out.

---

2 *Another flood* Possibly *another* with regard to the flood of words released in the last
   two scenes, but Morose's tendency to dramatize his afflictions by means of classical
   and other references suggests that *another* may mean 'second', the first being the
   flood of Genesis, vii.

7 s.d. *severally* each in turn.

11 *nomenclator* announcer of the names of guests (a sense coined by Jonson in *C.R.*,.
    V.x.5); punning here on 'clatter'. See note to I.ii.68.

13 *'tis decreed of me* judgement is passed on me, I am a condemned man (H&S, who
    compare Latin *actum est de me*).
    and if.

HAUGHTY

I' faith, Master Morose, would you steal a marriage thus, in the
midst of so many friends, and not acquaint us? Well, I'll kiss
you, notwithstanding the justice of my quarrel. You shall give
me leave, mistress, to use a becoming familiarity with your   20
husband.

EPICOENE

Your ladyship does me an honour in it, to let me know he is so
worthy your favour; as you have done both him and me grace
to visit so unprepared a pair to entertain you.

MOROSE

Compliment! Compliment!   25

EPICOENE

But I must lay the burden of that upon my servant here.

HAUGHTY

It shall not need, Mistress Morose; we will all bear, rather than
one shall be oppressed.

MOROSE

I know it, and you will teach her the faculty, if she be to learn it.
                    [*The collegiates talk apart with* TRUEWIT]

HAUGHTY

Is this the silent woman?   30

CENTAURE

Nay, she has found her tongue since she was married, Master
Truewit says.

HAUGHTY

Oh, Master Truewit! 'Save you. What kind of creature is your
bride here? She speaks, methinks!

TRUEWIT

Yes, madam, believe it, she is a gentlewoman of very absolute   35
behaviour and of a good race.

HAUGHTY

And Jack Daw told us she could not speak.

TRUEWIT

So it was carried in plot, madam, to put her upon this old
fellow, by Sir Dauphine, his nephew, and one or two more of us;

---

17   *steal a marriage* get married secretly (a stock phrase).
25   *Compliment* See I.i.121 and note.
29   *faculty . . . it* ability (to bear [sexual] burdens) if she has not learned it already; taking
     up the sexual sense of *oppressed*, 'ravished' (Latin *opprimere*).
35   *absolute* perfect.

261

but she is a woman of an excellent assurance, and an extra-   40
ordinary happy wit and tongue. You shall see her make rare
sport with Daw ere night.

HAUGHTY

And he brought us to laugh at her!

TRUEWIT

That falls out often, madam, that he that thinks himself the
master-wit is the master-fool. I assure your ladyship, ye cannot   45
laugh at her.

HAUGHTY

No, we'll have her to the college: and she have wit, she shall be
one of us! Shall she not, Centaure? We'll make her a collegiate.

CENTAURE

Yes, faith, madam, and Mavis and she will set up a side.

TRUEWIT

Believe it, madam, and Mistress Mavis, she will sustain her part.   50

MAVIS

I'll tell you that when I have talked with her and tried her.

HAUGHTY

Use her very civilly, Mavis.

MAVIS

So I will, madam.

[MAVIS *walks apart with* EPICOENE]

MOROSE

Blessed minute, that they would whisper thus ever.

TRUEWIT

In the meantime, madam, would but your ladyship help to vex   55
him a little: you know his disease, talk to him about the wedding-
ceremonies, or call for your gloves, or –

HAUGHTY

Let me alone. Centaure, help me. Master bridegroom, where are
you?

MOROSE

Oh, it was too miraculously good to last!   60

---

42   *with* of, at the expense of.
44–5 *he . . . fool* Adapting the proverb 'Who seem most crafty prove oft times most fools'
      (Middleton, *A Trick to Catch the Old One*, V.ii.193).
49   *a side* a partnership in cards (perhaps metaphorical here).
57, 62 *gloves . . . scarfs* Presented to guests at weddings.
58   *Let me alone* i.e. you can trust me for that.

HAUGHTY

We see no ensigns of a wedding here, no character of a bridal:
where be our scarfs and our gloves? I pray you give 'em us. Let's
know your bride's colours and yours at least.

CENTAURE

Alas, madam, he has provided none.

MOROSE

Had I known your ladyship's painter, I would.   65

HAUGHTY

He has given it you, Centaure, i' faith. But do you hear, Master
Morose, a jest will not absolve you in this manner. You that have
sucked the milk of the court, and from thence have been brought
up to the very strong meats and wine of it, been a courtier from
the biggin to the night-cap, as we may say, and you to offend in   70
such a high point of ceremony as this, and let your nuptials
want all marks of solemnity! How much plate have you lost
today – if you had but regarded your profit – what gifts, what
friends, through your mere rusticity?

MOROSE

Madam –   75

HAUGHTY

Pardon me, sir, I must insinuate your errors to you. No gloves?
No garters? No scarfs? No epithalamium? No masque?

DAW

Yes, madam, I'll make an epithalamium, I promised my
mistress, I have begun it already: will your ladyship hear it?

---

61   *ensigns* tokens.
63   *colours* Bride and groom each had their colour, which was worn by their respective
      friends.
65   *painter* cosmetician.
66   *given it you* paid you out, given you what for.
69   *strong meats* Greek στερεας τροφης, solid food, as opposed to easily digested food
      such as milk; see *OED*, 'strong', a., 9.d; *wine* introduces a pun on a less learned sense
      of 'strong'.
70   *biggin* baby-bonnet.
72   *solemnity* observance of ceremony.
74   *mere* absolute.
76   *insinuate* Latin *insinuare* means 'introduce, make known', but the English sense 'hint
      obliquely' is funnier, since this is the opposite of what Haughty proceeds to do.
77   *garters* After the ceremony the young men and bridesmaids would strive to possess
      the bride's garters.
      epithalamium Nuptial song in honour of the bride and groom; glossed in detail by
      Jonson in *Hym.*, 435–43.

HAUGHTY

Ay, good Jack Daw. 80

MOROSE

Will it please your ladyship command a chamber and be private
with your friend? You shall have your choice of rooms to retire
to after; my whole house is yours. I know it hath been your
ladyship's errand into the city at other times, however now you
have been unhappily diverted upon me; but I shall be loath to 85
break any honourable custom of your ladyship's. And therefore,
good madam –

EPICOENE

Come, you are a rude bridegroom, to entertain ladies of honour
in this fashion.

CENTAURE

He is a rude groom indeed. 90

TRUEWIT

By that light, you deserve to be grafted, and have your horns
reach from one side of the island to the other. – [*Aside to*
MOROSE] Do not mistake me, sir; I but speak this to give the
ladies some heart again, not for any malice to you.

MOROSE

Is this your bravo, ladies? 95

TRUEWIT

As God help me, if you utter such another word, I'll take
mistress bride in and begin to you in a very sad cup, do you see?
Go to, know your friends and such as love you.

---

81   *chamber* bedchamber.
82   *friend* lover (i.e. Daw).
84   *errand* purpose of going (i.e. an assignation).
90   *groom* (i) bridegroom; (ii) servant, lackey.
91   *grafted* Grafted with foreign stock, i.e. made a cuckold, with a consequent 'growth'
      of horns.
95   *bravo* hired thug.
97   *begin . . . cup* drink your health in a very unpleasant manner.
98   *Go to* common expression of reproof.

ACT III, SCENE vii

[*Enter*] CLERIMONT [*with* MUSICIANS]

CLERIMONT

By your leave, ladies. Do you want any music? I have brought
you variety of noises. Play, sirs, all of you.

Music of all sorts

MOROSE

Oh, a plot, a plot, a plot, a plot upon me! This day I shall be their
anvil to work on, they will grate me asunder. 'Tis worse than the
noise of a saw.   5

CLERIMONT

No, they are hair, rosin, and guts. I can give you the receipt.

TRUEWIT

Peace, boys.

CLERIMONT

Play, I say.

TRUEWIT

Peace, rascals. – You see who's your friend now, sir? Take courage,
put on a martyr's resolution. Mock down all their attemptings   10
with patience. 'Tis but a day, and I would suffer heroically.
Should an ass exceed me in fortitude? No. You betray your
infirmity with your hanging dull ears, and make them insult:
bear up bravely and constantly.

LA FOOLE [*with servants*] *passes over sewing the meat*
[*followed by* MISTRESS OTTER]

Look you here, sir, what honour is done you unexpected by your   15

---

2   *noises* bands of musicians, and glancing at the normal sense (cf. II.vi.34).
4   *grate* (i) annoy, harass; (ii) grind; (iii) make grating noises.
6   *hair . . . guts* Which produce the noise from a violin: strings of gut, a bow of
     horsehair, rosin to rub on the bow.
     receipt formula, recipe.
11   *with* by means of.
12   *ass* The type of patient endurance – but also of stupidity.
13   *infirmity* weakness.
     insult scornfully exult.
14   *constantly* steadfastly.
     s.d. *sewing the meat* directing the serving of the food.

nephew: a wedding-dinner come, and a knight-sewer before it,
for the more reputation; and fine Mistress Otter, your neighbour, in the rump or tail of it.

MOROSE

Is that Gorgon, that Medusa come? Hide me, hide me!

TRUEWIT

I warrant you, sir, she will not transform you. Look upon her   20
with a good courage. Pray you entertain her and conduct your
guests in. No? – Mistress bride, will you entreat in the ladies?
Your bridegroom is so shamefaced here –

EPICOENE

Will it please your ladyship, madam?

HAUGHTY

With the benefit of your company, mistress.   25

EPICOENE

Servant, pray you perform your duties.

DAW

And glad to be commanded, mistress.

CENTAURE

How like you her wit, Mavis?

MAVIS

Very prettily absolutely well.

MISTRESS OTTER [*Trying to take precedence*]

'Tis my place.   30

MAVIS

You shall pardon me, Mistress Otter.

MISTRESS OTTER

Why, I am a collegiate.

MAVIS

But not in ordinary.

MISTRESS OTTER

But I am.

MAVIS

We'll dispute that within.   35

[*Exit* DAW *with ladies*]

19   *Medusa* The most terrible of the three Gorgons.
20   *transform* i.e. turn to stone; see note to II.iv.13.
21   *entertain* receive.
23   *shamefaced* shy, bashful.
29   *Very . . . well* 'Prettily' modifies the rest of the phrase, giving an affected example of
      'compliment'; cf. *B.F.*, III.iv.80.
33   *in ordinary* see note to II.iii.83.

CLERIMONT

Would this had lasted a little longer.

TRUEWIT

And that they had sent for the heralds.

[*Enter* OTTER]

Captain Otter, what news?

OTTER

I have brought my bull, bear, and horse in private, and yonder
are the trumpeters without, and the drum, gentlemen.   40

The drum and trumpets sound

MOROSE

Oh, oh, oh!

OTTER

And we will have a rouse in each of 'em anon, for bold Britons,
i' faith.

[*They sound again*]

MOROSE

Oh, oh, oh!   [*Exit* MOROSE]

ALL

Follow, follow, follow!   45

[*Exeunt*]

---

37   *heralds* Since they determine questions of precedence, and *heralds* (of a rather dif-
        ferent sort) blow trumpets.
42   *rouse* Full draught of liquor; often marked by a fanfare, as in *Hamlet*, I.iv.6–8, where
        there is '*A flourish of trumpets, and two pieces goes off*'.
45   *Follow* a hunting-cry.

ACT IV, SCENE i

[Enter] TRUEWIT, CLERIMONT

TRUEWIT

Was there ever poor bridegroom so tormented? or man, indeed?

CLERIMONT

I have not read of the like in the chronicles of the land.

TRUEWIT

Sure, he cannot but go to a place of rest after all this purgatory.

CLERIMONT

He may presume it, I think.

TRUEWIT

The spitting, the coughing, the laughter, the neezing, the fart-   5
ing, dancing, noise of the music, and her masculine and loud
commanding and urging the whole family, makes him think he
has married a Fury.

CLERIMONT

And she carries it up bravely.

TRUEWIT

Ay, she takes any occasion to speak: that's the height on't.   10

CLERIMONT

And how soberly Dauphine labours to satisfy him that it was
none of his plot!

TRUEWIT

And has almost brought him to the faith i' the article.

[Enter DAUPHINE]

Here he comes. – Where is he now? What's become of him,
Dauphine?   15

DAUPHINE

Oh, hold me up a little, I shall go away i' the jest else. He has got

---

5 *neezing* sneezing.
7 *urging . . . family* driving all the servants.
8 *Fury* One of the ferocious female beings sent from Tartarus to avenge wrong or
   punish crime.
9 *carries . . . bravely* keeps it up splendidly.
13 *faith . . . article* Referring to the Articles of Faith, the 39 statements to which Church
   of England ministers must subscribe.
16 *go . . . jest* die laughing.

on his whole nest of night-caps, and locked himself up i' the
top o' the house, as high as ever he can climb from the noise. I
peeped in at a cranny and saw him sitting over a cross-beam o'
the roof, like him o' the saddler's horse in Fleet Street, upright;   20
and he will sleep there.

CLERIMONT

But where are your collegiates?

DAUPHINE

Withdrawn with the bride in private.

TRUEWIT

Oh, they are instructing her i' the college grammar. If she have
grace with them, she knows all their secrets instantly.   25

CLERIMONT

Methinks the Lady Haughty looks well today, for all my dispraise
of her i' the morning. I think I shall come about to thee again,
Truewit.

TRUEWIT

Believe it, I told you right. Women ought to repair the losses time
and years have made i' their features with dressings. And an   30
intelligent woman, if she know by herself the least defect, will be
most curious to hide it; and it becomes her. If she be short, let
her sit much, lest when she stands she be thought to sit. If she
have an ill foot, let her wear her gown the longer and her shoe
the thinner. If a fat hand and scald nails, let her carve the less,   35
and act in gloves. If a sour breath, let her never discourse fasting,
and always talk at her distance. If she have black and rugged
teeth, let her offer the less at laughter, especially if she laugh
wide and open.

---

17   *nest* set of objects of diminishing sizes fitting one inside the other.

20   *him . . . horse* The model of a horse and rider outside a saddler's shop. Cf. *E.M I.*,
    V.v.49–51, where Clement calls Bobadill and Matthew the 'signe o' the Souldier, and
    picture o' the *Poet* (but, both so false, I will not ha' you hang'd out at my dore till
    midnight)'.

27   *come . . . thee* come round to your opinion (*OED*'s first example).

30   *dressings* Personal decorations. Jonson's coinage, translating Ovid's *munditiis*.

31   *by* about.

32   *curious* careful (suggested by Ovid's *cura*).

35   *scald* scaly, scabbed (*scaber*, Ovid).

35–6   *let . . . gloves* 'Act' at this date meant specifically 'gesture', as could *carve* (as well as
    'carve the meat at table'). Cf. Hamlet's advice to the players: 'do not saw the air too
    much with your hand, thus' (III.ii.4–5).

36   *fasting* Ovid has *jejuna*, i.e. while her stomach is empty (when the breath is sourest).

CLERIMONT

Oh, you shall have some women, when they laugh, you would   40
think they brayed, it is so rude, and –

TRUEWIT

Ay, and others that will stalk i' their gait like an ostrich, and take
huge strides. I cannot endure such a sight. I love measure i' the
feet and number i' the voice: they are gentlenesses that oft-times
draw no less than the face.   45

DAUPHINE

How cam'st thou to study these creatures so exactly? I would
thou wouldst make me a proficient.

TRUEWIT

Yes, but you must leave to live i' your chamber, then, a month
together upon *Amadis de Gaule* or *Don Quixote*, as you are wont,
and come abroad where the matter is frequent, to court, to   50
tiltings, public shows and feasts, to plays, and church sometimes: thither they come to show their new tires too, to see and
to be seen. In these places a man shall find whom to love, whom
to play with, whom to touch once, whom to hold ever. The variety
arrests his judgement. A wench to please a man comes not down   55
dropping from the ceiling, as he lies on his back droning a
tobacco-pipe. He must go where she is.

DAUPHINE

Yes, and be never the near.

TRUEWIT

Out, heretic! That diffidence makes thee worthy it should be so.

43   *measure* due proportion in moving.
44   *number* harmonious rhythm.
       gentlenesses graces.
45   *draw* attract.
47   *proficient* learner (as opposed to one who is perfect).
48   *leave* cease.
49   *Amadis . . . Quixote* Romances which Jonson regarded as frivolous entertainments,
       'publique Nothings ; / Abortives of the fabulous, darke cloyster, / Sent out to poison
       courts, and infest manners' (*N.I.*, I.vi.126–8).
50   *abroad . . . frequent* away from home where the subject-matter is plentiful.
51   *tiltings* jousts (at this date mock-combats for courtly entertainment).
55   *arrests* In law, to *arrest a judgement* is to stay proceedings after a verdict, on the
       ground of error (*OED*, v., 5.d, earliest example 1768); translating Ovid's *judicium
       morata est*.
56   *droning* sucking, as though playing a bagpipe (*OED*); glancing at *drone* = act indo-
       lently, idle away the time.
58   *near* nearer, comparative of *nigh*.

CLERIMONT

He says true to you, Dauphine. 60

DAUPHINE

Why?

TRUEWIT

A man should not doubt to overcome any woman. Think he can vanquish 'em, and he shall; for though they deny, their desire is to be tempted. Penelope herself cannot hold out long. Ostend, you saw, was taken at last. You must persever and hold to your 65 purpose. They would solicit us, but that they are afraid. Howsoever, they wish in their hearts we should solicit them. Praise 'em, flatter 'em, you shall never want eloquence or trust; even the chastest delight to feel themselves that way rubbed. With praises you must mix kisses too. If they take them, they'll take 70 more. Though they strive, they would be overcome.

CLERIMONT

Oh, but a man must beware of force.

TRUEWIT

It is to them an acceptable violence, and has oft-times the place of the greatest courtesy. She that might have been forced, and you let her go free without touching, though she then seem 75 to thank you, will ever hate you after; and glad i' the face, is assuredly sad at the heart.

CLERIMONT

But all women are not to be taken all ways.

TRUEWIT

'Tis true. No more than all birds or all fishes. If you appear learned to an ignorant wench, or jocund to a sad, or witty to a 80 foolish, why, she presently begins to mistrust herself. You must approach them i' their own height, their own line; for the contrary makes many that fear to commit themselves to noble and

---

62 *doubt to* doubt that he may.
63 *deny* Say no. 'Maids say nay and take it' (Tilley, M34).
64 *Penelope . . . Ostend* Ancient and modern examples of steadfast resistance. The wife of Odysseus put off her suitors for twenty years until her husband returned from Troy; the Belgian port fell to the Spanish in September 1604 after a three-year siege.
68 *want . . . trust* lack eloquence in yourself, or trust from your audience.
71 *strive . . . would be* struggle . . . wish to be.
74 *and* if.
78 *all ways* ed. (alwaies F).
81 *presently* at once.
82 *height . . . line* The metaphor is, appropriately, from fencing (referring to the 'high' and 'low' ward, and the angle of the sword).

worthy fellows run into the embraces of a rascal. If she love wit, give verses, though you borrow 'em of a friend, or buy 'em, to have good. If valour, talk of your sword, and be frequent in the mention of quarrels, though you be staunch in fighting. If activity, be seen o' your barbary often, or leaping over stools, for the credit of your back. If she love good clothes or dressing, have your learned council about you every morning, your French tailor, barber, linener, *et cetera*. Let your powder, your glass, and your comb be your dearest acquaintance. Take more care for the ornament of your head than the safety, and wish the commonwealth rather troubled than a hair about you. That will take her. Then if she be covetous and craving, do you promise anything, and perform sparingly; so shall you keep her in appetite still. Seem as you would give, but be like a barren field that yields little, or unlucky dice to foolish and hoping gamesters. Let your gifts be slight and dainty, rather than precious. Let cunning be above cost. Give cherries at time of year, or apricots; and say they were sent you out o' the country, though you bought 'em in Cheapside. Admire her tires, like her in all fashions, compare her in every habit to some deity, invent excellent dreams to flatter her, and riddles; or, if she be a great one, perform always the second parts to her: like what she likes, praise whom she praises, and fail not to make the household and servants yours, yea, the whole family, and salute 'em by their names – 'tis but light cost if you can purchase 'em so – and make her physician your pensioner, and her chief woman. Nor will it be out of your gain to make love to her too, so she follow, not usher, her lady's pleasure. All blabbing is taken away when she comes to be a part of the crime.

85

90

95

100

105

110

. DAUPHINE

On what courtly lap hast thou late slept, to come forth so sudden and absolute a courtling?

---

87 *staunch* restrained.
88 *activity* physical exercise. *barbary* horse, of high quality Arab stock.
89 *back* A 'good back' implies sexual prowess; cf. IV.v.179.
100 *Let . . . cost* let your ingenuity be greater than your expense.
   at time of year in season.
104–5 *great one* person of rank.
105 *perform . . . parts* act a subordinate role (Latin *agere secundae partes*).
109 *make . . . pensioner* i.e. buy his support.
   woman maidservant.
110 *out . . . her* irrelevant to your interests to behave amorously towards.
114 *courtling* courtier (Jonson's coinage in *C.R.*, V.iv.33).

TRUEWIT

Good faith, I should rather question you, that are so heark'ning   115
after these mysteries. I begin to suspect your diligence, Dauphine.
Speak, art thou in love in earnest?

DAUPHINE

Yes, by my troth, am I; 'twere ill dissembling before thee.

TRUEWIT

With which of 'em, I pray thee?

DAUPHINE

With all the collegiates.   120

CLERIMONT

Out on thee! We'll keep you at home, believe it, i' the stable, and
you be such a stallion.

TRUEWIT

No; I like him well. Men should love wisely, and all women:
some one for the face, and let her please the eye; another for the
skin, and let her please the touch; and third for the voice, and let   125
her please the ear; and where the objects mix, let the senses so
too. Thou wouldst think it strange if I should make 'em all in
love with thee afore night!

DAUPHINE

I would say thou hadst the best philtre i' the world, and couldst
do more than Madam Medea or Doctor Forman.   130

TRUEWIT

If I do not, let me play the mountebank for my meat while I live,
and the bawd for my drink.

DAUPHINE

So be it, I say.

---

124   *some one* a certain one.
130   *Medea* The classical enchantress who helped Jason win the Golden Fleece, and
restored his father Aeson's youth.
    Forman Simon Forman (1552–1611), well-known London astrologer, quack, and
supplier of love-philtres to the court; see A.L. Rowse's biography (1974).

ACT IV, SCENE ii

[*Enter*] OTTER [*carrying his cups*], DAW, LA FOOLE

OTTER
Oh lord, gentlemen, how my knights and I have missed you here!

CLERIMONT
Why, captain, what service, what service?

OTTER
To see me bring up my bull, bear, and horse to fight.

DAW
Yes, faith, the captain says we shall be his dogs to bait 'em.   5

DAUPHINE
A good employment.

TRUEWIT
Come on, let's see a course then.

LA FOOLE
I am afraid my cousin will be offended if she come.

OTTER
Be afraid of nothing. Gentlemen, I have placed the drum and
the trumpets and one to give 'em the sign when you are ready.   10
Here's my bull for myself, and my bear for Sir John Daw, and my
horse for Sir Amorous. Now, set your foot to mine, and yours to
his, and –

LA FOOLE
Pray God my cousin come not.

OTTER
Saint George and Saint Andrew, fear no cousins. Come, sound,   15
sound! *Et rauco strepuerunt cornua cantu.*

> [*Drum and trumpets sound. They drink*]

---

3   *service* in the military sense: employment, duty.
4   *to fight* The animal-baiting metaphors continue to l. 65.
7   *course* (i) (drinking-) round; (ii) in bull- and bear-baiting, a bout between the baited
     animal and the dogs; cf. *Macbeth*, V.vii.1–2.
12   *set . . . mine* The stance in drinking-bouts; cf. the ballad 'Uptails All': 'set your foote
     to my foote, & up tails all' (H&S).
15   *fear no cousins* Adapting the proverb 'Fear no colours' (Tilley, C520).
16   *Et . . . cantu* 'The horns blared out with hoarse note' (Virgil, *Aeneid*, VIII, 2).

TRUEWIT
Well said, captain, i' faith; well fought at the bull.

CLERIMONT
Well held at the bear.

TRUEWIT
'Loo, 'loo, captain!

DAUPHINE
Oh, the horse has kicked off his dog already.   20

LA FOOLE
I cannot drink it, as I am a knight.

TRUEWIT
Gods so! Off with his spurs, somebody.

LA FOOLE
It goes again my conscience. My cousin will be angry with it.

DAW
I ha' done mine.

TRUEWIT
You fought high and fair, Sir John.   25

CLERIMONT
At the head.

DAUPHINE
Like an excellent bear-dog.

CLERIMONT [*Aside to* DAW]
You take no notice of the business, I hope.

DAW [*Aside to* CLERIMONT]
Not a word, sir; you see we are jovial.

OTTER
Sir Amorous, you must not equivocate. It must be pulled down,   30
for all my cousin.

CLERIMONT [*Aside to* LA FOOLE]
'Sfoot, if you take not your drink, they'll think you are dis-
contented with something; you'll betray all if you take the least
notice.

LA FOOLE [*Aside to* CLERIMONT]
Not I, I'll both drink and talk then.   35

---

17   *Well said* well done.
19   *'Loo* (Low F). A cry to urge on dogs; cf. *Troilus andCressida*, V.vii.10 (here the early
      texts have 'lowe').
22   *Off . . . spurs* i.e. deprive him of his knighthood.

OTTER

You must pull the horse on his knees, Sir Amorous. Fear no
cousins: *jacta est alea.*

TRUEWIT [*Aside to* DAUPHINE *and* CLERIMONT]

Oh, now he's in his vein, and bold. The least hint given him of
his wife now will make him rail desperately.

CLERIMONT

Speak to him of her.   40

TRUEWIT

Do you, and I'll fetch her to the hearing of it.   [*Exit*]

DAUPHINE

Captain he-Otter, your she-Otter is coming, your wife.

OTTER

Wife! Buz! *Titivilitium.* There's no such thing in nature. I confess, gentlemen, I have a cook, a laundress, a house-drudge, that
serves my necessary turns and goes under that title; but he's an   45
ass that will be so uxorious to tie his affections to one circle.
Come, the name dulls appetite. Here, replenish again: another
bout. Wives are nasty, sluttish animals.   [*Fills the cups*]

DAUPHINE

Oh captain!

OTTER

As ever the earth bare, *tribus verbis.* Where's Master Truewit?   50

DAW

He's slipped aside, sir.

CLERIMONT

But you must drink and be jovial.

DAW

Yes, give it me.

LA FOOLE

And me too.

DAW

Let's be jovial.   55

---

37   *jacta est alea* 'The die is cast': Caesar's remark on crossing the Rubicon.
39   *desperately* recklessly.
43   *Buz* exclamation of impatience or contempt.
      Titivilitium A worthless trifle, bagatelle. Coined by Plautus, *Casino*, 347.
46   *to . . . circle* Like a donkey driving a rotary mill.
48   *animals* (*animalls* F). F usually italicizes only proper, foreign, or technical words;
      possibly a mistake for Latin *animalia;* cf. l. 65.
50   *tribus verbis* in three (i.e. few) words.
51   *slipped* Used of dogs in hunting and coursing.

LA FOOLE

As jovial as you will.

OTTER

Agreed. Now you shall ha' the bear, cousin, and Sir John Daw the horse, and I'll ha' the bull still. Sound, Tritons o' the Thames. *Nunc est bibendum, nunc pede libero* –

[*They drink.*]

MOROSE *speaks from above, the trumpets sounding*

MOROSE

Villains, murderers, sons of the earth, and traitors, what do you there?   60

CLERIMONT

Oh, now the trumpets have waked him we shall have his company.

OTTER

A wife is a scurvy clogdogdo, an unlucky thing, a very foresaid bear-whelp, without any good fashion or breeding: *mala bestia*.   65

His wife is brought out to hear him [*by* TRUEWIT]

DAUPHINE

Why did you marry one then, captain?

OTTER

A pox – I married with six thousand pound, I. I was in love with that. I ha' not kissed my Fury these forty weeks.

CLERIMONT

The more to blame you, captain.

TRUEWIT

Nay, Mistress Otter, hear him a little first.   70

OTTER

She has a breath worse than my grandmother's, *profecto.*

---

58   *Tritons* classical sea-gods, commonly depicted blowing shell-trumpets.
59   *Nunc . . . libero* 'Now is the time for drinking, now with free foot . . . ' The first line of Horace's ode (I.xxxvii) on the downfall of Cleopatra, the type of the man-destroying female.
60   *sons . . . earth* bastards, i.e. low-born knaves (Latin *terrae filii*).
64   *clogdogdo* Baffling. Perhaps, if *foresaid* = 'aforesaid', Bear Garden slang for 'bear-whelp without "fashion or breeding".' Other editors suggest 'clog fit for a dog', i.e. the weight or *trash* placed round a dog's neck when training it, and gloss *foresaid* as either 'predictable, i.e. certain to be bad', or = *forsaid*, 'forbidden'.
65   *mala bestia* evil beast.
71   *profecto* truly.

MISTRESS OTTER

Oh treacherous liar! Kiss me, sweet Master Truewit, and prove him a slandering knave.

TRUEWIT

I'll rather believe you, lady.

OTTER

And she has a peruke that's like a pound of hemp made up in shoe-threads. 75

MISTRESS OTTER

Oh viper, mandrake!

OTTER

A most vile face! And yet she spends me forty pound a year in mercury and hogs' bones. All her teeth were made i' the Black-friars, both her eyebrows i' the Strand, and her hair in Silver 80 Street. Every part o' the town owns a piece of her.

MISTRESS OTTER

I cannot hold.

OTTER

She takes herself asunder still when she goes to bed, into some twenty boxes, and about next day noon is put together again, like a great German clock; and so comes forth and rings a 85 tedious larum to the whole house, and then is quiet again for an hour, but for her quarters. – Ha' you done me right, gentlemen?

MISTRESS OTTER

No, sir, I'll do you right with my quarters, with my quarters.

She falls upon him and beats him

---

77   *mandrake* poisonous plant, the root of which was thought to resemble a human figure, hence a common term of abuse.

77–85   The most elaborate and imaginative of Jonson's imitations of a passage in Martial, imitated previously in *C.R.*, IV.i.145–9, and *Sej.*, I, 307–10; the places are chosen as amusingly the right ones to remedy black teeth, coarse eyebrows, and grey hair. For a brilliantly savage later treatment, cf. Swift's 'A Beautiful Young Nymph Going to Bed'.

79   *mercury . . . hogs' bones* 'Crude mercurie . . . with the jaw-bones of a sow' are the ingredients of the Perfumer's fucus in *C.R.*, V.iv.403–4.

80–1   *Silver Street* Where Shakespeare once lodged, in Cheapside.

85   *like . . . clock* A frequent comparison in Jacobean drama, deriving from *Love's Labour's Lost*, III.i.190–2: 'A woman, that is like a German clock, / Still a-repairing, ever out of frame, / And never going aright'. Tilley, W658, gives examples from Dekker, Middleton, and Fletcher.

86   *larum* chime, alarm (of a clock).

87   *quarters* (i) quarter-hours; (ii) living-quarters.
       done me right matched me drink for drink (a set phrase).

88   *quarters* strokes, blows (in fencing and fighting with staves).

OTTER

Oh hold, good princess!

TRUEWIT

Sound, sound. 90

[Drum and trumpets sound]

CLERIMONT

A battle, a battle.

MISTRESS OTTER

You notorious stinkardly bearward, does my breath smell?

OTTER

Under correction, dear princess. Look to my bear and my horse,
gentlemen.

MISTRESS OTTER

Do I want teeth and eyebrows, thou bull-dog? 95

TRUEWIT

Sound, sound still.

[They sound again]

OTTER

No, I protest, under correction –

MISTRESS OTTER

Ay, now you are under correction, you protest; but you did not
protest before correction, sir. Thou Judas, to offer to betray thy
princess! I'll make thee an example – 100

MOROSE *descends with a long sword*

MOROSE

I will have no such examples in my house, Lady Otter.

MISTRESS OTTER

Ah!

[She runs off, followed by DAW and LA FOOLE]

MOROSE

Mistress Mary Ambree, your examples are dangerous. – Rogues,
hell-hounds, Stentors, out of my doors, you sons of noise and

---

93 *Under correction* cf. III.i.9.

98 *protest* avow.

103 *Mary Ambree* A modern Amazon; according to a popular ballad, she dressed up and
fought as a soldier at the siege of Ghent in 1584.

104 *Stentors* Stentor was a Greek herald at Troy whose 'iron voice' was as loud as the
shout of fifty men (*Iliad*, V, 785–6).

tumult, begot on an ill May-day, or when the galley-foist is   105
afloat to Westminster!

[Drives out the MUSICIANS]

A trumpeter could not be conceived but then!

DAUPHINE

What ails you, sir?

MOROSE

They have rent my roof, walls, and all my windows asunder,
with their brazen throats.   *[Exit]*   110

TRUEWIT

Best follow him, Dauphine.

DAUPHINE

So I will.   *[Exit]*

CLERIMONT

Where's Daw and La Foole?

OTTER

They are both run away, sir. Good gentlemen, help to pacify my
princess, and speak to the great ladies for me. Now must I go lie   115
with the bears this fortnight, and keep out o' the way till my
peace be made, for this scandal she has taken. Did you not see
my bull-head, gentlemen?

CLERIMONT

Is't not on, captain?

TRUEWIT

No: – *[Aside to* CLERIMONT] but he may make a new one, by   120
that is on.

OTTER

Oh, here 'tis. And you come over, gentlemen, and ask for Tom
Otter, we'll go down to Ratcliffe, and have a course i' faith, for

---

105   *ill May-day* The immediate reference is to the 'Ill' or 'Evil' May-day of 1517, when
the London apprentices attacked wealthy foreign merchants; but as Partridge notes,
any 1 May, with its maypole dancing and merrymaking, would be an ill day to a
man who hated noise.
       galley-foist State barge which once a year brought the new Lord Mayor to be sworn
in at Westminster. A contemporary account quoted by H&S mentions 'drumming,
and piping, and trumpetting' accompanying the celebrations.

117   *scandal* offence.

119   *on* (i) on the cup; (ii) on your shoulders (suggesting, because of the bull's horns,
that Otter is a cuckold).

120–1   *by that* by copying the one that.

122   *And . . . over* if you come across the Thames (to the Bankside).

123   *Ratcliffe* A seafaring area downriver in Stepney, where Dol and Subtle plan to escape
to in *Alch.*
       course cf. l. 7.

all these disasters. There's *bona spes* left.

TRUEWIT

Away, captain, get off while you are well. 125

[*Exit* OTTER]

CLERIMONT

I am glad we are rid of him.

TRUEWIT

You had never been, unless we had put his wife upon him. His humour is as tedious at last, as it was ridiculous at first.

ACT IV, SCENE iii

[*Enter*] HAUGHTY, MISTRESS OTTER, MAVIS, DAW, LA FOOLE, CENTAURE, EPICOENE.
[TRUEWIT *and* CLERIMONT *move aside and observe*]

HAUGHTY

We wondered why you shrieked so, Mistress Otter.

MISTRESS OTTER

Oh God, madam, he came down with a huge long naked weapon in both his hands, and looked so dreadfully! Sure, he's beside himself.

MAVIS

Why, what made you there, Mistress Otter? 5

MISTRESS OTTER

Alas, Mistress Mavis, I was chastising my subject, and thought nothing of him.

DAW [*To* EPICOENE]

Faith, mistress, you must do so too. Learn to chastise. Mistress Otter corrects her husband so, he dares not speak but under correction. 10

LA FOOLE

And with his hat off to her: 'twould do you good to see.

---

124   *bona spes* From Cicero, *In Catilinam*, II, 25: 'Good hope fights against despair of all things' (Beaurline).

5   *made you* were you doing.

HAUGHTY

In sadness, 'tis good and mature counsel: practise it, Morose. I'll
call you Morose still now, as I call Centaure and Mavis: we four
will be all one.

CENTAURE

And you'll come to the college and live with us? 15

HAUGHTY

Make him give milk and honey.

MAVIS

Look how you manage him at first, you shall have him ever
after.

CENTAURE

Let him allow you your coach and four horses, your woman, your
chambermaid, your page, your gentleman-usher, your French 20
cook, and four grooms.

HAUGHTY

And go with us to Bedlam, to the china-houses, and to the
Exchange.

CENTAURE

It will open the gate to your fame.

HAUGHTY

Here's Centaure has immortalized herself with taming of her 25
wild male.

MAVIS

Ay, she has done the miracle of the kingdom.

EPICOENE

But ladies, do you count it lawful to have such plurality of servants, and do 'em all graces?

HAUGHTY

Why not? Why should women deny their favours to men? Are 30
they the poorer, or the worse?

DAW

Is the Thames the less for the dyer's water, mistress?

---

12   *In sadness* seriously.

13   *Morose* The masculine form of address.

17   *manage* train, handle (said of horses).

22   *Bedlam* See note to II.ii.30.

       china-houses . . . Exchange Cf. I.iii.31–2.

24   *open . . . fame* Cf. Centaure's similarly unfortunate ambiguity at ll. 43–4.

32–3   *Is . . . torches* Daw and La Foole's arguments are mechanical clichés, as Truewit
ironically indicates; cf. 'To cast water into the Thames' and 'One candle can light
many more' (Tilley, W106, C45). They also introduce, unwittingly, ideas of (sexual)

LA FOOLE
Or a torch for lighting many torches?

TRUEWIT [*Aside*]
Well said, La Foole; what a new one he has got!

CENTAURE
They are empty losses women fear in this kind.   35

HAUGHTY
Besides, ladies should be mindful of the approach of age, and let
no time want his due use. The best of our days pass first.

MAVIS
We are rivers that cannot be called back, madam: she that now
excludes her lovers may live to lie a forsaken beldame in a frozen
bed.   40

CENTAURE
'Tis true, Mavis; and who will wait on us to coach then? or write,
or tell us the news then? make anagrams of our names, and
invite us to the cockpit, and kiss our hands all the play-time, and
draw their weapons for our honours?

HAUGHTY
Not one.   45

DAW
Nay, my mistress is not altogether unintelligent of these things;
here be in presence have tasted of her favours.

CLERIMONT [*Aside*]
What a neighing hobby-horse is this!

EPICOENE
But not with intent to boast 'em again, servant. And have you
those excellent receipts, madam, to keep yourselves from bearing   50
of children?

HAUGHTY
Oh yes, Morose. How should we maintain our youth and beauty
else? Many births of a woman make her old, as many crops make
the earth barren.

pollution; in sexual slang *water* meant semen, *torch* penis, and *burn* infect with
venereal disease.
34   *new one* i.e. new expression.
39   *beldame* crone.
41   *wait on* escort.
50   *receipts* preparations, mixtures.

ACT IV, SCENE iv

[*Enter*] MOROSE, DAUPHINE; [*they speak apart*]

MOROSE

Oh my cursed angel, that instructed me to this fate!

DAUPHINE

Why, sir?

MOROSE

That I should be seduced by so foolish a devil as a barber will
make!

DAUPHINE

I would I had been worthy, sir, to have partaken your counsel;   5
you should never have trusted it to such a minister.

MOROSE

Would I could redeem it with the loss of an eye, nephew, a
hand, or any other member.

DAUPHINE

Marry, God forbid, sir, that you should geld yourself to anger
your wife.   10

MOROSE

So it would rid me of her! And that I did supererogatory
penance, in a belfry, at Westminster Hall, i' the cockpit, at the
fall of a stag, the Tower Wharf – what place is there else? –
London Bridge, Paris Garden, Belinsgate, when the noises are at
their height and loudest. Nay, I would sit out a play that were   15
nothing but fights at sea, drum, trumpet, and target!

---

1   *instructed* directed.
12   *Westminster Hall* Its shops and law-courts drew noisy crowds.
      i' the cockpit F corr. (in a Cock-pit F uncorr.). See note to I.i.166.
13   *fall . . . stag* Accompanied by the clamour of hounds and huntsmen's horns.
14   *London Bridge* The bridge-piers obstructing the stream made the water roar loudly;
      cf. Middleton and Rowley's *A Fair Quarrel*, IV.iv.46.
      Paris Garden Centre for bear-baiting and other noisy sports; cf. III.i.14.
      Belinsgate Billingsgate, wharf east of London Bridge specializing in fish and fruit,
      supposedly built by King Belin; its fishwives made it a byword for coarse and raucous
      language.
15–16 *play . . . sea* Such as Heywood and Rowley's *Fortune by Land and Sea* (1607), an
      episodic romance drama of the sort Jonson despised.
16   *target* shield.

DAUPHINE

I hope there shall be no such need, sir. Take patience, good uncle.
This is but a day, and 'tis well worn too now.

MOROSE

Oh, 'twill be so forever, nephew, I foresee it, forever. Strife and
tumult are the dowry that comes with a wife.   20

TRUEWIT

I told you so, sir, and you would not believe me.

MOROSE

Alas, do not rub those wounds, Master Truewit, to blood again;
'twas my negligence. Add not affliction to affliction. I have per-
ceived the effect of it, too late, in Madam Otter.

EPICOENE [*Coming forward*]

How do you, sir?   25

MOROSE

Did you ever hear a more unnecessary question? As if she did
not see! Why, I do as you see, empress, empress.

EPICOENE

You are not well, sir! You look very ill! Something has distempered you.

MOROSE

Oh horrible, monstrous impertinencies! Would not one of these   30
have served? Do you think, sir? Would not one of these have
served?

TRUEWIT

Yes, sir, but these are but notes of female kindness, sir; certain
tokens that she has a voice, sir.

MOROSE

Oh, is't so? Come, and't be no otherwise – what say you?   35

EPICOENE

How do you feel yourself, sir?

MOROSE

Again that!

TRUEWIT

Nay, look you, sir: you would be friends with your wife upon
unconscionable terms, her silence –

---

24   *effect* fulfilment, embodiment.
30   *impertinencies* irrelevances.
33   *notes* marks.
     kindness punning on the sense 'natural tendency, behaviour according to kind'.
39   *unconscionable* unreasonably demanding.

EPICOENE

They say you are run mad, sir.   40

MOROSE

Not for love, I assure you, of you; do you see?

EPICOENE

Oh lord, gentlemen! Lay hold on him for God's sake. What shall
I do? Who's his physician – can you tell – that knows the state of
his body best, that I might send for him? Good sir, speak. I'll
send for one of my doctors else.   45

MOROSE

What, to poison me, that I might die intestate and leave you
possessed of all?

EPICOENE

Lord, how idly he talks, and how his eyes sparkle! He looks
green about the temples! Do you see what blue spots he has?

CLERIMONT

Ay, it's melancholy.   50

EPICOENE

Gentlemen, for heaven's sake counsel me. Ladies! Servant, you
have read Pliny and Paracelsus: ne'er a word now to comfort
a poor gentlewoman? Ay me! What fortune had I to marry a
distracted man?

DAW

I'll tell you, mistress –   55

TRUEWIT [Aside]

How rarely she holds it up!

[TRUEWIT *and* CLERIMONT *prevent* MOROSE *from leaving*]

MOROSE

What mean you, gentlemen?

EPICOENE

What will you tell me, servant?

DAW

The disease in Greek is called μανία, in Latin *insania, furor, vel*

---

50   *melancholy* Perhaps in the original Greek sense, 'frenzy, madness' (H&S). In Eliza-
      bethan psychology the term indicated an excess of bile in the mixture of the four
      humours, causing irascibility and broodiness.
52   *Pliny* First-century Roman author of the encyclopedic *Historia Naturalis*.
      Paracelsus Famous Swiss scientist (1493–1541); the first to introduce chemistry to
      the study of medicine.
59–61 μανία . . . *fanaticus* Emptily repetitive: 'madness . . . insanity, frenzy, or melancholic
      ecstasy . . . a going out of one's mind, when a man from being melancholy becomes
      mad'. Daw's next speech only extends the tautology.

ecstasis melancholia, that is, *egressio,* when a man *ex melancholico*   60
evadit fanaticus.

MOROSE

Shall I have a lecture read upon me alive?

DAW

But he may be but *phreneticus* yet, mistress, and *phrenetis* is only
delirium or so –

EPICOENE

Ay, that is for the disease, servant; but what is this to the cure?   65
We are sure enough of the disease.

MOROSE

Let me go!

TRUEWIT

Why, we'll entreat her to hold her peace, sir.

MOROSE

Oh no, labour not to stop her. She is like a conduit-pipe that will
gush out with more force when she opens again.   70

HAUGHTY

I'll tell you, Morose, you must talk divinity to him altogether, or
moral philosophy.

LA FOOLE

Ay, and there's an excellent book of moral philosophy, madam,
of Reynard the Fox and all the beasts, called *Doni's Philosophy.*

CENTAURE

There is indeed, Sir Amorous La Foole.   75

MOROSE

Oh misery!

LA FOOLE

I have read it, my Lady Centaure, all over to my cousin here.

MISTRESS OTTER

Ay, and 'tis a very good book as any is of the moderns.

DAW

Tut, he must have Seneca read to him, and Plutarch and the
ancients; the moderns are not for this disease.   80

---

62   *have . . . alive* i.e. be treated as a specimen in an anatomy class.
63   *mistress* ed. (mistris? F).
65   *is this to* has this got to do with.
74   *Doni's Philosophy* A collection of oriental beast fables translated into Italian by Doni
        and into English by Thomas North, with the title *The Moral Philosophy of Doni*
        (1570): La Foole is clearly as mesmerized by titles as Daw. The fable of Reynard is
        not included.

CLERIMONT

Why, you discommended them too today, Sir John.

DAW

Ay, in some cases; but in these they are best, and Aristotle's *Ethics*.

MAVIS

Say you so, Sir John? I think you are deceived: you took it upon trust.   85

HAUGHTY

Where's Trusty, my woman? I'll end this difference. I prithee, Otter, call her. Her father and mother were both mad when they put her to me.

> [*Exit* MISTRESS OTTER]

MOROSE

I think so. – Nay, gentlemen, I am tame. This is but an exercise, I know, a marriage ceremony, which I must endure.   90

HAUGHTY

And one of 'em – I know not which – was cured with *The Sick Man's Salve*, and the other with Greene's *Groat's-worth of Wit*.

TRUEWIT

A very cheap cure, madam.

HAUGHTY

Ay, it's very feasible.

> [*Enter* MISTRESS OTTER *with* TRUSTY]

MISTRESS OTTER

My lady called for you, Mistress Trusty; you must decide a con-   95
troversy.

HAUGHTY

Oh, Trusty, which was it you said, your father or your mother, that was cured with *The Sick Man's Salve*?

TRUSTY

My mother, madam, with the *Salve*.

---

88   *put . . . me* placed her in my charge.
89   *exercise* Several senses are involved: (i) performance of a ceremony; (ii) training, as
      of an animal (cf. *tame*); (iii) disciplinary suffering, trial. Sense (iii) was often used
      of saints and martyrs, and thus fits Morose's view of his plight; cf. I.i.154,
      III.vii.9–11.
91–2 *The . . . Salve* Religious tract by Thomas Becon urging patience and humility in time
      of illness; seventeen editions appeared between 1561 and 1632.
92   *Greene's . . . Wit* Robert Greene's popular admonitory and confessional pamphlet
      (1592), written on his deathbed.
94   *feasible* practicable.

TRUEWIT

Then it was *The Sick Woman's Salve.*   100

TRUSTY

And my father with the *Groat's-worth of Wit.* But there was other
means used: we had a preacher that would preach folk asleep
still; and so they were prescribed to go to church by an old
woman that was their physician, thrice a week –

EPICOENE

To sleep?   105

TRUSTY

Yes, forsooth; and every night they read themselves asleep on
those books.

EPICOENE

Good faith, it stands with great reason. I would I knew where to
procure those books.

MOROSE

Oh!   110

LA FOOLE

I can help you with one of 'em, Mistress Morose, the *Groat's-
worth of Wit.*

EPICOENE

But I shall disfurnish you, Sir Amorous. Can you spare it?

LA FOOLE

Oh, yes, for a week or so; I'll read it myself to him.

EPICOENE

No, I must do that, sir; that must be my office.   115

MOROSE

Oh, oh!

EPICOENE

Sure, he would do well enough, if he could sleep.

MOROSE

No, I should do well enough if you could sleep. Have I no friend
that will make her drunk? or give her a little ladanum, or opium?

TRUEWIT

Why, sir, she talks ten times worse in her sleep.   120

MOROSE

How!

103   *still* always.
113   *disfurnish you* deprive you (of the little wit you have).
119   *ladanum* laudanum (Jonson characteristically reverts to the classical, as opposed to
       the medieval, Latin form).

CLERIMONT

Do you not know that, sir? Never ceases all night.

TRUEWIT

And snores like a porcpisce.

MOROSE

Oh, redeem me, fate, redeem me, fate! For how many causes
may a man be divorced, nephew?   125

DAUPHINE

I know not truly, sir.

TRUEWIT

Some divine must resolve you in that, sir, or canon lawyer.

MOROSE

I will not rest, I will not think of any other hope or comfort,
till I know.

                    [*Exeunt* MOROSE *and* DAUPHINE]

CLERIMONT

Alas, poor man.   130

TRUEWIT

You'll make him mad indeed, ladies, if you pursue this.

HAUGHTY

No, we'll let him breathe now a quarter of an hour or so.

CLERIMONT

By my faith, a large truce.

HAUGHTY

Is that his keeper that is gone with him?

DAW

It is his nephew, madam.   135

LA FOOLE

Sir Dauphine Eugenie.

CENTAURE

He looks like a very pitiful knight –

DAW

As can be. This marriage has put him out of all.

LA FOOLE

He has not a penny in his purse, madam –

DAW

He is ready to cry all this day.   140

---

123   *porcpisce* porpoise (Latin *porcus piscis*, pig fish).
127   *canon lawyer* lawyer specializing in ecclesiastical law.
134   *keeper* i.e. as though Morose were a lunatic.

LA FOOLE

A very shark, he set me i' the nick t'other night at primero.

TRUEWIT [*Aside*]

How these swabbers talk!

CLERIMONT [*Aside*]

Ay, Otter's wine has swelled their humours above a spring-tide.

HAUGHTY

Good Morose, let's go in again. I like your couches exceeding
well: we'll go lie and talk there.   145

EPICOENE

I wait on you, madam.

> [*Exeunt* HAUGHTY, CENTAURE, MAVIS,
> TRUSTY, LA FOOLE *and* DAW]

TRUEWIT

'Slight, I will have 'em as silent as signs, and their posts too, ere
I ha' done. Do you hear, lady bride? I pray thee – now, as thou
art a noble wench, continue this discourse of Dauphine within;
but praise him exceedingly. Magnify him with all the height   150
of affection thou canst – I have some purpose in't – and but
beat off these two rooks, Jack Daw and his fellow, with any discontentment hither, and I'll honour thee forever.

EPICOENE

I was about it here. It angered me to the soul to hear 'em begin
to talk so malapert.   155

TRUEWIT

Pray thee perform it, and thou winn'st me an idolater to thee
everlasting.

EPICOENE

Will you go in and hear me do it?

TRUEWIT

No, I'll stay here. Drive 'em out of your company, 'tis all I ask;
which cannot be any way better done than by extolling Dauphine, 160
whom they have so slighted.

---

141   *shark* predatory cheat, sharper (Jonson's coinage).
       set . . . nick Implying 'cleaned me out'; to *set* is to bet against, and the *nick*, in the dice
       game of hazard, the predetermined winning score. *Primero* is a card game: La Foole
       is muddling his terms.
142   *swabbers* louts (*OED*'s first example of this sense).
152–3 *discontentment* annoyance, vexation.
154   *about it* setting about it.
155   *malapert* impudently.

EPICOENE

I warrant you; you shall expect one of 'em presently.   [*Exit*]

CLERIMONT

What a cast of kastrils are these, to hawk after ladies thus?

TRUEWIT

Ay, and strike at such an eagle as Dauphine.

CLERIMONT

He will be mad when we tell him. Here he comes.   165

ACT IV, SCENE v

[*Enter*] DAUPHINE

CLERIMONT

Oh sir, you are welcome.

TRUEWIT

Where's thine uncle?

DAUPHINE

Run out o' doors in's night-caps to talk with a casuist about his divorce. It works admirably.

TRUEWIT

Thou wouldst ha' said so and thou hadst been here! The ladies   5
have laughed at thee most comically since thou went'st, Dauphine.

CLERIMONT

And asked if thou wert thine uncle's keeper?

TRUEWIT

And the brace of baboons answered yes, and said thou wert a pitiful poor fellow and didst live upon posts, and hadst nothing

---

163   *cast of kastrils* Pair of kestrels (which were cast off in pairs). *Kestrel*, like the cognate *coistrel*, 'base fellow', was a term of contempt; cf. I.iv.68 and note.

3   *casuist* theologian or other person who resolves cases of conscience or doubtful questions regarding duty or conduct (*OED*'s first example of the word).

6   *comically* (i) satirically, derisively (as though Dauphine were a comic character); (ii) in a comical manner. *OED*'s first example of the word.

7   *if . . . keeper* Cf. 'Am I my brothers keper?' (Genesis, iv.9, Geneva Bible).

9   *upon posts* by running errands.

but three suits of apparel and some few benevolences that lords   10
ga' thee to fool to 'em and swagger.

DAUPHINE

Let me not live, I'll beat 'em. I'll bind 'em both to grand
madam's bed-posts and have 'em baited with monkeys.

TRUEWIT

Thou shalt not need, they shall be beaten to thy hand, Dauphine.
I have an execution to serve upon 'em I warrant thee shall serve;   15
trust my plot.

DAUPHINE

Ay, you have many plots! So you had one to make all the
wenches in love with me.

TRUEWIT

Why, if I do not yet afore night, as near as 'tis, and that they do
not every one invite thee and be ready to scratch for thee, take   20
the mortgage of my wit.

CLERIMONT

'Fore God, I'll be his witness; thou shalt have it, Dauphine; thou
shalt be his fool forever if thou dost not.

TRUEWIT

Agreed. Perhaps 'twill be the better estate. Do you observe this
gallery, or rather lobby, indeed? Here are a couple of studies, at   25
each end one: here will I act such a tragicomedy between the
Guelphs and the Ghibellines, Daw and La Foole. Which of 'em
comes out first will I seize on. You two shall be the chorus
behind the arras, and whip out between the acts and speak. If

10   *three suits* like a servant; cf. III.i.35.
14   *to thy hand* For you, without exertion on your part; cf. *Antony and Cleopatra*, IV.xiv.
      28–9: 'What thou wouldst do / Is done unto thy hand'.
15   *execution* legal writ enforcing a judgement.
19   *night* evening.
20   *scratch for* struggle fiercely to obtain (*OED*, v., 6.b); also literally: scratch each other.
22–3 *thou . . . fool* Truewit will be Dauphine's jester and butt.
24   *better estate* Picking up *mortgage*: better for Dauphine to receive Truewit as his fool
      than the ladies as his lovers.
26   *tragicomedy* A new type of drama introduced by Beaumont and Fletcher about the
      time *Epicoene* was written. The suggestion is that Daw and La Foole lack the dignity
      requisite to tragedy, and that such a hybrid unclassical form deserves such idiotic
      protagonists, as well as they it.
27   *Guelphs . . . Ghibellines* Papal and imperial factions which fought for power in
      medieval Italy. H&S note a reference to a lost play of this title, a 'tearing Tragaedy full
      of fights and skirmishes'.
29   *arras* Thick tapestry hung across a recess at the back of the stage; handy for hiding
      behind, as Polonius found in *Hamlet*.

I do not make 'em keep the peace for this remnant of the day,   30
if not of the year, I have failed once – I hear Daw coming. Hide,
and do not laugh, for God's sake.

[DAUPHINE *and* CLERIMONT *hide*]

[*Enter* DAW]

DAW

Which is the way into the garden, trow?

TRUEWIT

Oh, Jack Daw! I am glad I have met with you. In good faith, I
must have this matter go no further between you. I must ha'   35
it taken up.

DAW

What matter, sir? Between whom?

TRUEWIT

Come, you disguise it: Sir Amorous and you. If you love me,
Jack, you shall make use of your philosophy now, for this once,
and deliver me your sword. This is not the wedding the   40
Centaurs were at, though there be a she-one here. The bride has
entreated me I will see no blood shed at her bridal; you saw her
whisper me erewhile.   [*Takes his sword*]

DAW

As I hope to finish Tacitus, I intend no murder.

TRUEWIT

Do you not wait for Sir Amorous?   45

DAW

Not I, by my knighthood.

TRUEWIT

And your scholarship too?

DAW

And my scholarship too.

TRUEWIT

Go to, then I return you your sword, and ask you mercy; but put
it not up, for you will be assaulted. I understood that you had   50

33   *trow* do you think.
35   *matter* dispute (cf. *Hamlet*, II.ii.193–4).
36   *taken up* made up.
40–1   *This . . . at* At the marriage of Pirithous, King of the Lapiths, and Hippodamia a
       bloody fight broke out when a Centaur tried to rape the bride (*Metamorphoses*, XII,
       210 ff.).
44   *Tacitus* The Roman historian was a prolific author.
49–50 *put . . . up* do not sheathe it.

apprehended it, and walked here to brave him, and that you had
held your life contemptible in regard of your honour.

DAW

No, no, no such thing, I assure you. He and I parted now as good
friends as could be.

TRUEWIT

Trust not you to that visor. I saw him since dinner with another   55
face: I have known many men in my time vexed with losses, with
deaths, and with abuses, but so offended a wight as Sir Amorous
did I never see, or read of. For taking away his guests, sir, today,
that's the cause, and he declares it behind your back with such
threat'nings and contempts. He said to Dauphine you were the   60
arrant'st ass –

DAW

Ay, he may say his pleasure.

TRUEWIT

And swears you are so protested a coward that he knows you
will never do him any manly or single right, and therefore he
will take his course.   65

DAW

I'll give him any satisfaction, sir – but fighting.

TRUEWIT

Ay, sir, but who knows what satisfaction he'll take? Blood he
thirsts for, and blood he will have; and whereabouts on you he
will have it, who knows but himself?

DAW

I pray you, Master Truewit, be you a mediator.   70

TRUEWIT

Well, sir, conceal yourself then in this study till I return.

He puts him up

Nay, you must be content to be locked in; for, for mine own
reputation, I would not have you seen to receive a public disgrace, while I have the matter in managing. Gods so, here he
comes! Keep your breath close, that he do not hear you sigh. –   75
In good faith, Sir Amorous, he is not this way; I pray you be

51   *brave* defy.
55   *visor* mask.
57   *wight* Person. Truewit uses the archaic word to help evoke an atmosphere of
      romantic chivalry (cf. 'read of').
59   *cause* subject of dispute, as at l. 154.
63   *protested* declared.
64   *do . . . right* grant him the right to meet you man-to-man in an honourable duel.

merciful, do not murder him; he is a Christian as good as you; you are armed as if you sought a revenge on all his race. Good Dauphine, get him away from this place. I never knew a man's choler so high but he would speak to his friends, he would hear reason. – Jack Daw. Jack Daw! Asleep? 80

[*Brings* DAW *out*]

DAW

Is he gone, Master Truewit?

TRUEWIT

Ay, did you hear him?

DAW

Oh God, yes.

TRUEWIT [*Aside*]

What a quick ear fear has! 85

DAW

But is he so armed, as you say?

TRUEWIT

Armed? Did you ever see a fellow set out to take possession?

DAW

Ay, sir.

TRUEWIT

That may give you some light to conceive of him; but 'tis nothing to the principal. Some false brother i' the house has 90 furnished him strangely. Or, if it were out o' the house, it was Tom Otter.

DAW

Indeed, he's a captain, and his wife is his kinswoman.

TRUEWIT

He has got somebody's old two-hand sword, to mow you off at the knees. And that sword hath spawned such a dagger! – But 95 then he is so hung with pikes, halberds, petronels, calivers, and

---

85   *What . . . has* Proverbial: 'Fear has a quick ear' (Tilley, F134).
87   *take possession*, i.e. of his property, a mission which often required force, or the threat of it.
90   *principal* original, La Foole himself.
      false brother treacherous associate.
91   *strangely* exceptionally, i.e. with many kinds of weapons.
94   *two-hand sword* A large, fearsome, antiquated weapon, swung from side to side rather like a scythe. Clement comes close to mowing Brainworm off at the knees with one in *E.M.I.*, V.iii.36.
96   *petronels* large pistols or carbines used by cavalry.
      calivers light muskets.

muskets, that he looks like a justice of peace's hall; a man of two
thousand a year is not sessed at so many weapons as he has on.
There was never fencer challenged at so many several foils. You
would think he meant to murder all Saint Pulchre's parish. If he   100
could but victual himself for half a year in his breeches, he is
sufficiently armed to overrun a country.

DAW

Good lord, what means he, sir! I pray you, Master Truewit, be
you a mediator.

TRUEWIT

Well, I'll try if he will be appeased with a leg or an arm; if not,   105
you must die once.

DAW

I would be loath to lose my right arm, for writing madrigals.

TRUEWIT

Why, if he will be satisfied with a thumb or a little finger, all's
one to me. You must think I'll do my best.

DAW

Good sir, do.   110

He puts him up again, and then
[DAUPHINE *and* CLERIMONT] *come forth*

CLERIMONT

What hast thou done?

TRUEWIT

He will let me do nothing, man, he does all afore me; he offers
his left arm.

CLERIMONT

His left wing, for a Jack Daw.

DAUPHINE

Take it by all means.   115

TRUEWIT

How! Maim a man forever for a jest? What a conscience hast thou?

---

97   *justice . . . hall* Commonly hung with weapons ancient and modern.
98   *sessed* Assessed; i.e. to be able to provide so many when required by the monarch.
99   *at . . . foils* to fence with so many different types of sword.
100   *Pulchre's* Or Sepulchre's, a large and crowded parish in north-west London.
101   *breeches* La Foole is wearing the fashionable continental breeches with enormous
         stuffed legs, known as 'slops'.
106   *once* a common intensive: once for all, in short.
110   s.d. *come* ed. (*came* F).

DAUPHINE

Tis no loss to him: he has no employment for his arms but to
eat spoon-meat. Beside, as good maim his body as his reputation.

TRUEWIT

He is a scholar and a Wit, and yet he does not think so. But he
loses no reputation with us, for we all resolved him an ass before.   120
To your places again.

CLERIMONT

I pray thee let me be in at the other a little.

TRUEWIT

Look, you'll spoil all: these be ever your tricks.

CLERIMONT

No, but I could hit of some things that thou wilt miss, and thou
wilt say are good ones.   125

TRUEWIT

I warrant you. I pray forbear, I'll leave it off else.

DAUPHINE

Come away, Clerimont.

[*They hide*]

[*Enter* LA FOOLE]

TRUEWIT

Sir Amorous!

LA FOOLE

Master Truewit.

TRUEWIT

Whither were you going?   130

LA FOOLE

Down into the court to make water.

TRUEWIT

By no means, sir; you shall rather tempt your breeches.

LA FOOLE

Why, sir?

---

118   *spoon-meat* baby-food.
119   *so* That his body might as well be maimed.
120   *resolved him* decided he was.
122   *in at* involved in (the fooling of). *OED* does not cite this expression before 1814,
       when it gives 'in at the kill' (Supplement, 'kill', sb., 2.b). In view of the play's hunting
       and baiting imagery, this association would be highly appropriate.
124   *hit of* light upon.
132   *tempt* make trial of.

TRUEWIT [*Opening the other door*]
  Enter here if you love your life.
LA FOOLE
  Why? Why?   135
TRUEWIT
  Question till your throat be cut, do; dally till the enraged soul
  find you.
LA FOOLE
  Who's that?
TRUEWIT
  Daw it is; will you in?
LA FOOLE
  Ay, ay, I'll in; what's the matter?   140
TRUEWIT
  Nay, if he had been cool enough to tell us that, there had been
  some hope to atone you, but he seems so implacably enraged.
LA FOOLE
  'Slight, let him rage. I'll hide myself.
TRUEWIT
  Do, good sir. But what have you done to him within that should
  provoke him thus? You have broke some jest upon him afore the   145
  ladies –
LA FOOLE
  Not I, never in my life broke jest upon any man. The bride was
  praising sir Dauphine, and he went away in snuff, and I followed
  him, unless he took offence at me in his drink erewhile, that I
  would not pledge all the horse-full.   150
TRUEWIT
  By my faith, and that may be, you remember well; but he walks
  the round up and down, through every room o' the house, with
  a towel in his hand, crying, 'Where's La Foole? Who saw La
  Foole?' And when Dauphine and I demanded the cause, we can
  force no answer from him but 'Oh revenge, how sweet art thou!   155
  I will strangle him in this towel' – which leads us to conjecture

---

142   *atone* set 'at one', reconcile.
145   *broke . . . him* cracked some joke at his expense.
147   *never* The colloquial omission of 'I' is paralleled in *E.M.I.*, IV.vii.97.
148   *in snuff* in a huff.
149   *unless* lest, in case.
151–2 *walks the round* A military metaphor from the patrol which goes round a camp or
       fortress to check that the sentries are vigilant (H&S).

that the main cause of his fury is for bringing your meat today,
with a towel about you, to his discredit.

LA FOOLE

Like enough. Why, and he be angry for that, I'll stay here till his
anger be blown over.   160

TRUEWIT

A good becoming resolution, sir. If you can put it on o' the
sudden.

LA FOOLE

Yes, I can put it on. Or I'll away into the country presently.

TRUEWIT

How will you get out o' the house, sir? He knows you are i' the
house, and he'll watch you this se'en-night but he'll have you.   165
He'll outwait a sergeant for you.

LA FOOLE

Why then I'll stay here.

TRUEWIT

You must think how to victual yourself in time then.

LA FOOLE

Why, sweet Master Truewit, will you entreat my cousin Otter
to send me a cold venison pasty, a bottle or two of wine, and a   170
chamber-pot?

TRUEWIT

A stool were better, sir, of Sir A-jax his invention.

LA FOOLE

Ay, that will be better indeed; and a pallet to lie on.

TRUEWIT

Oh, I would not advise you to sleep by any means.

LA FOOLE

Would you not, sir? Why then I will not.   175

TRUEWIT

Yet there's another fear –

---

161   *put . . . on* (i) adopt; (ii) feign.
163   *presently* at once.
165   *watch* keep watch for.
166   *sergeant* Sheriff's officer. 'All the vacation hee lies imboagde behinde the lattice of
      some . . . Ale-house, and if he spy his prey out he leaps' (Overbury, 'A Sargeant',
      Characters, 1618, sig. N6^V).
172   *A-jax* Referring to Sir John Harington's treatise on the flushing toilet, *The Meta-
      morphosis of Ajax* (1596), with its pun on 'a jakes'.
173   *pallet* straw mattress.

LA FOOLE

Is there, sir? What is't?

TRUEWIT

No, he cannot break open this door with his foot, sure.

LA FOOLE

I'll set my back against it, sir. I have a good back.

TRUEWIT

But then if he should batter. 180

LA FOOLE

Batter! If he dare, I'll have an action of batt'ry against him.

TRUEWIT

Cast you the worst. He has sent for powder already, and what he
will do with it, no man knows; perhaps blow up the corner o' the
house where he suspects you are. Here he comes! In, quickly.

He feigns as if one were present, to fright the other,
who is run in to hide himself

I protest, Sir John Daw, he is not this way. What will you do? 185
Before God, you shall hang no petard here. I'll die rather. Will
you not take my word? I never knew one but would be satisfied.
– Sir Amorous, there's no standing out. He has made a petard of
an old brass pot, to force your door. Think upon some satisfaction or terms to offer him. 190

LA FOOLE [*Within*]

Sir, I'll give him any satisfaction. I dare give any terms.

TRUEWIT

You'll leave it to me then?

LA FOOLE

Ay, sir. I'll stand to any conditions.

[TRUEWIT] *calls forth* CLERIMONT *and* DAUPHINE

TRUEWIT

How now, what think you, sirs? Were't not a difficult thing to
determine which of these two feared most? 195

CLERIMONT

Yes, but this fears the bravest; the other a whiniling dastard, Jack
Daw. But La Foole, a brave heroic coward! And is afraid in a

---

182   *Cast* forecast, anticipate.
186   *petard* bomb used to breach walls and blow down gates.
188   *standing out* resisting.
193   s.d. TRUEWIT ed. (*He* F).
196   *whiniling* whimpering.

great look and a stout accent. I like him rarely.

CLERIMONT

TRUEWIT

Had it not been pity these two should ha' been concealed?

CLERIMONT

Shall I make a motion?   200

TRUEWIT

Briefly. For I must strike while 'tis hot.

CLERIMONT

Shall I go fetch the ladies to the catastrophe?

TRUEWIT

Umh? Ay, by my troth.

DAUPHINE

By no mortal means. Let them continue in the state of ignorance, and err still; think 'em wits and fine fellows as they have   205
done. 'Twere sin to reform them.

TRUEWIT

Well, I will have 'em fetched, now I think on't, for a private purpose of mine; do, Clerimont, fetch 'em, and discourse to 'em all
that's past, and bring 'em into the gallery here.

DAUPHINE

This is thy extreme vanity now; thou think'st thou wert undone   210
if every jest thou mak'st were not published.

TRUEWIT

Thou shalt see how unjust thou art presently. Clerimont, say it
was Dauphine's plot.

[*Exit* CLERIMONT]

Trust me not if the whole drift be not for thy good. There's a
carpet i' the next room; put it on, with this scarf over thy face   215
and a cushion o' thy head, and be ready when I call Amorous.
Away.

[*Exit* DAUPHINE]

– John Daw!   [*Brings* DAW *out of his study*]

DAW

What good news, sir?

TRUEWIT

Faith, I have followed and argued with him hard for you. I   220
told him you were a knight and a scholar, and that you knew

200   *motion* proposal.
202   *catastrophe* dénouement (as in a play; cf. ll. 6, 17–18, 26–9).
211   *published* made generally known, as at l. 286.
215   *carpet* tablecloth of thick wool.

fortitude did consist *magis patiendo quam faciendo, magis ferendo quam feriendo.*

DAW

It doth so indeed, sir.

TRUEWIT

And that you would suffer, I told him: so at first he demanded,   225
by my troth, in my conceit too much.

DAW

What was it, sir?

TRUEWIT

Your upper lip, and six o' your fore-teeth.

DAW

'Twas unreasonable.

TRUEWIT

Nay, I told him plainly, you could not spare 'em all. So after long   230
argument – *pro et con*, as you know – I brought him down to
your two butter-teeth, and them he would have.

DAW

Oh, did you so? Why, he shall have 'em.

[*Enter above* HAUGHTY, CENTAURE, MAVIS, MISTRESS OTTER,
EPICOENE, TRUSTY, *and* CLERIMONT]

TRUEWIT

But he shall not, sir, by your leave. The conclusion is this, sir:
because you shall be very good friends hereafter, and this never   235
to be remembered or upbraided, besides that he may not boast
he has done any such thing to you in his own person, he is to
come here in disguise, give you five kicks in private, sir, take
your sword from you, and lock you up in that study, during
pleasure. Which will be but a little while, we'll get it released   240
presently.

DAW

Five kicks? He shall have six, sir, to be friends.

222–3   *magis . . . feriendo* 'More in suffering than in doing, more in enduring than in
striking'. Quoted elsewhere (see H&S), but the source is unknown.
226   *conceit* opinion.
232   *butter-teeth* front teeth.
234–7   *sir: . . . person* ed. (sir, . . . person: F).
236   *upbraided* brought up as a ground for reproach.
239–40   *during pleasure* for as long as he pleases.

TRUEWIT

Believe me, you shall not overshoot yourself to send him that word by me.

DAW

Deliver it, sir. He shall have it with all my heart, to be friends. 245

TRUEWIT

Friends? Nay, and he should not be so, and heartily too, upon these terms, he shall have me to enemy while I live. Come, sir, bear it bravely.

DAW

Oh God, sir, 'tis nothing.

TRUEWIT

True. What's six kicks to a man that reads Seneca? 250

DAW

I have had a hundred, sir.

TRUEWIT

Sir Amorous! No speaking one to another, or rehearsing old matters.

DAUPHINE *comes forth and kicks him*

DAW

One, two, three, four, five. I protest, Sir Amorous, you shall have six. 255

TRUEWIT

Nay, I told you, you should not talk. Come, give him six, and he will needs,

[DAUPHINE *kicks him again*]

Your sword.

[DAW *gives* TRUEWIT *his sword*]

Now return to your safe custody: you shall presently meet afore the ladies, and be the dearest friends one to another. 260

[DAW *goes into his study*]

– Give me the scarf; now thou shalt beat the other barefaced. Stand by.

[*Exit* DAUPHINE]

– Sir Amorous!

[*Brings out* LA FOOLE]

243   *overshoot yourself to* overreach yourself if you.
250   *Seneca* The stoic philosopher. Cf. I.i.55 and note.
252–3 *old matters* former quarrels.
256   *you, you* ed. (you F).
262   *by* ed. (by F) to one side.

LA FOOLE

What's here? A sword!

TRUEWIT

I cannot help it, without I should take the quarrel upon myself;   265
here he has sent you his sword –

LA FOOLE

I'll receive none on't.

TRUEWIT

And he wills you to fasten it against a wall, and break your head
in some few several places against the hilts.

LA FOOLE

I will not: tell him roundly. I cannot endure to shed my own   270
blood.

TRUEWIT

Will you not?

LA FOOLE

No. I'll beat it against a fair flat wall, if that will satisfy him; if
not, he shall beat it himself for Amorous.

TRUEWIT

Why, this is strange starting off when a man undertakes for you!   275
I offered him another condition: will you stand to that?

LA FOOLE

Ay, what is't?

TRUEWIT

That you will be beaten in private.

LA FOOLE

Yes. I am content, at the blunt.

TRUEWIT

Then you must submit yourself to be hoodwinked in this scarf,   280
and be led to him, where he will take your sword from you, and

---

265   *without* unless.
269   *several* different.
      hilts Because the hilt comprises several parts, pommel, handle, and shell, it was often
      spoken of as plural.
270   *roundly* plainly.
274   *for Amorous* 'For all Amorous cares' is preferable to 'on Amorous's behalf; cf. V.i.81.
275   *starting off* swerving aside, shying away (said of horses).
      undertakes makes himself answerable.
279   *at the blunt*, i.e. with the flat of the sword; strictly the phrase means to fence with
      capped sword-points.
280   *hoodwinked* (i) blindfolded; (ii) duped.

make you bear a blow over the mouth, gules, and tweaks by the
nose *sans nombre.*

LA FOOLE

I am content. But why must I be blinded?

TRUEWIT

That's for your good, sir: because if he should grow insolent   285
upon this and publish it hereafter to your disgrace – which I
hope he will not do – you might swear safely and protest he never
beat you, to your knowledge.

LA FOOLE

Oh, I conceive.

TRUEWIT

I do not doubt but you'll be perfect good friends upon't, and   290
not dare to utter an ill thought one of another in future.

LA FOOLE

Not I, as God help me, of him.

TRUEWIT

Nor he of you, sir. If he should – Come, sir.

[Blindfolds him]

– All hid, Sir John.

DAUPHINE *enters to tweak him*

LA FOOLE

Oh, Sir John, Sir John! Oh, o-o-o-o-o-Oh –   295

[DAUPHINE takes his sword]

TRUEWIT

Good Sir John, leave tweaking, you'll blow his nose off.

[Exit DAUPHINE with the two swords]

'Tis Sir John's pleasure you should retire into the study.

[Unbinds LA FOOLE's eyes and shuts him in]

Why, now you are friends. All bitterness between you, I hope, is

282   *bear* (i) endure; (ii) in heraldry, carry, display.
282–3   *a blow . . . nombre* In ironic correspondence to I.iv.35–8. La Foole's new coat-of-
        arms will be a bloody mouth surrounded by numberless tweaked noses. Cf. *Hamlet*,
        III.i.571–4: 'Am I a coward? / Who . . . / Tweaks me by the nose?'.
283   *nombre* ed. (*numbre* F).
285   *insolent* arrogant, overbearing, as at V.ii.58.
294   *All hid* The cry in hide-and-seek; '[he] cryes all-hidde as boyes do' (Dekker, *Satiro-
        mastix*, V.ii.154).

buried; you shall come forth by and by Damon and Pythias upon't, and embrace with all the rankness of friendship that   300
can be.

Enter DAUPHINE

I trust we shall have 'em tamer i' their language hereafter. Dauphine, I worship thee. – God's will, the ladies have surprised us!

ACT IV, SCENE vi

[*Enter from above*] HAUGHTY, CENTAURE, MAVIS,
MISTRESS OTTER, EPICOENE, TRUSTY, [*and* CLERIMONT,]
having discovered part of the past scene above

HAUGHTY

Centaure, how our judgements were imposed on by these adulterate knights!

CENTAURE

Nay, madam, Mavis was more deceived than we; 'twas her commendation uttered 'em in the college.

MAVIS

I commended but their wits, madam, and their braveries. I never   5
looked toward their valours.

HAUGHTY

Sir Dauphine is valiant, and a wit too, it seems.

MAVIS

And a Bravery too.

HAUGHTY

Was this his project?

299   *Damon and Pythias* A type of loyal friendship. Pythias, sentenced to death by the
      King of Syracuse, returned to save his friend Damon, who had gone bail for him, and
      was reprieved for his fidelity.
300   *rankness* (i) abundance; (ii) foulness.
303   *surprised* caught unawares (spoken for the ladies' benefit).

1–2   *adulterate* counterfeit.
   4   *uttered 'em* made them known.
   5   *braveries* fine clothes.
   8   *Bravery* cf. I.i.70.

MISTRESS OTTER
So Master Clerimont intimates, madam.   10
HAUGHTY
Good Morose, when you come to the college, will you bring him
with you? He seems a very perfect gentleman.
EPICOENE
He is so, madam, believe it.
CENTAURE
But when will you come, Morose?
EPICOENE
Three or four days hence, madam, when I have got me a coach   15
and horses.
HAUGHTY
No, tomorrow, good Morose; Centaure shall send you her coach.
MAVIS
Yes, faith, do, and bring Sir Dauphine with you.
HAUGHTY
She has promised that, Mavis.
MAVIS
He is a very worthy gentleman in his exteriors, madam.   20
HAUGHTY
Ay, he shows he is judicial in his clothes.
CENTAURE
And yet not so superlatively neat as some, madam, that have
their faces set in a brake!
HAUGHTY
Ay, and have every hair in form!
MAVIS
That wear purer linen than ourselves, and profess more neat-   25
ness than the French hermaphrodite!

---

21   *judicial* a ludicrous mistake: not 'like a judge' but 'judicious'.
22   *superlatively* exaggeratedly.
23   *in a brake* in an immovable expression of countenance; cf. V.iii.18. Another image
      from horses: a *brake* was a frame for the horse's hoof while being shod.
25   *profess* practise.
26   *French hermaphrodite* Mavis may only be indicating a type (the English tended to
      envy the French for being ahead of them in fashion while despising them for being
      effeminate), but she may also be making a historical reference: possibly to the
      hermaphrodite said to be on show in London in Beaumont's *The Knight of the Burn-
      ing Pestle* (*c.* 1607–10), III.276; or perhaps, as Beaurline suggests, to Henry III of
      France (d. 1589), a notorious transvestite satirized in Thomas Arthus's *Isle des
      Hermaphrodites* (1605).

EPICOENE

Ay, ladies, they, what they tell one of us, have told a thousand,
and are the only thieves of our fame, that think to take us with
that perfume or with that lace, and laugh at us unconscionably
when they have done.   30

HAUGHTY

But Sir Dauphine's carelessness becomes him.

CENTAURE

I could love a man for such a nose!

MAVIS

Or such a leg!

CENTAURE

He has an exceeding good eye, madam!

MAVIS

And a very good lock!   35

CENTAURE

Good Morose, bring him to my chamber first.

MISTRESS OTTER

Please your honours to meet at my house, madam?

TRUEWIT [*Aside to* DAUPHINE]

See how they eye thee, man! They are taken, I warrant thee.

HAUGHTY [*Approaching* TRUEWIT *and* DAUPHINE]

You have unbraced our brace of knights here, Master Truewit.

TRUEWIT

Not I, madam, it was Sir Dauphine's engine; who, if he have   40
disfurnished your ladyship of any guard or service by it, is able
to make the place good again in himself.

HAUGHTY

There's no suspicion of that, sir.

CENTAURE

God so, Mavis, Haughty is kissing.

MAVIS

Let us go too and take part.   45

HAUGHTY

But I am glad of the fortune – beside the discovery of two such

28   *fame* reputation.
35   *lock* see note to III.v.62.
39   *unbraced* disarmed, implying 'exposed, disgraced'.
40   *engine* device.
41   *service* glancing at the amatory sense; cf. *servant* = lover.
43   *suspicion* affectedly for 'doubt'.
46   *discovery* uncovery, exposure.

empty caskets – to gain the knowledge of so rich a mine of virtue
as Sir Dauphine.

CENTAURE

We would be all glad to style him of our friendship, and see him
at the college. 50

MAVIS

He cannot mix with a sweeter society, I'll prophesy, and I hope
he himself will think so.

DAUPHINE

I should be rude to imagine otherwise, lady.

TRUEWIT [*Aside to* DAUPHINE]

Did not I tell thee, Dauphine? Why, all their actions are governed
by crude opinion, without reason or cause; they know not why 55
they do anything; but as they are informed, believe, judge, praise,
condemn, love, hate, and in emulation one of another, do all
these things alike. Only, they have a natural inclination sways
'em generally to the worst, when they are left to themselves. But
pursue it, now thou hast 'em. 60

HAUGHTY

Shall we go in again, Morose?

EPICOENE

Yes, madam.

CENTAURE

We'll entreat Sir Dauphine's company.

TRUEWIT

Stay, good madam, the interview of the two friends, Pylades and
Orestes: I'll fetch 'em out to you straight. 65

HAUGHTY

Will you, Master Truewit?

DAUPHINE

Ay, but, noble ladies, do not confess in your countenance
or outward bearing to 'em any discovery of their follies, that we
may see how they will bear up again, with what assurance and
erection. 70

HAUGHTY

We will not, Sir Dauphine.

49   *style . . . friendship* affectedly for 'call him one of our friends'.
64   *Stay* remain for.
64–5 *Pylades and Orestes* In the tragedies of Aeschylus and Euripides, Pylades is the loyal
       friend who helps Orestes revenge the murder of his father, Agamemnon.
70   *erection* Uprightness, confidence of bearing. The sexual pun is appropriate after the
       ritual castration (Beaurline).

CENTAURE [*and*] MAVIS
Upon our honours, Sir Dauphine.

TRUEWIT
Sir Amorous, Sir Amorous! The ladies are here.

LA FOOLE [*Within*]
Are they?

TRUEWIT
Yes, but slip out by and by as their backs are turned and meet Sir   75
John here, as by chance, when I call you. – Jack Daw!

DAW [*Within*]
What say you, sir?

TRUEWIT
Whip out behind me suddenly, and no anger i' your looks to
your adversary. – Now, now!

> [LA FOOLE *and* DAW *come out of their studies*
> *and salute each other*]

LA FOOLE
Noble Sir John Daw! Where ha' you been?   80

DAW
To seek you, Sir Amorous.

LA FOOLE
Me! I honour you.

DAW
I prevent you, sir.

CLERIMONT
They have forgot their rapiers!

TRUEWIT
Oh, they meet in peace, man.   85

DAUPHINE
Where's your sword, Sir John?

CLERIMONT
And yours, Sir Amorous?

DAW
Mine? My boy had it forth to mend the handle, e'en now.

LA FOOLE
And my gold handle was broke too, and my boy had it forth.

DAUPHINE
Indeed, sir? How their excuses meet!   90

83   *prevent* anticipate, forestall.
89   *had it forth* took it away from here.

CLERIMONT

What a consent there is i' the handles!

TRUEWIT

Nay, there is so i' the points too, I warrant you.

MISTRESS OTTER

Oh me! Madam, he comes again, the madman! Away!

[*Exeunt hastily* HAUGHTY, CENTAURE, EPICOENE, MAVIS,
MISTRESS OTTER, TRUSTY, DAW, *and* LA FOOLE]

ACT IV, SCENE vii

[*Enter*] MOROSE [*with a sword in each hand;*]
he had found the two swords drawn within

MOROSE

What make these naked weapons here, gentlemen?

TRUEWIT

Oh, sir! Here hath like to been murder since you went! A couple
of knights fallen out about the bride's favours. We were fain to
take away their weapons, your house had been begged by this
time else –   5

MOROSE

For what?

CLERIMONT

For manslaughter, sir, as being accessary.

MOROSE

And for her favours?

TRUEWIT

Ay, sir, heretofore, not present. Clerimont, carry 'em their swords
now. They have done all the hurt they will do.   10

[*Exit* CLERIMONT *with the swords*]

---

92   *points* (i) sword-points, which both have been afraid to use; (ii) various points of
their excuses.

3   *fain* obliged.
4   *begged* begged for by some courtier in anticipation of the confiscation of Morose's
property as that of a criminal.
9   *heretofore* i.e. past ones.

DAUPHINE

Ha' you spoke with a lawyer, sir?

MOROSE

Oh no! There is such a noise i' the court that they have frighted
me home with more violence than I went! Such speaking and
counter-speaking, with their several voices of citations, appella-
tions, allegations, certificates, attachments, intergatories, refer-   15
ences, convictions, and afflictions indeed among the doctors
and proctors, that the noise here is silence to't! A kind of calm
midnight!

TRUEWIT

Why, sir, if you would be resolved indeed, I can bring you hither
a very sufficient lawyer and a learned divine, that shall enquire   20
into every least scruple for you.

MOROSE

Can you, Master Truewit?

TRUEWIT

Yes, and are very sober grave persons, that will dispatch it in a
chamber, with a whisper or two.

MOROSE

Good sir, shall I hope this benefit from you, and trust myself   25
into your hands?

TRUEWIT

Alas, sir! Your nephew and I have been ashamed, and oft-times
mad, since you went, to think how you are abused. Go in, good
sir, and lock yourself up till we call you; we'll tell you more anon,
sir.   30

MOROSE

Do your pleasure with me, gentlemen; I believe in you, and that
deserves no delusion –

TRUEWIT

You shall find none, sir

[*Exit* MOROSE]

– but heaped, heaped plenty of vexation.

DAUPHINE

What wilt thou do now, Wit?   35

15   *attachments* writs of arrest.
        intergatories interrogatories.
15–16   *references* submissions.
16–17   *doctors . . . proctors* barristers . . . attorneys.
21   *scruple* uncertainty, doubt.
28   *mad* furious.

TRUEWIT

Recover me hither Otter and the barber if you can, by any means, presently.

DAUPHINE

Why? To what purpose?

TRUEWIT

Oh, I'll make the deepest divine and gravest lawyer out o' them two for him –   40

DAUPHINE

Thou canst not, man; these are waking dreams.

TRUEWIT

Do not fear me. Clap but a civil gown with a welt o' the one, and a canonical cloak with sleeves o' the other, and give 'em a few terms i' their mouths; if there come not forth as able a doctor and complete a parson for this turn as may be wished, trust not   45
my election. And I hope, without wronging the dignity of either profession, since they are but persons put on, and for mirth's sake, to torment him. The barber smatters Latin, I remember.

DAUPHINE

Yes, and Otter too.

TRUEWIT

Well then, if I make 'em not wrangle out this case to his no   50
comfort, let me be thought a Jack Daw, or La Foole, or anything worse. Go you to your ladies, but first send for them.

DAUPHINE

I will.

[*Exeunt*]

---

42   *fear* doubt.
       welt border (here, of fur)
46   *election* ability to make choices, judgement.
46–8 *without . . . sake* Jonson is referring to, and guarding against a recurrence of, the trouble caused by his satire on lawyers in *Poet.*, I.ii.117 ff; cf. the Apologetical Dialogue, 81–2, and *Satiromastix*, IV.iii.184–8.
48, 50 *smatters Latin . . . wrangle out* OED's first examples of these usages.

ACT V, SCENE i

[*Enter*] LA FOOLE, CLERIMONT, DAW

LA FOOLE
Where had you our swords, Master Clerimont?

CLERIMONT
Why, Dauphine took 'em from the madman.

LA FOOLE
And he took 'em from our boys, I warrant you.

CLERIMONT
Very like, sir.

LA FOOLE
Thank you, good Master Clerimont. Sir John Daw and I are   5
both beholden to you.

CLERIMONT
Would I knew how to make you so, gentlemen.

DAW
Sir Amorous and I are your servants, sir.

[*Enter* MAVIS]

MAVIS
Gentlemen, have any of you a pen and ink? I would fain write
out a riddle in Italian for Sir Dauphine to translate.   10

CLERIMONT
Not I, in troth, lady, I am no scrivener.

DAW
I can furnish you, I think, lady.

[*Exeunt* DAW *and* MAVIS]

CLERIMONT
He has it in the haft of a knife, I believe!

LA FOOLE
No, he has his box of instruments.

CLERIMONT
Like a surgeon!   15

LA FOOLE
For the mathematics: his squire, his compasses, his brass pens,
and black lead, to draw maps of every place and person where
he comes.

16   *squire* square.

315

CLERIMONT

How, maps of persons!

LA FOOLE

Yes, sir, of Nomentack, when he was here, and of the Prince of   20
Moldavia, and of his mistress, Mistress Epicoene.

CLERIMONT

Away! He has not found out her latitude, I hope.

LA FOOLE

You are a pleasant gentleman, sir.

[*Enter* DAW]

CLERIMONT

Faith, now we are in private, let's wanton it a little and talk waggishly. Sir John, I am telling Sir Amorous here that you two   25
govern the ladies; where'er you come, you carry the feminine
gender afore you.

DAW

They shall rather carry us afore them, if they will, sir.

CLERIMONT

Nay, I believe that they do, withal; but that you are the prime
men in their affections, and direct all their actions –   30

DAW

Not I; Sir Amorous is.

LA FOOLE

I protest Sir John is.

DAW

As I hope to rise i' the state, Sir Amorous, you ha' the person.

LA FOOLE

Sir John, you ha' the person, and the discourse too.

DAW

Not I, sir. I have no discourse – and then you have activity beside.   35

20   *Nomentack* Red Indian brought from Virginia to England in 1608 and sent back in
        May 1609.
23   *pleasant* humorous, jocular.
26   *ladies;* ed. (ladies, F).
26–7 *you . . . afore you* A punning jibe at the knights' effeminacy.
28   *They . . . them* Waggishly referring to the male's superincumbency during coition.
29   *Nay . . . withal* Glancing at the collegiates' masculinity.
33, 34 *person* Daw is apparently saying, affectedly, 'it is you who are'. La Foole understands
        him to mean, or puns weakly on, 'presence, attractiveness'.
35   *activity* gymnastic skill.

LA FOOLE

> I protest, Sir John, you come as high from Tripoli as I do every
> whit, and lift as many joined stools and leap over 'em, if you
> would use it –

CLERIMONT

> Well, agree on't together, knights, for between you you divide
> the kingdom or commonwealth of ladies' affections: I see it and   40
> can perceive a little how they observe you, and fear you, indeed.
> You could tell strange stories, my masters, if you would, I know.

DAW

> Faith, we have seen somewhat, sir.

LA FOOLE

> That we have: vellet petticoats and wrought smocks or so.

DAW

> Ay, and –   45

CLERIMONT

> Nay, out with it, Sir John; do not envy your friend the pleasure
> of hearing, when you have had the delight of tasting.

DAW

> Why – a – do you speak, Sir Amorous.

LA FOOLE

> No, do you, Sir John Daw.

DAW

> I' faith, you shall.   50

LA FOOLE

> I' faith, you shall.

DAW

> Why, we have been –

LA FOOLE

> In the great bed at Ware together in our time. On, Sir John.

DAW

> Nay, do you, Sir Amorous.

---

36   *come . . . Tripoli* 'To vault and tumble with activity. It was, I believe, first applied to
      the tricks of an ape or monkey, which might be supposed to come from that part of
      the world' (Nares). A more obvious explanation of the phrase, which Jonson uses
      elsewhere (cf. Epigram CXV), is a pun on *trip*.

38   *use* practise.

40   *commonwealth* Implying that Daw and La Foole's women are shared by everyone.

44   *vellet . . . smocks* Worn by high-class prostitutes; cf. *B.F.*, IV.vi.19–20.

53   *great . . . Ware* Famous bed at the Saracen's Head, Ware, made about 1580, 7½ feet
      high and nearly 11 feet square, sleeping twelve people; mentioned in *Twelfth Night*,
      III.ii.47–8. Now in the Victoria and Albert Museum.

CLERIMONT.

And these ladies with you, knights? 55

LA FOOLE

No, excuse us, sir.

DAW

We must not wound reputation.

LA FOOLE

No matter; they were these, or others. Our bath cost us fifteen
pound, when we came home.

CLERIMONT

Do you hear, Sir John, you shall tell me but one thing truly, as 60
you love me.

DAW

If I can, I will, sir.

CLERIMONT

You lay in the same house with the bride here?

DAW

Yes, and conversed with her hourly, sir.

CLERIMONT

And what humour is she of? Is she coming and open, free? 65

DAW

Oh, exceeding open, sir. I was her servant, and Sir Amorous was
to be.

CLERIMONT

Come, you have both had favours from her? I know and have
heard so much.

DAW

Oh no, sir. 70

LA FOOLE

You shall excuse us, sir: we must not wound reputation.

CLERIMONT

Tut, she is married now, and you cannot hurt her with any report,
and therefore speak plainly: how many times, i' faith? Which of
you led first? Ha?

LA FOOLE

Sir John had her maidenhead, indeed. 75

---

58   *bath* La Foole seems to mean a medicinal bath for treating lice or venereal disease,
      and absurdly offers this as a boast.
65   *coming and open* For the innuendoes cf. *E.M.I.*, IV.x.74, where Cob asks his wife,
      'doe you let [your doors] lie open for all commers?'.
66   *servant* cf. The Persons of the Play, l. 6.

DAW

Oh, it pleases him to say so, sir, but Sir Amorous knows what's what as well.

CLERIMONT

Dost thou i' faith, Amorous?

LA FOOLE

In a manner, sir.

CLERIMONT

Why, I commend you, lads. Little knows Don Bridegroom of   80
this. Nor shall he, for me.

DAW

Hang him, mad ox.

CLERIMONT

Speak softly: here comes his nephew, with the Lady Haughty.
He'll get the ladies from you, sirs, if you look not to him in time.

LA FOOLE

Why, if he do, we'll fetch 'em home again, I warrant you.   85

[*Exeunt*]

ACT V, SCENE ii

[*Enter*] HAUGHTY, DAUPHINE

HAUGHTY

I assure you, Sir Dauphine, it is the price and estimation of your
virtue only that hath embarked me to this adventure, and I could
not but make out to tell you so; nor can I repent me of the act,
since it is always an argument of some virtue in ourselves that
we love and affect it so in others.   5

---

80   *Don* The Spanish title for 'Master' was often used contemptuously or jocularly,
somewhat the way we now use 'Comrade' (Partridge).

82   *mad ox* Crazy fool, and suggesting 'maddened cuckold', because of the ox's horns.

1   *price* value, worth. The near synonimity with 'estimation' is symptomatic of Haughty's
extravagant language; cf. the similarly redundant couplings at ll. 5, 10, 14–15, and
Dauphine's ironic play on 'price' at l. 6.

3   *make out* make shift, contrive (*OED* has no other example before 1776).

4   *argument* proof, token.

5   *affect* love.

DAUPHINE

Your ladyship sets too high a price on my weakness.

HAUGHTY

Sir, I can distinguish gems from pebbles –

DAUPHINE

Are you so skilful in stones?

HAUGHTY

And howsoever I may suffer in such a judgement as yours, by
admitting equality of rank or society with Centaure or Mavis –   10

DAUPHINE

You do not, madam; I perceive they are your mere foils.

HAUGHTY

Then are you a friend to truth, sir. It makes me love you the
more. It is not the outward but the inward man that I affect. They
are not apprehensive of an eminent perfection, but love flat and
dully.   15

CENTAURE [*Within*]

Where are you, my Lady Haughty?

HAUGHTY

I come presently, Centaure. – My chamber, sir, my page shall
show you; and Trusty, my woman, shall be ever awake for you;
you need not fear to communicate anything with her, for she is
a Fidelia. I pray you wear this jewel for my sake, Sir Dauphine.   20

[*Enter* CENTAURE]

Where's Mavis, Centaure?

CENTAURE

Within, madam, a-writing. I'll follow you presently. I'll but speak
a word with Sir Dauphine.

[*Exit* HAUGHTY]

DAUPHINE

With me, madam?

CENTAURE

Good Sir Dauphine, do not trust Haughty, nor make any credit   25
to her, whatever you do besides. Sir Dauphine, I give you this
caution, she is a perfect courtier and loves nobody but for her
uses, and for her uses she loves all. Besides, her physicians give
her out to be none o' the clearest – whether she pay 'em or no,

8   *stones* (i) gemstones; (ii) testicles.
11   *foils* (i) settings for a jewel; (ii) contrasts which show one off to advantage.
20   *Fidelia* Latin for 'trusty'; also a common name for a heroine in popular romances.
25–6   *make . . . to* put any faith in (Latin *fidem facere*). More loose tautological language.

heav'n knows; and she's above fifty too, and pargets! See her in   30
a forenoon. Here comes Mavis, a worse face than she! You would
not like this by candlelight. If you'll come to my chamber one o'
these mornings early, or late in an evening, I'll tell you more.

[*Enter* MAVIS]

Where's Haughty, Mavis?
MAVIS
Within, Centaure.   35
CENTAURE
What ha' you there?
MAVIS
An Italian riddle for Sir Dauphine. – You shall not see it i' faith,
Centaure. – Good Sir Dauphine, solve it for me. I'll call for it anon.
[*Exeunt* MAVIS *and* CENTAURE]

[*Enter* CLERIMONT]

CLERIMONT
How now, Dauphine? How dost thou quit thyself of these
females?   40
DAUPHINE
'Slight, they haunt me like fairies, and give me jewels here;
I cannot be rid of 'em.
CLERIMONT
Oh, you must not tell though.
DAUPHINE
Mass, I forgot that; I was never so assaulted. One loves for virtue,
and bribes me with this. Another loves me with caution, and so   45
would possess me. A third brings me a riddle here, and all are
jealous and rail each at other.

30   *pargets* Plasters (herself with make-up); more usually used of roughcasting walls
      than face-painting.
32   *by candlelight* Even by candlelight, by which all women are said to look attractive; cf.
      Tilley, W682, and 'An Epigram on the Court Pucelle', 32: 'Her face there's none can
      like by Candle light'.
37–8 *You . . . Centaure* Bracketed in F, which may indicate that Mavis says this to herself,
      or as a tart aside to Centaure, or merely that this is a temporary diversion in the
      main flow of the speech.
39   *quit . . . of* (i) acquit yourself with; (ii) rid yourself of.
43   *you . . . tell* 'Fairies treasure . . . reveal'd, brings on the blabbers, mine' (Massinger,
      The Fatal Dowry, IV.i.191–2; *Plays and Poems*, ed. P. Edwards and C. Gibson, Oxford,
      1976).
45   *this* this jewel.
      caution warning advice.

CLERIMONT

A riddle? Pray' le' me see't? *He reads the paper*
'Sir Dauphine, I chose this way of intimation for privacy. The
ladies here, I know, have both hope and purpose to make a 50
collegiate and servant of you. If I might be so honoured as to
appear at any end of so noble a work, I would enter into a fame
of taking physic tomorrow and continue it four or five days
or longer, for your visitation. Mavis.' – By my faith, a subtle one!
Call you this a riddle? What's their plain dealing, trow? 55

DAUPHINE

We lack Truewit to tell us that.

CLERIMONT

We lack him for somewhat else too: his knights *reformados* are
wound up as high and insolent as ever they were.

DAUPHINE

You jest.

CLERIMONT

No drunkards, either with wine or vanity, ever confessed such 60
stories of themselves. I would not give a fly's leg in balance
against all the women's reputations here, if they could be but
thought to speak truth; and for the bride, they have made their
affidavit against her directly –

DAUPHINE

What, that they have lien with her? 65

CLERIMONT

Yes, and tell times and circumstances, with the cause why and
the place where. I had almost brought 'em to affirm that they had
done it today.

DAUPHINE

Not both of 'em.

CLERIMONT

Yes, faith; with a sooth or two more I had effected it. They 70
would ha' set it down under their hands.

---

52   *enter . . . fame* affectedly for 'begin a rumour'.
54 · *visitation* A smart quibble: 'the action or practice of visiting sick or distressed persons
      as a work of charity or pastoral care' (*OED*, sb., 3).
57   *reformados* Officers of disbanded companies who retained their rank; hence 'hollow,
      spurious'. Punning also on *reformed*.
65   *lien* lain.
70   *sooth . . . it* Probably 'with one or two more exclamations of "sooth" (= really,
      indeed)'. *OED*'s gloss, 'flattery, blandishment' (sb., 8), seems mistaken. Neither of its
      other two examples is precisely parallel, and one may be the verb *soothe* oddly
      spelled.

DAUPHINE

Why, they will be our sport, I see, still! whether we will or no.

ACT V, SCENE iii

[*Enter*] TRUEWIT

TRUEWIT

Oh, are you here? Come, Dauphine. Go call your uncle presently. I have fitted my divine and my canonist, dyed their beards
and all; the knaves do not know themselves, they are so exalted
and altered. Preferment changes any man. Thou shalt keep one
door and I another, and then Clerimont in the midst, that he   5
may have no means of escape from their cavilling when they
grow hot once. And then the women – as I have given the bride
her instructions – to break in upon him i' the *l'envoy*. Oh, 'twill
be full and twanging! Away, fetch him.

[*Exit* DAUPHINE]

[*Enter* CUTBEARD *disguised as a canon lawyer,*
OTTER *as a divine*]

Come, master doctor and master parson, look to your parts now   10
and discharge 'em bravely; you are well set forth, perform it as
well. If you chance to be out, do not confess it with standing still
or humming or gaping one at another, but go on and talk aloud
and eagerly, use vehement action, and only remember your
terms, and you are safe. Let the matter go where it will: you have 15
many will do so. But at first be very solemn and grave like your
garments, though you loose yourselves after and skip out like a
brace of jugglers on a table. Here he comes! Set your faces, and
look superciliously while I present you.

---

4   *keep* guard.
8   *l'envoy* conclusion. Literally, concluding stanza of a poem or ballad, hence 'full and
      twanging'.
11   *bravely* worthily, finely.
12   *be out* forget your words.
14   *action* rhetorical gestures as an accompaniment to speech.
15   *terms* i.e. technical Latin terms.
      matter substance, content (of your discussion).

[*Enter* DAUPHINE *and* MOROSE]

MOROSE

Are these the two learned men?   20

TRUEWIT

Yes, sir; please you salute 'em?

MOROSE

Salute 'em? I had rather do anything than wear out time so
unfruitfully, sir. I wonder how these common forms, as 'God
save you' and 'You are welcome', are come to be a habit in our
lives! Or 'I am glad to see you'! when I cannot see what the profit   25
can be of these words, so long as it is no whit better with him
whose affairs are sad and grievous that he hears this salutation.

TRUEWIT

'Tis true, sir; we'll go to the matter then. Gentlemen, master
doctor and master parson, I have acquainted you sufficiently
with the business for which you are come hither. And you are   30
not now to inform yourselves in the state of the question, I
know. This is the gentleman who expects your resolution, and
therefore, when you please, begin.

OTTER

Please you, master doctor.

CUTBEARD

Please you, good master parson.   35

OTTER

I would hear the canon law speak first.

CUTBEARD

It must give place to positive divinity, sir.

MOROSE

Nay, good gentlemen, do not throw me into circumstances. Let
your comforts arrive quickly at me, those that are. Be swift in
affording me my peace, if so I shall hope any. I love not your   40
disputations or your court tumults. And that it be not strange
to you, I will tell you. My father, in my education, was wont to
advise me that I should always collect and contain my mind, not
suff'ring it to flow loosely; that I should look to what things
were necessary to the carriage of my life, and what not, em-   45
bracing the one and eschewing the other. In short, that I should

30–1   *are not now* do not need.
37   *positive* practical, as opposed to theoretical or speculative (*OED*).
38   *circumstances* circumstantialities; suggested by *ne me in longae orationis ambages
       coniiciatis* in the Latin translation of Libanius.

endear myself to rest and avoid turmoil, which now is grown to
be another nature to me. So that I come not to your public
pleadings or your places of noise; not that I neglect those things
that make for the dignity of the commonwealth, but for the   50
mere avoiding of clamours and impertinencies of orators, that
know not how to be silent. And for the cause of noise am I now
a suitor to you. You do not know in what a misery I have been
exercised this day, what a torrent of evil! My very house turns
round with the tumult! I dwell in a windmill! The perpetual   55
motion is here, and not at Eltham.

TRUEWIT

Well, good master doctor, will you break the ice? Master parson
will wade after.

CUTBEARD

Sir, though unworthy, and the weaker, I will presume.

OTTER

'Tis no presumption, *domine* doctor.   60

MOROSE

Yet again!

CUTBEARD

Your question is, for how many causes a man may have *divor-
tium legitimum*, a lawful divorce. First, you must understand the
nature of the word divorce, *a divertendo* –

MOROSE

No excursions upon words, good doctor; to the question briefly. 65

CUTBEARD

I answer then, the canon law affords divorce but in few cases,
and the principal is in the common case, the adulterous case.
But there are *duodecim impedimenta*, twelve impediments – as
we call 'em – all which do not *dirimere contractum*, but *irritum
reddere matrimonium*, as we say in the canon law, not take away 70
the bond, but cause a nullity therein.

---

49   *neglect* do not care about (Latin *negligo*).
51   *impertinencies* F corr. (pertinencies F uncorr.) irrelevances.
54   *exercised* 'harassed, afflicted', but *in* rather than *with* suggests additional senses:
       trained; disciplined in suffering, like a martyr; cf. IV.iv.89 and note.
55–6 *perpetual motion* Famous perpetual motion machine invented by a Dutch scientist,
       Cornelius Drebbel, on display at Eltham Palace, where Drebbel, who had come to
       live in London about 1609/10, was probably staying; described and illustrated in W.
       B. Rye, *England as Seen by Foreigners in the Days of . . . James I*, 1885, pp. 232–42.
60   *domine* master.
64   *a divertendo* (it is derived) from 'separating'.
65   *briefly* at once.

MOROSE

I understood you before; good sir, avoid your impertinency of translation.

OTTER

He cannot open this too much, sir, by your favour.

MOROSE

Yet more!   75

TRUEWIT

Oh, you must give the learned men leave, sir. To your impediments, master doctor.

CUTBEARD

The first is *impedimentum erroris*.

OTTER

Of which there are several species.

CUTBEARD

Ay, as *error personae*.   80

OTTER

If you contract yourself to one person, thinking her another.

CUTBEARD

Then, *error fortunae*.

OTTER

If she be a beggar, and you thought her rich.

CUTBEARD

Then, *error qualitatis*.

OTTER

If she prove stubborn or headstrong, that you thought obedient.   85

MOROSE

How? Is that, sir, a lawful impediment? One at once, I pray you, gentlemen.

OTTER

Ay, *ante copulam*, but not *post copulam*, sir.

CUTBEARD

Master parson says right. *Nec post nuptiarum benedictionem*. It doth indeed but *irrita reddere sponsalia*, annul the contract;   90
after marriage it is of no obstancy.

---

74   *open* expound.
79   *species* Italicized in F, so possibly the three-syllable Latin word.
86   *One at once* Speak one at a time, as in *Alch.*, V.v.21–2.
89   *Nec . . . benedictionem* and not after the blessing of the marriage.
91   *obstancy* oppositional force (Latin *obstantia*). *OED*'s only example.

TRUEWIT

Alas, sir, what a hope are we fall'n from, by this time!

CUTBEARD

The next is *conditio*: if you thought her free-born, and she prove
a bondwoman, there is impediment of estate and condition.

OTTER

Ay, but master doctor, those servitudes are *sublatae* now, among   95
us Christians.

CUTBEARD

By your favour, master parson –

OTTER

You shall give me leave, master doctor.

MOROSE

Nay, gentlemen, quarrel not in that question; it concerns not my
case: pass to the third.   100

CUTBEARD

Well then, the third is *votum*. If either party have made a vow of
chastity. But that practice, as master parson said of the other,
is taken away among us, thanks be to discipline. The fourth is
cognatio: if the persons be of kin within the degrees.

OTTER

Ay. Do you know what the degrees are, sir?   105

MOROSE

No, nor I care not, sir; they offer me no comfort in the question,
I am sure.

CUTBEARD

But there is a branch of this impediment may, which is *cognatio
spiritualis*. If you were her godfather, sir, then the marriage is
incestuous.   110

OTTER

That comment is absurd and superstitious, master doctor. I cannot endure it. Are we not all brothers and sisters, and as much
akin in that as godfathers and god-daughters?

MOROSE

Oh me! To end the controversy, I never was a godfather, I never
was a godfather in my life, sir. Pass to the next.   115

---

92   *time* i.e. timing.
95   *servitudes* Otter flings his law-terms about wildly: this one strictly refers to landed
      property (H&S).
      sublatae abolished.
103   *discipline* the Church's rules for conduct.
104   *degrees* degrees of consanguinity within which marriage is not allowed.

CUTBEARD

The fifth is *crimen adulterii*: the known case. The sixth, *cultus disparitas*, difference of religion: have you ever examined her what religion she is of?

MOROSE

No, I would rather she were of none, than be put to the trouble of it! 120

OTTER

You may have it done for you, sir.

MOROSE

By no means, good sir; on to the rest. Shall you ever come to an end, think you?

TRUEWIT

Yes, he has done half, sir. – On to the rest. – Be patient and expect, sir. 125

CUTBEARD

The seventh is *vis*: if it were upon compulsion or force.

MOROSE

Oh no, it was too voluntary, mine; too voluntary.

CUTBEARD

The eighth is *ordo*: if ever she have taken holy orders.

OTTER

That's superstitious too.

MOROSE

No matter, master parson: would she would go into a nunnery 130 yet.

CUTBEARD

The ninth is *ligamen*: if you were bound, sir, to any other before.

MOROSE

I thrust myself too soon into these fetters.

CUTBEARD

The tenth is *publico honestas*, which is *inchoata quaedam affinitas*.

OTTER

Ay, or *affinitas orta ex sponsalibus*, and is but *leve impedimentum*. 135

MOROSE

I feel no air of comfort blowing to me in all this.

---

116   *crimen adulterii* the crime of adultery.
      case (i) instance; (ii) vagina (a common pun).
134   *publico honestas* public reputation.
      inchoata . . . affinitas some (previous) uncompleted relationship by marriage.
135   *affinitas . . . sponsalibus* relationship arising from a betrothal
      leve slight.

CUTBEARD

The eleventh is *affinitas ex fornicatione*.

OTTER

Which is no less *vera affinitas* than the other, master doctor.

CUTBEARD

True, *quae oritur ex legitimo matrimonio*.

OTTER

You say right, venerable doctor. And *nascitur ex eo, quod per*   140
conjugium duae personae efficiuntur una caro —

MOROSE

Heyday, now they begin!

CUTBEARD

I conceive you, master parson. *Ita per fornicationem aeque est*
verus pater, qui sic generat —

OTTER

Et vere filius qui sic generatur —   145

MOROSE

What's all this to me?

CLERIMONT [*Aside*]

Now it grows warm.

CUTBEARD

The twelfth and last is *si forte coire nequibis*.

OTTER

Ay, that is *impedimentum gravissimum*. It doth utterly annul and
annihilate, that. If you have *manifestam frigiditatem*, you are   150
well, sir.

TRUEWIT

Why, there is comfort come at length, sir. Confess yourself but a
man unable, and she will sue to be divorced first.

OTTER

Ay, or if there be *morbus perpetuus et insanabilis*, as paralysis,
elephantiasis, or so –   155

137   *affinitas ex fornicatione* relationship arising from fornication.
138   *vera* true.
139   *quae . . . matrimonio* (than that) which arises from legal marriage.
140–1   *nascitur . . . caro* it springs from this, that through physical union two people are
        made one flesh.
143–4   *Ita . . . general* Thus he is equally a true father who begets through fornication.
145   *Et . . . generatur* and he truly a son who is thus begotten.
148   *si . . . nequibis* if it chances that you are unable to copulate.
149   *gravissimum* very weighty.
150   *manifestam frigiditatem* evident frigidity.
154   *morbus . . . insanabilis* a continuous and incurable disease.

DAUPHINE

Oh, but *frigiditas* is the fairer way, gentlemen.

OTTER

You say troth, sir, and as it is in the canon, master doctor.

CUTBEARD

I conceive you, sir.

CLERIMONT [*Aside*]

Before he speaks.

OTTER

That 'a boy or child under years is not fit for marriage because   160
he cannot *reddere debitum*'. So your *omnipotentes* –

TRUEWIT [*Aside to* OTTER]

Your *impotentes*, you whoreson lobster.

OTTER

Your *impotentes*, I should say, are *minime apti ad contrahenda matrimonium*.

TRUEWIT [*Aside to* OTTER]

Matrimonium! We shall have most unmatrimonial Latin with   165
you: *matrimonia*, and be hanged.

DAUPHINE [*Aside to* TRUEWIT]

You put 'em out, man.

CUTBEARD

But then there will arise a doubt, master parson, in our case,
post matrimonium: that *frigiditate praeditus* – do you conceive
me, sir?   170

OTTER

Very well, sir.

CUTBEARD

Who cannot *uti uxore pro uxore*, may *habere eam pro sorore*.

OTTER

Absurd, absurd, absurd, and merely apostatical.

CUTBEARD

You shall pardon me, master parson, I can prove it.

161   *reddere debitum* render what is required.
162   *lobster* 'An opprobrious name (? for a red-faced man)' (*OED*, which cites three other
        examples, all close in date).
163–4   *minime . . . matrimonium* least suited to contracting marriages
165   *unmatrimonial* Because the grammatical inflexions are not correctly 'married'.
167   *put 'em out* Specifically at this date, 'make them forget their words'; cf. *As You Like
        It*, IV.i.76.
169   *frigiditate praeditus* one who is frigid (lit. 'equipped with').
172   *uti . . . sorore* use a wife as a wife, may keep her as a sister.
173   *merely apostatical* absolutely heretical.

OTTER

You can prove a will, master doctor, you can prove nothing else.   175
Does not the verse of your own canon say, *Haec socianda vetant
conubia, facta retractant* –

CUTBEARD

I grant you, but how do they *retractare*, master parson?

MOROSE

Oh, this was it I feared.

OTTER

In aeternum, sir.   180

CUTBEARD

That's false in divinity, by your favour.

OTTER

'Tis false in humanity to say so. Is he not *prorsus inutilis ad
thorum*? Can he *praestare fidem datam*? I would fain know.

CUTBEARD

Yes: how if he do *convalere*?

OTTER

He cannot *convalere*, it is impossible.   185

TRUEWIT [*To* MOROSE]

Nay, good sir, attend the learned men; they'll think you neglect
'em else.

CUTBEARD

Or if he do *simulare* himself *frigidum, odio uxoris*, or so?

OTTER

I say he is *adulter manifestus* then.

DAUPHINE

They dispute it very learnedly, i' faith.   190

OTTER

And *prostitutor uxoris*, and this is positive.

MOROSE

Good sir, let me escape.

TRUEWIT

You will not do me that wrong, sir?

176–7   *Haec . . . retractant* these things forbid joinings together in marriage, and after
marriages have been made annul them.

180   *In aeternum* forever.

182–3   *prorsus . . . thorum* utterly useless for marriage (Otter's blinder for *torum*).

183   *praestare . . . datum* fulfil the promise given.

184   *convalere* recover.

188   *simulare . . . uxoris* pretend to be frigid, out of hatred for his wife.

189   *adulter manifestus* a manifest adulterer.

191   *prostitutor uxoris* the prostitutor of his wife.

OTTER

And therefore, if he be *manifeste frigidus*, sir –

CUTBEARD

Ay, if he be *manifeste frigidus*, I grant you –   195

OTTER

Why, that was my conclusion.

CUTBEARD

And mine too.

TRUEWIT

Nay, hear the conclusion, sir.

OTTER

Then *frigiditatis causa* –

CUTBEARD

Yes, *causa frigiditatis* –   200

MOROSE

Oh, mine ears!

OTTER

She may have *libellum divortii* against you.

CUTBEARD

Ay, *divortii libellum* she will sure have.

MOROSE

Good echoes, forbear.

OTTER

If you confess it.   205

CUTBEARD

Which I would do, sir –

MOROSE

I will do anything –

OTTER

And clear myself *in foro conscientiae* –

CUTBEARD

Because you want indeed –

MOROSE

Yet more?   210

OTTER

Exercendi potestate.

194   *manifeste* manifestly.
200   *causa* on the ground of.
202   *libellum divortii* a petition of divorce.
208   *in foro conscientiae* at the bar of conscience; a law proverb (H&S).
209   *want* lack.
211   *Exercendi potestate* the power of putting into effect.

ACT V, SCENE iv

[*Enter*] EPICOENE, HAUGHTY, CENTAURE, MAVIS,
MISTRESS OTTER, DAW, LA FOOLE

EPICOENE

I will not endure it any longer! Ladies, I beseech you help me.
This is such a wrong as never was offered to poor bride before.
Upon her marriage-day, to have her husband conspire against
her, and a couple of mercenary companions to be brought in for
form's sake, to persuade a separation! If you had blood or virtue   5
in you, gentlemen, you would not suffer such earwigs about a
husband, or scorpions to creep between man and wife –

MOROSE

Oh the variety and changes of my torment!

HAUGHTY

Let 'em be cudgelled out of doors by our grooms.

CENTAURE

I'll lend you my footman.   10

MAVIS

We'll have our men blanket 'em i' the hall.

MISTRESS OTTER

As there was one at our house, madam, for peeping in at the
door.

DAW

Content, i' faith.

TRUEWIT

Stay, ladies and gentlemen, you'll hear before you proceed?   15

MAVIS

I'd ha' the bridegroom blanketed too.

CENTAURE

Begin with him first.

HAUGHTY

Yes, by my troth.

---

4   *companions* fellows (contemptuous), as at l. 131.
6   *earwigs* ear whisperers, parasites.
11   *blanket* toss in a blanket (*OED*'s first example).

MOROSE

Oh mankind generation!

DAUPHINE

Ladies, for my sake forbear. 20

HAUGHTY

Yes, for Sir Dauphine's sake.

CENTAURE

He shall command us.

LA FOOLE

He is as fine a gentleman of his inches, madam, as any is about
the town, and wears as good colours when he list.

TRUEWIT [*Aside to* MOROSE]

Be brief, sir, and confess your infirmity, she'll be afire to be quit 25
of you; if she but hear that named once, you shall not entreat
her to stay. She'll fly you like one that had the marks upon him.

MOROSE

Ladies, I must crave all your pardons –

TRUEWIT

Silence, ladies.

MOROSE

For a wrong I have done to your whole sex in marrying this fair 30
and virtuous gentlewoman –

CLERIMONT

Hear him, good ladies.

MOROSE

Being guilty of an infirmity which, before I conferred with these
learned men, I thought I might have concealed –

TRUEWIT

But now being better informed in his conscience by them, he is 35
to declare it and give satisfaction by asking your public forgiveness.

19   *mankind* Unnaturally masculine, virago-like, as in H. Smith, *A Preparative to
      Marriage*, 1591, pp. 61–2: 'A mankind woman is a monster, that is, halfe a woman
      and halfe a man'. The sense is related to *mankeen* or *mankind* = furious, savage (used
      of animals inclined to attack men).
23   *of his inches* valiant; cf. 'a tall fellow of thy hands' in *The Winter's Tale*, V.ii.64.
      Probably with a (unconscious) bawdy quibble: 'according to thy inches' in *B.F.*,
      I.iii.66, refers punningly to the length of the penis.
24   *colours* heraldic colours, insignia of a knight. La Foole is thinking of, or (if he has them
      on) drawing the attention of the ladies to, his own gaudy colours; cf. I.iv.35–8.
26   *you;* ed. (you, F).
27   *marks* Surely 'marks of impotency'. Other editors gloss 'plague-marks'.

MOROSE

I am no man, ladies.

ALL

How!

MOROSE

Utterly unabled in nature, by reason of frigidity, to perform the   40
duties or any the least office of a husband.

MAVIS

Now out upon him, prodigious creature!

CENTAURE

Bridegroom uncarnate.

HAUGHTY

And would you offer it, to a young gentlewoman?

MISTRESS OTTER

A lady of her longings?   45

EPICOENE

Tut, a device, a device, this, it smells rankly, ladies. A mere comment of his own.

TRUEWIT

Why, if you suspect that, ladies, you may have him searched.

DAW

As the custom is, by a jury of physicians.

LA FOOLE

Yes, faith, 'twill be brave.   50

MOROSE

Oh me, must I undergo that!

MISTRESS OTTER

No, let women search him, madam: we can do it ourselves.

MOROSE

Out on me, worse!

EPICOENE

No, ladies, you shall not need, I'll take him with all his faults.

MOROSE

Worst of all!   55

CLERIMONT

Why, then 'tis no divorce, doctor, if she consent not?

43   *uncarnate* i.e. without flesh and blood. Centaure's coinage, from *incarnate*.
44   *offer it* attempt to do such a thing.
45   *longings* (i) belongings, wealth, as in the phrase 'a man of his havings'; (ii) (sexual)
       longings.
46–7   *comment* invention, fiction (Latin *commentum*).
48   *searched* examined.

335

CUTBEARD

No, if the man be *frigidus,* it is *de parte uxoris* that we grant *libellum divortii,* in the law.

OTTER

Ay, it is the same in theology.

MOROSE

Worse, worse than worst! 60

TRUEWIT

Nay, sir, be not utterly disheartened, we have yet a small relic of hope left, as near as our comfort is blown out. [*Aside to* CLERIMONT] Clerimont, produce your brace of knights. – What was that, master parson, you told me *in errore qualitatis,* e'en now? [*Aside to* DAUPHINE] Dauphine, whisper the bride that 65 she carry it as if she were guilty and ashamed.

OTTER

Marry, sir, *in errore qualitatis* – which master doctor did forbear to urge – if she be found *corrupta,* that is, vitiated or broken up, that was *pro virgine desponsa,* espoused for a maid –

MOROSE

What then, sir? 70

OTTER

It doth *dirimere contractum* and *irritum reddere* too.

TRUEWIT

If this be true, we are happy again, sir, once more. Here are an honourable brace of knights that shall affirm so much.

DAW

Pardon us, good Master Clerimont.

LA FOOLE

You shall excuse us, Master Clerimont. 75

CLERIMONT

Nay, you must make it good now, knights, there is no remedy; I'll eat no words for you nor no men: you know you spoke it to me?

DAW

Is this gentleman-like, sir?

---

62   *as near . . . out* Cf. V.iii.136.
63   *produce . . . knights* Clerimont must in V.iii or earlier in this scene have whispered to Truewit Daw and La Foole's claim to have slept with Epicoene, and arranged this piece of business with him; cf. l. 196, 'unexpected'.
68   *vitiated* deflowered.
71   *dirimere . . . reddere* dissolve the contract and render it null and void.

TRUEWIT [*Aside to* DAW]

    Jack Daw, he's worse than Sir Amorous, fiercer a great deal.   80
    [*Aside to* LA FOOLE] Sir Amorous, beware, there be ten Daws in
    this Clerimont.

LA FOOLE

    I'll confess it, sir.

DAW

    Will you, Sir Amorous? Will you wound reputation?

LA FOOLE

    I am resolved.   85

TRUEWIT

    So should you be too, Jack Daw: what should keep you off?
    She is but a woman, and in disgrace. He'll be glad on't.

DAW

    Will he? I thought he would ha' been angry.

CLERIMONT

    You will dispatch, knights; it must be done, i' faith.

TRUEWIT

    Why, an' it must, it shall, sir, they say. They'll ne'er go back.   90
    [*Aside to* DAW *and* LA FOOLE] Do not tempt his patience.

DAW

    It is true indeed, sir.

LA FOOLE

    Yes, I assure you, sir.

MOROSE

    What is true, gentlemen? What do you assure me?

DAW

    That we have known your bride, sir –   95

LA FOOLE

    In good fashion. She was our mistress, or so –

CLERIMONT

    Nay, you must be plain, knights, as you were to me.

OTTER

    Ay, the question is, if you have *carnaliter* or no.

LA FOOLE

    Carnaliter? What else, sir?

OTTER

    It is enough: a plain nullity.   100

EPICOENE

    I am undone, I am undone!

    98   *carnaliter* carnally.

MOROSE
Oh, let me worship and adore you, gentlemen!

EPICOENE
I am undone!

MOROSE
Yes, to my hand, I thank these knights. Master parson, let me
thank you otherwise. [*Gives* OTTER *money*] 105

CENTAURE
And ha' they confessed?

MAVIS
Now out upon 'em, informers!

TRUEWIT
You see what creatures you may bestow your favours on, madams.

HAUGHTY
I would except against 'em as beaten knights, wench, and not
good witnesses in law. 110

MISTRESS OTTER
Poor gentlewoman, how she takes it!

HAUGHTY
Be comforted, Morose, I love you the better for't.

CENTAURE
So do I, I protest.

CUTBEARD
But, gentlemen, you have not known her since *matrimonium*?

DAW
Not today, master doctor. 115

LA FOOLE
No, sir, not today.

CUTBEARD
Why, then I say, for any act before, the *matrimonium* is good
and perfect, unless the worshipful bridegroom did precisely,
before witness, demand if she were *virgo ante nuptias*.

EPICOENE
No, that he did not, I assure you, master doctor. 120

---

104   *to my hand* See note to IV.v.14.
109   *except against* object to.
109–10 *not good witnesses* Until the mid-sixteenth century a recreant knight 'was no longer
       accounted *liber et legalis homo*; and being by the event supposed to be forsworn, he
       was never put upon a jury, or admitted as a witness in any cause' (Gifford).
118   *precisely* expressly.
119   *virgo . . . nuptias* a virgin before the wedding.

CUTBEARD

If he cannot prove that, it is *ratum conjugium,* notwithstanding the premises. And they do no way *impedire.* And this is my sentence, this I pronounce.

OTTER

I am of master doctor's resolution too, sir, if you made not that demand *ante nuptias.* 125

MOROSE

Oh my heart! Wilt thou break? Wilt thou break? This is worst of all worst worsts! that hell could have devised! Marry a whore! and so much noise!

DAUPHINE

Come, I see now plain confederacy in this doctor and this parson, to abuse a gentleman. You study his affliction. I pray be gone, 130 companions. And gentlemen, I begin to suspect you for having parts with 'em. Sir, will it please you hear me?

MOROSE

Oh, do not talk to me, take not from me the pleasure of dying in silence, nephew.

DAUPHINE

Sir, I must speak to you. I have been long your poor despised 135 kinsman, and many a hard thought has strengthened you against me; but now it shall appear if either I love you or your peace, and prefer them to all the world beside. I will not be long or grievous to you, sir. If I free you of this unhappy match absolutely and instantly after all this trouble, and almost in your 140 despair now –

MOROSE

It cannot be.

DAUPHINE

Sir, that you be never troubled with a murmur of it more, what shall I hope for or deserve of you?

MOROSE

Oh, what thou wilt, nephew! Thou shalt deserve me and have 145 me.

DAUPHINE

Shall I have your favour perfect to me, and love hereafter?

---

121   *ratum conjugium* a valid marriage.
126–7   *This . . . worsts* Echoing St John Chrysostom's Ὦ κακὸν κακων κακιβτου, 'O this is worst, of all worsts worst' (Upton).
130   *study* seek, aim at; punning on scholarly study.

MOROSE

That and anything beside. Make thine own conditions. My whole
estate is thine. Manage it, I will become thy ward.

DAUPHINE

Nay, sir, I will not be so unreasonable. 150

EPICOENE

Will Sir Dauphine be mine enemy too?

DAUPHINE

You know I have been long a suitor to you, uncle, that out of
your estate, which is fifteen hundred a year, you would allow me
but five hundred during life, and assure the rest upon me after,
to which I have often by myself and friends tendered you a writ- 155
ing to sign, which you would never consent or incline to. If you
please but to effect it now –

MOROSE

Thou shalt have it, nephew. I will do it, and more.

DAUPHINE

If I quit you not presently and forever of this cumber, you shall
have power instantly, afore all these, to revoke your act, and I will 160
become whose slave you will give me to forever.

MOROSE

Where is the writing? I will seal to it, that, or to a blank, and
write thine own conditions.

EPICOENE

Oh me, most unfortunate wretched gentlewoman!

HAUGHTY

Will Sir Dauphine do this? 165

EPICOENE

Good sir, have some compassion on me. [*Weeps*]

MOROSE

Oh, my nephew knows you belike; away, crocodile!

CENTAURE

He does it not, sure, without good ground.

DAUPHINE

Here, sir.

[*Gives him papers*]

---

159   *presently* ed. (presently? F) at once.
       cumber encumbrance, load of care.
167   *belike* very likely.
       crocodile Thought to weep as it took its prey; hence applied to someone who uses a
       show of grief to hide a malicious purpose.

MOROSE

Come, nephew, give me the pen. I will subscribe to anything,   170
and seal to what thou wilt, for my deliverance. Thou art my
restorer. Here, I deliver it thee as my deed. If there be a word in
it lacking or writ with false orthography, I protest before – I will
not take the advantage.

[Returns papers]

DAUPHINE

Then here is your release, sir: *He takes off* EPICOENE*'s peruke*   175
you have married a boy: a gentleman's son that I have brought
up this half year at my great charges, and for this composition
which I have now made with you. – What say you, master doctor?
This is *justum impedimentum,* I hope, *error personae?*

OTTER

Yes, sir, *in primo gradu.*   180

CUTBEARD

In primo gradu.

DAUPHINE

I thank you, good Doctor Cutbeard and Parson Otter.

He pulls off their beards and disguise

You are beholden to 'em, sir, that have taken this pains for you;
and my friend, Master Truewit, who enabled 'em for the business. Now you may go in and rest, be as private as you will, sir.   185
I'll not trouble you till you trouble me with your funeral, which
I care not how soon it come.

[Exit MOROSE*]*

Cutbeard, I'll make your lease good. Thank me not but with your
leg, Cutbeard. And Tom Otter, your princess shall be reconciled
to you. – How now, gentlemen! Do you look at me?   190

CLERIMONT

A boy.

DAUPHINE

Yes, Mistress Epicoene.

---

173   *protest before* — Declare in advance. Gifford and all later editors take F's dash to
represent the omission of an oath, and substitute 'heaven' or 'God'. This seems unlikely. F makes good sense (leading to 'will not'), the use of the dash within speeches
is common in the text, blasphemies are frequent (e.g. 'Before God', IV.v,186), and the
Act against Abuses of Players (1606), which is cited to explain the omission, was not
concerned with printed plays.

177   *composition* contract, settlement, particularly of a financial kind.

180   *in primo gradu* in the first or highest degree.

188   *make . . . good* i.e. honour Morose's promise at II.v.81.

TRUEWIT

Well, Dauphine, you have lurched your friends of the better half
of the garland, by concealing this part of the plot! But much
good do it thee, thou deserv'st it, lad. And Clerimont, for thy   195
unexpected bringing in these two to confession, wear my part of
it freely. Nay, Sir Daw and Sir La Foole, you see the gentlewoman
that has done you the favours! We are all thankful to you, and so
should the womankind here, specially for lying on her, though
not with her! You meant so, I am sure? But that we have stuck it   200
upon you today in your own imagined persons, and so lately, this
Amazon, the champion of the sex, should beat you now thriftily
for the common slanders which ladies receive from such cuckoos
as you are. You are they that, when no merit or fortune can make
you hope to enjoy their bodies, will yet lie with their reputations   205
and make their fame suffer. Away, you common moths of these
and all ladies' honours. Go, travel to make legs and faces, and
come home with some new matter to be laughed at: you deserve
to live in an air as corrupted as that wherewith you feed rumour.

[*Exeunt* DAW *and* LA FOOLE]

Madams, you are mute upon this new metamorphosis! But here   210
stands she that has vindicated your fames. Take heed of such
insectae hereafter. And let it not trouble you that you have discovered any mysteries to this young gentleman. He is, a'most, of

193 *lurched* cheated, robbed; as often at this date, though Jonson (or Truewit) may be
      consciously echoing *Coriolanus* (*c.* 1608), II.ii.101: 'He lurch'd all swords of the
      garland'. Shakespeare scholars tend to regard the parallel as 'another of [Jonson's]
      gibes at Shakespeare' (*Riverside Shakespeare*, p. 1392).
199 *on* i.e. about.
200 *But* were it not.
      stuck it fastened the lie.
201–2 *this Amazon* Mistress Otter.
202 *thriftily* soundly.
203 *cuckoos* fools; and referring to the cuckoo's laying its eggs in other birds' nests.
206–7 *moths . . . honours* Cf. *The Revenger's Tragedy*, I.iv.32, 'that moth to honour' (said of
      the violator of another man's wife).
207 *travel* (trauaile F). Both 'travel' and 'travail'. F's form represents the contemporary
      pronunciation of both words.
      make . . . faces i.e. learn new styles of facial expression and making bows; cf.
      Overbury's 'An Affected Traveller': '[He] is a speaking fashion; he hath taken paines
      to be ridiculous, and hath seen more then he hath perceived. His attire speakes
      French or *Italian*, and *his gate* cryes *Behold mee* . . . He chooseth rather to tell lyes
      then not wonders' (*Characters*, 1614, sig. El^v).
208 *matter* (i) subject; (ii) pus (cf. *corrupted*).
212 *insectae* The substitution of the incorrect feminine form of the plural, in place of
      neuter *insecta*, is probably not a blunder (H&S), but a jibe at the knights' effeminacy.

years, and will make a good visitant within this twelvemonth. In the meantime we'll all undertake for his secrecy, that can 215 speak so well of his silence. [*Coming forward*] Spectators, if you like this comedy, rise cheerfully, and now Morose is gone in, clap your hands. It may be that noise will cure him, at least please him.

[*Exeunt*]

THE END

218   *that noise* i.e. *that* noise, of applause.

EPICOENE

This comedy was first
acted in the year
1609

By the Children of her Majesty's
Revels

The principal comedians were

Nathan Field	William Barksted
Giles Carey	William Penn
Hugh Attawell	Richard Allin
John Smith	John Blaney

With the allowance of the Master of Revels

The principal comedians. The columns are headed by the two most senior members of the troupe. Field (1587–1633), one of the most famous players of the time, was Jonson's 'Schollar & he had read to him the Satyres of Horace & some Epigrames of Martiall' (*Conversations with Drummond,* H&S, I, 317). He acted in at least three other plays by Jonson, *C.R.* (1600), *Poet.* (1601), and *B.F.* (1614). In V.iii of this last play Cokes speaks of 'Your best *Actor.* Your *Field'.* Barksted is not known as an actor before 1609. In 1607 he published a narrative poem, *Mirrha,* and about 1610 he probably completed Marston's last play, *The Insatiate Countess.* Nothing is heard of Carey, Penn, Attawell or Blaney prior to 1609. Carey joined an adult company in 1611, the other three probably some years later; see E. Nunzeger, *A Dictionary of Actors . . . before 1642,* New Haven and London, 1929. Nothing is known about Allin or Smith. Contemporary ascriptions give the part of Morose to Barksted and La Foole to Attawell: see J.A. Riddell, 'Some Actors in Ben Jonson's Plays', *Shakespeare Studies,* V (1969), 285–98.

Master of Revels. Who licensed plays for performance. Sir George Buc had held the post since 1608.

THE
ALCHEMIST.

VVritten
by
BEN. IONSON.

———Neque, me vt miretur turba, laboro:
Contentus paucis lectoribus.

LONDON,
Printed by *Thomas Snodham*, for *Walter Burre*,
and are to be sold by *Iohn Stepneth*, at the
West-end of Paules.
1612.

The original title-page of the 1612 Quarto.

DEDICATION

TO THE LADY, MOST
DESERVING HER NAME,
AND BLOOD:
Mary,

LADY WROTH   5

MADAM,

In the age of sacrifices, the truth of religion was not in the greatness, and fat of the offerings, but in the devotion, and zeal of the sacrificers: else, what could a handful of gums have done in the sight of a hecatomb? Or, how might I appear at this altar,   10
except with those affections, that no less love the light and witness, than they have the conscience of your virtue? If what I offer bear an acceptable odour, and hold the first strength, it is your value of it, which remembers, where, when, and to whom it was kindled. Otherwise, as the times are, there comes rarely forth that   15
thing, so full of authority, or example, but by assiduity and custom, grows less, and loses. This, yet, safe in your judgment (which is a Sidney's) is forbidden to speak more; lest it talk, or look like one of the ambitious faces of the time: who, the more they paint, are the less themselves.   20

Your Ladyship's true honourer,

Ben Jonson.

2–3   DESERVING ... BLOOD most aequall with vertue, and her Blood: The Grace, and Glory .
       of women Q.
4–5   Mary, LADY WROTH daughter of Robert Sidney, first Earl of Leicester, and niece of
       Sir Philip Sidney; she married Sir Robert Wroth in 1604. The name was also spelled
       'Worth' – hence 'deserving her name'.
7–12   from Seneca, De Beneficiis, i.vi.2.
9   gums incense.
10   hecatomb huge public sacrifice.
10–12 Or, how ... virtue? Or how, yet, might a grateful minde be furnish'd against the
       iniquitie of Fortune; except, when she fail'd it, it had power to impart it selfe? A way
       found out, to ouercome euen those, whom Fortune hath enabled to returne most,
       since they, yet leaue themselues more. In this assurance am I planted; and stand with
       those affections at this Altar, as shall no more auoide the light and witnesse, then
       they do the conscience of your vertue Q.
12   conscience consciousness.
14   value of it, which valew, that Q.
15   as the times are in these times Q.   16 assiduity daylinesse Q.
17   This, yet But this Q.   19 paint use make up.

TO THE READER

If thou beest more, thou art an understander, and then I trust thee. If thou art one that takest up, and but a pretender, beware at what hands thou receivest thy commodity; for thou wert never more fair in the way to be cozened (than in this age) in poetry, especially in plays: wherein, now, the concupiscence of dances and antics so reigneth, as to run away 5 from nature, and be afraid of her, is the only point of art that tickles the spectators. But how out of purpose, and place, do I name art? When the professors are grown so obstinate contemners of it, and presumers on their own naturals, as they are deriders of all diligence that way, and, by simple mocking at the terms, when they understand not the things, 10 think to get off wittily with their ignorance. Nay, they are esteemed the more learned, and sufficient for this, by the multitude, through their excellent vice of judgment. For they commend writers, as they do fencers, or wrestlers; who if they come in robustiously, and put for it with a great deal of violence, are received for the braver fellows: when 15 many times their own rudeness is the cause of their disgrace, and a little touch of their adversary gives all that boisterous force the foil. I deny not, but that these men, who always seek to do more than enough, may some time happen on something that is good, and great; but very seldom: and when it comes it doth not recompense the rest of their ill. It 20 sticks out perhaps, and is more eminent, because all is sordid, and vile about it: as lights are more discerned in a thick darkness, than a faint shadow. I speak not this, out of a hope to do good on any man, against his will; for I know, if it were put to the question of theirs, and mine, the worse would find more suffrages: because the most favour com- 25 mon errors. But I give thee this warning, that there is a great difference between those, that (to gain the opinion of copie) utter all they can, however unfitly; and those that use election, and a mean. For it is only the disease of the unskilful, to think rude things greater than polished: or scattered more numerous than composed. 30

This preface is taken from Q. It was not included in F. A more expanded version of these views (which derive from Quintilian) can be found in Jonson's *Discoveries* (*H. & S.* viii, esp. pp. 583, 586–7).

1   *more* i.e. more than a reader.
9   *naturals* what nature has given them (with a pun on 'fools').
15 *braver* finer.
27 *copie* copiousness
    all they can all they know (ken).
28 *those that use election, and a mean* those that employ discrimination and moderation.

THE PERSONS OF THE PLAY

SUBTLE, *The Alchemist*
FACE, *The Housekeeper*
DOL COMMON, *Their Colleague*
DAPPER, *A Clerk*
DRUGGER, *A Tobaccoman* 5
LOVEWIT, *Master of the House*
EPICURE MAMMON, *A Knight*
SURLY, *A Gamester*
TRIBULATION, *A Pastor of Amsterdam*
ANANIAS, *A Deacon there* 10
KASTRIL, *The Angry Boy*
DAME PLIANT, *His Sister: A Widow*
Neighbours
Officers
Mutes 15

THE SCENE

LONDON [inside Lovewit's house and in the street outside]

PLAY Comoedie Q.
5 *Tobaccoman* tobacco was a new and fashionable commodity and tobacco sellers a new breed of tradesmen. See John Earle, *Microcosmography* (1628) for the 'character' of *A Tobacco Seller*.
11 *KASTRIL* an obsolete spelling of 'kestril'. As an 'angry boy' he is one of a type of pugnacious men about town.
15 *Mutes* non-speaking parts, e.g. the Parson of V.v.118.
16–17 *THE SCENE LONDON* F; not in Q.

THE ARGUMENT

T he sickness hot, a master quit, for fear,
H is house in town: and left one servant there.
E ase him corrupted, and gave means to know
A cheater, and his punk; who, now brought low,
L eaving their narrow practice, were become   5
C ozeners at large: and, only wanting some
H ouse to set up, with him they here contract,
E ach for a share, and all begin to act.
M uch company they draw, and much abuse,
I n casting figures, telling fortunes, news,   10
S elling of flies, flat bawdry, with the stone:
T ill it, and they, and all in fume are gone.

1   *sickness* plague.
4   *punk* whore.
10   *casting figures* drawing up horoscopes.
11   *stone* the Philosopher's Stone.
12   *fume* smoke.

PROLOGUE

Fortune, that favours fools, these two short hours
   We wish away; both for your sakes, and ours,
Judging spectators: and desire in place,
   To th'author justice, to ourselves but grace.
Our scene is London, 'cause we would make known,   5
   No country's mirth is better than our own,
No clime breeds better matter, for your whore,
   Bawd, squire, imposter, many persons more,
Whose manners, now called humours, feed the stage:
   And which have still been subject, for the rage   10
Or spleen of comic writers. Though this pen
   Did never aim to grieve, but better men;
Howe'er the age, he lives in, doth endure
   The vices that she breeds, above their cure.
But, when the wholesome remedies are sweet,   15
   And, in their working, gain, and profit meet,
He hopes to find no spirit so much diseased,
   But will, with such fair correctives be pleased.
For here, he doth not fear, who can apply.
   If there be any, that will sit so nigh   20
Unto the stream, to look what it doth run,
   They shall find things, they'd think, or wish, were done;
They are so natural follies, but so shown.
   As even the doers may see, and yet not own.

---

7   *for* William Empson observes that this must mean 'as providing' and not 'because'
       (*'The Alchemist* and the Critics', 1970, in *Jonson: Every Man in his Humour and The*
       Alchemist: a Casebook, ed. R. V. Holdsworth).
8   *squire* pimp.
9   *now called humours* According to medieval psychologists an individual's temperament
       was determined by the balance and proportion of four bodily humours: blood,
       phlegm, red bile and black bile. These in turn reflect the balance of the four elements:
       air, water, fire and earth. A 'humour' thence came to mean any bent of personality.
       Jonson protests against the misuse of this term (as an excuse for fashionably interesting
       foibles) in his induction to *Every Man Out of his Humour*, 110–17.
10   *for* to Q.
12   *better* a verb.
19   *apply* interpret veiled allusions.

ACT I, SCENE i

[Inside Lovewit's house]

[Enter] FACE, SUBTLE, DOL COMMON

FACE
  Believ't, I will.
SUBTLE   Thy worst. I fart at thee.
DOL
  Ha' you your wits? Why gentlemen! For love–
FACE
  Sirrah, I'll strip you –
SUBTLE   What to do? Lick figs
  Out at my –
FACE   Rogue, rogue, out of all your sleights.
DOL
  Nay, look ye! Sovereign, General, are you madmen?   5
SUBTLE
  O, let the wild sheep loose.
                              [Threatens FACE *with phial]*
                        I'll gum your silks
  With good strong water, an' you come.
DOL   Will you have
  The neighbours hear you? Will you betray all?
  Hark, I hear somebody.
FACE   Sirrah –
SUBTLE   I shall mar
  All that the tailor has made, if you approach.   10
FACE
  You most notorious whelp, you insolent slave
  Dare you do this?
SUBTLE   Yes faith, yes faith.
FACE   Why! Who
  Am I, my mongrel? Who am I?
SUBTLE   I'll tell you,
  Since you know not yourself –
FACE   Speak lower, rogue.

---

  3   *figs* piles, the *ficus morbus.*
  6   *gum* stiffen.
  10 *All that the tailor has made* this establishes that Face's persona has been manufactured.

SUBTLE

Yes. You were once (time's not long past) the good,   15
Honest, plain, livery-three-pound-thrum; that kept
Your master's worship's house, here, in the Friars,
For the vacations –

FACE   Will you be so loud?

SUBTLE

Since, by my means, translated suburb-Captain.

FACE

By your means, Doctor Dog?

SUBTLE   Within man's memory,   20
All this, I speak of.

FACE   Why, I pray you, have I
Been countenanced by you? Or you, by me?
Do but collect, sir, where I met you first.

SUBTLE

I do not hear well.

FACE   Not of this, I think it.
But I shall put you in mind, sir, at Pie Corner,   25
Taking your meal of steam in, from cooks' stalls,
Where, like the father of hunger, you did walk
Piteously costive, with your pinched-horn-nose,
And your complexion, of the Roman wash,
Stuck full of black, and melancholic worms,   30
Like powder corns, shot, at th'artillery-yard.

---

16   *livery-three-pound-thrum* 'livery' is a servant's garb, 'three-pound' is probably Face's
      annual wage, and 'thrum' is waste thread – the loose end of a weaver's warp. The
      whole compound suggests that Face was a lowly menial..

17   *the Friars* Blackfriars in London, between St. Paul's and the river; site of the Blackfriars
      theatre and also of Jonson's home for a time.

18   *vacations* between the four terms of the Law-Courts: Hilary (11th–31st January),
      Easter (mid-April–8th May), Trinity (22nd May–12th June), and Michaelmas
      (2nd–25th November). There was a lull in London activity during vacations.

19   *translated* transformed into.

23   *collect* recollect.

25   *Pie Corner* a place in nearby Smithfield, noted for cooks' shops.

26   *Taking your meal of steam in* Martial, *Epigrams*, I.xcii. 7–10.

27   *father of hunger* Catullus, xxi.1, 'pater esuritionum'.

29   *of the Roman wash* a 'wash' is a dye. The Roman wash may be dark like an Italian, or
      red like the Scarlet Whore of Babylon, as the Roman Church was portrayed.

31   *powder corns* grains of gunpowder.
      artillery-yard the exercise yard of the Honourable Artillery Company at Teasel Close
      (now Artillery Lane). It was also used by the City Trainband (a home guard).

SUBTLE

    I wish, you could advance your voice, a little.

FACE

    When you went pinned up, in the several rags
    You'd raked, and picked from dunghills, before day,
    Your feet in mouldy slippers, for your kibes,   35
    A felt of rug, and a thin threaden cloak,
    That scarce would cover your no-buttocks –

SUBTLE   So, sir!

FACE

    When all your alchemy, and your algebra,
    Your minerals, vegetals, and animals,
    Your conjuring, cozening, and your dozen of trades,   40
    Could not relieve your corps, with so much linen
    Would make you tinder, but to see a fire;
    I ga' you countenance, credit for your coals,
    Your stills, your glasses, your materials,
    Built you a furnace, drew you customers   45
    Advanced all your black arts; lent you, beside,
    A house to practise in –

SUBTLE   Your master's house?

FACE

    Where you have studied the more thriving skill
    Of bawdry, since.

SUBTLE   Yes, in your master's house.

    You, and the rats, here, kept possession.   50
    Make it not strange. I know, y'were one, could keep
    The buttr'y-hatch still locked, and save the chippings,
    Sell the dole-beer to aqua-vitae-men,
    The which, together with your Christmas vails,
    At post and pair, your letting out of counters,   55

---

  35   *kibes* chilblains.
36–7   see Martial I.xcii, 7–8.
  36   *felt of rug* rough wool hat.   *threaden* made of thread.
  39   *vegetals* vegetable substances.
  41   *corps* body.
  52   *buttr'y-hatch* the buttery was where drink was stored.
  53   *aqua-vitae-men* liquor dealers.
  54   *Christmas vails* Christmas boxes, tips.
  55   *post and pair* a card game.
            letting out of counters As in roulette now, counters (then usually metal) were used in place of coin for gambling. Face would be tipped for supplying these.

Made you a pretty stock, some twenty marks,
And gave you credit, to converse with cobwebs,
Here, since your mistress' death hath broke up house.

FACE
You might talk softlier, rascal.

SUBTLE   No, you scarab,
I'll thunder you, in pieces. I will teach you   60
How to beware, to tempt a fury again
That carries tempest in his hand, and voice.

FACE
The place has made you valiant.

SUBTLE   No, your clothes.
Thou vermin, have I ta'en thee, out of dung,
So poor, so wretched, when no living thing   65
Would keep thee company, but a spider, or worse?
Raised thee from brooms, and dust, and wat'ring-pots?
Sublimed thee, and exalted thee, and fixed thee
I' the third region, called our state of grace?
Wrought thee to spirit, to quintessence, with pains   70
Would twice have won me the philosopher's work?
Put thee in words, and fashion? Made thee fit
For more than ordinary fellowships?
Given thee thy oaths, thy quarrelling dimensions?
Thy rules, to cheat at horse-race, cock-pit, cards,   75
Dice, or whatever gallant tincture else?
Made thee a second, in mine own great art?
And have I this for thank? Do you rebel?
Do you fly out, i' the projection?

59   *scarab* dung beetle.
68   *Sublimed* Converted into vapour to remove impurities.
     exalted Alchemical exaltation is a process of purification and concentration.
     fixed stabilized.
69   *third region* the upper, and purest, region of the air.
     our state of grace the high state of grace Q.
70   *quintessence* the 'fifth essence' of which heavenly bodies are composed and which is
     latent in substances composed of the four material elements.
71   *philosopher's work* Philosopher's Stone.
72–4 *Put thee . . . dimensions* Taught you how to speak and dress; enabled you to enter
     company a) better than average b) beyond what you would find at cheap eating
     houses (ordinaries); taught you how to swear and on what grounds you may quarrel.
75   *cock-pit* cock-fighting.
76   *gallant tincture* touch of gallantry; *tincture* is an alchemical term.
79   *projection* the moment of alchemical transformation when the Philosopher's Stone
     interpenetrates qualities with the matter to be changed.

Would you be gone, now?

DOL   Gentlemen, what mean you?   80

Will you mar all?

SUBTLE   Slave, thou hadst had no name –

DOL

Will you undo yourselves, with civil war?

SUBTLE

Never been known, past *equi clibanum*,

The heat of horse-dung, under ground, in cellars,

Or an ale-house, darker than deaf John's: been lost   85

To all mankind, but laundresses, and tapsters,

Had not I been.

DOL   Do you know who hears you, Sovereign?

FACE

Sirrah –

DOL   Nay, General, I thought you were civil –

FACE

I shall turn desperate, if you grow thus loud.

SUBTLE

And hang thyself, I care not.

FACE   Hang thee, collier,   90

And all thy pots, and pans, in picture I will,

Since thou hast moved me –

DOL   (O, this'll o'erthrow all.)

FACE

Write thee up bawd, in Paul's; have all thy tricks

Of coz'ning with a hollow coal, dust, scrapings,

---

83   *equi clibanum* lit. 'horse's oven' – horse dung was used by alchemists when a moderate heat was desired.

85   *deaf John's* an alehouse (unidentified).

90   *Hang thee, collier* cf. *Twelfth Night* III.iv.119, 'Hang him, foul collier!' (of the devil). It was commonplace to associate colliers with the infernal. Subtle's smoky appearance would suggest the remark.

91   *in picture* Face threatens to expose Subtle with a public advertisement.

93   *Paul's* St. Paul's Cathedral (not the one now standing); a popular meeting place for secular purposes of social and business exchange. In Dekker's *The Dead Tearme* (1608) Paul's steeple complains 'am I like a common Mart where all Commodities . . . are to be bought and solde' (E^r).

94   *coz'ning with a hollow coal* Chaucer describes this trick in the *Canon's Yeoman's Tale*, 1159–64. Silver filings are placed inside a hollow coal which is then sealed with wax. When the wax melts molten silver appears amongst the coals to convince prospective clients of the 'alchemist's' prowess.

Searching for things lost, with a sieve, and shears,   95
Erecting figures, in your rows of houses,
And taking in of shadows, with a glass,
Told in red letters: and a face, cut for thee,
Worse than Gamaliel Ratsey's.

DOL   Are you sound?
Ha' you your senses, masters?

FACE   I will have   100
A book, but barely reckoning thy impostures,
Shall prove a true philosopher's stone, to printers.

SUBTLE
Away, you trencher-rascal.

FACE   Out you dog-leech,
The vomit of all prisons –

DOL   Will you be
Your own destructions, gentlemen?

FACE   Still spewed out   105
For lying too heavy o' the basket.

SUBTLE   Cheater.

FACE
Bawd.

SUBTLE Cow-herd.

FACE   Conjurer.

SUBTLE   Cut-purse.

FACE   Witch.

DOL   O me!
We are ruined! Lost! Ha' you no more regard
To your reputations? Where's your judgment? 'Slight,
Have yet, some care of me, o' your republic –   110

---

95   *sieve, and shears* the points of shears are stuck into the rim of a sieve to form a dowsing
     instrument for divination.
96   *Erecting figures* See *Argument* 10.
97   *glass* a crystal or beryl ball which is supposedly entered by angels which can be
     discerned and understood by a *speculatrix.*
98   *red letters: and a face, cut for thee* eye-catching rubric headings and a wood-cut portrait.
99   *Gamaliel Ratsey* a highwayman, hanged in 1605. He worked in a hideous mask,
     probably referred to here.
103 *trencher-rascal* meal-scrounger.
104 *dog-leech* dog-doctor (i.e. quack).
106 *For lying too heavy o' the basket* For taking an unfairly large helping from the
     communal basket of scraps for prisoners.
109 *'Slight* 'God's light'.
110 *republic* Lat. 'common thing', i.e. Dol.

FACE

    Away this brach. I'll bring thee, rogue, within
    The statute of sorcery, *tricesimo tertio,*
    Of Harry the Eighth: ay, and (perhaps) thy neck
    Within a noose, for laund'ring gold, and barbing it.

DOL

    You'll bring your head within a coxcomb, will you?   115
       She catcheth out FACE *his sword: and breaks* SUBTLE*'s glass*
    And you, sir, with your menstrue, gather it up.
    S'death, you abominable pair of stinkards,
    Leave off your barking, and grow one again,
    Or, by the light that shines, I'll cut your throats.
    I'll not be made a prey unto the marshal,   120
    For ne'er a snarling dog-bolt o' you both.
    Ha' you together cozened all this while,
    And all the world, and shall it now be said
    You've made most courteous shift, to cozen yourselves?
    [*To* FACE] You will accuse him? You will bring him in   125
    Within the statute? Who shall take your word?
    A whoreson, upstart, apocryphal captain,
    Whom not a puritan, in Blackfriars, will trust
    So much, as for a feather! [*To* SUBTLE] And you, too,
    Will give the cause, forsooth? You will insult,   130
    And claim a primacy, in the divisions?
    You must be chief? As if you, only, had

---

111   *brach* bitch.

112–13 *tricesimo tertio . . . Eighth* This act (classified as 33 Henry VIII c.8) was passed in 1541 and forbade, *inter alia*, invocations to find gold or silver and divinations to discover lost or stolen goods. It was repealed in 1863.

114   *laundering . . . barbing* washing gold coins in acid to dissolve some of the surface was known as 'laundering'; 'barbing' involved clipping the edges. Tampering with coin was a capital offence.
       it not in Q.

115   *You'll bring your head . . . you?* You're determined to be a fool? The coxcomb (which Dol counterposes to the noose [114]) was the traditional fool's headdress.

116   *menstrue* solvent.

120   *marshal* provost-marshal, in charge of prisons.

121   *dog-bolt* a blunt-headed arrow. Here used figuratively and with an associative logic from 'snarling'.

127   *apocryphal* fictional.

128–9 *Blackfriars . . . feather!* Many Puritans lived in Blackfriars. Surprisingly they were the principal purveyors of feathers and plumes – a fact that let them in for much satire.

The powder to project with? And the work
Were not begun out of equality?
The venture tripartite? All things in common?   135
Without priority? 'Sdeath, you perpetual curs,
Fall to your couples again, and cozen kindly,
And heartily, and lovingly, as you should,
And lose not the beginning of a term,
Or, by this hand, I shall grow factious too,   140
And take my part, and quit you.

FACE   'Tis his fault,
He ever murmurs, and objects his pains,
And says, the weight of all lies upon him.

SUBTLE

Why, so it does.

DOL   How does it? Do not we
Sustain our parts?

SUBTLE   Yes, but they are not equal.   145

DOL

Why, if your part exceed today, I hope
Ours may, tomorrow, match it.

SUBTLE   Ay, they may.

DOL

May, murmuring mastiff? Ay, and do. Death on me!
Help me to throttle him.

SUBTLE   Dorothy, mistress Dorothy,
'Ods precious, I'll do anything. What do you mean?   150

DOL

Because o' your fermentation, and cibation?

SUBTLE

Not I, by heaven –

DOL   Your Sol, and Luna – [*To* FACE] help me.

133   *powder to project with* Here used figuratively for criminal inventiveness.
136   *'Sdeath* 'God's death'.
137   *couples* the word used for a pair of hunting dogs working together.
       cozen kindly deceive amicably (with a pun on 'act like relatives').
139   *term* of the law courts. The four terms were periods of great business and social
       activity and provided opportunities for swindlers.
142   *objects* 'puts forward' (a Latinism).
148   *Death on me* Gods will Q.
150   *'Ods precious* 'God's precious [blood]'.
151   *fermentation . . . cibation* the sixth and seventh processes of alchemy.
152   *Sol, and Luna* gold and silver; each metal was associated with a planet.

SUBTLE
    Would I were hanged then. I'll conform myself.
DOL
    Will you, sir, do so then, and quickly: swear.
SUBTLE
    What should I swear?
DOL   To leave your faction, sir.   155
    And labour, kindly, in the common work.
SUBTLE
    Let me not breathe, if I meant ought, beside.
    I only used those speeches, as a spur
    To him.
DOL   I hope we need no spurs, sir. Do we?
FACE
    'Slid, prove today, who shall shark best.
SUBTLE   Agreed.   160
DOL
    Yes, and work close, and friendly.
SUBTLE   'Slight, the knot
    Shall grow the stronger, for this breach, with me.
DOL
    Why so, my good baboons! Shall we go make
    A sort of sober, scurvy, precise neighbours,
    (That scarce have smiled twice, sin' the king came in)   165
    A feast of laughter, at our follies? Rascals,
    Would run themselves from breath, to see me ride,
    Or you t'have but a hole, to thrust your heads in,
    For which you should pay ear-rent? No, agree.
    And may Don Provost ride a-feasting, long,   170
    In his old velvet jerkin, and stained scarves
    (My noble Sovereign, and worthy General)

155   *faction* quarrel.
160   *'Slid* 'God's [eye] lid'.
       shark swindle.
164   *sort of* set of.
       precise puritanical; strict in religious observance.
165   *sin' the king came in* i.e. since 1603.
167–9 *to see ... ear-rent* to see me displayed in a cart as a prostitute and you pilloried and
       your ears cut off. (Dee's assistant Kelley lost both ears as a punishment for coining).
170   *Don Provost* Provost-marshal 'who is often both Informer, Judge, and Executioner ...
       [and] punishes disorderlie Souldiors, Coyners, Free-booters, highway robbers ... '
       Cotgrave, *A Dictionary of the French and English Tongues*, London, 1611. Dol here
       evokes the hangman, entitled to the clothes of his victims.

Ere we contribute a new crewel garter
To his most worsted worship.

SUBTLE   Royal Dol!
Spoken like Claridiana, and thy self!   175

FACE

For which, at supper, thou shalt sit in triumph,
And not be styled Dol Common, but Dol Proper,
Dol Singular: the longest cut, at night,
Shall draw thee for his Dol Particular.   [*A bell rings*]

SUBTLE

Who's that? One rings. To the window, Dol. Pray heaven,   180
The master do not trouble us, this quarter.

FACE

O, fear not him. While there dies one, a week,
O'the plague, he's safe, from thinking toward London.
Beside, he's busy at his hop-yards, now:
I had a letter from him. If he do,   185
He'll send such word, for airing o' the house
As you shall have sufficient time, to quit it:
Though we break up a fortnight, 'tis no matter.

SUBTLE

Who is it, Dol?

DOL   A fine young quodling.

FACE   O,
My lawyer's clerk, I lighted on, last night,   190
In Holborn, at the Dagger. He would have
(I told you of him) a familiar,
To rifle with, at horses, and win cups.

DOL

O, let him in.

SUBTLE   Stay. Who shall do't?

173–4   *crewel garter . . . worsted worship* two puns playing on 'crewel' (yarn and 'cruel') and
         'worsted' (dressed in worsted and 'thwarted').
  175   *Claridiana* heroine of Diego Ortuñez del Calahorra's *Caballero del Sol*, a popular
         romance first translated as *The Mirror of Princely Deeds and Knighthood*, 1578.
177–9   *Common . . . Proper . . . Singular . . . Particular* grammatical categories used to indicate
         Dol's sexual range.
  178   *longest cut* they will draw straws for Dol.
  189   *quodling* an unripe apple; youth.
  191   *Dagger* the Dagger tavern was famous for pies and frumety. It was perhaps also a
         gambling house.
  192   *familiar* spirit.
  193   *rifle* gamble (raffle).

FACE   Get you   195
   Your robes on. I will meet him, as going out.
DOL
   And what shall I do?
FACE   Not be seen, away.
   Seem you very reserved.

                                         [*Exit* DOL]
SUBTLE   Enough.   [*Exit* SUBTLE]
FACE   God be w'you, sir.
   I pray you, let him know that I was here.
   His name is Dapper. I would gladly have stayed, but –

ACT I, SCENE ii

DAPPER [*Within*]
   Captain, I am here.
FACE   Who's that? He's come, I think, Doctor.

       [*Enter* DAPPER]

   Good faith, sir, I was going away.
DAPPER   In truth,
   I am very sorry, Captain.
FACE   But I thought
   Sure, I should meet you.
DAPPER   Ay, I am very glad.
   I had a scurvy writ, or two, to make,   5
   And I had lent my watch last night, to one
   That dines, today, at the sheriff's: and so was robbed
   Of my pass-time.

      [*Enter* SUBTLE *in doctor's robes*]

       Is this the cunning-man?
FACE
   This is his worship.

    6   *watch* a desirable status-commodity.

DAPPER	Is he a Doctor?	
FACE	Yes.	
DAPPER		

And ha' you broke with him, Captain?

FACE	Ay.	
DAPPER		And how?

FACE

Faith, he does make the matter, sir, so dainty,
I know not what to say –

DAPPER   Not so, good Captain.

FACE

Would I were fairly rid on't, believe me.

DAPPER

Nay, now you grieve me, sir. Why should you wish so?
I dare assure you. I'll not be ungrateful.

FACE

I cannot think you will, sir. But the law
Is such a thing – and then, he says, Read's matter
Falling so lately –

DAPPER   Read? He was an ass,
And dealt, sir, with a fool.

FACE   It was a clerk, sir.

DAPPER

A clerk?

FACE   Nay, hear me, sir, you know the law
Better, I think –

DAPPER   I should, sir, and the danger.
You know I showed the statute to you?

FACE   You did so.

DAPPER

And will I tell, then? By this hand, of flesh,
Would it might never write good court-hand, more,

10

15

20

---

10   *broke* broached the matter.
11   *he does . . . dainty* he treats it with such fastidious caution.
17   *Read's matter* In 1608 Simon Read, a Southwark doctor, was given a pardon for having (in November 1607) invoked three spirits in order to discover a thief.
19   *a fool* presumably Tobias Matthews who had been robbed and called upon Read's assistance.
22   *the statute* see I.i.112.
24   *court-hand* a much abbreviated (and therefore hard to read) style of writing used in the law courts.

If I discover. What do you think of me, 25
That I am a *Chiause*?
FACE   What's that?
DAPPER   The Turk was, here –
As one would say, do you think I am a Turk?
FACE
I'll tell the Doctor so.
DAPPER   Do, good sweet Captain.
FACE
Come, noble Doctor, 'pray thee, let's prevail,
This is the gentleman, and he is no *Chiause*. 30
SUBTLE
Captain, I have returned you all my answer.
I would do much, sir, for your love – but this
I neither may, nor can.
FACE   Tut, do not say so.
You deal, now, with a noble fellow, Doctor,
One that will thank you, richly, and he's no *Chiause*: 35
Let that, sir, move you.
SUBTLE   Pray you, forbear –
FACE   He has
Four angels, here –
SUBTLE   You do me wrong, good sir.
FACE
Doctor, wherein? To tempt you, with these spirits?
SUBTLE
To tempt my art, and love, sir, to my peril.
'Fore heaven, I scarce can think you are my friend, 40
That so would draw me to apparent danger.
FACE
I draw you? A horse draw you, and a halter,

25   *discover* reveal.
26   *Chiause* in July 1607 a Turk named Mustafa arrived in England declaring himself
      ambassador from the Sultan, though he used only the title 'Chaush' (messenger).
      The Levant merchants were fooled into entertaining him at great cost and 'to play
      the Chaush . . . seems to have become a popular synonym for imposture'. *The Travels
      of Sir John Sanderson in the Levant*, ed. Sir W. Foster, London, 1931, p. xxxv.
37   *angels* gold coins bearing a picture of the Archangel Michael combatting a dragon.
      The word – conjoining the spiritual and the pecuniary – was much played upon, as
      here.
38   *spirits* continues the play on 'angels'.
42   *A horse draw you* i.e. in a cart to be hanged.

You, and your flies together –
DAPPER   Nay, good Captain.
FACE
That know no difference of men.
SUBTLE   Good words, sir.
FACE
Good deeds, sir, Doctor Dogs-meat. 'Slight I bring you   45
No cheating Clim o' the Cloughs, or Claribels,
That look as big as five-and-fifty, and flush,
And spit out secrets, like hot custard –
DAPPER   Captain.
FACE
Nor any melancholic under-scribe,
Shall tell the Vicar: but, a special gentle,   50
That is the heir to forty marks, a year,
Consorts with the small poets of the time,
Is the sole hope of his old grandmother,
That knows the law, and writes you six fair hands,
Is a fine clerk, and has his cyph'ring perfect,   55
Will take his oath, o' the Greek Testament
If need be, in his pocket: and can court
His mistress, out of Ovid.
DAPPER   Nay, dear Captain.
FACE
Did you not tell me, so?
DAPPER   Yes, but I'd ha' you
Use master Doctor, with some more respect.   60

---

45   *Dogs-meat* Dogges-mouth Q.
46   *Clim o' the Cloughs . . . Claribels* Clim of the Clough, 'an archer good ynough' (*Ballad of Adam Bell*) and an outlaw. Nashe uses his name for the devil in *Pierce Pennilesse* (1592). Sir Claribel pursues the False Florimell in Spenser's *Faerie Queene* IV.ix.
47   *as big as five-and-fifty, and flush* all 55 cards in the same suit – an unbeatable hand in Primero.
50   *Vicar* Vicar general, acting for the bishop in ecclesiastical courts.
     gentle gentleman.
54   *six fair hands* six styles of handwriting; probably those cited in John de Beau Chesne and John Baildon's *A Booke containing divers sortes of hands, as well the English as French secretarie with the Italian, Roman, Chancelry & Court hands*, London, 1571.
55   *cyph'ring* book-keeping.
56   *Testament* This is the Q reading; in F it is changed to 'Xenophon' which makes no sense except to highlight the absurdities to which censorship leads.
58   *Ovid* If he courted out of the *Amores* he would be quite forward.

FACE

    Hang him proud stag, with his broad velvet head.
    But, for your sake, I'd choke, ere I would change
    An article of breath, with such a puck-fist –
    Come let's be gone.

SUBTLE   Pray you, le' me speak with you.

DAPPER

    His worship calls you, Captain.

FACE   I am sorry,   65

    I e'er embarked myself, in such a business.

DAPPER

    Nay, good sir. He did call you.

FACE   Will he take, then?

SUBTLE

    First, hear me –

FACE   Not a syllable, 'less you take.

SUBTLE

    Pray ye, sir –

FACE   Upon no terms, but an *assumpsit*

SUBTLE

    Your humour must be law.   *He takes the money*

FACE   Why now, sir, talk.

    Now, I dare hear you with mine honour. Speak.   70

    So may this gentleman too.

SUBTLE   Why, sir –

FACE   No whispering.

SUBTLE

    'Fore heaven, you do not apprehend the loss
    You do yourself, in this.

FACE   Wherein? For what?

SUBTLE

    Marry, to be so importunate for one,   75

    That, when he has it, will undo you all:

    He'll win up all the money i' the town.

61   *proud stag . . . velvet head* Subtle is wearing a doctor's velvet hat whose texture is like
      that of the plush on a stag's antlers.

63   *puck-fist* puff-ball (i.e. wind-bag).

69   *assumpsit* legal term; lit. 'he has taken'; a voluntary, oral contract sealed with some
      form of payment.

FACE
  How!

SUBTLE Yes. And blow up gamester, after gamester,
  As they do crackers, in a puppet-play.
  If I do give him a familiar,   80
  Give you him all you play for; never set him:
  For he will have it.

FACE   You're mistaken, Doctor.
  Why, he does ask one but for cups, and horses,
  A rifling fly: none o' your great familiars.

DAPPER
  Yes, Captain, I would have it, for all games.   85

SUBTLE
  I told you so.

FACE   'Slight, that's a new business!
  I understood you, a tame bird, to fly
  Twice in a term, or so; on Friday nights,
  When you had left the office: for a nag,
  Of forty, or fifty shillings.

DAPPER   Ay, 'tis true, sir,   90
  But I do think, now, I shall leave the law,
  And therefore –

FACE   Why, this changes quite the case!
  D'you think, that I dare move him?

DAPPER   If you please, sir,
  All's one to him, I see.

FACE   What! For that money?
  I cannot with my conscience. Nor should you   95
  Make the request, methinks.

DAPPER   No, sir, I mean
  To add consideration.

FACE   Why, then, sir,
  I'll try. Say, that it were for all games, Doctor?

SUBTLE
  I say, then, not a mouth shall eat for him

78   *blow up* ruin.
79   *crackers* fireworks.
81   *set him* lay a wager with him.
87   *I understood you* I thought you meant.
97   *consideration* payment.
99–100   *not a mouth . . . o' the score* because of him no gambler in town will be able to eat
       unless they chalk it up on the slate.

At any ordinary, but o' the score,   100
That is a gaming mouth, conceive me.

FACE   Indeed!

SUBTLE

He'll draw you all the treasure of the realm,
If it be set him.

FACE   Speak you this from art?

SUBTLE

Ay, sir, and reason too: the ground of art.
He's o' the only best complexion,   105
The Queen of Fairy loves.

FACE   What! Is he!

SUBTLE   Peace.

He'll overhear you. Sir, should she but see him –

FACE

  What?

SUBTLE   Do not you tell him.

FACE   Will he win at cards too?

SUBTLE

The spirits of dead Holland, living Isaac,
You'd swear, were in him: such a vigorous luck   110
As cannot be resisted. 'Slight he'll put
Six o' your gallants, to a cloak, indeed.

FACE

A strange success, that some man shall be born to!

SUBTLE

He hears you, man –

DAPPER   Sir, I'll not be ingrateful.

FACE

Faith, I have a confidence in his good nature: 115
You hear, he says, he will not be ingrateful.

SUBTLE

Why, as you please, my venture follows yours.

FACE

Troth, do it, Doctor. Think him trusty, and make him.
He may make us both happy in an hour:

100   *ordinary* eating house.
103   *art* occult knowledge.
109   *dead Holland, living Isaac* John and Isaac Holland were the first Dutch alchemists.
111–12   *put . . . to a cloak* he'll reduce six gallants to nothing but their cloaks.
117   *my venture . . . yours* I'll risk it if you will.
119   *happy* rich (the Latin *beatus* translates as both).

Win some five thousand pound, and send us two on't. 120

DAPPER
Believe it, and I will, sir.

FACE   And you shall, sir.
You have heard all?

DAPPER   No, what was't? Nothing, I sir.

                                FACE *takes him aside*

FACE
Nothing?

DAPPER   A little, sir.

FACE   Well, a rare star
Reigned, at your birth.

DAPPER   At mine, sir? No.

FACE   The Doctor
Swears that you are –

SUBTLE   Nay, Captain, you'll tell all, now. 125

FACE
Allied to the Queen of Fairy.

DAPPER   Who? That I am?
Believe it, no such matter –

FACE   Yes, and that
Yo' were born with a caul o' your head.

DAPPER   Who says so?

FACE   Come.
You know it well enough, though you dissemble it.

DAPPER
I'fac, I do not. You are mistaken.

FACE   How! 130
Swear by your fac? And in a thing so known
Unto the Doctor? How shall we, sir, trust you
I' the other matter? Can we ever think,
When you have won five, or six thousand pound,
You'll send us shares in't, by this rate?

DAPPER   By Jove, sir, 135
I'll win ten thousand pound, and send you half.
I'fac's no oath.

SUBTLE   No, no, he did but jest.

---

128   *born with a caul* a sign of good luck.
130   *I'fac* In faith.
135   *Jove* Gad Q.
137   *I'fac's* fac is Q.

FACE
> Go to. Go, thank the Doctor, He's your friend
> To take it so.

DAPPER   I thank his worship.

FACE   So?
> Another angel.

DAPPER   Must I?

FACE   Must you? 'Slight,   140
> What else is thanks? Will you be trivial?

>   [*Gives money* to SUBTLE]
>   Doctor,
> When must he come, for his familiar?

DAPPER
> Shall I not ha' it with me?

SUBTLE   O, good sir!
> There must a world of ceremonies pass,
> You must be bathed, and fumigated, first;   145
> Besides, the Queen of Fairy does not rise,
> Till it be noon.

FACE   Not, if she danced, tonight.

SUBTLE
> And she must bless it.

FACE   Did you never see
> Her royal Grace, yet?

DAPPER   Whom?

FACE   Your aunt of Fairy?

SUBTLE
> Not, since she kissed him, in the cradle, Captain,   150
> I can resolve you that.

FACE   Well, see her Grace,
> Whate'er it cost you, for a thing that I know!
> It will be somewhat hard to compass: but,
> How ever, see her. You are made, believe it,
> If you can see her. Her Grace is a lone woman,   155
> And very rich, and if she take a fancy,
> She will do strange things. See her, at any hand.

---

138   *He's* He is Q.
141   *trivial* petty.
147   *tonight* last night.
151   *resolve you that* answer that for you.
152   *for* on account of.

'Slid, she may hap to leave you all she has!
It is the Doctor's fear.

DAPPER   How will't be done, then?

FACE

Let me alone, take you no thought. Do you   160
But say to me, Captain, I'll see her Grace.

DAPPER

Captain, I'll see her Grace.

FACE   Enough.   *One knocks without*

SUBTLE   Who's there?

Anon. [*To* FACE] (Conduct him forth, by the back way.)
Sir, against one o'clock, prepare yourself.
Till when you must be fasting; only, take   165
Three drops of vinegar, in, at your nose;
Two at your mouth; and one, at either ear;
Then, bathe your fingers' ends; and wash your eyes;
To sharpen your five senses; and, cry *hum*,
Thrice; and then *buz*, as often; and then, come.   170

FACE

Can you remember this?

DAPPER   I warrant you.

FACE

Well, then, away. 'Tis, but your bestowing
Some twenty nobles, 'mong her Grace's servants;
And, put on a clean shirt: you do not know
What grace her Grace may do you in clean linen.   175

                            [*Exeunt*]

ACT I, SCENE iii

[*Enter*] SUBTLE

SUBTLE [*To* DRUGGER]

Come in. [*He turns and calls out*]
        (Good wives, I pray you forbear me, now.
Troth I can do you no good, till afternoon.)

---

174   *clean shirt* Fairies are traditionally particular about cleanliness.

1   *Good wives* This is addressed to some putative clients outside.

[*Enter* DRUGGER]

What is your name, say you, Abel Drugger?
DRUGGER   Yes, sir.
SUBTLE
  A seller of tobacco?
DRUGGER   Yes, sir.
SUBTLE   'Umh.
  Free of the Grocers?
DRUGGER   Ay, and't please you.
SUBTLE   Well –   5
  Your business, Abel?
DRUGGER   This, and't please your worship,
  I am a young beginner, and am building
  Of a new shop, and't like your worship; just,
  At corner of a street: (here's the plot on't.)
  And I would know, by art, sir, of your worship,   10
  Which way I should make my door, by necromancy.
  And, where my shelves. And, which should be for boxes.
  And, which for pots. I would be glad to thrive, sir.
  And, I was wished to your worship, by a gentleman,
  One Captain Face, that says you know men's planets,   15
  And their good angels, and their bad.
SUBTLE   I do,
  If I do see 'em –

[*Enter* FACE]

FACE   What! My honest Abel?
  Thou art well met, here!
DRUGGER   Troth, sir, I was speaking,
  Just, as your worship came here, of your worship.
  I pray you, speak for me to master Doctor.   20
FACE
  He shall do anything. Doctor, do you hear?
  This is my friend, Abel, an honest fellow,
  He lets me have good tobacco, and he does not

---

5 *Free of the Grocers* a member of the Grocers' guild or company.
9 *plot* groundplan.
14 *wished to* recommended.

Sophisticate it, with sack-lees, or oil,
Nor washes it in muscadel, and grains,   25
Nor buries it, in gravel, under ground,
Wrapped up in greasy leather, or pissed clouts:
But keeps it in fine lily-pots, that opened,
Smell like conserve of roses, or French beans.
He has his maple block, his silver tongs,   30
Winchester pipes, and fire of juniper.
A neat, spruce-honest-fellow, and no gold-smith.

SUBTLE

He's a fortunate fellow, that I am sure on –

FACE

Already, sir, ha' you found it? Lo' thee Abel!

SUBTLE

And, in right way toward riches –

FACE   Sir.

SUBTLE   This summer,   35
He will be of the clothing of his company:
And, next spring, called to the scarlet. Spend what he can.

FACE

What, and so little beard?

SUBTLE   Sir, you must think,
He may have a receipt, to make hair come.

---

24   *Sophisticate . . . oil* William Barclay records, 'Some . . . haue *Tabacco* from *Florida*
      indeede, but because either it is exhausted of spiritualitie, or the radicall humor is
      spent, and wasted, or it hath gotten moysture by the way, or it hath been dried for
      expedition in the Sunne, or carried too negligently, they sophisticate and farde the
      same in sundrie sortes with blacke spice, *Galanga, aqua vitae*, Spanish wine, Anise
      seeds, oyle of Spicke and such like.' *Nepenthes, or the vertues of Tabacco*, Edinburgh,
      1614, A4^V–A5.
25   *muscadel* a fragrant white wine.
      grains spice.
27   *pissed clouts* rags dampened with urine.
30–1 *maple block . . . silver tongs, Winchester pipes . . . fire of juniper* the maple block is for
      shredding the tobacco leaf; the silver tongs for holding hot coals; Winchester made
      famously good tobacco pipes; the fire of Juniper wood (very long-burning) enables
      customers to light their pipes in Abel's shop which, typically, is arranged for the
      consumption, as well as purchase, of tobacco.
32   *gold-smith* usurer.
36   *of the clothing of his company* i.e. Drugger will be made a livery-man of his company.
      Each of the trade guilds and companies had a distinctive livery.
37   *called to the scarlet* be made a sheriff.
38   *and so little beard?* and so young?

But he'll be wise, preserve his youth, and fine for't: 40
His fortune looks for him, another way.

FACE
'Slid, Doctor, how canst thou know this so soon?
I am amused at that!

SUBTLE   By a rule, Captain,
In metoposcopy, which I do work by,
A certain star i'the forehead, which you see not.   45
Your chestnut, or your olive-coloured face
Does never fail: and your long ear doth promise.
I knew't, by certain spots too, in his teeth,
And on the nail of his mercurial finger.

FACE
Which finger's that?

SUBTLE   His little finger. Look.   50
Y'were born upon a Wednesday?

DRUGGER   Yes, indeed, sir.

SUBTLE
The thumb, in chiromanty, we give Venus;
The forefinger to Jove; the midst, to Saturn;
The ring to Sol; the least, to Mercury:
Who was the lord, sir, of his horoscope,   55
His house of life being Libra, which foreshowed,
He should be a merchant, and should trade with balance.

FACE
Why, this is strange! Is't not, honest Nab?

SUBTLE
There is a ship now, coming from Ormus,

---

40 *fine for't* H.&S. read this as meaning 'pay the fine for refusing office'; but it may
    simply mean 'and be fine because of it'.
43 *amused* amazed; bewildered.
44 *metoposcopy* the art of reading character from physiognomy.
46–7 *Your chestnut . . . fail* 'The colours of the Body, and especially of the face denote the
    Humour and inclination of the person . . . Those that be chestnut or olive colour are
    Jovialists and honest people, open without painting or cheating', R. Sanders,
    Physionomie and Chiromancie, Metoposcopie, London, 1653, pp. 166–7.
49 *mercurial finger* the little finger; each finger is assigned a separate planet in J. B. Porta's
    Coelestis Physiognomoniae, Naples, 1603, lib. v, cap. xiii.
52 *chiromanty* palmistry.
54–7 *the least . . . balance* Libra is ruled, not by Mercury, but by Venus. But Mercury is a
    more encouraging ruling planet for the aspiring business man. (Jonson's own sign,
    Gemini, is ruled by Mercury).
57 *trade with balance* the scales are the sign of Libra.
59 *Ormus* Hormuz on the Persian Gulf, source of much spice.

That shall yield him, such a commodity   60
Of drugs – [*looking at plan*]
          this is the west, and this the south?

DRUGGER
  Yes, sir.

SUBTLE And those are your two sides?

DRUGGER   Ay, sir.

SUBTLE
  Make me your door, then, south; your broad side, west:
  And, on the east side of your shop, aloft,
  Write *Mathlai, Tarmiel,* and *Baraborat*;   65
  Upon the north part, *Rael, Velel, Thiel.*
  They are the names of those mercurial spirits,
  That do fright flies from boxes.

DRUGGER   Yes, sir.

SUBTLE   And
  Beneath your threshold, bury me a loadstone
  To draw in gallants, that wear spurs: the rest,   70
  They'll seem to follow.

FACE   That's a secret, Nab!

SUBTLE
  And, on your stall, a puppet, with a vice,
  And a court-fucus, to call city-dames.
  You shall deal much, with minerals.

DRUGGER   Sir, I have,
  At home, already –

SUBTLE   Ay, I know, you have arsenic,   75
  Vitriol, sal-tartar, argaile, alkali,
  Cinoper: I know all. This fellow, Captain
  Will come, in time, to be a great distiller,

65–6 *Mathlai . . . . Thiel* quoted from the *Heptameron, seu Elementa magica Pietri Abano Philosophi* (appended to Cornelius Agrippa's *De Occulta Philosophia* Paris?, no date).

67 *mercurial* Mercurian Q.

68 *fright flies from boxes* protect your stores from flies.

69 *loadstone* magnet.

71 *seem* be seen (a Latinism, *videri*).

72 *vice* wire mechanism for operating the puppet.

73 *fucus* cosmetic; one used at court would be desirable to socially-aspiring city women.

76 *Vitriol* Sulphuric acid.
     sal-tartar carbonate of potash.
     argaile cream of tartar.
     alkali caustic soda.

77 *Cinoper* Red mercuric sulphide.

And give a say (I will not say directly,
But very fair) at the philosopher's stone.   80

FACE
Why, how now, Abel! Is this true?

DRUGGER   Good Captain,
What must I give?

FACE   Nay, I'll not counsel thee.
Thou hear'st, what wealth (he says, spend what thou canst)
Th'art like to come to.

DRUGGER   I would gi' him a crown.

FACE
A crown! And toward such a fortune? Heart,   85
Thou shalt rather gi' him thy shop. No gold about thee?

DRUGGER
Yes, I have a portague, I ha' kept this half year.

FACE
Out on thee, Nab; 'Slight, there was such an offer –
'Shalt keep't no longer, I'll gi'it him for thee?
Doctor, Nab prays your worship, to drink this:
                                    [Gives money to SUBTLE]
                                    and swears   90
He will appear more grateful, as your skill
Does raise him in the world.

DRUGGER   I would entreat
Another favour of his worship.

FACE   What is't, Nab?

DRUGGER
But, to look over, sir, my almanack,
And cross out my ill days, that I may neither   95
Bargain, nor trust upon them.

FACE   That he shall, Nab.
Leave it, it shall be done, 'gainst afternoon.

SUBTLE
And a direction for his shelves.

FACE   Now, Nab?
Art thou well pleased, Nab?

79   *give a say* make a try for.
87   *portague* a Portuguese gold coin.
95   *ill days* days that are astrologically inauspicious.
97   *'gainst* by.

DRUGGER   Thank, sir, both your worships.

FACE   Away.

[*Exit* DRUGGER]

Why, now, you smoky persecutor of nature!   100
Now, do you see, that something's to be done,
Beside your beech-coal, and your corsive waters,
Your crosslets, crucibles, and cucurbites?
You must have stuff, brought home to you, to work on?
And, yet, you think, I am at no expense,   105
In searching out these veins, then following 'em,
Then trying 'em out. 'Fore God, my intelligence
Costs me more money, than my share oft comes to,
In these rare works.

SUBTLE   You are pleasant, sir.

[*Enter*] DOL

                                          How now?

ACT I, SCENE iv

FACE

What says, my dainty Dolkin?

DOL   Yonder fish-wife
Will not away. And there's your giantess,
The bawd of Lambeth.

SUBTLE   Heart, I cannot speak with 'em.

DOL

Not, afore night, I have told 'em, in a voice,
Thorough the trunk, like one of your familiars.   5
But I have spied Sir Epicure Mammon –

SUBTLE   Where?

102   *beech-coal* beech wood made the best charcoal.
       corsive corrosive.
103   *crosslets* melting pots.
       cucurbites gourd-shaped retorts used in distillation.
107   *intelligence* information.

3   *Lambeth* noted for prostitutes and thieves.
5   *Thorough the trunk* i.e. through a speaking tube.

DOL

Coming along, at the far end of the lane,
Slow of his feet, but earnest of his tongue,
To one, that's with him.

SUBTLE   Face, go you, and shift.

[*Exit* FACE]

Dol, you must presently make ready too –   10

DOL

Why, what's the matter?

SUBTLE   O, I did look for him
With the sun's rising: marvel, he could sleep!
This is the day, I am to perfect for him
The *magisterium*, our great work, the stone;
And yield it, made, into his hands: of which,   15
He has, this month, talked, as he were possessed.
And, now, he's dealing pieces on't, away.
Methinks, I see him, entering ordinaries,
Dispensing for the pox; and plaguey-houses,
Reaching his dose; walking Moorfields for lepers;   20
And offering citizens' wives pomander-bracelets,
As his preservative, made of the elixir;
Searching the spittle, to make old bawds young;
And the highways, for beggars, to make rich:
I see no end of his labours. He will make   25
Nature ashamed of her long sleep: when art,
Who's but a step-dame, shall do more, than she,
In her best love to mankind, ever could.
If his dream last, he'll turn the age, to gold.

[*Exeunt*]

---

9   *shift* change.
14   *magisterium* master work.
16   *possessed* possess'd on't Q.
17   *dealing . . . away* giving parts of it away (in imagination).
20   *Reaching* offering.
     Moorfields a stretch of reclaimed marshland which in Jonson's time was being laid
     out in parks. It was noted for beggars, and lepers were allowed to beg there.
21   *pomander-bracelets* a pomander was a perfumed ball carried as a protection against
     infection (and smells).
23   *spittle* hospital.
27   *step-dame* The debate as to the respective roles of Art and Nature was a commonplace.
     See, e.g., *The Winter's Tale*, IV. iv.79–102.

ACT II, SCENE i

[*Enter*] MAMMON, SURLY

MAMMON

Come on, sir. Now, you set your foot on shore
In *novo orbe*; here's the rich Peru:
And there within, sir, are the golden mines,
Great Solomon's Ophir! He was sailing to't,
Three years, but we have reached it in ten months.   5
This is the day, wherein, to all my friends,
I will pronounce the happy word, be rich.
This day, you shall be *spectatissimi*.
You shall no more deal with the hollow die,
Or the frail card. No more be at charge of keeping   10
The livery-punk, for the young heir, that must
Seal, at all hours, in his shirt. No more
If he deny, ha' him beaten to't, as he is
That brings him the commodity. No more
Shall thirst of satin, or the covetous hunger   15
Of velvet entrails, for a rude-spun cloak,

1–5   *Now, you set your foot . . . ten months* Mammon is promising Surly a 'new world' of wealth.
        The discovery of the Americas by Renaissance voyagers became a potent metaphor for
        much non-topographical experience of the time. Solomon was believed to have possessed
        the Philosopher's Stone and to have fetched his wealth 'once in three years' from
        Ophir (*I Kings* x.22).
2   *novo orbe* the new world, i.e. America; both a metaphor for wealth and its source
        (through imports).
        Peru synonym for great wealth; the location of El Dorado.
8   *spectatissimi* (Lat.) very much regarded.
9   *hollow die* loaded dice (hollowed and then weighted with lead).
10–14   *No more . . . commodity* An allusion to the 'commodity swindle' (described in Greene's
        Defence of Coney-Catching, The Works of Robert Greene, ed. A. B. Grosart, London
        1881–6, vol. xi, p. 53) by which a borrower was constrained to take all or part of a
        loan in the form of often unsaleable goods (see III.iv.87–99). The 'livery-punk' is a
        prostitute ('livery' implies that she is part of the regular retinue) who, by compromising
        the young heir in *déshabille*, furthers the money-lender's attempts to make him 'seal'
        such an unprofitable bargain.
11   *the young* my yong Q.
16   *velvet entrails* velvet linings. The contemporary fashion for 'slashing' the top layer of
        fabric to allow the contrasting inner stuff to show through could be disturbingly
        reminiscent of gaping wounds. See Lovelace's 'La Bella Bona Roba' 'whose white-
        sattin upper coat of skin/[Is] Cut upon velvet rich incarnadin'.

To be displayed at Madam Augusta's, make
The sons of sword, and hazard fall before
The golden calf, and on their knees, whole nights,
Commit idolatry with wine, and trumpets: 20
Or go a-feasting, after drum and ensign.
No more of this. You shall start up young viceroys,
And have your punks, and punketees, my Surly.
And unto thee, I speak it first, be rich.
Where is my Subtle there? Within ho?

FACE   *Within*   Sir.   25
He'll come to you, by and by.

MAMMON   That's his fire-drake,
His lungs, his Zephyrus, he that puffs his coals,
Till he firk nature up, in her own centre.
You are not faithful, sir. This night, I'll change
All, that is metal, in thy house, to gold.   30
And, early in the morning, will I send
To all the plumbers, and the pewterers,
And buy their tin, and lead up: and to Lothbury,
For all the copper.

SURLY   What, and turn that too?

MAMMON
Yes, and I'll purchase Devonshire, and Cornwall,   35
And make them perfect Indies! You admire now?

SURLY
No faith.

---

17   *Madam Augusta* presumably a brothel madam.
18   *The sons of sword, and hazard* thugs and gamblers.
19   *golden calf* a false idol (*Exodus* xxxii).
22   *start up* generate.
23   *punketees* little whores.
26   *fire-drake* fiery dragon or meteor; here used figuratively for fire-maker.
27   *lungs* bellows; i.e. assistant.   *Zephyrus* the west wind personified.
28   *firk* stir.
29   *faithful* trusting.
30   *thy* my Q (the F reading may be an error).
33   *Lothbury* 'This streete is possessed for the most part by Founders, that cast Candlestickes, Chafingdishes, Spice mortars and such like Copper or Laton workes.' John Stow, *A Survey of London*, ed. C. L. Kingsford, Oxford, 1908, p. 277.
35   *Devonshire, and Cornwall* the site of tin and copper mines.
36   *perfect Indies* the West Indies, thought to be rich in 'spice and mine' (Donne, 'The Sun Rising').
       admire are struck.

MAMMON But when you see th'effects of the great med'cine!
 Of which one part projected on a hundred
 Of Mercury, or Venus, or the Moon,
 Shall turn it, to as many of the Sun;   40
 Nay, to a thousand, so *ad infinitum*:
 You will believe me.

SURLY   Yes, when I see't, I will.
 But, if my eyes do cozen me so (and I
 Giving 'em no occasion) sure, I'll have
 A whore, shall piss 'em out, next day.

MAMMON   Ha! Why?   45
 Do you think, I fable with you? I assure you,
 He that has once the flower of the sun,
 The perfect ruby, which we call elixir,
 Not only can do that, but by its virtue,
 Can confer honour, love, respect, long life,   50
 Give safety, valour: yea, and victory,
 To whom he will. In eight, and twenty days,
 I'll make an old man, of fourscore, a child.

SURLY
 No doubt, he's that already.

MAMMON   Nay, I mean,
 Restore his years, renew him, like an eagle,   55
 To the fifth age; make him get sons, and daughters,
 Young giants; as our philosophers have done
 (The ancient patriarchs afore the flood)
 But taking, once a week, on a knife's point,
 The quantity of a grain of mustard, of it: 60
 Become stout Marses, and beget young Cupids.

SURLY
 The decayed Vestals of Pict-Hatch would thank you,

39–40   *Mercury . . . the Sun* Mercury is quicksilver; Venus stands for copper, the moon for
     silver and the sun for gold.
47–8   *flower of the sun . . . perfect ruby . . . elixir* all synonyms for the Philosopher's Stone.
55   *like an eagle* 'Thy youth is renewed like the eagle's', *Psalms* ciii.5.
56   *the fifth age* 'The *fifth* age, named *Mature Manhood,* hath . . . fifteen yeares of
     continuance, and therefore makes his progress so far as six and fifty yeares' (quoted
     from *The Treasury of Ancient and Modern Times,* 1613, by Malone on *As You Like It,*
     II.vii.151).
58   *ancient patriarchs* The longevity of the Patriarchs was attributed to their knowledge
     of alchemy.
62–3   *The decayed Vestals of Pict-Hatch* Pict-Hatch (just south of where Goswell Road and
     Old Street now meet) was a haunt of prostitutes. Vestals were traditionally virgin

That keep the fire alive, there.
MAMMON   'Tis the secret
Of nature, naturized 'gainst all infections,
Cures all diseases, coming of all causes,   65
A month's grief, in a day; a year's, in twelve:
And, of what age soever, in a month.
Past all the doses, of your drugging Doctors.
I'll undertake, withal, to fright the plague
Out o' the kingdom, in three months.
SURLY   And I'll   70
Be bound, the players shall sing your praises, then,
Without their poets.
MAMMON   Sir, I'll do't. Meantime,
I'll give away so much, unto my man,
Shall serve th' whole city, with preservative,
Weekly, each house his dose, and at the rate –   75
SURLY
As he that built the waterwork, does with water?
MAMMON
You are incredulous.
SURLY   Faith, I have a humour,
I would not willingly be gulled. Your stone
Cannot transmute me.
MAMMON   Pertinax, Surly,
Will you believe antiquity? Records?   80
I'll show you a book, where Moses, and his sister,
And Solomon have written, of the art;
Ay, and a treatise penned by Adam.
SURLY   How!

temple servers. The fire maintained by these vestals is presumably that of venereal
infection.
64   *nature, naturized* Scholastic philosophy distinguished between creating nature (*natura
naturans*) and created nature (*natura naturata*). The stone is part of creat*ed* nature.
71–2 *the players . . . poets* The London theatres were closed while the plague was rife because
they were thought to be places of infection and also to invite infection as retribution
for the immorality they housed. The players would sing Mammon's praises if they
found themselves in work again.
76   *the waterwork* probably the pump-house built by Bevis Bulmer at Broken Wharf in
1594. This supplied Cheapside and Fleet Street with water from the Thames.
77   *I have a humour* It is my temperament.
81–3 *Moses . . . Adam* Mammon is not alone in his attribution of alchemical lore to Moses,
Solomon and Adam. See *H.&S.* for references.

MAMMON

O' the philosopher's stone, and in High Dutch.

SURLY

Did Adam write, sir, in High Dutch?

MAMMON   He did: 85

Which proves it was the primitive tongue.

SURLY   What paper?

MAMMON

On cedar board.

SURLY   O that, indeed (they say)

Will last 'gainst worms.

MAMMON   'Tis like your Irish wood,

'Gainst cobwebs. I have a piece of Jason's fleece, too,

Which was no other, than a book of alchemy,   90

Writ in large sheepskin, a good fat ram-vellum.

Such was Pythagoras' thigh, Pandora's tub;

And, all that fable of Medea's charms,

The manner of our work: the bulls, our furnace,

Still breathing fire; our *argent-vive*, the dragon;   95

The dragon's teeth, mercury sublimate,

That keeps the whiteness, hardness, and the biting;

And they are gathered, into Jason's helm,

(Th' alembic) and then sowed in Mars his field,

And, thence, sublimed so often, till they are fixed.   100

---

84   *High Dutch* hoch Deutsch (high German); Joannes Goropius Becanus, a Flemish
      physician, claimed that German was the original language and that the early Germans
      were not at the Tower of Babel. He declared this in a treatise called *Hermathena* (c.
      1580).

87–8   *cedar board . . . Irish wood* Cedar wood was known for its durability, Irish wood for
       its ability to repel spiders and insects.

89   *Jason's fleece* 'Cornelius Agrippa maketh mention of some Philosophers that held the
      skinne of the sheepe that bare the golden fleece, to be nothing but a booke of Alcumy
      written vpon it', *The Works of Thomas Nashe*, ed. R. B. McKerrow, Oxford, 1966, iii,
      221.

92   *Pythagoras' thigh* supposedly golden (*Diogenes Laertius*, viii.i). Martin Delrio associates
      both this and Pandora's box (*tub*) with alchemy in his *Disquisitiones Magicae*, 1599.

93–100 *that fable . . . are fixed* In order to gain the golden fleece Jason had to yoke and plough
        with two brazen-footed, fire-breathing bulls. He then had to sow dragons' teeth
        which sprang up as armed warriors. Medea, his witch-lover, taught him how to cope.

95   *argent-vive* quicksilver.

96   *mercury sublimate* chloride of mercury – a corrosive (hence the 'biting').

99   *alembic* distilling apparatus.
      Mars his field an old genitive form (= Mars' field) Mars stands for iron.

Both this, th' Hesperian garden, Cadmus' story,
Jove's shower, the boon of Midas, Argus' eyes,
Boccace his Demogorgon, thousands more,
All abstract riddles of our stone. How now?

ACT II, SCENE ii

[*Enter*] FACE [*dressed as bellows-man to them*]

MAMMON
Do we succeed? Is our day come? And holds it?
FACE
The evening will set red, upon you, sir;
You have colour for it, crimson: the red ferment
Has done his office. Three hours hence, prepare you
To see projection.
MAMMON   Pertinax, my Surly,   5
Again, I say to thee, aloud: be rich.
This day, thou shalt have ingots: and, tomorrow,
Give lords th'affront. Is it, my Zephyrus, right?
Blushes the bolt's head?
FACE   Like a wench with child, sir,
That were, but now, discovered to her master.   10

---

101   *th' Hesperian garden* site of golden apples guarded by a dragon.
       Cadmus' story Cadmus founded Thebes on the spot where he killed a dragon, then
       planted its teeth which sprang up as warriors. All but five of these warriors killed
       each other.
102   *Jove's shower* Jove entered Danae as a shower of gold.
       the boon of Midas Bacchus gave Midas the dubious gift of turning all he touched to
       gold.
       Argus' eyes Argus was a dog with a hundred eyes whom Juno set to guard the woman-
       heifer Io whom her husband, Jupiter, loved.
103   *Boccace his Demogorgon* a primeval god named by Boccaccio in his *Genealogica
       Deorum*. Demogorgon is also mentioned by Milton and Spenser.
104   *abstract riddles* allegories.

  3   *red ferment* 'Red is last in the work of *Alkimy*', Norton, *Ordinal*, in *T.C.B.*, p. 56;
       'ferment' is leaven.
  8   *Give lords th'affront* look lords in the eye as their equal.
  9   *bolt's head* 'a globular flask with a long cylindrical neck' (*OED*); it 'blushes' as it reddens.

385

MAMMON

Excellent witty Lungs! My only care is,
Where to get stuff, enough now, to project on,
This town will not half serve me.

FACE   No, sir? Buy
The covering off o' churches.

MAMMON   That's true.

FACE   Yes.

Let 'em stand bare, as do their auditory.   15
Or cap 'em, new, with shingles.

MAMMON   No, good thatch:
Thatch will lie light upo' the rafters, Lungs.
Lungs, I will manumit thee, from the furnace;
I will restore thee thy complexion, Puff,
Lost in the embers; and repair this brain,   20
Hurt wi' the fume o' the metals.

FACE   I have blown, sir,
Hard, for your worship; thrown by many a coal,
When 'twas not beech; weighed those I put in, just,
To keep your heat still even; these bleared eyes
Have waked, to read your several colours, sir,   25
Of the pale citron, the green lion, the crow,
The peacock's tail, the plumed swan.

MAMMON   And, lastly,
Thou hast descried the flower, the *sanguis agni?*

FACE

Yes, sir.

MAMMON Where's master?

FACE   At's prayers, sir, he,

---

13   *Buy* Take Q.
15   *auditory* congregation (who remove their hats).
16   *shingles* slats of wood used like roof tiles.
18   *manumit* release.
23   *When 'twas not beech* In Lyly's *Gallathea* the alchemist says, 'I may have onely Beechen coales', II.ii.78.
26–7   *pale citron . . . swan* Each of these items names a colour and stage in the alchemical process: 'Pale, and Black, wyth falce Cityrne, unparfyt Whyte & Red, Pekoks fethers in color gay, the Raynbow whych shall overgoe/The Spottyd Panther wyth the Lyon greene, the Crowys byll bloe as lede;/These shall appere before the parfyt Whyte', Ripley, *Compound of Alchymie*, in *T.C.B.*, p. 188.
28   *sanguis agni* 'blood of the lamb' (Lat.); a red indicating successful projection. The term has Christian, sacrificial connotations.

Good man, he's doing his devotions,   30
  For the success.
MAMMON   Lungs, I will set a period,
  To all thy labours: thou shalt be the master
  Of my seraglio.
FACE   Good, sir.
MAMMON   But do you hear?
  I'll geld you, Lungs.
FACE   Yes, sir.
MAMMON   For I do mean
  To have a list of wives, and concubines,   35
  Equal with Solomon; who had the stone
  Alike, with me: and I will make me, a back
  With the elixir, that shall be as tough
  As Hercules, to encounter fifty a night.
  Th'art sure, thou saw'st it blood?
FACE   Both blood, and spirit, sir.   40
MAMMON
  I will have all my beds, blown up; not stuffed:
  Down is too hard. And then, mine oval room,
  Filled with such pictures, as Tiberius took
  From Elephantis: and dull Aretine
  But coldly imitated. Then, my glasses,   45
  Cut in more subtle angles, to disperse,
  And multiply the figures, as I walk
  Naked between my *succubae*. My mists
  I'll have of perfume, vapoured 'bout the room,
  To lose ourselves in; and my baths, like pits   50
  To fall into: from whence, we will come forth,
  And roll us dry in gossamer, and roses.
  (Is it arrived at ruby?) – Where I spy
  A wealthy citizen, or rich lawyer,
  Have a sublimed pure wife, unto that fellow   55

33   *seraglio* harem; seraglia Q, F.
41   *beds, blown up* Lampridius, *Elagabalus*, xxv.
43–4 Suetonius, *Tiberius*, cap. xliii.
44   *Aretine* Pietro Aretino (1492–1550); Italian poet whose *Sonnetti Lussuriosi* (1523)
       illustrated by Giulio Romano were notorious erotica of their time.
45   *glasses* Seneca, *Naturales Quaestiones*, I.xvi, refers to Hostius Quadra's use of mirrors
       to arouse himself.
48   *succubae* demons assuming female form in order to have sexual intercourse with
       humans.

I'll send a thousand pound, to be my cuckold.

FACE

And I shall carry it?

MAMMON   No. I'll ha' no bawds,
But fathers, and mothers. They will do it best.
Best of all others. And, my flatterers
Shall be the pure, and gravest of Divines,   60
That I can get for money. My mere fools,
Eloquent burgesses, and then my poets,
The same that writ so subtly of the fart,
Whom I will entertain, still, for that subject.
The few, that would give out themselves, to be   65
Court, and town stallions, and, eachwhere, belie
Ladies, who are known most innocent, for them;
Those will I beg, to make me eunuchs of:
And they shall fan me with ten ostrich tails
Apiece, made in a plume, to gather wind.   70
We will be brave, Puff, now we ha' the med'cine.
My meat, shall all come in, in Indian shells,
Dishes of agate, set in gold, and studded,
With emeralds, sapphires, hyacinths, and rubies.
The tongues of carps, dormice, and camels' heels,   75
Boiled i' the spirit of Sol, and dissolved pearl,
(Apicius' diet, 'gainst the epilepsy)
And I will eat these broths, with spoons of amber,
Headed with diamant, and carbuncle.
My footboy shall eat pheasants, calvered salmons,   80

58–9   *They will . . . all others* not in Q.
  60   *the pure, and gravest* purest and gravest.
        pure best Q.
  62   *burgesses* members of Parliament.
  63   *that writ . . . of the fart* perhaps the anonymous author of 'The fart Censured in the
        Parliament House' – a ballad commemorating an event in 1607. But Jonson himself
        wrote much of farts in 'The Famous Voyage'.
  74   *hyacinths* not the flowers but precious blue stones.
  75   *tongues of carps* 'The tongues of *Carps* are noted to be choice and costly meat', Isaac
        Walton, *The Compleat Angler* (1653), Oxford, 1935, p. 149.
        dormice The Romans ate them (Apicius gives a recipe), and the practice has lately
        been revived in England by a firm hoping to catch the novelty delicacy market.
        camels' heels Lampridius, *Elagabalus*, xx, tells how this emperor ate these 'in imitation
        of Apicius' – he also ate the beards of mullets.
  77   *Apicius* the Roman author of *Artis Magiricae* (The Art of Cooking).
  80   *calvered* a culinary process only applicable to fresh firm fish.

Knots, godwits, lampreys: I myself will have
The beards of barbels, served, instead of salads;
Oiled mushrooms; and the swelling unctuous paps
Of a fat pregnant sow, newly cut off,
Dressed with an exquisite, and poignant sauce;   85
For which, I'll say unto my cook, there's gold,
Go forth, and be a knight.

FACE   Sir, I'll go look
A little, how it heightens.

MAMMON   Do.

                                [*Exit* FACE]

                    My shirts
I'll have of taffeta-sarsnet, soft, and light
As cobwebs; and for all my other raiment   90
It shall be such, as might provoke the Persian;
Were he to teach the world riot, anew.
My gloves of fishes', and birds' skins, perfumed
With gums of paradise, and eastern air –

SURLY
And do you think to have the stone, with this?   95

MAMMON
No, I do think, t' have all this, with the stone.

SURLY
Why, I have heard, he must be *homo frugi,*
A pious, holy, and religious man,
One free from mortal sin, a very virgin.

MAMMON
That makes it, sir, he is so. But I buy it.   100
My venture brings it me. He, honest wretch,
A notable, superstitious, good soul,

---

81   *Knots* a species of snipe.
       godwits marsh birds, similar to curlews.
       lampreys eel-shaped fish.
82   *barbels* a species of carp with fleshy filaments hanging from its mouth. See note to
       line 75.
85   *poignant* piquant.
89   *taffeta-sarsnet* a fine soft silk.
91   *the Persian* Sardanapalus, king of Nineveh 9 B.C. – of legendary luxury.
94   *gums of paradise* incense from the middle East (where the Garden of Eden had
       supposedly been).
97–9 *homo frugi . . . virgin* Piety, purity and a lack of material ambition are prerequisite
       to alchemical success.

Has worn his knees bare, and his slippers bald,
With prayer, and fasting for it: and, sir, let him
Do it alone, for me, still. Here he comes, 105
Not a profane word, afore him: 'tis poison.

ACT II, SCENE iii

[*Enter*] SUBTLE [*to them*]

MAMMON
Good morrow, Father.
SUBTLE   Gentle son, good morrow,
    And, to your friend, there. What is he, is with you?
MAMMON
    An heretic, that I did bring along,
    In hope, sir, to convert him.
SUBTLE   Son, I doubt
    You're covetous, that thus you meet your time 5
    I' the just point: prevent your day, at morning.
    This argues something, worthy of a fear
    Of importune, and carnal appetite.
    Take heed, you do not cause the blessing leave you,
    With your ungoverned haste. I should be sorry, 10
    To see my labours, now, e'en at perfection,
    Got by long watching, and large patience,
    Not prosper, where my love, and zeal hath placed 'em.
    Which (heaven I call to witness, with yourself,
    To whom, I have poured my thoughts) in all my ends, 15
    Have looked no way, but unto public good,
    To pious uses, and dear charity,
    Now grown a prodigy with men. Wherein
    If you, my son, should now prevaricate,
    And, to your own particular lusts, employ 20

 4   *doubt* fear.
 6   *I' the just point* punctually, on the dot.
     prevent anticipate.
12   *watching* waking.
18   *Now* No Q, F.
19   *prevaricate* walk crookedly (Lat. *praevaricari*).

So great, and catholic a bliss: be sure,
A curse will follow, yea, and overtake
Your subtle, and most secret ways.

MAMMON   I know, sir,
You shall not need to fear me. I but come,
To ha' you confute this gentleman.

SURLY   Who is,   25
Indeed, sir, somewhat costive of belief
Toward your stone: would not be gulled.

SUBTLE   Well, son,
All that I can convince him in, is this,
The work is done: bright Sol is in his robe.
We have a med'cine of the triple soul,   30
The glorified spirit. Thanks be to heaven,
And make us worthy of it. **Ulen Spiegel**.

FACE [*Within*]
Anon, sir.

[*Enter* FACE]

SUBTLE   Look well to the register,
And let your heat, still, lessen by degrees,
To the aludels.

FACE   Yes, sir.

SUBTLE   Did you look   35
O' the bolt's head yet?

FACE   Which, on D, sir?

SUBTLE   Ay.

21 *catholic* general (as opposed to 'particular', line 20).
25 SURLY SVB. Q.
29 *bright Sol is in his robe* Sol (the sun), the planet governing gold, is ready to officiate.
30 *triple soul* according to scholastic thought there are three kinds of soul: the vegetable
    (capable of growth), the animal (capable of reproduction) and the intellectual (capable
    of thought). Humans are possessed of all three and are linked to the angels by their
    intellectual souls.
32 **Ulen Spiegel** lit. 'Owl-glass'; Til Eulen Spiegel is the hero of several German jest books.
    He is a practical joker. William Copeland's *Howle glass* was published in England
    between 1548 and 1560.
33 *register* a contrivance – usually consisting of moveable metal plates – for regulating
    the passage of air, heat and smoke.
35 *aludels* pear-shaped vessels, open at either end; used for sublimation.
36 *on D* Face gives the impression of a number of different operations going on
    concurrently, each distinguished by a letter of the alphabet.

What's the complexion?

FACE   Whitish.

SUBTLE   Infuse vinegar,
To draw his volatile substance, and his tincture:
And let the water in glass E be filtered,
And put into the gripe's egg. Lute him well;   40
And leave him closed in *balneo*.

FACE   I will, sir.   [*Exit* FACE]

SURLY
What a brave language here is? Next to canting?

SUBTLE
I have another work; you never saw, son,
That, three days since, passed the philosopher's wheel,
In the lent heat of Athanor; and's become   45
Sulphur o' nature.

MAMMON   But 'tis for me?

SUBTLE   What need you?
You have enough in that is perfect.

MAMMON   O, but –

SUBTLE
Why, this is covetise!

MAMMON   No, I assure you,
I shall employ it all, in pious uses,
Founding of colleges, and grammar schools,   50
Marrying young virgins, building hospitals,
And now, and then, a church.

[*Enter* FACE]

SUBTLE   How now?

FACE   Sir, please you,

---

37   *complexion* colour.
38, 40   *his . . . him* The use of the personal pronoun is in keeping with the alchemists' belief
       that all matter is animate.
40   *gripe's egg* an egg-shaped pot (a 'gripe' is a vulture).
     Lute stop up the gaps with lute (clay).
41   *in balneo* in a bath (of boiling water or hot sand).
42   *canting* Cant was the private (though much publicised) language of thieves.
44   *philosopher's wheel* alchemical cycle.
45   *lent* slow (Lat.).
     Athanor a 'digesting furnace' maintaining a low, constant heat.
46   *Sulphur o' nature* pure sulphur in an immutable state.

Shall I not change the filter?
SUBTLE   Marry, yes.
And bring me the complexion of glass B.

[*Exit* FACE]

MAMMON
Ha' you another?
SUBTLE   Yes, son, were I assured   55
Your piety were firm, we would not want
The means to glorify it. But I hope the best:
I mean to tinct C in sand-heat, tomorrow,
And give him imbibition.
MAMMON   Of white oil?
SUBTLE

No, sir, of red. F is come over the helm too,   60
I thank my Maker, in S. Mary's bath,
And shows *lac virginis*. Blessed be heaven.
I sent you of his faeces there, calcined.
Out of that calx, I ha' won the salt of mercury.
MAMMON
By pouring on your rectified water?   65
SUBTLE
Yes, and reverberating in Athanor.

[*Enter* FACE]

How now? What colour says it?
FACE   The ground black, sir.
MAMMON
That's your crow's head?
SURLY   Your cockscomb's, is't not?

58   *sand-heat* i.e. in a sand bath.
59   *imbibition* steeping in liquid.
59–60 *white . . . red* Mercury is 'white', sulphur 'red'; the oils would be derivatives of these.
61   *S. Mary's bath* the 'bain Marie' of modern cooking.
62   *lac virginis* 'Mercurial Water, the Dragon's Tail: it washes and coagulates without any
     manual labour', Ruland, *A Lexicon of Alchemy*, Frankfurt, 1612.
63   *faeces* sediment.
     calcined reduced to a powder having had its humidity drawn out by heat.
64   *calx* the powdery result of calcining.
     salt oxide.
65   *rectified* distilled.
66   *reverberating* being heated by reflected heat.
68   *crow's head* blackness resulting from calcination.

SUBTLE
  No, 'tis not perfect, would it were the crow.
  That work wants something.
SURLY   (O, I looked for this.   70
  The hay is a-pitching.)
SUBTLE   Are you sure, you loosed 'em
  I' their own menstrue?
FACE   Yes, sir, and then married 'em,
  And put 'em in a bolt's head, nipped to digestion,
  According as you bade me; when I set
  The liquor of Mars to circulation,   75
  In the same heat.
SUBTLE   The process, then, was right.
FACE
  Yes, by the token, sir, the retort broke,
  And what was saved, was put into the pelican,
  And signed with Hermes' seal.
SUBTLE   I think 'twas so.
  We should have a new amalgama.
SURLY   (O, this ferret   80
  Is rank as any pole-cat.)
SUBTLE   But I care not.
  Let him e'en die; we have enough beside,
  In embrion. H has his white shirt on?
FACE   Yes, sir,
  He's ripe for inceration: he stands warm,
  In his ash-fire. I would not, you should let   85
  Any die now, if I might counsel, sir,

71   *The hay is a-pitching* A 'hay' is a net 'pitched' or set in front of rabbits' burrows.
      The metaphor is from the language of coney-catching.
71–2 *loosed . . . menstrue* dissolved them in the fluid distilled from them.
73   *nipped* sealed.
      digestion slow extraction of soluble substances through 'cooking' in a digesting oven.
75   *liquor of Mars* molten iron.
78   *pelican* an alembic with a tubular head and two curved spouts, each of which re-
      enter the vessel (like a pelican wounding its own breast).
79   *signed with Hermes' seal* hermetically sealed.
80   *amalgama* mixture of metals with mercury.
80–1 *ferret . . . pole-cat* The images sustain the coney-catching metaphor; pole-cats are
      smellier than ferrets.
83   *In embrion* In their early stages.
83   *has his white shirt on* has turned white.
84   *inceration* bringing the substances to the consistency of soft wax.

For luck's sake to the rest. It is not good.

MAMMON

   He says right.

SURLY   (Ay, are you bolted?)

FACE   Nay, I know't, sir,

   I have seen th' ill fortune. What is some three ounces

   Of fresh materials?

MAMMON   Is't no more?

FACE   No more, sir,   90

   Of gold, t'amalgam, with some six of mercury.

MAMMON

   Away, here's money. What will serve?

FACE   Ask him, sir.

MAMMON

   How much?

SUBTLE   Give him nine pound: you may gi' him ten.

SURLY

   Yes, twenty, and be cozened, do.

MAMMON   There 'tis.

SUBTLE

   This needs not. But that you will have it, so,   95

   To see conclusions of all. For two

   Of our inferior works, are at fixation.

   A third is in ascension. Go your ways.

   Ha' you set the oil of Luna in kemia?

FACE

   Yes, sir.

SUBTLE   And the philosopher's vinegar?

FACE   Ay.   [*Exit* FACE]   100

SURLY

   We shall have a salad.

MAMMON   When do you make projection?

SUBTLE

   Son, be not hasty. I exalt our med'cine,

---

88   *bolted* entered the snare (another coney-catching image).

97   *fixation* the process of reducing a volatile substance to a stable form.

99   *oil of Luna* white elixir.

       kemia from the Greek χυμέια: alchemy; here it probably implies entrance into the whole process.

100 *philosopher's vinegar* either mercury or a corrosive vinegar made of mead.

101 *salad* a salad dressing from the oil and vinegar; the term was actually used by alchemists.

By hanging him in *balneo vaporoso;*
And giving him solution; then congeal him;
And then dissolve him; then again congeal him;   105
For look, how oft I iterate the work,
So many times, I add unto his virtue.
As, if at first, one ounce convert a hundred,
After his second loose, he'll turn a thousand;
His third solution, ten; his fourth, a hundred.   110
After his fifth, a thousand thousand ounces
Of any imperfect metal, into pure
Silver, or gold, in all examinations,
As good, as any of the natural mine.
Get you your stuff here, against afternoon,   115
Your brass, your pewter, and your andirons.

MAMMON
Not those of iron?

SUBTLE   Yes, you may bring them, too.
We'll change all metals.

SURLY   I believe you, in that.

MAMMON
Then I may send my spits?

SUBTLE   Yes, and your racks.

SURLY
And dripping pans, and pot-hangers, and hooks?   120
Shall he not?

SUBTLE   If he please.

SURLY   To be an ass.

SUBTLE
How, sir!

MAMMON This gent'man, you must bear withal.
I told you, he had no faith.

SURLY   And little hope, sir,
But, much less charity, should I gull my self.

---

103   *balneo vaporoso* a contrivance for suspending vessels in steam.
106–7 *how oft . . . virtue* the potency of the stone is increased each time I subject it to the
       process of dissolution and congelation.
108   *convert* turn into.
109   *loose* dissolution.
116   *andirons* metal supports for logs in a fire; fire-dogs.
123–4 *faith . . . hope . . . charity* the Cardinal Virtues and all necessary to alchemical success.

SUBTLE

    Why, what have you observed, sir, in our art,   125

    Seems so impossible?

SURLY   But your whole work, no more.

    That you should hatch gold in a furnace, sir,

    As they do eggs, in Egypt!

SUBTLE   Sir, do you

    Believe that eggs are hatched so?

SURLY   If I should?

SUBTLE

    Why, I think that the greater miracle.   130

    No egg, but differs from a chicken, more,

    Than metals in themselves.

SURLY   That cannot be.

    The egg's ordained by nature, to that end:

    And is a chicken in *potentia*.

SUBTLE

    The same we say of lead, and other metals,   135

    Which would be gold, if they had time.

MAMMON   And that

    Our art doth further.

SUBTLE   Ay, for 'twere absurd

    To think that nature, in the earth, bred gold

    Perfect, i' the instant. Something went before.

    There must be remote matter.

SURLY   Ay, what is that?   140

SUBTLE

    Marry, we say –

MAMMON   Ay, now it heats: stand Father.

    Pound him to dust –

SUBTLE   It is, of the one part,

    A humid exhalation, which we call

    Materia liquida, or the unctuous water;

    On th' other part, a certain crass, and viscous   145

---

128   *eggs, in Egypt* Pliny mentions eggs hatching on dung-hills in Egypt (*Nat. Hist.*, x.lxxv.153).

131–76 *No egg . . . metals* Subtle's argument is taken, in places almost verbatim, from Martin Delrio's *Disquisitiones Magicae*, 1599.

140.   *remote matter* the first matter.

144   *unctuous* oily.

145   *crass* dense.

Portion of earth; both which, concorporate,
Do make the elementary matter of gold:
Which is not, yet, *propria materia*,
But common to all metals, and all stones.
For, where it is forsaken of that moisture 150
And hath more dryness, it becomes a stone;
Where it retains more of the humid fatness,
It turns to sulphur, or to quicksilver:
Who are the parents of all other metals.
Nor can this remote matter, suddenly, 155
Progress so from extreme, unto extreme,
As to grow gold, and leap o'er all the means.
Nature doth, first, beget th' imperfect; then
Proceeds she to the perfect. Of that airy,
And oily water, mercury is engendered; 160
Sulphur o' the fat, and earthy part: the one
(Which is the last) supplying the place of male,
The other of the female, in all metals.
Some do believe hermaphrodeity,
That both do act, and suffer. But, these two 165
Make the rest ductile, malleable, extensive.
And, even in gold, they are; for we do find
Seeds of them, by our fire, and gold in them:
And can produce the species of each metal
More perfect thence, than nature doth in earth. 170
Beside, who doth not see, in daily practice,
Art can beget bees, hornets, beetles, wasps,
Out of the carcasses, and dung of creatures;
Yea, scorpions, of an herb, being ritely placed:
And these are living creatures, far more perfect, 175
And excellent, than metals.

146   *concorporate* fused into a single body.
148   *propria materia* a specific substance.
165   *do act, and suffer* are active and passive; this division of all things into active and
        passive, male and female, light and dark, accords with the ancient Chinese divisions
        of Yang and Yin.
166   *extensive* able to be stretched out.
169   *species* essence or form.
172–3   *Art . . . creatures* This was widely believed.
174   *ritely placed* Delrio has 'rite posita': 'placed in accordance with the rites'; an audience
        would only hear 'rightly'. The herb is basil.
176   *metals* metall Q.

MAMMON   Well said, Father!
  Nay, if he take you in hand, sir, with an argument,
  He'll bray you in a mortar.
SURLY   Pray you, sir, stay.
  Rather, than I'll be brayed, sir, I'll believe,
  That alchemy is a pretty kind of game,   180
  Somewhat like tricks o' the cards, to cheat a man,
  With charming.
SUBTLE   Sir?
SURLY   What else are all your terms,
  Whereon no one o' your writers 'grees with other?
  Of your elixir, your *lac virginis*,
  Your stone, your med'cine, and your chrysosperm,   185
  Your sal, your sulphur, and your mercury,
  Your oil of height, your tree of life, your blood,
  Your marcasite, your tutty, your magnesia,
  Your toad, your crow, your dragon, and your panther,
  Your sun, your moon, your firmament, your adrop,   190
  Your lato, azoch, zernich, chibrit, heautarit,
  And then, your red man, and your white woman,
  With all your broths, your menstrues, and materials,
  Of piss, and eggshells, women's terms, man's blood,
  Hair o' the head, burnt clouts, chalk, merds, and clay,   195

---

178   *bray* pound.
182–207   *What else . . . allegories* also from Delrio.
185   *chrysosperm* seed of gold.
187   *tree of life* Philosopher's Stone.
      blood redness.
188   *marcasite* crystalised iron pirites.
      tutty impure zinc oxide (collected from chimneys).
189   *toad . . . crow . . . panther* all colours which appear at different stages of the work; the
      dragon is mercury.
190   *firmament* blue.
      adrop lead.
191   *lato* latten; a compound similar to brass.
      azoch mercury (Arabic *az-zaug*).
      zernich trisulphide of arsenic.
      chibrit sulphur.
      heautarit mercury.
194   *eggshells* According to Aubrey, John Dee 'used to distill Egge-shells, and 'twas from
      hence that Ben. Johnson had his hint of the *Alkimist*, whom he meant', *Brief Lives*,
      ed. O. L. Dick, Harmondsworth, 1972, p. 249.
      women's terms menstrual blood.
195   *clouts* rags.   *merds* faeces.

Powder of bones, scalings of iron, glass,
And worlds of other strange ingredients,
Would burst a man to name?

SUBTLE   And all these, named
Intending but one thing: which art our writers
Used to obscure their art.

MAMMON   Sir, so I told him,   200
Because the simple idiot should not learn it,
And make it vulgar.

SUBTLE   Was not all the knowledge
Of the Egyptians writ in mystic symbols?
Speak not the Scriptures, oft, in parables?
Are not the choicest fables of the poets,   205
That were the fountains, and first springs of wisdom,
Wrapped in perplexed allegories?

MAMMON   I urged that,
And cleared to him, that Sisyphus was damned
To roll the ceaseless stone, only, because
He would have made ours common.

DOL *is seen*

Who is this?   210

SUBTLE
God's precious – What do you mean? Go in, good lady,
Let me entreat you.

[*Exit* DOL]

Where's this varlet?

[*Enter* FACE]

FACE   Sir?
SUBTLE
You very knave! Do you use me, thus?

201–7   *simple idiot . . . allegories* cf. Henry Reynolds on the rationale of hieroglyphs, 'that
high and Mysticall matters should by riddles and enigmaticall knotts be kept inuiolate
from the prophane Multitude', *Mythomystes* in *Critical Essays of the Seventeenth
Century*, ed. J. E. Spingarn, Oxford, 1957, vol. I, p. 156.

208   *Sisyphus* condemned to an eternity of rolling a boulder up a hill in Hades; the boulder
always rolls back when the summit is reached.

210   *common* This word punningly cues in Dol.

FACE   Wherein, sir?
SUBTLE
   Go in, and see, you traitor. Go.

                                        [*Exit* FACE]
MAMMON   Who is it, sir?
SUBTLE
   Nothing, sir. Nothing.
MAMMON   What's the matter? Good, sir!   215
   I have not seen you thus distempered. Who is 't?
SUBTLE
   All arts have still had, sir, their adversaries,
   But ours the most ignorant.

                        FACE *returns*

                        What now?
FACE
   'Twas not my fault, sir, she would speak with you.
SUBTLE
   Would she, sir? Follow me.   [*Exit* SUBTLE]
MAMMON   Stay, Lungs.
FACE   I dare not, sir.   220
MAMMON
   Stay man, what is she?
FACE   A lord's sister, sir.
MAMMON
   How! Pray thee stay?
FACE   She's mad, sir, and sent hither –
   (He'll be mad too.
MAMMON   I warrant thee.) Why sent hither?
FACE
   Sir, to be cured.
SUBTLE [*Within*]   Why, rascal!
FACE   Lo you. Here, sir.   *He goes out*
MAMMON
   'Fore God, a Bradamante, a brave piece.   225
SURLY
   Heart, this is a bawdy-house! I'll be burnt else.

221–2   Q transposed in F.
   225   *Bradamante* a woman knight in Ariosto's *Orlando Furioso.*

MAMMON

    O, by this light, no. Do not wrong him. He's
    Too scrupulous, that way. It is his vice.
    No, he's a rare physician, do him right.
    An excellent Paracelsian! And has done   230
    Strange cures with mineral physic. He deals all
    With spirits, he. He will not hear a word
    Of Galen, or his tedious recipes.

[Enter] FACE *again*

    How now, Lungs!
FACE   Softly, sir, speak softly. I meant
    To ha' told your worship all. This must not hear.   235
MAMMON
    No, he will not be gulled; let him alone.
FACE
    You're very right, sir, she is a most rare scholar;
    And is gone mad, with studying Broughton's works.
    If you but name a word, touching the Hebrew,
    She falls into her fit, and will discourse   240
    So learnedly of genealogies,
    As you would run mad, too, to hear her, sir.
MAMMON
    How might one do t'have conference with her, Lungs?
FACE
    O, divers have run mad upon the conference.
    I do not know, sir: I am sent in haste,   245
    To fetch a vial.
SURLY   Be not gulled, Sir Mammon.
MAMMON
    Wherein? Pray ye, be patient.
SURLY   Yes, as you are.
    And trust confederate knaves, and bawds, and whores.

230   *Paracelsian* a follower of Paracelsus (1493–1541) whose holistic medical theories
      involved the application of chemical principles. He was believed to have learned the
      secret of the Philosopher's Stone while in Constantinople.
238   *Broughton* Hugh Broughton (1549–1612), a puritan and rabbinical scholar. His
      idiolect is referred to in *Volpone*: SIR POL. Is not his language rare? PER. But alchemy,/I
      never heard the like – or Broughton's books. (II.ii.112–13).
241   *genealogies* Broughton attempted to settle Old Testament chronology in *A Concent
      of Scripture*, 1590, from which Dol quotes in IV.v.74–6.

MAMMON
  You are too foul, believe it. Come here, **Ulen**.
  One word.
FACE   I dare not, in good faith.
MAMMON   Stay, knave.   250
FACE
  He's extreme angry, that you saw her, sir.
MAMMON
  [*Gives money*] Drink that. What is she, when she's out of her fit?
FACE
  O, the most affablest creature, sir! So merry!
  So pleasant! She'll mount you up, like quicksilver,
  Over the helm; and circulate, like oil,   255
  A very vegetal: discourse of state,
  Of mathematics, bawdry, anything –
MAMMON
  Is she no way accessible? No means,
  No trick, to give a man a taste of her – wit –
  Or so? **Ulen**!
FACE   I'll come to you again, sir,   [Exit FACE]   260
MAMMON
  Surly, I did not think, one o' your breeding
  Would traduce personages of worth.
SURLY   Sir Epicure,
  Your friend to use: yet, still, loth to be gulled.
  I do not like your philosophical bawds.
  Their stone is lechery enough, to pay for,   265
  Without this bait.
MAMMON   'Heart, you abuse yourself.
  I know the lady, and her friends, and means,
  The original of this disaster. Her brother
  Has told me all.
SURLY   And yet, you ne'er saw her
  Till now?
MAMMON O, yes, but I forgot. I have (believe it)   270

---

249   **Ulen** Zephyrus, thus marginally glossed in Q.
255   *helm* See II.i.98; the head of the penis is also implied.
256   *vegetal* See I.i.39; here emphasis is on Dol's liveliness.
259–60 *her – wit –/Or so?* her – /Wit? or so? Q.
260   **Ulen** not in Q.
268   *original* source.

One of the treacherous'st memories, I do think,
Of all mankind.

SURLY   What call you her, brother?

MAMMON   My lord –
He wi' not have his name known, now I think on't.

SURLY

A very treacherous memory!

MAMMON   O' my faith –

SURLY

Tut, if you ha' it not about you, pass it,   275
Till we meet next.

MAMMON   Nay, by this hand, 'tis true.
He's one I honour, and my noble friend,
And I respect his house.

SURLY   Heart! Can it be,
That a grave sir, a rich, that has no need,
A wise sir, too, at other times, should thus   280
With his own oaths, and arguments, make hard means
To gull himself? And, this be your elixir,
Your *lapis mineralis*, and your lunary,
Give me your honest trick, yet, at primero,
Or gleek; and take your *lutum sapientis*,   285
Your *menstruum simplex*: I'll have gold, before you,
And, with less danger of the quicksilver;
Or the hot sulphur.

[*Enter* FACE]

FACE *To* SURLY   Here's one from Captain Face, sir,

---

272   SURLY svb. Q, F.
275   *pass it* leave it.
283   *lapis mineralis* mineral stone.
       lunary the plant now known as honesty; in alchemy this would be associated with
       the moon's metal, silver.
284   *primero* a card game; the best hand of four cards is the 'prime'.
285   *gleek* a card game for three players.
       lutum sapientis 'the philosopher's lute'– a quick-drying paste used to seal vessels
       quickly.
286   *menstruum simplex* simple solvent.
287–8 *less danger . . . sulphur* Quicksilver was used in the treatment of venereal disease which
       Surly suggests Mammon is likely to contract in this place; sulphur is a remedy for skin
       infections.

Desires you meet him i' the Temple Church,
Some half hour hence, and upon earnest business.   290
                                   He whispers MAMMON
Sir, if you please to quit us, now; and come,
Again, within two hours: you shall have
My master busy examining o' the works;
And I will steal you in, unto the party,
That you may see her converse. [*To* SURLY] Sir, shall I say,   295
You'll meet the Captain's worship?
SURLY   Sir, I will.
(But, by attorney, and to a second purpose.
Now, I am sure, it is a bawdy house;
I'll swear it, were the Marshal here, to thank me:
The naming this Commander, doth confirm it.   300
Don Face! Why, he's the most authentic dealer
I' these commodities! The Superintendent
To all the quainter traffickers, in town.
He is their Visitor, and does appoint
Who lies with whom; and at what hour; what price;   305
Which gown; and in what smock; what fall; what tire.
Him will I prove, by a third person, to find
The subleties of this dark labyrinth:
Which if I do discover, dear Sir Mammon,
You'll give your poor friend leave, though no philosopher,   310
To laugh: for you that are, 'tis thought, shall weep.)
FACE
Sir. He does pray, you'll not forget.
SURLY   I will not, sir.
Sir Epicure, I shall leave you?
MAMMON   I follow you, straight.
                                          [*Exit* SURLY]
FACE
But do so, good sir, to avoid suspicion.

---

289   *Temple Church* the official church for law students and – like St. Paul's – a centre for
      gossip and meetings.
295   *converse* the word has a sexual sense.
297   *by attorney* not in my own person.
303   *quainter traffickers* prostitutes; 'quaint' used to mean cunt.
304   *Visitor* official inspector
306   *fall* falling band or veil.
307   *prove* test (Lat. *probare*).

This gent'man has a parlous head.

MAMMON   But wilt thou, 𝕬𝖑𝖊𝖓.   315
Be constant to thy promise?

FACE   As my life, sir.

MAMMON
And wilt thou insinuate what I am? And praise me?
And say I am a noble fellow?

FACE   O, what else, sir?
And, that you'll make her royal, with the stone,
An Empress; and yourself King of Bantam.   320

MAMMON
Wilt thou do this?

FACE   Will I, sir?

MAMMON   Lungs, my Lungs!
I love thee.

FACE   Send your stuff, sir, that my master
May busy himself, about projection.

MAMMON
Th'hast witched me, rogue: take, [*Gives money*] go.

FACE   Your jack, and all, sir.

MAMMON
Thou art a villain – I will send my jack;   325
And the weights too. Slave, I could bite thine ear.
Away, thou dost not care for me.

FACE   Not I, sir?

MAMMON
Come, I was born to make thee, my good weasel;
Set thee on a bench: and, ha' thee twirl a chain
With the best lord's vermin, of 'em all.

FACE   Away, sir.   330

MAMMON
A Count, nay, a Count Palatine –

FACE   Good sir, go.

MAMMON
– Shall not advance thee, better: no, nor faster.

                                   [*Exit* MAMMON]

315   *parlous* difficult to deal with, risky, cunning.   𝕬𝖑𝖊𝖓 not in Q.
320   *Bantam* a city in north Java, once capital of a Mohammedan empire and legendary
       for its magnificence.
324   *jack* a machine for turning a spit (driven by weights).
331   *Count Palatine* originally a count attached to an imperial palace with supreme judicial
       authority; later, a count permitted supreme jurisdiction of his province.

ACT II, SCENE iv

[*Enter*] SUBTLE, DOL [*to* FACE]

SUBTLE
  Has he bit? Has he bit?
FACE   And swallowed too, my Subtle.
  I ha' given him line, and now he plays, i' faith.
SUBTLE
  And shall we twitch him?
FACE   Thorough both the gills.
  A wench is a rare bait, with which a man
  No sooner's taken, but he straight firks mad.   5
SUBTLE
  Dol, my Lord Whats'hum's sister, you must now
  Bear yourself **statelich**.
DOL   O, let me alone.
  I'll not forget my race, I warrant you.
  I'll keep my distance, laugh, and talk aloud;
  Have all the tricks of a proud scurvy lady,   10
  And be as rude's her woman.
FACE   Well said, Sanguine.
SUBTLE
  But will he send his andirons?
FACE   His jack too;
  And's iron shoeing-horn: I ha' spoke to him. Well,
  I must not lose my wary gamester, yonder.
SUBTLE
  O Monsieur Caution, that will not be gulled?   15
FACE
  Ay, if I can strike a fine hook into him, now,
  The Temple Church, there I have cast mine angle.
  Well, pray for me. I'll about it.

2   *line . . . plays* the image is from angling.
5   *firks mad* falls into transports of madness.
7   **statelich** in a stately way (Dutch, or German); the Netherlands wars, in which Jonson
    served, brought many such words into England.
11 *Sanguine* Those in whom the sanguine (bloody) humour is predominant are opti-
    mistic, bold and amorous.
17 *angle* fishing line.

One knocks

SUBTLE   What, more gudgeons!

Dol, scout, scout; stay Face, you must go to the door:

Pray God, it be my Anabaptist. Who is't, Dol?   20

DOL [*Looking out*]

I know him not. He looks like a gold-end-man.

SUBTLE

Gods so! 'Tis he, he said he would send. What call you him?

The sanctified Elder, that should deal

For Mammon's jack, and andirons! Let him in.

Stay, help me off, first, with my gown. Away   25

Madam, to your withdrawing chamber.

[*Exit* DOL]

Now,

In a new tune, new gesture, but old language.

This fellow is sent, from one negotiates with me

About the stone, too; for the holy Brethren

Of Amsterdam, the exiled Saints: that hope   30

To raise their discipline, by it. I must use him

In some strange fashion, now, to make him admire me.

ACT II, SCENE v

[*Enter*] ANANIAS [*to them*]

SUBTLE

Where is my drudge?

FACE   Sir.

SUBTLE   Take away the recipient,

And rectify your menstrue, from the phlegma.

---

18   *gudgeons* small, freshwater fish, used as bait but themselves easily caught.

20   *Anabaptist* member of the non-conformist sect of Anabaptists who advocated adult baptism, community of goods and no authority other than the Scriptures. They originated on the Continent in the 1520s and began to arrive in England in the 1530s (in 1535 a proclamation against their heresy was issued).

21   *gold-end-man* a buyer and seller of old gold.

29–30   *holy Brethren . . . Saints* The Anabaptists attempted to take control of several Dutch cities, including Amsterdam; they fled to England to escape the consequent persecutions.

2   *phlegma* watery distillate.

Then pour it, o' the Sol, in the cucurbite,
And let 'em macerate, together.

FACE   Yes, sir.
And save the ground?

SUBTLE   No. *Terra damnata*   5
Must not have entrance, in the work. Who are you?

ANANIAS
A faithful Brother, if it please you.

SUBTLE   What's that?
A Lullianist? A Ripley? *Filius artis?*
Can you sublime, and dulcify? Calcine?
Know you the *sapor pontic? Sapor styptic?*   10
Or, what is homogene, or heterogene?

ANANIAS
I understand no heathen language, truly.

SUBTLE
Heathen,you Knipper-Doling? Is *Ars sacra,*
Or *chrysopoeia,* or *spagyrica,*
Or the pamphysic, or panarchic knowledge,   15
A heathen language?

ANANIAS   Heathen Greek, I take it.

---

4   *macerate* soften by soaking.
5   *the ground* the sediment which remains after distillation.
     Terra damnata damned earth.
8   *Lullianist* follower of Raymond Lull (1235–1315), Spanish missionary, deviser of
     mnemonic schemes and (reputedly) alchemist; many alchemical works are attributed
     to him.
     Ripley follower of George Ripley (d. *c.* 1490), author of *The Compound of Alchemy*
     (in *T.C.B.*); he did much to popularise in England works attributed to Lull.
     Filius artis a 'son of the art' (Lat.); Subtle pretends to misunderstand Ananias'
     description of himself as 'A faithful Brother'.
9   *dulcify* sweeten by dissolving the salt from a substance.
10   *sapor pontic? Sapor styptic?* Nine 'sapors' (tastes) were distinguished by alchemists;
     five are created by heat and four (including pontic and stiptic) by cold.
     styptick stipstick Q, F.
13   *Knipper-Doling* Bernard Knipperdollinck was a leading Anabaptist and instrumental
     in the occupation of Münster in 1534 where the Anabaptists established a 'Kingdom
     of God' under the rule of John of Leyden.
     Ars sacra the sacred art.
14   *chrysopoeia* gold-making (Greek).
     spagyrica a word supposedly coined by Paracelsus from the Greek σπαω (to stretch
     and rend) and αγειρω) (to collect together); it signifies the Paracelsian method of
     alchemy by separation and combination.
15   *pamphysic, or panarchic knowledge* knowledge of all nature or all power.

SUBTLE

How? Heathen Greek?

ANANIAS   All's heathen, but the Hebrew.

SUBTLE

Sirrah, my varlet, stand you forth, and speak to him
Like a philosopher: answer, i' the language.
Name the vexations, and the martyrizations   20
Of metals, in the work.

FACE   Sir, Putrefaction,
Solution, Ablution, Sublimation,
Cohobation, Calcination, Ceration, and
Fixation.

SUBTLE   This is heathen Greek, to you, now?
And when comes Vivification?

FACE   After Mortification.   25

SUBTLE

What's Cohobation?

FACE   'Tis the pouring on
Your *Aqua Regis*, and then drawing him off,
To the trine circle of the seven spheres.

SUBTLE

What's the proper passion of metals?

FACE   Malleation.

---

17   *All's heathen, but the Hebrew* Hebrew was believed by some to be the unfallen language
        that Adam first used.
19   *i' the language* in the language of alchemy.
20   *vexations* contortions.
        martyrizations various processes of reduction to which the metals are subjected; the
        metaphor suits the hearer.
21   *Putrefaction* Breaking down.
        Ablution Washing.
23   *Cohobation* Repeated distillation.
        Ceration the same as inceration; see II.iii.84.
25   *Vivification* the process of extracting a pure substance from a compound.
        Mortification Breaking down of substance.
27   *Aqua Regis* 'King's Water'; a mixture of vitriol and hydrochloric acid; it is so named
        because it is able to dissolve the 'noble' metals.
28   *the trine circle of the seven spheres:* 'Know, too, that no solution will take place in your
        electrum unless it thrice runs perfectly through the sphere of seven planets', *The
        Hermetic and Alchemical Writings of Paracelsus*, ed. A. E. Waite, 2 vols, London 1894,
        vol. ii, p. 105.
29   *passion* again, the religious dimension of this word fits it to the hearer.

SUBTLE

    What's your *ultimum supplicium auri?*

FACE   *Antimonium.*   30

SUBTLE

    This 's heathen Greek, to you? And, what's your mercury?

FACE

    A very fugitive, he will be gone, sir.

SUBTLE

    How know you him?   By his viscosity,

    His oleosity, and his suscitability.

SUBTLE

    How do you sublime him?   With the calce of eggshells,   35

    White marble, talc.

SUBTLE   Your *magisterium,* now?

    What's that?

FACE   Shifting, sir, your elements,

    Dry into cold, cold into moist, moist in –

    To hot, hot into dry.

SUBTLE   This 's heathen Greek to you, still?

    Your *lapis philosophicus?*

FACE   'Tis a stone, and not   40

    A stone; a spirit, a soul, and a body:

    Which, if you do dissolve, it is dissolved,

    If you coagulate, it is coagulated,

    If you make it to fly, it flieth.

SUBTLE   Enough.

                                   [*Exit* FACE]

    This 's heathen Greek, to you? What are you, sir?   45

ANANIAS

    Please you, a servant of the exiled Brethren,

    That deal with widows' and with orphans' goods;

---

30   *ultimum supplicium auri* extreme punishment for gold.
       Antimonium antimony – a slight alloy which destroys the malleability of gold.
34   *oleosity* oiliness.
       suscitability excitability.
35   *calce* calx (i.e. powder).
37–9   *Shifting . . . dry* F. H. Mares (in the Revels edition of the play) suggests that this
       may be the 'philosopher's wheel' of II.iii.44. The process involves placing substances
       into their opposing elements in order to reduce them to their essences.

And make a just account, unto the Saints:
A Deacon.
SUBTLE   O, you are sent from master Wholesome,
Your teacher?
ANANIAS   From Tribulation Wholesome,   50
Our very zealous Pastor.
SUBTLE   Good. I have
Some orphans' goods to come here.
ANANIAS   Of what kind, sir?
SUBTLE
Pewter, and brass, andirons, and kitchen ware,
Metals, that we must use our med'cine on:
Wherein the Brethren may have a penn'orth,   55
For ready money.
ANANIAS   Were the orphans' parents
Sincere professors?
SUBTLE   Why do you ask?
ANANIAS   Because
We then are to deal justly, and give (in truth)
Their utmost value.
SUBTLE   'Slid, you'd cozen, else,
And, if their parents were not of the faithful?   60
I will not trust you, now I think on 't,
Till I ha' talked with your Pastor. Ha you brought money
To buy more coals?
ANANIAS   No, surely.
SUBTLE   No? How so?
ANANIAS
The Brethren bid me say unto you, sir.
Surely, they will not venture any more   65
Till they may see projection.
SUBTLE   How!
ANANIAS   You've had,
For the instruments, as bricks, and loam, and glasses,
Already thirty pound; and, for materials,
They say, some ninety more: and, they have heard, since,
That one, at Heidelberg, made it, of an egg,   70

---

48   *Saints* Ananias is anticipating the mass canonization of the brethren.
57   *professors* of the Anabaptist faith.
70   *Heidelberg* believed to be the centre of alchemy.

And a small paper of pin-dust.

SUBTLE   What's your name?

ANANIAS

My name is Ananias.

SUBTLE   Out, the varlet
That cozened the Apostles! Hence, away,
Flee Mischief; had your holy Consistory
No name to send me, of another sound;   75
Than wicked Ananias? Send your Elders,
Hither, to make atonement for you, quickly.
And gi' me satisfaction; or out goes
The fire: and down th' alembics, and the furnace,
Piger Henricus, or what not. Thou wretch,   80
Both Sericon, and Bufo, shall be lost,
Tell 'em. All hope of rooting out the Bishops,
Or th' Antichristian Hierarchy shall perish,
If they stay threescore minutes. The Aqueity,
Terreity, and Sulphureity   85
Shall run together again, and all be annulled,
Thou wicked Ananias.

                                          [*Exit* ANANIAS]

                    This will fetch 'em,
And make 'em haste towards their gulling more.
A man must deal like a rough nurse, and fright
Those, that are froward, to an appetite.   90

---

71   *pin-dust* metallic dust produced in the manufacture of pins (Germany was ahead
      of England in this; pins were not produced in England until 1626).

72–3 *Ananias . . . Apostles* see *Acts* v.1–11.

74   *Consistory* assembly.

76   *Elders* high-ranking church officers.

80   *Piger Henricus* a 'lazy Henry': a multiple furnace fired by a single, central fire.

81   *Sericon, and Bufo* red and black tincture ('Bufo' is 'the toad').

82–3 *All hope . . . Hierarchy* Many saw the retention of bishops in the Church of England
      as a residue of popery.

84–6 *The Aqueity . . . annulled* all the work of separation and purification will be undone.

90   *froward* hard to please.

ACT II, SCENE vi

[*Enter*] DRUGGER, FACE [*dressed as Captain to* SUBTLE]

FACE

He's busy with his spirits, but we'll upon him.

SUBTLE

How now! What mates? What Bayards ha' we here?

FACE

I told you, he would be furious. Sir, here's Nab,

Has brought you another piece of gold, to look on:

[*To* DRUGGER] (We must appease him. Give it me) and prays you,⠀⠀⠀5

You would devise (what is it Nab?)

DRUGGER⠀⠀⠀⠀⠀⠀⠀⠀⠀⠀⠀⠀⠀⠀⠀A sign, sir.

FACE

Ay, a good lucky one, a thriving sign, Doctor.

SUBTLE

I was devising now.

FACE [*To* SUBTLE]⠀⠀⠀('Slight, do not say so,

He will repent he ga' you any more.)

What say you to his constellation, Doctor?⠀⠀⠀⠀⠀⠀⠀⠀⠀10

The Balance?

SUBTLE⠀⠀⠀⠀⠀No, that way is stale, and common.

A townsman, born in Taurus, gives the bull;

Or the bull's head: in Aries, the ram.

A poor device. No, I will have his name

Formed in some mystic character; whose radii,⠀⠀⠀⠀⠀⠀⠀15

Striking the senses of the passers-by,

Shall, by a virtual influence, breed affections,

That may result upon the party owns it:

As thus –

FACE⠀⠀⠀⠀⠀Nab!

SUBTLE⠀⠀⠀⠀⠀⠀⠀He first shall have a bell, that's Abel;

⠀2⠀⠀*Bayards* Bayard was a common name for a horse (see Chaucer, *Troilus and Criseyde*
⠀⠀⠀⠀I, 218.
⠀11⠀⠀*Balance* Libra.
⠀12⠀⠀*gives* uses as his sign.
⠀15⠀⠀*radii* emanations.
⠀17⠀⠀*virtual influence* influence of its power.⠀⠀*affections* inclinations.
19–24⠀⠀Subtle is constructing a rebus of Drugger's name. Rebuses (which originated in

And, by it, standing one, whose name is Dee,   20
In a rug gown; there's D and Rug, that's Drug:
And, right anenst him, a dog snarling *Er*;
There's Drugger, Abel Drugger. That's his sign.
And here's now mystery, and hieroglyphic.

FACE
Abel, thou art made.

DRUGGER   Sir, I do thank his worship.   [*Bows*]   25

FACE
Six o' thy legs more, will not do it, Nab.
He has brought you a pipe of tobacco, Doctor.

DRUGGER   Yes, sir:
I have another thing, I would impart –

FACE
Out with it, Nab.

DRUGGER   Sir, there is lodged, hard by me,
A rich young widow –

FACE   Good! A *bona roba*?   30

DRUGGER
But nineteen, at the most.

FACE   Very good, Abel.

DRUGGER
Marry, she's not in fashion, yet; she wears
A hood: but 't stands a cop.

FACE   No matter, Abel.

DRUGGER
And, I do, now and then give her a fucus –

FACE
What! Dost thou deal, Nab?

SUBTLE   I did tell you, Captain.   35

DRUGGER

France) were popular at the time. Camden mentions a man who expressed 'Rose
Hill I love well' by painting the border of his gown with a rose, a hill, a loaf and a
well (*Remains*, 1623, p. 145).

20   *Dee* John Dee (1527–1608); an eminent occultist patronised by Queen Elizabeth.
25   FACE not in Q.
26   *legs* bows.
30   *bona roba* fine woman; prostitute.
33   *a cop* on the head (a hat would have been more fashionable than a hood, but at least
      she wears her hood *like* a hat).
34   *fucus* a cosmetic; Face pretends to understand 'fuck'.
35   *deal* do business (with sexual sense of 'get down to it').

And physic too sometime, sir: for which she trusts me
With all her mind. She's come up here, of purpose
To learn the fashion.
FACE   Good (his match too!) on, Nab.
DRUGGER
And she does strangely long to know her fortune.
FACE
God's lid, Nab, send her to the Doctor, hither.   40
DRUGGER
Yes, I have spoke to her of his worship, already:
But she's afraid, it will be blown abroad
And hurt her marriage.
FACE   Hurt it? 'Tis the way
To heal it, if 'twere hurt; to make it more
Followed, and sought: Nab, thou shalt tell her this.   45
She'll be more known, more talked of, and your widows
Are ne'er of any price till they be famous;
Their honour is their multitude of suitors:
Send her, it may be thy good fortune. What?
Thou dost not know.
DRUGGER   No, sir, she'll never marry   50
Under a knight. Her brother has made a vow.
FACE
What, and dost thou despair, my little Nab,
Knowing, what the Doctor has set down for thee,
And, seeing so many, o' the city, dubbed?
One glass o' thy water, with a Madam, I know,   55
Will have it done, Nab. What's her brother? A knight?
DRUGGER
No, sir, a gentleman, newly warm in his land, sir,
Scarce cold in his one and twenty; that does govern
His sister, here: and is a man himself
Of some three thousand a year, and is come up   60
To learn to quarrel, and to live by his wits,
And will go down again, and die i' the country.
FACE

---

54   *dubbed* knighted; James I notoriously raised money by selling knighthoods to the new
      rich.
57   *newly warm in* who has just gained.

How! To quarrel?

DRUGGER   Yes, sir, to carry quarrels,
    As gallants do, and manage 'em, by line.

FACE
    'Slid, Nab! The Doctor is the only man   65
    In Christendom for him. He has made a table,
    With mathematical demonstrations,
    Touching the art of quarrels. He will give him
    An instrument to quarrel by. Go, bring 'em, both:
    Him, and his sister. And, for thee, with her   70
    The Doctor haply may persuade. Go to.
    Shalt give his worship, a new damask suit
    Upon the premises.

SUBTLE   O, good Captain.

FACE   He shall,
    He is the honestest fellow, Doctor. Stay not,
    No offers, bring the damask, and the parties.   75

DRUGGER
    I'll try my power, sir.

FACE   And thy will too, Nab.

SUBTLE
    'Tis good tobacco this! What is't an ounce?

FACE
    He'll send you a pound, Doctor.

SUBTLE   O, no.

FACE   He will do't.
    It is the goodest soul. Abel, about it.
    (Thou shalt know more anon. Away, be gone.)   80

                                    [*Exit* DRUGGER]

    A miserable rogue, and lives with cheese,
    And has the worms. That was the cause indeed
    Why he came now. He dealt with me, in private,
    To get a med'cine for 'em.

SUBTLE   And shall, sir. This works.

FACE
    A wife, a wife, for one on's, my dear Subtle: 85
    We'll e'en draw lots, and he, that fails, shall have

64   *by line* by rules.
66   *table* diagram, visual scheme.
74   *Stay not* Say not Q.
85   *on's* of us.

417

The more in goods, the other has in tail.

SUBTLE
Rather the less. For she may be so light
She may want grains.

FACE   Ay, or be such a burden,
A man would scarce endure her, for the whole.   90

SUBTLE
Faith, best let's see her first, and then determine.

FACE
Content. But Dol must ha' no breath on't.

SUBTLE   Mum.
Away, you to your Surly yonder, catch him.

FACE
Pray God, I ha' not stayed too long.

SUBTLE   I fear it.

[*Exeunt*]

---

87   *in tail* puns on 1) genital satisfaction ('tail' is still used in this sense) and 2) entail –
a settlement of succession to an estate.

89   *grains* A grain is the smallest unit of weight, based upon a grain of corn or wheat.

ACT III, SCENE i

[*In the street outside Lovewit's house*]

[*Enter*] TRIBULATION, ANANIAS

TRIBULATION
These chastisements are common to the Saints,
And such rebukes we of the Separation
Must bear, with willing shoulders, as the trials
Sent forth, to tempt our frailties.

ANANIAS   In pure zeal,
I do not like the man: he is a heathen.   5
And speaks the language of Canaan, truly.

TRIBULATION
I think him a profane person, indeed.

ANANIAS   He bears
The visible mark of the Beast, in his forehead.
And for his stone, it is a work of darkness,
And, with philosophy, blinds the eyes of man.   10

TRIBULATION
Good Brother, we must bend unto all means,
That may give furtherance, to the holy cause.

ANANIAS
Which his cannot: the sanctified cause
Should have a sanctified course.

TRIBULATION   Not always necessary.
The children of perdition are, oft-times,   15
Made instruments even of the greatest works.
Beside, we should give somewhat to man's nature,

2–4   *we of the . . . Sent forth* th'Elect must beare, with patience;/They are the exercises of
      the Spirit,/And sent Q.
  2   *Separation* The Anabaptists believed themselves to be the elect, separate from all
      others.
  6   *the language of Canaan* as opposed to Hebrew or their Puritan idiolect; 'In that day
      shall five cities in the land of Egypt speak the language of Canaan', *Isaiah* xix.18.
  8   *mark of the Beast Revelation* xvi.2, xix.20.
15–16 *The children . . . works* This concept of evil being, in spite of itself, an agent for good
      was a familiar one. Shakespeare's Richard III is an example.
 17   *give* concede.

419

The place he lives in, still about the fire,
And fume of metals, that intoxicate
The brain of man, and make him prone to passion.   20
Where have you greater atheists, than your cooks?
Or more profane, or choleric than your glassmen?
More antichristian, than your bell-founders?
What makes the Devil so devilish, I would ask you,
Satan, our common enemy, but his being   25
Perpetually about the fire, and boiling
Brimstone, and arsenic? We must give, I say,
Unto the motives, and the stirrers up
Of humours in the blood. It may be so.
When as the work is done, the stone is made,   30
This heat of his may turn into a zeal,
And stand up for the beauteous discipline,
Against the menstruous cloth, and rag of Rome.
We must await his calling, and the coming
Of the good spirit. You did fault, t' upbraid him   35
With the Brethren's blessing of Heidelberg, weighing
What need we have, to hasten on the work,
For the restoring of the silenced Saints,
Which ne'er will be, but by the philosopher's stone.
And, so a learned Elder, one of Scotland,   40
Assured me; *aurum potabile* being
The only med'cine, for the civil magistrate,
T' incline him to a feeling of the cause:
And must be daily used, in the disease.

ANANIAS

I have not edified more, truly, by man;   45
Not since the beautiful light, first, shone on me:
And I am sad, my zeal hath so offended.

TRIBULATION

Let us call on him, then.

---

18   *still* always.

33   *rag of Rome* The Puritans identified the Church of Rome with the scarlet-clad woman
of *Revelation* xvii. Here the red surplice worn by Roman bishops is identified with
rags stained with menstrual blood. The alchemists also used a *menstruum*; the words
could be taken in three different ways (alchemical, theological, gynaecological)
according to the situation of the hearer.

38   *the silenced Saints* puritan clergy excommunicated for non-conformity after the
Hampton Court conference of 1604; they were known as the 'silenced ministers'.

41   *aurum potabile* drinkable gold; bribery is intended here.

ANANIAS   The motion's good,
  And of the spirit; I will knock first: [*Knocks*]
                           Peace be within.

ACT III, SCENE ii

[*Inside Lovewit's house*]

[*Enter*] SUBTLE

SUBTLE

  O, are you come? 'Twas time. Your threescore minutes
  Were at the last thread, you see; and down had gone
  Furnus acediae, turris circulatorius:
  Lembic, bolt's head, retort, and pelican
  Had all been cinders. Wicked Ananias!   5
  Art thou returned? Nay then, it goes down, yet.

TRIBULATION

  Sir, be appeased, he is come to humble
  Himself in spirit, and to ask your patience,
  If too much zeal hath carried him, aside,
  From the due path.

SUBTLE   Why, this doth qualify!   10

TRIBULATION

  The Brethren had no purpose, verily,
  To give you the least grievance: but are ready
  To lend their willing hands, to any project
  The spirit, and you direct.

SUBTLE   This qualifies more!

TRIBULATION

  And, for the orphans' goods, let them be valued,   15
  Or what is needful, else, to the holy work,

---

48   *motion* intention.

 3   *Furnus acediae* 'the furnace of sloth'; the same as the 'lazy Henry' of II.v.80.
       turris circulatorius circulating tower; an apparatus for continuous circulation and
       refinement.
 4   *Lembic* alembic.
10   *qualify* mitigate.

It shall be numbered: here, by me, the Saints
Throw down their purse before you.

SUBTLE   This qualifies, most!
Why, thus it should be, now you understand.
Have I discoursed so unto you, of our stone?   20
And, of the good that it shall bring your cause?
Showed you, (beside the main of hiring forces
Abroad, drawing the Hollanders, your friends,
From th' Indies, to serve you, with all their fleet)
That even the med'cinal use shall make you a faction,   25
And party in the realm? As, put the case,
That some great man in state, he have the gout,
Why, you but send three drops of your elixir,
You help him straight: there you have made a friend.
Another has the palsy, or the dropsy,   30
He takes of your incombustible stuff,
He's young again: there you have made a friend.
A lady, that is past the feat of body,
Though not of mind, and hath her face decayed
Beyond all cure of paintings, you restore   35
With the oil of talc; there you have made a friend:
And all her friends. A lord, that is a leper,
A knight, that has the bone-ache, or a squire
That hath both these, you make 'em smooth, and sound,
With a bare fricace of your medicine: still,   40
You increase your friends.

TRIBULATION   Ay, 'tis very pregnant.

SUBTLE
And, then, the turning of this lawyer's pewter
To plate, at Christmas –

ANANIAS   Christ-tide, I pray you.

SUBTLE
Yet, Ananias?

17   *by me* in my person;.
25–6 *That even . . . realm* You'll become a force to be reckoned with in the country merely
      through the influence you'll gain from its medical effects.
33   *feat of body* copulation.
35   *paintings* cosmetics; painting Q.
36   *oil of talc* white elixir used by alchemists; this contrasts with the cosmetic used to
      whiten the skin.
40   *fricace* rubbing.
41   *pregnant* persuasive; full of sense.

ANANIAS   I have done.

SUBTLE   Or changing

His parcel gilt, to massy gold. You cannot   45
But raise you friends. Withal, to be of power
To pay an army, in the field, to buy
The king of France, out of his realms; or Spain,
Out of his Indies: what can you not do,
Against lords spiritual, or temporal,   50
That shall oppone you?

TRIBULATION   Verily, 'tis true.

We may be temporal lords, ourselves, I take it.

SUBTLE

You may be anything, and leave off to make
Long-winded exercises: or suck up,
Your ha, and hum, in a tune. I not deny,   55
But such as are not graced, in a state,
May, for their ends, be adverse in religion,
And get a tune, to call the flock together:
For (to say sooth) a tune does much, with women,
And other phlegmatic people, it is your bell.   60

ANANIAS

Bells are profane: a tune may be religious.

SUBTLE

No warning with you? Then, farewell my patience.
'Slight, it shall down: I will not be thus tortured.

TRIBULATION

I pray you, sir.

SUBTLE   All shall perish. I have spoke it.

TRIBULATION

Let me find grace, sir, in your eyes; the man   65
He stands corrected: neither did his zeal
(But as yourself) allow a tune, somewhere.
Which, now, being toward the stone, we shall not need.

SUBTLE

No, nor your holy vizard, to win widows

---

45   *parcel gilt* partly gilded stuff.
51   *oppone* oppose.   55   *I not* I do not.
61   *Bells are profane* Bells had popish associations.
63   *it shall down* i.e. the alchemical apparatus.
69–97   *No, nor . . . the disciple* Subtle continues to expose the Anabaptists' craft and hypocrisy to the audience while Ananias and Tribulation remain oblivious.
69   *holy vizard* pious appearance.

To give you legacies; or make zealous wives   70
To rob their husbands, for the common cause:
Nor take the start of bonds, broke but one day,
And say, they were forfeited, by providence.
Nor shall you need, o'er-night, to eat huge meals,
To celebrate your next day's fast the better: 75
The whilst the Brethren, and the Sisters, humbled,
Abate the stiffness of the flesh. Nor cast
Before your hungry hearers, scrupulous bones,
As whether a Christian may hawk, or hunt;
Or whether, matrons, of the holy assembly,   80
May lay their hair out, or wear doublets:
Or have that idol Starch, about their linen.

ANANIAS

It is, indeed, an idol.

TRIBULATION   Mind him not, sir.
I do command thee, spirit (of zeal, but trouble)
To peace within him. Pray you, sir, go on.   85

SUBTLE

Nor shall you need to libel 'gainst the prelates,
And shorten so your ears, against the hearing
Of the next wire-drawn grace. Nor, of necessity,
Rail against plays, to please the alderman,
Whose daily custard you devour. Nor lie   90

---

72   *take the start* take advantage of.
77   *Abate the stiffness of the flesh* We (but not Ananias and Tribulation) should hear the
      sexual innuendo here.
78   *scrupulous bones* trivial bones of contention.
79   *hawk . . . hunt* 'I neuer read of any, in the volume of the sacred scripture, that was
      a good man and a Hunter', Stubbes, *The Anatomie of the Abuses in England in
      Shakespeare's Youth*, ed. Furnivall, 1877–9, part i, p. 181.
81   *lay their hair out, or wear doublets* 'Then followeth the trimming and tricking of
      their heds in laying out their hair to the shewe, which of force must be curled, frisled
      and crisped, laid out (a World to see!) on wreathes & borders from one eare to an
      other' (ibid. p. 67) and (re. *Deuteronomy* xxii.5) 'The Women also there haue dublets
      & Ierkins, as men haue heer . . . & though this be a kinde of attire appropriate onely
      to man, yet they blush not to wear it' (ibid. p. 73).
82   *that idol Starch* 'The deuils liquore, I mean *Starch*' (ibid. p. 70).
84–5 *I do . . . him* Tribulation is attempting to placate the troubled spirit that possesses
      Ananias.
87   *shorten so your ears* have your ears cut off or clipped as a punishment.
88   *wire-drawn grace* extended prayer (grace) before eating.
90   *custard* a kind of open pie; a bit like *quiche*.

With zealous rage, till you are hoarse. Not one
Of these so singular arts. Nor call yourselves,
By names of Tribulation, Persecution,
Restraint, Long-Patience, and such like, affected
By the whole family, or wood of you,   95
Only for glory, and to catch the ear
Of the disciple.
TRIBULATION   Truly, sir, they are
Ways, that the godly Brethren have invented,
For propagation of the glorious cause,
As very notable means, and whereby, also,   100
Themselves grow soon, and profitably famous.
SUBTLE
O, but the stone, all's idle to it! Nothing!
The art of angels, nature's miracle,
The divine secret, that doth fly in clouds,
From east to west: and whose tradition   105
Is not from men, but spirits.
ANANIAS   I hate traditions:
I do not trust 'em –
TRIBULATION   Peace.
ANANIAS   They are Popish, all.
I will not peace. I will not –
TRIBULATION   Ananias.
ANANIAS
Please the profane, to grieve the godly: I may not.
SUBTLE
Well, Ananias, thou shalt overcome.   110
TRIBULATION
It is an ignorant zeal, that haunts him, sir.
But truly, else, a very faithful Brother,
A botcher: and a man, by revelation,
That hath a competent knowledge of the truth.

---

95 *wood* a gathering of family trees; 'wood' also meant 'mad'– a good collective noun
    for extremists.
99 *glorious* holy Q.
106 *I hate traditions* Some Puritans recognised only the authority of the Bible and direct
    revelation. Traditions were associated with the Church of Rome and Judaism.
113 *botcher* probably used in the specialised sense of 'tailor'; John of Leyden, the
    Anabaptist 'King', had been a tailor and is called 'the botcher' by Thomas Nashe in
    his description of the occupation of Münster in *The Unfortunate Traveller*, ed. J. B.
    Steane, Harmondsworth, 1972, p. 277.

SUBTLE

    Has he a competent sum, there, i' the bag,   115

    To buy the goods, within? I am made guardian,

    And must, for charity, and conscience' sake,

    Now, see the most be made, for my poor orphan:

    Though I desire the Brethren, too, good gainers.

    There, they are, within. When you have viewed, and bought 'em,   120

    And ta'en the inventory of what they are,

    They are ready for projection; there's no more

    To do: cast on the med'cine, so much silver

    As there is tin there, so much gold as brass,

    I'll gi' it you in, by weight.

TRIBULATION   But how long time,   125

    Sir, must the Saints expect, yet?

SUBTLE   Let me see,

    How's the moon, now? Eight, nine, ten days hence

    He will be silver potate; then, three days,

    Before he citronize: some fifteen days,

    The *magisterium* will be perfected.   130

ANANIAS

    About the second day, of the third week,

    In the ninth month?

SUBTLE   Yes, my good Ananias.

TRIBULATION

    What will the orphans' goods arise to, think you?

SUBTLE

    Some hundred marks; as much as filled three cars,

    Unladed now: you'll make six millions of 'em   135

    But I must ha' more coals laid in.

TRIBULATION   How!

SUBTLE   Another load,

    And then we ha' finished. We must now increase

    Our fire to *ignis ardens*, we are past

    Fimus equinus, balnei, cineris,

---

128   *silver potate* liquid silver.

129   *citronize* turn yellow – a sign that the work is near completion.

134   *cars* carts.

135   *you'll* you shall Q.

138   *ignis ardens* the hottest fire.

139   *Fimus equinus* the lowest form of heat, produced by horse dung.

       balnei See II.iii.41.

       cineris the heat of ashes.

And all those lenter heats. If the holy purse   140
Should, with this draught, fall low, and that the Saints
Do need a present sum, I have a trick
To melt the pewter, you shall buy now, instantly,
And, with a tincture, make you as good Dutch dollars,
As any are in Holland.

TRIBULATION   Can you so?   145

SUBTLE
Ay, and shall bide the third examination.

ANANIAS
It will be joyful tidings to the Brethren.

SUBTLE
But you must carry it, secret.

TRIBULATION   Ay, but stay,
This act of coining, is it lawful?

ANANIAS   Lawful?
We know no magistrate. Or, if we did,   150
This 's foreign coin.

SUBTLE   It is no coining, sir.
It is but casting.

TRIBULATION   Ha? You distinguish well.
Casting of money may be lawful.

ANANIAS   'Tis, sir.

TRIBULATION
Truly, I take it so.

SUBTLE   There is no scruple,
Sir, to be made of it; believe Ananias: 155
This case of conscience he is studied in.

TRIBULATION
I'll make a question of it, to the Brethren.

ANANIAS
The Brethren shall approve it lawful, doubt not.
Where shall't be done.

Knock without

SUBTLE   For that we'll talk, anon.

---

140   *lenter* slower.
142   *have a trick* F2 *have trick* Q, F.
150   *We know no magistrate* Some Puritans would only accept Scriptural authority in civil
       matters.
151–2 *It is . . . casting* The casting of foreign coin was as much an offence as coining English
       counterfeits.

There's some to speak with me. Go in, I pray you, 160
And view the parcels. That's the inventory.
I'll come to you straight.

> [*Exeunt* ANANIAS, TRIBULATION]

Who is it? Face! Appear.

ACT III, SCENE iii

> [*Enter*] FACE [*dressed as Captain, to* SUBTLE]

SUBTLE
How now? Good prize?

FACE   Good pox! Yond' costive cheater
Never came on.

SUBTLE   How then?

FACE   I ha' walked the round,
Till now, and no such thing.

SUBTLE   And ha' you quit him?

FACE
Quit him? And hell would quit him too, he were happy.
'Slight, would you have me stalk like a mill-jade,   5
All day, for one, that will not yield us grains?
I know him of old.

SUBTLE   O, but to ha' gulled him,
Had been a mastery.

FACE   Let him go, black boy,
And turn thee, that some fresh news may possess thee.
A noble Count, a Don of Spain (my dear   10
Delicious compeer, and my party-bawd)
Who is come hither, private, for his conscience,
And brought munition with him, six great slops,

---

2   *walked the round* gone round the nave (of the Temple Church – also known as 'the round').
5   *mill-jade* a horse that works a mill by moving in circles.
8   *black boy* Subtle's face is darkened by the smoke of his business.
9   *turn thee* shift your attention.
11   *compeer* companion; mate.
      party-bawd part bawd, or 'bawd of my party'.
13   *slops* wide breeches.

Bigger than three Dutch hoys, beside round trunks
Furnished with pistolets, and pieces of eight,   15
Will straight be here, my rogue, to have thy bath
(That is the colour,) and to make his battery
Upon our Dol, our castle, our Cinque-Port,
Our Dover pier, our what thou wilt. Where is she?
She must prepare perfumes, delicate linen,   20
The bath in chief, a banquet, and her wit,
For she must milk his epididimis.
Where is the doxy?
SUBTLE   I'll send her to thee:
And but dispatch my brace of little John Leydens,
And come again myself.
FACE   Are they within then?   25
SUBTLE
Numbering the sum.
FACE   How much?
SUBTLE   A hundred marks, boy.
                                        [*Exit* SUBTLE]

FACE
Why, this 's a lucky day! Ten pounds of Mammon!
Three o' my clerk! A portague o' my grocer!
This o' the Brethren! Beside reversions,
And states, to come i' the widow, and my Count!   30

                    [*Enter* DOL]

My share, today, will not be bought for forty –
DOL   What?

---

14   *hoys* small sea vessels carrying passengers and goods around coastal waters.
      trunks trunk hose; knee breeches.
15   *pistolets* Spanish gold coins.
      pieces of eight Spanish dollars.
18–19 *Cinque-Port . . . Dover pier* one of the five ports on the South-East coast of England
      occupying vital defence positions. Dover is the chief. Dol is a Cinque-Port because
      she is constantly invaded. The portals of her body and five senses may also be implied.
      'Cinque' would have been pronounced 'sink'.
22   *milk* feele Q.
      epididimis 'A long narrow structure attached to the posterior border of the adjoining
      outer surface of the testicle' (*OED*); so 'milk his epididimis' = 'drain his balls'.
24   *John Leydens* John Leyden led the Anabaptist occupation of Münster in 1532–6.
29   *reversions* goods due in the future.

FACE

Pounds, dainty Dorothy, art thou so near?

DOL

Yes, say lord General, how fares our camp?

FACE

As, with the few, that had entrenched themselves
Safe, by their discipline, against a world, Dol: 35
And laughed, within those trenches, and grew fat
With thinking on the booties, Dol, brought in
Daily, by their small parties. This dear hour,
A doughty Don is taken, with my Dol;
And thou may'st make his ransom, what thou wilt,   40
My Dousabell: he shall be brought here, fettered
With thy fair looks, before he sees thee; and thrown
In a down-bed, as dark as any dungeon;
Where thou shalt keep him waking, with thy drum;
Thy drum, my Dol; thy drum; till he be tame   45
As the poor blackbirds were i' the great frost,
Or bees are with a basin: and so hive him
I' the swanskin coverlid, and cambric sheets,
Till he work honey, and wax, my little God's-gift.

DOL

What is he, General?

FACE   An *Adalantado,*   50
A grandee, girl. Was not my Dapper here, yet?

DOL

No.

FACE   Nor my Drugger?

DOL   Neither.

FACE   A pox on 'em,
They are so long a-furnishing! Such stinkards

---

33   *say . . . camp* the first line of Kyd's *The Spanish Tragedy* – a hugely popular play to which Jonson had written additions.

41   *Dousabell* (French) 'douce et belle': sweet and lovely.

44   *drum* belly; perhaps also suggesting the beat of sexual intercourse.

46   *the great frost* of 1607–8 when the Thames froze over; the blackbirds would have depended on humans for food.

47   *bees . . . basin* according to Virgil (*et al.*) swarming bees can be attracted by banging a metal basin (*Georgics* 4.64).

49   *wax* both noun (what Mammon will produce) and verb – 'to grow [erect]'. *God's-gift* Dorothea means 'God's gift' in Greek.

53   *a-furnishing* preparing; stocking up.

Would not be seen, upon these festival days.

[*Enter* SUBTLE]

How now! Ha' you done?
SUBTLE   Done. They are gone. The sum   55
Is here in bank, my Face. I would, we knew
Another chapman, now, would buy 'em outright.
FACE
'Slid, Nab shall do't, against he ha' the widow,
To furnish household.
SUBTLE   Excellent, well thought on,
Pray God, he come.
FACE   I pray, he keep away   60
Till our new business be o'erpast.
SUBTLE   But, Face,
How camest thou, by this secret Don?
FACE   A spirit
Brought me th' intelligence, in a paper, here,
As I was conjuring, yonder, in my circle
For Surly: I ha' my flies abroad. Your bath   65
Is famous, Subtle, by my means. Sweet Dol,
You must go tune your virginal, no losing
O' the least time. And, do you hear? Good action.
Firk, like a flounder; kiss, like a scallop, close:
And tickle him with thy mother-tongue. His great   70
Verdugoship has not a jot of language:
So much the easier to be cozened, my Dolly.
He will come here, in a hired coach, obscure,
And our own coachman, whom I have sent, as guide,

---

57   *chapman* merchant.
62   FACE F2; not in Q, F.
69   *Firk, like a flounder* The arching contortions of a flat fish out of water are suggested.
      kiss, like a scallop, close Editors refer to a Latin poem by the Emperor Gallienus containing the phrase 'non vincant oscula conchae' ('Don't let a clam's kisses win'). But Jonson wouldn't have needed this to remind him of the resemblance between shellfish and female genitals which has led many to find shellfish aphrodisiac.
70   *mother-tongue* i.e. what lies between the vaginal *labia*.
71   *Verdugoship Verdugo* is Spanish for 'hangman'.
      language English.
73   *obscure* concealed.

No creature else.   *One knocks*
                        Who's that?
SUBTLE   It i' not he?   75
FACE
    O no, not yet this hour.
SUBTLE   Who is't?
DOL [*Looking out*]   Dapper,
    Your clerk.
FACE   God's will, then, Queen of Fairy,
    On with your tire; and, Doctor, with your robes.
    Let's despatch him, for God's sake.
SUBTLE   'Twill be long.
FACE
    I warrant you, take but the cues I give you,   80
    It shall be brief enough. [*Looking out*] 'Slight, here are more!
    Abel, and I think, the angry boy, the heir,
    That fain would quarrel.
SUBTLE   And the widow?
FACE   No,
    Not that I see. Away.
                        [*Exit* SUBTLE, DOL. FACE *opens door*]
                    O sir, you are welcome.

ACT III, SCENE iv

[*Enter*] DAPPER [*to them*]

FACE
    The Doctor is within, a-moving for you;
    (I have had the most ado to win him to it)
    He swears, you'll be the darling o' the dice:
    He never heard her Highness dote, till now (he says.)
    Your aunt has given you the most gracious words,   5
    That can be thought on.
DAPPER   Shall I see her Grace?

---

79   *Let's* Lett's vs Q.
82   *angry boy* 'Angry boys', 'terrible boys' or, most commonly, 'roaring boys' were names
      given to well-heeled thugs.
4   (*he says.*) not in Q.

FACE

    See her, and kiss her, too.

          [*Enter* DRUGGER *and* KASTRIL]

             What? Honest Nab!
    Hast brought the damask?

DRUGGER   No, sir, here's tobacco.

FACE

    'Tis well done, Nab: thou'lt bring the damask too?

DRUGGER

    Yes, here's the gentleman, Captain, Master Kastril,   10
    I have brought to see the Doctor.

FACE   Where's the widow?

DRUGGER

    Sir, as he likes, his sister (he says) shall come.

FACE

    O, is it so? 'Good time. Is your name Kastril, sir?

KASTRIL

    Ay, and the best o' the Kastrils, I'd be sorry else,
    By fifteen hundred, a year. Where is this Doctor?   15
    My mad tobacco-boy, here, tells me of one,
    That can do things. Has he any skill?

FACE   Wherein, sir?

KASTRIL

    To carry a business, manage a quarrel, fairly,
    Upon fit terms.

FACE   It seems sir, you're but young
    About the town, that can make that a question!   20

KASTRIL

    Sir, not so young, but I have heard some speech
    Of the angry boys, and seen 'em take tobacco;
    And in his shop: and I can take it too.
    And I would fain be one of 'em, and go down
    And practise i' the country.

FACE   Sir, for the *duello*,   25

    8   DRUGGER *Nab* Q, F.
    9   *Nab* not in Q.
 18–19   *manage . . . terms* Quarrelling, like much else, had been systematised and made into a
        science at this period. In *As You Like It* Touchstone goes through the degrees of the lie
        (V.iv.90ff).
   25   *duello* duel.

The Doctor, I assure you, shall inform you,
To the least shadow of a hair: and show you,
An instrument he has, of his own making,
Wherewith, no sooner shall you make report
Of any quarrel, but he will take the height on't,   30
Most instantly; and tell in what degree,
Of safety it lies in, or mortality.
And, how it may be borne, whether in a right line,
Or a half-circle; or may, else, be cast
Into an angle blunt, if not acute: 35
All this he will demonstrate. And then, rules,
To give, and take the lie, by.

KASTRIL   How? To take it?

FACE

Yes, in oblique, he'll show you; or in circle:
But never in diameter. The whole town
Study his theorems, and dispute them, ordinarily,   40
At the eating academies.

KASTRIL   But, does he teach
Living, by the wits, too?

FACE   Anything, whatever.
You cannot think that subtlety, but he reads it.
He made me a Captain. I was a stark pimp,
Just o' your standing, 'fore I met with him: 45
It i' not two months since. I'll tell you his method.
First, he will enter you, at some ordinary.

KASTRIL

No, I'll not come there. You shall pardon me.

FACE   For why, sir?

KASTRIL

There's gaming there, and tricks.

FACE   Why, would you be
A gallant, and not game?

KASTRIL   Ay, 'twill spend a man.   50

---

32   *mortality* danger.
39   *in diameter* i.e. head-on; 'the lie direct'.
40–1 *ordinarily . . . academies* Jonson puns on the sense of 'ordinary' as eating house and
     reverses the expected epithets (study and disputation usually take place in academies,
     eating in ordinaries).
43   *reads* understands.
44   *stark* arrant, unmodified.
50   *spend a man* waste away a man's wealth.

FACE

    Spend you? It will repair you, when you are spent.
    How do they live by their wits, there, that have vented
    Six times your fortunes?

KASTRIL   What, three thousand a year!

FACE

    Ay, forty thousand.

KASTRIL   Are there such?

FACE   Ay, sir.

    And gallants, yet. Here's a young gentleman,   55
    Is born to nothing, forty marks a year,
    Which I count nothing. He's to be initiated,
    And have a fly o' the Doctor. He will win you
    By unresistable luck, within this fortnight,
    Enough to buy a barony. They will set him   60
    Upmost, at the Groom-porter's, all the Christmas!
    And, for the whole year through, at every place,
    Where there is play, present him with the chair;
    The best attendance, the best drink, sometimes
    Two glasses of canary, and pay nothing;   65
    The purest linen, and the sharpest knife,
    The partridge next his trencher: and, somewhere,
    The dainty bed, in private, with the dainty.
    You shall ha' your ordinaries bid for him,
    As playhouses for a poet; and the master   70
    Pray him, aloud, to name what dish he affects,
    Which must be buttered shrimps: and those that drink
    To no mouth else, will drink to his, as being
    The goodly, president mouth of all the board.

KASTRIL

    Do you not gull one?

FACE   'Od's my life! Do you think it?   75
    You shall have a cast commander, (can but get

---

58   *fly* see Argument, l. 11.
61   *Groom-porter* an officer in the royal household particularly concerned with gaming
       regulations.
64   *attendance* service.
65   *canary* canary wine.
71   *affects* desires.
75   *'Od's my life* God's my life Q.
76   *cast commander* unemployed officer.

In credit with a glover, or a spurrier,
For some two pair, of either's ware, aforehand)
Will, by most swift posts, dealing with him,
Arrive at competent means, to keep himself,   80
His punk, and naked boy, in excellent fashion.
And be admired for it.

KASTRIL   Will the Doctor teach this?

FACE

He will do more, sir, when your land is gone,
(As men of spirit hate to keep earth long)
In a vacation, when small money is stirring,   85
And ordinaries suspended till the term,
He'll show a perspective, where on one side
You shall behold the faces, and the persons
Of all sufficient young heirs, in town,
Whose bonds are current for commodity;   90
On th' other side, the merchants' forms, and others,
That, without help of any second broker,
(Who would expect a share) will trust such parcels:
In the third square, the very street, and sign
Where the commodity dwells, and does but wait   95
To be delivered, be it pepper, soap,
Hops, or tobacco, oatmeal, woad, or cheeses.
All which you may so handle, to enjoy,
To your own use, and never stand obliged.

KASTRIL

I' faith! Is he such a fellow?

FACE   Why, Nab here knows him.   100
And then for making matches, for rich widows,
Young gentlewomen, heirs, the fortunat'st man!
He's sent to, far, and near, all over England,
To have his counsel, and to know their fortunes.

KASTRIL

God's will, my suster shall see him.

FACE   I'll tell you, sir,   105

77   *spurrier* spur-maker.
79   *by most swift posts* with great speed.
81   *punk* prostitute, kept woman.   *naked boy* just that; 'catamite' is the grander term.
84   *As men . . . long* This has the logic of a natural law: earth descends, spirit rises.
87   *perspective* optical trick.
90   *commodity* see II.i.10–14.
97   *woad* a blue dye.

What he did tell me of Nab. It's a strange thing!
(By the way you must eat no cheese, Nab, it breeds melancholy:
And that same melancholy breeds worms) but pass it –
He told me, honest Nab, here, was ne'er at tavern,
But once in's life.

DRUGGER   Truth, and no more I was not.   110

FACE

And, then he was so sick –

DRUGGER   Could he tell you that, too?

FACE

How should I know it?

DRUGGER   In troth we had been a-shooting,
And had a piece of fat ram-mutton, to supper,
That lay so heavy o' my stomach –

FACE   And he has no head
To bear any wine; for, what with the noise o' the fiddlers,   115
And care of his shop, for he dares keep no servants –

DRUGGER

My head did so ache –

FACE   As he was fain to be brought home,
The Doctor told me. And then, a good old woman –

DRUGGER

(Yes, faith, she dwells in Sea-coal Lane) did cure me,
With sodden ale, and pellitory o' the wall: 120
Cost me but two pence. I had another sickness,
Was worse than that.

FACE   Ay, that was with the grief
Thou took'st for being 'sessed at eighteen pence,
For the waterwork.

107   *eat . . . melancholy* Milk and its products were thought to engender melancholy. In fact
       they stimulate the production of mucus and, if anything, promote a phlegmatic
       disposition.
109–26 *He told . . . the Doctor* Face's prompting shows him to know Dapper's story – and its
       wording – by heart.
119   *Sea-coal Lane* now Old Seacoal Lane, running from Farringdon Street to Fleet Lane.
       It was the home of fruiterers.
120   *sodden* boiled.
       pellitory o' the wall lichwort (of the same family as stinging nettle and hop); this
       bushy plant which grows in the cracks of walls is used in decoctions and infusions
       as a remedy for urinary disorders.
123   *'sessed* assessed (for a rate).
124   *the water-work* see II.i.76. The 'New River', an aqueduct, was under construction at
       the time the play was written.

DRUGGER In truth, and it was like
T'have cost me almost my life.
FACE   Thy hair went off?   125
DRUGGER
Yes, sir, 'twas done for spite.
FACE   Nay, so says the Doctor.
KASTRIL
Pray thee, tobacco-boy, go fetch my suster,
I'll see this learned boy, before I go:
And so shall she.
FACE   Sir, he is busy now:
But, if you have a sister to fetch hither,   130
Perhaps, your own pains may command her sooner;
And he, by that time, will be free.
KASTRIL   I go.   [*Exit* KASTRIL]
FACE
Drugger, she's thine: the damask.

                              [*Exit* DRUGGER]
                    (Subtle, and I
Must wrestle for her.) Come on, master Dapper.
You see, how I turn clients, here, away,   135
To give your cause dispatch. Ha' you performed
The ceremonies were enjoined you?
DAPPER   Yes, o' the vinegar,
And the clean shirt.
FACE   'Tis well: that shirt may do you
More worship than you think. Your aunt's afire,
But that she will not show it, t'have a sight on you.   140
Ha' you provided for her Grace's servants?
DAPPER
Yes, here are six score Edward shillings.
FACE   Good.
DAPPER
And an old Harry's sovereign.
FACE   Very good.
DAPPER
And three James shillings, and an Elizabeth groat,

126   *'twas done for spite* i.e. the excessive levy.
132   *go* go, Sir Q.
143   *old Harry's sovereign* a sovereign from the realm of either Henry VII or Henry VIII;
         worth only 10 shillings.
144   *James shillings* i.e. shillings from the present realm.   *groat* fourpence.

Just twenty nobles.

FACE O, you are too just. 145

I would you had had the other noble in Marys.

DAPPER

I have some Philip, and Marys.

FACE Ay, those same

Are best of all. Where are they? Hark, the Doctor.

ACT III, SCENE v

[*Enter*] SUBTLE *disguised like a Priest of Fairy* [*to them*]

SUBTLE

Is yet her Grace's cousin come?

FACE He is come.

SUBTLE

And is he fasting?

FACE Yes.

SUBTLE And hath cried *hum*?

FACE

Thrice, you must answer.

DAPPER Thrice.

SUBTLE And as oft *buz*?

FACE

If you have, say.

DAPPER I have.

SUBTLE Then, to her coz,

Hoping, that he hath vinegared his senses, 5

As he was bid, the Fairy Queen dispenses,

145 *nobles* worth 6 shillings and 8 pence.

147 *Philip, and Marys* These nobles had the heads of the two sovereigns facing each other. Face, true to his name, seems to want his coins to provide a portrait gallery. There was a slight, but insignificant reduction in the fineness of gold coins between the reigns of Mary and James, so Face's enthusiasm for the earlier coins is not based on greed for gold.

III.v *H.&S.* cite Edward Marchant's *The seuerall Notorious and lewd Cosenages of Iohn West, and Alice West, falsely called the King and Queen of Fayries*. These two were convicted in 1613 of practices very similar to those described in this scene. Jonson may well have heard of them.

By me, this robe, the petticoat of Fortune;
Which that he straight put on, she doth importune.
And though to Fortune near be her petticoat,
Yet, nearer is her smock, the Queen doth note: 10
And, therefore, even of that a piece she hath sent,
Which, being a child, to wrap him in, was rent;
And prays him, for a scarf, he now will wear it
                              They blind him with a rag
(With as much love, as then her Grace did tear it)
About his eyes, to show, he is fortunate.   15
And, trusting unto her to make his state,
He'll throw away all worldly pelf, about him;
Which that he will perform, she doth not doubt him.

FACE

She need not doubt him, sir. Alas, he has nothing,
But what he will part withall, as willingly,   20
Upon her Grace's word (throw away your purse)
                         He throws away, as they bid him
As she would ask it: (handkerchiefs, and all)
She cannot bid that thing, but he'll obey.
(If you have a ring, about you, cast it off,
Or a silver seal, at your wrist, her Grace will send   25
Her fairies here to search you, therefore deal
Directly with her Highness. If they find
That you conceal a mite, you are undone.)

DAPPER

Truly, there's all.

FACE   All what?

DAPPER   My money, truly.

FACE

Keep nothing, that is transitory, about you.   30
(Bid Dol play music.) Look, the elves are come

> DOL *enters with a cithern: they pinch him*

To pinch you, if you tell not truth. Advise you.

DAPPER

O, I have a paper with a spur-rial in't.

---

17   *pelf* property; stuff.
31   s.d. *cithern* ghittern; an instrument like a guitar.
33   *spur-rial* Edward IV noble with a blazing sun on the tail side, resembling the rowel of
     a spur.

FACE   *Ti, ti,*
  They knew't, they say.
SUBTLE   *Ti, ti, ti, ti,* he has more yet.
FACE
  Ti, ti-ti-ti. I' the tother pocket?
SUBTLE   *Titi, titi, titi, titi.*   35
  They must pinch him, or he will never confess, they say.
DAPPER
  O, O.
FACE   Nay, 'pray you hold. He is her Grace's nephew.
  Ti, ti, ti? What care you? Good faith, you shall care.
  Deal plainly, sir, and shame the fairies. Show
  You are an innocent.
DAPPER   By this good light, I ha' nothing.   40
SUBTLE
  Ti, ti, titi to ta. He does equivocate, she says:
  Ti, ti do ti, ti ti do, ti da. And swears by the light, when he is
     blinded.
DAPPER
  By this good dark, I ha' nothing but a half crown
  Of gold, about my wrist, that my love gave me;
  And a leaden heart I wore, sin' she forsook me.   45
FACE
  I thought, 'twas something. And, would you incur
  Your aunt's displeasure for these trifles? Come,
  I had rather you had thrown away twenty half crowns.
  You may wear your leaden heart still.
                              [DOL *looking out*]
                    How now?
SUBTLE
  What news, Dol?
DOL   Yonder's your knight, sir Mammon.   50
FACE
  God's lid, we never thought of him, till now.
  Where is he?
DOL   Here, hard by. He's at the door.
SUBTLE [*To* FACE]
  And, you are not ready, now? Dol, get his suit.
  He must not be sent back.

41   *equivocate* evade.
45   *leaden heart* an emblem of grief.

[Exit DOL]

FACE   O, by no means.
What shall we do with this same puffin, here,   55
Now he's o' the spit?
SUBTLE   Why, lay him back a while,
With some device.

[Enter DOL]

                    Ti, ti ti, ti ti ti. Would her Grace speak with me?
I come. Help, Dol.
                    He speaks through the keyhole, the other knocking
FACE   Who's there? Sir Epicure;
My master's i' the way. Please you to walk
Three or four turns, but till his back be turned,   60
And I am for you. Quickly, Dol.
                              [FACE *dresses as 'Lungs'*]
SUBTLE   Her Grace
Commends her kindly to you, master Dapper.
DAPPER
I long to see her Grace.
SUBTLE   She, now, is set
At dinner, in her bed; and she has sent you,
From her own private trencher, a dead mouse,   65
And a piece of gingerbread, to be merry withal,
And stay your stomach, lest you faint with fasting:
Yet, if you could hold out, till she saw you (she says)
It would be better for you.
FACE   Sir, he shall
Hold out, and 'twere this two hours, for her Highness;   70
I can assure you that. We will not lose
All we ha' done –
SUBTLE   He must nor see, nor speak
To anybody, till then.
FACE   For that, we'll put, sir,
A stay in 's mouth.
SUBTLE   Of what?
FACE   Of gingerbread.
Make you it fit. He that hath pleased her Grace,   75

56   *o' the spit* ready for roasting.
74   *stay* gag.

442

Thus far, shall not now crinkle, for a little.
Gape sir, and let him fit you.

[SUBTLE inserts gag]

SUBTLE   Where shall we now
Bestow him?
DOL   I' the privy.
SUBTLE   Come along, sir,
I now must show you Fortune's privy lodgings.
FACE
Are they perfumed? And his bath ready?
SUBTLE   All.   80
Only the fumigation's somewhat strong.
FACE
Sir Epicure, I am yours, sir, by and by.

[Exeunt SUBTLE, DOL, DAPPER]

---

76 *crinkle* shrink from his purpose.
77 *let him fit you* The term to 'fit' someone could have sinister undertones; e.g. *The
     Spanish Tragedy*, IV.i.70, 'Why then I'll fit you'.
78 *privy* private place; i.e. lavatory.

[*Enter*] MAMMON [*to* FACE]

FACE
O, sir, you're come i' the only, finest time –
MAMMON
Where's master?
FACE   Now preparing for projection, sir.
Your stuff will b' all changed shortly.
MAMMON   Into gold?
FACE
To gold, and silver, sir.
MAMMON   Silver, I care not for.
FACE
Yes, sir, a little to give beggars.
MAMMON   Where's the lady?   5
FACE
At hand, here. I ha' told her such brave things, o' you,
Touching your bounty and your noble spirit –
MAMMON   Hast thou?
FACE
As she is almost in her fit to see you.
But, good sir, no divinity i' your conference,
For fear of putting her in rage –
MAMMON   I warrant thee.   10
FACE
Six men will not hold her down. And then,
If the old man should hear, or see you –
MAMMON   Fear not.
FACE
The very house, sir, would run mad. You know it
How scrupulous he is, and violent,
'Gainst the least act of sin. Physic, or mathematics,   15
Poetry, state, or bawdry (as I told you)
She will endure, and never startle: but
No word of controversy.

6   *o'you* on you Q.
9   *divinity* theology.
16   *state* matters of state; politics.
17   *startle* be startled.

MAMMON   I am schooled, good **Ulen**.

FACE

And you must praise her house, remember that,
And her nobility.

MAMMON   Let me, alone: 20

No herald, no nor antiquary, Lungs,
Shall do it better. Go.

FACE   (Why, this is yet

A kind of modern happiness, to have
Dol Common for a great lady.)   [*Exit* FACE]

MAMMON   Now Epicure,

Heighten thyself, talk to her, all in gold;   25
Rain her as many showers, as Jove did drops
Unto his Danae: show the God a miser,
Compared with Mammon. What? The stone will do't.
She shall feel gold, taste gold, hear gold, sleep gold:
Nay, we will *concumbere* gold. I will be puissant,   30
And mighty in my talk to her! Here she comes.

[*Enter* FACE, DOL]

FACE

To him, Dol, suckle him. This is the noble knight,
I told your ladyship –

MAMMON   Madam, with your pardon,

I kiss your vesture.

DOL   Sir, I were uncivil

If I would suffer that, my lip to you, sir.   35

MAMMON

I hope, my lord your brother be in health, lady?

DOL

My lord, my brother is, though I no lady, sir.

FACE

(Well said my Guinea bird.)

MAMMON   Right noble madam –

18   **Ulen** Lungs Q.
23   *modern* commonplace (and so a play on Dol's name); the sense 'contemporary' was
      also present.
26–7   *Rain . . . Danae* See II.i.102.
30   *concumbere* lit. 'lie together' which Mammon seems to use as a transitive verb 'to generate'.
      puissant (Fr.) powerful; Mammon perhaps means 'potent'.
38   *Guinea bird* guinea hen and guinea bird were slang terms for prostitute.

FACE

    (O, we shall have most fierce idolatry!)

MAMMON

    'Tis your prerogative.

DOL   Rather your courtesy.   40

MAMMON

    Were there nought else t'enlarge your virtues, to me,

    These answers speak your breeding, and your blood.

DOL

    Blood we boast none, sir, a poor baron's daughter.

MAMMON

    Poor! And gat you? Profane not. Had your father

    Slept all the happy remnant of his life   45

    After the act, lain but there still, and panted,

    He'd done enough, to make himself, his issue,

    And his posterity noble.

DOL   Sir, although

    We may be said to want the gilt, and trappings,

    The dress of honour; yet we strive to keep   50

    The seeds, and the materials.

MAMMON   I do see

    The old ingredient, virtue, was not lost,

    Nor the drug money, used to make your compound.

    There is a strange nobility, i' your eye,

    This lip, that chin! Methinks you do resemble   55

    One o' the Austriac princes.

FACE   (Very like,

    Her father was an Irish costermonger.)

MAMMON

    The house of Valois, just, had such a nose.

    And such a forehead, yet, the Medici

    Of Florence boast.

DOL   Troth, and I have been likened   60

    To all these princes.

FACE   (I'll be sworn, I heard it.)

MAMMON

    I know not how. It is not any one,

51–3   *The seeds . . . compound* Dol and Mammon converse in alchemical metaphors.

57   *Irish costermonger* at that time many of the London street vendors were Irish.

58–9   *Valois . . . Medici* great European houses but not physiognomically marked. Mammon is name-dropping.

But e'en the very choice of all their features.

FACE

    (I'll in, and laugh.)   [*Exit* FACE]

MAMMON   A certain touch, or air,

    That sparkles a divinity, beyond   65

    An earthly beauty!

DOL   O, you play the courtier.

MAMMON

Good lady, gi' me leave –

DOL   In faith, I may not,

    To mock me, sir.

MAMMON   To burn i' this sweet flame:

    The Phoenix never knew a nobler death.

DOL

    Nay, now you court the courtier: and destroy   70

    What you would build. This art, sir, i' your words,

    Calls your whole faith in question.

MAMMON   By my soul –

DOL

    Nay, oaths are made o' the same air, sir.

MAMMON   Nature

    Never bestowed upon mortality,

    A more unblamed, a more harmonious feature: 75

    She played the stepdame in all faces, else.

    Sweet madam, le' me be particular –

DOL

    Particular, sir? I pray you, know your distance.

MAMMON

    In no ill sense, sweet lady, but to ask

    How your fair graces pass the hours? I see   80

    You're lodged, here, i' the house of a rare man,

    An excellent artist: but, what's that to you?

DOL

    Yes, sir. I study here the mathematics,

    And distillation.

MAMMON   O, I cry your pardon.

---

69   *Phoenix* a unique and legendary bird that builds its own funeral pyre at regular
     intervals and, from its own ashes, is born again.

70   *court the courtier* use elaborate courtly language.

78   *Particular* Mammon *could* mean 'let me go into more detail'; but Dol takes 'particular'
     to mean 'familiar', 'intimate'.

He's a divine instructor! Can extract   85
The souls of all things, by his art; call all
The virtues, and the miracles of the sun,
Into a temperate furnace: teach dull nature
What her own forces are. A man, the Emperor
Has courted, above Kelley: sent his medals,   90
And chains, t' invite him.
DOL   Ay, and for his physic, sir –
MAMMON
Above the art of Æsculapius,
That drew the envy of the Thunderer!
I know all this, and more.
DOL   Troth, I am taken, sir,
Whole, with these studies, that contemplate nature.   95
MAMMON
It is a noble humour. But, this form
Was not intended to so dark a use!
Had you been crooked, foul, of some coarse mould,
A cloister had done well: but, such a feature
That might stand up the glory of a kingdom,   100
To live recluse! – is a mere solecism,
Though in a nunnery. It must not be.
I muse, my lord your brother will permit it!
You should spend half my land first, were I he.
Does not this diamant better, on my finger,   105
Than i' the quarry?
DOL   Yes.
MAMMON   Why, you are like it.
You were created, lady, for the light!
Here, you shall wear it; take it, the first pledge
Of what I speak: to bind you, to believe me.

90   *Kelley* Edward Kelley (1555–95) who worked with John Dee as his 'scryer'.
91   *chains* These recall the fact that the Emperor Rudolph of Germany imprisoned Kelley
       for failing to produce the Philosopher's Stone.
92   *Æsculapius* son of Apollo and god of medicine. He was able to restore men to life
       until Jupiter ('the Thunderer') killed him with a thunderbolt in order that men
       should be immortal.
96–7; 105–8 Compare this specious argument with that used by Milton's Comus to the Lady
       (*Comus*, ll. 709–54).
101   *recluse* as a recluse.
       solecism error.
105   *diamant* diamond.
107   *the light* light Q.

DOL

 In chains of adamant?

MAMMON   Yes, the strongest bands.   110

 And take a secret, too. Here, by your side,

 Doth stand, this hour, the happiest man, in Europe.

DOL

 You are contented, sir?

MAMMON   Nay, in true being:

 The envy of princes, and the fear of states.

DOL

 Say you so, Sir Epicure!

MAMMON   Yes, and thou shalt prove it,   115

 Daughter of honour. I have cast mine eye

 Upon thy form, and I will rear this beauty,

 Above all styles.

DOL   You mean no treason, sir!

MAMMON

 No, I will take away that jealousy.

 I am the lord of the philosopher's stone,   120

 And thou the lady.

DOL   How sir! Ha' you that?

MAMMON

 I am the master of the mastery.

 This day, the good old wretch, here, o' the house

 Has made it for us. Now, he's at projection.

 Think therefore, thy first wish, now; let me hear it: 125

 And it shall rain into thy lap, no shower,

 But floods of gold, whole cataracts, a deluge,

 To get a nation on thee!

DOL   You are pleased, sir,

 To work on the ambition of our sex.

MAMMON

 I am pleased, the glory of her sex should know,   130

 This nook, here, of the Friars, is no climate

 For her, to live obscurely in, to learn

 Physic, and surgery, for the Constable's wife

---

110 *adamant* puns on 'a diamant'.
112 *in* of Q.
117–18 *I will rear . . . styles* I will see that this beauty becomes the type of all fashion.
122 *mastery* the *magisterium* or master-work.
131 *the Friars* Blackfriars.

449

Of some odd Hundred in Essex; but come forth,
And taste the air of palaces; eat, drink   135
The toils of emp'rics, and their boasted practice;
Tincture of pearl, and coral, gold, and amber;
Be seen at feasts, and triumphs; have it asked,
What miracle she is? Set all the eyes
Of court afire, like a burning glass,   140
And work 'em into cinders; when the jewels
Of twenty states adorn thee; and the light
Strikes out the stars; that, when thy name is mentioned,
Queens may look pale: and, we but showing our love,
Nero's Poppæa may be lost in story!   145
Thus, will we have it.
DOL   I could well consent, sir.
But, in a monarchy, how will this be?
The Prince will soon take notice; and both seize
You, and your stone: it being a wealth unfit
For any private subject.
MAMMON   If he knew it.   150
DOL
Yourself do boast it, sir.
MAMMON   To thee, my life.
DOL
O, but beware, sir! You may come to end
The remnant of your days, in a loathed prison,
By speaking of it.
MAMMON   'Tis no idle fear!
We'll therefore go with all, my girl, and live   155
In a free state; where we will eat our mullets,
Soused in high-country wines, sup pheasants' eggs,
And have our cockles, boiled in silver shells,
Our shrimps to swim again, as when they lived,

---

134   *Hundred* a subdivision of a county.
136   *The toils of emp'rics* the products of experimental endeavour.
145   *Nero's Poppæa* so desired by Nero that he had her husband and his own wife killed
      in order to possess her. But she died of a kick from Nero (a typical *lapsus* on
      Mammon's part). Her beauty – and her solicitude for it – were legendary. She is
      supposed to have kept 500 asses in order to be able to bathe daily in their milk.
      story history.
157   *high-country wines* wines from hill country; but 'high' also suggests their intoxicating
      effect.

In a rare butter, made of dolphins' milk,   160
Whose cream does look like opals: and, with these
Delicate meats, set ourselves high for pleasure,
And take us down again, and then renew
Our youth, and strength, with drinking the elixir,
And so enjoy a perpetuity   165
Of life, and lust. And, thou shalt ha' thy wardrobe,
Richer than Nature's, still, to change thyself,
And vary oftener, for thy pride, than she:
Or Art, her wise, and almost equal servant.

[*Enter* FACE]

FACE

Sir, you are too loud. I hear you, every word,   170
Into the laboratory. Some fitter place.
The garden, or great chamber above. How like you her?

MAMMON

Excellent! Lungs. There's for thee.   [*Gives money*]

FACE   But, do you hear?

Good sir, beware, no mention of the Rabbins.

MAMMON

We think not on 'em.

FACE   O, it is well, sir.

[*Exeunt* DOL, MAMMON]
Subtle!   175

---

160   *rare butter* As Geoffrey Hill remarks, this obvious oxymoron 'is a good, serious joke'
      (*The Lords of Limit*, 1984, p. 51).
166   *lust* both pleasure in general (the German *Lust*) and sexual pleasure in particular. It
      is one of the Deadly Sins.
167   *Richer than Nature's* See I.iv.27 n.; Shakespeare's Perdita would have considered such
      an attempt to outdo nature overweening and wrong.
168   *for thy pride* for your adornment.
174   *Rabbins* Rabbis; Hugh Broughton, from whose work Dol is to quote copiously, was
      expert in Judaic history and law.

ACT IV, SCENE ii

[Enter] SUBTLE *[to* FACE*]*

FACE
Dost thou not laugh?
SUBTLE   Yes. Are they gone?
FACE   All's clear.
SUBTLE
The widow is come.
FACE   And your quarrelling disciple?
SUBTLE
  Ay.
FACE   I must to my Captainship again, then.
SUBTLE
Stay, bring 'em in, first.
FACE   So I meant. What is she?
  A bonnibell?
SUBTLE   I know not.
FACE   We'll draw lots,   5
You'll stand to that?
SUBTLE   What else?
FACE   O, for a suit,
To fall now, like a curtain: flap.
SUBTLE   To th' door, man.
FACE
You'll ha' the first kiss, 'cause I am not ready.   *[Exit* FACE*]*
SUBTLE
Yes, and perhaps hit you through both the nostrils.
FACE *[Within]*
Who would you speak with?
KASTRIL *[Within]*   Where's the Captain?
FACE   Gone, sir.   10
About some business.
KASTRIL   Gone?
FACE   He'll return straight.
But master Doctor, his lieutenant, is here.

5   *bonnibell* (Fr.) 'bonne et belle', i.e. a good and pretty woman.
6   *suit* of clothes; Face needs to change into his captain's outfit.
9   *hit . . . nostrils* 'lead you through the nose'.

[Enter KASTRIL, DAME PLIANT, *Exit* FACE]

SUBTLE

    Come near, my worshipful boy, my *terrae fili,*
    That is, my boy of land; make thy approaches:
    Welcome, I know thy lusts, and thy desires,   15
    And I will serve, and satisfy 'em. Begin,
    Charge me from thence, or thence, or in this line;
    Here is my centre: ground thy quarrel.

KASTRIL   You lie.

SUBTLE

    How, child of wrath, and anger! The loud lie?
    For what, my sudden boy?

KASTRIL   Nay, that look you to,   20
    I am aforehand.

SUBTLE   O, this 's no true grammar,
    And as ill logic! You must render causes, child,
    Your first, and second intentions, know your canons,
    And your divisions, moods, degrees, and differences,
    Your predicaments, substance, and accident,   25
    Series extern, and intern, with their causes
    Efficient, material, formal, final,
    And ha' your elements perfect –

KASTRIL   What is this!
    The angry tongue he talks in?

SUBTLE   That false precept,
    Of being aforehand, has deceived a number;   30
    And made 'em enter quarrels, oftentimes,
    Before they were aware: and, afterward,
    Against their wills.

KASTRIL   How must I do then, sir?

SUBTLE

    I cry this lady mercy. She should, first,
    Have been saluted. I do call you lady,   35
    Because you are to be one, ere't be long,

                          He kisses her

---

13   *terrae fili* (Lat.) son of the soil.
17   *Charge* Accuse; attack.
18   *ground* establish.
22–8   *You must . . . perfect* Subtle applies the distinctions of logic to the art of quarrelling.
35   *saluted* kissed; greeted.

My soft, and buxom widow.

KASTRIL   Is she, i'faith?

SUBTLE

Yes, or my art is an egregious liar.

KASTRIL

How know you?

SUBTLE   By inspection, on her forehead,

And subtlety of her lip, which must be tasted   40

He kisses her again

Often, to make a judgement. 'Slight, she melts

Like a myrobalan! Here is, yet, a line

In *rivo frontis*, tells me, he is no knight.

PLIANT

What is he then, sir?

SUBTLE   Let me see your hand.

O, your *linea Fortunae* makes it plain;   45

And *stella* here, in *monte Veneris*:

But, most of all, *iunctura annularis*.

He is a soldier, or a man of art, lady:

But shall have some great honour, shortly.

PLIANT   Brother,

He's a rare man, believe me!

KASTRIL   Hold your peace.   50

[Enter FACE *dressed as Captain]*

Here comes the tother rare man. 'Save you Captain.

FACE

Good master Kastril. Is this your sister?

KASTRIL   Ay, sir.

Please you to kuss her, and be proud to know her?

FACE

I shall be proud to know you, lady.

PLIANT   Brother,

He calls me lady, too.

---

42 *myrobalan* fruit, like a plum.
43 *In rivo frontis* In the vein of the forehead.
45 *linea Fortunae* line of Fortune.
46 *stella . . . monte Veneris* star on the mount of Venus (at the base of the thumb).
47 *iunctura annularis* joint of the ring finger.
53 *kuss* kiss (Kastril also says 'suster').

KASTRIL   Ay, peace. I heard it.   55
                         [FACE *and* SUBTLE *talk aside*]

FACE
  The Count is come.

SUBTLE   Where is he?

FACE   At the door.

SUBTLE
  Why, you must entertain him.

FACE   What'll you do
  With these the while?

SUBTLE   Why, have 'em up, and show 'em
  Some fustian book, or the dark glass.

FACE   'Fore God,
  She is a delicate dab-chick! I must have her.   [*Exit* FACE]   60

SUBTLE
  Must you? Ay, if your fortune will, you must.
  [*To* KASTRIL] Come sir, the Captain will come to us presently.
  I'll ha' you to my chamber of demonstrations,
  Where I'll show you both the grammar, and logic,
  And rhetoric of quarrelling; my whole method,   65
  Drawn out in tables; and my instrument,
  That hath the several scale upon't, shall make you
  Able to quarrel, at a straw's breadth, by moonlight.
  And, lady, I'll have you look in a glass,
  Some half an hour, but to clear your eyesight,   70
  Against you see your fortune: which is greater,
  Than I may judge upon the sudden, trust me.
                     [*Exeunt* SUBTLE, KASTRIL, PLIANT]

---

59   *fustian* written in jargon or cant.
      dark glass crystal ball.
66   *Drawn out in tables* Tabulated.
71   *Against* In order that.

ACT IV, SCENE iii

[Enter] FACE

FACE

Where are you, Doctor?

SUBTLE *[Within]*   I'll come to you presently.

FACE

I will ha' this same widow, now I ha' seen her,
On any composition.

[Enter SUBTLE*]*

SUBTLE   What do you say?

FACE

Ha' you disposed of them?

SUBTLE   I ha' sent 'em up.

FACE

Subtle, in troth, I needs must have this widow.   5

SUBTLE

Is that the matter?

FACE   Nay, but hear me.

SUBTLE   Go to,

If you rebel once, Dol shall know it all.
Therefore be quiet, and obey your chance.

FACE

Nay, thou art so violent now – Do but conceive:
Thou art old, and canst not serve –

SUBTLE   Who, cannot I?   10

'Slight, I will serve her with thee, for a –

FACE   Nay,

But understand: I'll gi' you composition.

SUBTLE

I will not treat with thee: what, sell my fortune?
'Tis better than my birthright. Do not murmur.
Win her, and carry her. If you grumble, Dol   15

---

 3   *composition* deal.
10   *serve* a pun on the sense 'inseminate' (which adds a further dimension to 'conceive'
       in the previous line).
11   *'Slight* 'Sblood Q.
13   *treat* bargain.

Knows it directly.

FACE   Well sir, I am silent.

Will you go help, to fetch in Don, in state?   [*Exit* FACE]

SUBTLE

I follow you, sir: we must keep Face in awe,
Or he will overlook us like a tyrant.

      [*Enter* FACE,] SURLY *like a Spaniard*

Brain of a tailor! Who comes here? Don John!   20

SURLY

Señores, beso las manos, á vuestras mercedes.

SUBTLE

Would you had stooped a little, and kissed our *anos.*

FACE

Peace Subtle.

SUBTLE   Stab me; I shall never hold, man.

He looks in that deep ruff, like a head in a platter,
Served in by a short cloak upon two trestles!   25

FACE

Or, what do you say to a collar of brawn, cut down
Beneath the souse, and wriggled with a knife?

SUBTLE

'Slud, he does look too fat to be a Spaniard.

FACE

Perhaps some Fleming, or some Hollander got him
In d'Alva's time: Count Egmont's bastard.

SUBTLE   Don,   30

Your scurvy, yellow, Madrid face is welcome.

SURLY

Gratia.

---

19   *overlook* look over; lord it over.

20   *Don John* a common type-name for a Spaniard.

21   *Señores . . . mercedes* 'Gentlemen, I kiss your worships' hands'.

24–5   *He looks . . . trestles* cf. John Webster, *The White Devil*, 'He carries his face in's ruff, as I have seen a serving-man carry glasses in a cypress hat-band, monstrous steady, for fear of breaking' (III.i.75–7).

27   *souse* ear.   *wriggled* i.e. the knife has cut a zigzag pattern in the meat so that it looks pleated or folded like a ruff.

30   *d'Alva* Fernando Alvarez, Duke of Alva, governor of the Spanish Netherlands between 1567 and 1573.

       Count Egmont a Flemish patriot executed by d'Alva in 1568.

32   *Gratia* Thank you.

SUBTLE He speaks, out of a fortification.
Pray God, he ha' no squibs in those deep sets.

SURLY
Por Dios, Señores, muy linda casa!

SUBTLE
What says he?

FACE   Praises the house, I think,   35
I know no more but's action.

SUBTLE   Yes, the *casa*,
My precious Diego, will prove fair enough,
To cozen you in. Do you mark? You shall
Be cozened, Diego.

FACE   Cozened, do you see?
My worthy Donzel, cozened.

SURLY   *Entiendo.*   40

SUBTLE
Do you intend it? So do we, dear Don.
Have you brought pistolets? Or portagues?

He feels his pockets

My solemn Don? [*To* FACE] Dost thou feel any?

FACE   [*To* SUBTLE] Full.

SUBTLE
You shall be emptied, Don; pumped, and drawn,
Dry, as they say.

FACE   Milked, in troth, sweet Don.   45

SUBTLE
See all the monsters; the great lion of all, Don.

SURLY
Con licencia, se puede ver á esta señora?

SUBTLE
What talks he now?

FACE   O' the *Señora*.

32–3 *He speaks . . . sets* Surly is immured in his ruff and the pleats resemble the crenellations
of a fortress which could conceal explosives (squibs) in its recesses. The tubular
pattern of the ruff's edge would itself evoke gun-barrels pointing outward from
embrasures.

34 *Por Dios . . . casa* 'By God, gentlemen, a most charming house'.

40 *Donzel* little Don.
Entiendo I understand.

46 *monsters . . . lion* Lions were kept in the Tower of London as tourist attractions.
Monsters (freaks and prodigies of various sorts) were also objects of holiday viewing.

47 *Con . . . señora?* 'Is it possible, by your leave, to see the señora?'.

SUBTLE   O, Don,
  That is the lioness, which you shall see
  Also, my Don.
FACE   'Slid, Subtle, how shall we do?   50
SUBTLE
  For what?
FACE   Why, Dol's employed, you know.
SUBTLE   That's true!
  'Fore heaven I know not: he must stay, that's all.
FACE
  Stay? That he must not by no means.
SUBTLE   No, why?
FACE
  Unless you'll mar all. 'Slight, he'll suspect it.
  And then he will not pay, not half so well.   55
  This is a travelled punk-master, and does know
  All the delays: a notable hot rascal,
  And looks, already, rampant.
SUBTLE   'Sdeath, and Mammon
  Must not be troubled.
FACE   Mammon, in no case!
SUBTLE
  What shall we do then?
FACE   Think: you must be sudden.   60
SURLY
  Entiendo, que la señora es tan hermosa, que codicio tan
  á verla, como la bien aventuranza de mi vida.
FACE
  Mi vida? 'Slid, Subtle, he puts me in mind o' the widow.
  What dost thou say to draw her to't? Ha?
  And tell her, it is her fortune. All our venture   65
  Now lies upon 't. It is but one man more,
  Which on's chance to have her: and, beside,
  There is no maidenhead, to be feared, or lost.
  What dost thou think on't, Subtle?
SUBTLE   Who, I? Why –
FACE

---

60   *sudden* quick.
61–2   *Entiendo . . . vida* 'I understand that the señora is so beautiful that I long to see her
       as if she were my life's good fortune'.

The credit of our house too is engaged.   70

SUBTLE
You made me an offer for my share erewhile.
What wilt thou gi' me, i'faith?

FACE   O, by that light,
I'll not buy now. You know your doom to me.
E'en take your lot, obey your chance, sir; win her,
And wear her, out for me.

SUBTLE   'Slight. I'll not work her then.   75

FACE
It is the common cause, therefore bethink you.
Dol else must know it, as you said.

SUBTLE   I care not.

SURLY
Señores, porqué se tarda tanto?

SUBTLE
Faith, I am not fit, I am old.

FACE   That's now no reason, sir.

SURLY
Puede ser, de hacer burla de mi amor?   80

FACE
You hear the Don, too? By this air, I call.
And loose the hinges, Dol.

SUBTLE   A plague of hell –

FACE
Will you then do?

SUBTLE   You're a terrible rogue,
I'll think of this: will you, sir, call the widow?

FACE
Yes, and I'll take her too, with all her faults,   85
Now I do think on't better.

SUBTLE   With all my heart, sir,
Am I discharged o' the lot?

FACE   As you please.

SUBTLE   Hands.
                                    [*They shake hands*]

78   *Senores . . . tanto?* 'Gentlemen, why so much delay?'.
80   *Puede . . . amor?* 'Perhaps you are treating my love as a joke?'.
82   *loose the hinges* break our bond.

FACE

Remember now, that upon any change,
You never claim her.

SUBTLE   Much good joy, and health to you, sir.
Marry a whore? Fate, let me wed a witch first.   90

SURLY

Por estas honradas barbas —

SUBTLE   He swears by his beard.
Dispatch, and call the brother too.

[*Exit* FACE]

SURLY   *Tengo dúda Señores,*
Que no me hágan alguna traición.

SUBTLE

How, issue on? Yes, *praesto Señor.* Please you
Enthratha the *chambratha,* worthy Don;   95
Where if it please the Fates, in your *bathada*
You shall be soaked, and stroked, and tubbed, and rubbed:
And scrubbed, and fubbed, dear Don, before you go.
You shall, in faith, my scurvy baboon Don:
Be curried, clawed, and flawed, and tawed, indeed.   100
I will the heartilier go about it now,
And make the widow a punk, so much the sooner,
To be revenged on this impetuous Face:
The quickly doing of it is the grace.

[*Exeunt* SUBTLE, SURLY]

ACT IV, SCENE iv

[*Enter*] FACE, KASTRIL, DAME PLIANT

FACE

Come lady: I knew, the Doctor would not leave,
Till he had found the very nick of her fortune.

---

91   *Por . . . barbas* 'By this honoured beard . . . '
92–3   *Tengo . . . traición* 'I suspect, gentlemen, that you are practising some kind of treachery
        on me'.
100   *curried* tickled; rubbed down (as in 'curry comb').   *flawed* flayed.
        tawed beaten (like leather being made pliable for use).

2   *nick* hiding place.

KASTRIL

    To be a Countess, say you?

FACE   A Spanish Countess, sir.

PLIANT

    Why? Is that better than an English countess?

FACE

    Better? 'Slight, make you that a question, lady?   5

KASTRIL

    Nay, she is a fool, Captain, you must pardon her.

FACE

    Ask from your courtier, to your Inns of Court-man,

    To your mere milliner: they will tell you all,

    Your Spanish jennet is the best horse. Your Spanish

    Stoop is the best garb. Your Spanish beard   10

    Is the best cut. Your Spanish ruffs are the best

    Wear. Your Spanish pavan the best dance.

    Your Spanish titillation in a glove

    The best perfume. And, for your Spanish pike,

    And Spanish blade, let your poor Captain speak.   15

    Here comes the Doctor.

                    [*Enter* SUBTLE]

SUBTLE   My most honoured lady,

    (For so I am now to style you, having found

    By this my scheme, you are to undergo

    An honourable fortune, very shortly.)

    What will you say now, if some –

FACE   I ha' told her all, sir.   20

    And her right worshipful brother, here, that she shall be

    A Countess: do not delay 'em, sir. A Spanish Countess.

SUBTLE

    Still, my scarce worshipful Captain, you can keep

    No secret. Well, since he has told you, madame,

---

    3   FACE Q; not in F.

    9   *jennet* small Spanish horse.

  10   *Stoop* Bow.

  12   *pavan* a stately dance, introduced into England in the 16th century.

  13   *titillation* means of titillating – in this case scent.

14–15   *pike . . . blade* Toledo is still famous for its steel. The vogue for things Spanish at court
              was due to James' desire for a closer link with Spain.

  18   *scheme* planetary chart.   *undergo* There is a sexual innuendo here.

Do you forgive him, and I do.

KASTRIL   She shall do that, sir.   25
I'll look to't, 'tis my charge.

SUBTLE   Well then. Nought rests
But that she fit her love, now, to her fortune.

PLIANT
Truly, I shall never brook a Spaniard.

SUBTLE   No?

PLIANT
Never, sin' eighty-eight could I abide 'em,
And that was some three year afore I was born, in truth.   30

SUBTLE
Come, you must love him, or be miserable:
Choose, which you will.

FACE   By this good rush, persuade her,
She will cry strawberries else, within this twelvemonth.

SUBTLE
Nay, shads, and mackerel, which is worse.

FACE   Indeed, sir?

KASTRIL
God's lid, you shall love him, or I'll kick you.

PLIANT   Why?   35
I'll do as you will ha' me, brother.

KASTRIL   Do,
Or by this hand, I'll maul you.

FACE   Nay, good sir,
Be not so fierce.

SUBTLE   No, my enraged child,
She will be ruled. What, when she comes to taste
The pleasures of a Countess! To be courted –   40

FACE
And kissed, and ruffled!

SUBTLE   Ay, behind the hangings.

---

29   *eighty-eight* 1588, the year of the Armada. Dame Pliant's voice is typical of popular
      anti-Spanish sentiment of the time.

30   Which makes Dame Pliant nineteen.

32   *rush* Rushes were used as floor cover in houses and on theatre stages.

33   *cry strawberries* become a street fruit vendor.

34   *shads* a species of herring; Subtle suggests that it is worse to sell fish than fruit. 'Fish
      wife' is still a derogatory term.

41   *behind the hangings* Wall-hangings – like the arras in *Hamlet* – provided useful hiding-
      places in great houses.

FACE

    And then come forth in pomp!

SUBTLE   And know her state!

FACE

    Of keeping all th'idolators o' the chamber

    Barer to her, than at their prayers!

SUBTLE   Is served

    Upon the knee!

FACE   And has her pages, ushers,   45

    Footmen, and coaches –

SUBTLE   Her six mares –

FACE   Nay, eight!

SUBTLE

    To hurry her through London, to th' Exchange,

    Bedlam, the China-houses –

FACE   Yes, and have

    The citizens gape at her, and praise her tires!

    And my lord's goose-turd bands, that rides with her!   50

KASTRIL

    Most brave! By this hand, you are not my suster,

    If you refuse.

PLIANT   I will not refuse, brother.

                    [*Enter* SURLY]

SURLY

    Qué es esto, Señores, que no se venga?

    Esta tardanza me mata!

FACE   It is the Count come!

    The Doctor knew he would be here, by his art.   55

---

44   *Barer* of their hats (and perhaps more).

47   *th' Exchange* the New Exchange in the Strand – a fashionable meeting place where negotiations and purchases took place. It was opened in 1609.

48   *Bedlam* Bethlehem Royal Hospital for the insane. Viewing the inmates was considered a chic pastime.

      China-houses London shops where Oriental silks and porcelains were sold. These three places are also found grouped together as loci for fashionable living in *Epicoene*, IV.iii.22–3.

49   *tires* attires.

50   *goose-turd bands* collars of the fashionable goose-turd shade of green.

53–4   *Qué . . . mata* 'Why doesn't she come, gentlemen? This delay is killing me'.

SUBTLE
En galanta madama, Don! Galantissima!

SURLY
Por todos los dioses, la más acabada
Hermosura, que he visto en mi vida!

FACE
Is't not a gallant language, that they speak?

KASTRIL
An admirable language! Is't not French?   60

FACE
No, Spanish, sir.

KASTRIL   It goes like law-French,
And that, they say, is the courtliest language.

FACE   List, sir.

SURLY
El sol ha perdido su lumbre, con el
Resplandor, que trae esta dama. Válgame dios!

FACE
He admires your sister.

KASTRIL   Must not she make curtsey?   65

SUBTLE
'Ods will, she must go to him, man; and kiss him!
It is the Spanish fashion, for the women
To make first court.

FACE   'Tis true he tells you, sir:
His art knows all.

SURLY   *Porqué no se acude?*

KASTRIL
He speaks to her, I think?

FACE   That he does sir.   70

---

56   *En . . . Galantissima!* Subtle speaks a made-up Spanglish: 'A fine woman, Don, very
      fine!'
57–8 *Por . . . vida!* 'By all the gods, the most perfect beauty that I have seen in [all] my
      life!'
61   *law-French* a very corrupt derivation of Norman French, still used in law-courts at
      the date of the play though discontinued soon after.
62   *courtliest* in this case the language of the law-courts rather than the royal court.
      List listen.
63–4 *El . . . dios!* 'The sun has lost its light with the splendour that this lady bears, so help me
      God!'
69   *Porqué . . . acude?* 'Why doesn't she come?'

SURLY
> *Por el amor de dios, qué es esto, que se tarda?*

KASTRIL
> Nay, see: she will not understand him! Gull.
> Noddy.

PLIANT   What say you brother?

KASTRIL   Ass, my suster,
> Go kuss him, as the cunning man would ha' you, ,
> I'll thrust a pin i' your buttocks else.

FACE   O, no sir.   75

SURLY
> *Señora mía, mi persona muy indigna está*
> *Á llegar á tanta hermosura.*

FACE
> Does he not use her bravely?

KASTRIL   Bravely, i' faith!

FACE
> Nay, he will use her better.

KASTRIL   Do you think so?

SURLY
> *Señora, si sera servida, entremos.*   80

> [*Exeunt* SURLY, DAME PLIANT]

KASTRIL
> Where does he carry her?

FACE   Into the garden, sir;
> Take you no thought: I must interpret for her.

SUBTLE
> Give Dol the word.

> [*Exit* FACE]

>   Come, my fierce child, advance,
> We'll to our quarrelling lesson again.

KASTRIL   Agreed.
> I love a Spanish boy, with all my heart.   85

SUBTLE
> Nay, and by this means, sir, you shall be brother
> To a great Count.

---

71   *Por . . . tarda?* 'For the love of God, what is it that makes her delay?'
76–7 *Señora . . . hermosura* 'My lady, my person is wholly unworthy to approach such
         beauty.'
80   *Señora . . . entremos* 'Señora, if it is convenient, let us go in.' (There is a pun on 'serve'
         here.)
83   *the word* i.e. to begin her 'fit'.

KASTRIL   Ay, I knew that, at first.
  This match will advance the house of the Kastrils.
SUBTLE
  Pray God, your sister prove but pliant.
KASTRIL   Why,
  Her name is so: by her other husband.
SUBTLE   How!   90
KASTRIL
  The widow Pliant. Knew you not that?
SUBTLE   No faith, sir.
  Yet, by erection of her figure, I guessed it.
  Come, let's go practise.
KASTRIL   Yes, but do you think, Doctor,
  I e'er shall quarrel well?
SUBTLE   .   I warrant you.

                          [*Exeunt* SUBTLE, KASTRIL]

ACT IV, SCENE v

[*Enter*] DOL *in her fit of talking,* MAMMON

DOL
  For, after Alexander's death –
MAMMON   Good lady –
DOL
  That Perdicas, and Antigonus were slain,
  The two that stood, Seleuc', and Ptolomee –
MAMMON
  Madam.

87   *great Count* an aural quibble on 'cunt'.
92   *by erection of her figure* by the drawing of her horoscope. Subtle also suggests the
      erection which Dame Pliant's figure has aroused in him.

1–32   *after . . . Rome* Dol's diatribe is a patchwork of quotations from Hugh Broughton's *A
       Concent of Scripture* (1590) which attempts to answer questions of Old Testament
       chronology.
2–3   *Perdicas . . . Antigonus . . . Seleuc' . . . Ptolomee* the four generals of Alexander the Great,
       recipients of his divided empire. Alexander's empire was interpreted as one of the
       'four kingdoms' mentioned by Daniel in his interpretation of Nebuchadnezzar's dream.

DOL   Made up the two legs, and the fourth Beast.
That was Gog-north, and Egypt-south: which after   5
Was called Gog-Iron-leg, and South-Iron-leg –

MAMMON   Lady –

DOL

And then Gog-horned. So was Egypt, too.
Then Egypt-clay-leg, and Gog-clay-leg –

MAMMON   Sweet madam.

DOL

And last God-dust, and Egypt-dust, which fall
In the last link of the fourth chain. And these   10
Be stars in story, which none see, or look at –

MAMMON

What shall I do?

DOL   For, as he says, except
We call the Rabbins, and the heathen Greeks –

MAMMON

Dear lady.

DOL   To come from Salem, and from Athens,
And teach the people of Great Britain –

[*Enter* FACE *dressed as bellows-man*]

FACE   What's the matter, sir?   15

DOL

To speak the tongue of Eber, and Javan –

MAMMON   O,
She's in her fit.

DOL   We shall know nothing –

FACE   Death, sir,
We are undone.

DOL   Where, then, a learned linguist
Shall see the ancient used communion
Of vowels, and consonants –

FACE   My master will hear!   20

---

10   *the fourth chain* 'Fiue, as it were, chaines of time are in Scripture . . . the fourth chaine
containeth the continuance of Nebuchadnezars 70 yeares', Broughton, *Daniel his
Chaldie Visions and his Ebrew*, London, 1596, H2ᵛ.
14   *Salem* Jerusalem.
16   *Eber, and Javan* Hebrew and Gentile tongues.

DOL

A wisdom, which Pythagoras held most high –

MAMMON

Sweet honourable lady.

DOL   To comprise

All sounds of voices, in few marks of letters –

FACE

Nay, you must never hope to lay her now.

They speak together

DOL	FACE	
And so we may arrive by Talmud skill,	How did you put her into't?	
	MAMMON Alas I talked	25
And profane Greek, to raise the building up	Of a fifth monarchy I would erect,	
	With the philosopher's stone (by chance) and she	
Of Helen's house, against the Ismaelite,	Falls on the other four, straight.	
	FACE Out of Broughton!	
King of Thogarma, and his habergeons	I told you so. 'Slid stop her mouth.	
Brimstony, blue, and fiery; and the force	MAMMON Is't best?	
	FACE	
Of King Abaddon, and the Beast of Cittim:	She'll never leave else. If the old man hear her,	30
	We are but fæces, ashes.	
Which Rabbi David Kimchi, Onkelos,	SUBTLE [*Within*]	
	What's to do there?	
And Aben-Ezra do interpret Rome.	FACE O, we are lost. Now she hears him, she is quiet.	

Upon SUBTLE's *entry they disperse*
[*Exeunt* DOL *and* FACE]

MAMMON

Where shall I hide me?

25   *Talmud* the great rabbinical thesaurus.
25, 29   MAMMON MAN. F.
26   *fifth monarchy* the millennium; identified with the 'stone … cut out of the mountain without hands … that … brake in pieces the iron, the brass, the clay, the silver and the gold' of *Daniel* ii.45 – the fifth kingdom which will destroy the other four imaged by the clay-footed statue of Nebuchadnezzar's dream.
27   *With the* Which the Q.

SUBTLE   How! What sight is here!
Close deeds of darkness, and that shun the light!
Bring him again. Who is he? What, my son!   35
O, I have lived too long.
MAMMON   Nay good, dear Father,
There was no unchaste purpose.
SUBTLE   Not? And flee me,
When I come in?
MAMMON   That was my error.
SUBTLE   Error?
Guilt, guilt, my son. Give it the right name. No marvel,
If I found check in our great work within,   40
When such affairs as these were managing!
MAMMON
Why, have you so?
SUBTLE   It has stood still this half hour:
And all the rest of our less works gone back.
Where is the instrument of wickedness,
My lewd false drudge?
MAMMON   Nay, good sir, blame not him   45
Believe me, 'twas against his will, or knowledge.
I saw her by chance.
SUBTLE   Will you commit more sin,
T'excuse a varlet?
MAMMON   By my hope, 'tis true, sir.
SUBTLE
Nay, then I wonder less, if you, for whom
The blessing was prepared, would so tempt heaven: 50
And lose your fortunes.
MAMMON   Why, sir?
SUBTLE   This'll retard
The work, a month at least.
MAMMON   Why, if it do,
What remedy? But think it not, good Father:
Our purposes were honest.
SUBTLE   As they were,
So the reward will prove.

41   *managing* taking place.
42   *stood still* gone back Q.
43   *gone back* stand still Q.
51   *This'll retard* This will hinder Q.

A great crack and noise within
How now! Ay me.   55
God, and all saints be good to us. What's that?

[*Enter* FACE]

FACE

O sir, we are defeated! All the works
Are flown *in fumo*: every glass is burst.
Furnace, and all rent down! As if a bolt
Of thunder had been driven through the house.   60
Retorts, receivers, pelicans, boltheads,
All struck in shivers!
                        SUBTLE *falls down as in a swoon*
                Help, good, sir! Alas,
Coldness, and death invades him. Nay, sir Mammon,
Do the fair offices of a man! You stand,
As you were readier to depart, than he.   65
                                One knocks
Who's there? My lord her brother is come.
MAMMON   Ha, Lungs?
FACE

His coach is at the door. Avoid his sight,
For he's as furious, as his sister is mad.
MAMMON

Alas!
FACE   My brain is quite undone with the fume, sir,
I ne'er must hope to be mine own man again.   70
MAMMON

Is all lost, Lungs? Will nothing be preserved,
Of all our cost?
FACE   Faith, very little, sir.
A peck of coals, or so, which is cold comfort, sir.
MAMMON

O my voluptuous mind! I am justly punished.
FACE

And so am I, sir.
MAMMON   Cast from all my hopes –   75

---

58   *in fumo* in smoke.
61   *receivers* vessels used to retain distillates.

FACE
Nay, certainties, sir.

MAMMON   By mine own base affections.

                              SUBTLE *seems to come to himself*

SUBTLE
O, the curst fruits of vice, and lust!

MAMMON   Good father,
It was my sin. Forgive it.

SUBTLE   Hangs my roof
Over us still, and will not fall, O justice,
Upon us, for this wicked man!

FACE   Nay, look, sir,   80
You grieve him, now, with staying in his sight:
Good sir, the nobleman will come too, and take you,
And that may breed a tragedy.

MAMMON   I'll go.

FACE
Ay, and repent at home, sir. It may be,
For some good penance, you may ha' it, yet,   85
A hundred pound to the box at Bedlam –

MAMMON   Yes.

FACE
For the restoring such as ha' their wits.

MAMMON   I'll do't.

FACE
I'll send one to you to receive it.

MAMMON   Do.
Is no projection left?

FACE   All flown, or stinks, sir.

MAMMON
Will nought be saved, that's good for med'cine, thinkst thou?   90

FACE
I cannot tell, sir. There will be, perhaps,
Something, about the scraping of the shards,
Will cure the itch: though not your itch of mind, sir.
It shall be saved for you, and sent home. Good sir,
This way: for fear the lord should meet you.

                              [*Exit* MAMMON]

SUBTLE   Face.   95

86   *box* charity collection box.
93   *itch* a contagious pustular disease in which the skin is inflamed and itchy.

472

FACE
  Ay.
SUBTLE Is he gone?
FACE   Yes, and as heavily
  As all the gold he hoped for, were in his blood.
  Let us be light, though.
SUBTLE   Ay, as balls, and bound
  And hit our heads against the roof for joy:
  There's so much of our care now cast away.   100
FACE
  Now to our Don.
SUBTLE   Yes, your young widow, by this time
  Is made a Countess, Face: she's been in travail
  Of a young heir for you.
FACE   Good, sir.
SUBTLE   Off with your case,
  And greet her kindly, as a bridegroom should,
  After these common hazards.
FACE   Very well, sir.   105
  Will you go fetch Don Diego off, the while?
SUBTLE
  And fetch him over too, if you'll be pleased, sir:
  Would Dol were in her place, to pick his pockets now.
FACE
  Why, you can do it as well, if you would set to't.
  I pray you prove your virtue.
SUBTLE   For your sake, sir.   110
                    [*Exeunt* SUBTLE *and* FACE]

---

98   *balls* bubbles.
99–100 The final syllables of these lines would have rhymed in 17th-century pronunciation.
102   *travail* labour.
103   *case* disguise.
106   *fetch . . . off* keep him away.
107   *fetch . . . over* get one up on him.

ACT IV, SCENE vi

[*Enter*] SURLY, DAME PLIANT

SURLY

Lady, you see into what hands you are fall'n;
'Mongst what a nest of villians! And how near
Your honour was t'have catched a certain clap
(Through your credulity) had I but been
So punctually forward, as place, time,   5
And other circumstance would ha' made a man:
For you're a handsome woman: would y'were wise, too.
I am a gentleman, come here disguised,
Only to find the knaveries of this citadel,
And where I might have wronged your honour, and have not,   10
I claim some interest in your love. You are,
They say, a widow, rich: and I am a bachelor,
Worth nought: your fortunes may make me a man,
As mine ha' preserved you a woman. Think upon it,
And whether, I have deserved you, or no.

PLIANT   I will, sir.   15

SURLY

And for these household-rogues, let me alone,
To treat with them.

[*Enter* SUBTLE]

SUBTLE   How doth my noble Diego?
And my dear madam, Countess? Hath the Count
Been courteous, lady? Liberal? And open?
Donzell, methinks you look melancholic,   20
After your *coitum*, and scurvy! Truly,
I do not like the dulness of your eye:
It hath a heavy cast, 'tis upsee Dutch,
And says you are a lumpish whore-master,
Be lighter, I will make your pockets so.   25

He falls to picking of them

---

3   *clap* then, as now, gonorrhoea; but also used to mean any sudden stroke of misfortune.
16   SURLY SVB. F.
23   *upsee Dutch* from the Dutch *op zijn*: 'to be up'; i.e. a drinking term like 'bottoms up';
     here the phrase probably means something like 'drunk as a Dutchman'.

SURLY

Will you, Don bawd, and pickpurse? How now?

> [*Sets on him*]
> Reel you?

Stand up sir, you shall find since I am so heavy,
I'll gi' you equal weight.

SUBTLE   Help, murder!

SURLY   No, sir.

There's no such thing intended. A good cart,
And a clean whip shall ease you of that fear.   30
I am the Spanish Don, that should be cozened,
Do you see? Cozened? Where's your Captain Face?
That parcel-broker, and whole-bawd, all rascal.

> [*Enter* FACE *dressed as Captain*]

FACE

How, Surly!

SURLY   O, make your approach, good Captain.

I have found, from whence your copper rings, and spoons   35
Come now, wherewith you cheat abroad in taverns.
'Twas here, you learned t'anoint your boot with brimstone,
Then rub men's gold on't, for a kind of touch,
And say 'twas naught, when you had changed the colour,
That you might ha't for nothing? And this Doctor,   40
Your sooty, smoky-bearded compeer, he
Will close you so much gold, in a bolt's head,
And, on a turn, convey (i' the stead) another
With sublimed mercury, that shall burst i' the heat,
And fly out all *in fumo*? Then weeps Mammon: 45
Then swoons his worship. Or, he is the Faustus,

29–30   *cart . . . whip* To be whipped behind a cart was a common public punishment for prostitutes.

33   *parcel-broker* part-broker; 'broker' means 'pawnbroker'; probably a receiver of stolen goods.

37–9   *anoint . . . colour* Gold was tested by being rubbed against a touchstone on which it left a trace whose quality could be analysed.

40–5   *Doctor . . . in fumo* a trick by which the fraudulent alchemist pockets the gold (in a bolt's head) and replaces it with a similar container holding mercury which will then explode and give the appearance of the gold being lost in smoke.

41   *compeer* colleague.

46   *Faustus* Johann Faustus, the damned necromancer hero of Marlowe's *Doctor Faustus*.

[FACE *slips out*]

That casteth figures, and can conjure, cures
Plague, piles, and pox, by the ephemerides,
And holds intelligence with all the bawds,
And midwives of three shires? While you send in –   50
Captain, (what is he gone?) damsels with child,
Wives, that are barren, or, the waiting-maid
With the green sickness?

[SUBTLE *attempts to leave*]
Nay, sir, you must tarry
Though he be 'scaped; and answer, by the ears, sir.

ACT IV, SCENE vii

[*Enter*] FACE, KASTRIL [*to them*]

FACE

Why, now's the time, if ever you will quarrel
Well (as they say) and be a true-born child.
The Doctor, and your sister both are abused.

KASTRIL

Where is he? Which is he? He is a slave
Whate'er he is, and the son of a whore. Are you   5
The man, sir, I would know?

SURLY   I should be loath, sir,
To confess so much.

KASTRIL   Then you lie, i' your throat.

SURLY   How?

FACE

A very errant rogue, sir, and a cheater,
Employed here, by another conjurer,
That does not love the Doctor, and would cross him   10
If he knew how –

SURLY   Sir, you are abused.

48   *ephemerides* an almanac indicating planetary positions for astrological use.
53   *green sickness* an anaemic disease to which pubertal women are susceptible.
54   *by the ears* See I.i.169.

2   *true-born child* The sense 'nobly born' was still current.

KASTRIL   You lie:
  And 'tis no matter.
FACE   Well said, sir. He is
  The impudentest rascal –
SURLY   You are indeed. Will you hear me, sir?
FACE
  By no means: bid him be gone.
KASTRIL   Be gone, sir, quickly.
SURLY
  This's strange! Lady, do you inform your brother.   15
FACE
  There is not such a foist, in all the town,
  The Doctor had him, presently: and finds, yet,
  The Spanish Count will come, here. Bear up, Subtle.
SUBTLE
  Yes, sir, he must appear, within this hour.
FACE
  And yet this rogue, would come, in a disguise,   20
  By the temptation of another spirit,
  To trouble our art, though he could not hurt it.
KASTRIL   Ay,
  I know – Away, you talk like a foolish mauther.
                              [*Exit* DAME PLIANT]
SURLY
  Sir, all is truth, she says.
FACE   Do not believe him, sir:
  He is the lyingest swabber! Come your ways, sir.   25
SURLY
  You are valiant, out of company.
KASTRIL   Yes, how then, sir?

                        [*Enter* DRUGGER]

FACE
  Nay, here's an honest fellow too, that knows him,
  And all his tricks. (Make good what I say, Abel,)
  This cheater would ha' cozened thee o' the widow.
  He owes this honest Drugger, here, seven pound,   30

16   *foist* cheat, rogue.
23   *mauther* young woman.
25   *swabber* deck-hand.
26   *out of* because you are in.

He has had on him, in two-penny 'orths of tobacco.

DRUGGER

Yes sir. And he's damned himself, three terms, to pay me.

FACE

And what does he owe for *lotium?*

DRUGGER   Thirty shillings, sir:

And for six syringes.

SURLY   Hydra of villany!

FACE

Nay, sir, you must quarrel him out o' the house.

KASTRIL   I will.   35

Sir, if you get not out o' doors, you lie:

And you are a pimp.

SURLY   Why, this is madness, sir,

Not valour in you: I must laugh at this.

KASTRIL

It is my humour: you are a pimp, and a trig,

And an Amadis de Gaul, or a Don Quixote.   40

DRUGGER

Or a Knight o' the Curious Coxcomb. Do you see?

[*Enter* ANANIAS]

ANANIAS

Peace to the household.

KASTRIL   I'll keep peace, for no man.

ANANIAS

Casting of dollars is concluded lawful.

KASTRIL

Is he the Constable?

SUBTLE   Peace, Ananias.

FACE   No, sir.

---

32   *he's* he hath Q.
33   *lotium* stale urine used by barbers as a lye for the hair.
34   *Hydra* a monster whose many heads multiplied each time one was severed – a fitting
     epithet for Face.
39   *trig* coxcomb.
40   *Amadis de Gaul* the name of a Spanish or Portuguese romance written up by Garcia
     de Montalvo in the second half of the 15th century.
     Don Quixote eponymous hero of Cervantes' novel; the *Amadis de Gaul* is one of the
     few romances excused from burning in *Don Quixote*.
41   *Knight o' the Curious Coxcomb* a reference to Surly's extraordinary headgear.

KASTRIL
   Then you are an otter, and a shad, a whit,   45
   A very tim.
SURLY   You'll hear me, sir?
KASTRIL   I will not.
ANANIAS
   What is the motive?
SUBTLE   Zeal, in the young gentleman,
   Against his Spanish slops –
ANANIAS   They are profane,
   Lewd, superstitious, and idolatrous breeches.
SURLY
   New rascals!
KASTRIL   Will you be gone, sir?
ANANIAS   Avoid Satan,   50
   Thou art not of the light. That ruff of pride,
   About thy neck, betrays thee: and is the same
   With that, which the unclean birds, in seventy-seven,
   Were seen to prank it with, on divers coasts.
   Thou look'st like Antichrist, in that lewd hat.   55
SURLY
   I must give way.
KASTRIL   Be gone, sir.
SURLY   But I'll take
   A course with you –
ANANIAS   (Depart, proud Spanish fiend)
SURLY
   Captain, and Doctor –
ANANIAS   Child of perdition.
KASTRIL   Hence, sir.
                          [*Exit* SURLY]
   Did I not quarrel bravely?
FACE   Yes, indeed, sir.
KASTRIL
   Nay, and I give my mind to't, I shall do't.   60

45–6   *shad . . . whit . . . tim* The first of these is a small fish; the *OED* cites this passage in
       defining the other two as terms of abuse; they are Kastril's homemade insults; each
       has a diminutive sound.
52–4   *the same . . . coasts* Malcolm H. South argues that the 'unclean birds' are Catholic
       seminary priests trained on the Continent and returned to England wearing
       outlandish ruffs. 'The Vncleane Birds, in Seuenty-Seven: *The Alchemist*', *Studies in
       English Literature 1500–1900*, xiii (1973), pp. 331–43.

FACE

    O, you must follow, sir, and threaten him tame.

    He'll turn again else.

KASTRIL   I'll re-turn him, then.   [*Exit* KASTRIL]

FACE

    Drugger, this rogue prevented us, for thee:

    We had determined, that thou shouldst ha' come,

    In a Spanish suit, and ha' carried her so; and he   65

    A brokerly slave, goes, puts it on himself.

    Hast brought the damask?

DRUGGER   Yes sir.

FACE   Thou must borrow,

    A Spanish suit. Hast thou no credit with the players?

DRUGGER

    Yes, sir, did you never see me play the fool?

FACE

    I know not, Nab: thou shalt, if I can help it.   70

    Hieronymo's old cloak, ruff, and hat will serve,

    I'll tell thee more, when thou bring'st 'em.

                           [*Exit* DRUGGER]

            SUBTLE *hath whispered with him this while*

ANANIAS   Sir, I know

    The Spaniard hates the Brethren, and hath spies

    Upon their actions: and that this was one

    I make no scruple. But the holy Synod   75

    Have been in prayer, and meditation, for it.

    And 'tis revealed no less, to them, than me,

    That casting of money is most lawful.

SUBTLE   True.

    But here, I cannot do it; if the house

    Should chance to be suspected, all would out,   80

    And we be locked up, in the Tower, forever,

    To make gold there (for th' state) never come out:

    And, then, are you defeated.

---

  63   *prevented* forestalled.

67–8   *borrow . . . players* Stage costumes were augmented by court cast-offs so actors might
       have a supply of the Spanish clothes in fashion at Court.

  69   *did you never see me play the fool?* an illusion-breaking joke: the part of Drugger would
       have been taken by the leading comic actor in the company – Robert Armin in the first
       instance.

  71   *Hieronymo* the crazed, revenging hero of Kyd's *Spanish Tragedy*. It is possible that
       Jonson played this role.

ANANIAS   I will tell
  This to the Elders, and the weaker Brethren,
  That the whole company of the Separation   85
  May join in humble prayer again.
SUBTLE   (And fasting.)
ANANIAS
  Yea, for some fitter place. The peace of mind
  Rest with these walls.
SUBTLE   Thanks, courteous Ananias.

                                              [*Exit* ANANIAS]

FACE
  What did he come for?
SUBTLE   About casting dollars,
  Presently, out of hand. And so, I told him,   90
  A Spanish minister came here to spy,
  Against the faithful –
FACE   I conceive. Come Subtle,
  Thou art so down upon the least disaster!
  How wouldst th' ha' done, if I had not helped thee out?
SUBTLE
  I thank thee Face, for the angry boy, i' faith.   95
FACE
  Who would ha' looked, it should ha' been that rascal?
  Surly? He had dyed his beard, and all. Well, sir,
  Here's damask come, to make you a suit.
SUBTLE   Where's Drugger?
FACE
  He is gone to borrow me a Spanish habit,
  I'll be the Count, now.
SUBTLE   But where's the widow?   100
FACE
  Within, with my lord's sister: Madam Dol
  Is entertaining her.
SUBTLE   By your favour, Face,
  Now she is honest, I will stand again.
FACE
  You will not offer it?
SUBTLE   Why?

    96   *looked* realised; thought.
    104 *SUBTLE* SVR. F.

                          481

FACE   Stand to your word,
  Or – here comes Dol. She knows –
SUBTLE   You're tyrannous still.   105

[*Enter* DOL]

FACE
  Strict for my right. How now, Dol? Hast told her,
  The Spanish Count will come?
DOL   Yes, but another is come,
  You little looked for!
FACE   Who's that?
DOL   Your master:
  The master of the house.
SUBTLE   How, Dol!
FACE   She lies.
  This is some trick. Come, leave your quiblins, Dorothy.   110
DOL
  Look out, and see.
SUBTLE   Art thou in earnest?
DOL   'Slight,
  Forty o' the neighbours are about him, talking.
FACE
  'Tis he, by this good day.
DOL   'Twill prove ill day,
  For some on us.
FACE   We are undone, and taken.
DOL
  Lost, I am afraid.
SUBTLE   You said he would not come,   115
  While there died one a week, within the liberties.
FACE
  No: 'twas within the walls.
SUBTLE   Was't so? Cry you mercy:
  I thought the liberties. What shall we do now, Face?
FACE
  Be silent: not a word, if he call, or knock.
  I'll into mine old shape again, and meet him,   120

110   *quiblins* tricks.
116   *liberties* the area surrounding a town subject to municipal authority.

Of Jeremy, the butler. I' the mean time,
Do you two pack up all the goods, and purchase,
That we can carry i' the two trunks. I'll keep him
Off for today, if I cannot longer: and then
At night, I'll ship you both away to Ratcliff,   125
Where we'll meet tomorrow, and there we'll share.
Let Mammon's brass, and pewter keep the cellar:
We'll have another time for that. But, Dol,
Pray thee, go heat a little water, quickly,
Subtle must shave me. All my Captain's beard   130
Must off, to make me appear smooth Jeremy.
You'll do't?

SUBTLE   Yes, I'll shave you, as well as I can.

FACE

And not cut my throat, but trim me?

SUBTLE   You shall see, sir.

               [*Exeunt* SUBTLE, FACE, DOL]

---

122   *purchase* gains.
125   *Ratcliff* a riverside district of east London.
126   *there* then Q.

ACT V, SCENE i

[In the street outside Lovewit's house]

[Enter] LOVEWIT, NEIGHBOURS

LOVEWIT
  Has there been such resort, say you?
NEIGHBOUR 1   Daily, sir.
NEIGHBOUR 2
  And nightly, too.
NEIGHBOUR 3 ·   Ay, some as brave as lords.
NEIGHBOUR 4
  Ladies, and gentlewomen.
NEIGHBOUR 5   Citizens' wives.
NEIGHBOUR 1
  And knights.
NEIGHBOUR 6 In coaches.
NEIGHBOUR 2   Yes, and oyster-women.
NEIGHBOUR 1
  Beside other gallants.
NEIGHBOUR 3   Sailors' wives.
NEIGHBOUR 4   Tobacco-men.   5
NEIGHBOUR 5
  Another Pimlico!
LOVEWIT   What should my knave advance,
  To draw this company? He hung out no banners
  Of a strange calf, with five legs, to be seen?
  Or a huge lobster, with six claws?
NEIGHBOUR 6   No, sir.
NEIGHBOUR 3
  We had gone in then, sir.
LOVEWIT   He has no gift   10

---

  1   *resort* thronging of people.
  4   *oyster-women* female oyster sellers.
  6   *Pimlico* not the present Pimlico but a place in Hoxton (then Hogsden), east of the
       city, famous for pies and 'Pimlico' nut-brown ale.
       advance produce.
  8   *calf . . . legs* See *Bartholmew Fair*, V.iv.75–6, where this calf has matured to a bull.
       Such deformities were great money-spinners.

Of teaching i' the nose, that e'er I knew of!
You saw no bills set up, that promised cure
Of agues, or the toothache?
NEIGHBOUR 2   No such thing, sir.
LOVEWIT
Nor heard a drum struck, for baboons, or puppets?
NEIGHBOUR 5
Neither, sir.
LOVEWIT   What device should he bring forth now!   15
I love a teeming wit, as I love my nourishment.
Pray God he ha' not kept such open house,
That he hath sold my hangings, and my bedding:
I left him nothing else. If he have eat 'em,
A plague o' the moth, say I. Sure he has got   20
Some bawdy pictures, to call all this ging;
The Friar, and the Nun; or the new motion
Of the Knight's courser, covering the Parson's mare;
The boy of six year old, with the great thing:
Or 't may be, he has the fleas that run at tilt,   25
Upon a table, or some dog to dance?
When saw you him?
NEIGHBOUR 1   Who sir, Jeremy?
NEIGHBOUR 2   Jeremy butler?
We saw him not this month.
LOVEWIT   How!
NEIGHBOUR 4   Not these five weeks, sir.
NEIGHBOUR 1
These six weeks, at the least.
LOVEWIT   Y' amaze me, neighbours!
NEIGHBOUR 5
Sure, if your worship know not where he is,   30
He's slipped away.
NEIGHBOUR 6   Pray God, he be not made away!

---

11   *teaching i' the nose* i.e. with an impressive twang; la di da.
14   *drum struck* to 'drum up' a crowd.
21   *ging* gang; crowd.
22   *motion* puppet show.
24   *The boy . . . thing* 'but of all the sights that ever were in London since I married,
      methinks the little child that was so fair grown about the members was the prettiest'
      Francis Beaumont, *The Knight of the Burning Pestle*, III.273–5.
25   *at tilt* in a duel or tilting match.
29   *NEIGHBOUR 1* ed. Q, F omit 1.

LOVEWIT

Ha? It's no time to question, then.   *He knocks*

NEIGHBOUR 6   About

Some three weeks since, I heard a doleful cry,

As I sat up, a-mending my wife's stockings.

LOVEWIT

This's strange! That none will answer! Didst thou hear   35

A cry, saist thou?

NEIGHBOUR 6   Yes, sir, like unto a man

That had been strangled an hour, and could not speak.

NEIGHBOUR 2

I heard it too, just this day three weeks, at two o'clock

Next morning.

LOVEWIT   These be miracles, or you make 'em so!

A man an hour strangled, and could not speak,   40

And both you heard him cry?

NEIGHBOUR 3   Yes, downward, sir.

LOVEWIT

Thou art a wise fellow: give me thy hand I pray thee.

What trade art thou on?

NEIGHBOUR 3   A smith, and't please your worship.

LOVEWIT

A smith? Then, lend me thy help, to get this door open.

NEIGHBOUR 3

That I will presently, sir, but fetch my tools –   45

                    [*Exit* NEIGHBOUR 3]

NEIGHBOUR 1

Sir, best to knock again, afore you break it.

ACT V, SCENE ii

LOVEWIT

I will. [*Knocks*]

    [FACE, *clean-shaven as Jeremy, opens door*]

FACE   What mean you, sir?

---

1   The trick used in this scene resembles the one played by the servant Tranio on his master Theropides in Plautus' *Mostellaria*.

NEIGHBOURS 1, 2, 4   O, here's Jeremy!
FACE
   Good sir, come from the door.
LOVEWIT   Why! What's the matter?
FACE
   Yet farther, you are too near, yet.
LOVEWIT   I'the name of wonder!
   What means the fellow?
FACE   The house, sir, has been visited.
LOVEWIT
   What? With the plague? Stand thou then farther.
FACE   No, sir,   5
   I had it not.
LOVEWIT   Who had it then? I left
   None else, but thee, i'the house!
FACE   Yes, sir. My fellow,
   The cat, that kept the buttery, had it on her
   A week, before I spied it: but I got her
   Conveyed away, i'the night. And so I shut   10
   The house up for a month –
LOVEWIT   How!
FACE   Purposing then, sir,
   T'have burnt rose-vinegar, treacle, and tar,
   And, ha' made it sweet, that you should ne'er ha' known it:
   Because I knew the news would but afflict you, sir.
LOVEWIT
   Breathe less, and farther off. Why, this is stranger!   15
   The neighbours tell me all, here, that the doors
   Have still been open –
FACE   How, sir!
LOVEWIT   Gallants, men, and women,
   And of all sorts, tag-rag, been seen to flock here
   In threaves, these ten weeks, as to a second Hogsden,
   In days of Pimlico, and Eye-bright!
FACE   Sir,   20
   Their wisdoms will not say so!

19   *threaves* throngs.
     Hogsden Hoxton.
20   *Eye-bright* a drinking place which made its name before Pimlico. *H.&S.* quote '*Pimlico.*
     Or Runne Red-Cap: Eye-bright, (so fam'd of late for *Beere*)/Although thy *Name* be
     numbered heere,/Thine ancient Honors now runne low;/Thou art struck blind by
     Pimlyco.' Perhaps its famous beer contained the herb Eyebright (*Euphrasia*).

LOVEWIT   Today, they speak
  Of coaches, and gallants; one in a French hood,
  Went in, they tell me: and another was seen
  In a velvet gown, at the window! Divers more
  Pass in and out!
FACE   They did pass through the doors then,   25
  Or walls, I assure their eyesights, and their spectacles;
  For here, sir, are the keys: and here have been,
  In this my pocket, now, above twenty days!
  And for before, I kept the fort alone, there.
  But, that 'tis yet not deep i'the afternoon,   30
  I should believe my neighbours had seen double
  Through the black pot, and made these apparitions!
  For, on my faith, to your worship, for these three weeks,
  And upwards, the door has not been opened.
LOVEWIT   Strange!
NEIGHBOUR 1
  Good faith, I think I saw a coach!
NEIGHBOUR 2   And I too,   35
  I'd ha' been sworn!
LOVEWIT   Do you but think it now?
  And but one coach?
NEIGHBOUR 4   We cannot tell, sir: Jeremy
  Is a very honest fellow.
FACE   Did you see me at all?
NEIGHBOUR 1
  No. That we are sure on.
NEIGHBOUR 2   I'll be sworn o' that.
LOVEWIT
  Fine rogues, to have your testimonies built on!   40

[Enter NEIGHBOUR 3 *with his tools]*

NEIGHBOUR 3
  Is Jeremy come?
NEIGHBOUR 1   O, yes, you may leave your tools,
  We were deceived, he says.

---

24   *window* windore Q, F.
32   *apparitions* The English title of Plautus' *Mostellaria* is *The Haunted House.*
42   NEIGHBOUR 1 MEI Q.

NEIGHBOUR 2   He's had the keys:
And the door has been shut these three weeks.
NEIGHBOUR 3   Like enough.
LOVEWIT
   Peace, and get hence, you changelings.

                    [*Enter* SURLY *and* MAMMON]

FACE   Surly come!
   And Mammon made acquainted? They'll tell all.   45
   (How shall I beat them off? What shall I do?)
   Nothing's more wretched, than a guilty conscience.

ACT V, SCENE iii

SURLY
   No, sir, he was a great physician. This,
   It was no bawdy-house: but a mere chancel.
   You knew the lord, and his sister.
MAMMON   Nay, good Surly –
SURLY
   The happy word, 'be rich' –
MAMMON   Play not the tyrant –
SURLY
   Should be today pronounced, to all your friends.   5
   And where be your andirons now? And your brass pots?
   That should ha' been golden flagons, and great wedges?
MAMMON
   Let me but breathe. What! They ha' shut their doors,
   Me thinks!
                         MAMMON *and* SURLY *knock*
SURLY   Ay, now, 'tis holiday with them.
MAMMON   Rogues,
   Cozeners, imposters, bawds.

---

44   *changelings* those of unstable wits; so-called because they change their stories.
47   *Mostellaria* 544: 'Nihil est miserius quam animus hominis conscius'.

2   *chancel* the part of the church used for priestly offices.

FACE   What mean you, sir?   10
MAMMON
  To enter if we can.
FACE   Another man's house?
  Here is the owner, sir. Turn you to him,
  And speak your business.
MAMMON   Are you, sir, the owner?
LOVEWIT
  Yes, sir.
MAMMON And are those knaves, within, your cheaters?
LOVEWIT
  What knaves? What cheaters?
MAMMON   Subtle, and his Lungs.   15
FACE
  The gentleman is distracted, sir! No lungs,
  Nor lights ha' been seen here these three weeks, sir,
  Within these doors, upon my word!
SURLY   Your word,
  Groom arrogant?
FACE   Yes, sir, I am the housekeeper
  And know the keys ha' not been out o' my hands.   20
SURLY
  This's a new Face?
FACE   You do mistake the house, sir!
  What sign was't at?
SURLY   You rascal! This is one
  O' the confederacy. Come, let's get officers,
  And force the door.
LOVEWIT   Pray you stay, gentlemen.
SURLY
  No, sir, we'll come with warrant.
MAMMON   Ay, and then,   25
  We shall ha' your doors open.
                   [*Exeunt* SURLY, MAMMON]
LOVEWIT   What means this?
FACE
  I cannot tell, sir!

---

  16   *distracted* out of his wits.
16–17 *lungs . . . lights* puns on the anatomical sense of 'lights': entrails.
  22   *sign* Public eating houses, taverns and brothels all had signs like modern pub signs.

NEIGHBOUR 1   These are two o' the gallants,
That we do think we saw.
FACE   Two o' the fools?
You talk as idly as they. Good faith, sir,
I think the moon has crazed 'em all!

[*Enter* KASTRIL]

(O me,   30
The angry boy come too? He'll make a noise,
And ne'er away till he have betrayed us all.)

KASTRIL *knocks*

KASTRIL
What rogues, bawds, slaves, you'll open the door anon,
Punk, cockatrice, my suster. By this light
I'll fetch the marshal to you. You are a whore,   35
To keep your castle –
FACE   Who would you speak with, sir?
KASTRIL
The bawdy Doctor, and the cozening Captain,
And Puss my suster.
LOVEWIT   This is something, sure!
FACE
Upon my trust, the doors were never open, sir.
KASTRIL
I have heard all their tricks, told me twice over,   40
By the fat knight, and the lean gentleman.
LOVEWIT
Here comes another.

[*Enter* ANANIAS, TRIBULATION]

FACE   Ananias too?
And his pastor?
TRIBULATION   The doors are shut against us.

They beat too, at the door

ANANIAS
Come forth, you seed of sulphur, sons of fire,

---

30   *the moon* creator of lunacy.
34   *cockatrice* a serpent, usually identified with the death-glancing Basilisk. Here it is
     used partly for its association with 'cock' (it was often used for prostitutes).
44   *sulphur, sons of fire* Vipers, Sonnes of Belial Q.

Your stench, it is broke forth: abomination   45
Is in the house.

KASTRIL   Ay, my suster's there.

ANANIAS   The place,
It is become a cage of unclean birds.

KASTRIL
Yes, I will fetch the scavenger, and the constable.

TRIBULATION
You shall do well.

ANANIAS   We'll join, to weed them out.

KASTRIL
You will not come then? Punk, device, my suster!   50

ANANIAS
Call her not sister. She is a harlot, verily.

KASTRIL
I'll raise the street.

LOVEWIT   Good gentlemen, a word.

ANANIAS
Satan, avoid, and hinder not our zeal.

> [*Exeunt* ANANIAS, TRIBULATION, KASTRIL]

LOVEWIT
The world's turned Bedlam.

FACE   These are all broke loose,
Out of St. Katherine's, where they use to keep,   55
The better sort of mad folks.

NEIGHBOUR 1   All these persons
We saw go in, and out, here.

NEIGHBOUR 2   Yes, indeed, sir.

NEIGHBOUR 3
These were the parties.

---

45   *stench, it* wickednesse Q.
46   *Ay,* not in Q.
47   *cage . . . birds* see IV.vii. 53 and *Revelation* xviii.2.
48   *Yes* I (i.e. Ay) Q.
      scavenger officer responsible for keeping streets clean and orderly.
50   *Punk, device* perhaps by analogy with 'point-device' (faultlessly proper in dress). But 'device' may be an independent noun in his list of insults; in which case he is calling his sister a whore and a contraption.
53   *avoid* clear off.
55   *St. Katherine's* In fact the Hospital of St. Mary 'that was prouided for poore priests, and others, men and women in the City of London, that were fallen into frensie or losse of their memory' (Stow, ii, 143). This had been taken over by the Hospital of St. Katherine (on the north side of the Thames, just east of the Tower).

FACE   Peace, you drunkards. Sir,
  I wonder at it! Please you, to give me leave
  To touch the door, I'll try, and the lock be changed.   60

LOVEWIT
  It mazes me!

FACE   Good faith, sir, I believe,
  There's no such thing. 'Tis all *deceptio visus.*
  (Would I could get him away.)

                            DAPPER *cries out within*

DAPPER   Master Captain, master Doctor.

LOVEWIT
  Who's that?

FACE   (Our clerk within, that I forgot!) I know not, sir.

DAPPER
  For God's sake, when will her Grace be at leisure?

FACE   Ha!   65
  Illusions, some spirit o' the air: (his gag is melted,
  And now he sets out the throat.)

DAPPER   I am almost stifled –

FACE
  (Would you were altogether.)

LOVEWIT   'Tis i' the house.
  Ha! List.

FACE   Believe it, sir, i' the air!

LOVEWIT   Peace, you –

DAPPER
  Mine aunt's Grace does not use me well.

SUBTLE [*Within*]   You fool,   70
  Peace, you'll mar all.

FACE   Or you will else, you rogue.

LOVEWIT
  O, is it so? Then you converse with spirits!
  Come sir. No more o' your tricks, good Jeremy,
  The truth, the shortest way.

FACE   Dismiss this rabble, sir.
  What shall I do? I am catched.

LOVEWIT   Good neighbours,   75
  I thank you all. You may depart.

60   *and* either 'even if' or 'and see if'.
62   *deceptio visus* an optical illusion.
67   *sets out the throat* raises his voice.

[*Exeunt* NEIGHBOURS]
Come sir,
You know that I am an indulgent master:
And therefore, conceal nothing. What's your med'cine,
To draw so many several sorts of wild-fowl?

FACE

Sir, you were wont to affect mirth, and wit: 80
(But here's no place to talk on't i' the street.)
Give me but leave, to make the best of my fortune,
And only pardon me th'abuse of your house:
It's all I beg. I'll help you to a widow,
In recompense, that you shall gi' me thanks for,   85
Will make you seven years younger, and a rich one.
'Tis but your putting on a Spanish cloak,
I have her within. You need not fear the house,
It was not visited.

LOVEWIT   But by me, who came
Sooner than you expected.

FACE   It is true, sir.   90
'Pray you forgive me.

LOVEWIT   Well: let's see your widow.
[*Exeunt* LOVEWIT, FACE]

ACT V, SCENE iv

[*Inside Lovewit's house*]

[*Enter* SUBTLE, DAPPER]

SUBTLE

How! Ha' you eaten your gag?

DAPPER   Yes faith, it crumbled
Away i' my mouth.

SUBTLE   You ha' spoiled all then.

DAPPER   No,
I hope my aunt of Fairy will forgive me.

SUBTLE

Your aunt's a gracious lady: but in troth
You were to blame.

DAPPER   The fume did overcome me,   5
And I did do't to stay my stomach. 'Pray you
So satisfy her Grace. Here comes the Captain.

[*Enter* FACE]

FACE
How now! Is his mouth down?
SUBTLE   Ay! He has spoken!
FACE
(A pox, I heard him, and you too.) He's undone, then.
(I have been fain to say, the house is haunted   10
With spirits, to keep churl back.
SUBTLE   And hast thou done it?
FACE
Sure, for this night.
SUBTLE   Why, then triumph, and sing
Of Face so famous, the precious king
Of present wits.
FACE   Did you not hear the coil,
About the door?
SUBTLE   Yes, and I dwindled with it.)   15
FACE
Show him his aunt, and let him be dispatched:
I'll send her to you.   [*Exit* FACE]
SUBTLE   Well sir, your aunt her Grace,
Will give you audience presently, on my suit,
And the Captain's word, that you did not eat your gag,
In any contempt of her Highness.
DAPPER   Not I, in troth, sir.   20

[*Enter*] DOL *like the Queen of Fairy*

SUBTLE
Here she is come. Down o' your knees, and wriggle:
She has a stately presence. Good. Yet nearer,
And bid, God save you.
DAPPER   Madam.

---

7   s.d. *Enter* FACE who might now need a false beard since he was shaved at the end of
     Act IV (IV.vii.130–1).
8   *mouth down* gag gone.
11 *churl* countryman.
14 *coil* row.   23   *you* her Q.

SUBTLE   And your aunt.

DAPPER

And my most gracious aunt, God save your Grace.

DOL

Nephew, we thought to have been angry with you: 25
But that sweet face of yours, hath turned the tide,
And made it flow with joy, that ebbed of love.
Arise, and touch our velvet gown.

SUBTLE   The skirts,
And kiss 'em. So.

DOL   Let me now stroke that head,
Much, nephew, shalt thou win; much shalt thou spend;   30
Much shalt thou give away: much shalt thou lend.

SUBTLE

(Ay, much, indeed.) Why do you not thank her Grace?

DAPPER

I cannot speak, for joy.

SUBTLE   See, the kind wretch!
Your Grace's kinsman right.

DOL   Give me the bird.
Here is your fly in a purse, about your neck, cousin,   35
Wear it, and feed it, about this day se'ennight,
On your right wrist –

SUBTLE   Open a vein, with a pin,
And let it suck but once a week: till then,
You must not look on't.

DOL   No. And, kinsman,
Bear yourself worthy of the blood you come on.   40

SUBTLE

Her Grace would ha' you eat no more Woolsack pies,
Nor Dagger frume'ty.

DOL   Nor break his fast,
In Heaven, and Hell.

---

33   *kind* showing the affections of kin.
34   *bird* Dapper's fly-familiar is a bird in fairyland.
36   *se'ennight* week (seven nights).
41   *Woolsack pies* pies from the Woolsack tavern – probably the one outside Aldgate.
42   *Dagger frume'ty* See I.i.191.
43   *Heaven, and Hell* drinking places in Westminster, popular with lawyers' clerks. Hell
      had once been a debtor's prison.

SUBTLE She's with you everywhere!
　Nor play with costermongers, at mum-chance, tray-trip,
　God-make-you-rich, (whenas your aunt has done it:) but keep　　45
　The gallantest company, and the best games –
DAPPER　　　　　　　　　　　　　　　　　　Yes, sir.
SUBTLE
　Gleek and primero: and what you get, be true to us.
DAPPER
　By this hand, I will.
SUBTLE　　　　　　You may bring's a thousand pound,
　Before tomorrow night, (if but three thousand,
　Be stirring) an' you will.
DAPPER　　　　　　　　I swear, I will then.　　　　　　50
SUBTLE
　Your fly will learn you all games.
FACE [*Within*]　　　　　　　Ha' you done there?
SUBTLE
　Your grace will command him no more duties?
DOL　　　　　　　　　　　　No:
　But come, and see me often. I may chance
　To leave him three or four hundred chests of treasure,
　And some twelve thousand acres of Fairyland:　　　　　55
　If he game well, and comely, with good gamesters.
SUBTLE
　There's a kind aunt! Kiss her departing part.
　But you must sell your forty mark a year, now:
DAPPER
　Ay, sir, I mean.
SUBTLE　　　　　Or, gi't away: pox on't.
DAPPER
　I'll gi't mine aunt. I'll go and fetch the writings.　　　60

44　*mum-chance, tray-trip* dice games.
45　*God-make-you-rich* a kind of backgammon.
47　*Gleek and primero* See II.iii.284–5.
50　*an'* if Q.
　　an' you will should you feel like it.
51　*learn* teach.
55　*twelve* fiue Q.
56　*comely* (adv.) 'comelily'.
57　*her departing part* i.e. her backside.
58　*your* Q; you F.
59　*pox* A pox Q.
60　DAPPER FAC. Q, F.

SUBTLE

   'Tis well, away.

                                 [*Exit* DAPPER]

              [*Enter* FACE]

FACE   Where's Subtle?

SUBTLE   Here. What news?

FACE

   Drugger is at the door, go take his suit,

   And bid him fetch a parson, presently:

   Say, he shall marry the widow. Thou shalt spend

   A hundred pound by the service!

                         [*Exit* SUBTLE]

                    Now, queen Dol,   65

   Ha' you packed up all?

DOL   Yes.

FACE   And how do you like

   The lady Pliant?

DOL   A good dull innocent.

             [*Enter* SUBTLE]

SUBTLE

   Here's your Hieronimo's cloak, and hat.

FACE   Give me 'em.

SUBTLE

   And the ruff too?

FACE   Yes, I'll come to you presently.   [*Exit* FACE]

SUBTLE

   Now, he is gone about his project, Dol,   70

   I told you of, for the widow.

DOL   'Tis direct

   Against our articles.

SUBTLE   Well, we'll fit him, wench.

   Hast thou gulled her of her jewels, or her bracelets?

DOL

   No, but I will do't.

SUBTLE   Soon at night, my Dolly,

   When we are shipped, and all our goods aboard,   75

---

  64   *spend* have to spend; i.e. gain.

  72   *articles* of faith (their 'venture tripartite', I.i.135).

Eastward for Ratcliff; we will turn our course
To Brainford, westward, if thou saist the word:
And take our leaves of this o'erweening rascal,
This peremptory Face.

DOL   Content, I am weary of him.

SUBTLE
Th' hast cause, when the slave will run a-wiving, Dol,   80
Against the instrument, that was drawn between us.

DOL
I'll pluck his bird as bare as I can.

SUBTLE   Yes, tell her,
She must by any means, address some present
To th' cunning man; make him amends, for wronging
His art with her suspicion; send a ring;   85
Or chain of pearl; she will be tortured else
Extremely in her sleep, say: and ha' strange things
Come to her. Wilt thou?

DOL   Yes.

SUBTLE   My fine flitter-mouse,
My bird o'the night; we'll tickle it at the Pigeons,
When we have all, and may unlock the trunks,   90
And say, this's mine, and thine, and thine, and mine –

                                                        They kiss

                    [*Enter* FACE]

FACE
What now, a-billing?

SUBTLE   Yes, a little exalted
In the good passage of our stock-affairs.

FACE
Drugger has brought his parson, take him in, Subtle,
And send Nab back again, to wash his face.   95

SUBTLE
I will: and shave himself?

77   *Brainford* Brentford, in Middlesex.
81   *instrument* agreement.
88   *flitter-mouse* bat.
89   *tickle it* live it up.
      the Pigeons the Three Pigeons in Brentford market place (closed in 1916); John Lowin,
      the actor who played Mammon, kept it in the Commonwealth period.
92   *a-billing* A pun for the audience who have witnessed Dol and Subtle tot up their gains.
95   *Nab* him Q.

499

FACE   If you can get him.

                                                              [*Exit* SUBTLE]

DOL

You are hot upon it, Face, what e'er it is!

FACE

A trick, that Dol shall spend ten pound a month by.

                          [*Enter* SUBTLE]

  Is he gone?

SUBTLE   The chaplain waits you i'the hall, sir.

FACE

  I'll go bestow him.   [*Exit* FACE]

DOL   He'll now marry her, instantly.   100

SUBTLE

He cannot, yet, he is not ready. Dear Dol,
Cozen her of all thou canst. To deceive him
Is no deceit, but justice, that would break
Such an inextricable tie as ours was.

DOL

Let me alone to fit him.

                          [*Enter* FACE]

FACE   Come, my venturers,   105
  You ha' packed up all? Where be the trunks? Bring forth.

SUBTLE

  Here.

FACE   Let's see 'em. Where's the money?

SUBTLE   Here,
  In this.

FACE   Mammon's ten pound: eight score before.
  The Brethren's money, this. Drugger's, and Dapper's.
  What paper's that?

DOL   The jewel of the waiting maid's,   110
  That stole it from her lady, to know certain –

FACE

  If she should have precedence of her mistress?

---

  100   *bestow* conduct.
  102–4   *To deceive . . . ours was* The word order is Latinate and confusing. A more usual order
           would be 'To deceive him that would break such an inextricable tie as ours was, is
           no deceit, but justice'.

DOL   Yes.

FACE

  What box is that?

SUBTLE   The fish-wives' rings, I think:

  And th' ale-wives' single money. Is't not Dol?

DOL

  Yes: and the whistle, that the sailor's wife   115

  Brought you, to know, and her husband were with Ward.

FACE

  We'll wet it tomorrow: and our silver beakers,

  And tavern cups. Where be the French petticoats,

  And girdles, and hangers?

SUBTLE   Here, i' the trunk,

  And the bolts of lawn.

FACE   Is Drugger's damask, there?   120

  And the tobacco?

SUBTLE   Yes.

FACE   Give me the keys.

DOL

  Why you the keys!

SUBTLE   No matter, Dol: because

  We shall not open 'em, before he comes.

FACE

  'Tis true, you shall not open them, indeed:

  Nor have 'em forth. Do you see? Not forth, Dol.

DOL   No!   125

FACE

  No, my smock-rampant. The right is, my master

  Knows all, has pardoned me, and he will keep 'em.

  Doctor, 'tis true (you look) for all your figures:

  I sent for him, indeed. Wherefore, good partners,

---

114   *single money* small change.

116   *and* whether.

      Ward a notorious pirate. Andrew Barker, who had been made captive by him, published a pamphlet about his captor in 1609. Robert Daborne's play, *A Christian turn'd Turke: or the Tragicall Lives and Deaths of Two Famous Pyrates, Ward and Dansiker*, was acted in 1609 or 1610.

117   *wet it* i.e. wet our whistles.

119   *hangers* loops on sword belts from which swords could be hung.

120   *bolts* rolls.

128   *for all your figures* in spite of all your astrological charts; i.e. you never foresaw this.

129   *I sent . . . indeed* not true; Face is trying to 'save face'.

Both he, and she, be satisfied: for, here   130
Determines the indenture tripartite,
Twixt Subtle, Dol, and Face. All I can do
Is to help you over the wall, o' the back-side;
Or lend you a sheet, to save your velvet gown, Dol.
Here will be officers, presently; bethink you,   135
Of some course suddenly to scape the dock:
For thither you'll come else.

                                             Some knock

SUBTLE   Hark you, thunder.
You are a precious fiend!
OFFICERS [*Without*]   Open the door.
FACE
Dol, I am sorry for thee i' faith. But hear'st thou?
It shall go hard, but I will place thee somewhere: 140
Thou shalt ha' my letter to mistress Amo.
DOL   Hang you –
FACE
Or madam Cæsarean.
DOL   Pox upon you, rogue,
Would I had but time to beat thee.
FACE   Subtle,
Let's know where you set up next; I'll send you
A customer, now and then, for old acquaintance: 145
What new course ha' you?
SUBTLE   Rogue, I'll hang myself:
That I may walk a greater devil, than thou,
And haunt thee i' the flock-bed, and the buttery.

                               [*Exeunt* SUBTLE, FACE, DOL]

---

131   *Determines* terminates.
136   *dock* then a word for a rabbit hutch or cage – so part of 'coney-catching' cant.
         Dickens made the word familiar and the metaphor dead.
141–2 *mistress Amo . . . madam Cæsarean* invented names for brothel-keepers. 'Amo' is Latin
         for 'I love' and 'Cæsarean' implies abortion, and perhaps, since Q has 'Imperiall',
         suggests a Dominatrix.
142   *Caesarean* Imperiall Q.
145   *for* for the sake of.

ACT V, SCENE v

[*Enter*] LOVEWIT [*in Spanish costume,* PARSON]

LOVEWIT
What do you mean, my masters?
MAMMON [*Without*]   Open your door,
Cheaters, bawds, conjurers.
OFFICER [*Without*]   Or we'll break it open.
LOVEWIT
What warrant have you?
OFFICER [*Without*]   Warrant enough, sir, doubt not:
If you'll not open it.
LOVEWIT   Is there an officer, there?
OFFICER [*Without*]
Yes, two, or three for failing.
LOVEWIT   Have but patience,   5
And I will open it straight.

[*Enter* FACE]

FACE   Sir, ha' you done?
Is it a marriage? Perfect?
LOVEWIT   Yes, my brain.
FACE
Off with your ruff, and cloak then, be yourself, sir.
SURLY [*Without*]
Down with the door.
KASTRIL [*Without*]   'Slight, ding it open.
LOVEWIT   Hold.
Hold gentlemen, what means this violence?   10

[*Enter* MAMMON, SURLY, KASTRIL, ANANIAS,
TRIBULATION, OFFICERS]

MAMMON
Where is this collier?

5   *for failing* to avoid failing.
9   *ding* batter, push.
11   *collier* See I.i.90.

SURLY   And my Captain Face?

MAMMON

   These day-owls.

SURLY   That are birding in men's purses.

MAMMON

   Madam Suppository.

KASTRIL   Doxy, my suster.

ANANIAS   Locusts

   Of the foul pit.

TRIBULATION   Profane as Bel, and the Dragon.

ANANIAS

   Worse than the grasshoppers, or the lice of Egypt.   15

LOVEWIT .

   Good gentlemen, hear me. Are you officers,

   And cannot stay this violence?

OFFICER   Keep the peace.

LOVEWIT

   Gentlemen, what is the matter? Whom do you seek?

MAMMON

   The chemical cozener.

SURLY   And the Captain Pandar.

KASTRIL

   The nun my suster.

MAMMON   Madam Rabbi.

ANANIAS   Scorpions,   20

   And caterpillars.

LOVEWIT   Fewer at once, I pray you.

OFFICER

   One after another, gentlemen, I charge you,

   By virtue of my staff –

ANANIAS   They are the vessels

   Of pride, lust, and the cart.

---

12   *birding* bird-catching.

13   *Madam Suppository* 'Suppository' was a slang term for prostitute; perhaps also a sense of 'supposed madam' (like 'apocryphal captain').
      suster Q; sister F.

14   *Bel, and the Dragon* two false idols in *Apocrypha*.

15   *grasshoppers . . . lice* two of the plagues visited upon the Egyptians (*Exodus* vii–xii).

17   *stay* prevent.

20   *nun* a common irony (cf. *Hamlet*, III.i.121).

24   *pride, lust, and the cart* shame, and of dishonour Q.
      and the cart deserving of the cart.

LOVEWIT   Good zeal, lie still,
   A little while.
TRIBULATION Peace, Deacon Ananias.   25
LOVEWIT
   The house is mine here, and the doors are open:
   If there be any such persons, as you seek for,
   Use your authority, search on o' God's name.
   I am but newly come to town, and finding
   This tumult 'bout my door (to tell you true)   30
   It somewhat mazed me; till my man, here, (fearing
   My more displeasure) told me he had done
   Somewhat an insolent part, let out my house
   (Belike, presuming on my known aversion
   From any air o' the town, while there was sickness)   35
   To a Doctor, and a Captain: who, what they are,
   Or where they be, he knows not.

They enter

MAMMON   Are they gone?
LOVEWIT
   You may go in, and search, sir. Here, I find
   The empty walls, worse than I left 'em, smoked,
   A few cracked pots, and glasses, and a furnace,   40
   The ceiling filled with poesies of the candle:
   And **MADAM**, with a dildo, writ o' the walls.
   Only, one gentlewoman, I met here,
   That is within, that said she was a widow –
KASTRIL
   Ay, that's my suster. I'll go thump her. Where is she?   45
LOVEWIT
   And should ha' married a Spanish Count, but he,
   When he came to't, neglected her so grossly,
   That I, a widower, am gone through with her.

---

32   *he* ed.; not in Q, F.
41   *poesies of the candle* stains caused by candle smoke.
42   *MADAM* the typographical joke is from F.
     dildo artificial penis.
48   *am gone through with her* have gone through the marriage ceremony (with a suggestion
     of literal going through in consummation).

SURLY

How! Have I lost her then?

LOVEWIT   Were you the Don, sir?

Good faith, now, she does blame y'extremely, and says   50
You swore, and told her, you had ta'en the pains,
To dye your beard, and umbre o'er your face,
Borrowed a suit, and ruff, all for her love;
And then did nothing. What an oversight,
And want of putting forward, sir, was this!   55
Well fare an old harquebuzier, yet,
Could prime his powder, and give fire, and hit,
All in a twinkling.

MAMMON *comes forth*

MAMMON   The whole nest are fled!

LOVEWIT

What sort of birds were they?

MAMMON   A kind of choughs,

Or thievish daws, sir, that have picked my purse   60
Of eight score, and ten pounds, within these five weeks,
Beside my first materials; and my goods,
That lie i' the cellar: which I am glad they ha' left.
I may have home yet.

LOVEWIT   Think you so, sir?

MAMMON   Ay.

LOVEWIT

By order of law, sir, but not otherwise.   65

MAMMON

Not mine own stuff?

LOVEWIT   Sir, I can take no knowledge,

That they are yours, but by public means.
If you can bring certificate, that you were gulled of 'em,
Or any formal writ, out of a court,
That you did cozen yourself: I will not hold them.   70

MAMMON

I'll rather lose 'em.

---

52   *umbre* darken.
56   *harquebuzier* musketeer; armed with a harquebus (a kind of long-barrelled gun used
      in the army. Citizens did weapon-training drill at Mile-End Green and other open
      spaces. Justice Shallow reminisces about them in 2. *Henry IV*, III.ii.272 ff).

LOVEWIT   That you shall not, sir,
   By me, in troth. Upon these terms they are yours.
   What should they ha' been, sir, turned into gold all?
MAMMON   No.
   I cannot tell. It may be they should. What then?
LOVEWIT
   What a great loss in hope have you sustained?   75
MAMMON
   Not I, the commonwealth has.
FACE   Ay, he would ha' built
   The city new; and made a ditch about it
   Of silver, should have run with cream from Hogsden:
   That, every Sunday in Moorfields, the younkers,
   And tits, and tomboys should have fed on, *gratis*.   80
MAMMON
   I will go mount a turnip cart, and preach
   The end o' the world, within these two months. Surly,
   What! In a dream?
SURLY   Must I needs cheat myself,
   With that same foolish vice of honesty!
   Come let us go, and harken out the rogues.   85
   That Face I'll mark for mine, if e'er I meet him.
FACE
   If I can hear of him, sir, I'll bring you word,
   Unto your lodging: for in troth, they were strangers
   To me, I thought 'em honest, as myself, sir.
                      [*Exeunt* MAMMON, SURLY]

       They [TRIBULATION *and* ANANIAS] *come forth*

TRIBULATION
   'Tis well, the Saints shall not lose all yet. Go,   90
   And get some carts –
LOVEWIT   For what, my zealous friends?
ANANIAS
   To bear away the portion of the righteous,

---

76   *the commonwealth* Mammon has returned to his grandiloquent fantasies of
      philanthropy.
79   *younkers* youths (especially fashionable ones).
80   *tits, and tomboys* young girls and wild girls.
81   *turnip cart* a farm-wagon; the type of moveable platform employed by itinerant preachers.

Out of this den of thieves.

LOVEWIT   What is that portion?

ANANIAS

  The goods, sometimes the orphans', that the Brethren,
  Bought with their silver pence.

LOVEWIT   What, those i' the cellar,   95
  The knight Sir Mammon claims?

ANANIAS   I do defy
  The wicked Mammon, so do all the Brethren,
  Thou profane man. I ask thee, with what conscience
  Thou canst advance that idol, against us,
  That have the seal? Were not the shillings numbered,   100
  That made the pounds? Were not the pounds told out,
  Upon the second day of the fourth week,
  In the eighth month, upon the table dormant,
  The year, of the last patience of the Saints,
  Six hundred and ten?

LOVEWIT   Mine earnest vehement botcher,   105
  And Deacon also, I cannot dispute with you,
  But, if you get you not away the sooner,
  I shall confute you with a cudgel.

ANANIAS   Sir.

TRIBULATION

  Be patient Ananias.

ANANIAS   I am strong,
  And will stand up, well girt, against an host,   110
  That threaten Gad in exile.

LOVEWIT   I shall send you
  To Amsterdam, to your cellar.

ANANIAS   I will pray there,
  Against thy house: may dogs defile thy walls,
  And wasps, and hornets breed beneath thy roof,
  This seat of falsehood, and this cave of cozenage.   115

               [*Exeunt* ANANIAS, TRIBULATION]

---

99   *idol* Nemrod Q.
100   *the seal* Revelation ix.4.
103   *table dormant* permanent side-board.
104   *of the last patience of the Saints* i.e. this is the last millenium before Doomsday.
105   *botcher* See III.ii.113.
111   *Gad in exile* Genesis xlix.19.

DRUGGER *enters*

LOVEWIT
Another too?

DRUGGER   Not I sir, I am no Brother.

LOVEWIT

He beats him away

Away you Harry Nicholas, do you talk?

[*Exit* DRUGGER]

FACE
No, this was Abel Drugger.
          To the PARSON   Good sir, go,
And satisfy him; tell him, all is done:
He stayed too long a-washing of his face.   120
The Doctor, he shall hear of him at Westchester;
And of the Captain, tell him at Yarmouth: or
Some good port town else, lying for a wind.

[*Exit* PARSON]

If you get off the angry child, now, sir –

[*Enter* KASTRIL, DAME PLIANT]

KASTRIL *To his sister*
Come on, you ewe, you have matched most sweetly, ha' you not?   125
Did not I say, I would never ha' you tupped
But by a dubbed boy, to make you a lady tom?
'Slight, you are a mammet! O, I could touse you, now.
Death, mun' you marry with a pox?

LOVEWIT   You lie, boy;
As sound as you: and I am aforehand with you.

115–17   s.d.s *Drugger enters, and he beats him away* opposite 117–18 F.
   116   s.d. at 118 F.
   117   *Harry Nicholas* Hendrick Niclaes, Anabaptist mystic and leader of 'The Family of
          Love'. He came to England during Edward VI's reign. In 1580 Elizabeth issued a
          proclamation against the sect and their publications.
   121   *Westchester* Chester.
   124   *get* can get Q.
   126   *tupped* mated (continues the farmyard talk of l. 125).
   127   *dubbed boy* knight.
   128   *mammet* doll; idiot.
          touse tousle; shake.
   129   *mun' you* must you.
   130   *sound* pox-free.

KASTRIL   Anon?   130

LOVEWIT

    Come, will you quarrel? I will feize you, sirrah.

    Why do you not buckle to your tools?

KASTRIL   God's light!

    This is a fine old boy, as e'er I saw!

LOVEWIT

    What, do you change your copy, now? Proceed,

    Here stands my dove: stoop at her, if you dare.   135

KASTRIL

    'Slight I must love him! I cannot choose, i' faith!

    And I should be hanged for't. Suster, I protest,

    I honour thee, for this match.

LOVEWIT   O, do you so, sir?

KASTRIL

    Yes, and thou canst take tobacco, and drink, old boy,

    I'll give her five hundred pound more, to her marriage,   140

    Than her own state.

LOVEWIT   Fill a pipe-full, Jeremy.

FACE

    Yes, but go in, and take it, sir.

LOVEWIT   We will.

    I will be ruled by thee in anything, Jeremy.

KASTRIL

    'Slight, thou art not hidebound! Thou art a Jovy boy!

    Come let's in, I pray thee, and take our whiffs.   145

LOVEWIT

    Whiff in with your sister, brother boy.

                   [*Exeunt* KASTRIL, DAME PLIANT]

                         That master

    That had received such happiness by a servant,

    In such a widow, and with so much wealth,

    Were very ungrateful, if he would not be

    A little indulgent to that servant's wit,   150

    And help his fortune, though with some small strain

131   *feize* do for; flog; squeeze.
132   *buckle . . . tools* get on your weapons.
135   *stoop* a term from falconry, appropriate to Kastril (kestrel).
144   *Jovy boy* jovial fellow.
145   *I* not in Q.
      whiffs smokes.

Of his own candour. Therefore, gentlemen,
And kind spectators, if I have outstripped
An old man's gravity, or strict canon, think
What a young wife, and a good brain may do: 155
Stretch age's truth sometimes, and crack it too.
Speak for thyself, knave.

FACE   So I will, sir. Gentlemen,
My part a little fell in this last scene,
Yet 'twas *decorum*. And though I am clean
Got off, from Subtle, Surly, Mammon, Dol, 160
Hot Ananias, Dapper, Drugger, all
With whom I traded; yet I put myself
On you, that are my country: and this pelf,
Which I have got, if you do quit me, rests
To feast you often, and invite new guests. 165

THE END

152   *candour* whiteness of soul.
154   *canon* regularity.
159   *decorum* the classical principle of consistency and fittingness.
163   *my country* my jury (chosen from the neighbourhood).
164   *quit* acquit.

BARTHOLMEW FAYRE:

A COMEDIE,

ACTED IN THE YEARE, 1614.

By the Lady *ELIZABETHS* SERVANTS.

And then dedicated to King IAMES, of most *Blessed Memorie*;

By the Author, BENIAMIN IOHNSON.

Si foret in terris, rideret Democritus : *nam*
Spectaret populum ludis attentiùs ipsis,
Vt sibi præbentem, mimo spectacula plura.
Scriptores autem narrare putaret asello
Fabellam surdo. Hor.lib.2.Epist.1.

LONDON,
Printed by *I. B.* for ROBERT ALLOT, and are
to be sold at the signe of the *Beare*, in *Pauls*
Church-yard. 1631.

BARTHOLMEW FAYRE. The full form of the name *Bartholomew* occurs only once in the play, at l. i, 3, where, significantly, Littlewit is reading the licence for Cokes's marriage. Everywhere else the preferred form, preserved in this edition, is *Bartholmew* (probably pronounced *Bartlemy*), a spelling which persisted into the nineteenth century.

From 1120 till 1855 a great fair was held annually in Smithfield on 24 August, the feast of St Bartholomew.

the Lady ELIZABETHS SERVANTS. This company of players seems to have come into being in 1611, when a patent was issued to them on 27 April. After various vicissitudes, they established themselves at the newly built theatre called the Hope in the autumn of 1614. See Chambers, ii. 246–58.

Si foret . . . surdo. Quoted from Horace, *Epistles*, II.i. 194–200, with lines 195–6 omitted, *nam* for *seu*, and *asello* misprinted as *assello*. 'If Democritus were still in the land of the living, he would laugh himself silly, for he would pay far more attention to the audience than to the play, since the audience offers the more interesting spectacle. But as for the authors of the plays—he would conclude that they were telling their tales to a deaf donkey'. Characteristically, Jonson is telling his audience what he thinks of them and of the state of the drama.

I.B. The initials of the printer John Beale.

Pauls Church-yard. The churchyard of old St Paul's Cathedral was the centre of the book-trade in London in the sixteenth and early seventeenth centuries.

THE
PROLOGUE
TO
THE KING'S
MAJESTY

Your Majesty is welcome to a Fair;
Such place, such men, such language, and such ware,
You must expect; with these, the zealous noise
Of your land's Faction, scandalized at toys,
As babies, hobby-horses, puppet-plays,   5
And such like rage, whereof the petulant ways
Yourself have known, and have been vexed with long.
These for your sport, without particular wrong,
Or just complaint of any private man
Who of himself or shall think well or can,   10
The Maker doth present; and hopes tonight
To give you, for a fairing, true delight.

PROLOGUE. This prologue took the place of the Induction when the play was presented
before James I at court on 1 November 1614.
4 *your land's Faction* Ever since the breakdown of the Hampton Court Conference in 1604
   James I had been embroiled with the Puritans.
   toys trifles
5 *babies* dolls
6 *rage* mad folly
8 *particular wrong* injurious reference to any individual
11 *Maker* Author
12 *fairing* present given at or bought at a fair

THE PERSONS OF THE PLAY

JOHN LITTLEWIT, *a proctor*
[SOLOMON, *his man*]
WIN LITTLEWIT, *his wife*
DAME PURECRAFT, *her mother and a widow*
ZEAL-OF-THE-LAND BUSY, *her suitor, a Banbury man*　　　　5
WINWIFE, *his rival, a gentleman*
QUARLOUS, *his companion, a gamester*
BARTHOLMEW COKES, *an esquire of Harrow*
HUMPHREY WASP, *his man*
ADAM OVERDO, *a Justice of Peace*　　　　10
DAME OVERDO, *his wife*
GRACE WELLBORN, *his ward*
LANTERN LEATHERHEAD, *a hobby-horse-seller*
JOAN TRASH, *a gingerbread-woman*
EZEKIEL EDGWORTH, *a cutpurse*　　　　15
NIGHTINGALE, *a ballad-singer*
URSLA, *a pig-woman*
MOONCALF, *her tapster*
JORDAN KNOCKEM, *a horse-courser, and ranger o' Turnbull*
VAL CUTTING, *a roarer*　　　　20
CAPTAIN WHIT, *a bawd*
PUNK ALICE, *mistress o' the game*

---

1 *proctor* legal agent, attorney
2 SOLOMON, *his man* ed. (omitted F)
  a Banbury man Banbury, in Oxfordshire, was proverbially famous for its cheese, cakes, and ale, and, by the early seventeenth century, it had come to be regarded as a centre of Puritanism. Busy, a glutton as well as a Puritan, has been a baker (cf. I.iii, 101–11).
7 QUARLOUS combination of 'quarrellous' (= contentious) and 'parlous' (= dangerously clever)
  gamester (i) gambler (ii) rake (iii) inveterate jeerer
8 COKES dupe, simpleton
17 URSLA shortened form of Ursula, Latin for 'little she-bear'

...ler, expert in sharp practice
...ekeeper of Turnbull Street in London, the 'game' being the
...e street was notorious

...of uncertain meaning, also used by Jonson in *The Alchemist*

TROUBLE-ALL, *a madman*
[HAGGIS, BRISTLE,] *watchmen*
[POCHER, *a beadle*]   25
[A] COSTARD-MONGER
[A CORNCUTTER]
[A TINDERBOX-MAN]
[NORTHERN, *a*] *clothier*
[PUPPY, *a*] *wrestler*   30
[FILCHER, SHARKWELL,] *doorkeepers* [*at the puppet-shew*]
PUPPETS
[PASSENGERS]

The Scene: Smithfield

24 HAGGIS ... *beadle* ed. (WHTCHMEN, three. F)
26 A COSTARD-MONGER ed. (COSTARD-monger. F) costermonger (originally a vendor of costards, i.e., apples)
27 A CORNCUTTER ed. (omitted F)
28 A TINDERBOX-MAN ed. (MOVSETRAP-man. F)
29 NORTHERN, *a* ed. (CLOTHIER. F)
30 PUPPY, *a* ed. (WRESTLER. F)
31 FILCHER, SHARKWELL, *doorkeepers at the puppet-shew* ed. (DOORE-KEEPERS. F)
33 PASSENGERS ed. (PORTERS F)

THE INDUCTION ON THE STAGE

[*Enter*] STAGE-KEEPER

STAGE-KEEPER

Gentlemen, have a little patience, they are e'en upon coming,
instantly. He that should begin the play, Master Littlewit, the
Proctor, has a stitch new fallen in his black silk stocking; 'twill be
drawn up ere you can tell twenty. He plays one o' the Arches, that
dwells about the Hospital, and he has a very pretty part. But   5
for the whole play, will you ha' the truth on't?—I am looking, lest
the poet hear me, or his man, Master Brome, behind the arras—
it is like to be a very conceited scurvy one, in plain English.
When't comes to the Fair once, you were e'en as good go to
Virginia for anything there is of Smithfield. He has not hit the   10
humours, he does not know 'em; he has not conversed with the
Bartholmew-birds, as they say; he has ne'er a sword-and-buckler
man in his Fair, nor a little Davy to take toll o' the bawds there,
as in my time, nor a Kindheart, if anybody's teeth should
chance to ache in his play; nor a juggler with a well-educated ape   15
to come over the chain for the King of England, and back again
for the Prince, and sit still on his arse for the Pope and the King
of Spain! None o' these fine sights! Nor has he the canvas cut i'

---

 1 s.d. *STAGE-KEEPER* man employed to set and sweep the stage
    tell count
 4 *one o' the Arches* The Court of Arches, where Littlewit practises, was held in Bow Church
    and was the court of appeal from the diocesan courts.
    the Hospital. 'St. Bartlemew, in Smithfield, an hospital of great receipt and relief for the
    poor . . . is endowed by the citizens' benevolence' (Stow, 438).
 7 *his man, Master Brome* Richard Brome was for a time Jonson's 'faithful servant', learned
    from him how to write plays, and eventually became a dramatist in his own right. Jonson's
    tribute to him is printed in H & S, viii. 409.
    arras tapestry hanging
 8 *conceited* fanciful, unrealistic
10-11 *hit the humours* hit off the typical oddities of behaviour
 12 *Bartholmew-birds* roguish denizens of the Fair (cf. 'jail-birds')
    sword-and-buckler man ed. (Sword, and Buckler man F) swash-buckler, bragging bully
 13 *little Davy* Referred to in several works of the early seventeenth century, this individual
    seems to have been a professional bully.
 14 *Kindheart* An itinerant tooth-drawer who gave his name to Henry Chettle's pamphlet
    Kind-Harts Dreame (1593).

the night for a hobby-horse-man to creep in to his she-
neighbour and take his leap there! Nothing! No, an some writer   20
that I know had had but the penning o' this matter, he would ha'
made you such a jig-a-jog i' the booths, you should ha' thought
an earthquake had been i' the Fair! But these master-poets, they
will ha' their own absurd courses; they will be informed of
nothing. He has, sir-reverence, kicked me three or four times   25
about the tiring-house, I thank him, for but offering to put in
with my experience. I'll be judged by you, gentlemen, now, but
for one conceit of mine! Would not a fine pump upon the stage
ha' done well for a property now? And a punk set under upon
her head, with her stern upward, and ha' been soused by my   30
witty young masters o' the Inns o' Court? What think you o' this
for a shew, now? He will not hear o' this! I am an ass! I! And yet I
kept the stage in Master Tarlton's time, I thank my stars. Ho! an
that man had lived to have played in Bartholmew Fair, you
should ha' seen him ha' come in, and ha' been cozened i' the   35
cloth-quarter, so finely! And Adams, the rogue, ha' leaped and
capered upon him, and ha' dealt his vermin about as though
they had cost him nothing. And then a substantial watch to ha'

19 *hobby-horse-man* (i) seller of hobby-horses (ii) frequenter of hobby-horses (prostitutes)
20 *take his leap* technical term for the copulation of a stallion with a mare
    an if
22 *jig-a-jog* jogging motion (with sexual innuendo)
25 *sir-reverence* (originally 'save reverence') I apologize for mentioning it
26 *tiring-house* backstage area where the dressing-rooms were
    put in intervene, help him out
28 *conceit* bright idea
29 *punk* whore
30 *soused* soaked to the skin
31 *witty* clever, facetious
    young masters o' the Inns o' Court The Inns of Court—Lincoln's Inn, the Inner Temple,
    the Middle Temple, and Gray's Inn—where students studied the law, were virtually a
    third university.
33 *in Master Tarlton's time* Richard Tarlton, who died in 1588, was the most celebrated
    clown of his time. A member of the Queen's Men from the time of that company's
    foundation in 1583, he became something of a legend, and there were numerous stories
    and anecdotes about him.
35–6 *cozened i' the cloth-quarter* The cloth-quarter, originally the most important part of the
    Fair, was by the north wall of St Bartholomew's Church. An anecdote in the anonymous
    Tarltons Jests (1611) tells how the comedian was cheated of his clothes there.
36 *Adams* John Adams was another member of the Queen's Men at the same time as Tarlton
    (Chambers, ii. 296).
37 *vermin* fleas?

stolen in upon 'em, and taken 'em away with mistaking words, as
the fashion is in the stage practice.   40

[Enter] BOOK-HOLDER, SCRIVENER, *to him*

BOOK-HOLDER

How now? What rare discourse are you fallen upon, ha? Ha' you
found any familiars here, that you are so free? What's the
business?

STAGE-KEEPER

Nothing, but the understanding gentlemen o' the ground here
asked my judgement.   45

BOOK-HOLDER

Your judgement, rascal? For what? Sweeping the stage? Or
gathering up the broken apples for the bears within? Away,
rogue, it's come to a fine degree in these spectacles when such a
youth as you pretend to a judgement.

[Exit STAGE-KEEPER*]*

And yet he may, i' the most o' this matter i'faith; for the author   50
hath writ it just to his meridian, and the scale of the grounded
judgements here, his play-fellows in wit. Gentlemen, not for want
of a prologue, but by way of a new one, I am sent out to you here,
with a scrivener and certain articles drawn out in haste between
our author and you; which if you please to hear, and as they   55
appear reasonable, to approve of, the play will follow presently.
Read, scribe; gi' me the counterpane.

SCRIVENER

Articles of Agreement, indented, between the spectators or

---

39 *mistaking words* malapropisms (cf. Dogberry and Verges in *Much Ado About Nothing*)
41 s.d. *BOOK-HOLDER* prompter
42 *free* free of speech, forward
44 *understanding gentlemen o' the ground* A punning reference to the groundlings who stood
    under, i.e. below, the stage, in the pit.
47 *the bears within* The Hope Theatre, which opened in 1614, was both a playhouse and a
    bear-garden. The stage was removed on the days when bear-baiting was the entertainment
    offered.
49 *pretend* lay claim
51 *just to his meridian* exactly calculated to the limit of his understanding
    grounded (i) well-grounded, proficient (ii) standing on the ground, in the pit
57 *counterpane* other half of the indenture

hearers at the Hope on the Bankside, in the County of Surrey, on
the one party, and the author of *Bartholmew Fair*, in the said   60
place and county, on the other party, the one and thirtieth day of
October, 1614, and in the twelfth year of the reign of our
Sovereign Lord, James, by the grace of God King of England,
France, and Ireland; Defender of the Faith; and of Scotland the
seven and fortieth.   65

INPRIMIS, It is covenanted and agreed by and between the
parties above-said . . . and the said spectators and hearers, as well
the curious and envious as the favouring and judicious, as also the
grounded judgements and understandings, do for themselves
severally covenant and agree to remain in the places their money   70
or friends have put them in, with patience, for the space of two
hours and an half, and somewhat more. In which time the author
promiseth to present them, by us, with a new sufficient play
called *Bartholmew Fair*, merry, and as full of noise as sport, made
to delight all, and to offend none—provided they have either the   75
wit or the honesty to think well of themselves.

It is further agreed that every person here have his or their free-
will of censure, to like or dislike at their own charge; the author
having now departed with his right, it shall be lawful for any
man to judge his six penn'orth, his twelve penn'orth, so to his   80

59 *the Bankside* An area on the south side of the river Thames, and therefore not within the
    jurisdiction of the City of London, which, during the decade 1590–1600, became the
    theatrical centre.

67 *above-said . . . and* ed. (abouesaid, and F) It is very difficult to make sense of the long
    sentence 'It is . . . more.' (ll. 66–72) as it stands in the Folio. One expects the initial statement
    'It is . . . abovesaid', to be followed by 'that', as it is in each of the subsequent articles. The
    present editor assumes that the compositor has omitted a line of Jonson's manuscript.
    The difficulty can be got over in the theatre by having the actor mumble after 'above-
    said', much as lawyers often do in reading the preliminaries of a will or the like.

68 *curious* hypercritical
    envious hostile

73 *sufficient* up to standard, of good quality

78 *censure* judgement, criticism
    charge; ed. (charge, F)

79 *departed with* surrendered, parted with
    right, ed. (right: F)

80–1 *six penn'orth . . . half a crown.* The list of prices given here is remarkably high for the
    time, rather more than double what appears to have been normal. Chambers suggests
    (ii. 534) that a possible explanation is to be found in the fact that the play was 'not merely
    a new play, but a new play at a new house'.

eighteen pence, two shillings, half a crown, to the value of his place—provided always his place get not above his wit. And if he pay for half a dozen, he may censure for all them too, so that he will undertake that they shall be silent. He shall put in for censures here as they do for lots at the lottery; marry, if he drop 85
but sixpence at the door, and will censure a crown's worth, it is thought there is no conscience or justice in that.

It is also agreed that every man here exercise his own judgement, and not censure by contagion, or upon trust, from another's voice or face that sits by him, be he never so first in the 90
Commission of Wit; as also that he be fixed and settled in his censure, that what he approves or not approves today, he will do the same tomorrow, and if tomorrow, the next day, and so the next week, if need be; and not to be brought about by any that sits on the bench with him, though they indict and arraign plays 95
daily. He that will swear *Jeronimo* or *Andronicus* are the best plays yet, shall pass unexcepted at here as a man whose judgement shews it is constant, and hath stood still these five and twenty or thirty years. Though it be an ignorance, it is a virtuous and staid ignorance; and next to truth, a confirmed error does 100
well. Such a one the author knows where to find him.

It is further covenanted, concluded, and agreed that how great soever the expectation be, no person here is to expect more than he knows, or better ware than a Fair will afford; neither to look back to the sword-and-buckler age of Smithfield, but content 105

---

83   *so* provided
85   *the lottery* A lottery, under the patronage of the King, was opened in 1612 to provide funds for the colonization of Virginia.
89   *contagion* infectious influence
91   *the Commission of Wit* An imaginary body of critics empowered to examine and pass judgement on plays, poems, and the like.
94   *brought about* converted, made to change his mind
95   *bench* (i) bench of magistrates (ii) form on the stage occupied by the distinguished and fashionable
96   *Jeronimo or Andronicus* Thomas Kyd's *The Spanish Tragedy* (c. 1587) and Shakespeare's *Titus Andronicus* (1589–90?) had become very old-fashioned by 1614.
97   *unexcepted at* unobjected to
105 *the sword-and-buckler age of Smithfield* The 'field commonly called West-Smith field, was for many years called Ruffians hall, by reason it was the usuall place of Frayes and common fighting, during the time that Sword-and-Bucklers were in use . . . This manner of Fight was frequent with all men, untill the fight of Rapier and Dagger tooke place, and then suddenly the generall quarrell of fighting abated, which began about the 20 yeare of Queen *Elizabeth* . . .' (Stow, *Annals*, 1631, p. 1024 ab, quoted from Nashe, iv. 111).

himself with the present. Instead of a little Davy to take toll o' the bawds, the author doth promise a strutting horse-courser, with a leer drunkard, two or three to attend him, in as good equipage as you would wish. And then for Kindheart, the tooth-drawer, a fine oily pig-woman, with her tapster to bid you welcome, and 110
a consort of roarers for music. A wise Justice of Peace *meditant*, instead of a juggler with an ape. A civil cutpurse *searchant*. A sweet singer of new ballads *allurant*; and as fresh an hypocrite as ever was broached *rampant*. If there be never a servant-monster i' the Fair, who can help it? he says; nor a nest of antics? He is 115
loth to make Nature afraid in his plays, like those that beget Tales, Tempests, and such like drolleries, to mix his head with other men's heels, let the concupiscence of jigs and dances reign as strong as it will amongst you; yet if the puppets will please anybody, they shall be entreated to come in. 120

In consideration of which, it is finally agreed by the foresaid hearers and spectators that they neither in themselves conceal, nor suffer by them to be concealed, any state-decipherer, or politic picklock of the scene, so solemnly ridiculous as to search out who was meant by the gingerbread-woman, who by the 125
hobby-horse-man, who by the costard-monger, nay, who by their wares; or that will pretend to affirm, on his own inspired

108 *leer* sly
      equipage array
110 *pig-woman*, ed. (Pig-woman F)
      tapster ed. (Tapster, F)
111–14 *meditant. . . searchant. . . allurant* A series of mock heraldic terms modelled on such forms as *rampant*.
114 *servant-monster* A patent allusion to Caliban in Shakespeare's *The Tempest*, who is repeatedly addressed as 'servant-monster' by Stephano and Trinculo at the opening of III.ii.
115 *nest of antics* group of clowns
116–17 *Tales, Tempests* An obvious reference to *The Winter's Tale* and *The Tempest*.
117 *drolleries* comic entertainments of a fantastic kind
123 *state-decipherer* professional informer on the look-out for seditious matter
124 *politic picklock of the scene* Informers on the look-out for 'lewd, seditious, or slanderous matter' were, as Jonson knew to his cost, a menace that the playwright had to guard against. He had been imprisoned in 1597 for his share in the lost play *The Isle of Dogs*, and again in 1605 for his share in *Eastward Ho!*

ignorance, what Mirror of Magistrates is meant by the Justice, what great lady by the pig-woman, what concealed statesman by the seller of mousetraps, and so of the rest. But that such person or persons, so found, be left discovered to the mercy of the author, as a forfeiture to the stage and your laughter aforesaid; as also, such as shall so desperately or ambitiously play the fool by his place aforesaid, to challenge the author of scurrility because the language somewhere savours of Smithfield, the booth, and the pig-broth; or of profaneness because a madman cries, 'God quit you', or 'bless you'. In witness whereof, as you have preposterously put to your seals already, which is your money, you will now add the other part of suffrage, your hands. The play shall presently begin. And though the Fair be not kept in the same region that some here, perhaps, would have it, yet think that therein the author hath observed a special decorum, the place being as dirty as Smithfield, and as stinking every whit.

Howsoever, he prays you to believe his ware is still the same, else you will make him justly suspect that he that is so loth to look on a baby or an hobby-horse here, would be glad to take up a commodity of them, at any laughter or loss, in another place.

[*Exeunt*]

---

128 *Mirror of Magistrates* The phrase probably has a double meaning: (i) paragon of magistrates (ii) in allusion to George Whetstone's *A Mirour for Magestrates of Cyties* (1584), in which it is argued that a good magistrate should find out the truth for himself by visiting places of entertainment in disguise.

131 *discovered* revealed, exposed

134 *challenge* accuse

138 *preposterously* in reversed order, back to front
     put to affixed

139 *suffrage* approval
     hands (i) signatures (ii) applause

142 *decorum* sense of fitness

146-7 *to take up a commodity of them, at any laughter or loss, in another place* Jonson refers to a trick, designed to get round the law limiting interest to 10 per cent, which was commonly practised at the time. The moneylender, pleading that he was short of ready cash, would persuade his client to take part or the whole of the loan in the form of goods, such as 'lute-strings and brown paper'. He would then introduce the borrower to another businessman, with whom he was in collusion, prepared to buy these goods at a very large discount. Jonson is saying, in effect, that the spectator who is not willing to pay with laughter for the excellent play he is being offered will be forced into buying very inferior wares elsewhere and will expose himself to derision as a consequence.

ACT I, SCENE i

[Enter] LITTLEWIT

LITTLEWIT

A pretty conceit, and worth the finding! I ha' such luck to spin out
these fine things still, and like a silk-worm, out of myself. Here's
Master Bartholomew Cokes, of Harrow o'th'Hill, i'th'County of
Middlesex, Esquire, takes forth his licence to marry Mistress Grace
Wellborn of the said place and county. And when does he take it   5
forth? Today! The four-and-twentieth of August! Bartholmew day!
Bartholmew upon Bartholmew! There's the device! Who would
have marked such a leap-frog chance now? A very less than ames-
ace on two dice! Well, go thy ways, John Littlewit, Proctor John
Littlewit—one o' the pretty wits o' Paul's, the Little Wit of   10
London, so thou art called, and something beside. When a quirk
or a quiblin does scape thee, and thou dost not watch, and apprehend
it, and bring it afore the constable of conceit—there now, I speak
quib too—let 'em carry thee out o' the Archdeacon's court into

---

1 s.d. *Enter LITTLEWIT* ed. (LITTLE-WIT (*To him*) WIN. F). Following classical precedent,
Jonson lists all the characters taking part in a scene at the opening of that scene, irrespective
of when they actually enter, and he does not normally supply stage directions to mark
entrances and exits. The character who is first on the list makes the opening speech,
which has no speech prefix. In this edition that speech prefix is supplied. A new scene
begins when a fresh group of characters appears. It does not necessarily mark a break in
the action, which is usually, though not invariably, continuous within the act. Act I of
Bartholmew Fair is set in Littlewit's house.

2 *Here's* ed. (Her's F)

3 *Bartholomew* This is the only occasion on which the full form of this name occurs in the
play. Significantly, Littlewit is reading from an official legal document, where the full
form should be given.

7 *device* clever design

8 *leap-frog chance* chance of two interchangeable things appearing together
    very less truly slighter (with the word 'chance' understood)

8–9 *ames-ace* ambs-ace, double ace, lowest possible throw with two dice

10 *Paul's* The middle aisle of St Paul's was, in Jonson's day, the great meeting-place of
London. Merchants came there to do business, and the fashionable to exchange news
and gossip.

11 *quirk* quip

12 *quiblin* quibble, pun

13 *conceit* wit

14 *Archdeacon's court* The court of Arches, where Littlewit is employed.

his kitchen, and make a Jack of thee, instead of a John. There I am   15
again, la!

[*Enter*] *to him* WIN

Win, good morrow, Win. Ay, marry, Win! Now you look finely
indeed, Win! This cap does convince! You'd not ha' worn it,
Win, nor ha' had it velvet, but a rough country beaver with a
copper band, like the coney-skin woman of Budge Row? Sweet   20
Win, let me kiss it! And her fine high shoes, like the Spanish
lady! Good Win, go a little; I would fain see thee pace, pretty
Win! By this fine cap, I could never leave kissing on't.

WIN

Come, indeed la, you are such a fool, still!

LITTLEWIT

No, but half a one, Win; you are the tother half: man and wife make   25
one fool, Win.—Good!—Is there the proctor, or doctor indeed, i'
the diocese, that ever had the fortune to win him such a Win?—
There I am again!—I do feel conceits coming upon me more than
I am able to turn tongue to. A pox o' these pretenders to wit! your
Three Cranes, Mitre, and Mermaid men! Not a corn of true salt   30

---

15   *Jack* mechanical device for turning the spit when roasting meat (*OED*, sb., 7)
18   *does convince* is overwhelming, is a knock-out
19   *beaver* hat made of beaver's fur
20   *coney-skin woman* woman who sells rabbit-skins
     Budge Row A street, where the sellers of budge—a kind of fur, consisting of lamb's skin
     with the wool dressed outwards—had their shops.
21   *kiss it* kiss you (baby language)
21–2 *the Spanish lady* The only information we have about this person, who evidently caused
     quite a stir in the fashionable world, is contained in Jonson's next play *The Devil is an
     Ass* (1616). There she is described as
 An *English* widdow, who hath lately trauell'd,
 But shee's call'd the *Spaniard*; 'cause she came
 Latest from thence: and keepes the *Spanish* habit.
 Such a rare woman! (II.viii, 25-39)
 A list of her many accomplishments follows.
22   *go* walk
23   *on't* you (literally 'of it')
30   *Three Cranes, Mitre, and Mermaid* London taverns, much frequented by playwrights
     and poets. The Mermaid, Jonson's favourite haunt, was, according to Thomas Fuller,
     the scene of many 'wit-combats' between him and Shakespeare (H & S, i. 50. n.3).
     corn grain
30–1 *salt . . . mustard* sharp pungent wit

nor a grain of right mustard amongst them all. They may stand
for places or so, again the next witfall, and pay twopence in a
quart more for their canary than other men. But gi' me the man
can start up a Justice of Wit out of six-shillings beer, and give the
law to all the poets and poet-suckers i' town! Because they are the   35
players' gossips? 'Slid, other men have wives as fine as the players',
and as well dressed. Come hither, Win.   [*Kisses her*]

[ACT I,] SCENE ii

[Enter to them] WINWIFE

WINWIFE

Why, how now, Master Littlewit? Measuring of lips or moulding
of kisses? Which is it?

LITTLEWIT

Troth, I am a little taken with my Win's dressing here! Does't not
fine, Master Winwife? How do you apprehend, sir? She would not
ha' worn this habit. I challenge all Cheapside to shew such   5
another—Moorfields, Pimlico Path, or the Exchange, in a summer
evening—with a lace to boot, as this has. Dear Win, let Master
Winwife kiss you. He comes a-wooing to our mother, Win, and
may be our father perhaps, Win. There's no harm in him, Win.

31–2 *stand for* strive for (*OED*, Stand, *v.*, 71, † b., quoting *The Devil is an Ass*, I.vi, 36)
   32 *again* in anticipation of
        witfall the letting-fall of a jest or repartee (Horsman)
   33 *canary* light sweet wine from the Canary Islands
   34 *six-shillings beer* small beer sold at six shillings a barrel
   35 *poet-suckers* sucking poets, fledgling poets *town! Because* ed. (Towne, because F)
35–6 *Because . . . gossips?* Littlewit's mind suddenly reverts to the 'pretenders to wit', who, he
        thinks, give themselves airs.
   36 *gossips* familiar acquaintances
        'Slid by God's eyelid
    3 *Does't* looks it
    4 *How do you apprehend* Would you believe it
    5 *Cheapside* The mercers and haberdashers had their shops in this street.
    6 *Moorfields, Pimlico Path, or the Exchange* All places of resort for the citizens of London.
        Moorfields, to the north-east of the City walls, had been laid out as a park in 1606. Pimlico
        in the village of Hoxton was a house famous for its cakes and ale; and the New Exchange
        in the Strand, built in 1608-09, had milliners' and sempstresses' shops which made it
        attractive to women.

WINWIFE

None i' the earth, Master Littlewit. [*Kisses her*]　　　　10

LITTLEWIT

I envy no man my delicates, sir.

WINWIFE

Alas, you ha' the garden where they grow still! A wife here with a strawberry-breath, cherry-lips, apricot-cheeks, and a soft velvet head, like a melicotton.

LITTLEWIT

Good i'faith!—Now dullness upon me, that I had not that before　　15
him, that I should not light on't as well as he! Velvet head!

WINWIFE

But my taste, Master Littlewit, tends to fruit of a later kind: the sober matron, your wife's mother.

LITTLEWIT

Ay! We know you are a suitor, sir. Win and I both wish you well. By this licence here, would you had her, that your two names　　20
were as fast in it as here are a couple. Win would fain have a fine young father-i'-law with a feather, that her mother might hood it and chain it with Mistress Overdo. But you do not take the right course, Master Winwife.

WINWIFE

No? Master Littlewit, why?　　　　25

LITTLEWIT

You are not mad enough.

WINWIFE

How? Is madness a right course?

LITTLEWIT

I say nothing, but I wink upon Win. You have a friend, one Master Quarlous, comes here sometimes?

WINWIFE

Why, he makes no love to her, does he?　　　　30

LITTLEWIT

Not a tokenworth that ever I saw, I assure you. But—

11　*delicates* delights, delicacies

14　*melicotton* peach grafted on a quince

22–3　*hood it and chain it* shew an ostentatious pride in her husband's hood and chain (the marks of his office)

31　*tokenworth* Tokens were pieces of metal issued by tradesmen to overcome the shortage of small change. As they had no general currency, a 'tokenworth' signified 'the least possible amount'

WINWIFE

What?

LITTLEWIT

He is the more madcap o' the two. You do not apprehend me.

WIN

You have a hot coal i' your mouth now, you cannot hold.

LITTLEWIT

Let me out with it, dear Win.   35

WIN

I'll tell him myself.

LITTLEWIT

Do, and take all the thanks, and much good do thy pretty heart, Win.

WIN

Sir, my mother has had her nativity-water cast lately by the cunning
men in Cow-lane, and they ha' told her her fortune, and do ensure   40
her she shall never have happy hour, unless she marry within this
sennight; and when it is, it must be a madman, they say.

LITTLEWIT

Ay, but it must be a gentleman madman.

WIN

Yes, so the tother man of Moorfields says.

WINWIFE

But does she believe 'em?   45

LITTLEWIT

Yes, and has been at Bedlam twice since, every day, to enquire if
any gentleman be there, or to come there, mad!

WINWIFE

Why, this is a confederacy, a mere piece of practice upon her, by
these impostors!

---

37 *good do* ed. (do good F) good may it do

39 *nativity-water cast* Win seems to be confusing the casting (calculation) of a horoscope
with the casting (inspection) of urine for the diagnosis of disease.

39–40 *cunning men* fortune-tellers

40 *Cow-lane* The modern King Street.
   ensure assure

42 *sennight* period of seven nights, week.

46 *Bedlam* The hospital of St Mary of Bethlehem in Bishopsgate was a lunatic asylum.
   Citizens would go to visit it, much as they go to the Zoo today.

48 *confederacy* conspiracy
   mere sheer, downright
   practice trickery or imposture practised (*OED*, Practice, 7., citing this passage)

LITTLEWIT

I tell her so; or else say I that they mean some young madcap 50
gentleman, for the devil can equivocate as well as a shopkeeper,
and therefore would I advise you to be a little madder than
Master Quarlous, hereafter.

WINWIFE

Where is she? Stirring yet?

LITTLEWIT

Stirring! Yes, and studying an old elder, come from Banbury, a 55
suitor that puts in here at meal-tide, to praise the painful
brethren, or pray that the sweet singers may be restored; says a
grace as long as his breath lasts him! Sometime the spirit is so
strong with him it gets quite out of him, and then my mother,
or Win, are fain to fetch it again with malmsey, or *aqua* 60
coelestis.

WIN

Yes indeed, we have such a tedious life with him for his diet, and
his clothes too; he breaks his buttons and cracks seams at every
saying he sobs out.

LITTLEWIT

He cannot abide my vocation, he says. 65

WIN

No, he told my mother a proctor was a claw of the Beast, and that
she had little less than committed abomination in marrying me
so as she has done.

LITTLEWIT

Every line, he says, that a proctor writes, when it comes to be read

---

51 *equivocate* deal in ambiguities
56 *meal-tide* Littlewit is jeering at the Puritan habit of replacing 'mass', in words such as
    'Christmas', with 'tide' meaning 'time'. Cf. *The Alchemist*, III.ii, 43, where, when Subtle
    mentions 'Christ-masse', Ananias interjects: 'Christ-tide, I pray you'.
    painful diligent
57 *sweet singers . . . restored* In the Geneva version of the Bible (1560) David is called 'the
    sweet singer of Israel' (2 Samuel, xxiii. 1). The reference here is, however, to the Puritan
    ministers who had been deprived of their livings because they refused to conform to the
    constitution of the Church of England as set out in 1604.
60 *fetch it again* bring it back, i.e., revive him
60–1 *aqua coelestis* spirit distilled from wine, kind of brandy
62 *tedious* irksome
66 *the Beast* The Beast of the Apocalypse (Revelation, xiii) was equated by the Protestants
    generally, and especially by the Puritans, with Antichrist, identified as the Pope and the
    Church of Rome.

in the Bishop's court, is a long black hair, kembed out of the tail   70
of Antichrist.

WINWIFE

When came this proselyte?

LITTLEWIT

Some three days since.

ACT I, SCENE iii

[Enter to them] QUARLOUS

QUARLOUS

O sir, ha' you ta'en soil here? It's well a man may reach you after
three hours running, yet! What an unmerciful companion art
thou, to quit thy lodging at such ungentlemanly hours! None but
a scattered covey of fiddlers, or one of these rag-rakers in
dunghills, or some marrow-bone man at most, would have been   5
up when thou wert gone abroad, by all description. I pray thee
what ailest thou, thou canst not sleep? Hast thou thorns i' thy
eyelids, or thistles i' thy bed?

WINWIFE

I cannot tell. It seems you had neither i' your feet, that took this
pain to find me.   10

QUARLOUS

No, an I had, all the lime-hounds o' the City should have drawn
after you by the scent rather. Master John Littlewit! God save you,
sir. 'Twas a hot night with some of us, last night, John. Shall we
pluck a hair o' the same wolf today, Proctor John?

LITTLEWIT

Do you remember, Master Quarlous, what we discoursed on last   15
night?

---

70 *kembed* combed

 1 *ta'en soil* taken refuge (technical term used in deer-hunting)
4–5 *rag-rakers . . . marrow-bone man* equivalents of the modern rag-and-bone man
11 *lime-hounds* lyam-hounds, bloodhounds held on a lyam (leash)
11–12 *drawn after* tracked
13 *hot* hectic
14 *hair o' the same wolf* cf. 'hair of the dog that bit you'

QUARLOUS

Not I, John: nothing that I either discourse or do at those times.
I forfeit all to forgetfulness.

LITTLEWIT

No? Not concerning Win? Look you, there she is, and dressed as
I told you she should be. Hark you, sir, had you forgot?   20

QUARLOUS

By this head, I'll beware how I keep you company, John, when I
drink, an you have this dangerous memory! That's certain.

LITTLEWIT

Why, sir?

QUARLOUS

Why? [*To the rest*] We were all a little stained last night, sprinkled
with a cup or two, and I agreed with Proctor John here to come and   25
do somewhat with Win—I know not what 'twas—today; and he
puts me in mind on't now; he says he was coming to fetch me.—
Before truth, if you have that fearful quality, John, to remember
when you are sober, John, what you promise drunk, John, I shall
take heed of you, John. For this once, I am content to wink at you.   30
Where's your wife? Come hither, Win.

He kisseth her

WIN

Why, John! Do you see this, John? Look you! Help me, John.

LITTLEWIT

O Win, fie, what do you mean, Win? Be womanly, Win. Make an
outcry to your mother, Win? Master Quarlous is an honest
gentleman, and our worshipful good friend, Win; and he is Master   35
Winwife's friend, too. And Master Winwife comes a suitor to your
mother, Win, as I told you before, Win, and may perhaps be our
father, Win. They'll do you no harm, Win, they are both our
worshipful good friends. Master Quarlous! You must know Master
Quarlous, Win; you must not quarrel with Master Quarlous, Win.   40

---

17   *do* ed. (doe, F)
    times, ed. (times F)
19   *Win?* ed. (Win, F)
22   *drink* ed. (drunke F)
24   s.d. *To the rest* ed. (not in F). This direction seems necessary in view of Quarlous's
    reference to 'Proctor John here' (ll. 24–6).
    stained the worse for drink
30   *wink at you* overlook your indiscretion
36   *friend* ed. (friends F)

QUARLOUS

No, we'll kiss again and fall in.

LITTLEWIT

Yes, do, good Win.

WIN

I'faith you are a fool, John.

LITTLEWIT

A fool-John she calls me, do you mark that, gentlemen? Pretty
littlewit of velvet! A fool-John!   45

QUARLOUS

She may call you an apple-John, if you use this.

WINWIFE

Pray thee forbear, for my respect somewhat.

QUARLOUS

Hoy-day! How respective you are become o' the sudden! I fear
this family will turn you reformed too; pray you come about
again. Because she is in possibility to be your daughter-in-law,   50
and may ask you blessing hereafter, when she courts it to
Tottenham to eat cream—well, I will forbear, sir; but I'faith,
would thou wouldst leave thy exercise of widow-hunting
once, this drawing after an old reverend smock by the splay-
foot! There cannot be an ancient tripe or trillibub i' the town,   55
but thou art straight nosing it; and 'tis a fine occupation thou'lt
confine thyself to when thou hast got one—scrubbing a piece of

---

41 *fall in* (i) be reconciled (ii) copulate (cf. *Troilus and Cressida*, III.i, 96–7)
44 *fool-John* As Littlewit seems pleased with this appellation, he is probably taking 'fool' as
     the term of endearment that it could be in the early seventeenth century (cf. *King Lear*,
     V.iii, 305).
46 *apple-John* A kind of apple that was thought to be at its best when shrivelled and withered.
     It seems to have been regarded as symbolic of impotence (cf. *2 Henry IV*, II.iv, 3–10),
     and this sense fits well with Quarlous's jeer
     use this behave thus
48 *respective* concerned about good manners
51 *you blessing* ask you for your blessing
     courts it plays the courtier
51–2 *to Tottenham to eat cream* Tottenham Court was famed for its cream, cakes, and ale.
52 *cream—well* ed. (*creame. Well* F)
53 *exercise* regular occupation
54 *once* once for all
     drawing after tracking
     smock woman (derogatory)
54–5 *splay-foot* flat foot that turns outwards
55 *tripe or trillibub* bag of guts (literally 'entrails')

buff, as if thou hadst the perpetuity of Pannier-alley to stink in; or perhaps, worse, currying a carcass that thou hast bound thyself to alive. I'll be sworn, some of them, that thou art or hast been a suitor to, are so old as no chaste or married pleasure can ever become 'em. The honest instrument of procreation has, forty years since, left to belong to 'em. Thou must visit 'em, as thou wouldst do a tomb, with a torch, or three handfuls of link, flaming hot, and so thou mayst hap to make 'em feel thee, and after, come to inherit according to thy inches. A sweet course for a man to waste the brand of life for, to be still raking himself a fortune in an old woman's embers. We shall ha' thee, after thou hast been but a month married to one of 'em, look like the quartan ague and the black jaundice met in a face, and walk as if thou hadst borrowed legs of a spinner and voice of a cricket. I would endure to hear fifteen sermons a week for her, and such coarse and loud ones as some of 'em must be; I would e'en desire of Fate I might dwell in a drum, and take in my sustenance with an old broken tobacco-pipe and a straw. Dost thou ever think to bring thine ears or stomach to the patience of a dry grace as long as thy tablecloth, and droned out by thy son here, that might be thy father, till all the meat o' thy board has forgot it was that day i' the kitchen? Or to brook the noise made in a question of predestination, by the good labourers and painful eaters assembled together, put to 'em by the matron, your spouse, who moderates with a cup of wine, ever and anon, and a sentence out

60

65

70

75

80

---

58 *buff* (i) tough leather (ii) bare skin
    perpetuity perpetual tenure
    Pannier-alley A passage opening out of Pater Noster Row, where tripe and skins were sold.
59 *currying* (i) rubbing down (as with a horse) (ii) flattering
63 *left to belong* ceased to be of interest (*OED*, Belong, *v*., 2.)
64 *link* tow and pitch used for torches
66 *inherit* possess your share (of the old woman's fortune)
    inches size, length (of penis)
67 *brand* fire
70 *quartan ague* fever in which the paroxysm occurs every fourth day
71 *spinner* spider
72 *for* instead of
76 *patience* enduring, suffering
    dry (i) boring (ii) thirst-inducing (because of its length)
82 *moderates* acts as moderator, arbitrates
    sentence maxim, well-known quotation

of Knox between? Or the perpetual spitting before and after a
sober drawn exhortation of six hours, whose better part was the
'hum-ha-hum'? Or to hear prayers groaned out over thy iron   85
chests, as if they were charms to break 'em? And all this, for the
hope of two apostle-spoons, to suffer! And a cup to eat a caudle
in! For that will be thy legacy. She'll ha' conveyed her state, safe
enough from thee, an she be a right widow.

WINWIFE
Alas, I am quite off that scent now.   90

QUARLOUS
How so?

WINWIFE
Put off by a brother of Banbury, one that, they say, is come here,
and governs all already.

QUARLOUS
What do you call him? I knew divers of those Banburians when I
was in Oxford.   95

WINWIFE
Master Littlewit can tell us.

LITTLEWIT
Sir!—Good Win, go in, and if Master Bartholmew Cokes his man
come for the licence—the little old fellow—let him speak with
me.

[Exit WIN]

What say you, gentlemen?   100

WINWIFE
What call you the reverend elder you told me of—your Banbury
man?

LITTLEWIT
Rabbi Busy, sir. He is more than an elder, he is a prophet, sir.

QUARLOUS
O, I know him! A baker, is he not?

LITTLEWIT
He was a baker, sir, but he does dream now, and see visions; he   105
has given over his trade.

---

83 *Knox* The works of John Knox (c. 1505–1572) the Scottish reformer were popular among
    the Puritans.
87 *apostle-spoons* It was customary for the sponsors at a baptism to give the infant a set of
    silver spoons with the figure of an apostle on the handle of each
    caudle warm concoction given to invalids
88 *conveyed her state* made a legal conveyance of her estate to another

QUARLOUS

I remember that too—out of a scruple he took that, in spiced conscience, those cakes he made were served to bridales, maypoles, morrises, and such profane feasts and meetings. His Christen name is Zeal-of-the-land. 110

LITTLEWIT

Yes, sir, Zeal-of-the-land Busy.

WINWIFE

How! what a name's there!

LITTLEWIT

O, they have all such names, sir. He was witness for Win here—they will not be called godfathers—and named her Win-the-fight. You thought her name had been Winifred, did you not? 115

WINWIFE

I did indeed.

LITTLEWIT

He would ha' thought himself a stark reprobate, if it had.

QUARLOUS

Ay, for there was a blue-starch-woman o' the name, at the same time. A notable hypocritical vermin it is; I know him. One that stands upon his face more than his faith, at all times; ever in 120 seditious motion, and reproving for vain-glory; of a most lunatic conscience and spleen, and affects the violence of singularity in all he does.—He has undone a grocer here, in Newgate-market, that broked with him, trusted him with currants, as arrant a zeal as he; that's by the way.—By his 125 profession, he will ever be i' the state of innocence, though, and

---

107 *spiced* tender, scrupulous
108 *bridales* wedding feasts
109 *maypoles . . . meetings* The more rigid Protestants, not merely the Puritans, were strongly opposed to popular merry-makings such as these, because they saw them, quite rightly, as survivals of paganism.
 morrises morris dances
118 *blue-starch-woman* Laundress who used blue starch to whiten and set ruffs, which were associated with the sin of pride.
120 *stands upon his face* relies on his effrontery
120–1 *in seditious motion* causing trouble
124 *Newgate-market* Established for the sale of corn and meal, this market was, by Jonson's time, dealing in other kinds of foodstuff as well.
 broked ed. (broke F) did business. All other editors retain 'broke', but then have difficulty in explaining it. This editor thinks that Jonson wrote 'brokd', which the compositor turned into 'broke'.
125 *zeal* zealot

childhood; derides all antiquity; defies any other learning than inspiration; and what discretion soever years should afford him, it is all prevented in his original ignorance. Ha' not to do with him, for he is a fellow of a most arrogant and invincible dullness, 130 I assure you. Who is this?

ACT I, SCENE iv

[Enter to them] WASP, [WIN]

WASP

By your leave, gentlemen, with all my heart to you, and God you good morrow. Master Littlewit, my business is to you. Is this licence ready?

LITTLEWIT

Here, I ha' it for you in my hand, Master Humphrey.

WASP

That's well. Nay, never open or read it to me; it's labour in vain, 5 you know. I am no clerk, I scorn to be saved by my book; i'faith I'll hang first. Fold it up o' your word and gi' it me. What must you ha' for't?

LITTLEWIT

We'll talk of that anon, Master Humphrey.

WASP

Now, or not at all, good Master Proctor; I am for no anons, I 10 assure you.

LITTLEWIT

Sweet Win, bid Solomon send me the little black box within, in my study.

---

129 *prevented* balked, precluded

1 *God you* God give you
6 *to be saved by my book* Wasp is referring to the 'neck-verse', as it was called. Until 1827 anyone who could read a Latin verse (usually the beginning of the fifty-first psalm) printed in black-letter was exempted from sentence on his first conviction. Also known as 'benefit of clergy', since it was originally the privilege of exemption from trial before a secular court claimed by clergymen arraigned for felony, the neck-verse had saved Jonson's life in October 1598, when he was tried at the Old Bailey for killing the actor Gabriel Spencer in a duel.

WASP

Ay, quickly, good mistress, I pray you, for I have both eggs o' the
spit, and iron i' the fire.   15

[*Exit* WIN]

Say what you must have, good Master Littlewit.

LITTLEWIT

Why, you know the price, Master Numps.

WASP

I know? I know nothing, I. What tell you me of knowing, now I
am in haste? Sir, I do not know, and I will not know, and I scorn
to know; and yet, now I think on't, I will and do know as well as   20
another: you must have a mark for your thing here, and
eightpence for the box. I could ha' saved twopence i' that, an I
had bought it myself, but here's fourteen shillings for you. Good
Lord! How long your little wife stays! Pray God, Solomon, your
clerk, be not looking i' the wrong box, Master Proctor.   25

LITTLEWIT

Good i'faith! No, I warrant you, Solomon is wiser than so, sir.

WASP

Fie, fie, fie, by your leave, Master Littlewit, this is scurvy, idle,
foolish, and abominable, with all my heart; I do not like it.

WINWIFE

Do you hear? Jack Littlewit, what business does thy pretty head
think this fellow may have, that he keeps such a coil with?   30

QUARLOUS

More than buying of gingerbread i' the Cloister here, for that we
allow him, or a gilt pouch i' the Fair?

LITTLEWIT

Master Quarlous, do not mistake him. He is his master's both-
hands, I assure you.

14–15 *eggs o' the spit, and iron i' the fire* Two proverbial expressions (Tilley, E86 and 199) denoting
     haste.
  18 *nothing, I.* ed. (nothing. I, F)
18–19 *knowing, now I am in haste? Sir,* ed. (knowing? (now I am in hast) Sir, F)
  21 *mark* thirteen shillings and fourpence (two-thirds of a pound sterling)
  30 *keeps such a coil with* makes such a fuss about
  31 *the Cloister* The Cloisters of Christ Church, near to Smithfield, were used as a mart for
     various wares at the time of the Fair.
33–4 *both-hands* factotum

QUARLOUS

What? To pull on his boots, a mornings, or his stockings? Does   35
he?

LITTLEWIT

Sir, if you have a mind to mock him, mock him softly, and look
tother way; for if he apprehend you flout him once, he will fly at
you presently. A terrible testy old fellow, and his name is Wasp
too.   40

QUARLOUS

Pretty insect! Make much on him.

WASP

A plague o' this box, and the pox too, and on him that made it,
and her that went for't, and all that should ha' sought it, sent it,
or brought it! Do you see, sir?

LITTLEWIT

Nay, good Master Wasp.   45

WASP

Good Master Hornet, turd i' your teeth, hold you your tongue!
Do not I know you? Your father was a pothecary, and sold
glisters, more than he gave, I wusse.

[*Enter* WIN, *with the box*]

And turd i' your little wife's teeth too—here she comes— 'twill
make her spit, as fine as she is, for all her velvet-custard on her   50
head, sir.

LITTLEWIT

O! be civil, Master Numps.

WASP

Why, say I have a humour not to be civil; how then? Who shall
compel me? You?

LITTLEWIT

Here is the box now.   55

---

39 *presently* immediately
48 *glisters* clysters, enemas
    I wusse iwis, certainly, truly
50 *velvet-custard* velvet hat in the shape of a pie (custard)
53 *humour* inclination

WASP

Why, a pox o' your box, once again! Let your little wife stale in it, an she will. Sir, I would have you to understand, and these gentlemen too, if they please—

WINWIFE

With all our hearts, sir.

WASP

That I have a charge, gentlemen.   60

LITTLEWIT

They do apprehend, sir.

WASP

Pardon me, sir, neither they nor you can apprehend me yet.— You are an ass.—I have a young master; he is now upon his making and marring. The whole care of his well-doing is now mine. His foolish schoolmasters have done nothing but run up   65 and down the country with him to beg puddings and cake-bread of his tenants, and almost spoiled him; he has learned nothing but to sing catches and repeat *Rattle bladder rattle* and *O, Madge*. I dare not let him walk alone, for fear of learning of vile tunes, which he will sing at supper and in the sermon-times! If he   70 meet but a carman i' the street, and I find him not talk to keep him off on him, he will whistle him and all his tunes over at night in his sleep! He has a head full of bees! I am fain now, for this little time I am absent, to leave him in charge with a gentlewoman. 'Tis true she is a Justice of Peace his wife, and a   75 gentlewoman o' the hood, and his natural sister; but what may happen under a woman's government, there's the doubt. Gentlemen, you do not know him; he is another manner of piece than you think for! But nineteen year old and yet he is taller than either of you, by the head, God bless him!   80

56 *stale* piss (usually said of horses and cattle)

66 *puddings sausages*

66-7 *cake-bread* bread of a fine cake-like quality

68 *Rattle bladder rattle* Part of a proverbial piece of nonsense which ran: 'Three blue beans in a blue bladder, rattle, bladder, rattle' (Tilley, B124).

69 *O, Madge* A ballad about the barn-owl, which was known as Madge or Madge-howlet.

71 *carman* carter, carrier

73 *He has a head full of bees* Proverbial (Tilley, H255) for 'he is full of crazy notions' (cf. 'He has bees in his bonnet').

76 *o' the hood* of consequence

78-9 *another manner of piece* a different sort of person

QUARLOUS

Well, methinks this is a fine fellow!

WINWIFE

He has made his master a finer by this description, I should think.

QUARLOUS

'Faith, much about one; it's cross and pile; whether for a new
farthing.

WASP

I'll tell you, gentlemen—   85

LITTLEWIT

Will't please you drink, Master Wasp?

WASP

Why, I ha' not talked so long to be dry, sir. You see no dust or
cobwebs come out o' my mouth, do you? You'd ha' me gone,
would you?

LITTLEWIT

No, but you were in haste e'en now, Master Numps.   90

WASP

What an I were? So I am still, and yet I will stay too. Meddle you
with your match, your Win there; she has as little wit as her
husband it seems. I have others to talk to.

LITTLEWIT

She's my match indeed, and as little wit as I. Good!

WASP

We ha' been but a day and a half in town, gentlemen, 'tis true.   95
And yesterday i' the afternoon we walked London to shew the
city to the gentlewoman he shall marry, Mistress Grace. But afore
I will endure such another half day with him I'll be drawn with a
good gib-cat through the great pond at home, as his uncle
Hodge was! Why, we could not meet that heathen thing all day   100
but stayed him. He would name you all the signs over, as he

---

83 *cross and pile* heads and tails. Proverbial (Tilley, C835), French *croix et pile* (the two sides
    of a coin)

83–4 *whether for a new farthing* nothing in it, there is not a farthings-worth of difference
    ('whether' = 'no matter which of the two')

98–9 *drawn . . . home* The reference is to a rather primitive rustic joke. A bet is made with a
    foolish person that a gib-cat (tom-cat) will draw him through a pond. A rope is tied
    round him; the loose end is thrown across the pond; and the cat fastened to it with
    packthread. Those appointed to guide the cat then haul the victim through the water.

101 *stayed him* stopped him in his tracks

went, aloud; and where he spied a parrot or a monkey, there he was pitched with all the little long-coats about him, male and female. No getting him away! I thought he would ha' run mad o' the black boy in Bucklersbury that takes the scurvy, roguy 105 tobacco there.

LITTLEWIT

You say true, Master Mumps: there's such a one indeed.

WASP

It's no matter whether there be or no. What's that to you?

QUARLOUS

He will not allow of John's reading at any hand.

ACT I, SCENE v

[*Enter to them*] COKES, MISTRESS OVERDO, GRACE

COKES

O Numps! are you here, Numps? Look where I am, Numps! And Mistress Grace, too! Nay, do not look angerly, Numps. My sister is here, and all. I do not come without her.

WASP

What the mischief! Do you come with her? Or she with you?

COKES

We came all to seek you, Numps.   5

WASP

To seek me? Why, did you all think I was lost? Or run away with your fourteen shillingsworth of small ware here? Or that I had changed it i' the Fair for hobby-horses? 'Sprecious—to seek me!

---

103 *pitched* fixed
     long-coats children
105 *Bucklersbury* A street in London where herbalists, who also sold tobacco, had their shops.
     Cf. *The Merry Wives of Windsor*, III.iii, 63.
109 *reading* comment
     at any hand on any account

  4 *mischief!* ed. (mischiefe, F)
  8 *changed* exchanged
     'Sprecious By God's precious blood

MISTRESS OVERDO

Nay, good Master Numps, do you shew discretion, though he be
exorbitant, as Master Overdo says, an't be but for conservation   10
of the peace.

WASP

Marry gip, goody she-Justice, Mistress French-hood! Turd i'
your teeth; and turd i' your French-hood's teeth, too, to do you
service, do you see? Must you quote your Adam to me? You think
you are Madam Regent still, Mistress Overdo, when I am in   15
place? No such matter, I assure you; your reign is out when I am
in, dame.

MISTRESS OVERDO

I am content to be in abeyance, sir, and be governed by you. So
should he too, if he did well. But 'twill be expected you should
also govern your passions.   20

WASP

Will't so forsooth? Good Lord! How sharp you are! With being at
Bedlam yesterday? Whetstone has set an edge upon you, has he?

MISTRESS OVERDO

Nay, if you know not what belongs to your dignity, I do, yet, to
mine.

WASP

Very well, then.   25

COKES

Is this the licence, Numps? For love's sake, let me see't. I never
saw a licence.

WASP

Did you not so? Why, you shall not see't, then.

COKES

An you love me, good Numps.

---

10 *exorbitant* out of hand (like something that has gone out of orbit)
12 *Marry gip* An exclamatory oath which probably originated from 'By Mary Gipcy' ('by
    St Mary of Egypt'), but then became confused with 'Gip' meaning (i) gee-up (to a horse)
    and (ii) 'go along with you' (to a person).
    French-hood kind of hood fashionable among citizens' wives
22 *Whetstone* 'A whetstone cannot cut but yet it makes tools cut' was a proverbial saying
    (Tilley, W299), but there is also a reference here to a specific person. H & S suggest that
    Whetstone was probably 'the name of a keeper at the Bethlehem Hospital', but, in view
    of the context, it would seem far more likely that it was the name of a well-known inmate.
    Cf. 'the dullness of the fool is the whetstone of the wits' (*As You Like It*, I.ii, 49–50).

WASP

Sir, I love you, and yet I do not love you i' these fooleries. Set your   30
heart at rest; there's nothing in't but hard words. And what
would you see't for?

COKES

I would see the length and the breadth on't, that's all; and I will
see't now, so I will.

WASP

You sha' not see it here.   35

COKES

Then I'll see't at home, and I'll look upo' the case here.

WASP

Why, do so. [*Holds up the box*] A man must give way to him a
little in trifles, gentlemen. These are errors, diseases of youth,
which he will mend when he comes to judgement and knowledge
of matters. I pray you conceive so, and I thank you. And I pray   40
you pardon him, and I thank you again.

QUARLOUS

Well, this dry nurse, I say still, is a delicate man.

WINWIFE

And I am for the cosset, his charge! Did you ever see a fellow's
face more accuse him for an ass?

QUARLOUS

Accuse him? It confesses him one without accusing. What pity   45
'tis yonder wench should marry such a cokes!

WINWIFE

'Tis true.

QUARLOUS

She seems to be discreet, and as sober as she is handsome.

WINWIFE

Ay, and if you mark her, what a restrained scorn she casts upon
all his behaviour and speeches!   50

COKES

Well, Numps, I am now for another piece of business more,
the Fair, Numps, and then—

WASP

Bless me! deliver me! help! hold me! the Fair!

---

38 *trifles, gentlemen* ed. (trifles: Gentlemen F)
43 *cosset* spoilt child (literally 'lamb brought up by hand')
46 *cokes* ninny

COKES

> Nay, never fidge up and down, Numps, and vex itself. I am
> resolute Bartholmew in this. I'll make no suit on't to you. 'Twas 55
> all the end of my journey, indeed, to shew Mistress Grace my
> Fair. I call't my Fair because of Bartholmew: you know my name
> is Bartholmew, and Bartholmew Fair.

LITTLEWIT

> That was mine afore, gentlemen—this morning. I had that i'faith,
> upon his licence; believe me, there he comes after me. 60

QUARLOUS

> Come, John, this ambitious wit of yours, I am afraid, will do you
> no good i' the end.

LITTLEWIT

> No? Why sir?

QUARLOUS

> You grow so insolent with it, and overdoing, John, that if you
> look not to it, and tie it up, it will bring you to some obscure place 65
> in time, and there 'twill leave you.

WINWIFE

> Do not trust it too much, John; be more sparing, and use it but
> now and then. A wit is a dangerous thing in this age; do not
> overbuy it.

LITTLEWIT

> Think you so, gentlemen? I'll take heed on't hereafter. 70

WIN

> Yes, do, John.

COKES

> A pretty little soul, this same Mistress Littlewit! Would I might
> marry her.

GRACE

> [*Aside*] So would I, or anybody else, so I might scape you.

COKES

> Numps, I will see it, Numps, 'tis decreed. Never be melancholy 75
> for the matter.

---

54 *fidge* move restlessly, fidget
    itself yourself
64 *insolent* extravagant
69 *overbuy* pay too much for (by allowing it to get you into trouble)

WASP

Why, see it, sir, see it, do see it! Who hinders you? Why do you not go see it? 'Slid, see it.

COKES

The Fair, Numps, the Fair.

WASP

Would the Fair and all the drums and rattles in't were i' your 80
belly for me; they are already i' your brain. He that had the means to travel your head, now, should meet finer sights than any are i' the Fair, and make a finer voyage on't, to see it all hung with cockle-shells, pebbles, fine wheat-straws, and here and there a chicken's feather and a cobweb. 85

QUARLOUS

Good faith, he looks, methinks, an you mark him, like one that were made to catch flies, with his Sir Cranion legs.

WINWIFE

And his Numps, to flap 'em away.

WASP

God be w'you, sir. There's your bee in a box, and much good do't you. 90

[*Gives him the box, and offers to leave*]

COKES

Why, 'your friend and Bartholmew', an you be so contumacious.

QUARLOUS

What mean you, Numps?

WASP

I'll not be guilty, I, gentlemen.

MISTRESS OVERDO

You will not let him go, brother, and lose him?

COKES

Who can hold that will away? I had rather lose him than the 95
Fair, I wusse.

---

87   *Sir Cranion* daddy-long-legs
89   *God be w'you* God be with you (original form of 'good-bye')
91   *'your . . . Bartholmew'* ed. (your . . . *Bartholmew* F) farewell. Cokes is using a common form of subscribing a letter.
94   *lose* ed. (loose F)
95   *Who can hold that will away?* Proverbial (Tilley, H515); *that* = him who.
       lose ed. (loose F)

WASP

You do not know the inconvenience, gentlemen, you persuade to; nor what trouble I have with him in these humours. If he go to the Fair, he will buy of everything to a baby there; and household-stuff for that too. If a leg or an arm on him did not 100 grow on, he would lose it i' the press. Pray heaven I bring him off with one stone! And then he is such a ravener after fruit! You will not believe what a coil I had t'other day to compound a business between a Catherine-pear-woman and him about snatching! 'Tis intolerable, gentlemen. 105

WINWIFE

O! but you must not leave him now to these hazards, Numps.

WASP

Nay, he knows too well I will not leave him, and that makes him presume. Well, sir, will you go now? If you have such an itch i' your feet to foot it to the Fair, why do you stop? Am I your tarriers? Go, will you go! Sir, why do you not go? 110

COKES

O Numps! have I brought you about? Come, Mistress Grace, and sister, I am resolute Bat, i'faith, still.

GRACE

Truly, I have no such fancy to the Fair, nor ambition to see it; there's none goes thither of any quality or fashion.

COKES

O Lord, sir! You shall pardon me, Mistress Grace, we are enow of 115 ourselves to make it a fashion; and for qualities, let Numps alone, he'll find qualities.

[*Exeunt* COKES, WASP, GRACE, MISTRESS OVERDO]

99 *buy of everything to a baby there* buy some of everything there, down to and including a doll
102 *stone* testicle
103 *coil* trouble, fuss
110 *tarriers* hinderers
  will you go! ed. (will you goe? F) if you want to go
111 *about* round
114 *quality* social standing
116 *qualities* features of character
  let Numps alone leave it to Numps

QUARLOUS

What a rogue in apprehension is this! To understand her language no better!

WINWIFE

Ay, and offer to marry to her! Well, I will leave the chase of my 120 widow for today, and directly to the Fair. These flies cannot, this hot season, but engender us excellent creeping sport.

QUARLOUS

A man that has but a spoonful of brain would think so. Farewell, John.

[*Exeunt* QUARLOUS, WINWIFE]

LITTLEWIT

Win, you see 'tis in fashion to go to the Fair, Win. We must to the 125 Fair too, you and I, Win. I have an affair i' the Fair, Win, a puppet-play of mine own making—say nothing—that I writ for the motion-man, which you must see, Win.

WIN

I would I might, John, but my mother will never consent to such a—'profane motion' she will call it. 130

LITTLEWIT

Tut, we'll have a device, a dainty one.—Now, Wit, help at a pinch; good Wit, come; come, good Wit, an't be thy will.—I have it, Win, I have it i'faith, and 'tis a fine one. Win, long to eat of a pig, sweet Win, i' the Fair, do you see? i'the heart o' the Fair; not at Pie-corner. Your mother will do anything, Win, to satisfy 135 your longing, you know; pray thee long presently, and be sick o' the sudden, good Win. I'll go in and tell her. Cut thy lace i' the mean time, and play the hypocrite, sweet Win.

WIN

No, I'll not make me unready for it. I can be hypocrite enough, though I were never so strait-laced. 140

---

118 *rogue in apprehension* lack-brain, unintelligent beggar
128 *motion-man* puppet-master
130 *a—'profane motion' she* ed. (a prophane motion: she F)
135 *Pie-corner* The site of an old tavern, whose sign was a magpie, this place in West Smithfield was given over to cook-shops. It was at Pie-corner that Face first met Subtle 'Taking his meale of steeme in, from cookes stalls' (*The Alchemist*, I.i, 26).
139 *make me unready* undress
140 *strait-laced* (i) wearing a tightly laced bodice (ii) rigidly moral

LITTLEWIT

You say true. You have been bred i' the family, and brought up
to't. Our mother is a most elect hypocrite, and has maintained us
all this seven year with it, like gentlefolks.

WIN

Ay, let her alone, John; she is not a wise wilful widow for nothing,
nor a sanctified sister for a song. And let me alone too; I ha'   145
somewhat o' the mother in me; you shall see. Fetch her, fetch her!
Ah, ah!

[*Exit* LITTLEWIT]

ACT I, SCENE vi

[*Enter to her*] PURECRAFT, LITTLEWIT

PURECRAFT

Now the blaze of the beauteous discipline fright away this evil
from our house! How now, Win-the-fight, child, how do you?
Sweet child, speak to me.

WIN

Yes, forsooth.

PURECRAFT

Look up, sweet Win-the-fight, and suffer not the enemy to enter   5
you at this door; remember that your education has been with the
purest. What polluted one was it that named first the unclean
beast, pig, to you, child?

WIN

Uh, Uh!

LITTLEWIT

Not I, o' my sincerity, mother. She longed above three hours ere   10
she would let me know it. Who was it, Win?

---

143 *this seven year* The statement is endorsed by Purecraft's confession at V.ii, 47–56.
146 *mother* (i) female parent (ii) hysteria

1 *discipline* religious practice (of the Puritans)

WIN

A profane black thing with a beard, John.

PURECRAFT

O! resist it, Win-the-fight, it is the Tempter, the wicked Tempter; you may know it by the fleshly motion of pig. Be strong against it and its foul temptations in these assaults, whereby it broacheth   15
flesh and blood, as it were, on the weaker side; and pray against its carnal provocations, good child, sweet child, pray.

LITTLEWIT

Good mother, I pray you that she may eat some pig, and her bellyful, too; and do not you cast away your own child, and perhaps one of mine, with your tale of the Tempter. How do you,   20
Win? Are you not sick?

WIN

Yes, a great deal, John. Uh, uh!

PURECRAFT

What shall we do? Call our zealous brother Busy hither, for his faithful fortification in this charge of the adversary.

[*Exit* LITTLEWIT]

Child, my dear child, you shall eat pig, be comforted, my sweet   25
child.

WIN

Ay, but i' the Fair, mother.

PURECRAFT

I mean i' the Fair, if it can be any way made or found lawful.

[*Enter* LITTLEWIT]

Where is our brother Busy? Will he not come? Look up, child.

LITTLEWIT

Presently, mother, as soon as he has cleansed his beard. I found   30
him, fast by the teeth i' the cold turkey-pie i' the cupboard, with a great white loaf on his left hand, and a glass of malmsey on his right.

PURECRAFT

Slander not the brethren, wicked one.

[*Enter to them*] BUSY

14   *motion* prompting

LITTLEWIT

Here he is now, purified, mother.   35

PURECRAFT

O Brother Busy! your help here to edify and raise us up in a
scruple. My daughter Win-the-fight is visited with a natural
disease of women, called 'A longing to eat pig'.

LITTLEWIT

Ay sir, a Bartholmew pig, and in the Fair.

PURECRAFT

And I would be satisfied from you, religiously-wise, whether a   40
widow of the sanctified assembly, or a widow's daughter, may
commit the act without offence to the weaker sisters.

BUSY

Verily, for the disease of longing, it is a disease, a carnal disease,
or appetite, incident to women; and as it is carnal, and incident,
it is natural, very natural. Now pig, it is a meat, and a meat that is   45
nourishing, and may be longed for, and so consequently eaten; it
may be eaten; very exceeding well eaten. But in the Fair, and as a
Bartholmew-pig, it cannot be eaten, for the very calling it a
Bartholmew-pig, and to eat it so, is a spice of idolatry, and you
make the Fair no better than one of the high places. This, I take   50
it, is the state of the question. A high place.

LITTLEWIT

Ay, but in state of necessity, place should give place, Master
Busy—I have a conceit left, yet.

PURECRAFT

Good Brother Zeal-of-the-land, think to make it as lawful as you
can.   55

LITTLEWIT

Yes sir, and as soon as you can; for it must be, sir. You see the
danger my little wife is in, sir.

PURECRAFT

Truly, I do love my child dearly, and I would not have her
miscarry, or hazard her first fruits, if it might be otherwise.

---

36 *raise us up* in a scruple assist us in a question of conscience
49 *spice* kind, species
52 *place should give place* Littlewit is quibbling, taking Busy's 'high place' (in the Scriptural
    sense of a place of idolatrous worship and sacrifice) as 'high rank or position' and saying
    that a man in high place must yield precedence to a better man—a version of noblesse
    oblige. Cf. the proverb (Tilley, M238) 'Man honours the place, not the place the man'.

553

BUSY

Surely, it may be otherwise, but it is subject to construction, 60
subject, and hath a face of offence with the weak, a great face, a
foul face, but that face may have a veil put over it, and be
shadowed, as it were; it may be eaten, and in the Fair, I take it, in a
booth, the tents of the wicked. The place is not much, not very
much; we may be religious in midst of the profane, so it be eaten 65
with a reformed mouth, with sobriety, and humbleness; not
gorged in with gluttony, or greediness; there's the fear; for, should
she go there as taking pride in the place, or delight in the unclean
dressing, to feed the vanity of the eye, or the lust of the palate, it
were not well, it were not fit, it were abominable, and not good. 70

LITTLEWIT

Nay, I knew that afore, and told her on't. But courage, Win, we'll
be humble enough; we'll seek out the homeliest booth i' the Fair,
that's certain; rather than fail, we'll eat it o' the ground.

PURECRAFT

Ay, and I'll go with you myself, Win-the-fight, and my brother,
Zeal-of-the-land, shall go with us too, for our better consolation. 75

WIN

Uh, uh!

LITTLEWIT

Ay, and Solomon too, Win; the more the merrier, Win. [*Aside to*
WIN] We'll leave Rabbi Busy in a booth.— Solomon, my cloak.

[*Enter to them*] SOLOMON

SOLOMON

Here, sir.

BUSY

In the way of comfort to the weak, I will go and eat. I will eat 80
exceedingly, and prophesy. There may be a good use made of it,
too, now I think on't: by the public eating of swine's flesh, to

---

61 *face of offence* look of a stumbling-block
67 *fear* thing to be feared

profess our hate and loathing of Judaism whereof the brethren
stand taxed. I will therefore eat, yea, I will eat exceedingly.

LITTLEWIT

Good i'faith, I will eat heartily too, because I will be no Jew; I   85
could never away with that stiff-necked generation. And truly,
I hope my little one will be like me, that cries for pig so, i' the
mother's belly.

BUSY

Very likely, exceeding likely, very exceeding likely.

[*Exeunt*]

ACT II, SCENE i

[*Enter*] JUSTICE OVERDO, [*disguised as Mad Arthur of Bradley*]

OVERDO

Well, in Justice' name, and the King's, and for the
Commonwealth! Defy all the world, Adam Overdo, for a
disguise, and all story; for thou hast fitted thyself, I swear. Fain
would I meet the Lynceus now, that eagle's eye, that piercing
Epidaurian serpent as my Quintus Horace calls him, that could   5
discover a Justice of Peace, and lately of the Quorum, under this

---

83 *Judaism, whereof the brethren stand taxed* The Puritans were accused (taxed) of Judaism not
only because of the emphasis they placed on the Old Testament but also because, very much
to their credit, they were, first in Holland and then in England, more tolerant in their attitude
towards the Jews than other Christian sects were. It was Oliver Cromwell who allowed the
Jews to return to England from which they had been expelled by Edward I.

86 *away with* tolerate, put up with
stiff-necked generation stubborn race (cf. Deuteronomy, ix. 13, Acts, vii, 51, etc.)

2 *Commonwealth* common weal, general good
3 *fitted* perfectly furnished
4 *Lynceus* One of the Argonauts, famous for his extraordinarily keen eyesight.
4–5 *piercing Epidaurian serpent ... him* Horace writes:
   cur in amicorum vitiis tam cernis acutum
   quam aut aquila aut serpens Epidaurius? (*Satires*, I.iii. 26-7): 'Why, when you look into
   the failings of your friends, are you as sharp-sighted as an eagle or a serpent of Epidaurus?'
   Serpents, which were supposed to have very keen eyes, were sacred to Aesculapius, the
   god of medicine, who was worshipped in the form of a serpent at Epidaurus in Greece.
6 *Quorum* Certain justices, selected for their learning and ability, whose presence was
   necessary to constitute a bench of magistrates.

covering. They may have seen many a fool in the habit of a
Justice; but never till now a Justice in the habit of a fool. Thus
must we do, though, that wake for the public good; and thus
hath the wise magistrate done in all ages. There is a doing of right 10
out of wrong, if the way be found. Never shall I enough
commend a worthy worshipful man, sometime a capital
member of this city, for his high wisdom in this point, who
would take you, now the habit of a porter, now of a carman, now
of the dog-killer in this month of August, and in the winter of a 15
seller of tinder-boxes. And what would he do in all these shapes?
Marry, go you into every alehouse, and down into every cellar;
measure the length of puddings, take the gauge of black pots and
cans, ay, and custards, with a stick; and their circumference, with
a thread; weigh the loaves of bread on his middle finger. Then 20
would he send for 'em, home; give the puddings to the poor, the
bread to the hungry, the custards to his children; break the pots,
and burn the cans, himself; he would not trust his corrupt
officers; he would do't himself. Would all men in authority
would follow this worthy precedent! For, alas, as we are public 25
persons, what do we know? Nay, what can we know? We hear
with other men's ears; we see with other men's eyes; a foolish
constable or a sleepy watchman is all our information. He
slanders a gentleman, by the virtue of his place, as he calls it, and
we, by the vice of ours, must believe him; as, a while agone, they 30
made me, yea me, to mistake an honest zealous pursuivant for
a seminary, and a proper young Bachelor of Music for a bawd.
This we are subject to, that live in high place: all our intelligence

9 *wake* are vigilant, keep watch and ward
12 *capital* leading
12–13 *a worthy . . . city* David McPherson argues that one of Jonson's sources for Overdo was
an actual Lord Mayor of London, Thomas Middleton (no relation to the playwright).
Middleton, like Overdo, visited places of ill repute in disguise, and concerned himself
with weights and measures in the sale of food and drink. See 'The Origins of Overdo: A
Study in Jonsonian Invention', *MLQ*, 37 (1976), 221-33.
15 *dog-killer* Acting under the mistaken impression that dogs carried the infection, the city
fathers hired a dog-killer to exterminate all stray dogs in times of plague, thus freeing
the black rat, whose fleas were the true source of the infection, from its chief enemy.
27 *eyes*; ed. (eyes? F)
31 *pursuivant* state official having power to execute warrants for arrest
32 *seminary* Roman Catholic priest trained at one of the seminaries in Europe
33–4 *intelligence is idle* information is unreliable

is idle, and most of our intelligencers knaves; and, by your
leave, ourselves thought little better, if not arrant fools, for   35
believing 'em. I, Adam Overdo, am resolved therefore to spare
spy-money hereafter, and make mine own discoveries. Many are
the yearly enormities of this Fair, in whose courts of Pie-
powders I have had the honour, during the three days sometimes,
to sit as judge. But this is the special day for detection of   40
those foresaid enormities. Here is my black book for the purpose;
this the cloud that hides me; under this covert I shall see and not
be seen. On, Junius Brutus! And as I began, so I'll end: in
Justice' name, and the King's, and for the Commonwealth!

[Stands aside]

ACT II, SCENE ii

[Enter] LEATHERHEAD *[and]* TRASH

LEATHERHEAD

The Fair's pestilence dead, methinks. People come not abroad
today, whatever the matter is. Do you hear, Sister Trash, Lady o'
the Basket? Sit farther with your gingerbread-progeny there, and
hinder not the prospect of my shop, or I'll ha' it proclaimed i' the
Fair what stuff they are made on.   5

34   *intelligencers* spies, informers
38   *enormities* monstrous offences and irregularities
      of ed. (of of F)
38–9   *courts of Pie-powders* Summary courts held at fairs and markets to administer justice
      among the itinerant dealers and their customers. 'Pie-powders' (French pied-poudreux)
      = 'dustyfoot', 'wayfarer'.
42   *covert* disguise
43   *Junius Brutus* Lucius Junius Brutus, who drove the Tarquins out of Rome and founded
      the Roman Republic, is invoked by Overdo for two reasons: he disguised himself as an
      idiot in order to escape the vigilance of Tarquinius Superbus, and he sentenced his own
      sons to death when they conspired to restore the Tarquins, thus winning a reputation
      as an inflexible judge.

1   *pestilence* plaguily

TRASH

Why, what stuff are they made on, Brother Leatherhead? Nothing but what's wholesome, I assure you.

LEATHERHEAD

Yes, stale bread, rotten eggs, musty ginger, and dead honey, you know.

OVERDO

[*Aside*] Ay! have I met with enormity so soon?   10

LEATHERHEAD

I shall mar your market, old Joan.

TRASH

Mar my market, thou too-proud pedlar? Do thy worst. I defy thee; ay, and thy stable of hobby-horses. I pay for my ground as well as thou dost. An thou wrong'st me, for all thou art parcel-poet and an inginer, I'll find a friend shall right me, and make a   15
ballad of thee and thy cattle all over. Are you puffed up with the pride of your wares? Your arsedine?

LEATHERHEAD

Go to, old Joan, I'll talk with you anon; and take you down too afore Justice Overdo. He is the man must charm you; I'll ha' you i' the Pie-powders.   20

TRASH

Charm me? I'll meet thee face to face afore his worship when thou dar'st; and though I be a little crooked o' my body, I'll be found as upright in my dealing as any woman in Smithfield, I. Charm me!

OVERDO

[*Aside*] I am glad to hear my name is their terror yet; this is doing   25
of justice.

[*Enter to them*] PASSENGERS

LEATHERHEAD

What do you lack? What is't you buy? What do you lack? Rattles, drums, halberts, horses, babies o' the best? Fiddles o'th'finest?

10   s.p. OVERDO ed. (IVS. F)
14   *dost. An* ed. (dost, and F)
14-15   *parcel-poet* a bit of a poet, part-time poet
15   *inginer, I'll* ed. (Inginer. I'll F*); inginer* designer, contriver of shows
16   *cattle* wares
17   *arsedine* gold-coloured alloy used for ornamenting toys
19   *charm you* subdue your tongue (as though by magic)

Enter COSTARDMONGER [*followed by*] NIGHTINGALE

COSTARDMONGER
Buy any pears, pears, fine, very fine pears!
TRASH
Buy any gingerbread, gilt gingerbread!   30
NIGHTINGALE   [*Sings*]
   Hey, now the Fair's a filling!
   O, for a tune to startle
   The birds o' the booths here billing
   Yearly with old Saint Bartle!
   The drunkards they are wading,   35
   The punks and chapmen trading;
   Who'd see the Fair without his lading?
Buy any ballads, new ballads?

[*Enter*] URSLA

URSLA
Fie upon't! Who would wear out their youth and prime thus in
roasting of pigs, that had any cooler vocation? Hell's a kind of cold   40
cellar to't, a very fine vault, o' my conscience! What, Mooncalf!
MOONCALF
[*Within*] Here, Mistress.
NIGHTINGALE
How now, Ursla? In a heat, in a heat?
URSLA
[*To* MOONCALF] My chair, you false faucet you; and my
morning's draught, quickly, a bottle of ale to quench me,   45
rascal.—I am all fire and fat, Nightingale, I shall e'en melt away
to the first woman, a rib, again, I am afraid. I do water the ground
in knots as I go, like a great garden-pot; you may follow me by the
S's I make.

30 *gilt* given a golden appearance (cf. 'to take the gilt off the gingerbread')
35 *wading* half seas over
37 *lading* freight (of fairings)
44 *faucet* tap for a barrel
48 *knots* intricate figures of criss-cross lines

NIGHTINGALE

Alas, good Urs! Was Zekiel here this morning? 50

URSLA

Zekiel? What Zekiel?

NIGHTINGALE

Zekiel Edgworth, the civil cutpurse—you know him well enough—he that talks bawdy to you still. I call him my secretary.

URSLA

He promised to be here this morning, I remember.

NIGHTINGALE

When he comes, bid him stay. I'll be back again presently. 55

URSLA

Best take your morning's dew in your belly, Nightingale.

MOONCALF *brings in the chair*

Come, sir, set it here. Did not I bid you should get this chair let out o' the sides for me, that my hips might play? You'll never think of anything till your dame be rump-galled. 'Tis well, changeling; because it can take in your grasshopper's thighs, 60 you care for no more. Now you look as you had been i' the corner o' the booth, fleaing your breech with a candle's end, and set fire o' the Fair. Fill, stote, fill.

OVERDO

[*Aside*] This pig-woman do I know, and I will put her in for my second enormity. She hath been before me, punk, pinnace, and 65 bawd, any time these two and twenty years, upon record i' the Pie-powders.

URSLA

Fill again, you unlucky vermin.

MOONCALF

'Pray you be not angry, mistress; I'll ha' it widened anon.

URSLA

No, no, I shall e'en dwindle away to't ere the Fair be done, you 70 think, now you ha' heated me! A poor vexed thing I am. I feel

---

53 *secretary* confidant
60 *changeling* stupid or ugly child left by the fairies in place of one they have stolen
62 *fleaing* removing fleas from
63 *stote* (i) stoat (ii) stot (clumsy stupid person)
65 *pinnace* go-between

myself dropping already as fast as I can; two stone o' suet a day is
my proportion. I can but hold life and soul together with this—
here's to you, Nightingale—and a whiff of tobacco at most.
Where's my pipe now? Not filled? Thou arrant incubee!   75

NIGHTINGALE

Nay, Ursla, thou'lt gall between the tongue and the teeth with
fretting now.

URSLA

How can I hope that ever he'll discharge his place of trust—
tapster, a man of reckoning under me—that remembers nothing
I say to him?   80

                              [*Exit* NIGHTINGALE]

But look to't, sirrah, you were best. Threepence a pipeful I will ha'
made of all my whole half-pound of tobacco, and a quarter of a
pound of coltsfoot mixed with it too, to itch it out. I that have dealt
so long in the fire will not be to seek in smoke now. Then, six and
twenty shillings a barrel I will advance o' my beer, and fifty   85
shillings a hundred o' my bottle-ale; I ha' told you the ways how to
raise it. Froth your cans well i' the filling at length rogue, and jog
your bottles o' the buttock, sirrah; then skink out the first glass, ever,
and drink with all companies, though you be sure to be drunk;
you'll misreckon the better, and be less ashamed on't. But your true   90
trick, rascal, must be to be ever busy, and mistake away the bottles
and cans in haste before they be half drunk off, and never hear
anybody call, if they should chance to mark you, till you ha' brought
fresh, and be able to forswear 'em. Give me a drink of ale.

OVERDO

[*Aside*] This is the very womb and bed of enormity gross as   95
herself! This must all down for enormity, all, every whit on't.

                                                            One knocks

URSLA

Look who's there, sirrah! Five shillings a pig is my price— at least.
If it be a sow-pig, sixpence more. If she be a great bellied wife, and
long for't, sixpence more for that.

73 *proportion* estimate
75 *incubee* offspring of a woman and an incubus
83 *itch* eke
84 *to seek in* short of
85 *advance* raise the price
87 *at length* i.e., with the can held as far below the spigot as possible
88 *skink* pour

OVERDO

[*Aside*] *O tempora! O mores!* I would not ha' lost my   100
discovery of this one grievance for my place and worship o' the
bench. How is the poor subject abused here! Well, I will fall in
with her, and with her Mooncalf, and wind out wonders of
enormity.   [*Comes forward*]
By thy leave, goodly woman and the fatness of the Fair, oily as the   105
King's constable's lamp, and shining as his shoeing-horn! Hath
thy ale virtue, or thy beer strength, that the tongue of man may
be tickled, and his palate pleased in the morning? Let thy pretty
nephew here go search and see.

URSLA

What new roarer is this?   110

MOONCALF

O Lord, do you not know him, mistress? 'Tis mad Arthur of
Bradley, that makes the orations.—Brave master, old Arthur of
Bradley, how do you? Welcome to the Fair! When shall we hear
you again to handle your matters, with your back again a booth,
ha? I ha' been one o' your little disciples, i'my days!   115

OVERDO

Let me drink, boy, with my love, thy aunt here, that I may be
eloquent; but of thy best, lest it be bitter in my mouth, and my
words fall foul on the Fair.

URSLA

Why dost thou not fetch him drink? And offer him to sit?

MOONCALF

Is't ale or beer, Master Arthur?   120

---

100   *O tempora! O mores!* (Cicero, *In Catilinam*, I.i. 2) What an age! What manners!
103   *wind* ed. (winne F) smell, scent (*OED*, Wind, *v²*, c.). It is difficult to find any parallel for
        'win out' in the sense it should have here, whereas the hunting term 'wind out' fits what
        Overdo sees himself as doing and is consonant with the use of animal imagery in the
        play. Cf. Barry's *Ram Alley* (1607-08): 'No nose to smell, and winde out all your tricks'
        (II.i).
111-12   *mad Arthur of Bradley* The hero of an old song, going back at least as far as the mid-
        sixteenth century, called 'The Ballad of the Wedding of Arthur of Bradley'. Jonson endows
        him with a fondness for making orations in order to fit him for the role Overdo takes
        on.
114   *again* against
116   *aunt* gossip

OVERDO

Thy best, pretty stripling, thy best; the same thy dove drinketh, and thou drawest on holy-days.

URSLA

Bring him a sixpenny bottle of ale; they say a fool's handsel is lucky.

OVERDO

Bring both, child. Ale for Arthur, and beer for Bradley. Ale for   125
thine aunt, boy.

[*Exit* MOONCALF]

[*Aside*] My disguise takes to the very wish and reach of it. I shall, by the benefit of this, discover enough and more, and yet get off with the reputation of what I would be—a certain middling thing between a fool and a madman.   130

ACT II, SCENE iii

[*Enter*] KNOCKEM *to them*

KNOCKEM

What! my little lean Ursla! my she-bear! art thou alive yet? With thy litter of pigs to grunt out another Bartholmew Fair, ha?

URSLA

Yes, and to amble afoot, when the Fair is done, to hear you groan out of a cart, up the heavy hill.

KNOCKEM

Of Holborn, Ursla, meanst thou so? For what? For what, pretty   5
Urs?

URSLA

For cutting halfpenny purses, or stealing little penny dogs out o' the Fair.

KNOCKEM

O! good words, good words, Urs.

121 *dove* darling
123-4 *a fool's handsel is lucky* A well-known proverb (Tilley, F517); 'handsel' is the first money taken in a day.
127 *takes* works, succeeds

3-4 *groan . . . heavy hill* Criminals sentenced to hanging were conveyed by cart from Newgate Gaol, up Holborn Hill, to the gallows at Tyburn; 'heavy' = 'grievous', 'distressing'.

OVERDO

    [*Aside*] Another special enormity. A cutpurse of the sword, the   10
boot, and the feather! Those are his marks.

[Enter MOONCALF]

URSLA

    You are one of those horse-leeches that gave out I was dead, in
Turnbull Street, of a surfeit of bottle-ale and tripes?

KNOCKEM

    No, 'twas better meat, Urs: cows' udders, cows' udders!

URSLA

    Well, I shall be meet with your mumbling mouth one day.   15

KNOCKEM

    What? Thou'lt poison me with a neuft in a bottle of ale, wilt
thou? Or a spider in a tobacco-pipe, Urs? Come, there's no malice
in these fat folks. I never fear thee, an I can scape thy lean
Mooncalf here. Let's drink it out, good Urs, and no vapours!

[Exit URSLA]

OVERDO

    Dost thou hear, boy?—There's for thy ale, and the remnant for   20
thee.—Speak in thy faith of a faucet, now. Is this goodly person
before us here, this Vapours', a knight of the knife?

MOONCALF

    What mean you by that, Master Arthur?

OVERDO

    I mean a child of the horn-thumb, a babe of booty, boy, a cutpurse.

MOONCALF

    O Lord, sir! far from it. This is Master Dan Knockem— Jordan   25
the ranger of Turnbull. He is a horse-courser, sir.

---

12 *horse-leeches* (i) farriers (ii) large blood-sucking leeches (iii) rapacious predators

15 *meet with* quits with, revenged on

16 *neuft* newt

17–18 *there's no malice in these fat folks* A version of the proverb 'Fat folks are good-natured' (Tilley, F419).

19 *vapours* This word which is used extensively in the play, is defined by Jonson himself in the s.d. at IV.iv.25 as 'nonsense'. For Knockem, who employs it incessantly, it means whatever he wants it to mean—usually little or nothing. It seems, however, to have two main connotations: (i) fantastic notions (ii) a ridiculous urge to brag and quarrel.

24 *horn-thumb* Cutpurses protected their thumbs with a piece of horn, so that they did not cut themselves in the act of cutting a purse

25 *Jordan* chamber-pot

OVERDO

Thy dainty dame, though, called him cutpurse.

MOONCALF

Like enough, sir. She'll do forty such things in an hour, an you listen to her, for her recreation, if the toy take her i'the greasy kerchief. It makes her fat, you see. She battens with it.   30

OVERDO

[*Aside*] Here might I ha' been deceived now, and ha' put a fool's blot upon myself, if I had not played an after-game o' discretion.

URSLA *comes in again dropping*

KNOCKEM

Alas, poor Urs, this's an ill season for thee.

URSLA

Hang yourself, hackney-man.   35

KNOCKEM

How, how, Urs? Vapours? Motion breed vapours?

URSLA

Vapours! Never tusk, nor twirl your dibble, good Jordan, I know what you'll take to a very drop. Though you be captain o' the roarers, and fight well at the case of piss-pots, you shall not fright me with your lion-chap, sir, nor your tusks. You angry?   40 You are hungry. Come, a pig's head will stop your mouth and stay your stomach at all times.

---

29 *toy* whim
30 *kerchief* cloth used as head-cover, but here the head itself
32 *after-game* second game played to reverse the outcome of the first
33 s.d. *dropping* exhausted and dripping with sweat
36 *How, how, Urs? Vapours?* ed. (How? how? *Vrs*, vapours! F)
    Motion breed vapours? Does activity give rise to tantrums?
37 *Never tusk, nor twirl your dibble* An obscure and disputed passage; *OED* suggests that 'tusk' means 'show your teeth', and 'twirl your dibble' = 'twist your moustache'. It seems more likely, however, since Ursla goes on to refer to Jordan's 'lion-chap' and his 'tusks', that 'tusks' are the ends of the moustache and the 'dibble' a little spade beard; 'tusk' would then mean 'twist up the ends of your moustache', and 'twirl your dibble', 'twist your little beard around'.
39 *at the case of piss-pots* To 'fight at the case of pistols' was to fight with a pair of pistols; but Ursla cleverly replaces the expected 'pistols' with 'piss-pots'.
40 *lion-chap* lion's jaw

KNOCKEM

Thou art such another mad merry Urs still! Troth, I do make conscience of vexing thee now i' the dog-days, this hot weather, for fear of foundering thee i' the body, and melting down a 45 pillar of the Fair. Pray thee take thy chair again, and keep state; and let's have a fresh bottle of ale, and a pipe of tobacco; and no vapours. I'll ha' this belly o' thine taken up, and thy grass scoured, wench. Look! here's Ezekiel Edgworth, a fine boy of his inches as any is i' the Fair! Has still money in his purse, and will 50 pay all with a kind heart, and good vapours.

ACT II, SCENE iv

[*Enter*] *to them* EDGWORTH, NIGHTINGALE, CORNCUTTER, TINDERBOX-MAN, PASSENGERS

EDGWORTH

That I will, indeed, willingly, Master Knockem. [*To* MOONCALF] Fetch some ale and tobacco.

[*Exit* MOONCALF]

LEATHERHEAD

What do you lack, gentlemen? Maid, see a fine hobby-horse for your young master; cost you but a token a week his provender.

CORNCUTTER

Ha' you any corns i' your feet and toes? 5

TINDERBOX-MAN

Buy a mousetrap, a mousetrap, or a tormentor for a flea.

---

45 *foundering* causing a horse to break down by overworking it
46 *keep state* act like a queen
48 *taken up* reduced (farriers' terminology)
49 *scoured* purged out
49–51 *Look!... vapours* While Knockem is saying these words, Edgworth makes his way from the rear of the stage to the front, where Knockem and Ursla are. He is not regarded as being fully on stage until he joins them.

1 s.d. TINDERBOX-MAN Here, and in the s.p. of the one speech assigned to him (l. 6), the Tinderbox-man takes the place of the Mousetrap-man listed among the Persons of the Play, though mousetraps still appear to be his main stock in trade.
Knockem. ed. (Knockhum, F)
6 *tormentor* trap

TRASH

Buy some gingerbread.

NIGHTINGALE

Ballads, ballads! fine new ballads!

> *Hear for your love, and buy for your money!*
> *A delicate ballad o' 'The Ferret and the Coney';*   10
> *'A Preservative again the Punk's Evil';*
> *Another of 'Goose-green Starch and the Devil';*
> *'A Dozen of Divine Points' and 'The Godly Garters';*
> *'The Fairing of Good Counsel', of an ell and three quarters.*

What is't you buy?   15

> *'The Windmill blown down by the witch's fart!'*
> *Or 'Saint George, that O! did break the dragon's heart!'*

[*Enter* MOONCALF]

EDGWORTH

Master Nightingale, come hither, leave your mart a little.

NIGHTINGALE

O my secretary! What says my secretary?

OVERDO

Child o' the bottles, what's he? What's he?   20

---

9   *Hear . . . money* Cf. the proverbial 'not to be had for love or money' (Tilley, L484).

10   *The Ferret and the Coney* The swindler and the dupe (thieves' cant)

11   *Punk's Evil* venereal disease

12   *Goose-green* (more usually 'gooseturd-green') yellowish green
     Goose-green Starch and the Devil The story on which this 'goodly Ballad against Pride' was based is told by Philip Stubbes in his *Anatomie of Abuses* (1583). It concerns a proud young woman of Antwerp who, dissatisfied with the way in which her ruffs were starched, wished that the Devil might take her 'when she weare any of those Neckerchers again'. Thereupon, the Devil came to her in the likeness of a young man, set her ruffs beautifully, so that she fell in love with him, and then, in the act of kissing her, broke her neck (*The Anatomie of Abuses*, ed. Furnivall, 1877, i. 71-2).

13   *A Dozen of Divine Points* Twelve moral maxims, in the form of a ballad, 'sent by a gentlewoman to her lover for a new yeares gift'.
     The Godly Garters Probably the ballad which John Charlwood entered on the Stationers' Register on 20 October 1578 under the title 'A paire of garters for yonge men to weare that serve the Lord God and Lyve in his feare'.

14   *ell* forty-five inches

18   *mart* trade

20   *What's* ed. (what F)

MOONCALF

A civil young gentleman, Master Arthur, that keeps company
with the roarers, and disburses all still. He has ever money in his
purse. He pays for them, and they roar for him: one does good
offices for another. They call him the secretary, but he serves nobody.
A great friend of the ballad-man's, they are never asunder.   25

OVERDO

What pity 'tis so civil a young man should haunt this debauched
company! Here's the bane of the youth of our time apparent. A
proper penman, I see't in his countenance; he has a good clerk's
look with him, and I warrant him a quick hand.

MOONCALF

A very quick hand, sir.   [*Exit*]   30

EDGWORTH

(*This they whisper that* OVERDO *hears it not*)

All the purses and purchase I give you today by conveyance,
bring hither to Ursla's presently. Here we will meet at night in her
lodge, and share. Look you choose good places for your standing
i' the Fair, when you sing, Nightingale.

URSLA

Ay, near the fullest passages; and shift 'em often.   35

EDGWORTH

And i' your singing you must use your hawk's eye nimbly, and fly the
purse to a mark still—where 'tis worn and o' which side—that
you may gi' me the sign with your beak, or hang your head that
way i' the tune.

URSLA

Enough, talk no more on't. Your friendship, masters, is not now   40
to begin. Drink your draught of indenture, your sup of
covenant, and away. The Fair fills apace, company begins to
come in, and I ha' ne'er a pig ready yet.

23 *roar* behave noisily and riotously (to help the cutpurse)
31 *purchase* booty, stolen goods
    conveyance sleight of hand
35 *fullest passages* most crowded thoroughfares
36–7 *fly the purse to a mark* Indicate precisely where the purse is—an image taken from hawking.
40–1 *Your friendship . . . begin* A significant reminiscence of Chaucer's remark about the collusion
    between the Doctor and the apothecaries:
        'For ech of hem made other for to winne;
        Hir frendschipe nas nat newe to beginne.'
        (Prologue to *The Canterbury Tales*, 427-8)
41 *draught of indenture* pledge drunk on the signing of an agreement, with a pun on 'draft'

KNOCKEM

Well said! Fill the cups and light the tobacco. Let's give fire
i'th'works, and noble vapours.   45

EDGWORTH

And shall we ha' smocks, Ursla, and good whimsies, ha?

URSLA

Come, you are i' your bawdy vein! The best the Fair will afford,
Zekiel, if bawd Whit keep his word.

[*Enter* MOONCALF]

How do the pigs, Mooncalf?

MOONCALF

Very passionate, mistress; one on 'em has wept out an eye. Master   50
Arthur o' Bradley is melancholy here; nobody talks to him. Will
you any tobacco, Master Arthur?

OVERDO

No, boy, let my meditations alone.

MOONCALF

He's studying for an oration now.

OVERDO

[*Aside*] If I can, with this day's travail and all my policy, but   55
rescue this youth here out of the hands of the lewd man and the
strange woman, I will sit down at night and say with my friend
Ovid, *Iamque opus exegi, quod nec Iovis ira, nec ignis, etc.*

KNOCKEM

Here, Zekiel; here's a health to Ursla, and a kind vapour! Thou
hast money t' thy purse still, and store! How dost thou come by   60
it? Pray thee vapour thy friends some in a courteous vapour.

---

46 *smocks* wenches
   whimsies Also occurring in the form 'whimsbies', this is a variant on the vulgar 'quims',
   i.e., 'female genitalia', used as a synonym for 'whores'.
50 *passionate* sorrowful, sorry for themselves
55 *policy* shrewd contriving
57 *strange woman*, ed. (strange woman. F) harlot
58 *Iamque . . . ignis, etc.* Having completed his *Metamorphoses*, Ovid expresses, in the last
   nine lines of that work, his conviction that it will bring him immortal fame. The passage
   opens thus:
      Iamque opus exegi, quod nec Iovis ira, nec ignis,
      Nec poterit ferrum, nec edax abolere vetustas (xv. 871-2):
   'And now I have finished a work, which neither the anger of Jove, nor fire, nor sword,
   nor devouring time will ever destroy'.
60 *store* plenty

EDGWORTH

Half I have, Master Dan Knockem, is always at your service.

OVERDO

[*Aside*] Ha, sweet nature! What goshawk would prey upon such a lamb?

KNOCKEM

Let's see what 'tis, Zekiel, count it! [*to* MOONCALF] Come, fill   65
him to pledge me.

ACT II, SCENE v

[*Enter*] WINWIFE, QUARLOUS, *to them*

WINWIFE

We are here before 'em, methinks.

QUARLOUS

All the better; we shall see 'em come in now.

LEATHERHEAD

What do you lack, gentlemen, what is't you lack? A fine horse? A lion? A bull? A bear? A dog or a cat? An excellent fine Bartholmew-bird? Or an instrument? What is't you lack?   5

QUARLOUS

'Slid! here's Orpheus among the beasts, with his fiddle and all!

TRASH

Will you buy any comfortable bread, gentlemen?

QUARLOUS

And Ceres selling her daughter's picture in gingerwork!

WINWIFE

That these people should be so ignorant to think us chapmen for 'em! Do we look as if we would buy gingerbread? Or hobby-   10
horses?

6 *Orpheus among the beasts* According to Greek myth, Orpheus, the greatest poet and musician who ever lived, could charm beasts with the sound of his lyre.

7 *comfortable bread* bread that does the stomach good

8 *Ceres selling . . . gingerwork!* Ceres, goddess of the cornfield, was the mother of Proserpina. When her daughter was carried off to Hades by Pluto, Ceres wandered about for nine days seeking news of her before she discovered what had happened.

9 *chapmen* customers

QUARLOUS

Why, they know no better ware than they have, nor better
customers than come. And our very being here makes us fit to be
demanded, as well as others. Would Cokes would come! There
were a true customer for 'em.   15

KNOCKEM

[*To* EDGWORTH] How much is't? Thirty shillings? Who's
yonder? Ned Winwife? And Tom Quarlous, I think! Yes.— Gi'
me it all, gi' me it all.—Master Winwife! Master Quarlous! Will
you take a pipe of tobacco with us?—Do not discredit me now,
Zekiel.   20

WINWIFE

Do not see him! He is the roaring horse-courser. Pray thee let's
avoid him; turn down this way.

QUARLOUS

'Slud, I'll see him, and roar with him too, an he roared as loud as
Neptune. Pray thee go with me.

WINWIFE

You may draw me to as likely an inconvenience, when you   25
please, as this.

QUARLOUS

Go to then, come along. We ha' nothing to do, man, but to see
sights now.

KNOCKEM

Welcome, Master Quarlous, and Master Winwife! Will you take
any froth and smoke with us?   30

QUARLOUS

Yes, sir; but you'll pardon us if we knew not of so much
familiarity between us afore.

KNOCKEM

As what, sir?

QUARLOUS

To be so lightly invited to smoke and froth.

KNOCKEM

A good vapour! Will you sit down, sir? This is old Ursla's   35
mansion; how like you her bower? Here you may ha' your punk
and your pig in state, sir, both piping hot.

---

23   *'Slud* by God's blood
25   *as likely an inconvenience* as promising a piece of mischief (Spencer)

QUARLOUS
I had rather ha' my punk cold, sir.

OVERDO
[*Aside*] There's for me: punk! and pig!

URSLA   *She calls within*
What, Mooncalf, you rogue!   40

MOONCALF
By and by; the bottle is almost off, mistress. Here, Master
Arthur.

URSLA
[*Within*] I'll part you and your play-fellow there i' the guarded
coat, an you sunder not the sooner.

KNOCKEM
Master Winwife, you are proud, methinks; you do not talk, nor   45
drink. Are you proud?

WINWIFE
Not of the company I am in, sir, nor the place, I assure you.

KNOCKEM
You do not except at the company, do you? Are you in vapours,
sir?

MOONCALF
Nay, good Master Dan Knockem, respect my mistress' bower, as   50
you call it. For the honour of our booth, none o' your vapours
here.

URSLA   *She comes out with a fire-brand*
Why, you thin lean polecat you, an they have a mind to be i' their
vapours, must you hinder 'em? What did you know, vermin, if
they would ha' lost a cloak, or such a trifle? Must you be drawing   55
the air of pacification here, while I am tormented within, i'the
fire, you weasel?

MOONCALF
Good mistress, 'twas in the behalf of your booth's credit that I
spoke.

---

38   *cold* because a 'hot' punk would be one with venereal disease
41   *off* finished
43   *guarded* trimmed (with lace or braid)

URSLA

    Why, would my booth ha' broke if they had fallen out in't, sir? Or 60
would their heat ha' fired it? In, you rogue, and wipe the pigs, and
mend the fire, that they fall not, or I'll both baste and roast you
till your eyes drop out, like 'em. Leave the bottle behind you, and
be curst a while.

                                         [*Exit* MOONCALF]

QUARLOUS

    Body o' the Fair! what's this? Mother o' the bawds? 65

KNOCKEM

    No, she's mother o' the pigs, sir, mother o' the pigs!

WINWIFE

    Mother o' the Furies, I think, by her fire-brand.

QUARLOUS

    Nay, she is too fat to be a Fury, sure; some walking sow of
tallow!

WINWIFE

    An inspired vessel of kitchen-stuff!   *She drinks this while* 70

QUARLOUS

    She'll make excellent gear for the coach-makers here in
Smithfield to anoint wheels and axle-trees with.

URSLA

    Ay, ay, gamesters, mock a plain plump soft wench o' the
suburbs, do, because she's juicy and wholesome. You must ha'
your thin pinched ware, pent up i' the compass of a dog-collar— 75
or 'twill not do—that looks like a long laced conger set upright;
and a green feather, like fennel i' the joll on't.

---

60   *broke* (i) fallen to pieces (ii) gone bankrupt (punning on 'credit')
62   *baste . . . roast* beat (in addition to normal culinary meanings)
68   *too fat to be a Fury* Because 'Fat folks are good-natured' (Tilley, F419).
     sure; ed. (sure, F)
68–9 *walking sow of tallow* Large oblong mass of tallow endowed with the power of movement;
     cf. 'sow of lead', 'sow of iron' (*OED*, Sow, *sb.*¹ 6.a. and b.); a sow of lead weighed about
     300 lb.
70   *An inspired vessel of kitchen-stuff* A container full of dripping that has been given the
     breath of life, with an allusion to Genesis, ii. 7.
71   *gear* material, stuff
74   *suburbs* The suburbs of London, especially those on the South Bank, were notorious for
     their brothels; in the City itself prostitution was more strictly regulated.
76   *laced* (i) streaked (ii) slashed (ready for cooking)
77   *joll* head (of a fish)

KNOCKEM

    Well said, Urs, my good Urs! To 'em, Urs!

QUARLOUS

    Is she your quagmire, Dan Knockem? Is this your bog?

NIGHTINGALE

    We shall have a quarrel presently.   80

KNOCKEM

    How? Bog? Quagmire? Foul vapours! Hum'h!

QUARLOUS

    Yes, he that would venture for't, I assure him, might sink into
    her, and be drowned a week ere any friend he had could find
    where he were.

WINWIFE

    And then he would be a fortnight weighing up again.   85

QUARLOUS

    'Twere like falling into a whole shire of butter. They had need be
    a team of Dutchmen, should draw him out.

KNOCKEM

    Answer 'em, Urs. Where's thy Bartholmew-wit now? Urs, thy
    Bartholmew-wit?

URSLA

    Hang 'em, rotten, roguy cheaters! I hope to see 'em plagued one   90
    day—poxed they are already, I am sure—with lean playhouse
    poultry, that has the bony rump sticking out, like the ace of
    spades or the point of a partizan, that every rib of 'em is like the
    tooth of a saw; and will so grate 'em with their hips and shoulders
    as, take 'em altogether, they were as good lie with a hurdle.   95

QUARLOUS

    Out upon her, how she drips! She's able to give a man the
    sweating sickness with looking on her.

URSLA

    Marry look off, with a patch o' your face and a dozen i' your

---

79   *quagmire . . . bog* Horse-dealers kept a part of their yards in a very soft wet condition, so
      that horses with unsound legs could stand there without betraying their deficiencies.

85   *weighing up* raising up (of an anchor or sunken ship)

87   *Dutchmen* Popularly thought of as great consumers of butter.

91-2 *playhouse poultry* whores (cf. French *poules*) who frequented theatres

93   *partizan* long-handled spear

97   *sweating sickness* epidemic fever prevalent in the 15th and 16th centuries

98-9 *patch . . . breech* symptoms of venereal disease

breech, though they be o' scarlet, sir. I ha' seen as fine outsides as
either o' yours bring lousy linings to the broker's ere now, twice   100
a week.

QUARLOUS

Do you think there may be a fine new cucking-stool i' the Fair to
be purchased? One large enough, I mean. I know there is a pond
of capacity for her.

URSLA

For your mother, you rascal! Out, you rogue, you hedge-bird,   105
you pimp, you pannier-man's bastard you!

QUARLOUS

Ha, ha, ha!

URSLA

Do you sneer, you dog's-head, you trendle-tail? You look as you
were begotten atop of a cart in harvest-time, when the whelp was
hot and eager. Go snuff after your brother's bitch, Mistress   110
Commodity. That's the livery you wear. 'Twill be out at the
elbows shortly. It's time you went to't for the tother remnant.

KNOCKEM

Peace, Urs, peace, Urs!—They'll kill the poor whale and make oil
of her.—Pray thee go in.

URSLA

I'll see 'em poxed first, and piled, and double piled.   115

WINWIFE

Let's away; her language grows greasier than her pigs.

URSLA

Does't so, snotty-nose? Good Lord! are you snivelling? You were
engendered on a she-beggar in a barn when the bald thrasher,
your sire, was scarce warm.

WINWIFE

Pray thee let's go.   120

---

100   *bring lousy linings to the broker's* Either (i) bring lice-infested underclothes to the
  pawnbroker's, or (ii) bring the diseased contents of your breeches, i.e., sexual organs,
  to the bawd's. (Cf. *OED*, Lining, *vbl. sb.*¹, 1. b. and 3.) *broker's* ed. (Brokers F)
102   *cucking-stool* chair used for punishing scolds, who were fastened in it and then ducked
  in a pond
105   *hedge-bird* foot-pad, vagrant (one born under a hedge)
106   *pannier-man's* hawker's
108   *trendle-tail* cur, mongrel with a curly tail
111   *Commodity* (i) gain (ii) article for sale (whore)
115   *piled* (i) bald (from the pox) (ii) afflicted with piles (iii) threadbare, reduced to beggary

QUARLOUS

No, faith; I'll stay the end of her now. I know she cannot last long; I find by her similes she wanes apace.

URSLA

Does she so? I'll set you gone. Gi' me my pig-pan hither a little. I'll scald you hence, an you will not go.   [*Exit*]

KNOCKEM

Gentlemen, these are very strange vapours! And very idle   125
vapours, I assure you!

QUARLOUS

You are a very serious ass, we assure you.

KNOCKEM

Hum'h! Ass? And serious? Nay, then pardon me my vapour. I have a foolish vapour, gentlemen: any man that does vapour me the ass, Master Quarlous—   130

QUARLOUS

What then, Master Jordan?

KNOCKEM

I do vapour him the lie.

QUARLOUS

Faith, and to any man that vapours me the lie, I do vapour that.   [*Strikes him*]

KNOCKEM

Nay then, vapours upon vapours.   135

EDGWORTH, NIGHTINGALE

'Ware the pan, the pan, the pan! She comes with the pan, gentlemen.

URSLA *comes in with the scalding-pan. They fight. She falls with it.*

God bless the woman!

URSLA

Oh!

[*Exeunt* QUARLOUS, WINWIFE]

TRASH

What's the matter?   140

OVERDO

Goodly woman!

123   *set you gone* set you going
139   s.p. TRASH ed. (ERA. F)

MOONCALF

Mistress!

URSLA

Curse of hell that ever I saw these fiends! Oh! I ha' scalded my leg, my leg, my leg, my leg! I ha' lost a limb in the service! Run for some cream and salad oil, quickly. [*To* MOONCALF] Are you   145
under-peering, you baboon? Rip off my hose, an you be men, men, men.

MOONCALF

Run you for some cream, good mother Joan. I'll look to your basket.

[*Exit* TRASH]

LEATHERHEAD

Best sit up i' your chair, Ursla. Help, gentlemen.   150

[*They lift her up*]

KNOCKEM

Be of good cheer, Urs. Thou hast hindered me the currying of a couple of stallions here, that abused the good race-bawd o' Smithfield. 'Twas time for 'em to go.

NIGHTINGALE

I'faith, when the pan came. They had made you run else.— This had been a fine time for purchase, if you had ventured.   155

EDGWORTH

Not a whit, these fellows were too fine to carry money.

KNOCKEM

Nightingale, get some help to carry her leg out o' the air; take off her shoes. Body o' me, she has the malanders, the scratches, the crown-scab, and the quitter-bone i' the tother leg.

URSLA

Oh, the pox! Why do you put me in mind o' my leg thus, to make   160
it prick and shoot? Would you ha' me i' the Hospital afore my time?

KNOCKEM

Patience, Urs. Take a good heart; 'tis but a blister as big as a windgall. I'll take it away with the white of an egg, a little honey,

151 *currying* beating, dressing-down
152 *race-bawd* breeder of bawds, mother-bawd
155 *purchase* theft
156 *fine* smart, clever
158–9 *malanders . . . quitter-bone* These are all diseases of the leg and hoof in horses.
164 *windgall* soft tumour on a horse's leg

and hog's-grease. Ha' thy pasterns well rolled, and thou shalt   165
pace again by tomorrow. I'll tend thy booth and look to thy
affairs the while. Thou shalt sit i' thy chair, and give directions,
and shine Ursa major.

[*Exeunt* KNOCKEM *and* MOONCALF *with* URSLA *in her chair*]

ACT II, SCENE vi

[*Enter*] COKES, WASP, MISTRESS OVERDO, GRACE

OVERDO

These are the fruits of bottle-ale and tobacco! the foam of the one
and the fumes of the other! Stay, young man, and despise not the
wisdom of these few hairs that are grown grey in care of thee.

EDGWORTH

Nightingale, stay a little. Indeed I'll hear some of this!

COKES

Come, Numps, come, where are you? Welcome into the Fair,   5
Mistress Grace.

EDGWORTH

[*To* NIGHTINGALE] 'Slight, he will call company, you shall see,
and put us into doings presently.

OVERDO

Thirst not after that frothy liquor, ale; for who knows, when he
openeth the stopple, what may be in the bottle? Hath not a snail,   10
a spider, yea, a neuft been found there? Thirst not after it, youth;
thirst not after it.

COKES

This is a brave fellow, Numps, let's hear him.

164–5 *white . . . hog's-grease* Remedies used by farriers to deal with diseases in horses.
  165 *rolled* bandaged
  168 *Ursa major* the constellation of the Great Bear

   7 *'Slight* by God's light
  13 *brave* fine, capital

WASP

'Sblood, how brave is he? In a guarded coat? You were best truck with him; e'en strip, and truck presently; it will become 15 you. Why will you hear him? Because he is an ass, and may be akin to the Cokeses?

COKES

O, good Numps!

OVERDO

Neither do thou lust after that tawny weed, tobacco.

COKES

Brave words! 20

OVERDO

Whose complexion is like the Indian's that vents it!

COKES

Are they not brave words, sister?

OVERDO

And who can tell if, before the gathering and making up thereof, the alligarta hath not pissed thereon?

WASP

'Heart, let 'em be brave words, as brave as they will! An they were 25 all the brave words in a country, how then? Will you away yet? Ha' you enough on him? Mistress Grace, come you away, I pray you, be not you accessary. If you do lose your licence, or somewhat else, sir, with listening to his fables, say Numps is a witch, with all my heart, do, say so. 30

COKES

Avoid, i' your satin doublet, Numps.

OVERDO

The creeping venom of which subtle serpent, as some late writers affirm, neither the cutting of the perilous plant, nor the drying of it, nor the lighting or burning, can any way persway or assuage. 35

---

14 *brave* well dressed
15 *truck* make an exchange (of clothes)
16 *him?* ed. (him, F)
21 *vents* sells (*OED*, Vent, *v*.3, 1.)
24 *alligarta* alligator
30 *witch* wizard
31 *Avoid* go away, keep off (cf. 'Avoid, Satan')
32–3 *some late writers* The most famous of those who wrote to attack the use of tobacco was James I, whose *Counterblaste to Tobacco* had come out in 1604.
34 *persway* diminish

COKES

Good, i'faith! is't not, sister?

OVERDO

Hence it is that the lungs of the tobacconist are rotted, the liver spotted, the brain smoked like the backside of the pig-woman's booth here, and the whole body within, black as her pan you saw e'en now without.   40

COKES

A fine similitude that, sir! Did you see the pan?

EDGWORTH

Yes, sir.

OVERDO

Nay, the hole in the nose here of some tobacco-takers, or the third nostril, if I may so call it, which makes that they can vent the tobacco out like the ace of clubs, or rather the flower-de-lys,   45
is caused from the tobacco, the mere tobacco! when the poor innocent pox, having nothing to do there, is miserably and most unconscionably slandered.

COKES

Who would ha' missed this, sister?

MISTRESS OVERDO

Not anybody but Numps.   50

COKES

He does not understand.

EDGWORTH

[*Aside*] Nor you feel.   *He picketh his purse*

COKES

What would you have, sister, of a fellow that knows nothing but a basket-hilt and an old fox in't? The best music i' the Fair will not move a log.   55

EDGWORTH

[*Slipping the purse to* NIGHTINGALE] In to Ursla, Nightingale, and carry her comfort. See it told. This fellow was sent to us by fortune for our first fairing.

---

37 *tobacconist* smoker
43-4 *hole in the nose . . . third nostril* An effect of syphilis; but Overdo prefers to attribute it to smoking.
44 *vent* blow, exhale
54 *basket-hilt* hilt with a basket-like protection for the hand
     fox sword
57 *told* counted

[*Exit* NIGHTINGALE]

OVERDO

But what speak I of the diseases of the body, children of the Fair?

COKES

That's to us, sister. Brave i'faith!   60

OVERDO

Hark, O you sons and daughters of Smithfield! and hear what
malady it doth the mind: it causeth swearing, it causeth swaggering,
it causeth snuffling and snarling, and now and then a hurt.

MISTRESS OVERDO

He hath something of Master Overdo, methinks, brother.

COKES

So methought, sister, very much of my brother Overdo. And, 'tis   65
when he speaks.

OVERDO

Look into any angle o' the town—the Straits, or the
Bermudas—where the quarrelling lesson is read, and how do
they entertain the time but with bottle-ale and tobacco? The
lecturer is o' one side, and his pupils o' the other; but the   70
seconds are still bottle-ale and tobacco, for which the lecturer
reads and the novices pay. Thirty pound a week in bottle-ale!
forty in tobacco! and ten more in ale again! Then, for a suit to
drink in, so much, and, that being slavered, so much for
another suit, and then a third suit, and a fourth suit! and still the 75
bottle-ale slavereth, and the tobacco stinketh!

WASP

Heart of a madman! are you rooted here? Will you never away?
What can any man find out in this bawling fellow, to grow here

---

63   *snuffling* sniffing with contempt
67   *angle* corner
67–8   *the Straits, or the Bermudas* A disreputable district of narrow lanes and alleys near Charing
       Cross, frequented by criminals.
68   *the quarrelling lesson* The vogue for fencing and duelling with sword and dagger, which
       developed in the 1590s, led to the establishment of fencing academies and to the
       publication of such works of instruction as Vincentio Saviola's *Practise of the Rapier and
       Dagger* (1594-95), which dealt, among other things, with the right way to go about making
       a challenge. See *As You Like It*, V.iv, 45-97, where Touchstone makes splendid fun of it
       all.
69   *entertain* occupy, while away
71   *seconds* stand-bys, main supports
74   *slavered* soiled with saliva and sweat
77   *Will* ed. (well F)

for? He is a full handful higher sin' he heard him. Will you fix
here? And set up a booth, sir?   80

OVERDO

I will conclude briefly—

WASP

Hold your peace, you roaring rascal, I'll run my head i' your
chaps else. [*To* COKES] You were best build a booth, and
entertain him; make your will, an you say the word, and him
your heir! Heart, I never knew one taken with a mouth of a peck   85
afore. By this light, I'll carry you away o' my back, an you will not
come.   *He gets him up on pickpack*

COKES

Stay, Numps, stay, set me down. I ha' lost my purse, Numps. O
my purse! One o' my fine purses is gone.

MISTRESS OVERDO

Is't indeed, brother?   90

COKES

Ay, as I am an honest man; would I were an arrant rogue, else! A
plague of all roguy damned cutpurses for me!

WASP

Bless 'em with all my heart, with all my heart, do you see! Now,
as I am no infidel, that I know of, I am glad on't. Ay, I am; here's
my witness! do you see, sir? I did not tell you of his fables, I? No, 95
no, I am a dull malt-horse, I, I know nothing. Are you not justly
served, i' your conscience, now? Speak i' your conscience. Much
good do you with all my heart, and his good heart that has it, with
all my heart again.

EDGWORTH

[*Aside*] This fellow is very charitable; would he had a purse too! 100
But I must not be too bold all at a time.

COKES

Nay, Numps, it is not my best purse.

79 *him.* ed. (him, F)
83 *chaps* mouth, chops
84 *entertain* support, maintain
85 *a peck* the capacity of a peck
87 s.d. *pickpack* pick-a-back
91 *Ay, I* ed. (I I F)
96 *malt-horse* heavy horse used to pull brewers' drays

WASP

Not your best! Death! Why should it be your worst? Why should it be any, indeed, at all? Answer me to that. Gi' me a reason from you why it should be any.   105

COKES

Nor my gold, Numps; I ha' that yet. Look here else, sister.

[*Shews* MISTRESS OVERDO *his other purse*]

WASP

Why so, there's all the feeling he has!

MISTRESS OVERDO

I pray you have a better care of that, brother.

COKES

Nay, so I will, I warrant you. Let him catch this that catch can. I would fain see him get this, look you, here.   110

WASP

So, so, so, so, so, so, so, so! Very good.

COKES

I would ha' him come again now, and but offer at it. Sister, will you take notice of a good jest? I will put it just where th'other was, and if we ha' good luck, you shall see a delicate fine trap to catch the cutpurse nibbling.   115

EDGWORTH

[*Aside*] Faith, and he'll try ere you be out o' the Fair.

COKES

Come, Mistress Grace, prithee be not melancholy for my mischance; sorrow wi' not keep it, sweetheart.

GRACE

I do not think on't, sir.

COKES

'Twas but a little scurvy white money, hang it; it may hang the   120
cutpurse one day. I ha' gold left to gi' thee a fairing yet, as hard as the world goes. Nothing angers me but that nobody here looked like a cutpurse, unless 'twere Numps.

---

112   *offer at* make an attempt on
118   *wi' not keep it* Will not bring the purse back—a version of the proverb 'Sorrow will pay no debt' (Tilley, S660).
120   *white money* silver

WASP

How? I? I look like a cutpurse? Death! your sister's a cut-purse!
and your mother and father, and all your kin, were cutpurses!   125
And here is a rogue is the bawd o' the cutpurses, whom I will beat
to begin with.

They speak all together; and WASP *beats the justice*

OVERDO

Hold thy hand, child of wrath and heir of anger. Make it not
Childermas day in thy fury, or the feast of the French
Bartholmew, parent of the Massacre.   130

COKES

Numps, Numps!

MISTRESS OVERDO

Good Master Humphrey!

WASP

You are the Patrico, are you? the patriarch of the cutpurses? You
share, sir, they say; let them share this with you. Are you i' your
hot fit of preaching again? I'll cool you.   135

OVERDO

Murther, murther, murther!

[Exeunt]

ACT III, SCENE i

[Enter] WHIT, HAGGIS, BRISTLE, LEATHERHEAD, TRASH

WHIT

Nay, 'tish all gone now! Dish 'tish phen tou vilt not be phitin call,

---

129   *Childermas day* Feast of the Holy Innocents, 28 December
130   *French Bartholmew* A reference to the great massacre of Protestants in France on 24
        August 1572.
133   *Patrico* hedge-priest of the gypsies and vagabonds

  1   *'tish* 'Tis. The curious and outlandish spellings Jonson resorts to for Whit's speeches are
        intended to represent an Irish brogue, which Elizabethan Englishmen, like their modern
        counterparts, evidently found extremely funny. Jonson, understandably, is not consistent
        in his attempts to reproduce it phonetically. Every now and again he forgets about it and
        allows Whit to lapse into standard English forms.

Master Offisher! Phat ish a man te better to lishen out noishes for
tee an tou art in anoder 'orld—being very shuffishient noishes
and gallantsh too? One o' their brabblesh would have fed ush all
dish fortnight; but tou art so bushy about beggersh still, tou hast   5
no leishure to intend shentlemen, an't be.

HAGGIS

Why, I told you, Davy Bristle.

BRISTLE

Come, come, you told me a pudding, Toby Haggis; a matter of
nothing; I am sure it came to nothing! You said, 'Let's go to
Ursla's', indeed; but then you met the man with the monsters,   10
and I could not get you from him. An old fool, not leave seeing
yet?

HAGGIS

Why, who would ha' thought anybody would ha' quarrelled so
early? Or that the ale o' the Fair would ha' been up so soon?

WHIT

Phy, phat o'clock toest tou tink it ish, man?   15

HAGGIS

I cannot tell.

WHIT

Tou art a vishe vatchman, i' te mean teeme.

HAGGIS

Why, should the watch go by the clock, or the clock by the watch,
I pray?

BRISTLE

One should go by another, if they did well.   20

WHIT

Tou art right now! Phen didst tou ever know or hear of a
shuffishient vatchman but he did tell the clock, phat bushiness
soever he had?

---

4 *brabblesh* brabbles, brawls
6 *intend* pay any attention to
8 *a pudding* a lot of 'tripe', with a pun on 'Haggis'

BRISTLE

Nay, that's most true, a sufficient watchman knows what o'clock it is.   25

WHIT

Shleeping or vaking, ash well as te clock himshelf, or te Jack dat shtrikes him!

BRISTLE

Let's enquire of Master Leatherhead, or Joan Trash here. Master Leatherhead, do you hear, Master Leatherhead?

WHIT

If it be a Ledderhead, 'tish a very tick Ledderhead, tat sho mush   30
noish vill not piersh him.

LEATHERHEAD

I have a little business now, good friends, do not trouble me.

WHIT

Phat? Because o' ty wrought neet-cap and ty phelvet sherkin, man? Phy, I have sheen tee in ty ledder sherkin ere now, Mashter o' de hobby-horses, as bushy and as stately as tou sheem'st to be.   35

TRASH

Why, what an you have, Captain Whit? He has his choice of jerkins, you may see by that, and his caps too, I assure you, when he pleases to be either sick or employed.

LEATHERHEAD

God a mercy, Joan, answer for me.

WHIT

Away, be not sheen i' my company; here be shentlemen, and men   40
of vorship.

[Exeunt HAGGIS, BRISTLE]

26   *Jack* mechanical figure which strikes the bell on a public clock
34   *Phy*, ed. (phy? F)

ACT III, SCENE ii

[*Enter to them*] QUARLOUS, WINWIFE

QUARLOUS

We had wonderful ill luck to miss this prologue o' the purse, but
the best is we shall have five acts of him ere night. He'll be
spectacle enough! I'll answer for't.

WHIT

O Creesh! Duke Quarlous, how dosht tou? Tou dosht not know
me, I fear? I am te vishesht man, but Justish Overdo, in all   5
Bartholmew Fair now. Gi' me twelvepence from tee, I vill help tee
to a vife vorth forty marks for't, an't be.

QUARLOUS

Away, rogue; pimp, away!

WHIT

And she shall shew tee as fine cut-'ork for't in her shmock, too,
as tou cansht vish i'faith. Vilt tou have her, vorshipful Vinvife? I   10
vill help tee to her here, be an't be, in te pig-quarter, gi' me ty
twel'pence from tee.

WINWIFE

Why, there's twel'pence; pray thee wilt thou be gone?

WHIT

Tou art a vorthy man, and a vorshipful man still.

QUARLOUS

Get you gone, rascal.   15

WHIT

I do mean it, man. Prinsh Quarlous, if tou hasht need on me, tou
shall find me here at Ursla's. I vill see phat ale and punk ish i' te
pigshty for tee; bless ty good vorship!   [*Exit*]

QUARLOUS

Look who comes here! John Littlewit!

WINWIFE

And his wife, and my widow, her mother: the whole family.   20

4   *Creesh* Christ
5   *vishesht* wisest
8   *pimp*, ed, (Pimpe F)
9   *cut-'ork* 'cut work', lace
13 *gone?* ed. (gone. F)
14 *still* ever

[Enter] BUSY, LITTLEWIT, PURECRAFT, WIN

QUARLOUS

'Slight, you must gi' 'em all fairings now!

WINWIFE

Not I, I'll not see 'em.

QUARLOUS

They are going a feasting. What schoolmaster's that is with 'em?

WINWIFE

That's my rival, I believe, the baker!

BUSY

So, walk on in the middle way, fore-right; turn neither to the   25
right hand nor to the left. Let not your eyes be drawn aside with
vanity, nor your ear with noises.

QUARLOUS

O, I know him by that start!

LEATHERHEAD

What do you lack? What do you buy, pretty Mistress? a fine
hobby-horse, to make your son a tilter? a drum, to make him a   30
soldier? a fiddle, to make him a reveller? What is't you lack? Little
dogs for your daughters? or babies, male or female?

BUSY

Look not toward them, hearken not. The place is Smithfield, or
the field of smiths, the grove of hobby-horses and trinkets. The
wares are the wares of devils; and the whole Fair is the shop of   35
Satan! They are hooks and baits, very baits, that are hung out on
every side to catch you, and to hold you, as it were, by the gills,
and by the nostrils, as the fisher doth; therefore, you must not
look, nor turn toward them—the heathen man could stop his
ears with wax against the harlot o' the sea; do you the like, with   40
your fingers, against the bells of the Beast.

---

25 *fore-right* straight ahead
30 *tilter* (i) jouster (ii) lecher, rake
33–4 *Smithfield, or the field of smiths* The correct etymology is, in fact, as the earliest recorded
spelling 'Smethefelda' (*c*. 1145) shows, 'Smooth-field'.
39 *the heathen man . . . sea* Busy is somewhat muddled. Ulysses, 'the heathen man', had the
ears of his crew stopped with wax to prevent them from hearing the song of the Sirens,
and had himself lashed to the mast of his boat, so that he could hear the song but was
unable to respond to its invitation. (Homer, *The Odyssey*, xii.)

WINWIFE

What flashes comes from him!

QUARLOUS

O, he has those of his oven! A notable hot baker 'twas, when he
plied the peel. He is leading his flock into the Fair now.

WINWIFE

Rather driving 'em to the pens; for he will let 'em look upon   45
nothing.

[*Enter*] KNOCKEM, WHIT

KNOCKEM

Gentlewomen, the weather's hot! Whither walk you? Have a care
o' your fine velvet caps, the Fair is dusty.

> LITTLEWIT *is gazing at the sign; which is the Pig's Head*
> *with a large writing under it*

Take a sweet delicate booth, with boughs, here i' the way, and
cool yourselves i' the shade, you and your friends. The best pig   50
and bottle-ale i' the Fair, sir. Old Ursla is cook, there you may
read: the pig's head speaks it. Poor soul, she has had a stringhalt,
the maryhinchco; but she's prettily amended.

WHIT

A delicate show-pig, little mistress, with shweet sauce, and
crackling like de bay-leaf i' de fire, la! Tou shalt ha' de clean side   55
o' de table-clot and dy glass vashed with phatersh of Dame
Annessh Cleare.

LITTLEWIT

This's fine, verily, 'Here be the best pigs, and she does roast 'em
as well as ever she did', the pig's head says.

KNOCKEM

Excellent, excellent, mistress, with fire o' juniper and rosemary   60
branches! The oracle of the pig's head, that, sir.

---

42 *flashes* showy phrases
   comes The third person plural in -s is very common in Elizabethan English (see Abbott,
   333).
44 *peel* baker's shovel for putting loaves in the oven and pulling them out
49 *delicate* charming, delightful
52-3 *stringhalt, the maryhinchco* diseases affecting a horse's legs
54 *show-pig* sow-pig (as pronounced by Whit)
56-7 *phatersh of Dame Annessh Cleare* Waters from a spring in Hoxton called Dame Annis
   (Agnes) the clear

PURECRAFT

Son, were you not warned of the vanity of the eye? Have you forgot the wholesome admonition so soon?

LITTLEWIT

Good mother, how shall we find a pig if we do not look about for't? Will it run off o' the spit into our mouths, think you, as in   65
Lubberland, and cry, 'We, we'?

BUSY

No, but your mother, religiously wise, conceiveth it may offer itself by other means to the sense, as by way of steam, which I think it doth, here in this place. Huh, huh!

>   BUSY *scents after it like a hound*

Yes, it doth. And it were a sin of obstinacy, great obstinacy, high   70
and horrible obstinacy, to decline or resist the good titillation of the famelic sense, which is the smell. Therefore be bold (huh, huh, huh), follow the scent. Enter the tents of the unclean, for once, and satisfy your wife's frailty. Let your frail wife be satisfied; your zealous mother, and my suffering self, will also be satisfied.   75

LITTLEWIT

Come, Win, as good winny here as go farther and see nothing.

BUSY

We scape so much of the other vanities by our early entering.

PURECRAFT

It is an edifying consideration.

WIN

This is scurvy, that we must come into the Fair and not look on't.

LITTLEWIT

Win, have patience, Win, I'll tell you more anon.   80

KNOCKEM

Mooncalf, entertain within there; the best pig i' the booth, a pork-like pig. These are Banbury-bloods, o' the sincere stud, come a pig-hunting. Whit, wait, Whit, look to your charge.

>   [*Exit* WHIT]

---

66 *Lubberland* An imaginary country of plenty and idleness, also known as the Land of Cockaigne and, in German, as 'Schlaraffenland'.
72 *famelic* exciting hunger
76 *winny* stay
82 *sincere stud* true breed

BUSY

A pig prepare presently, let a pig be prepared to us.

[*Exeunt* BUSY, LITTLEWIT, WIN, PURECRAFT]

[*Enter*] MOONCALF, URSLA

MOONCALF

'Slight, who be these?   85

URSLA

Is this the good service, Jordan, you'd do me?

KNOCKEM

Why, Urs? Why, Urs? Thou'lt ha' vapours i' thy leg again
presently; pray thee go in; 't may turn to the scratches else.

URSLA

Hang your vapours, they are stale, and stink like you. Are these
the guests o' the game you promised to fill my pit withal today?   90

KNOCKEM

Ay, what ail they, Urs?

URSLA

Ail they? They are all sippers, sippers o' the City. They look as
they would not drink off two penn'orth of bottle-ale amongst
'em.

MOONCALF

A body may read that i' their small printed ruffs.   95

KNOCKEM

Away, thou art a fool, Urs, and thy Mooncalf too, i' your ignorant
vapours now! Hence! Good guests, I say, right hypocrites, good
gluttons. In, and set a couple o' pigs o' the board, and half a dozen
of the biggest bottles afore 'em, and call Whit. I do not love to
hear innocents abused: fine ambling hypocrites! and a stone-   100
puritan with a sorrel head and beard—good-mouthed gluttons,
two to a pig. Away!

[*Exit* MOONCALF]

URSLA

Are you sure they are such?

---

91   *what ail they* what's wrong with them
95   *small printed ruffs* Puritans wore small ruffs, very carefully set; 'in print' was a synonym
     for 'precise'.
100 *stone-puritan* lascivious male puritan (by analogy with *stone-horse = stallion*)
101 *sorrel* chestnut coloured (of horses)

KNOCKEM

O' the right breed; thou shall try 'em by the teeth, Urs. Where's
this Whit? 105

[*Enter* WHIT]

WHIT

Behold, man, and see, what a worthy man am ee!
With the fury of my sword, and the shaking of my beard,
I will make ten thousand men afeard.

KNOCKEM

Well said, brave Whit! In, and fear the ale out o' the bottles into
the bellies of the brethren and the sisters; drink to the cause, and 110
pure vapours.

[*Exeunt* KNOCKEM, WHIT, URSLA]

QUARLOUS

My roarer is turned tapster, methinks. Now were a fine time for
thee, Winwife, to lay aboard thy widow; thou'lt never be master
of a better season or place. She that will venture herself into the
Fair, and a pig-box, will admit any assault, be assured of that. 115

WINWIFE

I love not enterprises of that suddenness, though.

QUARLOUS

I'll warrant thee, then, no wife out o' the widows' hundred. If I
had but as much title to her as to have breathed once on that strait
stomacher of hers, I would now assure myself to carry her yet,
ere she went out of Smithfield. Or she should carry me, which 120

106–8 *Behold. . . afeard* Whit's lines smack of the traditional St George play, described by Thomas
Hardy in *The Return of the Native*, Bk. II, Ch. v.

109 *fear* frighten

110 *brethren and the sisters;* ed. (brethren, and the sisters F)

113 *lay aboard* make advances to (nautical term for the manoeuvre of bringing one ship
alongside another in order to board it)

117 *the widow's hundred* Since a hundred was a sub-division of the English shire, the meaning
would seem to be 'the widows' section of the community', but some topical allusion has
probably been lost.

119 *stomacher* ornamental covering for the chest worn by women under the lacing of the
bodice

120 *carry* win

were the fitter sight, I confess. But you are a modest undertaker,
by circumstances and degrees. Come, 'tis disease in thee, not
judgement. I should offer at all together.—Look, here's the poor
fool again that was stung by the wasp erewhile.

ACT III, SCENE iii

[Enter] OVERDO

OVERDO

I will make no more orations shall draw on these tragical
conclusions. And I begin now to think that, by a spice of
collateral justice, Adam Overdo deserved this beating. For I, the
said Adam, was one cause, a by-cause, why the purse was lost—
and my wife's brother's purse too—which they know not of yet.   5
But I shall make very good mirth with it at supper—that will be
the sport—and put my little friend Master Humphrey Wasp's
choler quite out of countenance, when, sitting at the upper end o'
my table, as I use, and drinking to my brother Cokes and Mistress
Alice Overdo, as I will, my wife, for their good affection to old   10
Bradley, I deliver to 'em it was I that was cudgelled, and shew 'em
the marks. To see what bad events may peep out o' the tail of
good purposes! The care I had of that civil young man I took
fancy to this morning—and have not left it yet—drew me to that
exhortation; which drew the company, indeed; which drew the   15
cutpurse; which drew the money; which drew my brother Cokes
his loss; which drew on Wasp's anger; which drew on my beating:
a pretty gradation! And they shall ha' it i' their dish, i'faith, at
night for fruit. I love to be merry at my table. I had thought once,

---

121 *undertaker* venturer, one who undertakes an enterprise
122 *circumstances* roundabout methods
123 *offer at all together* make an all-out attack, risk everything

1 *shall draw on* which will produce
3 *collateral* concomitant
4 *by-cause* secondary or incidental cause

at one special blow he ga' me, to have revealed myself. But 20
then—I thank thee, fortitude—I remembered that a wise man,
and who is ever so great a part o' the Commonwealth in himself,
for no particular disaster ought to abandon a public good design.
The husbandman ought not, for one unthankful year, to forsake
the plough; the shepherd ought not, for one scabbed sheep, to 25
throw by his tar-box; the pilot ought not, for one leak i' the
poop, to quit the helm; nor the alderman ought not, for one
custard more at a meal, to give up his cloak; the constable ought
not to break his staff and forswear the watch, for one roaring
night; nor the piper o' the parish— *ut parvis componere magna* 30
solebam—to put up his pipes, for one rainy Sunday. These are
certain knocking conclusions; out of which I am resolved,
come what come can—come beating, come imprisonment, come
infamy, come banishment, nay, come the rack, come the
hurdle, welcome all— I will not discover who I am till my due 35
time. And yet still all shall be, as I said ever, in Justice' name, and
the King's, and for the Commonwealth.

WINWIFE

What does he talk to himself, and act so seriously? Poor fool!

[*Exit* OVERDO]

QUARLOUS

No matter what. Here's fresher argument, intend that.

---

20 *myself.* ed. (my selfe? F)
22 *and who . . . himself* Overdo, thinking of himself and petty officers like him as statesmen,
appears to have in mind Cicero's contention (*De Re Publica*, I.iv and v) that the statesman
is at least the equal of the philosopher (the wise man); 'and who' = 'and anyone who'.
26 *tar-box* box used by shepherds to hold tar employed as a cure for skin diseases in sheep
27–8 *one custard more* i.e., an extra guest
28 *cloak* i.e., office (of which the cloak was the mark)
29 *roaring* tempestuous
30 *piper o' the parish* piper employed by the parish to play at church-ales and similar functions
30–1 *ut parvis . . . solebam* Virgil, *Eclogues*, i. 23, with *sic* instead of *ut*: 'thus it was my habit to
compare great things to small ones'.
32 *knocking* clinching, decisive
35 *hurdle* a kind of sledge on which traitors were dragged through the streets to their
execution
38 *What* For what reason, why
39 *fresher argument* more matter for a May morning
intend pay attention to

ACT III, SCENE iv

[*Enter to them*] COKES, MISTRESS OVERDO, GRACE, WASP

COKES

Come, Mistress Grace, come sister, here's more fine sights yet,
i'faith. God's lid, where's Numps?

LEATHERHEAD

What do you lack, gentlemen? What is't you buy? Fine rattles?
drums? Babies? Little dogs? And birds for ladies? What do you
lack?   5

COKES

Good honest Numps, keep afore, I am so afraid thou'lt lose
somewhat. My heart was at my mouth when I missed thee.

WASP

You were best buy a whip i' your hand to drive me.

COKES

Nay, do not mistake, Numps, thou art so apt to mistake; I would
but watch the goods. Look you now, the treble fiddle was e'en   10
almost like to be lost.

WASP

Pray you take heed you lose not yourself. Your best way were e'en
get up and ride for more surety. Buy a token's worth of great pins
to fasten yourself to my shoulder.

LEATHERHEAD

What do you lack, gentlemen? Fine purses, pouches, pin-cases,   15
pipes? What is't you lack? A pair o' smiths to wake you i' the
morning? Or a fine whistling bird?

COKES

Numps, here be finer things than any we ha' bought, by odds!
And more delicate horses, a great deal! Good Numps, stay, and
come hither.   20

---

16 *A pair o' smiths* Presumably a clock of some kind with a pair of 'Jacks' in the shape of
    smiths.

WASP

Will you scourse with him? You are in Smithfield; you may fit yourself with a fine easy-going street-nag for your saddle again Michaelmas term, do. Has he ne'er a little odd cart for you to make a caroche on i' the country, with four pied hobby-horses? Why the measles should you stand here with your train, cheaping 25 of dogs, birds, and babies? You ha' no children to bestow 'em on, ha' you?

COKES

No, but again I ha' children, Numps, that's all one.

WASP

Do, do, do, do! How many shall you have, think you? An I were as you, I'd buy for all my tenants, too. They are a kind o' civil 30 savages that will part with their children for rattles, pipes, and knives. You were best buy a hatchet or two, and truck with 'em.

COKES

Good Numps, hold that little tongue o' thine, and save it a labour. I am resolute Bat, thou know'st.

WASP

A resolute fool you are, I know, and a very sufficient coxcomb. 35 With all my heart—nay, you have it, sir, an you be angry—turd i' your teeth, twice, if I said it not once afore; and much good do you.

WINWIFE

Was there ever such a self-affliction? And so impertinent?

QUARLOUS

Alas! his care will go near to crack him; let's in and comfort him. 40

WASP

Would I had been set i' the ground, all but the head on me, and had my brains bowled at, or threshed out, when first I underwent this plague of a charge!

21 *scourse* barter, bargain
22 *again* against, in preparation for
24 *caroche* smart carriage
25 *cheaping of* bargaining for, asking the price of
28 *again* in anticipation of the time when
30–1 *civil savages* savages of a civilized country
40 *crack him* drive him crazy
41–2 *Would I . . . bowled at* Cf. *The Merry Wives of Windsor*, III.iv, 85-6, where Anne Page responds to the suggestion that she marry Dr Caius by saying:
Alas, I had rather be set quick i' th' earth,
And bowl'd to death with turnips.

QUARLOUS

How now, Numps! Almost tired i' your protectorship?
Overparted? Overparted? 45

WASP

Why, I cannot tell, sir; it may be I am. Does't grieve you?

QUARLOUS

No, I swear does't not, Numps, to satisfy you.

WASP

Numps? 'Sblood, you are fine and familiar! How long ha' we been
acquainted, I pray you?

QUARLOUS

I think it may be remembered, Numps. That? 'Twas since 50
morning, sure.

WASP

Why, I hope I know't well enough, sir; I did not ask to be told.

QUARLOUS

No? Why then?

WASP

It's no matter why. You see with your eyes now, what I said to you
today? You'll believe me another time? 55

QUARLOUS

Are you removing the Fair, Numps?

WASP

A pretty question! and a very civil one! Yes faith, I ha' my lading
you see, or shall have anon; you may know whose beast I am by
my burden. If the pannier-man's jack were ever better known
by his loins of mutton, I'll be flayed and feed dogs for him, when 60
his time comes.

WINWIFE

How melancholy Mistress Grace is yonder! Pray thee let's go
enter ourselves in grace with her.

---

45 *Overparted* Given a bigger part than you can play. Cf. *Love's Labour's Lost*, V.ii, 577-8,
where Costard remarks that Sir Nathaniel was 'a little o'erparted' in taking on the role
of Alexander the Great.

59 *jack* Jackass, male ass. Though *OED* cites no instance of 'jackass' prior to 1727, 'jack' was
used in the sixteenth century to denote the male of some animals and birds. That a jackass
is meant here is evident from the reference to 'beast' and 'burden' (ll. 58-9) and still
more from Wasp's promise to 'be flayed and feed dogs for [in place of] him, when his
time comes', since this is precisely what happened to dead horses and donkeys; they were
flayed and used as dog food.

60 *for* in place of

63 *grace* favour

COKES

Those six horses, friend, I'll have—

WASP

How!   65

COKES

And the three Jew's trumps; and half a dozen o' birds, and that drum—I have one drum already—and your smiths—I like that device o' your smiths very pretty well—and four halberts—and, le' me see, that fine painted great lady, and her three women for state, I'll have.   70

WASP

No, the shop; buy the whole shop, it will be best; the shop, the shop!

LEATHERHEAD

If his worship please.

WASP

Yes, and keep it during the Fair, bobchin.

COKES

Peace, Numps. Friend, do not meddle with him, an you be wise   75 and would shew your head above board; he will sting thorough your wrought night-cap, believe me. A set of these violins I would buy too, for a delicate young noise I have i' the country, that are every one a size less than another, just like your fiddles. I would fain have a fine young masque at my marriage,   80 now I think on't. But I do want such a number o' things. And Numps will not help me now, and I dare not speak to him.

TRASH

Will your worship buy any gingerbread, very good bread, comfortable bread?

COKES

Gingerbread! Yes, let's see.   *He runs to her shop*   85

---

66   *trumps* harps
70   *state* ceremonial shew
74   *bobchin* Defined by *OED* as 'one who bobs his chin', an action denoting folly, especially in the form of idle chatter.
76   *above board* in company
77   *thorough* through
78   *delicate* fine
      noise band of musicians
80   *masque* group of masquers

WASP

There's the tother springe!

LEATHERHEAD

Is this well, Goody Joan? To interrupt my market? In the midst? And
call away my customers? Can you answer this at the Pie-powders?

TRASH

Why, if his mastership have a mind to buy, I hope my ware lies as
open as another's! I may shew my ware as well as you yours.   90

COKES

Hold your peace; I'll content you both: I'll buy up his shop, and
thy basket.

WASP

Will you i'faith?

LEATHERHEAD

Why should you put him from it, friend?

WASP

Cry you mercy! You'd be sold too, would you? What's the price   95
on you? Jerkin and all, as you stand? Ha' you any qualities?

TRASH

Yes, goodman angry-man, you shall find he has qualities, if you
cheapen him.

WASP

God's so, so you ha' the selling of him! What are they? Will they
be bought for love or money?   100

TRASH

No indeed, sir.

WASP

For what then? Victuals?

TRASH

He scorns victuals, sir, he has bread and butter at home, thanks
be to God! And yet he will do more for a good meal, if the toy take
him i' the belly. Marry, then they must not set him at lower end.   105
If they do, he'll go away, though he fast. But put him atop o' the
table, where his place is, and he'll do you forty fine things. He has
not been sent for and sought out for nothing at your great city-

---

86 *springe* snare used to catch birds
96 *qualities* accomplishments
99 *God's so* form of *cazzo* (Italian for penis) used as an oath
    so, so you ed. (so, you F)
105 *lower end* (of the table) where inferior guests sat

suppers, to put down Coriat and Cokeley, and been laughed at
for his labour. He'll play you all the puppets i' the town over, and   110
the players, every company, and his own company too; he spares
nobody!

COKES

I'faith?

TRASH

He was the first, sir, that ever baited the fellow i' the bear's skin,
an't like your worship. No dog ever came near him since. And for   115
fine motions!

COKES

Is he good at those too? Can he set out a masque, trow?

TRASH

O Lord, master! sought to, far and near, for his inventions; and
he engrosses all, he makes all the puppets i' the Fair.

COKES

Dost thou, in troth, old velvet jerkin? Give me thy hand.   120

TRASH

Nay, sir, you shall see him in his velvet jerkin, and a scarf too, at
night, when you hear him interpret Master Littlewit's motion.

COKES

Speak no more, but shut up shop presently, friend. I'll buy both
it and thee too, to carry down with me, and her hamper beside.
Thy shop shall furnish out the masque, and hers the banquet. I   125

---

109   *Coriat* Thomas Coryate (1577?–1617) was a great traveller and, according to Jonson, a
    great bore. His best-known work, *Coryats Crudities* (1611), is an account of his 'trauells
    in France, Sauoy, Italy . . .the Grisons . . . Switzerland, some parts of high Germany, and
    the Netherlands'. When it was published, Jonson contributed some mock-commendatory
    verses to it, together with 'The Character' of the author.(H & S, viii. 373–8.)
    Cokeley A jester of the time, who seems to have improvised at entertainments. Jonson
    also refers to him in *The Devil is an Ass* (I.i, 93) and in his poem 'To Mime' (*Epigrams*,
    cxxix. 16).

114   *baited . . . bear's skin* According to Samuel Rowlands, in his *The Knave of Harts* (1612),
    an actor at the Fortune Theatre, playing the part of a bear, was 'wel-nye' killed by 'Some
    Butchers (playing Dogs)'.

116   *motions* puppet-shews

117   *set out* produce (in the theatrical sense), exhibit (*OED*, Set, *v.*, 149., h.)
    trow do you think

118   *sought* applied, resorted

119   *engrosses* monopolizes

121-2 *at night* this evening
    interpret ventriloquize

125   *banquet* dessert

cannot go less, to set out anything with credit. What's the price, at a word, o' thy whole shop, case and all, as it stands?

LEATHERHEAD

Sir, it stands me in six and twenty shillings sevenpence half-penny, besides three shillings for my ground.

COKES

Well, thirty shillings will do all, then! And what comes yours to?   130

TRASH

Four shillings and elevenpence, sir, ground and all, an't like your worship.

COKES

Yes, it does like my worship very well, poor woman, that's five shillings more. What a masque shall I furnish out for forty shillings—twenty pound Scotch! And a banquet of   135 gingerbread! There's a stately thing! Numps! Sister! And my wedding gloves too! That I never thought on afore. All my wedding gloves gingerbread! O me! what a device will there be, to make 'em eat their fingers' ends! And delicate brooches for the bridemen and all! And then I'll ha' this poesy put to 'em: 'For the   140 best grace', meaning Mistress Grace, my wedding poesy.

GRACE

I am beholden to you, sir, and to your Bartholmew-wit.

WASP

You do not mean this, do you? Is this your first purchase?

COKES

Yes faith, and I do not think, Numps, but thou'lt say, it was the wisest act that ever I did in my wardship.   145

WASP

Like enough! I shall say anything, I!

---

126 *I cannot go less* it's the least I can do
128 *stands me in* costs me, is worth to me
135 *twenty pound Scotch* When the Crowns of England and Scotland were united on the accession of James I to the throne of England, the Scots pound was valued at one-twelfth of a pound sterling, i.e., 1*s*. 8*d*.
137 *wedding gloves* It was customary to present gloves to the guests at a wedding.
140 *bridemen* male attendants on the bridegroom
      poesy posy, motto in metrical form
142 *Bartholmew-wit* foolish attempt to be witty, cheap witticism

ACT III, SCENE v

[*Enter to them*] OVERDO, EDGWORTH, NIGHTINGALE

OVERDO

[*Aside*] I cannot beget a project, with all my political brain, yet;
my project is how to fetch off this proper young man from his
debauched company. I have followed him all the Fair over, and
still I find him with this songster; and I begin shrewdly to suspect
their familiarity; and the young man of a terrible taint, poetry!   5
With which idle disease if he be infected, there's no hope of him
in a state-course. *Actum est* of him for a commonwealth's-man if
he go to't in rhyme once.

EDGWORTH

[*To* NIGHTINGALE] Yonder he is buying o' gingerbread. Set in
quickly, before he part with too much on his money.   10

NIGHTINGALE   [*Sings*]
   My masters and friends, and good people, draw near, etc.

COKES

Ballads! Hark, hark! Pray thee, fellow, stay a little. Good Numps,
look to the goods.   *He runs to the ballad-man*
What ballads hast thou? Let me see, let me see myself.

WASP

Why so! He's flown to another lime-bush. There he will flutter as   15
long more, till he ha' ne'er a feather left. Is there a vexation like
this, gentlemen? Will you believe me now? Hereafter shall I have
credit with you?

---

   1 *political* shrewd
   2 *fetch off* rescue, save
       proper excellent
   7 *state-course* career of public service (?)
       Actum est of it's all up with
       commonwealth's man good citizen
   8 *go to't* indulge
   9 *Set in* Begin, go to work
   15 *lime-bush* snare (literally, a bush smeared with birdlime)
   16 *more* moreover, again
   17 *now? Hereafter* ed. (now, hereafter? F)

QUARLOUS

Yes faith, shalt thou, Numps, and thou art worthy on't, for thou
sweatest for't. I never saw a young puny errant and his squire   20
better matched.

WINWIFE

Faith, the sister comes after 'em well, too.

GRACE

Nay, if you saw the Justice her husband, my guardian, you were
fitted for the mess. He is such a wise one his way—

WINWIFE

I wonder we see him not here.   25

GRACE

O! he is too serious for this place, and yet better sport than the
other three, I assure you, gentlemen, where'er he is, though't be
o' the bench.

COKES

How dost thou call it? *A Caveat against Cutpurses*! A good jest,
i'faith. I would fain see that demon, your cutpurse you talk of,   30
that delicate-handed devil. They say he walks here-about; I would
see him walk now. Look you, sister, here, here, let him come,
sister, and welcome.

He shews his purse boastingly

Ballad-man, does any cutpurses haunt hereabout? Pray thee raise
me one or two; begin and shew me one.   35

NIGHTINGALE

Sir, this is a spell against 'em, spick and span new; and 'tis made
as 'twere in mine own person, and I sing it in mine own defence.
But 'twill cost a penny alone, if you buy it.

---

20 *puny* ed. (Pimpe F) ninny, raw novice, French *béjaune*. Cf. Nashe in his *Christs Teares
    Over Jerusalem* (1593): 'I see others of them [whores] sharing halfe with the Baudes their
    Hostesses, & laughing at the Punies they haue lurched [cheated]' (Nashe, ii. 150. 34–36).
    It is hard to see how Cokes, or Wasp who matches him, or Mistress Overdo who resembles
    ('comes after') him, or Overdo who completes the foursome ('mess'), can properly be
    described as a 'pimp' in any recorded sense of that word. All four are, however, very
    emphatically 'punies'; and 'Punye', in Jonson's handwriting, might easily have been
    misread as 'Pimpe', especially if a tiny splutter of ink had fallen above the first stroke of
    the 'u'.
24 *mess* group of four persons who ate together (*OED*, Mess *sb*. II.4); cf. *Love's Labour's
    Lost*, IV.iii, 203: 'you three fools lack'd me fool to make up the mess'
26 *than the* ed. (then then the F)

COKES

No matter for the price. Thou dost not know me, I see; I am an
odd Bartholmew. 40

MISTRESS OVERDO

Has't a fine picture, brother?

COKES

O sister, do you remember the ballads over the nursery chimney
at home o' my own pasting up? There be brave pictures! Other
manner of pictures than these, friend.

WASP

Yet these will serve to pick the pictures out o' your pockets, you 45
shall see.

COKES

So I heard 'em say. Pray thee mind him not, fellow; he'll have an
oar in everything.

NIGHTINGALE

It was intended, sir, as if a purse should chance to be cut in my
presence, now, I may be blameless though; as by the sequel will 50
more plainly appear.

COKES

We shall find that i' the matter. Pray thee begin.

NIGHTINGALE

To the tune of *Paggington's Pound*, sir.

COKES [*Sings*]

Fa, la la la, la la la, fa la la la. Nay, I'll put thee in tune, and all!
Mine own country dance! Pray thee begin. 55

NIGHTINGALE

It is a gentle admonition, you must know, sir, both to the purse-
cutter and the purse-bearer.

COKES

Not a word more out o' the tune, an thou lov'st me. [*Sings*]
Fa, la la la, la la la, fa la la la. Come, when?

NIGHTINGALE [*Sings*]

My masters and friends, and good people, draw near, 60
And look to your purses, for that I do say;

---

45 *pictures* coins (stamped with the king's head)
50 *though* nevertheless
53 *Paggington's Pound* Also known as *Packington's Pound*, this old country-dance tune still
survives.
58 *out o'* extraneous to, not part of
61 *for that* because of what

COKES

Ha, ha, this chimes! Good counsel at first dash.

NIGHTINGALE

And though little money in them you do bear,
It cost more to get than to lose in a day.

(COKES

Good!)   65

You oft have been told,
Both the young and the old;
And bidden beware of the cutpurse so bold;
Then if you take heed not, free me from the curse,
Who both give you warning, for and the cutpurse.   70

(COKES

Well said! He were to blame that would not, i'faith.)

Youth, youth, thou hadst better been starved by thy nurse,
Than live to be hangèd for cutting a purse.

COKES

Good i'faith, how say you, Numps? Is there any harm i'this?

NIGHTINGALE

It hath been upbraided to men of my trade,   75
That oftentimes we are the cause of this crime.

(COKES

The more coxcombs they that did it, I wusse.)

Alack and for pity, why should it be said?
As if they regarded or places, or time.
Examples have been   80
Of some that were seen,
In Westminster Hall, yea the pleaders between;

---

62 *chimes* rings true, goes well
    at first dash from the start

70 *for and* and moreover

75-6 *It hath . . . crime* The accusation had been made by Robert Greene in his *The Third and Last Part of Cony-Catching* (1592), where one of the stories is very similar to the action of this scene. See *Three Elizabethan Pamphlets*, ed. G. R. Hibbard (London, 1951), pp. 49–51; or *The Elizabethan Underworld*, ed. A. V. Judges (London, 1930) pp. 189–190.

82 *In Westminster Hall* The courts of Common Pleas, of the King's Bench, and of Chancery all sat in the great hall of the Palace of Westminster. H & S note that Thomas Dekker, in his *Iests to make you Merie* (1607), 'has a story of a foreman of the jury, taking pity on a young man who had picked a purse, got him acquitted; the man "in recompence presently vpon his discharge, paying his fees, came to the place where this Juror was, and pickt his pocket"' (H & S, x. 199).

> *Then why should the judges be free from this curse,*
> *More than my poor self, for cutting the purse?*

(COKES

  God a mercy for that! Why should they be more free indeed?)   85
> *Youth, youth, thou hadst better been starved by thy nurse,*
> *Than live to be hangèd for cutting a purse.*

COKES

  That again, good ballad-man, that again!

>   *He sings the burden with him*

  O rare! I would fain rub mine elbow now, but I dare not pull out
my hand. On, I pray thee. He that made this ballad shall be poet   90
to my masque.

NIGHTINGALE

> *At Worcester 'tis known well, and even i' the jail,*
> *A knight of good worship did there shew his face,*
> *Against the foul sinners, in zeal for to rail,*
> *And lost* (ipso facto) *his purse in the place.*   95

(COKES

  Is it possible?)

>   *Nay, once from the seat*
>   *Of judgement so great,*
> *A judge there did lose a fair pouch of velvet.*

(COKES

  I'faith?)   100
> *O Lord for thy mercy, how wicked or worse*
> *Are those that so venture their necks for a purse!*
> *Youth, youth, etc.*

---

  89   *rub mine elbow* (as a sign of glee)

97–9   *Nay . . . velvet* The allusion is to a story preserved by Cresacre More in his *The Life and
Death of Sir Thomas Moore* (1631), pp. 115–17. It tells how More grew tired of hearing one
of the Justices at Newgate upbraid victims of purse-cutting for not keeping their purses
more warily and thus encouraging cutpurses in their activities. Accordingly, he got in
touch with a cutpurse who was about to be tried, and promised to stand his friend 'if he
would cut that Iustice's purse, whilst he sate . . . on the Benche'. The cutpurse agreed.
Coming before the Bench, he asked to speak privately with the Justice, and, while
whispering to him, cut his purse. This he handed to More, who then restored it to its
owner, telling him not to be so censorious in future. The incident is dramatized, with
some alteration, in *Sir Thomas More*, the play in which Shakespeare probably had a hand.
See *Sir Thomas More*, I.ii, in *The Shakespeare Apocrypha*, ed. C. F. Tucker Brooke (Oxford,
1918), pp. 387–90.

COKES   [*Sings the burden with him again*]
    Youth, youth, etc.
Pray thee stay a little, friend. Yet o' thy conscience, Numps,   105
speak; is there any harm i' this?

WASP

To tell you true, 'tis too good for you, 'less you had grace to
follow it.

OVERDO

[*Aside*] It doth discover enormity, I'll mark it more; I ha'
not liked a paltry piece of poetry so well a good while.   110

COKES

    Youth, youth, etc.
Where's this youth now? A man must call upon him, for his own
good, and yet he will not appear. Look here, here's for him;
handy-dandy, which hand will he have?
                    He shews his purse
On, I pray thee, with the rest. I do hear of him, but I cannot see   115
him, this Master Youth, the cutpurse.

NIGHTINGALE

    At plays and at sermons, and at the sessions,
    'Tis daily their practice such booty to make:
    Yea, under the gallows, at executions,
    They stick not the stare-abouts' purses to take—   120
    Nay, one without grace,
    At a far better place,
    At court, and in Christmas, before the King's face.

(COKES

That was a fine fellow! I would have him, now.)
    Alack then for pity, must I bear the curse,   125
    That only belongs to the cunning cutpurse?

---

105 *stay* pause, break off
     friend. Yet ed. (friend, yet F)
107 *'less* unless
114 *handy-dandy* take your choice (from a children's game of guessing in which hand an
     object is hidden)
121–3 *Nay . . . face* The cutpurse in question, John Selman, picked a purse during a celebration
     of the sacrament in the King's Chapel at the Palace of Whitehall on Christmas Day 1611.
     He was hanged for it on 7 January 1612.
122 *a far better* ed. (a better F)

COKES

But where's their cunning now, when they should use it? They are all chained now, I warrant you.

Youth, youth, thou hadst better, etc.

The rat-catcher's charm! Are all fools and asses to this? A pox 130 on 'em, that they will not come! that a man should have such a desire to a thing and want it.

QUARLOUS

'Fore God, I'd give half the Fair, an 'twere mine, for a cutpurse for him, to save his longing.

COKES

Look you, sister, here, here, where is't now? which pocket is't in, 135 for a wager?

He shews his purse again

WASP

I beseech you leave your wagers, and let him end his matter, an't may be.

COKES

O, are you edified, Numps?

OVERDO

[*Aside*] Indeed he does interrupt him too much. There Numps 140 spoke to purpose.

COKES

Sister, I am an ass, I cannot keep my purse?

[He shews his purse] again

On, on, I pray thee, friend.

[While COKES *listens to the song]* EDGWORTH *gets up to him, and tickles him in the ear with a straw twice, to draw his hand out of his pocket*

---

130 *The rat-catcher's charm!* Cf. *As You Like It*, III.ii, 163–5, where Rosalind says, referring to Orlando's verses: 'I was never so berhym'd since Pythagoras' time that I was an Irish rat, which I can hardly remember'. The Irish peasantry held the superstitious belief that their bards could kill rats or drive them away by the use of magical verses.

charm! Are . . . this? ed. (charme, are ... this! F). The Folio punctuation does not make sense. Cokes, frustrated by the failure of the cutpurses to appear, puts their reluctance down to the effect of the ballad, which has, he says, scared them off and made fools and asses of them; 'this' is in apposition to 'charm'.

132 *to* for

want be unable to get

137 *matter* business, performance

142 *purse?* ed. (purse: F)

NIGHTINGALE

> *But O, you vile nation of cutpurses all,*
> *Relent and repent, and amend and be sound,* 145
> *And know that you ought not, by honest men's fall,*
> *Advance your own fortunes, to die above ground;*

(WINWIFE

Will you see sport? Look, there's a fellow gathers up to him, mark.)

> *And though you go gay,* 150
> *In silks as you may,*
> *It is not the highway to heaven, as they say.*

(QUARLOUS

Good, i'faith! O, he has lighted on the wrong pocket.)

> *Repent then, repent you, for better, for worse;*
> *And kiss not the gallows for cutting a purse.* 155

(WINWIFE

He has it! 'Fore God, he is a brave fellow; pity he should be detected.)

> *Youth, youth, thou hadst better been starved by thy nurse,*
> *Than live to be hangèd for cutting a purse.*

ALL

An excellent ballad! an excellent ballad! 160

EDGWORTH

Friend, let me ha' the first, let me ha' the first, I pray you.

[*He slips the purse to* NIGHTINGALE]

COKES

Pardon me, sir. First come, first served; and I'll buy the whole bundle too.

WINWIFE

That conveyance was better than all, did you see't? He has given the purse to the ballad-singer. 165

QUARLOUS

Has he?

EDGWORTH

Sir, I cry you mercy; I'll not hinder the poor man's profit; pray you, mistake me not.

---

145 *Relent* Abandon your wicked ways
147 *above ground* on the scaffold

COKES

Sir, I take you for an honest gentleman, if that be mistaking. I met
you today afore. Ha! humh! O God! my purse is gone, my purse,   170
my purse, etc.

WASP

Come, do not make a stir, and cry yourself an ass thorough the
Fair afore your time.

COKES

Why, hast thou it, Numps? Good Numps, how came you by it? I
mar'l!   175

WASP

I pray you seek some other gamester to play the fool with. You
may lose it time enough, for all your Fair-wit.

COKES

By this good hand, glove and all, I ha' lost it already, if thou hast
it not; feel else. And Mistress Grace's handkercher, too, out o' the
tother pocket.   180

WASP

Why, 'tis well; very well, exceeding pretty and well.

EDGWORTH

Are you sure you ha' lost it, sir?

COKES

O God! yes; as I am an honest man, I had it but e'en now, at
'Youth, youth'.

NIGHTINGALE

I hope you suspect not me, sir.   185

EDGWORTH

Thee? that were a jest indeed! Dost thou think the gentleman is
foolish? Where hadst thou hands, I pray thee? Away, ass, away.

[*Exit* NIGHTINGALE]

OVERDO

[*Aside and beginning to go*] I shall be beaten again if I be spied.

EDGWORTH

Sir, I suspect an odd fellow, yonder, is stealing away.

---

169 *gentleman, . . . mistaking.* ed. (Gentleman; . . . mistaking, F)
172 *thorough* throughout, from end to end of
175 *mar'l* marvel
176 *gamester* playmate

MISTRESS OVERDO

Brother, it is the preaching fellow! You shall suspect him. He was 190
at your tother purse, you know!—Nay, stay, sir, and view the
work you ha' done; an you be beneficed at the gallows, and
preach there, thank your own handiwork.

COKES

Sir, you shall take no pride in your preferment: you shall be
silenced quickly. 195

OVERDO

What do you mean, sweet buds of gentility?

COKES

To ha' my pennyworths out on you, bud! No less than two purses
a day serve you? I thought you a simple fellow when my man
Numps beat you i' the morning, and pitied you—

MISTRESS OVERDO

So did I, I'll be sworn, brother. But now I see he is a lewd and 200
pernicious enormity, as Master Overdo calls him.

OVERDO

[*Aside*] Mine own words turned upon me, like swords.

COKES

Cannot a man's purse be at quiet for you i' the master's pocket,
but you must entice it forth and debauch it?

WASP

Sir, sir, keep your 'debauch' and your fine Bartholmew-terms to 205
yourself, and make as much on 'em as you please. But gi'me this
from you i' the mean time. I beseech you see if I can look to this.
[*Tries to take the box*]

COKES

Why, Numps?

WASP

Why? Because you are an ass, sir. There's a reason the shortest way,
an you will needs ha' it. Now you ha' got the trick of losing, you'd 210
lose your breech an 'twere loose. I know you, sir. Come, deliver.

---

190   *shall* ought to, have every reason to
192–3   *an you . . . there* If you, who are so given to preaching, suffer a hanging as your church
living—a reference to the speeches of repentance which were a common feature of
executions at the time.
197   *pennyworths* revenge
204   *debauch it* induce it to desert

WASP *takes the licence from him*

You'll go and crack the vermin you breed now, will you? 'Tis very fine! Will you ha' the truth on't? They are such retchless flies as you are, that blow cutpurses abroad in every corner; your foolish having of money makes 'em. An there were no wiser than 215 I, sir, the trade should lie open for you, sir, it should i'faith, sir. I would teach your wit to come to your head, sir, as well as your land to come into your hand, I assure you, sir.

WINWIFE

Alack, good Numps.

WASP

Nay, gentlemen, never pity me, I am not worth it. Lord send me 220 at home once, to Harrow o' the Hill again; if I travel any more, call me Coriat, with all my heart.

   [*Exeunt* WASP, COKES, MISTRESS OVERDO, *with* OVERDO]

QUARLOUS

Stay, sir, I must have a word with you in private. Do you hear?

EDGWORTH

With me, sir? What's your pleasure, good sir?

QUARLOUS

Do not deny it. You are a cutpurse, sir; this gentleman here, and 225 I, saw you; nor do we mean to detect you, though we can sufficiently inform ourselves toward the danger of concealing you; but you must do us a piece of service.

EDGWORTH

Good gentlemen, do not undo me; I am a civil young man, and but a beginner, indeed. 230

---

211 s.d. WASP *takes the licence from him (*at l. 208 in F)
213 *retchless* heedless
214 *blow* beget (as a fly deposits its eggs and breeds maggots)
215–16 *An there . . . I* If I might have my way without interference
  216 *the trade . . . you* you would be apprenticed to some trade
  226 *nor do we* and yet we do not
    detect expose, inform on
  227 *toward* about
  229 *civil* orderly, respectable

QUARLOUS

> Sir, your beginning shall bring on your ending, for us. We are
> no catchpoles nor constables. That you are to undertake is this:
> you saw the old fellow with the black box here?

EDGWORTH

> The little old governor, sir?

QUARLOUS

> That same. I see you have flown him to a mark already. I would   235
> ha' you get away that box from him, and bring it us.

EDGWORTH

> Would you ha' the box and all, sir? Or only that that is in't? I'll get
> you that, and leave him the box to play with still—which will be
> the harder o' the two—because I would gain your worships' good
> opinion of me.   240

WINWIFE

> He says well, 'tis the greater mastery, and 'twill make the more
> sport when 'tis missed.

EDGWORTH

> Ay, and 'twill be the longer a-missing, to draw on the sport.

QUARLOUS

> But look you do it now, sirrah, and keep your word, or—

EDGWORTH

> Sir, if ever I break my word with a gentleman, may I never read   245
> word at my need. Where shall I find you?

QUARLOUS

> Somewhere i' the Fair, hereabouts. Dispatch it quickly.
>
> > [*Exit* EDGWORTH]
>
> I would fain see the careful fool deluded! Of all beasts, I love the
> serious ass: he that takes pains to be one, and plays the fool with
> the greatest diligence that can be.   250

---

231 *for us* for all we care
232 *That* That which, what
234 *governor* tutor
235 *flown him to a mark* identified him (cf. II. iv, 36–7)
241 *mastery* feat, exercise of skill
246 *word* the neck-verse (cf. I, iv, 6–7)
249 *ass: he* ed. (Asse. He F)

GRACE

Then you would not choose, sir, but love my guardian, Justice
Overdo, who is answerable to that description in every hair of him.

QUARLOUS

So I have heard. But how came you, Mistress Wellborn, to be his
ward, or have relation to him, at first?

GRACE

Faith, through a common calamity: he bought me, sir. And now   255
he will marry me to his wife's brother, this wise gentleman that
you see, or else I must pay value o' my land.

QUARLOUS

'Slid, is there no device of disparagement, or so? Talk with some
crafty fellow, some picklock o' the Law. Would I had studied a
year longer i' the Inns of Court, an't had been but i' your case!   260

WINWIFE

[*Aside*] Ay, Master Quarlous, are you proffering?

GRACE

You'd bring but little aid, sir.

WINWIFE

[*Aside*] I'll look to you i'faith, gamester.—An unfortunate
foolish tribe you are fallen into, lady; I wonder you can endure 'em.

GRACE

Sir, they that cannot work their fetters off must wear 'em.   265

WINWIFE

You see what care they have on you, to leave you thus.

GRACE

Faith, the same they have of themselves, sir. I cannot greatly
complain, if this were all the plea I had against 'em.

WINWIFE

'Tis true! But will you please to withdraw with us a little, and
make them think they have lost you? I hope our manners ha'   270

255   *he bought me* Grace is the victim of one of the major abuses of the age. The Court of
      Wards, established under Henry VIII, administered the estates of all wards of the crown,
      i.e., minors and lunatics inheriting from tenants of the King. The Court had the power
      to sell the guardianship, including control of the ward's marriage, to anyone it pleased
      for ready cash. See Joel Hurstfield, *The Queen's Wards* (1958), *passim*.

257   *or else . . . land* If the ward refused to accept the spouse chosen by the guardian, the
      guardian was entitled to recover the value of the marriage from the ward.

258   *disparagement* Disparagement was involved, and the match could not go forward, if the
      guardian sought to wed his ward to one of inferior rank.

261   *proffering* making an offer, making advances

263   *look to* keep an eye on, beware of

been such hitherto, and our language, as will give you no cause to
doubt yourself in our company.

GRACE

Sir, I will give myself no cause; I am so secure of mine own
manners as I suspect not yours.

QUARLOUS

Look where John Littlewit comes. 275

WINWIFE

Away, I'll not be seen by him.

QUARLOUS

No, you were not best, he'd tell his mother, the widow.

WINWIFE

Heart, what do you mean?

QUARLOUS

Cry you mercy, is the wind there? Must not the widow be named?

[*Exeunt* GRACE, WINWIFE, QUARLOUS]

ACT III, SCENE vi

[*Enter to them*] LITTLEWIT, WIN

LITTLEWIT

Do you hear, Win, Win?

WIN

What say you, John?

LITTLEWIT

While they are paying the reckoning, Win, I'll tell you a thing,
Win: we shall never see any sights i' the Fair, Win, except you
long still, Win. Good Win, sweet Win, long to see some hobby- 5
horses, and some drums, and rattles, and dogs, and fine devices,
Win. The bull with the five legs, Win, and the great hog. Now you
ha' begun with pig, you may long for anything, Win, and so for
my motion, Win.

---

272 *doubt* have fears for
273 *secure of* confident in
274 *manners* moral code of behaviour
277 *were not best* had best not
279 *is the wind there* is that the case (proverbial, Tilley, W421)

WIN

But we sha' not eat o' the bull and the hog, John. How shall I long   10
then?

LITTLEWIT

O yes, Win! You may long to see as well as to taste, Win. How did
the pothecary's wife, Win, that longed to see the anatomy, Win?
Or the lady, Win, that desired to spit i' the great lawyer's mouth
after an eloquent pleading? I assure you they longed, Win. Good   15
Win, go in, and long.

> [*Exeunt* LITTLEWIT, WIN]

TRASH

I think we are rid of our new customer, Brother Leatherhead, we
shall hear no more of him.

> *They plot to be gone*

LEATHERHEAD

All the better. Let's pack up all, and be gone, before he find us.

TRASH

Stay a little, yonder comes a company; it may be we may take   20
some more money.

[*Enter*] KNOCKEM, BUSY

KNOCKEM

Sir, I will take your counsel, and cut my hair, and leave vapours.
I see that tobacco, and bottle-ale, and pig, and Whit, and very
Ursla herself, is all vanity.

BUSY

Only pig was not comprehended in my admonition, the rest   25
were. For long hair, it is an ensign of pride, a banner, and the
world is full of those banners, very full of banners. And bottle-ale
is a drink of Satan's, a diet-drink of Satan's, devised to puff us up,
and make us swell in this latter age of vanity, as the smoke of
tobacco to keep us in mist and error. But the fleshly woman,   30
which you call Ursla, is above all to be avoided, having the marks
upon her of the three enemies of man: the World, as being in the
Fair; the Devil, as being in the fire; and the Flesh, as being herself.

13   *anatomy* skeleton
14   *to spit. . . mouth* (as a form of reward and encouragement—proverbial, Tilley, M1255
     and M1259)
26   *For* As for
28   *diet-drink* medicine
33   *and the* ed. (and and the F)

[*Enter*] PURECRAFT

PURECRAFT

Brother Zeal-of-the-land, what shall we do? My daughter, Win-
the-fight, is fallen into her fit of longing again.   35

BUSY

For more pig? There is no more, is there?

PURECRAFT

To see some sights, i' the Fair.

BUSY

Sister, let her fly the impurity of the place swiftly, lest she partake
of the pitch thereof. Thou art the seat of the Beast, O Smithfield,
and I will leave thee. Idolatry peepeth out on every side of thee.   40

KNOCKEM

An excellent right hypocrite! Now his belly is full, he falls a-
railing and kicking, the jade. A very good vapour! I'll in, and joy
Ursla with telling how her pig works; two and a half he ate to his
share. And he has drunk a pailful. He eats with his eyes, as well as
his teeth.   [*Exit*]   45

LEATHERHEAD

What do you lack, gentlemen? What is't you buy? Rattles, drums,
babies—

BUSY

Peace, with thy apocryphal wares, thou profane publican—thy
bells, thy dragons, and thy Toby's dogs. Thy hobby-horse is an
idol, a very idol, a fierce and rank idol; and thou the   50
Nebuchadnezzar, the proud Nebuchadnezzar of the Fair, that
sett'st it up, for children to fall down to and worship.

LEATHERHEAD

Cry you mercy, sir, will you buy a fiddle to fill up your noise?

[*Enter* LITTLEWIT, WIN]

LITTLEWIT

Look, Win; do look o' God's name, and save your longing. Here
be fine sights.   55

---

48 *apocryphal* sham, spurious (the Puritans rejected the Apocrypha completely)
     publican heathen, excommunicated person
48–9 *thy bells . . . Toby's dogs.* See *Tobit*, v. 16 and *Bel and the Dragon*, in the Apocrypha.
51 *Nebuchadnezzar* King of Babylon who set up a golden idol (Daniel, iii)
53 *noise?* ed. (noise. F)

PURECRAFT

Ay, child, so you hate 'em, as our brother Zeal does, you may look
on 'em.

LEATHERHEAD

Or what do you say to a drum, sir?

BUSY

It is the broken belly of the Beast, and thy bellows there are his
lungs, and these pipes are his throat, those feathers are of his tail,   60
and thy rattles the gnashing of his teeth.

TRASH

And what's my gingerbread, I pray you?

BUSY

The provender that pricks him up. Hence with thy basket of
popery, thy nest of images, and whole legend of ginger-work.

LEATHERHEAD

Sir, if you be not quiet the quicklier, I'll ha' you clapped fairly by   65
the heels, for disturbing the Fair.

BUSY

The sin of the Fair provokes me, I cannot be silent.

PURECRAFT

Good brother Zeal!

LEATHERHEAD

Sir, I'll make you silent, believe it.

LITTLEWIT

I'd give a shilling you could, i' faith, friend.   70

LEATHERHEAD

Sir, give me your shilling; I'll give you my shop if I do not, and I'll
leave it in pawn with you, i' the mean time.

LITTLEWIT

A match i' faith; but do it quickly then.

[*Exit* LEATHERHEAD]

58   *drum*, ed. (Drumme. F)

63   *pricks him up* makes him high-spirited (proverbial, Tilley, P615)

64   *images . . . legend of ginger-work* The Puritans were, of course, strongly opposed to the
     use of images in churches—some of Trash's wares are, presumably, in the shape of St
     Bartholomew—and they regarded *The Golden Legend*, the great mediaeval collection of
     saints' lives, as a pack of lies

70   *shilling you could*, ed. (shilling, you could F) shilling if you could

BUSY   *He speaks to the widow*
Hinder me not, woman. I was moved in spirit, to be here, this day,
in this Fair, this wicked and foul Fair—and fitter may it be called   75
a foul than a Fair—to protest against the abuses of it, the foul
abuses of it, in regard of the afflicted saints, that are troubled, very
much troubled, exceedingly troubled, with the opening of the
merchandise of Babylon again, and the peeping of popery upon
the stalls here, here in the high places. See you not Goldylocks, the   80
purple strumpet, there? in her yellow gown, and green sleeves? the
profane pipes, the tinkling timbrels? A shop of relics!
LITTLEWIT
Pray you forbear, I am put in trust with 'em.
BUSY
And this idolatrous grove of images, this flasket of idols! which I
will pull down—   85
                              Overthrows the gingerbread
TRASH
O my ware, my ware, God bless it.
BUSY
—in my zeal, and glory to be thus exercised.

                    LEATHERHEAD *enters with officers*

LEATHERHEAD
Here he is. Pray you lay hold on his zeal; we cannot sell a whistle,
for him, in tune. Stop his noise first!
BUSY
Thou canst not; 'tis a sanctified noise. I will make a loud and most   90
strong noise, till I have daunted the profane enemy. And for this
cause—
LEATHERHEAD
Sir, here's no man afraid of you, or your cause. You shall swear
it, i' the stocks, sir.

75 *be called* ed. (be a called F)
77 *saints* Puritans
84 *flasket* long shallow basket
89 *for* because of
93-4 *swear it* do your swearing

BUSY

    I will thrust myself into the stocks, upon the pikes of the land.   95

LEATHERHEAD

    Carry him away.

PURECRAFT

    What do you mean, wicked men?

BUSY

    Let them alone; I fear them not.

             [*Exeunt officers with* BUSY, *followed by* PURECRAFT]

LITTLEWIT

    Was not this shilling well ventured, Win, for our liberty? Now we
    may go play, and see over the Fair, where we list, ourselves. My   100
    mother is gone after him, and let her e'en go, and loose us.

WIN

    Yes, John, but I know not what to do.

LITTLEWIT

    For what, Win?

WIN

    For a thing I am ashamed to tell you, i'faith, and 'tis too far to go
    home.   105

LITTLEWIT

    I pray thee be not ashamed, Win. Come, i'faith thou shall not be
    ashamed. Is it anything about the hobby-horse-man? An't be,
    speak freely.

WIN

    Hang him, base bobchin, I scorn him. No, I have very great
    what-sha-callum, John.   110

LITTLEWIT

    O! Is that all, Win? We'll go back to Captain Jordan, to the pig-
    woman's, Win. He'll help us, or she with a dripping pan, or an
    old kettle, or something. The poor greasy soul loves you, Win.
    And after we'll visit the Fair all over, Win, and see my puppet
    play, Win. You know it's a fine matter, Win.   115

             [*Exeunt* LITTLEWIT, WIN]

---

95 *thrust myself . . . upon the pikes* rush to destruction (like a martyr)
110 *what-sha-callum* need to make water

LEATHERHEAD

Let's away. I counselled you to pack up afore, Joan.

TRASH

A pox of his Bedlam purity! He has spoiled half my ware. But the best is: we lose nothing if we miss our first merchant.

LEATHERHEAD

It shall be hard for him to find, or know us, when we are translated, Joan.   120

[*Exeunt*]

ACT IV, SCENE i

[*Enter*] TROUBLE-ALL, BRISTLE, HAGGIS, COKES, OVERDO

TROUBLE-ALL

My masters, I do make no doubt but you are officers.

BRISTLE

What then, sir?

TROUBLE-ALL

And the King's loving and obedient subjects.

BRISTLE

Obedient, friend? Take heed what you speak, I advise you: Oliver Bristle advises you. His loving subjects, we grant you; but not his   5 obedient, at this time, by your leave; we know ourselves a little better than so; we are to command, sir, and such as you are to be obedient. Here's one of his obedient subjects, going to the stocks, and we'll make you such another, if you talk.

TROUBLE-ALL

You are all wise enough i' your places, I know.   10

BRISTLE

If you know it, sir, why do you bring it in question?

---

118 *miss* avoid meeting, keep clear of merchant customer
119–20 *are translated* (i) have moved elsewhere (ii) have disguised ourselves

4–5 *Oliver Bristle* At III. i, 7, Haggis called him 'Davy Bristle', but Jonson appears to have
    forgotten this.
   7 *than so* than that

TROUBLE-ALL

I question nothing, pardon me. I do only hope you have warrant
for what you do, and so, quit you, and so, multiply you.

He goes away again

HAGGIS

What's he?—Bring him up to the stocks there. Why bring you
him not up? 15

[TROUBLE-ALL] *comes again*

TROUBLE-ALL

If you have Justice Overdo's warrant, 'tis well; you are safe; that is
the warrant of warrants. I'll not give this button for any man's
warrant else.

BRISTLE

Like enough, sir. But let me tell you, an you play away your
buttons thus, you will want 'em ere night; for any store I see 20
about you, you might keep 'em, and save pins, I wusse.

[TROUBLE-ALL] *goes away*

OVERDO

[*Aside*] What should he be, that doth so esteem and advance my
warrant? He seems a sober and discreet person! It is a comfort to
a good conscience to be followed with a good fame in his
sufferings. The world will have a pretty taste by this, how I can 25
bear adversity; and it will beget a kind of reverence toward me,
hereafter, even from mine enemies, when they shall see I carry my
calamity nobly, and that it doth neither break me nor bend me.

HAGGIS

Come, sir, here's a place for you to preach in. Will you put in
your leg? 30

They put him in the stocks

13 *quit you . . . you* God reward you and increase your family
20-1 *night; . . . you,* ed. (night, . . . you: F)
20 *store* plenty, abundant supply
22 *should* might, can
advance extol (*OED*, Advance *v.*, 12)
30 *leg* The stocks used here secure the victim by one leg only, not two, as was more normal.
See also the s.d. at IV.vi, 69.

OVERDO

That I will, cheerfully.

BRISTLE

O' my conscience, a seminary! He kisses the stocks.

COKES

Well, my masters, I'll leave him with you. Now I see him
bestowed, I'll go look for my goods, and Numps.

HAGGIS

You may, sir, I warrant you. Where's the tother bawler? Fetch   35
him too. You shall find 'em both fast enough.

[*Exit* COKES]

OVERDO

[*Aside*] In the midst of this tumult, I will yet be the author of
mine own rest, and, not minding their fury, sit in the stocks in
that calm as shall be able to trouble a triumph.

[TROUBLE-ALL] *comes again*

TROUBLE-ALL

Do you assure me upon your words? May I undertake for you, if   40
I be asked the question, that you have this warrant?

HAGGIS

What's this fellow, for God's sake?

TROUBLE-ALL

Do but shew me 'Adam Overdo', and I am satisfied.   *Goes out*

BRISTLE

He is a fellow that is distracted, they say—one Trouble-all. He
was an officer in the court of Pie-powders here last year, and put   45
out on his place by Justice Overdo.

OVERDO

Ha!

BRISTLE

Upon which he took an idle conceit, and's run mad upon't. So
that, ever since, he will do nothing but by Justice Overdo's

---

32 *seminary* recusant (cf. II. i, 32)
38 *rest* (i) tranquillity of mind (ii) arrest
39 *trouble* mar
46 *on* of
48 *took an idle conceit* became the victim of a groundless delusion

warrant: he will not eat a crust, nor drink a little, nor make him   50
in his apparel ready. His wife, sir-reverence, cannot get him make
his water, or shift his shirt, without his warrant.

OVERDO

[*Aside*] If this be true, this is my greatest disaster! How am I
bound to satisfy this poor man, that is, of so good a nature to me,
out of his wits, where there is no room left for dissembling!   55

[TROUBLE-ALL] *comes in*

TROUBLE-ALL

If you cannot shew me 'Adam Overdo', I am in doubt of you. I
am afraid you cannot answer it.   *Goes again*

HAGGIS

Before me, neighbour Bristle, and now I think on't better, Justice
Overdo is a very parantory person.

BRISTLE

O! are you advised of that? And a severe justicer, by your leave.   60

OVERDO

[*Aside*] Do I hear ill o' that side, too?

BRISTLE

He will sit as upright o' the bench, an you mark him, as a candle
i' the socket, and give light to the whole court in every business.

HAGGIS

But he will burn blue, and swell like a boil, God bless us, an he be
angry.   65

BRISTLE

Ay, and he will be angry too, when 'has list, that's more; and
when he is angry, be it right or wrong, he has the law on's side
ever. I mark that too.

50–1 *make him in his apparel ready* get dressed
  51 *shift* change
  54 *is,* ed. (is F)
      of as a consequence of
  57 *answer it* give a satisfactory answer
  58 *Before me* Upon my word
  59 *parantory* peremptory
  60 *are you advised* have you taken note
  66 *'has list* ed. (his list F) feels so inclined

OVERDO

> [*Aside*] I will be more tender hereafter. I see compassion may
> become a Justice, though it be a weakness, I confess, and nearer a   70
> vice than a virtue.

HAGGIS

> Well, take him out o' the stocks again. We'll go a sure way to
> work; we'll ha' the ace of hearts of our side, if we can.

> > *They take the Justice out*

[*Enter*] POCHER, BUSY, PURECRAFT

POCHER

> Come, bring him away to his fellow there. Master Busy, we shall
> rule your legs, I hope, though we cannot rule your tongue.   75

BUSY

> No, minister of darkness, no, thou canst not rule my tongue; my
> tongue it is mine own, and with it I will both knock and mock
> down your Bartholmew-abhominations, till you be made a
> hissing to the neighbour parishes round about.

HAGGIS

> Let him alone, we have devised better upon't.   80

PURECRAFT

> And shall he not into the stocks then?

BRISTLE

> No, mistress, we'll have 'em both to Justice Overdo, and let him
> do over 'em as is fitting. Then I, and my gossip Haggis, and my
> beadle Pocher are discharged.

PURECRAFT

> O, I thank you, blessed, honest men!   85

BRISTLE

> Nay, never thank us, but thank this madman that comes here, he
> put it in our heads.

[TROUBLE-ALL] *comes again*

73 *of* on
79 *Bartholmew-abhominations* This spelling of 'abomination', very common in the sixteenth
  century, arose from the mistaken view that the word was derived from 'ab homine',
  meaning 'inhuman'. Jonson, who knew better, puts this form of the word in Busy's
  mouth as a further indication of the preacher's ignorance.
80 *hissing* object of scorn and opprobrium (cf. Jeremiah, xix. 8)
84 *discharged* freed of responsibility

PURECRAFT

Is he mad? Now heaven increase his madness, and bless it, and
thank it! Sir, your poor handmaid thanks you.

TROUBLE-ALL

Have you a warrant? An you have a warrant, shew it.   90

PURECRAFT

Yes, I have a warrant out of the Word, to give thanks for
removing any scorn intended to the brethren.

TROUBLE-ALL

It is Justice Overdo's warrant that I look for; if you have not that,
keep your word, I'll keep mine. Quit ye, and multiply ye.

[*Exeunt all but* TROUBLE-ALL]

ACT IV, SCENE ii

[*Enter to him*] EDGWORTH, NIGHTINGALE

EDGWORTH

Come away, Nightingale, I pray thee.

TROUBLE-ALL

Whither go you? Where's your warrant?

EDGWORTH

Warrant for what, sir?

TROUBLE-ALL

For what you go about; you know how fit it is. An you have no
warrant, bless you, I'll pray for you, that's all I can do.   *Goes out*   5

EDGWORTH

What means he?

NIGHTINGALE

A madman that haunts the Fair; do you not know him? It's
marvel he has not more followers after his ragged heels.

88   *it!* ed. (it, F)
91   *the Word* the Bible

EDGWORTH

Beshrew him, he startled me; I thought he had known of our plot.
Guilt's a terrible thing! Ha' you prepared the costard-monger?   10

NIGHTINGALE

Yes, and agreed for his basket of pears. He is at the corner here,
ready. And your prize, he comes down, sailing, that way, all
alone, without his protector. He is rid of him, it seems.

EDGWORTH

Ay, I know. I should ha' followed his protectorship for a feat I am
to do upon him; but this offered itself so i' the way, I could not   15
let it scape. Here he comes. Whistle. Be this sport called 'Dorring
the Dottrel'.

[Enter] COKES

NIGHTINGALE   *Whistles*

Wh, wh, wh, wh, etc.

[Enter] COSTARD-MONGER

COKES

By this light, I cannot find my gingerbread-wife, nor my hobby-
horse-man, in all the Fair, now, to ha' my money again. And I do   20
not know the way out on't, to go home for more. Do you hear,
friend, you that whistle, what tune is that you whistle?

NIGHTINGALE

A new tune I am practising, sir.

COKES

Dost thou know where I dwell, I pray thee? Nay, on with thy tune;
I ha' no such haste for an answer. I'll practice with thee.   25

COSTARD-MONGER

Buy any pears, very fine pears, pears fine.

NIGHTINGALE *sets his foot afore him,*
and he falls with his basket

9   *Beshrew* Curse, A plague on
11   *agreed* settled on a price
12   *prize* prey (Cokes is seen as a ship to be captured)
15   *i' the way* invitingly, opportunely
16–17 *Dorring the Dottrel*. Hoaxing the simpleton. 'To dor' was 'to make a fool of', and the dottrel is
       a kind of plover proverbial for its foolishness (Tilley, D364) in allowing itself to be easily caught.
       The fatuous Norfolk squire in Jonson's next play, *The Devil is an Ass*, is called Fitz-Dottrel.
20   *again* back

627

COKES

God's so! A muss, a muss, a muss, a muss!

COSTARD-MONGER

Good gentleman, my ware, my ware! I am a poor man. Good sir, my ware.

NIGHTINGALE

Let me hold your sword, sir, it troubles you. 30

COKES

Do, and my cloak, an thou wilt, and my hat, too.

> COKES *falls a-scrambling*
> *whilst they run away with his things*

EDGWORTH

A delicate great boy! Methinks he out-scrambles 'em all. I cannot persuade myself but he goes to grammar-school yet, and plays the truant today.

NIGHTINGALE

Would he had another purse to cut, Zekiel! 35

EDGWORTH

Purse! A man might cut out his kidneys, I think, and he never feel 'em, he is so earnest at the sport.

NIGHTINGALE

His soul is half-way out on's body at the game.

EDGWORTH

Away, Nightingale, that way!

> [*Exit* NIGHTINGALE *with sword, cloak, and hat*]

COKES

I think I am furnished for Cather'ne pears, for one undermeal. 40 Gi' me my cloak.

COSTARD-MONGER

Good gentleman, give me my ware.

COKES

Where's the fellow I ga' my cloak to? My cloak? and my hat? Ha! God's lid, is he gone? Thieves, thieves! Help me to cry, gentlemen.

> *He runs out*

EDGWORTH

Away, costermonger, come to us to Ursla's. 45

---

27 *muss* scramble
31 s.d. COKES *falls . . . things* (at l. 30 in F)
40 *undermeal* afternoon meal, snack

[*Exit* COSTARD-MONGER]

Talk of him to have a soul? 'Heart, if he have any more than a
thing given him instead of salt, only to keep him from stinking,
I'll be hanged afore my time, presently. Where should it be, trow?
In his blood? He has not so much to'ard it in his whole body as
will maintain a good flea. And if he take this course, he will not   50
ha' so much land left as to rear a calf within this twelvemonth.
Was there ever green plover so pulled? That his little overseer
had been here now, and been but tall enough, to see him steal
pears in exchange for his beaver-hat and his cloak thus. I must
go find him out next, for his black box, and his patent, it seems   55
he has, of his place; which I think the gentleman would have a
reversion of, that spoke to me for it so earnestly.   [*Exit*]

He [COKES] *comes again*

COKES

Would I might lose my doublet, and hose too, as I am an honest
man, and never stir, if I think there be anything but thieving and
coz'ning i' this whole Fair. Bartholmew Fair, quoth he! An ever   60
any Bartholmew had that luck in't that I have had, I'll be
martyred for him, and in Smithfield too. I ha' paid for my pears.
A rot on 'em, I'll keep 'em no longer.   *Throws away his pears*
You were choke-pears to me. I had been better ha' gone to
mum-chance for you, I wusse. Methinks the Fair should not   65
have used me thus, an 'twere but for my name's sake. I would not
ha' used a dog o' the name so. O, Numps will triumph now!

46–7 *Talk . . . stinking* An allusion to the notion that just as salt preserves meat so the soul
      prevents man from going rotten, which he does, of course, when the soul leaves the body.
      H & S aptly quote Herrick's epigram:
          The body's salt, the soule is; which when gon,
          The flesh soone sucks in putrifaction. (*Works*, ed. L. C. Martin, Oxford, 1956, p. 332.)
  52 *pulled* plucked clean
  55 *patent, it seems* ed. (Patent (it seemes) F)
55–7 *patent . . . reversion of* Edgworth thinks the box contains a document confirming Wasp
      in his position as Cokes's tutor, and that Quarlous wants the document in order to make
      sure of taking over Wasp's position.
  62 *martyred . . . Smithfield too* A reference to the Smithfield Martyrs, the Protestants who
      were burned there during the reign of Mary Tudor.
  64 *choke-pears* (i) coarse unpalatable pears (ii) a harsh reproof
  65 *mum-chance* dicing game popular among costermongers
      for instead of

TROUBLE-ALL *comes again*

Friend, do you know who I am? Or where I lie? I do not myself,
I'll be sworn. Do but carry me home, and I'll please thee, I ha'
money enough there. I ha' lost myself, and my cloak and my hat,   70
and my fine sword, and my sister, and Numps, and Mistress
Grace, a gentlewoman that I should ha' married, and a cut-work
handkercher she ga' me, and two purses, today. And my bargain
o' hobby-horses and gingerbread, which grieves me worst of all.

TROUBLE-ALL

By whose warrant, sir, have you done all this?   75

COKES

Warrant? Thou art a wise fellow indeed—as if a man need a
warrant to lose anything with.

TROUBLE-ALL

Yes, Justice Overdo's warrant a man may get and lose with, I'll
stand to't.

COKES

Justice Overdo? Dost thou know him? I lie there, he is my   80
brother-in-law, he married my sister. Pray thee shew me the way;
dost thou know the house?

TROUBLE-ALL

Sir, shew me your warrant. I know nothing without a warrant,
pardon me.

COKES

Why, I warrant thee. Come along, thou shalt see I have wrought   85
pillows there, and cambric sheets, and sweet bags too. Pray thee
guide me to the house.

TROUBLE-ALL

Sir, I'll tell you. Go you thither yourself first alone; tell your
worshipful brother your mind; and but bring me three lines of his
hand, or his clerk's, with 'Adam Overdo' underneath. Here I'll   90
stay you, I'll obey you, and I'll guide you presently.

---

68 *lie* lodge
69 *carry* escort, take
    please satisfy, reward
72 *cut-work* embroidered
85 *thee. Come along,* ed. (thee, come along: F)
    wrought embroidered
86 *sweet bags,* bags containing fragrant herbs to perfume the linen
91 *stay* wait for

COKES

> [*Aside*] 'Slid, this is an ass, I ha' found him. Pox upon me, what do I talking to such a dull fool?—Farewell. You are a very coxcomb, do you hear?

TROUBLE-ALL

> I think I am. If Justice Overdo sign to it, I am, and so we are all.   95
> He'll quit us all, multiply us all.

>   [*Exeunt*]

ACT IV, SCENE iii

> [*Enter*] GRACE. *They* (QUARLOUS, WINWIFE) *enter with their
> swords drawn*

GRACE

> Gentlemen, this is no way that you take. You do but breed one another trouble and offence, and give me no contentment at all. I am no she that affects to be quarrelled for, or have my name or fortune made the question of men's swords.

QUARLOUS

> 'Slood, we love you.   5

GRACE

> If you both love me, as you pretend, your own reason will tell you but one can enjoy me; and to that point there leads a directer line than by my infamy, which must follow if you fight. 'Tis true—I have professed it to you ingenuously— that, rather than to be yoked with this bridegroom is appointed me, I would take   10
> up any husband, almost, upon any trust; though Subtlety would say to me—I know—he is a fool, and has an estate, and I might

92 *found him* discovered his true character, sized him up

3 *affects* likes
6 *pretend* claim
10 *is* who is
10-11 *take up* accept
11 *almost*, ed. (almost F)
   upon any trust without further investigation of his credentials
12 *he* Cokes

govern him, and enjoy a friend beside. But these are not my aims. I must have a husband I must love, or I cannot live with him. I shall ill make one of these politic wives! 15

WINWIFE

Why, if you can like either of us, lady, say which is he, and the other shall swear instantly to desist.

QUARLOUS

Content, I accord to that willingly.

GRACE

Sure you think me a woman of an extreme levity, gentlemen, or a strange fancy, that, meeting you by chance in such a place as 20 this, both at one instant, and not yet of two hours' acquaintance, neither of you deserving afore the other of me, I should so forsake my modesty, though I might affect one more particularly, as to say, 'This is he', and name him.

QUARLOUS

Why, wherefore should you not? What should hinder you? 25

GRACE

If you would not give it to my modesty, allow it yet to my wit; give me so much of woman, and cunning, as not to betray myself impertinently. How can I judge of you, so far as to a choice, without knowing you more? You are both equal and alike to me, yet; and so indifferently affected by me, as each of you might be 30 the man, if the other were away; for you are reasonable creatures; you have understanding and discourse; and if fate send me an understanding husband, I have no fear at all but mine own manners shall make him a good one.

QUARLOUS

Would I were put forth to making for you, then. 35

GRACE

It may be you are; you know not what's toward you. Will you

13 *friend* lover
15 *politic* scheming
26 *wit* intelligence
27 *cunning* knowledge of the world
28 *impertinently* unbecomingly
30 *indifferently affected* impartially regarded
31 *away; for* ed. (away. For F)
32 *discourse* the ability to reason
35 *put forth to making* apprenticed to be trained
36 *toward* in store for

consent to a motion of mine, gentlemen?

WINWIFE

Whatever it be, we'll presume reasonableness, coming from you.

QUARLOUS

And fitness, too.

GRACE

I saw one of you buy a pair of tables, e'en now.   40

WINWIFE

Yes, here they be, and maiden ones too, unwritten in.

GRACE

The fitter for what they may be employed in. You shall write,
either of you, here a word or a name, what you like best, but of
two or three syllables at most. And the next person that comes
this way—because Destiny has a high hand in business of this   45
nature—I'll demand which of the two words he or she doth
approve; and, according to that sentence, fix my resolution, and
affection, without change.

QUARLOUS

Agreed, my word is conceived already.

WINWIFE

And mine shall not be long creating after.   50

GRACE

But you shall promise, gentlemen, not to be curious to know
which of you it is, is taken; but give me leave to conceal that till
you have brought me, either home, or where I may safely tender
myself.

WINWIFE

Why, that's but equal.   55

QUARLOUS

We are pleased.

---

37 *motion* proposal, suggestion
40 *tables* writing tablets
43 *either* each
    what you like best whichever you prefer
45–6 *because Destiny . . . nature* Alluding to one or more proverbs: 'Marriage is destiny' (Tilley,
    M682); 'Marriage and magistrate be destinies of heaven' (Tilley, M680); and the familiar
    'Wedding and hanging go by destiny' (Tilley, W232).
52 *is, is taken* ed. (is, taken F)
53–4 *tender myself* offer myself for acceptance
55 *but equal* fair enough

GRACE

Because I will bind both your endeavours to work together, friendly and jointly, each to the other's fortune, and have myself fitted with some means to make him that is forsaken a part of amends.

60

QUARLOUS

These conditions are very courteous. Well, my word is out of the *Arcadia*, then: 'Argalus'.

WINWIFE

And mine out of the play: 'Palemon'.

TROUBLE-ALL *comes again*

TROUBLE-ALL

Have you any warrant for this, gentlemen?

QUARLOUS ⎫
WINWIFE ⎭

Ha?

65

TROUBLE-ALL

There must be a warrant had, believe it.

WINWIFE

For what?

TROUBLE-ALL

For whatsoever it is, anything indeed, no matter what.

QUARLOUS

'Slight, here's a fine ragged prophet, dropped down i' the nick!

TROUBLE-ALL

Heaven quit you, gentlemen.

70

QUARLOUS

Nay, stay a little. Good lady, put him to the question.

GRACE

You are content, then?

---

59 *forsaken* rejected, refused
    a part of some
63 *Argalus* A character in Sir Philip Sidney's *Arcadia*, whose love for Parthenia forms one
    of the episodes in that work.
64 *Palemon* Either Palamon in *The Two Noble Kinsmen* by Shakespeare and Fletcher, first
    performed in 1613, or Palaemon in Samuel Daniel's *The Queen's Arcadia,* played at Christ
    Church, Oxford, on 30 August 1605, during the course of a royal visit to the University.
69 *i' the nick* at exactly the right moment

WINWIFE }
QUARLOUS }

Yes, yes.

GRACE

Sir, here are two names written—

TROUBLE-ALL

Is Justice Overdo one?   75

GRACE

How, sir? I pray you read 'em to yourself—it is for a wager between these gentlemen—and, with a stroke or any difference, mark which you approve best.

TROUBLE-ALL

They may be both worshipful names for aught I know, mistress, but Adam Overdo had been worth three of 'em, I assure you, in   80 this place; that's in plain English.

GRACE

This man amazes me! I pray you, like one of 'em, sir.

TROUBLE-ALL

I do like him there, that has the best warrant. Mistress, to save your longing, and multiply him, it may be this.

> [*He marks the book*]

But I am aye still for Justice Overdo, that's my conscience. And   85 quit you.

> [*Exit*]

WINWIFE

Is't done, lady?

GRACE

Ay, and strangely as ever I saw! What fellow is this, trow?

QUARLOUS

No matter what, a fortune-teller we ha' made him. Which is't, which is't?   90

---

75 *Justice* ed. (*Iudice* F)
76 *to yourself* silently
77 *difference* distinguishing mark
83 *warrant.* ed. (warrant, F)
84 *and multiply him* Ed. (and (multiply him) F)
85 *aye* ed. (I F)
    conscience conviction
90 *is't?* ed. (is't. F)

GRACE

Nay, did you not promise, not to enquire?

[*Enter*] EDGWORTH

QUARLOUS

'Slid, I forgot that, pray you pardon me. Look, here's our Mercury come; the licence arrives i' the finest time, too! 'Tis but scraping out Cokes his name, and 'tis done.

WINWIFE

How now, lime-twig? Hast thou touched?   95

EDGWORTH

Not yet, sir; except you would go with me, and see't, it's not worth speaking on. The act is nothing, without a witness. Yonder he is, your man with the box, fallen into the finest company, and so transported with vapours. They ha' got in a northern clothier, and one Puppy, a western man, that's come to wrestle   100 before my Lord Mayor anon, and Captain Whit, and one Val Cutting, that helps Captain Jordan to roar, a circling boy; with whom your Numps is so taken that you may strip him of his clothes, if you will. I'll undertake to geld him for you; if you had but a surgeon ready, to sear him. And Mistress Justice, there, is   105 the goodest woman! She does so law 'em all over, in terms of

93 *Mercury* As well as being the messenger of the gods, Mercury was also the god of thieves.
95 *lime-twig* thief, one whose fingers are 'limed' so that things stick to them.
    touched? ed. (touch'd F) carried out the theft
96 *sir;* ed. (Sir, F)
    except unless
99 *vapours. They* ed. (vapours, they F)
100 *a western man* Cornwall was famous for its wrestlers.
101 *before my Lord Mayor* Wrestling in the presence of the Lord Mayor was a regular feature of Bartholmew Fair on the afternoon of the opening day.
102 *a circling boy* Since no other example of this term is known, it is difficult to say precisely what it means. Cutting is evidently a 'roarer'; he makes use of a circle for quarrelling purposes (see IV.iv, 109–16); and he 'gives the lie in circle', i.e., circuitously, indirectly (*OED*, Circle, *sb.*, †24., quoting from *The Alchemist*, III.iv, 38–9). The last of these activities is probably the reason for the term.
106 *goodest* most important
    law ed. (loue F) argue with, lay down the law to. It is difficult to see how one can 'love . . . in terms of justice, and the style of authority'. Nor is it what Mistress Overdo does at IV.iv, 119–22. Nashe, in *Nashes Lenten Stuffe* (1599), launches a vigorous attack on lawyers' jargon, and then continues: 'I stand lawing heere' (Nashe, iii. 216. 16). Mistress Overdo also 'stands lawing'. If Jonson wrote 'lawe', as this editor believes he did, a compositor might easily read it as 'loue'.

justice, and the style of authority, with her hood upright, that—
that I beseech you come away, gentlemen, and see't.

QUARLOUS

'Slight, I would not lose it for the Fair. What'll you do, Ned?

WINWIFE

Why, stay here about for you; Mistress Wellborn must not be   110
seen.

QUARLOUS

Do so, and find out a priest i' the mean time; I'll bring the
licence.—Lead, which way is't?

EDGWORTH

Here, sir, you are o' the backside o' the booth already, you may
hear the noise.   115

[*Exeunt*]

ACT IV, SCENE iv

[*Enter*] KNOCKEM, NORTHERN, PUPPY, CUTTING, WHIT,
WASP, MISTRESS OVERDO

KNOCKEM

Whit, bid Val Cutting continue the vapours for a lift, Whit, for a
lift.

NORTHERN

I'll ne mare, I'll ne mare, the eale's too meeghty.

KNOCKEM

How now, my Galloway Nag, the staggers? Ha! Whit, gi' him a
slit i' the forehead. Cheer up, man; a needle and thread to stitch   5

197–8 *upright, that—that* ed. (upright—that F)
  198 *come away* come along

    1 *for a lift* in preparation for a theft
    3 *ne mare . . . too meeghty* No more, the ale's too mighty. Jonson's attempt to represent
       the northern dialect.
    4 *the staggers* disease of horses, marked by a staggering gait
       Galloway Nag Breed of small horses from the south-west of Scotland, noted for their
       hardiness and powers of endurance.
  4–7 *gi' him . . . grains* The cure recommended in Jonson's day for a horse suffering from the
       staggers.

his ears. I'd cure him now, an I had it, with a little butter, and garlic, long-pepper, and grains. Where's my horn? I'll gi' him a mash, presently, shall take away this dizziness.

PUPPY

Why, where are you, zurs? Do you vlinch, and leave us i' the zuds, now?   10

NORTHERN

I'll ne mare, I is e'en as vull as a paiper's bag, by my troth, I.

PUPPY

Do my northern cloth zhrink i' the wetting, ha?

KNOCKEM

Why, well said, old flea-bitten, thou'lt never tire, I see.

They fall to their vapours again

CUTTING

No, sir, but he may tire, if it please him.

WHIT

Who told dee sho? that he vuld never teer, man?   15

CUTTING

No matter who told him so, so long as he knows.

KNOCKEM

Nay, I know nothing, sir, pardon me there.

[*Enter*] EDGWORTH, QUARLOUS

EDGWORTH

They are at it still, sir, this they call vapours.

WHIT

He shall not pardon dee, captain, dou shalt not be pardoned. Pre'de shweetheart, do not pardon him.   20

CUTTING

'Slight, I'll pardon him, an I list, whosoever says nay to't.

QUARLOUS

Where's Numps? I miss him.

7 *long-pepper* very strong kind of pepper
  grains refuse of malt
  horn drenching-horn
9 *vlinch* flinch (as pronounced in the West Country), weaken in your drinking
9–10 *i' the zuds* (literally, in the suds) i.e., in trouble
11 *paiper's* piper's
12 *Do my . . . wetting* The complaint that Northern cloth shrank easily was a common one.
13 *flea-bitten . . . tire* 'A flea-bitten horse never tires' was a proverb (Tilley, H640). 'Flea-bitten' refers to the horse's colour—dappled.

WASP

Why, I say nay to't.

QUARLOUS

O there he is!

KNOCKEM

To what do you say nay, sir?   25

Here they continue their game of vapours, which is nonsense:
every man to oppose the last man that spoke,
whether it concerned him, or no

WASP

To anything, whatsoever it is, so long as I do not like it.

WHIT

Pardon me, little man, dou musht like it a little.

CUTTING

No, he must not like it at all, sir; there you are i' the wrong.

WHIT

I tink I be; he musht not like it, indeed.

CUTTING

Nay, then he both must and will like it, sir, for all you.   30

KNOCKEM

If he have reason, he may like it, sir.

WHIT

By no meansh, captain, upon reason, he may like nothing upon
reason.

WASP

I have no reason, nor I will hear of no reason, nor I will look for
no reason, and he is an ass that either knows any, or looks for't   35
from me.

CUTTING

Yes, in some sense you may have reason, sir.

WASP

Ay, in some sense, I care not if I grant you.

WHIT

Pardon me, thou ougsht to grant him nothing, in no shensh, if
dou do love dyshelf, angry man.   40

WASP

Why then, I do grant him nothing; and I have no sense.

CUTTING

'Tis true, thou hast no sense indeed.

---

25   s.d. *Here they . . . no* (at l. 22 in F)

WASP

'Slid, but I have sense, now I think on't better, and I will grant him anything, do you see?

KNOCKEM

He is i' the right, and does utter a sufficient vapour. 45

CUTTING

Nay, it is no sufficient vapour, neither, I deny that.

KNOCKEM

Then it is a sweet vapour.

CUTTING

It may be a sweet vapour.

WASP

Nay, it is no sweet vapour, neither, sir; it stinks, and I'll stand to't.

WHIT

Yes, I tink it doesh shtink, captain. All vapour doesh shtink. 50

WASP

Nay, then, it does not stink, sir, and it shall not stink.

CUTTING

By your leave, it may, sir.

WASP

Ay, by my leave, it may stink; I know that.

WHIT

Pardon me, thou knowesht nothing; it cannot by thy leave, angry man. 55

WASP

How can it not?

KNOCKEM

Nay, never question him, for he is i' the right.

WHIT

Yesh, I am i' de right, I confesh it; so ish de little man too.

WASP

I'll have nothing confessed that concerns me. I am not i' the right, nor never was i' the right, nor never will be i' the right, while I am 60 in my right mind.

CUTTING

Mind? Why, here's no man minds you, sir, nor anything else.

They drink again

PUPPY

Vriend, will you mind this that we do?

QUARLOUS

Call you this vapours? This is such belching of quarrel as I never
heard. Will you mind your business, sir? 65

EDGWORTH

You shall see, sir.

NORTHERN

I'll ne mair, my waimb warks too mickle with this aueady.

EDGWORTH

Will you take that, Master Wasp, that nobody should mind you?

WASP

Why? What ha' you to do? Is't any matter to you?

EDGWORTH

No, but methinks you should not be unminded, though. 70

WASP

Nor I wu' not be, now I think on't; do you hear, new
acquaintance, does no man mind me, say you?

CUTTING

Yes, sir, every man here minds you, but how?

WASP

Nay, I care as little how as you do; that was not my question.

WHIT

No, noting was ty question; tou art a learned man, and I am a 75
valiant man, i'faith la; tou shalt speak for me, and I vill fight for tee.

KNOCKEM

Fight for him, Whit? A gross vapour; he can fight for himself.

WASP

It may be I can, but it may be I wu' not, how then?

CUTTING

Why, then you may choose.

WASP

Why, and I'll choose whether I'll choose or no. 80

KNOCKEM

I think you may, and 'tis true; and I allow it for a resolute vapour.

WASP

Nay, then I do think you do not think, and it is no resolute
vapour.

___

65 *mind your business* get on with your job (of stealing the licence)
67 *waimb warks too mickle* stomach is too upset
69 *What ha' you to do* What business of yours is it
70 *unminded* left unnoticed

CUTTING

Yes, in some sort he may allow you.

KNOCKEM

In no sort, sir, pardon me, I can allow him nothing. You mistake 85
the vapour.

WASP

He mistakes nothing, sir, in no sort.

WHIT

Yes, I pre dee now, let him mistake.

WASP

A turd i' your teeth! Never pre dee me, for I will have nothing
mistaken. 90

KNOCKEM

Turd, ha, turd? A noisome vapour! Strike, Whit.

They fall by the ears
[EDGWORTH *steals the licence from the box, and exit*]

MISTRESS OVERDO

Why gentlemen, why gentlemen, I charge you upon my
authority, conserve the peace. In the King's name, and my
husband's, put up your weapons; I shall be driven to commit you
myself, else. 95

QUARLOUS

Ha, ha, ha!

WASP

Why do you laugh, sir?

QUARLOUS

Sir, you'll allow me my Christian liberty. I may laugh, I hope.

CUTTING

In some sort you may, and in some sort you may not, sir.

KNOCKEM

Nay, in some sort, sir, he may neither laugh, nor hope, in this 100
company.

WASP

Yes, then he may both laugh and hope in any sort, an't please
him.

---

84 *sort* (i) sense (ii) company
s.d. *They fall by the ears* They fight
94 *commit you* send you to prison

QUARLOUS

Faith, and I will then, for it doth please me exceedingly.

WASP

No exceeding neither, sir. 105

KNOCKEM

No, that vapour is too lofty.

QUARLOUS

Gentlemen, I do not play well at your game of vapours, I am not
very good at it, but—

CUTTING

Do you hear, sir? I would speak with you in circle!

He draws a circle on the ground

QUARLOUS

In circle, sir? What would you with me in circle? 110

CUTTING

Can you lend me a piece, a Jacobus, in circle?

QUARLOUS

'Slid, your circle will prove more costly than your vapours, then.
Sir, no, I lend you none.

CUTTING

Your beard's not well turned up, sir.

QUARLOUS

How, rascal? Are you playing with my beard? I'll break circle with 115
you.

They draw all, and fight

PUPPY ⎫
NORTHERN ⎭

Gentlemen, gentlemen!

KNOCKEM

Gather up, Whit, gather up, Whit. Good vapours!

[*Exeunt* KNOCKEM *and* WHIT *with the cloaks*]

---

105 *exceeding* excess, going too far

109 *Do you . . . with you* The drawing of the circle is an indirect challenge, which Quarlous
fails to understand. Cutting then asks for the loan of a Jacobus, knowing that it will be
refused and thus provide the pretext for the final insult, his playing with Quarlous's
beard which precipitates the fight.

111 *Jacobus* gold coin, 'sovereign', issued by James I

MISTRESS OVERDO

What mean you? Are you rebels, gentlemen? Shall I send out a sergeant-at-arms, or a writ o' rebellion, against you? I'll commit   120
you, upon my womanhood, for a riot, upon my justice-hood, if you persist.

[*Exeunt* QUARLOUS, CUTTING]

WASP

Upon your justice-hood? Marry, shit o' your hood! You'll commit? Spoke like a true Justice of Peace's wife, indeed, and a fine female lawyer! Turd i' your teeth for a fee, now.   125

MISTRESS OVERDO

Why, Numps, in Master Overdo's name, I charge you.

WASP

Good Mistress Underdo, hold your tongue.

MISTRESS OVERDO

Alas! poor Numps.

WASP

Alas! And why alas from you, I beseech you? Or why poor Numps, Goody Rich? Am I come to be pitied by your   130
tuftaffeta now? Why, mistress, I knew Adam, the clerk, your husband, when he was Adam Scrivener, and writ for two pence a sheet, as high as he bears his head now, or you your hood, dame.

The watch comes in [*accompanied by* WHIT]

What are you, sir?

BRISTLE

We be men, and no infidels. What is the matter here, and the   135
noises? Can you tell?

WASP

Heart, what ha' you to do? Cannot a man quarrel in quietness, but he must be put out on't by you? What are you?

---

120   *commit* (i) send to prison (ii) fornicate
130   *Goody* Goodwife
131   *tuftaffeta* a kind of taffeta with a pile or nap arranged in tufts (*OED*)
132   *Adam Scrivener* There may be an allusion here to Chaucer's little poem 'Chaucers Wordes unto Adam, his own Scriveyn', reproving Adam for his carelessness in copying.
133   s.d. *accompanied by* WHIT ed. (not in F). Whit's entry here, like his exit at 118, is demanded by his collusion with the Watch established in III.i.
138   *put out on't* debarred from doing it

BRISTLE

Why, we be His Majesty's Watch, sir.

WASP

Watch? 'Sblood, you are a sweet watch, indeed. A body would   140
think, an you watched well o' nights, you should be contented to
sleep at this time o' day. Get you to your fleas, and your flock-
beds, you rogues, your kennels, and lie down close.

BRISTLE

Down? Yes, we will down, I warrant you.—Down with him in
His Majesty's name, down, down with him, and carry him away,   145
to the pigeon-holes.

[WASP *is arrested*]

MISTRESS OVERDO

I thank you, honest friends, in the behalf o' the Crown, and the
peace, and in Master Overdo's name, for suppressing enormities.

WHIT

Stay, Bristle, here ish a noder brashe o' drunkards, but very
quiet, special drunkards, will pay dee five shillings very well. Take   150
'em to dee, in de graish o' God: one of 'em does change cloth for
ale in the Fair here, te toder ish a strong man, a mighty man, my
Lord Mayor's man, and a wrestler. He has wreshled so long with
the bottle, here, that the man with the beard hash almosht
streek up hish heelsh.   155

BRISTLE

'Slid, the Clerk o' the Market has been to cry him all the Fair
over, here, for my Lord's service.

WHIT

Tere he ish, pre de taik him hensh, and make ty best on him.

[*Exit watch with* WASP, NORTHERN, PUPPY]

141   *watched* (i) stayed awake (ii) did your duties as watchmen
146   *pigeon-holes* stocks
149   *brashe* ed. (brash F) brace
154   *the man with the beard* A kind of drinking-jug, pot-bellied but with a narrow neck
      decorated with a bearded face.
155   *streek up hish heelsh* struck up his heels, i.e., overthrown him
156   *cry* summon
157   *Lord's* Lord Mayor's

How now, woman o' shilk, vat ailsh ty shweet faish? Art tou
melancholy? 160

MISTRESS OVERDO

A little distempered with these enormities. Shall I entreat a
courtesy of you, Captain?

WHIT

Entreat a hundred, velvet voman, I vill do it, shpeak out.

MISTRESS OVERDO

I cannot with modesty speak it out, but—

[*She whispers to him*]

WHIT

I vill do it, and more, and more, for dee. What Ursla, an't be 165
bitch, an't be bawd, an't be!

[*Enter*] URSLA

URSLA

How now, rascal? What roar you for, old pimp?

WHIT

Here, put up de cloaks, Ursh, de purchase. Pre dee now, shweet
Ursh, help dis good brave voman to a Jordan, an't be.

URSLA

'Slid, call your Captain Jordan to her, can you not? 170

WHIT

Nay, pre dee leave dy consheits, and bring the velvet woman to
de—

URSLA

I bring her? Hang her! Heart, must I find a common pot for every
punk i' your purlieus?

WHIT

O good voordsh, Ursh; it ish a guest o' velvet, i' fait la! 175

URSLA

Let her sell her hood, and buy a sponge, with a pox to her. My
vessel? Employed, sir. I have but one, and 'tis the bottom of an
old bottle. An honest proctor and his wife are at it within. If she'll
stay her time, so.

161 *distempered with* upset by
167 *for, old pimp?* ed. (for? old Pimpe. F)
168 *purchase.* ed. (purchase, F) booty
174 *your purlieus* the brothel areas
176–7 *her. My vessel? Employed, sir.* ed. (her, my vessell, employed Sir. F)

WHIT

    As soon ash tou cansht, shweet Ursh. Of a valiant man I tink I am   180
the patientsh man i' the world, or in all Smithfield.

[Enter KNOCKEM*]*

KNOCKEM

    How now, Whit? Close vapours? stealing your leaps? Covering
in corners, ha?

WHIT

    No fait, Captain, dough tou beesht a vishe man, dy vit is a mile
hence now. I vas procuring a shmall courtesy for a woman of   185
fashion here.

MISTRESS OVERDO

    Yes, Captain, though I am Justice of Peace's wife, I do love men
of war, and the sons of the sword, when they come before my
husband.

KNOCKEM

    Say'st thou so, filly? Thou shalt have a leap presently, I'll horse   190
thee myself else.

URSLA

    Come, will you bring her in now? And let her take her turn?

WHIT

    Gramercy, good Ursh, I tank dee.

MISTRESS OVERDO

    Master Overdo shall thank her.   *[Exit]*

ACT IV, SCENE v

[Enter to them] LITTLEWIT, WIN

LITTLEWIT

    Good Gammer Urs, Win and I are exceedingly beholden to you,
and to Captain Jordan, and Captain Whit. Win, I'll be bold to

---

182 *Covering* (technical term for a stallion mating with a mare) copulating
192 *take* ed. (talke F)

leave you i' this good company, Win, for half an hour or so, Win, while I go and see how my matter goes forward, and if the puppets be perfect. And then I'll come and fetch you, Win.   5

WIN

Will you leave me alone with two men, John?

LITTLEWIT

Ay, they are honest gentlemen, Win, Captain Jordan and Captain Whit, they'll use you very civilly, Win. God b'w'you, Win.   [*Exit*]

URSLA

What's her husband gone?   10

KNOCKEM

On his false gallop, Urs, away.

URSLA

An you be right Bartholmew-birds, now shew yourselves so. We are undone for want of fowl i' the Fair here. Here will be Zekiel Edgworth, and three or four gallants with him at night, and I ha' neither plover nor quail for 'em. Persuade this between you two,   15
to become a bird o' the game, while I work the velvet woman within, as you call her.

KNOCKEM

I conceive thee, Urs! Go thy ways.

[*Exit* URSLA]

Dost thou hear, Whit? Is't not pity my delicate dark chestnut here—with the fine lean head, large forehead, round eyes, even   20
mouth, sharp ears, long neck, thin crest, close withers, plain back, deep sides, short fillets, and full flanks; with a round belly, a plump buttock, large thighs, knit knees, straight legs, short pasterns, smooth hoofs, and short heels—should lead a dull honest woman's life, that might live the life of a lady?   25

WHIT

Yes, by my fait and trot, it is, Captain. De honesht woman's life is a scurvy dull life, indeed, la!

---

5   *be perfect* know their parts, are word-perfect
11 *false gallop* ed. (false, gallop F) canter, with a quibble on 'false' = 'unwise'
13 *fowl* 'birds', wenches
15 *neither plover nor quail* no wenches at all
18 *ways.* ed. (waies, F)
21 *plain* flat
25 *honest* (i) respectable (ii) chaste
       lady (i) woman of rank (ii) 'lady of pleasure'

WIN

How, sir? Is an honest woman's life a scurvy life?

WHIT

Yes, fait, shweetheart, believe him, de leef of a bondwoman! But
if dou vilt harken to me, I vill make tee a free-woman, and a lady;   30
dou shalt live like a lady, as te captain saish.

KNOCKEM

Ay, and be honest too, sometimes; have her wires, and her
tires, her grcen gowns, and velvet petticoats.

WHIT

Ay, and ride to Ware and Romford i' dy coash, shee de players,
be in love vit 'em; sup vit gallantsh, be drunk, and cost de noting.   35

KNOCKEM

Brave vapours!

WHIT

And lie by twenty on 'em, if dou pleash, shweetheart.

WIN

What, and be honest still? That were fine sport.

WHIT

'Tish common, shweetheart, tou may'st do it, by my hand. It shall
be justified to ty husband's faish, now: tou shalt be as honesht as   40
the skin between his hornsh, la!

KNOCKEM

Yes, and wear a dressing, top and topgallant, to compare with e'er
a husband on 'em all, for a fore-top. It is the vapour of spirit, in

32   *wires* frames of wire used to stiffen ruffs and to support the hair
33   *tires* head-dresses and dresses in general
     green gowns KNOCKEM is quibbling; 'to give a wench a green gown' was to seduce her
     by rolling her over in the grass. Hence green gowns came to be associated with prostitutes.
34   *Ware and Romford* Ware, famous for its 'great bed' (eleven feet square), and Romford
     were notorious as places of assignation within easy reach of London.
38   *still? That* ed. (still, that F)
39   *it,* ed. (it F)
40-1 *as honesht . . . hornsh.* 'As honest as the skin between his brows' was, and still is, proverbial
     (Tilley, S506), but Whit substitutes the horns of the cuckold for 'brows'.
42-3 *dressing . . . fore-top* The elaborate head-dresses and 'hair-dos' of the time are described
     in nautical terms, comparing the effect to that of a ship under full sail, by Shakespeare
     in *The Merry Wives of Windsor,* III.in, 46-9, and by Nashe in his *Christs Teares Over
     Jerusalem,* where he writes: 'Theyr heads, with theyr top and top gallant Lawne baby-
     caps, and Snow-resembled siluer curlings, they make a playne Puppet stage of (Nashe,
     ii. 137. 31-3). Got up in this fashion, Knockem says, Win's head will be a fit match for her
     husband's horns (foretop).

the wife, to cuckold, nowadays, as it is the vapour of fashion, in
the husband, not to suspect. Your prying cat-eyed citizen is an   45
abominable vapour.

WIN

Lord, what a fool have I been!

WHIT

Mend then, and do everyting like a lady hereafter; never know ty
husband from another man.

KNOCKEM

Nor any one man from another, but i' the dark.   50

WHIT

Ay, and then it ish no dishgrash to know any man.

[*Enter* URSLA]

URSLA

Help, help here!

KNOCKEM

How now? What vapour's there?

URSLA

O, you are a sweet ranger, and look well to your walks! Yonder is
your punk of Turnbull, Ramping Alice, has fallen upon the poor   55
gentlewoman within, and pulled her hood over her ears, and her
hair through it.

ALICE *enters, beating the Justice's wife*

MISTRESS OVERDO

Help, help, i' the King's name!

ALICE

A mischief on you! They are such as you are that undo us and
take our trade from us, with your tuftaffeta haunches.   60

KNOCKEM

How now, Alice!

ALICE

The poor common whores can ha' no traffic for the privy rich

48 *Mend* Reform yourself
59 *undo* ruin
60 *tuftaffeta haunches* artificial haunches made of silk and designed to improve the figure
62 *for* because of
    privy clandestine

ones. Your caps and hoods of velvet call away our customers,
and lick the fat from us.

URSLA

Peace, you foul ramping jade, you—   65

ALICE

Od's foot, you bawd in grease, are you talking?

KNOCKEM

Why, Alice, I say.

ALICE

Thou sow of Smithfield, thou.

URSLA

Thou tripe of Turnbull.

KNOCKEM

Catamountain vapours, ha!   70

URSLA

You know where you were tawed lately, both lashed and
slashed you were in Bridewell.

ALICE

Ay, by the same token, you rid that week, and broke out the
bottom o' the cart, night-tub.

KNOCKEM

Why, lion face, ha! Do you know who I am? Shall I tear ruff, slit   75
waistcoat, make rags of petticoat, ha? Go to, vanish, for fear of
vapours. Whit,a kick, Whit, in the parting vapour.

                              [*They kick* ALICE *out*]

Come, brave woman, take a good heart, thou shall be a lady too.

---

63   *velvet* ed. (veluet, F)
64   *lick the fat from us* 'To lick the fat from one's lips' was proverbial (Tilley F80) for depriving
     one of one's best customers.
66   *in grease* fat, in prime condition for killing
70   *Catamountain* wildcat, ferocious
71   *tawed* flogged
72   *slashed* cut with the scourge
     Bridewell The London prison, where sexual offenders in particular were confined and
     punished.
73   *rid* rode in the cart for whores
74   *night-tub* tub for excrement or night-soil
76   *waistcoat* When worn without a gown over it, the waistcoat was the mark of a prostitute,
     who was sometimes called a 'waistcoateer'
     petticoat, ha? ed. (petticoat? ha! F)

WHIT

Yes fait, dey shall all both be ladies, and write Madam. I vill do't
myself for dem. *Do* is the vord, and *D* is the middle letter of   80
Madam, DD, put 'em together and make deeds, without which all
words are alike, la!

KNOCKEM

'Tis true. Ursla, take 'em in, open thy wardrobe, and fit 'em to
their calling. Green gowns, crimson petticoats, green women! My
Lord Mayor's green women! guests o' the game, true bred. I'll   85
provide you a coach, to take the air in.

WIN

But do you think you can get one?

KNOCKEM

O, they are as common as wheelbarrows where there are great
dunghills. Every pettifogger's wife has 'em; for first he buys a
coach, that he may marry, and then he marries that he may be   90
made cuckold in't. For if their wives ride not to their cuckolding,
they do 'em no credit. 'Hide and be hidden, ride and be ridden',
says the vapour of experience.

[*Exeunt* URSLA, WIN, MISTRESS OVERDO]

ACT IV, SCENE vi

[*Enter to them*] TROUBLE-ALL

TROUBLE-ALL

By what warrant does it say so?

KNOCKEM

Ha! mad child o' the Pie-powders, art thou there? Fill us a fresh
can, Urs, we may drink together.

TROUBLE-ALL

I may not drink without a warrant, Captain.

79   *write* sign themselves, style themselves
80   *green women . . . green women* (i) loose women, whores (ii) female equivalents of the
     'green men', i.e., men dressed in green to represent wild men of the woods or woodwoses,
     as they were called, who were a common feature of the Lord Mayor's Show.
89   *pettifogger* lawyer of inferior status
92   *ridden* mounted sexually by a man

 3   *we* which we

KNOCKEM

    'Slood, thou'll not stale without a warrant, shortly. Whit, give   5
    me pen, ink and paper. I'll draw him a warrant presently.

TROUBLE-ALL

    It must be Justice Overdo's!

KNOCKEM

    I know, man. Fetch the drink, Whit.

WHIT

    I pre dee now, be very brief, Captain; for de new ladies stay for
    dee.   10

KNOCKEM

    O, as brief as can be; here 'tis already. 'Adam Overdo'.

TROUBLE-ALL

    Why, now I'll pledge you, Captain.

KNOCKEM

    Drink it off. I'll come to thee, anon, again.

                                      [Exeunt]

                [Enter] QUARLOUS, EDGWORTH

QUARLOUS   *To the cutpurse*

    Well, sir. You are now discharged; beware of being spied,
    hereafter.   15

EDGWORTH

    Sir, will it please you, enter in here at Ursla's, and take part of
    a silken gown, a velvet petticoat, or a wrought smock. I am
    promised such, and I can spare any gentleman a moiety.

QUARLOUS

    Keep it for your companions in beastliness, I am none of 'em, sir.
    If I had not already forgiven you a greater trespass, or thought you   20
    yet worth my beating, I would instruct your manners to whom you
    made your offers. But go your ways, talk not to me, the hangman
    is only fit to discourse with you; the hand of beadle is too merciful
    a punishment for your trade of life.

                                    [Exit EDGWORTH*]*

---

   5 *stale* urinate
 16 *will it* if it will
      take part partake
 18 *moiety* share, portion
21-2 *I would . . . offers* I would teach you proper behaviour towards the man to whom you
      make your offers

I am sorry I employed this fellow, for he thinks me such: *Facinus*   25
quos inquinat, aequat. But it was for sport. And would I make it
serious, the getting of this license is nothing to me, without other
circumstances concur. I do think how impertinently I labour, if
the word be not mine that the ragged fellow marked; and what
advantage I have given Ned Winwife in this time now of   30
working her, though it be mine. He'll go near to form to her
what a debauched rascal I am, and fright her out of all good
conceit of me. I should do so by him, I am sure, if I had the
opportunity. But my hope is in her temper yet; and it must
needs be next to despair, that is grounded on any part of a   35
woman's discretion. I would give, by my troth, now, all I could
spare, to my clothes and my sword, to meet my tattered
soothsayer again, who was my judge i' the question, to know
certainly whose word he has damned or saved. For, till then, I live
but under a reprieve. I must seek him. Who be these?   40

Enter WASP *with the officers*

WASP
Sir, you are a Welsh cuckold, and a prating runt, and no
constable.
BRISTLE
You say very well. Come, put in his leg in the middle roundel,
and let him hole there.
WASP
You stink of leeks, metheglin, and cheese, you rogue.   45

---

25   *such* such a one as he is
25-6   *Facinus quos inquinat, aequat.* 'Crime puts those it corrupts on the same footing' (Lucan, *Pharsalia*, v. 290).
26   *would I make it serious* if I wanted to take it seriously
28   *impertinently* pointlessly
31   *working* influencing
        form state explicitly
33   *conceit* opinion
34   *temper* character
37   *to* down to but not including
41   *runt* ignoramus
43   *roundel* round hole (of the stocks)
45   *metheglin* Welsh mead
        cheese, you ed. (cheese. You F)

BRISTLE

Why, what is that to you, if you sit sweetly in the stocks in the mean time? If you have a mind to stink too, your breeches sit close enough to your bum. Sit you merry, sir.

QUARLOUS

How now, Numps?

WASP

It is no matter how; pray you look off.   50

QUARLOUS

Nay, I'll not offend you, Numps. I thought you had sat there to be seen.

WASP

And to be sold, did you not? Pray you mind your business, an you have any.

QUARLOUS

Cry you mercy, Numps. Does your leg lie high enough?   55

[*Enter*] HAGGIS, OVERDO, BUSY

BRISTLE

How now, neighbour Haggis, what says Justice Overdo's worship to the other offenders?

HAGGIS

Why, he says just nothing. What should he say? Or where should he say? He is not to be found, man. He ha' not been seen i' the Fair, here, all this livelong day, never since seven o'clock i' the   60 morning. His clerks know not what to think on't. There is no court of Pie-powders yet. Here they be returned.

BRISTLE

What shall be done with 'em, then, in your discretion?

HAGGIS

I think we were best put 'em in the stocks, in discretion—there they will be safe in discretion—for the valour of an hour, or   65 such a thing, till his worship come.

---

63   *discretion* opinion
64–5 *in discretion . . . in discretion* (i) as an act of prudence (ii) in separation. The proverb 'Discretion is the better part of valour' (Tilley, D354) seems to be in Haggis's muddled mind, since he goes on to speak of 'valour' (= space, length).
65   *valour* length (literally, value or quantity)

BRISTLE

It is but a hole matter if we do, neighbour Haggis. Come, sir, here
is company for you. Heave up the stocks.

WASP

[*Aside*] I shall put a trick upon your Welsh diligence, perhaps.

As they open the stocks, WASP *puts his shoe on his hand,*
and slips it in for his leg

BRISTLE

Put in your leg, sir.   70

QUARLOUS

What, Rabbi Busy! Is he come?

They bring BUSY *and put him in*

BUSY

I do obey thee; the lion may roar, but he cannot bite. I am glad to
be thus separated from the heathen of the land, and put apart in
the stocks, for the holy cause.

WASP

What are you, sir?   75

BUSY

One that rejoiceth in his affliction, and sitteth here to prophesy
the destruction of Fairs and May-games, Wakes, and Whitsun-
ales, and doth sigh and groan for the reformation of these abuses.

[*They put* OVERDO *in the stocks*]

WASP

And do you sigh and groan too, or rejoice in your affliction?   80

OVERDO

I do not feel it, I do not think of it, it is a thing without me.
Adam, thou art above these batteries, these contumelies. *In te*
manca ruit fortuna, as thy friend Horace says; thou art one,

77–8 *Whitsun-ales* Parish festivals held at Whitsuntide and given over to feasting, sports, and
merrymaking, Whitsun ales were opposed by the Puritans.

81 *it is a thing without me* Overdo expresses the Stoic doctrine that no external factors can
have any effect on the man who is conscious of his own virtue.

82 *batteries* series of heavy blows

82–3 *In te manca ruit fortuna* Fortune maims herself when she attacks you (Horace, *Satires,*
II.vii. 88).

Quem neque pauperies, neque mors, neque vincula terrent. And
therefore, as another friend of thine says—I think it be thy friend   85
Persius—*Non te quaesiveris extra.*

QUARLOUS

What's here? A stoic i' the stocks? The fool is turned
philosopher.

BUSY

Friend, I will leave to communicate my spirit with you, if I hear
any more of those superstitious relics, those lists of Latin, the   90
very rags of Rome, and patches of Popery.

WASP

Nay, an you begin to quarrel, gentlemen, I'll leave you. I ha' paid
for quarrelling too lately. Look you, a device, but shifting in a
hand for a foot. God b'w'you.   *He gets out*

BUSY

Wilt thou then leave thy brethren in tribulation?   95

WASP

For this once, sir.   [*Exit*]

BUSY

Thou art a halting neutral—stay him there, stop him—that will
not endure the heat of persecution.

BRISTLE

How now, what's the matter?

BUSY

He is fled, he is fled, and dares not sit it out.   100

BRISTLE

What, has he made an escape? Which way? Follow, neighbour
Haggis.

[*Exit* HAGGIS]

[*Enter*] PURECRAFT

PURECRAFT

O me! In the stocks! Have the wicked prevailed?

---

84   *Quem . . . terrent* Whom neither poverty, nor death, nor shackles can affright (ibid., 84).
86   *Non . . . extra* Look to no one outside yourself (Persius, *Satires,* i. 7).
87   *A stoic . . . stocks* The association of Stoics with stocks (= senseless things) was a fairly
     common witticism (cf. *The Taming of the Shrew,* I.i, 31).
89   *leave* cease
90   *lists* strips, selvages, shreds
93–4   *but shifting in a hand for a foot* merely slipping in a hand in place of a foot

BUSY

    Peace, religious sister, it is my calling, comfort yourself, an
extraordinary calling, and done for my better standing, my surer   105
standing, hereafter.

The madman enters

TROUBLE-ALL

    By whose warrant, by whose warrant, this?

QUARLOUS

    O, here's my man dropped in, I looked for.

OVERDO

    Ha!

PURECRAFT

    O good sir, they have set the faithful here to be wondered at; and   110
provided holes for the holy of the land.

TROUBLE-ALL

    Had they warrant for it? Shewed they Justice Overdo's hand? If
they had no warrant, they shall answer it.

[*Enter* HAGGIS]

BRISTLE

    Sure you did not lock the stocks sufficiently, neighbour Toby!

HAGGIS

    No? See if you can lock 'em better.   115

BRISTLE

    They are very sufficiently locked, and truly, yet something is in
the matter.

TROUBLE-ALL

    True, your warrant is the matter that is in question; by what
warrant?

BRISTLE

    Madman, hold your peace; I will put you in his room else, in the   120
very same hole, do you see?

QUARLOUS

    How? Is he a madman?

108   *man* ed. (man! F)
     I whom I

TROUBLE-ALL

Shew me Justice Overdo's warrant, I obey you.

HAGGIS

You are a mad fool, hold your tongue.

TROUBLE-ALL

In Justice Overdo's name, I drink to you, and here's my warrant.   125

Shews his can

[*Exeunt* HAGGIS, BRISTLE]

OVERDO

[*Aside*] Alas, poor wretch! How it earns my heart for him!

QUARLOUS

[*Aside*] If he be mad, it is in vain to question him. I'll try, though.—Friend, there was a gentlewoman shewed you two names, some hour since, Argalus and Palemon, to mark in a book. Which of 'em was it you marked?   130

TROUBLE-ALL

I mark no name but Adam Overdo; that is the name of names; he only is the sufficient magistrate; and that name I reverence. Shew it me.

QUARLOUS

[*Aside*] This fellow's mad indeed. I am further off now than afore.

OVERDO

[*Aside*] I shall not breathe in peace till I have made him some   135
amends.

QUARLOUS

[*Aside*] Well, I will make another use of him, is come in my head: I have a nest of beards in my trunk, one something like his.

[*Exit*]

The watchmen come back again

BRISTLE

This mad fool has made me that I know not whether I have locked the stocks or no; I think I locked 'em.   140

TROUBLE-ALL

Take Adam Overdo in your mind, and fear nothing.

123 *warrant,* ed. (warrant. F)
126 *earns* grieves
128 *though.—Friend,* ed. (though, friend: F)
138 *nest* set, collection *trunk* trunk-hose, baggy padded breeches reaching to the knee
139 *I have* ed. (I I haue F)

BRISTLE

'Slid, madness itself, hold thy peace, and take that.

TROUBLE-ALL

Strikest thou without a warrant? Take thou that.

The madman fights with 'em, and they leave open the stocks

BUSY

We are delivered by miracle. Fellow in fetters, let us not refuse the means; this madness was of the spirit. The malice of the enemy hath mocked itself. 145

[*Exeunt* BUSY, OVERDO]

PURECRAFT

Mad do they call him! The world is mad in error, but he is mad in truth. I love him o' the sudden—the cunning man said all true—and shall love him more and more. How well it becomes a man to be mad in truth! O, that I might be his yoke-fellow, and be mad with him! What a many should we draw to madness in truth with us! 150

[*Exit*]

The watch, missing them, are affrighted

BRISTLE

How now? All scaped? Where's the woman? It is witchcraft! Her velvet hat is a witch, o' my conscience, or my key, t'one! The madman was a devil, and I am an ass; so bless me, my place, and mine office! 155

[*Exeunt*]

143 s.d. *The madman . . . stocks* (at l. 142 in F)
154 *t'one* the one or the other

ACT V, SCENE i

[*Enter*] LEATHERHEAD, FILCHER, SHARKWELL

LEATHERHEAD

Well, Luck and Saint Bartholmew! Out with the sign of our
invention, in the name of Wit, and do you beat the drum the
while. All the foul i' the Fair, I mean all the dirt in Smithfield —
that's one of Master Littlewit's carwhitchets now—will be thrown
at our banner today, if the matter does not please the people. O the   5
motions that I, Lantern Leatherhead, have given light to, i' my
time, since my Master Pod died! *Jerusalem* was a stately thing, and
so was *Nineveh*, and *The City of Norwich*, and *Sodom and
Gomorrah*, with the rising o' the prentices, and pulling down the
bawdy-houses there, upon Shrove Tuesday; but *The Gunpowder*   10
Plot, there was a get-penny! I have presented that to an eighteen-,
or twenty-pence audience, nine times in an afternoon. Your home-
born projects prove ever the best, they are so easy, and familiar.
They put too much learning i' their things nowadays; and that, I
fear, will be the spoil o' this. Littlewit? I say, Micklewit! if not too   15
mickle! Look to your gathering there, Goodman Filcher.

s.d. LEATHERHEAD ed. (LANTHORNE. F) From this point onwards to the end of the
play Leatherhead is almost consistently LANTHORNE or LANTERNE in stage directions
and LAN. in speech prefixes. Transformed from hobby-horse-seller into puppet-master
and suitably disguised for the new role, he has taken on another identity which prevents
Cokes from recognizing him. See his whispered request to Littlewit at V.iii, 46.

1–2 *sign of our invention* painted cloth depicting the subject of the puppet-shew

4   *carwhitchets* puns

6   *motions* puppet-shews

7   *my Master Pod* F has the marginal note 'Pod *was a Master of motions before him*'. Jonson
also refers to Pod in *Every Man Out of His Humour* (IV.v, 62) and in two of his *Epigrams*,
xcvii and cxxix.

7–9 *Jerusalem . . . Gomorrah*. The destruction of Jerusalem by the Romans, the fall of Nineveh
in which Jonah and the whale figured prominently, the building of Norwich, and the
destruction of Sodom and Gomorrah were common themes for puppet-shews.

9   *prentices*, ed. (premises; F)

9–10 *rising . . . Shrove Tuesday* The apprentices of London made a regular habit of wrecking
brothels and playhouses on Shrove Tuesday.

11   *get-penny* draw, profitable operation

13   *projects* designs
     familiar readily understood

15   *spoil* spoiling, ruination

16   *mickle* great
     gathering collecting of entrance money (technical theatrical term)

FILCHER
I warrant you, sir.
LEATHERHEAD
An there come any gentlefolks, take twopence apiece, Sharkwell.
SHARKWELL
I warrant you, sir; threepence an we can.

[Exeunt]

ACT V, SCENE ii

The Justice [OVERDO] *comes in like a porter*

OVERDO
This later disguise, I have borrowed of a porter, shall carry me out
to all my great and good ends; which, however interrupted, were
never destroyed in me. Neither is the hour of my severity yet
come, to reveal myself, wherein, cloud-like, I will break out in
rain and hail, lightning and thunder, upon the head of enormity.   5
Two main works I have to prosecute first: one is to invent some
satisfaction for the poor kind wretch who is out of his wits for my
sake; and yonder I see him coming. I will walk aside, and project
for it.

[Enter] WINWIFE, GRACE

WINWIFE
I wonder where Tom Quarlous is, that he returns not; it may be   10
he is struck in here to seek us.
GRACE
See, here's our madman again.

[Enter] QUARLOUS, PURECRAFT. QUARLOUS, *in the habit of the
madman, is mistaken by* MISTRESS PURECRAFT

1–2 *carry me out to* enable me to achieve
   6 *prosecute first*: ed. (prosecute: first, F)
      invent find, devise
   8 *project* think of some plan
  11 *is struck* has turned

QUARLOUS

[*Aside*] I have made myself as like him as his gown and cap will
give me leave.

PURECRAFT

Sir, I love you, and would be glad to be mad with you in truth.   15

WINWIFE

[*Aside*] How? My widow in love with a madman?

PURECRAFT

Verily, I can be as mad in spirit as you.

QUARLOUS

By whose warrant? Leave your canting. [*To* GRACE]
Gentlewoman, have I found you?—Save ye, quit ye, and multiply
ye.—Where's your book? 'Twas a sufficient name I marked, let   20
me see't, be not afraid to shew't me.

                He desires to see the book of MISTRESS GRACE

GRACE

What would you with it, sir?

QUARLOUS

Mark it again, and again, at your service.

GRACE

Here it is, sir; this was it you marked.

QUARLOUS

Palemon! Fare you well, fare you well.   25

WINWIFE

How, Palemon!

GRACE

Yes, faith, he has discovered it to you now, and therefore 'twere
vain to disguise it longer; I am yours, sir, by the benefit of your
fortune.

WINWIFE

And you have him, Mistress, believe it, that shall never give you   30
cause to repent her benefit, but make you rather to think that in
this choice she had both her eyes.

---

18 *canting* Puritan jargon
28 *benefit* favour, kindness
32 *she had both her eyes* Winwife is referring to the proverb 'Fortune is blind (= blindfolded)'
(Tilley, F604).

GRACE

I desire to put it to no danger of protestation.

[Exeunt GRACE, WINWIFE]

QUARLOUS

Palemon the word, and Winwife the man!

PURECRAFT

Good sir, vouchsafe a yoke-fellow in your madness; shun not one   35
of the sanctified sisters, that would draw with you, in truth.

QUARLOUS

Away! You are a herd of hypocritical proud ignorants, rather wild
than mad; fitter for woods, and the society of beasts, than houses,
and the congregation of men. You are the second part of the
society of canters, outlaws to order and discipline, and the only   40
privileged church-robbers of Christendom. Let me alone.
Palemon the word, and Winwife the man!

PURECRAFT

[*Aside*] I must uncover myself unto him, or I shall never enjoy
him, for all the cunning men's promises.—Good sir, hear me, I
am worth six thousand pound; my love to you is become my   45
rack; I'll tell you all, and the truth, since you hate the hypocrisy
of the parti-coloured brotherhood. These seven years, I have
been a wilful holy widow only to draw feasts and gifts from my
entangled suitors. I am also, by office, an assisting sister of the
deacons, and a devourer, instead of a distributor, of the alms. I   50
am a special maker of marriages for our decayed brethren with
our rich widows, for a third part of their wealth, when they are

33 *put . . . protestation* An allusion to the proverb 'Too much protesting makes the truth
suspected' (Tilley, P614); cf. *Hamlet*, III.ii, 225: 'The lady doth protest too much,
methinks'.

34 *man!* ed. (man? F)

39–40 *second. . . canters* The first part of the society of canters would be those who spoke thieves'
cant, i.e., the rogues and vagabonds of the time. Thomas Harman, in his *A Caveat or
Warning for Common Cursitors* (1566), provides some specimens of this cant. The
pamphlet is edited by A. V. Judges in his *The Elizabethan Underworld*, London, 1930

45 *you is* ed. (you, is F)

46 *truth,* ed. (truth: F)

47 *parti-coloured* of several colours, i.e., inconsistent

married, for the relief of the poor elect; as also our poor
handsome young virgins' with our wealthy bachelors or
widowers, to make them steal from their husbands, when I have   55
confirmed them in the faith, and got all put into their custodies.
And if I ha' not my bargain, they may sooner turn a scolding drab
into a silent minister than make me leave pronouncing
reprobation and damnation unto them. Our elder, Zeal-of-the-
land, would have had me; but I know him to be the capital knave   60
of the land, making himself rich by being made feoffee in trust to
deceased brethren, and cozening their heirs by swearing the
absolute gift of their inheritance. And thus, having eased my
conscience, and uttered my heart with the tongue of my love —
enjoy all my deceits together, I beseech you. I should not have   65
revealed this to you, but that in time I think you are mad; and I
hope you'll think me so too, sir.

QUARLOUS
Stand aside, I'll answer you presently.

He considers with himself of it

Why should not I marry this six thousand pound, now I think
on't? And a good trade too, that she has beside, ha? The tother   70
wench, Winwife is sure of; there's no expectation for me there!
Here I may make myself some saver yet, if she continue mad;
there's the question. It is money that I want; why should I not
marry the money, when 'tis offered me? I have a licence and all;
it is but razing out one name and putting in another. There's no   75
playing with a man's fortune! I am resolved! I were truly mad, an
I would not!—Well, come your ways, follow me; an you will be
mad, I'll shew you a warrant!

He takes her along with him

---

54 *virgins'* ed. (Virgins, F), i.e., virgins' marriages
58 *into* ed. (in to F)
   silent minister One of the Puritan clergy who had been put out of their livings as a result
   of the Hampton Court conference of 1604. Cf. I.ii, 57 and note.
61 *feoffee in trust* trustee invested with a freehold estate in land (*OED*)
65 *together, I* ed. (together. I F)
66 *in time* not too late
67 *sir.* ed. (Sir? F)
68 s.d. *considers* ed. (*consider* F)
71 *Winwife* ed. (*Winwife,* F)
72 *saver* compensation for loss (gambler's term)

PURECRAFT

Most zealously, it is that I zealously desire.

The Justice calls him

OVERDO

Sir, let me speak with you   80

QUARLOUS

By whose warrant?

OVERDO

The warrant that you tender and respect so: Justice Overdo's! I
am the man, friend Trouble-all, though thus disguised, as the
careful magistrate ought, for the good of the republic in the
Fair, and the weeding out of enormity. Do you want a house, or   85
meat, or drink, or clothes? Speak; whatsoever it is, it shall be
supplied you. What want you?

QUARLOUS

Nothing but your warrant.

OVERDO

My warrant? For what?

QUARLOUS

To be gone, sir.   90

OVERDO

Nay, I pray thee stay. I am serious, and have not many words nor
much time to exchange with thee; think what may do thee good.

QUARLOUS

Your hand and seal will do me a great deal of good; nothing else
in the whole Fair, that I know.

OVERDO

If it were to any end, thou should'st have it willingly.   95

QUARLOUS

Why, it will satisfy me—that's end enough—to look on. An you
will not gi' it me, let me go.

---

82 *tender* have regard for
83-4 *as the careful magistrate ought* as befits the watchful magistrate
84 *republic* state, commonwealth
86 *Speak; whatsoever* ed. (speake whatsoeuer F)
96 *me—that's end enough—to* ed. (me, that's end enough, to F)
     on at

OVERDO

Alas! thou shall ha' it presently. I'll but step into the scrivener's hereby, and bring it. Do not go away.

The Justice [OVERDO] *goes out*

QUARLOUS

Why, this madman's shape will prove a very fortunate one, I   100
think! Can a ragged robe produce these effects? If this be the wise Justice, and he bring me his hand, I shall go near to make some use on't.

The Justice [OVERDO] *returns.*

He is come already!

OVERDO

Look thee! here is my hand and seal, 'Adam Overdo'. If there be   105
anything to be written above in the paper, that thou want'st now, or at any time hereafter, think on't. It is my deed, I deliver it so. Can your friend write?

QUARLOUS

Her hand for a witness, and all is well.

OVERDO

With all my heart.   *He urgeth* MISTRESS PURECRAFT   110

QUARLOUS

[*Aside*] Why should not I ha' the conscience to make this a bond of a thousand pound now? Or what I would else?

OVERDO

Look you, there it is; and I deliver it as my deed again.

QUARLOUS

Let us now proceed in madness.

He takes her in with him

OVERDO

Well, my conscience is much eased; I ha' done my part. Though   115
it doth him no good, yet Adam hath offered satisfaction! The

---

28   s.d. *The Justice* [OVERDO] *returns* ed. (*and returns.* F)
29   *ha' the conscience* have the effrontery (*OED*, Conscience, 12.)
30   *pound now?* ed. (pound? now, F)

sting is removed from hence. Poor man, he is much altered with
his affliction, it has brought him low! Now for my other work:
reducing the young man I have followed so long in love, from
the brink of his bane to the centre of safety. Here, or in some   120
such-like vain place, I shall be sure to find him. I will wait the
good time.

ACT V, SCENE iii

[*Enter*] COKES, SHARKWELL, FILCHER

COKES

How now? What's here to do? Friend, art thou the Master of the
Monuments?

SHARKWELL

'Tis a motion, an't please your worship.

OVERDO

[*Aside*] My fantastical brother-in-law, Master Bartholmew
Cokes!   5

COKES

A motion, what's that?   *He reads the bill*
'The ancient modern history of *Hero and Leander*, otherwise
called *The Touchstone of True Love*, with as true a trial of
friendship between Damon and Pythias, two faithful friends o'

---

119 *reducing* leading back
120 *bane* destruction, ruin
122 *good time* propitious moment

  1 *to do* going on
1–2 *Master of the Monuments* Exactly what Cokes has in mind is not clear. He obviously takes
      Sharkwell for an official in charge of effigies, perhaps seeing him, as H & S suggest, as
      the equivalent of the guide who took people around Westminster Abbey.
  4 *fantastical* fanciful, unpredictable

the Bankside'? Pretty i'faith! What's the meaning on't? Is't an   10
interlude? or what is't?

FILCHER
Yes, sir. Please you come near, we'll take your money within.
The boys o' the Fair follow him [COKES]

COKES
Back with these children; they do so follow me up and down.

[*Enter*] LITTLEWIT

LITTLEWIT
By your leave, friend.

FILCHER
You must pay, sir, an you go in.   15

LITTLEWIT
Who, I? I perceive thou know'st not me. Call the master o' the
motion.

SHARKWELL
What, do you not know the author, fellow Filcher? You must take
no money of him; he must come in *gratis*. Master Littlewit is a
voluntary; he is the author.   20

LITTLEWIT
Peace, speak not too loud; I would not have any notice taken that
I am the author, till we see how it passes.

COKES
Master Littlewit, how dost thou?

LITTLEWIT
Master Cokes! you are exceeding well met. What, in your doublet
and hose, without a cloak or a hat?   25

7-10   *The ancient . . . Bankside* The puppet play, like the 'tedious brief scene of young
Pyramus/And his love Thisby; very tragical mirth' in *A Midsummer Night's Dream*, is a
burlesque of the kind of interlude (l. 11) that was popular in the early years of Elizabeth's
reign, and, in particular, of Richard Edwards's *The Excellent Comedie of two the moste
faithfullest Freendes, Damon and Pithias*. 'Newly Imprinted' in 1571, this work is described
in the Prologue to it (l. 38) as a 'tragical comedy'. Marlowe's *Hero and Leander*, which
is brutally travestied by Littlewit, had first appeared in print in 1598 and had proved
enormously popular. It had also been burlesqued, in prose, by Nashe, in his *Nashes
Lenten Stuffe* (1599); see Nashe, iii. 195–201.

11   *interlude* play
20   *voluntary* volunteer, amateur, one who serves without pay
22   *passes* goes down, is received

COKES

I would I might never stir, as I am an honest man, and by that fire; I have lost all i' the Fair, and all my acquaintance too. Didst thou meet anybody that I know, Master Littlewit? My man Numps, or my sister Overdo, or Mistress Grace? Pray thee, Master Littlewit, lend me some money to see the interlude here. 30 I'll pay thee again, as I am a gentleman—if thou'lt but carry me home, I have money enough there.

LITTLEWIT

O sir, you shall command it. What, will a crown serve you?

COKES

I think it will. What do we pay for coming in, fellows?

FILCHER

Twopence, sir. 35

COKES

Twopence? There's twelvepence, friend. Nay, I am a gallant, as simple as I look now, if you see me with my man about me, and my artillery, again.

LITTLEWIT

Your man was i' the stocks e'en now, sir.

COKES

Who, Numps? 40

LITTLEWIT

Yes, faith.

COKES

For what i'faith? I am glad o' that. Remember to tell me on't anon; I have enough now! What manner of matter is this, Master Littlewit? What kind of actors ha' you? Are they good actors?

[Enter] LEATHERHEAD

27 *fire* probably refers to the fire in Ursla's booth, but could be the fire of hell
31 *gentleman—if* ed. {Gentleman. If F)
34 *will. What* ed. (well, what F)
36-7 *as simple as* humble though
38 *artillery* full equipment
42 *i'faith?* ed. (i'faith, F)
45 *Pretty youths . . . 'em* Probably an allusion to the Children of the Chapel Royal, for whom Edwards, their Master, wrote *Damon and Pithias*; though it could refer to the Boys' Companies which enjoyed a great revival in the early seventeenth century.

LITTLEWIT

Pretty youths, sir, all children, both old and young, here's the   45
master of 'em—

LEATHERHEAD whispers to LITTLEWIT

LEATHERHEAD

Call me not Leatherhead, but Lantern.

LITTLEWIT

—Master Lantern, that gives light to the business.

COKES

In good time, sir! I would fain see 'em, I would be glad to
drink with the young company. Which is the tiring-house?   50

LEATHERHEAD

Troth sir, our tiring-house is somewhat little; we are but
beginners yet, pray pardon us; you cannot go upright in't.

COKES

No? Not now my hat is off? What would you have done with me
if you had had me, feather and all, as I was once today? Ha' you
none of your pretty impudent boys, now, to bring stools, fill   55
tobacco, fetch ale, and beg money, as they have at other houses?
Let me see some o' your actors.

LITTLEWIT

Shew him 'em, shew him 'em. Master Lantern, this is a gentleman
that is a favourer of the quality.

OVERDO

[*Aside*] Ay, the favouring of this licentious quality is the   60
consumption of many a young gentleman; a pernicious enormity.

He [LEATHERHEAD] *brings them out in a basket*

---

47   *Call me . . . Lantern* Leatherhead does not wish to be recognized by Cokes, whom he
has swindled.

49   *In good time* Well met

49–50 *glad to drink* ed. (glad drinke F)

51   *tiring-house* area at the back of the stage where the actors dressed (attired) themselves

52   *go upright* walk without stooping

54–6 *Ha' you . . . houses* There is a splendid satirical account of the way in which the young
fops who sat on the stage behaved in Thomas Dekker's *The Gull's Horn-Book* (1609);
see *Thomas Dekker*, ed. E. D. Pendry, London, 1967, pp. 98–102.

59   *quality* acting profession

61   *consumption* financial ruin

COKES

What, do they live in baskets?

LEATHERHEAD

They do lie in a basket, sir, they are o' the small players.

COKES

These be players minors, indeed. Do you call these players?

LEATHERHEAD

They are actors, sir, and as good as any, none dispraised, for 65
dumb shows: indeed, I am the mouth of 'em all!

COKES

Thy mouth will hold 'em all. I think one Taylor would go near to
beat all this company, with a hand bound behind him.

LITTLEWIT

Ay, and eat 'em all, too, an they were in cake-bread.

COKES

I thank you for that, Master Littlewit, a good jest! Which is your 70
Burbage now?

LEATHERHEAD

What mean you by that, sir?

COKES

Your best actor. Your Field?

LITTLEWIT

Good i'faith! You are even with me, sir.

LEATHERHEAD

This is he that acts young Leander, sir. He is extremely beloved of 75
the womenkind, they do so affect his action, the green
gamesters that come here; and this is lovely Hero; this with the

---

66 *mouth* interpreter, voice
67 *one Taylor* There may be as many as three allusions here: (i) to the notion that tailors
are cowardly, enshrined in the proverb 'Nine tailors make a man' (Tilley, T23); (ii) to
the actor Joseph Taylor, a member of the company that first played *Bartholmew Fair*;
(iii) to John Taylor, the water-poet as he was called, who had challenged William Fennor,
a pamphleteer and hack-writer, to a combat of wit at the Hope Theatre in October 1614.,
Fennor, having accepted the challenge, failed to show up.
69 *eat 'em all* Tailors were popularly supposed to have enormous appetites.
in cake-bread made of cake-bread
71 *Burbage* Richard Burbage, who died in 1619, was the leading player of the King's Men,
Shakespeare's company, and the most celebrated actor of the time.
73 *Field* Nathan Field (1587-1619?) was the chief actor of the Lady Elizabeth's Servants when
they put on *Bartholmew Fair*. A dramatist as well as a player, Field was on very good
terms with Jonson.
76 *affect his action* like his acting (with a quibble on 'action' = 'sexual activity')

beard, Damon; and this, pretty Pythias. This is the ghost of King
Dionysius in the habit of a scrivener, as you shall see anon, at
large.   80

COKES

Well, they are a civil company, I like 'em for that. They offer not
to fleer, nor jeer, nor break jests, as the great players do. And
then there goes not so much charge to the feasting of 'em, or
making 'em drunk, as to the other, by reason of their littleness.
Do they use to play perfect? Are they never flustered?   85

LEATHERHEAD

No, sir, I thank my industry and policy for it; they are as well-
governed a company, though I say it—And here is young
Leander, is as proper an actor of his inches, and shakes his head
like an hostler.

COKES

But do you play it according to the printed book? I have read   90
that.

LEATHERHEAD

By no means, sir.

COKES

No? How then?

LEATHERHEAD

A better way, sir. That is too learned and poetical for our
audience. What do they know what Hellespont is? 'Guilty of true   95
love's blood'? Or what Abydos is? Or 'the other Sestos hight'?

76–7 *green gamesters* young loose wenches
   79 *the habit of a scrivener* cf. V. iv, 284
79–80 *at large* in full
   81 *Well*, ed. (Well F)
   82 *fleer* gibe, laugh mockingly
      great adult, full-grown
   85 *perfect* word-perfect
   88 *of his inches* for his size
88–89 *shakes . . . hostler* There may be an allusion here to the actor William Ostler, a member
      of the King's Men.
   90 *the printed book* Marlowe's *Hero and Leander* (1598) and, with Chapman's continuation
      of it, 1598, 1600, 1606, 1609, 1613. The first four lines run thus:
         On Hellespont, guilty of true love's blood,
         In view and opposite two cities stood,
         Sea-borderers, disjoin'd by Neptune's might:
         The one Abydos, the other Sestos hight.
   94 *sir. That* ed. (Sir, that F)
   96 *hight* called

COKES

Th'art i' the right, I do not know myself.

LEATHERHEAD

No, I have entreated Master Littlewit to take a little pains to reduce it to a more familiar strain for our people.

COKES

How, I pray thee, good Master Littlewit?   100

LITTLEWIT

It pleases him to make a matter of it, sir. But there is no such matter, I assure you. I have only made it a little easy, and modern for the times, sir, that's all. As, for the Hellespont, I imagine our Thames here; and then Leander I make a dyer's son, about Puddle Wharf; and Hero a wench o' the Bankside, who   105 going over one morning to Old Fish Street, Leander spies her land at Trig Stairs, and falls in love with her. Now do I introduce Cupid having metamorphosed himself into a drawer, and he strikes Hero in love with a pint of sherry. And other pretty passages there are o' the friendship, that will delight you, sir, and   110 please you of judgement.

COKES

I'll be sworn they shall. I am in love with the actors already, and I'll be allied to them presently.—They respect gentlemen, these fellows.—Hero shall be my fairing. But which of my fairings? Le'me see—i'faith, my fiddle! and Leander my fiddle-stick. Then   115 Damon my drum, and Pythias my pipe, and the ghost of Dionysius my hobby-horse. All fitted.

---

103   *modern* up-to-date
105   *Puddle Wharf* Between Blackfriars and Paul's Stairs, it was one of the water-gates of London.
106   *Old Fish Street* As the name implies, the centre of the fish trade in Jonson's London.
107   *Trig Stairs* Stairs leading down to the Thames next to Puddle Wharf.
108   *drawer* tapster
109   *with* by means of
        sherry. And ed. (Sherry, and F)
113   *be allied to them* make them members of my family
116   *pipe,* ed. (Pipe F)

ACT V, SCENE iv

[*Enter*] *to them* WINWIFE, GRACE

WINWIFE

Look, yonder's your Cokes gotten in among his playfellows; I
thought we could not miss him at such a spectacle.

GRACE

Let him alone, he is so busy he will never spy us.

LEATHERHEAD

Nay, good sir.

COKES *is handling the puppets*

COKES

I warrant thee, I will not hurt her, fellow; what, dost think me   5
uncivil? I pray thee be not jealous; I am toward a wife.

LITTLEWIT

Well, good Master Lantern, make ready to begin, that I may fetch
my wife; and look you be perfect, you undo me else i' my
reputation.

LEATHERHEAD

I warrant you, sir. Do not you breed too great an expectation of   10
it among your friends; that's the only hurter of these things.

LITTLEWIT

No, no, no.   [*Exit*]

COKES

I'll stay here and see; pray thee let me see.

WINWIFE

How diligent and troublesome he is!

GRACE

The place becomes him, methinks.   15

OVERDO

[*Aside*] My ward, Mistress Grace, in the company of a stranger? I
doubt I shall be compelled to discover myself before my time!

---

5 *what,* ed. (what F)
6 *toward* about to marry
14 *diligent and troublesome* diligently troublesome (hendiadys)
17 *doubt* fear

[*Enter*] KNOCKEM, WHIT, EDGWORTH, WIN, MISTRESS OVERDO
[*the ladies masked*]

The door-keepers speak

FILCHER
Twopence apiece, gentlemen, an excellent motion.

KNOCKEM
Shall we have fine fireworks and good vapours?

SHARKWELL
Yes, Captain, and waterworks too.   20

WHIT
I pree dee take a care o' dy shmall lady there, Edgworth; I will
look to dish tall lady myself.

LEATHERHEAD
Welcome, gentlemen; welcome, gentlemen.

WHIT
Predee, mashter o' de' monshtersh, help a very sick lady here to a
chair to shit in.   25

LEATHERHEAD
Presently, sir.

They bring MISTRESS OVERDO *a chair*

WHIT
Good fait now, Ursla's ale and *aqua vitae* ish to blame for't. Shit
down, shweetheart, shit down and shleep a little.

EDGWORTH
[*To* WIN] Madam, you are very welcome hither.

KNOCKEM
Yes, and you shall see very good vapours.   30

OVERDO   *By* EDGWORTH
[*Aside*] Here is my care come! I like to see him in so good
company; and yet I wonder that persons of such fashion should
resort hither!

19 *vapours?* ed. (vapours! F)
20 *waterworks* a pageant exhibited on the water (much of the puppet shew is supposed to
    take place on the Thames)
31 s.d. *By* Referring to

676

EDGWORTH
>This is a very private house, madam.

The cutpurse courts MISTRESS LITTLEWIT

LEATHERHEAD
>Will it please your ladyship sit, madam?   35

WIN
>Yes, goodman. They do so all-to-be-madam me, I think they
>think me a very lady!

EDGWORTH
>What else, madam?

WIN
>Must I put off my mask to him?

EDGWORTH
>O, by no means.   40

WIN
>How should my husband know me, then?

KNOCKEM
>Husband? an idle vapour. He must not know you, nor you him;
>there's the true vapour.

OVERDO
>[*Aside*] Yea, I will observe more of this. [*To* WHIT] Is this a lady,
>friend?   45

WHIT
>Ay, and dat is anoder lady, shweetheart. If dou hasht a mind to
>'em, give me twelvepence from tee, and dou shalt have eder-
>oder on 'em!

OVERDO
>Ay? [*Aside*] This will prove my chiefest enormity, I will follow
>this.   50

EDGWORTH
>Is not this a finer life, lady, than to be clogged with a husband?

---

34 *private house* Edgworth quibbles on (i) house that affords us privacy (ii) private playhouse,
   i.e., one that was, unlike the public theatres such as the Globe or the Hope, entirely
   roofed in. It was also more expensive than the public theatres.
36 *all-to-be-madam me* persist in calling me madam
47–8 *eder-oder* one or the other

WIN

Yes, a great deal. When will they begin, trow, in the name o' the motion?

EDGWORTH

By and by, madam, they stay but for company.

KNOCKEM

Do you hear, puppet-master, these are tedious vapours; when   55
begin you?

LEATHERHEAD

We stay but for Master Littlewit, the author, who is gone for his wife; and we begin presently.

WIN

That's I, that's I.

EDGWORTH

That was you, lady, but now you are no such poor thing.   60

KNOCKEM

Hang the author's wife, a running vapour! Here be ladies will stay for ne'er a Delia o' 'em all.

WHIT

But hear me now, here ish one o' de ladish ashleep. Stay till she but vake, man.

[Enter] to them WASP

The door-keepers again

WASP

How now, friends? What's here to do?   65

FILCHER

Twopence apiece, sir, the best motion in the Fair.

WASP

I believe you lie. If you do, I'll have my money again, and beat you.

WINWIFE

Numps is come!

52 *trow* do you think
62 *a Delia* Delia is the name of the lady to whom Samuel Daniel addressed his sonnet sequence *Delia*, first published in 1592. Probably an anagram of 'ideal', the name is here synonymous with 'self-important lady'.
69 s.p. *WINWIFE* ed. (WIN. F)

WASP

Did you see a master of mine come in here, a tall young squire of   70
Harrow o' the Hill, Master Bartholmew Cokes?

FILCHER

I think there be such a one within.

WASP

Look he be, you were best; but it is very likely. I wonder I found him
not at all the rest. I ha' been at the Eagle, and the Black Wolf, and the
Bull with the five legs and two pizzles—he was a calf at Uxbridge   75
Fair, two years agone—and at the Dogs that dance the morris, and
the Hare o' the tabor, and missed him at all these! Sure this must
needs be some fine sight that holds him so, if it have him.

COKES

Come, come, are you ready now?

LEATHERHEAD

Presently, sir.   80

WASP

Hoyday, he's at work in his doublet and hose. Do you hear, sir?
Are you employed, that you are bare-headed and so busy?

COKES

Hold your peace, Numps; you ha' been i' the stocks, I hear.

WASP

Does he know that? Nay, then the date of my authority is out; I
must think no longer to reign, my government is at an end. He   85
that will correct another must want fault in himself.

WINWIFE

Sententious Numps! I never heard so much from him before.

LEATHERHEAD

Sure Master Littlewit will not come. Please you take your place,
sir, we'll begin.

COKES

I pray thee do, mine ears long to be at it, and my eyes too. O Numps,   90
i' the stocks, Numps? Where's your sword, Numps?

WASP

I pray you intend your game, sir, let me alone.

74–7 *the Eagle . . . tabor* Various attractions at the Fair. The 'Bull with five legs', first mentioned
at III.vi, 7, has now acquired an extra pizzle (penis) and has been joined by some other
animals, including a hare that plays on the tabor.

84 *date of my authority is out* term of my authority is up

86 *want* be free from

92 *intend* pay attention to

COKES

> Well then, we are quit for all. Come, sit down, Numps; I'll
> interpret to thee. Did you see Mistress Grace? It's no matter
> neither now I think on't, tell me anon. 95

WINWIFE

> A great deal of love and care he expresses.

GRACE

> Alas! Would you have him to express more than he has? That
> were tyranny.

COKES

> Peace, ho! now, now.

LEATHERHEAD

> *Gentles, that no longer your expectations may wander,* 100
> *Behold our chief actor, amorous Leander,*
> *With a great deal of cloth lapped about him like a scarf,*
> *For he yet serves his father, a dyer at Puddle Wharf,*
> *Which place we'll make bold with, to call it our Abydus,*
> *As the Bankside is our Sestos, and let it not be denied us.* 105
> *Now, as he is beating, to make the dye take the fuller,*
> *Who chances to come by but fair Hero in a sculler;*
> *And seeing Leander's naked leg and goodly calf,*
> *Cast at him, from the boat, a sheep's eye and a half.*
> *Now she is landed, and the sculler come back;* 110
> *By and by you shall see what Leander doth lack.*

PUPPET LEANDER

> *Cole, Cole, old Cole.*

LEATHERHEAD   *That is the sculler's name without control.*

PUPPET LEANDER

> *Cole, Cole, I say, Cole.*

LEATHERHEAD   *We do hear you.*

PUPPET LEANDER   *Old Cole.*

---

93   *quit* even (with one another)
101   *Leander,* ed. (Leander. F)
    amorous Leander The words are Marlowe's (*Hero and Leander*, i. 51).
106   *fuller* more completely
109   *Cast . . . eye* 'He casts a sheep's eye at her' was proverbial (Tilley, S323) and still is.
112   *Cole* often used as the name for a pander
    without control The normal meaning of this phrase is 'freely', but here 'beyond all
    contradiction' would seem more to the point.
113   *We do hear you* ed. (roman in F)

LEATHERHEAD
>Old coal? Is the dyer turned collier? How do you sell?

PUPPET LEANDER
>A pox o' your manners, kiss my hole here, and smell. 115

LEATHERHEAD
>Kiss your hole, and smell? There's manners indeed.

PUPPET LEANDER
>Why, Cole, I say, Cole.

LEATHERHEAD   It's the sculler you need!

PUPPET LEANDER
>Ay, and be hanged.

LEATHERHEAD   Be hanged? Look you yonder;
>Old Cole, you must go hang with Master Leander.

PUPPET COLE
>Where is he?

PUPPET LEANDER Here, Cole. What fairest of fairs 120
>Was that fare that thou landedst but now at Trig Stairs?

COKES
What was that, fellow? Pray thee tell me, I scarce understand 'em.

LEATHERHEAD
>Leander does ask, sir, what fairest of fairs
>Was the fare that he landed, but now, at Trig Stairs.

PUPPET COLE
>It is lovely Hero.

PUPPET LEANDER   Nero?

PUPPET COLE   No, Hero.

LEATHERHEAD   It is lovely Hero 125
>Of the Bankside, he saith, to tell you truth without erring,
>Is come over into Fish Street to eat some fresh herring.
>Leander says no more, but as fast as he can,
>Gets on all his best clothes, and will after to the Swan.

COKES
Most admirable good, is't not? 130

LEATHERHEAD
>Stay, sculler.

---

114   *collier* (i) seller of coal (ii) term of abuse, because coal-sellers were black from their trade and were notorious cheats
  How At what price
121   *at* ed. (a F)
124   *that he* ed. (thhe F)
125   *is lovely Hero* ed. (is Hero. F)

PUPPET COLE   *What say you?*
LEATHERHEAD   *You must stay for Leander,*
     And carry him to the wench.
PUPPET COLE   *You rogue, I am no pander.*
COKES
     He says he is no pander. 'Tis a fine language; I understand it now.
LEATHERHEAD
     Are you no pander, Goodman Cole? Here's no man says you are.   135
     You'll grow a hot Cole, it seems, pray you stay for your fare.
PUPPET COLE
     Will he come away?
LEATHERHEAD   *What do you say?*
PUPPET COLE   *I'd ha' him come away.*
LEATHERHEAD
     Would you ha' Leander come away? Why pray, sir, stay.
     You are angry, Goodman Cole. I believe the fair maid
     Came over w' you o' trust. Tell us, sculler, are you paid?   140
PUPPET COLE
     Yes, Goodman Hogrubber o' Pickt-hatch.
LEATHERHEAD
     How? Hogrubber o' Pickt-hatch?
PUPPET COLE   *Ay, Hogrubber o' Pickt-hatch.*
     Take you that.   The puppet strikes him over the pate
LEATHERHEAD   *O, my head!*
PUPPET COLE   *Harm watch, harm catch.*
COKES
     'Harm watch, harm catch,' he says. Very good i'faith! The sculler
     had like to ha' knocked you, sirrah.   145
LEATHERHEAD
     Yes, but that his fare called him away.
PUPPET LEANDER
     Row apace, row apace, row, row, row, row, row.
LEATHERHEAD
     You are knavishly loaden, sculler, take heed where you go.

---

140 *paid?* ed. (paid. F)
141 *Hogrubber o' Pickt-hatch* Hogrubber seems to have been a derisive term for a swineherd,
     while Pickt-hatch was a very unsavoury area of London, the haunt of thieves and
     prostitutes. It looks as though Leatherhead is being accused of bestiality.
144 *Harm watch, harm catch* if you do harm, you suffer harm (proverbial, Tilley, H167)
145 *had like to ha' knocked* seemed on the point of beating

PUPPET COLE

Knave i' your face, Goodman Rogue.

PUPPET LEANDER   *Row, row, row, row, row, row.*

COKES

He said 'knave i' your face,' friend.   150

LEATHERHEAD

Ay, sir, I heard him. But there's no talking to these watermen,
they will ha' the last word.

COKES

God's my life! I am not allied to the sculler yet. He shall be
Dauphin my boy. But my fiddle-stick does fiddle in and out too
much. I pray thee speak to him on't; tell him I would have him   155
tarry in my sight more.

LEATHERHEAD

I pray you be content; you'll have enough on him, sir.

Now gentles, I take it, here is none of you so stupid,
But that you have heard of a little god of love, called Cupid;
Who out of kindness to Leander, hearing he but saw her,   160
This present day and hour, doth turn himself to a drawer.
And because he would have their first meeting to be merry,
He strikes Hero in love to him, with a pint of sherry.
Which he tells her from amorous Leander is sent her,
Who after him into the room of Hero doth venter.   165

PUPPET JONAS

A pint of sack, score a pint of sack i' the Coney.

                 Puppet Leander goes into MISTRESS HERO's room

COKES

Sack? You said but e'en now it should be sherry.

PUPPET JONAS

Why so it is; sherry, sherry, sherry.

COKES

'Sherry, sherry, sherry.' By my troth he makes me merry. I must
have a name for Cupid too. Let me see. Thou mightest help me   170

151-2   *watermen, they will ha' the last word* a variant on the proverbial 'Women will have the
        last word' (Tilley, W723)

154   *my fiddle-stick* i.e., Leander (cf. V. iii, 115)
      Dauphin my boy Also referred to by Edgar in *King Lear* (III.iv, 99) as 'Dolphin my boy',
      this snatch (from some lost ballad or song?) still remains unexplained.

165   *venter* venture

166   *the Coney.* Rooms in Elizabethan inns were named not numbered.

167   *Sack? . . . sherry* Cokes loses no opportunity of demonstrating his ignorance. Sack was
      the name by which all white wines, including sherry, were called.

now, an thou wouldest, Numps, at a dead lift, but thou art
dreaming o' the stocks still! Do not think on't, I have forgot it.
'Tis but a nine days' wonder, man; let it not trouble thee.

WASP

I would the stocks were about your neck, sir; condition I hung by
the heels in them, till the wonder wore off from you, with all my   175
heart.

COKES

Well said, resolute Numps!—But hark you, friend, where is the
friendship, all this while, between my drum, Damon, and my
pipe, Pythias?

LEATHERHEAD

You shall see by and by, sir.   180

COKES

You think my hobby-horse is forgotten too. No, I'll see 'em all
enact before I go; I shall not know which to love best, else.

KNOCKEM

This gallant has interrupting vapours, troublesome vapours,
Whit, puff with him.

WHIT

No, I pre dee, Captain, let him alone. He is a child i'faith, la!   185

LEATHERHEAD

Now gentles, to the friends, who in number are two,
And lodged in that ale-house in which fair Hero does do.
Damon, for some kindness done him the last week,
Is come fair Hero, in Fish Street, this morning to seek.
Pythias does smell the knavery of the meeting,   190
And now you shall see their true friendly greeting.

PUPPET PYTHIAS

You whoremasterly slave, you!

COKES

'Whoremasterly slave, you?' Very friendly and familiar, that.

---

171 *at a dead lift* at a pinch (proverbial, Tilley, L271)
173 *a nine days' wonder* (proverbial, Tilley, W728)
174 *condition* on condition that
175 *wore* ed. (were F). Cf. 'These few days' wonder will be quickly worn' (2 *Henry VI*, II.iv,
     69).
177 *said,* ed. (said F)
181 *my hobby-horse is forgotten* A much-quoted line from some lost song; cf. *Hamlet*, III.ii,
     130.
184 *puff with* bully, quarrel with
187 *do* work

PUPPET DAMON   *Whoremaster i' thy face,*
    Thou hast lien with her thyself, I'll prove't i' this place.

COKES
    Damon says Pythias has lien with her himself, he'll prove't in this   195
    place.

LEATHERHEAD
    They are whoremasters both, sir, that's a plain case.

PUPPET PYTHIAS
    You lie like a rogue.

LEATHERHEAD   *Do I lie like a rogue?*

PUPPET PYTHIAS
    A pimp and a scab.

LEATHERHEAD   *A pimp and a scab?*
    I say between you, you have both but one drab.   200

PUPPET DAMON
    You lie again.

LEATHERHEAD   *Do I lie again?*

PUPPET DAMON
    Like a rogue again.

LEATHERHEAD   *Like a rogue again?*

PUPPET PYTHIAS
    And you are a pimp again.

COKES
    And you are a pimp again, he says.   205

PUPPET DAMON   *And a scab again.*

COKES
    And a scab again, he says.

LEATHERHEAD
    And I say again, you are both whoremasters again,
    And you have both but one drab again.

                                        They fight

PUPPET DAMON ⎫
PUPPET PYTHIAS ⎬
    Dost thou, dost thou, dost thou?

LEATHERHEAD
    What, both at once?

PUPPET PYTHIAS   *Down with him, Damon.*

PUPPET DAMON
    Pink his guts, Pythias.

---

199   *scab* scoundrel
210   *Pink* pierce, stab

LEATHERHEAD   *What, so malicious?*   210
  Will ye murder me, masters both, i' mine own house?
COKES
  Ho! well acted my drum, well acted my pipe, well acted still!
WASP
  Well acted, with all my heart!
LEATHERHEAD
  Hold, hold your hands.
COKES
  Ay, both your hands, for my sake! for you ha' both done well.   215
PUPPET DAMON
  Gramercy, pure Pythias.
PUPPET PYTHIAS   *Gramercy, dear Damon.*
COKES
  Gramercy to you both, my pipe, and my drum.
PUPPET PYTHIAS ⎫
PUPPET DAMON ⎬
  Come now we'll together to breakfast to Hero.
LEATHERHEAD
  'Tis well, you can now go to breakfast to Hero,
  You have given me my breakfast, with a 'hone and 'honero.   220
COKES
  How is it, friend, ha' they hurt thee?
LEATHERHEAD   O no!
  Between you and I, sir, we do but make shew.
    Thus, gentles, you perceive, without any denial,
    'Twixt Damon and Pythias here, friendship's true trial.
    Though hourly they quarrel thus, and roar each with other,   225
    They fight you no more than does brother with brother.
    But friendly together, at the next man they meet
    They let fly their anger, as here you might see't.
COKES
  Well, we have seen't, and thou hast felt it, whatsoever thou sayest.
  What's next? What's next?   230

214 *Hold* ed. (Hld F)
215 *for* ed. (for. F)
218 *to Hero* with Hero
220 *me my* ed. (*mmy* F)
      a 'hone and 'honero An Irish and Scottish exclamation of grief, from the Irish and Gaelic
      'ochòin', meaning 'alas'.
221 *is it* ed. (is't F)
230 *sayest.* ed. (sayest, F)

LEATHERHEAD

>*This while young Leander with fair Hero is drinking,*
>*And Hero grown drunk, to any man's thinking!*
>*Yet was it not three pints of sherry could flaw her,*
>*Till Cupid, distinguished like Jonas the drawer,*
>*From under his apron, where his lechery lurks,* 235
>*Put love in her sack. Now mark how it works.*

PUPPET HERO

>*O Leander, Leander, my dear, my dear Leander,*
>*I'll for ever be thy goose, so thou'lt be my gander.*

COKES

Excellently well said, fiddle! She'll ever be his goose, so he'll be her gander; was't not so? 240

LEATHERHEAD

Yes, sir, but mark his answer, now.

PUPPET LEANDER

>*And sweetest of geese, before I go to bed,*
>*I'll swim o'er the Thames, my goose, thee to tread.*

COKES

Brave! he will swim o'er the Thames and tread his goose tonight, he says. 245

LEATHERHEAD

Ay, peace, sir, they'll be angry if they hear you eaves-dropping, now they are setting their match.

PUPPET LEANDER

>*But lest the Thames should be dark, my goose, my dear friend,*
>*Let thy window be provided of a candle's end.*

PUPPET HERO

>*Fear not, my gander, I protest I should handle* 250
>*My matters very ill, if I had not a whole candle.*

PUPPET LEANDER

>*Well then, look to't, and kiss me to boot.*

LEATHERHEAD

>*Now here come the friends again, Pythias and Damon,*
>*And under their cloaks they have of bacon a gammon.*

---

233 *flaw her,* ed. (*flaw her.* F) make her drunk (earliest example in *OED* 1673)
234 *distinguished* dressed, disguised
236 *sack* (i) sherry (ii) loose gown
246 *they'll* ed. (the'll F)
247 *setting their match* fixing a time for their (amorous) encounter
250 *not,* ed. (*not* F)

DAMON *and* PYTHIAS *enter*

PUPPET PYTHIAS
> Drawer, fill some wine here.

LEATHERHEAD   *How, some wine there?*   255
> *There's company already, sir, pray forbear!*

PUPPET DAMON
> *'Tis Hero.*

LEATHERHEAD Yes, but she will not be taken,
> *After sack and fresh herring, with your Dunmow-bacon.*

PUPPET PYTHIAS
> *You lie, it's Westfabian.*

LEATHERHEAD   *Westphalian, you should say.*

PUPPET DAMON
> *If you hold not your peace, you are a coxcomb, I would say.*   260
>   LEANDER and HERO are kissing

PUPPET (PYTHIAS)
> *What's here? What's here? Kiss, kiss upon kiss.*

LEATHERHEAD
> *Ay, wherefore should they not? What harm is in this?*
> *'Tis Mistress Hero.*

PUPPET DAMON   *Mistress Hero's a whore.*

LEATHERHEAD
> *Is she a whore? Keep you quiet, or, sir knave, out of door.*

PUPPET DAMON
> *Knave out of door?*

PUPPET HERO   *Yes, knave, out of door.*   265

PUPPET DAMON
> *Whore out of door.*

PUPPET HERO   *I say, knave, out of door.*

Here the PUPPETS quarrel and fall together by the ears

PUPPET DAMON
> *I say, whore, out of door.*

---

258 *Dunmow-bacon* 'To fetch a flitch of bacon from Dunmow' was synonymous with marital fidelity (Tilley, F375), since the village of Dunmow, in Essex, gives a flitch of bacon to the couple who can show that they have not quarrelled since they were married. Leatherhead's point is that after her meal Hero will be feeling lecherous.

259 *Westphalian* Westphalia, in Germany, was famous for its bacon and ham.

PUPPET PYTHIAS   *Yea, so say I too.*

PUPPET HERO
> *Kiss the whore o' the arse.*

LEATHERHEAD   *Now you ha' something to do:*
> *You must kiss her o' the arse, she says.*

PUPPET DAMON, ⎱
PUPPET PYTHIAS ⎰   *So we will, so we will*

       [They kick her]

PUPPET HERO
> *O my haunches, O my haunches, hold, hold!*

LEATHERHEAD   *Stand'st thou still?*   270
> *Leander, where art thou? Stand'st thou still like a sot,*
> *And not offer'st to break both their heads with a pot?*
> *See who's at thine elbow there! Puppet Jonas and Cupid.*

PUPPET JONAS
> *Upon 'em, Leander, be not so stupid.*

            They fight

PUPPET LEANDER
> *You goat-bearded slave!*

PUPPET DAMON   *You whoremaster knave!*   275

PUPPET LEANDER
> *Thou art a whoremaster.*

PUPPET JONAS   *Whoremasters all.*

LEATHERHEAD
> *See, Cupid with a word has ta'en up the brawl.*

KNOCKEM
> These be fine vapours!

COKES
> By this good day they fight bravely! Do they not, Numps?

WASP
> Yes, they lacked but you to be their second, all this while.   280

LEATHERHEAD
> *This tragical encounter, falling out thus to busy us,*
> *It raises up the ghost of their friend Dionysius,*
> *Not like a monarch, but the master of a school,*

282–3 *Dionysius . . . school* According to some accounts, Dionysius the younger, tyrant of Syracuse (367-343 B.C.) became a schoolmaster after his abdication.

In a scrivener's furred gown, which shews he is no fool.
For therein he hath wit enough to keep himself warm. 285
'O Damon,' he cries, 'and Pythias, what harm
Hath poor Dionysius done you in his grave,
That after his death you should fall out thus, and rave,
And call amorous Leander whoremaster knave?'

PUPPET DIONYSIUS
I cannot, I will not, I promise you, endure it. 290

ACT V, SCENE v

[*Enter*] *to them* BUSY

BUSY

Down with Dagon, down with Dagon! 'Tis I, will no longer endure your profanations.

LEATHERHEAD

What mean you, sir?

BUSY

I will remove Dagon there, I say, that idol, that heathenish idol, that remains, as I may say, a beam, a very beam, not a beam of the 5 sun, nor a beam of the moon, nor a beam of a balance, neither a house-beam, nor a weaver's beam, but a beam in the eye, in the eye of the brethren; a very great beam, an exceeding great beam; such as are your stage-players, rhymers, and morris-dancers, who have walked hand in hand, in contempt of the brethren, and 10 the cause; and been borne out by instruments of no mean countenance.

LEATHERHEAD

Sir, I present nothing but what is licensed by authority.

285   *wit enough . . . warm* proverbial (Tilley, K10)

1   *Dagon* The national god of the Philistines, represented as half man and half fish, was regarded as the very type of an idol. Hence comes Busy's ridiculous equation of the puppets, whom he sees as idols, with Dagon. See I Samuel, v.
      will who will, and I will
6   *beam of a balance* transverse bar from the ends of which the scales of a balance are suspended
7   *weaver's beam* cylinder in a loom
7   *a beam in the eye* alluding to the figure of the mote and the beam (Matthew, vii. 3-5)
11   *borne out* supported
      instruments agents (of the devil)
12   *countenance* position, rank

BUSY

Thou art all licence, even licentiousness itself, Shimei!

LEATHERHEAD

I have the Master of the Revels' hand for't, sir.   15

BUSY

The Master of Rebels' hand, thou hast—Satan's! Hold thy peace;
thy scurrility shut up thy mouth; thy profession is damnable, and
in pleading for it, thou dost plead for Baal. I have long opened my
mouth wide, and gaped, I have gaped as the oyster for the tide,
after thy destruction, but cannot compass it by suit, or dispute; so   20
that I look for a bickering, ere long, and then a battle.

KNOCKEM

Good Banbury-vapours.

COKES

Friend, you'd have an ill match on't if you bicker with him here;
though he be no man o' the fist, he has friends that will go to cuffs
for him. Numps, will not you take our side?   25

EDGWORTH

Sir, it shall not need; in my mind, he offers him a fairer course—
to end it by disputation!—Hast thou nothing to say for thyself, in
defence of thy quality?

LEATHERHEAD

Faith, sir, I am not well studied in these controversies between
the hypocrites and us. But here's one of my motion, Puppet   30
Dionysius, shall undertake him, and I'll venture the cause on't.

14 *Shimei* Shimei, who cursed David, had, according to David himself, God's authority
    (licence) for doing it (II Samuel, xvi. 5-13).
15 *Master of the Revels* An officer of the court who was responsible for, among other things,
    the licensing of plays.
17 *thy scurrility shut up* let thy scurrility shut up
18 *Baal* The heathen god of the Midianites whose altar was cast down by Gideon (Judges,
    vi. 25-32), Busy sees himself as a Gideon.
19 *gaped as the oyster for the tide* proverbial (Tilley, 0114)
21 *bickering* skirmish
23 *here*; ed. (here, F)
25 *him.* ed. (him, F)
26 *need*; ed. (need, F)
28 *quality* profession
31 *undertake him* take him on

COKES

Who? My hobby-horse? Will he dispute with him?

LEATHERHEAD

Yes, sir, and make a hobby-ass of him, I hope.

COKES

That's excellent! Indeed he looks like the best scholar of 'em all.
Come, sir, you must be as good as your word, now.   35

BUSY

I will not fear to make my spirit and gifts known! Assist me, zeal,
fill me, fill me, that is, make me full.

WINWIFE

What a desperate, profane wretch is this! Is there any ignorance
or impudence like his? To call his zeal to fill him against a puppet?

GRACE

I know no fitter match than a puppet to commit with an   40
hypocrite!

BUSY

First, I say unto thee, idol, thou hast no calling.

PUPPET DIONYSIUS

You lie, I am called Dionysius.

LEATHERHEAD

The motion says you lie, he is called Dionysius i' the matter, and
to that calling he answers.   45

BUSY

I mean no vocation, idol, no present lawful calling.

PUPPET DIONYSIUS

Is yours a lawful calling?

LEATHERHEAD

The motion asketh if yours be a lawful calling.

---

40 s.p. *GRACE* ed. (QVA. F). As Waith points out, Quarlous is not on stage. Having made his
exit at V.ii, 114, he does not return until the opening of V.vi. A misreading of 'GRA.' as
'QVA.' by the compositor is the likeliest explanation of the mistake.
    commit do battle

41 *no calling* As Busy explains at l. 46, he means 'no lawful occupation'. The Puritans, and
opponents of the stage in general, took the view that acting was not a genuine occupation
at all; and they had the law on their side, for the player was liable to arrest as a rogue and
a vagabond, unless he could show that he was in the service of the court or of some great
man. It was for this reason that each acting company secured the patronage of a member
of the royal family, or of a noble, and called themselves 'The Lord Chamberlain's Men',
'The Lady Elizabeth's Servants', and the like.

44 *matter* puppet-play, text

BUSY

Yes, mine is of the spirit.

PUPPET DIONYSIUS

Then idol is a lawful calling. 50

LEATHERHEAD

He says, then idol is a lawful calling! For you called him idol, and your calling is of the spirit.

COKES

Well disputed, hobby-horse!

BUSY

Take not part with the wicked, young gallant. He neigheth and hinnyeth, all is but hinnying sophistry. I call him idol again. Yet, 55 I say, his calling, his profession is profane; it is profane, idol.

PUPPET DIONYSIUS

It is not profane!

LEATHERHEAD

It is not profane, he says.

BUSY

It is profane.

PUPPET DIONYSIUS

It is not profane. 60

BUSY

It is profane.

PUPPET DIONYSIUS

It is not profane.

LEATHERHEAD

Well said, confute him with 'not', still. You cannot bear him down with your base noise, sir.

BUSY

Nor he me with his treble creaking, though he creak like the 65 chariot wheels of Satan. I am zealous for the cause—

LEATHERHEAD

As a dog for a bone.

BUSY

And I say it is profane, as being the page of Pride, and the waiting-woman of Vanity.

---

54 *wicked*, ed. (wicked F)
65 *creaking* speaking in a strident tone

PUPPET DIONYSIUS

Yea? What say you to your tire-women, then?   70

LEATHERHEAD

Good.

PUPPET DIONYSIUS

Or feather-makers i' the Friars, that are o' your faction of faith?
Are not they, with their perukes, and their puffs, their fans, and
their huffs, as much pages of Pride, and waiters upon Vanity?
What say you? What say you? What say you?   75

BUSY

I will not answer for them.

PUPPET DIONYSIUS

Because you cannot, because you cannot. Is a bugle-maker a
lawful calling? Or the confect-maker's?—Such you have there. —Or
your French fashioner? You'd have all the sin within
yourselves, would you not? would you not?   80

BUSY

No, Dagon.

PUPPET DIONYSIUS

What then, Dagonet? Is a puppet worse than these?

BUSY

Yes, and my main argument against you is that you are an
abomination; for the male among you putteth on the apparel of
the female, and the female of the male.   85

PUPPET DIONYSIUS

You lie, you lie, you lie abominably.

COKES

Good, by my troth, he has given him the lie thrice.

70   *tire-women* dressmakers
72   *feather-makers i' the Friars* The traders in feathers, who lived in the Blackfriars area, also
     happened to be Puritans. The contradiction between their occupation, ministering to
     vanity, and their religious leanings did not escape their opponents.
73   *puffs* soft protuberant mass of material on the dress
74   *huffs* paddings used to raise the shoulders of dresses
77   *bugle-maker* maker of tube-shaped glass beads
78   *confect-maker's* that of the maker of sweetmeats
79   *fashioner* tailor or dressmaker
82   *Dagonet* King Arthur's fool
83–5 *an abomination . . . male* This 'old stale argument against the players', used long before
     1614 and long after it, is based on Deuteronomy, xxii. 5: 'The woman shall not wear that
     which pertaineth unto a man, neither shall a man put on a woman's garment: for all
     that do so are abomination unto the Lord thy God'. The text was indeed an inviting
     weapon for the enemies of a theatre in which all female roles were played by boys.

PUPPET DIONYSIUS

*It is your old stale argument against the players, but it will not hold
against the puppets, for we have neither male nor female amongst
us. And that thou may'st see, if thou wilt, like a malicious purblind
zeal as thou art!*   90

The PUPPET *takes up his garment*

EDGWORTH

By my faith, there he has answered you, friend, by plain
demonstration.

PUPPET DIONYSIUS

*Nay, I'll prove, against e'er a Rabbin of 'em all, that my standing
is as lawful as his; that I speak by inspiration, as well as he; that I*   95
*have as little to do with learning as he; and do scorn her helps as
much as he.*

BUSY

I am confuted, the cause hath failed me.

PUPPET DIONYSIUS

Then be converted, be converted.

LEATHERHEAD

Be converted, I pray you, and let the play go on!   100

BUSY

Let it go on. For I am changed, and will become a beholder with
you!

COKES

That's brave i'faith. Thou hast carried it away, hobby-horse. On
with the play!

The JUSTICE *discovers himself*

OVERDO

Stay. Now do I forbid, I, Adam Overdo! Sit still, I charge you.   105

COKES

What, my brother-i'-law!

GRACE

My wise guardian!

EDGWORTH

Justice Overdo!

94   *standing* profession
103   *carried it away* won

OVERDO

It is time to take enormity by the forehead, and brand it; for I
have discovered enough.   110

ACT V, SCENE vi

[*Enter*] *to them,* QUARLOUS (*like the madman*), PURECRAFT

QUARLOUS

Nay, come, Mistress bride. You must do as I do now. You must
be mad with me, in truth. I have here Justice Overdo for it.

OVERDO

Peace, good Trouble-all; come hither, and you shall trouble
none. I will take the charge of you and your friend too. (*To the
cutpurse and* MISTRESS LITTLEWIT) You also, young man, shall   5
be my care, stand there.

EDGWORTH

Now mercy upon me.

The rest are stealing away

KNOCKEM

Would we were away, Whit! These are dangerous vapours; best
fall off with our birds, for fear o' the cage.

OVERDO

Stay, is not my name your terror?   10

WHIT

Yesh faith, man, and it ish for tat we would be gone, man.

[*Enter*] LITTLEWIT

---

1   s.d. *Enter to them,* QUARLOUS (*like the madman*), PURECRAFT ed. (*To them,* QVARLOVS.
    (*like the Man-man*) PVRECRAFT. (*a while after*) IOHN. *to them* TROVBLE-ALL. VRSLA.
    NIGHTIGALE. F). Since Quarlous is speaking to Dame Purecraft as he enters, it is clear
    that the words *a while after* are intended to apply to John Littlewit, who does not appear
    until l. 11.
4   *too.* ed. (too, F)
5   *man,* ed. (man F)
8   *Whit!* ed. (*Whit,* F)
9   *fall off* withdraw
    cage gaol
11 *gone,* ed. (gone F)

LITTLEWIT

O gentlemen, did you not see a wife of mine? I ha' lost my little
wife, as I shall be trusted, my little pretty Win. I left her at the
great woman's house in trust yonder, the pig-woman's, with
Captain Jordan and Captain Whit, very good men, and I cannot   15
hear of her. Poor fool, I fear she's stepped aside. Mother, did you
not see Win?

OVERDO

If this grave matron be your mother, sir, stand by her, *et digito
compesce labellum*; I may perhaps spring a wife for you anon.
Brother Bartholmew, I am sadly sorry to see you so lightly given,   20
and such a disciple of enormity, with your grave governor
Humphrey. But stand you both there in the middle place; I will
reprehend you in your course. Mistress Grace, let me rescue you
out of the hands of the stranger.

WINWIFE

Pardon me, sir, I am a kinsman of hers.   25

OVERDO

Are you so? Of what name, sir?

WINWIFE

Winwife, sir.

OVERDO

Master Winwife? I hope you have won no wife of her, sir. If
you have, I will examine the possibility of it at fit leisure. Now
to my enormities! Look upon me, O London! and see me, O   30
Smithfield! the example of Justice, and Mirror of Magistrates; the
true top of formality, and scourge of enormity. Hearken unto
my labours and but observe my discoveries; and compare
Hercules with me, if thou dar'st, of old; or Columbus, Magellan,
or our countryman Drake of later times. Stand forth you weeds   35
of enormity and spread. (*To* BUSY) First, Rabbi Busy, thou
superlunatical hypocrite. (*To* LANTERN) Next, thou other
extremity, thou profane professor of puppetry, little better than

16   *fool* sweet
     stepped aside gone astray
18–19 *et digito compesce labellum* Adapted from Juvenal (*Satires*, i. 160): 'and check any
     movement of your lips with your finger', i.e., 'don't give yourself away'.
19   *spring* put up (as a partridge is 'put up' from cover)
23   *course* turn
32   *formality* legal procedure
36   *enormity and spread* ed. (enormity, and spread F) wide-spread enormity (hendiadys)

poetry. (*To the horse-courser, and cutpurse*) Then thou strong debaucher, and seducer of youth—witness this easy and honest   40
young man. (*Then* CAPTAIN WHIT *and* MISTRESS LITTLEWIT) Now thou esquire of dames, madams, and twelvepenny ladies; now my green madam herself of the price. Let me unmask your ladyship.

LITTLEWIT

O my wife, my wife, my wife!   45

OVERDO

Is she your wife? *Redde te Harpocratem!*

Enter TROUBLE-ALL [*followed by* URSLA *and* NIGHTINGALE]

TROUBLE-ALL

By your leave, stand by, my masters, be uncovered.

URSLA

O stay him, stay him! Help to cry, Nightingale. My pan, my pan!

OVERDO

What's the matter?

NIGHTINGALE

He has stolen Gammer Ursla's pan.   50

TROUBLE-ALL

Yes, and I fear no man but Justice Overdo.

OVERDO

Ursla? Where is she? O the sow of enormity, this! (*To* URSLA *and* NIGHTINGALE) Welcome. Stand you there; you, songster, there.

URSLA

An please your worship, I am in no fault. A gentleman stripped   55
him in my booth, and borrowed his gown and his hat; and he ran away with my goods here for it.

OVERDO

(*To* QUARLOUS) Then this is the true madman, and you are the enormity!

---

40 *easy* compliant, credulous
46 *Redde te Harpocratem* Transform yourself into Harpocrates (the god of silence, born with his finger on his lips).
47 *by*, ed. (by F)
    be uncovered take off your hats (as a sign of respect)
53 *you*, ed. (you F)
55 *in no fault* not to blame

QUARLOUS

You are i' the right, I am mad but from the gown outward.   60

OVERDO

Stand you there.

QUARLOUS

Where you please, sir.

                MISTERSS OVERDO *is sick, and her husband is silenced*

MISTRESS OVERDO

O lend me a basin, I am sick, I am sick. Where's Master Overdo?
Bridget, call hither my Adam.

OVERDO

How?   65

WHIT

Dy very own wife, i'fait, worshipful Adam.

MISTRESS OVERDO

Will not my Adam come at me? Shall I see him no more then?

QUARLOUS

Sir, why do you not go on with the enormity? Are you oppressed
with it? I'll help you. Hark you, sir, i' your ear— your 'innocent
young man', you have ta'en such care of all this day, is a cutpurse,   70
that hath got all your brother Cokes his things, and helped you to
your beating and the stocks. If you have a mind to hang him now,
and shew him your magistrate's wit, you may; but I should think
it were better recovering the goods, and to save your estimation
in pardoning him. I thank you, sir, for the gift of your ward,   75
Mistress Grace; look you, here is your hand and seal, by the way.
Master Winwife, give you joy, you are Palemon, you are
possessed o' the gentlewoman, but she must pay me value, here's

64 *Bridget* The most probable explanation of the mention of this character, not heard of
    elsewhere in the play, is that Mistress Overdo, waking from her drunken stupor, imagines
    herself at home and calls a servant of this name.

67 *at* to

68 *oppressed with* overwhelmed by
    estimation reputation
    in pardoning him ed. (inh im F). The Folio reading does not make sense. The purely
    conjectural insertion of 'pardoning', on the assumption that the compositor omitted it,
    as he omitted other words, balances 'recovering the goods' and fits in with the conclusion
    of the comedy. 'Pardon' is not an unusual word at the end of a Jonsonian comedy. Justice
    Clement tells Brainworm that he 'deserues to bee pardon'd for the wit o' the offence'
    (*Every Man in His Humour*, V.iii, 113–14), and Face asks for, and receives, Lovewit's
    pardon (*The Alchemist*, V.iii, 83).

77 *Winwife*, ed. (Win-wife F)

78 *pay me value* Because Quarlous is now Grace's guardian.

warrant for it. And honest madman, there's thy gown and cap again; I thank thee for my wife. (*To the widow*) Nay, I can be mad, sweetheart, when I please, still; never fear me. And careful Numps, where's he? I thank him for my licence.   80

WASP

How!

QUARLOUS

'Tis true, Numps.

WASP

I'll be hanged then.   WASP *misseth the licence*   85

QUARLOUS

Look i' your box, Numps. [*To* OVERDO] Nay, sir, stand not you fixed here, like a stake in Finsbury to be shot at, or the whipping post i' the Fair, but get your wife out o' the air, it will make her worse else. And remember you are but Adam, flesh and blood! You have your frailty. Forget your other name of Overdo, and invite us all to supper. There you and I will compare our 'discoveries', and drown the memory of all enormity in your biggest bowl at home.   90

COKES

How now, Numps, ha' you lost it? I warrant 'twas when thou wert i' the stocks. Why dost not speak?   95

WASP

I will never speak, while I live, again, for aught I know.

OVERDO

Nay, Humphrey, if I be patient, you must be so too. [*To them all*] This pleasant conceited gentleman hath wrought upon my judgement, and prevailed. I pray you take care of your sick friend, Mistress Alice, and, my good friends all—   100

QUARLOUS

And no enormities.

OVERDO

I invite you home with me to my house, to supper. I will have none fear to go along, for my intents are *ad correctionem, non ad destructionem; ad aedificandum, non ad diruendum.* So lead on.

81 *fear me* fear for me, doubt it
86 *Look* ed. (Loke F)
87 *a stake ... shot at* Finsbury Fields were a place of recreation for the citizens of London, and one of its attractions was archery contests.
97 s.d. *To them all* ed. (not in F)
98 *pleasant conceited* merrily disposed
103–4 *ad ... diruendum.* To correct, not destroy; to build up, not to tear down.

COKES

Yes, and bring the actors along, we'll ha' the rest o' the play at   105
home.

[*Exeunt*]

THE END

THE EPILOGUE

Your Majesty hath seen the play, and you
   Can best allow it from your ear and view.
You know the scope of writers, and what store
   Of leave is given them, if they take not more,   5
And turn it into licence. You can tell
   If we have used that leave you gave us well;
Or whether we to rage or licence break,
   Or be profane, or make profane men speak.
This is your power to judge, great sir, and not   10
   The envy of a few. Which if we have got,
We value less what their dislike can bring,
   If it so happy be, t' have pleased the King.

2 *allow* sanction, license
3 *store* ed. (*store*, F)
8 *speak*. ed. (*speake*? F)

NOTES ON THE TEXTS

VOLPONE

This edition is a modern-spelling text based on facsimiles of Jonson's 1607 quarto *Volpone* and 1616 folio *Works*, both of which I believe he supervised carefully, though not fanatically. F appears to be based on a copy of Q marked, presumably by Jonson, with minor revisions. Ordinarily this would lend greatest weight to F, which is how editors of *Volpone* (with the exception of Henry de Vocht's little-known 1936 version) have tended to proceed. But revisions are not always improvements, and Jonson was surely a sharper playwright around 1606, as he began his string of great comedies, than he was approaching 1616, with *Barthlomew Fair* his only recent play, and no theatrical successes in his remaining decades.

Some of F's corrections are indeed corrections, its punctuation is often more expressive, and some changes may have emerged from performance. But the fresh wisdom of the genius at the start of his remarkable comic period deserves more respect than Jonson himself or some of his editors have given it. Furthermore, some changes apparently arose from tightened censorship rather than artistic reconsideration.

And, in truth, the differences between Q and F (about a hundred substantive changes, not counting small corrections and shifts in punctuation) are quite minor, and do not suggest any coherent change in view, any basic differences in intention – unless we attribute to Jonson rather than to compositors the re-punctuation in the rape scene that arguably renders Celia commandingly rational in F, rather than breathlessly desperate as in Q (in performance, Siobhan McKenna's defiance of Ralph Richardson epitomized the implications of F, as Rosalind Iden's panic over Donald Wolfit's attack epitomized the implications of Q). Not even the myopia of an editor, and the accompanying narcissism of small differences among editions, can justify an absolute preference between the Q and F texts of *Volpone*, which are here therefore conflated to provide the best possible communication of this biting and hilarious play, with all its verbal and moral complexities, to a general modern audience.

With that goal in mind, I have worked as Jonson evidently did, using corrected versions of Q as a basis susceptible to small revisions: mostly modernization of spelling and punctuation, along with selective endorsements of revisions Jonson himself offered in F, and a few emendations (especially where authorized by the 1640 Second Folio) of what appear to be minor errors that slipped through both editions. Unlike previous editors, I have favoured the Q text of Jonson's Dedicatory Epistle, since it presumably reflects his thoughts at the time the play was composed, and certainly reflects the date at the end of the letter, more accurately than the F revision. The showy and archaic complexity of Jonson's syntax (in either version), evidently designed to flatter his university audience, makes this Epistle so difficult that I have placed it at the end of the text, rather than the beginning, to avoid discouraging modern readers before they reach the delights of the play proper. Several commendatory Latin and English poems from fellow-authors such as John Donne and Francis Beaumont also preceded the text – Jonson clearly designed Q to exalt himself as a literary artist – but must be omitted from this edition.

At the beginning of each scene, the original texts list all the characters who appear in that scene; I have replaced that group listing with individual entrances at the likeliest moment in the text. These and other added stage directions appear in square brackets, and readers and performers are encouraged to reconsider them. Aside from the group entrance listings, and parentheses around lines to be whispered aside from one character to another, Q provides no stage directions; all unbracketed stage directions here come from F, which was more intent on reflecting the theatrical experience than on presenting a literary credential.

I have sought to retain some impression of Jonson's characteristic verbal rhythms, which he conveyed by elisional apostrophes and heavy punctuation, especially in F. Modern usage generally dictates exchanging Jonson's colons and semicolons, as when Mosca remarks, 'There, he is farre enough; he can hear nothing: / And, for his father, I can keepe him off (F, III.vii.17–18); occasionally the original texts use a colon in place of a modern exclamation point. Otherwise, however, this edition retains (to an unusual degree) Jonson's elaborate punctuation, which provides a valuable guide at times to sense for the reader, at other times to performance for the actor. A comma often represents the space, the lightly emphatic pause (between a predicate and its objective or subjective clause), in which a modern speaker would insert 'that', as when Corbaccio offers a drug by claiming to 'know, it cannot but most gently worke' (Q, I.iv.16), or when Mosca describes Celia's 'soft lip, / Would tempt you to eternity of kissing!' (Q, I.v.111–12). At other times the comma provides a pause for dramatic effect: modern writers (indeed, most modern editors) would remove at least the second of the commas in Mosca's almost pornographic description of Celia as 'a beauty, ripe, as harvest' (Q, I.v.109); but Jonson's commas suggest the provocative pauses that give Mosca's description the quality of a cumulative, developing series of thoughts; 'ripe' works by itself, before becoming subsumed into the conventional comparison. The same effect explains the even more peculiar insistence of commas when Mosca evokes, for Voltore, the wealth supposedly awaiting him upon Volpone's death: 'When you do come to swim, in golden lard, / Up to the armes, in honey' (Q, I.iii.70–1); for an editor to decide, merely for the sake of eliminating commas, that the swimming should be associated only with the lard, and the immersion separately with the honey, is a waste of Mosca's mesmerizing artistry, and Jonson's behind it.

The mid-sentence question marks of Mosca's 'Am not I here? whom you have made? your creature?' (Q, I.v.78) demand preservation for similar reasons: the phrases are each separate expressive units, as well as finally blending into a single sentence that, normally punctuated, would be less than the sum of its parts. Ironically, editors have inadvertently made Jonson seem old-fashioned by over-eagerly modernizing the oddities of his syntax and punctuation which, in their original form, reveal exactly the process of a human subjectivity spontaneously and realistically developing from moment to moment that Jonson's drama is commonly accused of lacking.

ROBERT N. WATSON

EPICOENE

The earliest-known text of *Epicoene*, and the only one with authority, is
that contained in the folio *Works* of 1616, printed by William Stansby.
The present edition is based on a copy of this text in the Bodleian Library,
shelf mark Douce I, 302, collated against the editions of Herford and
Simpson, Beaurline, and Partridge.

There is a faint possibility that the folio was preceded by a quarto of
1612, which has since been lost. Gifford said he had seen such a quarto in
his edition of Jonson in 1816, and his claim is lent some colour by the
Stationers' Register, which has an entry dated 28 September 1612
transferring the publishing rights in the play from John Brown and John
Busby to Walter Burre. Burre may then have brought out a quarto, as he did
with *The Alchemist* in the same year. It seems more likely, however, that
Gifford was mistaken. Recent textual scholars have argued, very plausibly,
that the folio *Epicoene* was set from manuscript rather than printed copy,
and this would have been an odd choice had a quarto been available.

Stansby's manuscript was clearly authorial. The Dedication, the style
of act and scene division imitated from editions of classical dramatists,
the carefully explanatory stage-directions (e.g., II.i.9, IV.vi.1, IV.vii.1), all
point to the same meticulous preparation of copy which Jonson carried
out for the other plays in the folio. The printing was, after a shaky start,
equally careful. The compositors introduced a thin scattering of errors,
but scarcely any of any substance. The most serious to escape notice were
'Thy' for 'They' at I.i.92, and 'alwaies' for 'all ways' at IV.i.78. Unlike most
previous editors, I think F is correct at II.ii.121, III.iii.29, and IV.v.147;
I am not quite so sure about V.iv.173. At I.ii.18, 'more', the General Editor
suggests emending to 'mere', an attractive reading, but I can parallel this
use of 'more' but not the use of 'portent' which the emendation requires.
Conversely, F's '*came*' at IV.v.110 s.d., which I emend to '*come*', may be
correct: an instance, as at IV.vii.1, of Jonson slipping into the past-tense
style of direction he employs in his masques.

One major irregularity in the printing needs to be noted. Gathering Yy
(the prologues and the play to II.ii.55) exists in two states, the second a
resetting in entirely new type. What seems to have happened was that
Stansby and/or Jonson noticed, after a number of sheets of the gathering
had been printed, both that the compositors had made many blunders,
and that the speech-prefix DAV., for Dauphine, was liable to be confused
with DAW. for Daw, who was due to appear in the next scene. They decided
to scrap all twelve type-pages and set them up afresh, with DAV. altered to

DAVP. Jonson also took the opportunity to make some substantial local changes. He added an explanatory comment beneath the title of the second prologue and a marginal gloss at I.i.32. In the text of the play he added words at I.ii.30 and substituted them at I.i.160 and II.ii.30. These last three revisions, together with the variant at I.i.92 and the stop-press corrections at II.iii.51 and IV.iv.12, contradict his statement in the Dedication that 'There is not a line or a syllable . . . changed from the simplicity of the first copy'. Only major discrepancies between the two states are noted below. H&S, IX, 21–30, give a complete list, but the wrong way round, since, as Gerritsen and Beaurline have shown, their identification of which of the two settings is the later was mistaken.

In the present edition Jonson's marginal stage-directions have been incorporated into the text, and additions to them enclosed in square brackets. Departures from the copy text, in readings which affect sense, have been noted at the foot of the page. Two of Jonson's conventions of presentation in the folio have been silently amended: the custom of not supplying a speech-prefix for the character who speaks first in the scene, and 'massed' entries, i.e., the listing at the start of each scene of all the characters who appear in it, irrespective of whether they enter at that point or not. F's frequent use of brackets, indicating either an aside, or an interjected remark, or a temporary diversion of thought within a speech, has been considerably reduced. Spelling has been modernized, but occasionally – as in other New Mermaid editions of Jonson — an obsolete form has been retained in order to preserve some special intention of the author. Thus, the consciously odd spelling 'modes-tee' at II.iii.35 points up Daw's 'chiming' rhymes; 'kastrils' (IV.iv.163) puns on 'cast'; and 'vellet' is distinguished in F from 'velvet', for reasons of colloquialism or euphony. Jonson's deliberate signalling of a Latin root (e.g., 'porcpisce', 'moniments', 'tyrans') has also been preserved. Punctuation is a more difficult problem. Jonson's rhetorical style of pointing, marking stresses and pauses rather than units of meaning, is likely to seem intolerably heavy to a modern reader, particularly in a prose text. What a modernizing editor must therefore do, it seems to me, is judge every case separately and decide when an important nuance is in danger of being lost. Following this principle, I have, for example, retained the comma after 'it' at V.iv.44 and the exclamation mark after 'worsts' at V.iv.127, since they help convey the speakers' breathless outrage; and removed the comma after 'marriage' at IV.iv.138 – after some hesitation, since a portentous emphasis may be intended. The result is probably superior to the blanket imposition of a lighter system, but a degree of arbitrariness is an inevitable penalty.

R. V. HOLDSWORTH

THE ALCHEMIST

The Alchemist was first printed in quarto (Q) in 1612 and then included in the folio (F) edition of Jonson's *Works* in 1616. Jonson supervised the publication of both editions and it is likely that the copy text used for F was a corrected edition of Q. A second folio edition of the *Works* (F2) came out in 1640 and included some emendations. The present edition is based on F in all but a few details and all substantive variations from Q are recorded in the textual notes. Many of these variations stem from the tightening of regulations in the intervening years over the uttering of religious material on stage. Hence oaths which might be found blasphemous were emended in F to pagan or secular equivalents. For instance, 'God's will' (Q) becomes 'Death on me' in F (I.i.148). I have retained all these emendations (though there is a case for scrapping them) except one, at I.ii.56, which makes no sense outside the context of censorship.

Jonson's comprehensible punctuation in F has largely been retained, including the brackets which often indicate a *sotto voce* or an aside. Spelling – except when the word was archaic or odd at the time – has been modernized. Jonson's liberal use of capitals and italics has been abandoned here – with some regret since the typography of F gives an edge to many words which, while not necessarily specialist, smack of jargon or restricted use. I have, however, retained Jonson's use of black-letter type for German words - too good a visual joke to miss. All editorial stage directions are in square brackets; any others are as in F. In F block entries of all participants precede each scene with the name of the first speaker at the beginning. Here entries are supplied as the action requires and all speech prefixes are ranged on the left. (Jonson distributes the prefixes within the line where a metrical line is shared by more than one character.)

ELIZABETH COOK

BARTHOLMEW FAIR

The sole authority for the text of *Bartholmew Fair* is the folio printed by John Beale, in 1631, for Robert Allot. This folio also included *The Devil is an Ass*, first played in 1616, and *The Staple of News*, first played in 1626. However, no publication, so far as is known, followed on the printing. In July 1637 Mary Allot, whose husband had died, transferred her rights in *Bartholmew Fair* and *The Staple of News* – *The Devil is an Ass* appears to have been overlooked – to John Legatt and Andrew Crooke. They, in turn, though no record of the transaction survives, would seem to have sold the sheets of the 1631 printing to Richard Meighen, who issued them, in 1640, with a new title-page, describing the three plays as 'The Second Volume' of Jonson's 'Workes'.

The collation of *Bartholmew Fair* in the folio text of 1631 is A1 blank; A2 recto, the title-page; A2 verso, blank; A3 recto, the Prologue; A3 verso, the Persons of the Play; A4 recto to A6 verso, the Induction; B to M in fours, paged 1 to 88, with pages 12, 13, and 31 wrongly numbered as 6, 3, and 13 respectively, the text of the play and the Epilogue.

The copy for the text was, as the massed entries at the beginning of each scene and the rhetorical punctuation indicate, almost certainly a carefully prepared manuscript in Jonson's own hand. He was, therefore, justifiably very annoyed when Beale did a thoroughly bad job on it. In a letter he wrote to the Earl of Newcastle, when sending him a copy of *The Devil is an Ass*, he mentions that he has already sent a copy of *Bartholmew Fair*, but that he cannot extract a copy of *The Staple of News* from Beale, whom he calls 'the Lewd Printer'. He also complains that as a consequence of Beale's 'delayes and vexation, I am almost become blind' (H & S, i, 211). It was probably Beale's incompetence, and his own inability to force the printer into putting things right, that led Jonson, whose standards of accuracy were high, to drop the project of publishing a second volume of his Works, with the result that the three plays were not issued until three years after his death in 1637.

In setting up the play Beale and his men committed one common error after another, and, to make matters even worse, some kind of accident happened to the forme containing L2 recto (V.iii.76–117) and L3 verso (V.iv.79–117), so that it had to be reset. Most of their mistakes fall into definite groups. First, there is a fine crop of misprints. They begin, appropriately enough, on the title-page, where, in the penultimate line of the quotation from Horace, '*asello*' appears as '*assello*'. They continue in

'The Persons of the Play' with 'whtchmen' (1. 24) for 'watchmen', thence into the Induction, where 'Soueraigne' (l. 63) is turned into 'Soueragine', and so on into the main body of the play right down to the final scene, which gives 'fot' (l. 11) instead of 'for'. This last error, due to foul case, is one of a number of such: 'wirh' for 'with' (III.v.10), 'Heatt' for 'Heart' (III.v.278), and 'rhe' for 'the' (IV.vi.38). Similarly, there are several instances of *c* for *e*: 'Licencc' for 'Licence' (I.ii.20), 'shce' for 'shee' (I.ii.41), 'fatnessc' for 'fatnesse' (II.ii.105), and so on. Secondly, letters are omitted, giving 'Her's' for 'Here's' (I.i.2), 'littl' for 'little' (I.iv.103), 'scury' for 'scuruy' (I.iv.105), and the like. Thirdly, words are printed in the wrong order, for instance, 'do good' for 'good do' (I.ii.37). Fourthly, words are omitted. A clear example is 'is, taken' for 'is, is taken' (IV.iii.52), but as some of my emendations indicate, there are, I think, others. Fifthly, there is much pointless repetition of words: 'of of' for 'of' (II.i.38), 'then then' for 'then' (III.v.26), 'and and' for 'and' (III.vi.33). Sixthly, words are misspaced, beginning with 'hiseighteene' for 'his eighteene' (Ind. 81); and, finally, there are, in my opinion, a number of minim errors: 'drunke' for 'drinke' (I.iii.22) seems an obvious case.

Jonson, we know, was very careful indeed about his punctuation, which is designed to assist the actor's delivery of the lines. It is rhetorical, that is to say, the stops are intended primarily to denote the duration of pauses rather than the grammatical units into which a sentence falls. The heavier the stop, the longer the pause is to be. Beale, however, seems to have worked on the principle that one stop is as good as another. As early as I.i.21, he prints 'And. her' for 'And, her' or possibly 'And her'; and from this point onwards goes his own way, often producing sentences which have neither a rhetorical nor a grammatical basis.

In the present edition printer's errors of the obvious kind have been silently corrected, but all departures of substance from the copy text have been noted at the foot of the page on which they occur. All additions to the copy text, with the one exception of the speech prefix before the opening speech in each scene (see the note to the stage direction at the beginning of I.i), are enclosed in square brackets. The spelling has been modernized; but colloquial forms, such as 'o' the', meaning 'of the' or 'on the', and the like, have been retained. So have the abbreviated forms of personal names ('Bartholmew' for 'Bartholomew', 'Ursla' for 'Ursula', etc.). The punctuation presented a special problem. Jonson's rhetorical pointing is, in any case, disconcerting to the modern reader. When blurred and confused by the bunglings of Beale, it becomes very difficult indeed. It has therefore been replaced by modern punctuation. This policy has meant that on some occasions one possible sense has been suppressed in favour of another. In such cases the original pointing is given at the foot of the page.

The edition is based on a photocopy of the British Museum copy of the three plays of 1631 with the press-mark 642.1.29.

G. R. HIBBARD